Superstition
and the
Press

Superstition and the Press

by

Curtis D. MacDougall

Prometheus Books

700 East Amherst St. Buffalo, New York 14215

Library of Congress Card Catalog No. 83-61115
ISBN: 0-87975-211-4
     0-87975-212-2 pbk.

Contents

Introduction

Will Rogers, the sage cowboy from Oklahoma, used to say, "All I know is what I read in the newspapers." This book documents what anyone whose only source of information is newspapers would know about contemporary superstitions.

I have drawn information only from newspapers, citing most references specifically. Even when there is no direct attribution what is said was learned from newspapers and not from magazines or books. I did check a few facts in reference books, examples being the name of the French king during Nostradamus' lifetime and the outcome of the George Freeman-Muhammad Ali fight in *Information Please Almanac* and the exact Doomsday dates set by the Millerites in the Encyclopaedia Britannica.

When *Life, Newsweek, Time* or some other magazine is mentioned, usually it is because some newspaper referred to the article in question or someone sent me tne clipping. I have not subscribed to any of these magazines for at least a quarter-century. In a few instances, I made notes from magazines I read while waiting in the outer office of a doctor or dentist.

Doubtless, since I have been a journalist all my life, I am not a typical newspaper reader. Who is? My raw material is what I clipped and filed from the papers to which I subscribed, the Chicago papers, *National Observer* and, at intervals, the *New York Times*. One of my sons, A. Kent, was a reporter for the *Wall Street Journal* for ten years and still reads it while on the business page staff of the *Los Angeles Times*. He knows what interests me and clips from those two and other periodicals. Another son, Gordon P., a longtime Washington lawyer, does the same and my lawyer daughter, Priscilla Ruth, formerly of New York and now a resident of Madison, Wis., subscribes to the Madison and Milwaukee papers and reads other Wisconsin newspapers she encounters in her statewide travels for the Wisconsin Education Association Council.

I believe I come close to a 100 percent sample for the past three decades of what appeared on my subject in Chicago, New York, Washington and

Los Angeles newspapers.

Several former students have been aware of my interests and have helped swell my files. By far the most important is Mervin Block of CBS in New York. He loaned me hundreds of clippings, mostly from New York papers other than the *Times*. Others who have made it impossible to overlook extra important incidents have been Dr. Gene Burd, associate professor of journalism at the University of Texas in Austin; Edward Peeks, business-labor editor of the *Charleston* (W. Va.) *Gazette;* Leon Baden, copy-desk editor, *Harrisburg* (Pa.) *Evening News;* Lawrence Rember, Oklahoma City lawyer and journalist; and Dr. Daniel Thornburgh, director of the Department of Journalism at Eastern Illinois University, Charleston. Others to whom I am grateful for clippings and articles include the following: Dr. Warren Agee, professor of journalism, University of Georgia; Dr. Robert Blanchard, chairman of the Department of Journalism at Trinity University, San Antonio, Tex.; James Carty, professor of journalism, Bethany College, W. Va.; Dr. Harry Heath, director of the School of Journalism, Oklahoma State University; Charles-Gene McDaniel, professor of journalism, Roosevelt University; Diane Monk, formerly *Chicago Daily News* reporter; Doris Klein, Cocoa Beach, Fla. journalist and Howard Fibich, news editor, *Milwaukee Journal.*

For typing and clerical help as well as miscellaneous tasks and advice I am grateful to my wife, Genevieve Rockwood MacDougall, my daughter, Bonnie Cottrell, and my granddaughters, Jennifer and Stephanie Cottrell. I'm most grateful to Doris Doyle, Prometheus Books, the best book editor I've ever encountered.

Because someone "borrowed" my copy of the report of the University of Colorado Unidentified Flying Objects Project, I wrote to my former student Dr. Herbert Strentz, dean of the School of Journalism at Drake University, who worked with Dr. Edward U. Condon, director of the project, and produced a doctoral dissertation at Northwestern University on the press' handling of the phenomenon. That dissertation is now available through Arcturus Press, 263 N. Bailstron Avenue, Scotia, NY 12302.

I also wrote to Don Bishoff, a former student now editor of the *Eugene* (Ore.) *Register-Guard,* about a Bigfoot story; he sent me clippings of several stories pertaining to my study. Also on request ex-student William Pride, news editor of the *Denver Post,* sent me that paper's articles about the Mission Light International cult of Miharaj Ji, formerly headquartered in the *Post*'s circulation area. Also John L. Perry, a former student until recently the *Clearwater* (Fla.) *Sun* editor, sent me that paper's coverage of the Scientologists headquartered in that city.

Joe Nickell of Lexington, Ky. wrote to me about a story I included in my book *Hoaxes,* and during an exchange of letters and telephone calls I told him what I was doing. He then supplied me with more material on the Shroud of Turin, on which he is an expert, and also sent me about 20 clippings on other matters from Toronto newspapers.

Richard Kendrick, another former student, sent me clippings from his paper, the *Waukegan News-Sun,* of the series Roger Simon, now a *Chicago Sun-Times* columnist, did on the existence of Satanic clubs in Lake County, Ill.

When the press associations reported that a soothsayer in the state of Washington had foreseen a train–school bus wreck somewhere in Wyoming resulting in the deaths of several children, I wrote Prof. Ernest Linford of the University of Wyoming journalism faculty to ask if any Wyoming paper ran the story. One did and I thank Linford, former *Salt Lake Tribune* editorial writer, for a copy of it.

James Heavey, ex-student and editorial writer on the now defunct *Washington Star,* checked to confirm my suspicion that both the *Star* and *Post* abandoned coverage of the Potomac Monster after about a week without any final chapter.

That was the situation, over and over again, hundreds of examples in this book prove. A haunted house, poltergeist, land or sea monster and similar stories, unless someone is quick to take advantage of them for commercial purposes, are one-day sensations or maybe a few extra days if a posse is searching for a ghost, monster or other intruder. It is very frustrating never to find out if the beast was caught after sober reputable citizens had testified to its existence. Such failures to follow up or complete a story are those of the media for which I am not to blame. A lesson to be learned from this study is that to be fully informed one cannot rely entirely on the press. I cannot vouch for the accuracy of any of the news stories about which this book is written. My purpose is only to record what a reader thinks he knows.

The only extra expenditure I had for newspapers was for a week's subscription to the *Bismarck* (N.D.) *Herald* to check on the Bigfoot scare on nearby Indian reservations that had been mentioned in several newspapers in other parts of the country. Both the *Portland Oregonian* and *Atlanta Constitution* refused to send me back copies but did give me the dates of issues pertinent to a Scientology trial in the former and the black boy murders in the latter. I was unable to obtain research assistance in both cases.

Strangely it is almost impossible to get information from most of the organized groups active in promoting belief in the unexplained or intent on continuing investigations. Letters are returned because the addresses given in the newspapers were incorrect or no longer valid. Among those with which it was impossible for me to correspond were: Yeti Research Society, St. Petersburg, Fla.; Ozark Regional Commission, Little Rock, Ark.; Academy of Applied Science, Belmont, Mass.; Vampire Research Center, Elmhurst, N.Y.; Citizens Freedom Foundation, Denver; Spiritualist Counterfeits Project, Berkeley, Calif.; Basilica of Guadalupe, Mexico City; Edward Ben "Crazy" Olson, Madison, Wis.; Spiritualist Assembly, Lily Dale, N.Y.; Central Premonitions Registry, New York City.

I also obtained no responses from the Information Department of the Smithsonian Institution, Washington, D.C.; Prof. Barry Singer of California State University at Long Beach; Montauk Marine Basin, Montauk, N.Y.; Associated Press, Vancouver, Canada; Sheriff, Eureka, Calif.; Mayor Margaret Hill, Antelope, Ore. and Illinois Repr. Betty J. Hoxey, Springfield.

I did hear from Peter Byrne of the Bigfoot Information Center, Wood River, Ore. and Hayden Hewes of the International Bureau for Unidentified Flying Objects, Edmond, Okla., the latter, however, only after Lawrence Rember interviewed him on my behalf.

I have solicited information for 22 other books and have never encountered such a lack of response before. I don't think I suddenly lost the ability to compose a good letter. Perhaps if the response had been different I would have expanded the book to give whatever followup information I could obtain. In such a case it would have been necessary to extend the writing beyond the two years I have devoted to it and probably to publish the finished product in two or more volumes. But then the narrative would not be an accurate description of what the ordinary reader of newspapers learned from them.

I also have had considerable correspondence with Kendrick Frazier, editor of the *Skeptical Inquirer,* and found helpful his article "How to Cover 'Psychics' and the Paranormal" in the April 1982 *Bulletin* of the American Society of Newspapers Editors.

And I had a correspondence debate with my former student, employee, and longtime valued personal friend, Curtis G. Fuller, founder and publisher of *Fate,* who also sent me "Starbaby," by Dennis Rawlins, published in the October 1981 issue, in support of the so-called Mars effect, and "Irrational Behavior: A Critique of the Humanist's Crusade Against Psi Research" by Theodore, Robert and W. Teed Rockwell, and other material adversely critical of Paul Kurtz's Committee for the Scientific Investigation of Claims of the Paranormal.

I have attached no bibliography to this book. Over the years I have read scores, perhaps hundreds of books on hoaxes, mass hysteria, public-opinion formation and all kinds of superstitions. Three that I read shortly before beginning work on this book, and to which I refer, are *Flim-Flam!* by James Randi, *Cults of Unreason* by Christopher Evans and *Myths of the Space Age* by Daniel Cohen. Some articles worthy of mention are: "Mysterious Phenomena: The New Obsession" in Editorial Research Reports for Jan. 29, 1978; "Flapdoodle Writ Large: Astrology in Magazines" by Mervin Block in *Columbia Journalism Review* for Summer 1969; "In Search of the Gullible: The Media and Their Reports on the Paranormal" by Andrew Skolnick, a Columbia University Graduate School of Journalism thesis, 1981; "Everything You Always Wanted to Know About How Newspapers Perpetuate Superstitions" by Andrew M. Maday; a proposal for a Ph.D. dissertation on "The Horoscope Column" by Frances Elizabeth Butler at

American University, Dec. 29, 1967; "Media Hypo Boosts Occultism" by Robert C. Owen in the *Christian Science Monitor* for Feb. 25, 1981; and public-opinion seminar reports at the Medill School of Journalism of Northwestern University by Jerry Poole, now editorial writer for the *Daily Oklahoman,* Oklahoma City, and Mason Miller, now a communications scientist, Cooperative State Research Service, U.S. Department of Agriculture.

I also subscribe to the *Humanist,* the *Skeptical Inquirer* and *Free Inquiry* magazines.

Hardly a day passes that I do not add to my files a newspaper clipping or other material related to the subject matter of this book. As I write in late July 1983, much journalistic attention is being given to the beating death of a 12-year-old boy, called "bad" by "Prophet" William Lewis on whose religious commune near South Haven, Mich. the child died. And Jennifer Booth is resurrecting, in the *Dallas Times-Herald,* "Mystery of the Shroud: Age-Old Hoax or Venerated Relic; Scientists Put It to Test."

So, unfortunately, it seems that this book will be outdated before it appears and that it never could be kept up to date except by constant revision. It is hoped that the readers will do just that.

1

Horoscopes

During World War II the British Secret Service hired a noted astrologer, a Hungarian refugee named Louis DeWohl, to cast Adolf Hitler's horoscope and then, day by day, determine what the führer's astrologer probably was advising him. At war's end it was learned that the Nazis had imprisoned Hitler's stargazer in 1941 when the practice of astrology was forbidden throughout the Reich.

Perhaps Adolf Hitler did lose confidence in soothsayers. Throughout history, many heads of government, warriors and other celebrities have consulted and relied upon them heavily. Astrologers were constantly consulted as the barbarians threatened Athens, Rome and Constantinople. The prophecies of Nostradamus for the benefit of Henry II of France still are quoted by the true believers. There might not have been a successful Bolshevik revolution if the Romanoffs had paid less attention to the evil Rasputin.

According to posthumous biographies it has been revealed that many prominent American industrialists and bankers, including J. P. Morgan, consulted astrologers as did some denizens of the White House. In recent and contemporary times quite a few movie stars have publicly espoused astrology. Marlene Dietrich, about the most confirmed believer, is known to have sought an interview with U Thant, secretary-general of the United Nations, to advise him that a date set for a special session of the U.N. General Assembly was astrologically unsound.

As defined by the Associated Press in a July 28, 1968 story from Hollywood, astrology is based on an ancient theory that movements of celestial bodies—stars, planets, the sun—influence human affairs. Astrology is about as old as civilization itself. Archeologists have found astrological maxims on clay tablets dating from 3000 B.C. in excavations near the site of the ancient city of Babylon. Astrology originated as a religion in Mesopotamia, probably among the Sumerians, and gave birth to the world's oldest science, astronomy. At the time and for centuries thereafter Earth was believed to be flat and the center of the universe. The sky was thought to be like an inverted bowl covering it and the stars were fixed points of light on the back of the dome. Chaldeans, in southern Babylonia, erected towers used by priests to chart the apparent passage of the sun and moon along the same "heavenly path" every day which they called Anu's Way. The overwhelming majority of the heavenly bodies seemed to be fixed in space, but the five planets visible to the naked eye—Mercury, Mars, Venus, Saturn and Jupiter—the "wanderers," were erratic in their behavior. They were the planets that came to be the supposed homes of the gods.

Anu's Way developed into the zodiac which persists today. It is an imaginary belt across the sky showing the relative positions of the sun, moon, planets and constellations. It separates the sky into 12 equal parts, each encompassing a "sign" standing for one of the major constellations. A Chaldean cuneiform tablet dated 419 B.C. is the oldest document bearing the names of the signs: Aquarius, Aries, Capricorn, Gemini, Leo, Libra, Pisces, Scorpio, Sagittarius and three renamed by the Romans, Cancer, Taurus and Virgo.

In a full-page article, "Astrology: It's 'In' Now, But Does it Work?" in the *National Observer* for Feb. 17, 1969, Daniel St. Albin Greene wrote:

> By 3000 B.C. the Babylonian priests were translating their heavenly observations into predictions of human events. This led ultimately to the practice of forecasting their rulers' futures by figuring out how the sky looked at the time of the royal births. Thus the horoscope was born.
>
> The Chaldeans originated astrology, the Greeks and Romans popularized it and developed horoscopy to the baroque system it is today. A horoscope is a diagram, in the shape of a wheel with 12 spokes, that is cast to show the relative positions of the planets and the Zodiacal Signs (Constellations) at the exact moment of birth or at any moment, for that matter historic events, signing of contracts and so on. The 12 equal wedges, each holding a sign of the zodiac, are called houses. Each house is supposed to exercise influence over certain phases of human life; the Eighth House, for instance, covers legacies, death and sex. Moreover, by a puzzling classification that typifies astrological logic, each of the 12 signs relates to a trait, a part of the body or a human experience.

The Greeks introduced the horoscope for ordinary citizens, the first such personal horoscope probably being cast about 500 B.C. To cast a horoscope is not easy. One must know the place and date of birth, preferably the hour and exact minute. In his article "Astrology's Astonishing Comeback," in the *Chicago Tribune* magazine for Feb. 25, 1968, Daniel Cohen wrote: "There are a really staggering number of influences that must be taken into account, and, to make matters worse, there is no general agreement as to how these influences should be weighed or even exactly what they are. It often happens that two astrologers looking at the same horoscope will come up with completely different predictions about what the future holds for the individual."

In his *National Observer* article Daniel St. Albin Greene elaborated: "Some astrologers contend that since the horoscope reveals only general tendencies and potentials, making specific predictions from it is a risky business at best. Even so, few astrologers can resist the temptation to translate their analyses into prophecies."

To which should be added the comment of Tom Buckley in "The Signs Are Right for Astrology," in the *New York Times Magazine* for Dec. 15, 1968: "The language of astrology is ambiguous. Furthermore, it's the language of our likenesses. In the same way that you can look into a textbook of abnormal psychology and have no trouble identifying with every one of the cases, the characteristics described by astrology as being typical of people born under this or that sign of the zodiac are, in fact, to one degree or another, typical of everyone."

There is no unanimity of opinion as to whether all humans or only a gifted few possess the ability to prophesy. Philip Nobile put the question to Hans Holzer, a prominent parapsychologist. The answer, contained in the article "Checking Up on the Prophets" in the *Chicago Sun-Times Midwest Magazine* for Jan. 14, 1973, was in part: "Many people have proved the ability to foretell the future in a detailed, accurate way. This ability is part of human nature and not supernatural and exists in larger degrees in some and lesser degrees in others." Holzer said 10 percent accuracy in predictions is good but admitted that many psychics "live under the illusion that they have extra talents."

Astrology was introduced into Rome about 100 B.C. and enjoyed almost immediate popularity. Astrologers gave advice to those who wagered on chariot races in the Colosseum, and it has been rumored that one stargazer warned Julius Caesar to beware the Ides of March. True or false, astrology survived despite the strong opposition of the Christian church, especially from St. Augustine. In 1543 astrology became an anachronism when Copernicus published *De Revolutionibus* to contend that the sun, not Earth, was the center of the universe. During the next two centuries many scientists, mainly Galileo, Kepler, Brahe and Newton, confirmed Copernicus' studies. Myths regarding the origin and nature of man as well as of the world were put in jeopardy by geologists, anthropologists, archeologists, physicists, botanists, biologists and others.

"And so, why suddenly has astrology, seemingly dead and discredited except among the hagridden, the ignorant and the extraordinarily credulous, captured the imagination of the avant-garde?" as Buckley put it. There are about as many answers as there are people attempting to give them. Buckley himself gave the astrologers' explanation: "science, particularly space exploration and biological research, is proving the ancient nonesuch to be true after all. Those who see the United States on the verge of the apocalypse recall that corrupt and decaying nations turn to the supernatural in their last hours. . . . Then again it may be a question of fads, possibly related to the periodic reappearance of comets . . ." Buckley quoted Dr. Donald Kaplan that the present popularity of astrology "stemmed in part from the fact that its formal systematized procedures comprise a parody of true science." Greene explained that, according to the seers, we are entering the Age of Aquarius "and yesterday's hangups are passé. In this expansive, turned-on age of widening horizons, they say, the renascence of astrology was inevitable." And Cohen wrote:

> The core of an astrologer's popularity stems from the fact that he can offer something that no astronomer or any other scientists can give—reassurance. In an uncertain time, when religion, morals and ethics are shattered so regularly that one hardly notices that they are gone, the astrologer holds out a vision of a world ruled by forces that operate with clockwork regularity.
>
> In addition astrology is glorifying. Instead of feeling himself a mere slave in the hands of different or hostile forces, the believer is uplifted by his connection with the cosmos. . . . The sort of misty character analysis that astrologers engage in cannot be considered proof at all. Who can object to a flattering description of themselves? One astrologer told me that under my hard exterior I was a sensitive person. How was I to reply to a statement like that? Could I say, "No I am really a hardheaded clod"?

Several writers have quoted those who say that belief in astrology has therapeutic value. A zodiac devotee is quoted as saying, "With astrology one can blame the stars when things go wrong. Isn't that a lovely feeling?" It is certainly as good as scapegoating a parent or someone else under instruction from a Freudian practitioner.

Astrologer Mary Orser foresees the day when psychologists will routinely consult the zodiac in treating patients, Lloyd G. Carter wrote for the UPI after interviewing her on the West Coast. The *New York News-World* used the story Aug. 19, 1978.

Whatever the reason, astrology has been booming for the past quarter-century. Whereas before World War II only about 200 daily newspapers had horoscopes, today about 1,200 of the nation's 1,750 dailies have them. Because no accreditation or registration is required, anyone can call oneself an astrologer. So it is difficult to estimate the number who do so. In *Chicago Today* for March 21, 1971, Sammye Johnson gave the figures as 10,000 full-time and 175,000 part-time astrologers. The article was entitled "The Occult," with the subhead, "The lure of the future waxes strong, and its prophets are profiting." Johnson concluded, "Interest in the occult has become a mass movement in the United States." In the *Chicago Daily News* for June 14, 1969, Larry and Laura Green put it, "The occult is making its biggest comeback since Salem." Daniel St. Albin Greene noted that at least 5 million Americans plan their lives by horoscopes. They pay prices that range from $5 to $500 or more to make astrology a multi-million dollar business. A Gallup poll showed that 32 million Americans believe the stars influence people's lives and foretell events. That is 22 percent of the adult population; 24 percent read an astrology column daily and 77 percent know which astrological sign is associated with their birthdays. The *New York Times* had the story Oct. 19, 1975. Jane Wilson's review of Michel Gauquelin's *The Scientific Basis of Astrology* appeared in the *Chicago Tribune's Book World* for April 6, 1969. In 1963, in the homeland of the author of the book, 58 percent of the Frenchmen polled knew their birth signs and 54 percent thought that astrologers were scientists. In her review Wilson wrote:

> Astrology, or the horoscopes which are its product, is a multi-million dollar business in the U.S. today. The basic unit ranges from the syndicated newspaper columns of all-purpose generalized predictions, to the $50 private chart drawn up for the individual, after several hours of complicated calculations, by a professional astrologer. For the middle-income stargazer there is now the $20 computerized horoscope. Future plans of this recent industry include horoscopes programmed for corporations—with the date of incorporation taken as date of birth and special charts for the use of personnel directors. Bosses may soon want to know of a prospective employee as Napoleon did of his generals: Is he lucky?

The *New York Times* expressed dismay over the commercialization of astrology columns by means of the computer in an editorial by Anne-Marie Schiro in the issue of May 9, 1979.

Diana Milesko-Pytel explained in her article "Occult Craze Growing Like the Devil," in the *Chicago Daily News* for July 20, 1974:

> Some people say [the growing interest] is because we are on the threshold of the new Aquarian Age [announced in the musical "Hair"] which is an age of freedom and begins around the year 2000. We are moving out of the age of Pisces, they tell us, which was the age of law and of Christianity.
>
> Others who pooh-pooh such belief as hocus pocus, say the new spiritual pastime is the sign of a weak society, and they cite Rome and its many gods as an example of such decadence before a fall.

Many adherents to each view are quoted in the article.

Astrology was the leitmotif of the rock musical *Hair*. Tom Buckley revealed in his *New York Times Magazine* article, "The Signs Are Right for Astrology," Dec. 15, 1968 that it probably was the first show to list an astrologer in its program. That person, Maria Crummere, was consulted regarding every important decision management made. One cast member, Sally Eaton, had her obstetrician induce labor so her son would be born a Taurus as was her father. The event came off as scheduled except that the mother had forgotten to take Daylight Saving Time into consideration, making her calculations incorrect. On Nov. 15, 1970, the *New York Times* ran a story by Joan Cook about Margaret Harris, the first woman—let alone the first black woman—to be conductor of a major Broadway musical, *Hair*. One paragraph of the story reads:

> A child of Virgo in the Age of Aquarius, she managed to overcome potential astrological difficulties with the cast saying, "I'm Virgo but the moon is in Aries and the rising sun is in Aquarius."

The *Detroit Free Press* thought the public deserved to be informed about the background of a local newscaster, Norman Crim. So it ran his picture March 3, 1981 and revealed that he occasionally gets advice from psychic Joan Durham. Crim was quoted as saying he was impressed by some of the seer's prophecies, including one that the number 622 would play an important role in his life. It is the street number for the Channel 4 studio in Detroit with which Crim is associated.

Similar editorial judgment caused the insertion of the fact that Ervin Nyiregyhazi was born a "Capricorn on the cusp of Aquarius" in the profile "Curmudgeon of the Keyboard," by Bill Zakariasen in the *New York Daily News* of April 22, 1979.

An early warning to employers to refrain from using astrological data when hiring was sounded by Dr. Roy A. Doty, a psychologist who addressed the Chicago Production Congress. According to Arthur J. Snider, who covered the address for the *Chicago Daily News* of March 17, 1947, Doty warned employers "to beware the employment director who says, 'I can tell if he's the man we want the minute he walks through the door.'" Doty condemned "pseudo-sciences such as astrology and numerology."

After covering a biennial convention of the American Federation of Astrologers, John Peterson wrote from San Francisco for the *National Observer* of Aug. 24, 1974: "The emphasis was on trying to provide a scientific basis for the art." Carol Wilson, a noted Indiana astrologer, said, "Astrology is basically the story of man's growth"; but Robert Cooper, the federation's executive secretary, said, "The exact system of astrology has not been found."

Owen S. Rachleff, an associate professor of humanities at New York University, is called the Martin Luther of astrology for saying the charts used by astrologers are obsolete because about 2,000 years ago the earth shifted in relation to the stars. Judy Moore interviewed him for the *Chicago Sun-Times* of Nov. 13, 1973. He told her that the positions of the zodiac constellations have shifted at least one month.

In further attempts to understand the epidemic of gullibility the *Houston Chronicle* Jan. 20, 1974 conjectured that Americans were "edgy" because of economic problems and the approach of the comet Kohoutek. From New York May 29, 1977 the UPI reported on the findings of an 18-month study funded by the National Science Foundation: "Support and admira-

tion for science is waning. At the existential level we are all superstitious."
Sydney J. Harris wrote in his syndicated column for Oct. 30, 1968: ". . . for
we know (unconsciously) that our lives hang by a thread . . . We retain a
need to placate the gods, to get on the good side of destiny . . ."

So, as Daniel St. Albin Greene put it, "It is now hip to study astrology."
The Inner Vision School, the Time Pattern Research Institute, the Astrological Metaphysical Institute of Hollywood, Astrological Research Associates, the Astrological Guild of America, the American Federation of
Astrologers and other schools and groups provide information, instruction
and guidance. There are abundant bookstores with shelves of books and
magazines catering to the astrological public.

In addition, Buckley pointed out, "There are astrology cookbooks, an
astrology marriage guide, astrology for teen-agers, and an astrological
dating service. Tiffany offers cocktail glasses with signs of the zodiac.
Next-door Bonwit Teller is promoting the Horoscopic Record of the Month
Club . . . Inevitably an I.B.M. 36 computer has been programmed with 19
million pieces of horoscopic information by an organization that calls itself
Time Pattern Research Institute."

"Everything from jewelry to jobs has been keyed to zodiac themes,"
Sammye Johnson wrote, "More than $200 million is spent by some 40
million starry-eyed Americans on bulls, goats, crabs and scorpions."

Among the many blatant examples of the extent to which newspapers
take advantage of the upsurge of interest in the supernatural were two
features in the *Chicago Daily News* for April 13 and May 8, 1968. The first
was an interview by Diane Monk with Marsha Lane, who travels the
country to encourage horoscope parties as a major part of her duty as
marketing consultant for Old Charter Kentucky Bourbon. The basic idea
behind horoscopes for entertainment is that "the hostess sets the mood for
her party. Plans for an Aries party, for instance, are based on the astrologer's characterization of Aries as 'creative, energetic, impulsive and
enthusiastic.' "

There was no attempt to conceal Lane's purpose to advertise bourbon,
but Carl Byoir & Associates, the public relations firm handling the account, was not mentioned. Regarding the inspiration for the two-page
article "What recipe's in the stars for you?" by Isabel DuBois, the paper's
home-economics editor, answered my query at the time: "Sorry to blow
your theory to a cocked hat. The idea of keying a dozen ground beef recipes
to the zodiac was my own. I assure you that none of our ideas originate in
advertising or in advertising agencies." This I knew was not so because I
possess news releases and promotional literature supplied by advertisers
or their agencies. Also, a member of the *News* staff informed me, "Our
women's editor will take anything a p.r. agency feeds her."

At about the same time a reporter did considerable research prepara-
tory to writing a general story on the increase of interest in astrology. The
editor, however, "wasn't in the least bit interested in a serious story. What

he wanted was something with celebrity names in it—to be used as an indirect promotion for the daily horoscope the paper carries."

Other examples of Marsha Lane's success in obtaining free newspaper publicity were "Planning a Party? Better Check the Stars" by Dolores Alexander in *Newsday* for March 11, 1968 and "Astrological Party Giving" by Ellen Schlafly in the *St. Louis Post-Dispatch* for March 18, 1968. Both were illustrated with photographs of Lane and were almost identical in content.

When two French-cooking authorities, Marie Geberg and Monique Maine, with the aid of a food naturalist and three astrologers, published *La Cuisine Astrologique,* the *Washington Post* devoted almost an entire page Feb. 14, 1982 to an English translation of the advice for all cooks and gourmets according to their zodiac signs. In his introduction, John Rosson said: "A thorough knowledge of the astrology of food could confer the very essence of power and influence, to say nothing of making us social giants." And he explained that the book "tells us what dishes we 'love,' which we 'hate,' which are good for us, which bad and even what colors of food we prefer." For example, paragraphs directed to Gemini read: "The 'table's entertainer.' Not really interested in food; doesn't even know what he's eating. Doesn't go to a restaurant to eat or to a table for nourishment. Wants to know first of all, 'What are we here for?' Plays with the silverware and makes designs on the tablecloth . . . Will scatter shells from nuts all over the table, eventually forgetting to eat at all . . . If he or she must eat, preferences run to eggs, fish, chicken and lamb. Never garlic and seldom onions . . ."

This spread counteracted the space given Eve Zibert's series on Feb. 10, 17 and 24, 1980. "Just as a person's color preference and career choice is influenced by his horoscope, so is his taste in food." Of Gemini she wrote: ". . . versatile, perceptive, sensitive and informal; can also be restless, expedient, superficial and compromising . . . A joyous eater. It's hard to go wrong for his taste. He is one of the strongest fans of ethnic foods, even of that bastard variety euphemistically known as carry-out Chinese. Apt to keep pantry stocked with jars of little pepper sausages and anchovies . . . experiments with mixed menus . . ."

As for color, Fran Smith began her March 19, 1980 column, "Color vibrates. Astrologically you vibrate to your own color. Regardless of prior conditioning or habit, it's the one color in which you feel/look your finest, whether it's a sweater, a dress or an umbrella. Quite simply, you're in perfect rhythm with it." There followed information for all about what their favorite colors should be. Geminis, for instance, were told: "Your color key: effervescent. Your basic color is yellow. And then sometimes it's blue" and so forth and so on.

The spread of the commercialization of astrological advice-giving has meant business success for Kathleen Johnson, the object of a profile by Reuters, the British news agency, on Feb. 11, 1975. Headquartered in New

York, Johnson has 160 or more clients, including 15 corporations, the owner of a radio station, a record company, a managing consulting firm, a former hotel owner and a real estate company, all of whom paid from $100 to $500 for a prognostication.

The astrology business as a sideline also proved profitable for actress Arlene Dahl, whose 90-second astrological message was sold to 100 radio stations whose followers heard a few words of advice for every sign of the zodiac—"positive tips on how to use the day to advantage," Bess Winakor reported in the *Chicago Sun-Times* for Feb. 22, 1972.

A hopeful indication that not everyone is gullible was a paragraph in Kenneth R. Clark's "About People" column for UPI Nov. 13, 1979: "Philip A. Tanne is a Gemini and an astrologer will tell you that means he's interested in the occult. He is—'has been for the past three years—and he's concluded after all that study that astrology is bunk.' Says the University of Virginia professor who's writing a book on the subject: 'In the past 2,500 years or so science has been working to understand the universe as we understand it today. In astrology nothing has changed.' "

Another journalist with a healthy iconoclastic attitude is Harriet Van Horne, who reviewed Linda Goodman's *Love Signs* Dec. 4, 1978, in the *New York Post*. Van Horne terms astrology, belief in which the book promotes, "the silliest anti-intellectual theory of our time." And she added: "Our national preoccupation with astrology speaks ill for public education, scientists warn us." She quoted still another columnist, George Will, as saying that people who are willing to believe that the movements of the planets affect the character and success of people are (1) negating the influence of heredity, environment, and free will and (2) placing themselves in the same pew with witches, fortune tellers, voodoo priests, and flat-earth fanatics. "When You Wish Upon A Star: An Astrological Guide to Gift-Giving" in the *Chicago Daily News* for Feb. 6, 1977, was a full-page spread of an article by the psychic Laurie Brady. Typical of the help the zodiac can give in buying Christmas gifts was: "Geminis are versatile, on-the-go and the kind who never stop. Any labor-saving device would be good since Geminis don't like housework" and so forth for another 150 words.

"A Brief Case of Zodiac Shopping" was two pages of advice in the *New York Daily News* for Dec. 14, 1980. The editorial introduction read: "If you believe our fates lie in the stars, or if you just want to have some fun, here follows an insightful look at astrological shopping for women. Of course, we guarantee nothing." The advice for Geminis was typical: "Best color: yellow. She likes separates and coordinates and the changes she gets switching them about. If your favorite Gemini runs true to a type (say sophisticated or preppie, or young and naive) she'll get a huge charge if you shift gears on her. Perfume: Le parfum Qui Vous Metamorphous by Jean Laporte (sold only at Bloomingdale's)."

The headline, "Zodiac a Sign of the Time in Carpeting" suggests the nature of a story in the *Chicago Daily News* for Oct. 11–12, 1969. During those years of exaggerated publicity, the *Chicago Sun-Times* almost outdid its sister publication. Typical space grabbers were: "Fashion on an Astrology Kick," in the Family magazine section for June 10, 1968; "Vassar's Going to the Stars," by Carolyn Splear, with illustrations of how some women have makeups to follow the astrological approach, issue of March 11, 1969; "Jewelry's Success Written in the Stars" by Eugene Sheppard with illustrations of rings, bracelets and other items of jewelry shaped to resemble zodiac signs, issue of May 16, 1969; "Father's Gift Is in the Stars," by Elaine Taylor-Gordon, a guide to Father's Day gift purchasing, issue of June 16, 1970; and "Astrology Goes to the Dogs," by Mark Fineman, advice on how to select a congenial pet, based on an interview with Libby Collins, a Lake Forest astrologer, in *Suburban Week* for May 10–11, 1976. This was reminiscent of a half-page feature, "Dogs Go to the Humans," by Tony Weitzel, based on an interview with Mildred Best, who said it is possible to determine a dog's temperament by its horoscope, issue of Oct. 1, 1955.

The rival *Chicago Tribune* published "Zodiac Determines Travel Horoscope," by Marie Mattson who explained the warnings of the Chinese zodiac about what years are best for travel, issue of Feb. 13, 1972, and "An Astrological Guide to Perfect Gifts for Everyone," by Mary Daniels who said a Lear jet or a Honda motorcycle is the best gift for an Aries, whereas Aquarians like best autographed copies of autobiographies by famous persons, issue of Dec. 1, 1974.

In *This Week* for Feb. 23, 1969 Jess Stearn wrote about "Heavenly Houses," an account of how a New York architect, Robert Bruce Cousins, conceived of living quarters to suit the stars dwelling in them. For example, the dwelling for Cancer, the family-loving sign, is traditional style tri-level. It features large kitchen-dining areas, attic and "a protected terrace on the upper level which enables the moon, the governing planet of Cancer, to shine into the master bedroom and living room."

How to be "At Home in Your Astral House" was explained by Nancy Adams in the *Chicago Sunday Tribune* for March 3, 1974. On the authority of two astrologers, Michelle Carleton and Denise Alleman, she told how the fourth house in your birth sign may influence the decorating of your terrestrial home. For example, "Most Virgo homes have a lot of Early American furniture—upholstered chairs with maple finished arms . . . a living room that's untouchable, a museum exhibition lookalike, without the ropes."

"Is Astrology a $100 Million Hoax?" with the overline "Under the sign of the $," by Mort Weisinger in *Parade* for June 6, 1973, was one of the very few journalistic efforts written with some skepticism. However, it extols the business success of stargazers, names most of the prominent practitioners and their most famous clients and cites some of the notable errors of the seers as well as their hits.

As one evidence of the galloping popularity of astrology, Weisinger mentioned a new service, horoscopes by telephone. In Denver an experimental Dial Your Stars service pulled 1.25 million calls in five weeks. Richard J. Meislin explained this new development in "Horoscopes by Phone" for the *New York Times* of Oct. 18, 1976.

The first commercial test experiment approved by the Federal Communications Commission was operated by Field Electronic Publishing in more than 25 bars, restaurants, hospitals, and other locations where horoscopes are broadcast along with news and features, according to Gary Wisby in the *Chicago Sun-Times* for Sept. 8, 1981. On Jan. 7, 1982 the same newspaper devoted three full pages of its Food section to "Eating On A Cosmic Scale." The first page contained colored reproductions of all twelve zodiac signs with short horoscopic information. For example: "Capricon (Dec. 22–Jan. 19): Firm believers in the right of self-expression Capricorns are often just ahead of the pack in terms of trends. But pragmatism is their strong suit, so down-to-earth cooking with foods in season is the proper way to appease their appetite. Since they are inclined to overindulge in eating and drinking, make sure there is ample food. Their sense of drama as well as their powerful emotions make it appear that Capricorns run hot or cold but they will run hot on foods that grow under the ground. After all, they are an earth sign." There followed on page 2 a recipe for Capricorn's winter vegetable casserole.

It's that kind of information that converts to the cause have been conditioned to want and accept; and the daily newspaper owes some of its prosperity to its performance of the service. The papers tell subscribers what their general characteristics are, what the long-term forecast is and, especially, what is proper day-by-day behavior.

Many papers have run series by noted astrologers to describe the characteristics of the 12 different types of men and women. Sometimes the experts don't exactly agree but they are always entertaining. In her series that ran Oct. 5 to 17, 1969, in *Chicago Today,* Linda Goodman described the Virgo man as "the true individualist, constantly seeking perfection tho he is far from perfect." She warned, "Don't pin your hopes on a Virgo man if your heart is hungry for romantic dreams and fairytales or you'll find yourself on a starvation diet." And, "Do you visualize the Virgo girl as a gently virginal maiden, pure as the driven snow? If you do then you are about to have that illusion shattered."

In a similar series that began Sept. 16, 1973 in the *Chicago Tribune* Mary Daniels quoted the Chicago astrologer Katherine deJersey: "One does not enter into a relationship with a Virgo man lightly. . . Virgo is the technician, the intellectual, the perfectionist. Virgoans can be most unkind with their cutting criticism, but they never seem to be aware that they're hurting others badly . . . Because the Virgo man is so meticulous he will often sort of draw back from sex. You must have an intellect to please a Virgo man."

In still another series in the *Chicago Tribune* from Sept. 1. to Oct. 8, 1974, Mary Daniels quoted deJersey, that the Virgo woman is "the brains of the zodiac, too smart to grow old. She is meticulous, blames others when things are in disarray and is inclined to be old-maidish." Dec. 29, 1974 Daniels used a page to summarize deJersey's forecasts for 1975. For Virgons, she wrote: "Uranus in Saturn is going to mean Virgo people will stretch their minds and their thinking will become more flexible. Jupiter moves into Aries in mid March. Ordinarily that would bring legal or financial settlements, Miss deJersey says, but Saturn blocks Jupiter's financial bonanzas will be held up until October, when it is better in general for Virgons. They've been having splotchy times of it these last few years and the immediate future doesn't look much better. There will be disappointments in love and romance throughout the summer, plus financial disappointments in connection with them."

Just how all this works—the chemistry and physics of the effect the constellations have on millions of people born during the period of one month—nobody, certainly not any newspaper, has tried to explain. The *Skeptical Inquirer,* however, has had several articles telling of the negative results of tests to determine how widespread certain traits are among those who are supposed to have been influenced similarly by the positions of the stars. One of the most important was a four-part report in the Winter 1979–80 issue on the claims of the French Michel and Françoise Gauquelin that there is a correlation between the position of Mars at the time of birth of future sports champions. In one article, Paul Kurtz, Marvin Zelen and George Abell said their study of American sports champions invalidated the Gauquelins' conclusions of a "Mars Effect." There followed a heated controversy. Dennis Rawlins wrote an article, "Starbaby," for the October 1981 issue of *Fate,* in which he charged that the American tests were faulty and the results distorted. He was removed from the editorial board of the *Skeptical Inquirer* by Editor Kendrick Frazier, who had received a letter of resignation from Rawlins, and was not reelected to the committee's Executive Council. He was, however, given space for an article, "Remus Extremus," in the Winter 1981–82 issue of *Skeptical Inquirer,* which was accompanied by a statement from the Executive Council of the Committee for the Scientific Investigation of Claims of the Paranormal and a brief comment by Kurtz and Abell.

In a four-part series that began Jan. 4, 1981, in the *Chicago Sun-Times,* Fran Smith gave day-by-day advice based on what the stars foretold. Virgons were told that because for all 1981 Saturn moves through their solar second house, "rewards will tumble in from more than one source . . . Watch what you do with what you get from Jupiter. For Saturn demands a detailed accounting of all things, incoming and outgoing," and so on. Favorable days and periods are cited. The total impression given is that of a fatalistic, preordained future, a gigantic game being played by a superior player with all the moves planned in advance for eternity. Doesn't seem to be much validity to William Ernest Henley's boast in *Invictus,* "I am the master of my fate; I am the captain of my soul."

June 7, 1981 the *Sun-Times* gave two pages to "Sun Signs in the Sunshine," Fran Smith's "three month cycle of summer holds trends for each sign." Typically she advised: "The summer months affect the sun signs differently. [Summer] activates the individual nature of each sign," etc. Virgo men are told that "all summertime activity must, in some way, be good for you; even when the activity itself has been planned by someone else, you'll find (or manufacture) the good in it. And nothing is wasted."

Oct. 11, 1981 Smith advised that even children born under the same sign can be different and that vital to all is parental love. Mothers and fathers are reminded of their babies' astrological influences and are advised to act accordingly. For instance Virgons are told: "Symbolized by the virgin this sweet child wants only to do the right thing. . . . In schools goes to great lengths to understand everything . . . tendency exists to criticize others (really self) while protecting self from past mistakes," etc. Dr. Spock and all other pediatricians can go out of business as stargazers eliminate the need for them.

Under such headings as "Forecast for Tomorrow" (Rita Del Mar), "Your Stars Today" (Marion Drew), "Horoscope" (Jeane Dixon), "Astrological Forecast" (Sydney Omarr), and "Zodiac Guide" (Cullen Moore), newspapers run daily horoscope columns. Scientifically curious, with as open a mind as possible, I sought to ascertain the potential value to me of a daily horoscope. Specifically, I investigated what the two seers who enlighten the readership of the two Chicago daily newspapers would prophesy for me, an Aquarius (Jan. 20 to Feb. 19) for a given day, July 24, 1978. This is the pertinent part of my Sept. 7, 1978, column in *Chicago Skyline:*

The astrological forecast by Sydney Omarr in the *Sun-Times* follows: "Obtain valid hint from Capricorn message. You locate 'escape hatch.' You are able to utilize knowledge. You receive accolade from neighbor or relative. Your message gets across in meaningful manner. Yes, this trip is necessary."

Naturally it was then necessary to read what the soothsayer had to say about Capricorn (Dec. 22 to Jan. 19): "Foundations solid, despite increased activity, diversions. Element of luck or timing rides with you. Cheerful atmosphere at social function lifts spirit. Gemini, Sagittarius persons figure in scenario."

Possibly the foregoing makes sense to somebody else. To me it is just gibberish. From the perspective of July 25: I obtained no hint, valid or otherwise, from the Capricorn paragraph. I located no "escape hatch," whatever that means.

I'll concede that I used knowledge as does everyone else. I sent nobody a message, meaningful or otherwise. Neither did I contemplate or take a trip. I received no accolade from neighbor or relative or anyone else. I attended no social function with or without a cheerful atmosphere, and my spirits didn't lift noticeably.

The Capricorn horoscope, which supposedly contains a hint for me, is just as unintelligible. What foundation? What activity? What diversion? What timing? So that my spirits wouldn't sag too much, in the spirit of the open-minded researcher, I sought the word of the dean (or is it deaness?) of all the soothsayers, Jeane Dixon, whose living derives in part from the onetime world's greatest newspaper, the *Chicago Tribune*. Said the prophet about what would befall me on July 24, 1978:

"Aquarius (Jan. 20 to Feb. 19): Approach routine tasks with enthusiasm, creativity. Hard work likely to pay off. Superiors are impressed. Concentration level good."

What all of this resembles is the paper inside a fortune cookie or the small piece of cardboard you get when you weigh yourself on a public scale. The ghastly truth, however, is that these forecasters are taken seriously by millions. More important, they probably take themselves seriously.

Devotees want to be told not only about themselves but, perhaps even more important, about the objects of their hero or heroine worship, mostly entertainers of stage and screen, popular musicians, prominent athletes and important public figures. It fortifies worshipers in their own faith in the stars to know that those who make the front-page headlines also have confidence in the zodiac. And everyone in a position to do so—authors, editors, broadcasters and others—do their best to give the public, as they say, what it wants.

In "Why Churchill Had an Astrologer" in *This Week* for Nov. 1, 1959, Christine Hotchkiss not only told the story of how the British Secret Service employed an astrologer to inform them what Adolf Hitler's stargazer probably was advising him, but in addition revealed what the horoscopes of several World War II leaders contained. Franklin D. Roosevelt, for instance, was called "a true humanitarian," a man of great energy interested in the idea of power and possessed of a "magnetic personality and ability to sway the masses." One wonders why it was necessary to consult the inanimate stars to learn those facts.

At least a hundred of the best known personalities in Hollywood consult astrologers at prices ranging from $3 to $100 a phone call or visit according to Joe Hyams in "Why Is Hollywood Horoscope Happy?" in *This Week* for April 22, 1962. "They ask for advice on such matters as what to eat, what to wear, where to live, when to make love," he wrote. Among the amusing anecdotes Hyams related was one that concerned Marilyn Monroe who was told by the famous Carroll Righter, astrologer, that she was born under the same sign as Rosalind Russell, Judy Garland and Rosemary Clooney. Monroe replied: "I know nothing of these people. I was born under the same sign as Ralph Waldo Emerson, Queen Victoria and Walt Whitman."

In her article "Astrology Boom: the Sky's the Limit," in *Parade* for Feb. 9, 1969, Linda Gutstein related that the marriage of Frank Sinatra and Mia Farrow broke up because he did not think much of astrology whereas she was a devotee. Gutstein quoted the teacher of an astrology class studying Mia's horoscope, "It's not the astrologer's fault if things don't turn out. It depends on whether the person responds."

"Psychics Are Flourishing in Southern California, Gaining Social Acceptance Among Middle Class" was a good summary of what Robert Lindsey wrote from Hollywood for the *New York Times* Dec. 15, 1976. It dealt mainly with Kabrina Kinkade and was explicit in naming people who visited psychics and the advice they received. Psychic study groups are widespread, and at least 100 men and women work fulltime at fees of $250 an hour or more.

Tom Smothers put up $175,000 to have Clark Cable's signature restored to the wall outside Earl Carroll's Vanities, the Hollywood hotspot of the depression days. However, the date for the restoration, Dec. 3, 1968, was selected by an astrologer. Gable had opened the nighclub on New Year's Eve in 1938. The club ran into hard times and changed hands more than once in the years to follow.

In Kup's *Chicago Sun-Times* column for Feb. 19, 1981, Irving Kupcinet revealed that a prominent guest at the party honoring Phyllis Diller on the occasion of the Oscar awards, was Katherine deJersey of Chicago, astrologer "without whom the comedian makes very few decisions." Similar statements have been made about many other actors and actresses, including Bette Davis, Robert Cummings, Peter Lawford, Susan Hayward, Le Roi Jones, Marlene Dietrich, Zsa Zsa Gabor and Jackie Gleason, according to an article in the June 3, 1973 *Parade*.

Katherine deJersey, the Chicago astrologer who specializes in marital counseling, had an easy time of it with former first lady Betty Ford. In the *Chicago Tribune* for Aug. 25, 1974 Mary Daniels reported that deJersey considers the Fords a better match than might be expected since she is an Aries—dynamic, expecting goals to be reached immediately if not sooner—whereas her husband is a "soft shelled" Crab, a Cancer—intuitive, good at dealing with people but basically slow, sensitive, and emotional.

During the baseball season of 1972, Dee Taylor wrote a series of what the stars told about local players. Her piece on Bill North of the Cubs began:

Bill North, May 15, 1948; Taurus-Cancer. This young healthy specimen of a man is an interesting mixture of lion and pussycat. He's really more Leo in temperament than Taurus or Cancer, and this gives tremendous drive, aggressiveness and stubbornness to his earthy nature, making him run between timidity and showiness. Bill appears rather conservative, cautious and "set in his ways," then he does a complete about face, "turns on" and comes out on center stage. He loves splender in all things, and when fully mature had the potential for a nobility of his own. He certainly has pride and a cat-like regal bearing that makes his movement a beauty to behold on the field.

Not just what celebrities are like but what they are destined to do is forecast by the journalistic experts on prognostication who also predict events. "What's in Store for These People?" the *New York Post* asked Jan. 6, 1981 and then gave a page to the predictions of 12 psychics who looked ahead until 2001 in *The Book of Predictions* by David Wallechinsky, Amy Wallace, and Irving Wallace. Already one of the dozen celebrities has doublecrossed the seers. They said the now-deceased Moshe Dayan would become Israel's prime minister before 2000. By that year, according to the stargazers, Henry Kissinger will be a United States senator, Yassir Arafat will be assassinated and Billy Graham will have changed his opinion of homosexuals.

Despite the dismal record of those who use the stars in their guesswork (98.8 percent of all *National Enquirer* predictions were wrong, according to the *Chicago Tribune* for Jan. 5, 1981), newspapers almost always report their predictions and activities as straight and important news. Here's some of the record.

French newspapers published the forecasts of the nation's leading astrologers, the UP reported from Paris Dec. 26, 1939: the war would end in 1940 and Adolf Hitler would be assassinated.

New York's *PM* used a story from Denver on July 14, 1942 that A. M. Ziegler, executive secretary of the Astro Scientists, announced at a convention: Hitler died in 1940; Göring died more recently; Himmler, Gestapo chief, was now the No. 1 Nazi; the war would end in 1942 when "an earthquake, a tidal wave or both" would swallow the Axis armies near Jerusalem.

The *Washington Post* gave an entire column June 28, 1949 to a UPI story from New Orleans listing the New Year predictions of Dr. John E. Kieffer, Tulane University political scientist, who explained his method: (1) build an intensified background of the history of governments; (2) subscribe to and read thoroughly the publications distributed by the embassies of various countries and (3) balance the information. So without help from the stars he was able to declare that there would be no war in 1949 between the Sovet Union and the United States.

William D. Laffler wrote enough copy Sept. 13, 1961 for the UPI in New York to fill two columns of a standard-sized newspaper about the prowess of the British astrologer Maurice Woodruff. Despite his arcane verbiage, he seemed to be predicting that England would produce a superweapon, Castro, Nehru or Nasser would be assassinated, Khrushchev would be ousted and the Cleveland Indians would win the 1961 World Series.

When a reader asked Robin Adams Sloan how the seers made out for 1972, he answered in his Gossip Column in the *New York News* for Jan. 28, 1973: "One of the world's most famous astrologers, Maurice Woodruff, turned out to have a very cloudy crystal ball. He said Nixon would barely scrape into office, a Red plot would shake world capitals, Yugoslavia would worry about Tito's health . . . Mrs. Gandhi would lose the premiership of India . . ."

When Woodruff died Dorothy Manners wrote in her syndicated column for Feb. 8, 1973, that at a Hollywood party en route to Singapore, where he had a fatal heart attack, his friends recalled some of his successful predictions, such as Lucille Ball's serious accident while skiing and the death of Aristotle Onassis' son.

The *Chicago Daily News* gave about the same amount of space Dec. 20, 1967 to an interview by Eleanor Lambert of Xavora Pove (real name Rosemary Riccardo, née Schultz from Sandusky, Ohio). In her astrological role she predicted perfection of a device to communicate with denizens of other planets, air pollution to be solved by a simple electronic device, and mankind to learn how to make hair grow thick and stay in and more of the same.

Not to be outdone United Features Syndicate Feb. 10, 1968 distributed a full-length story about Katina Theodission, onetime astrologer for the British royal family who came to the United States to *found* and be research director of the Time Pattern Research Institute at Valley Stream, N.Y. Having fed 18 million pieces of astrological information into an IBM 360 computer, she made it possible to produce a complete horoscope in 60 seconds, whereas 60 hours otherwise would be needed. And so she predicted that President Johnson would be reelected in 1968 over Nelson Rockefeller, a cancer cure would be found, life would be created in the laboratory before 1971 and so on.

In the *Midwest Magazine* supplement to the *Chicago Sun-Times,* May 19, 1968, Linda Rockey prefaced a zodiac chart of the presidential hopefuls that year with a biographical sketch of Nickey Carlton, who revealed she became a convert to astrology "at a time in my life when religion wasn't giving me all the answers. Astrology has the answers—it provides an explanation of existence." A sample of astrological truth, as she saw it, is her comment on Richard M. Nixon: "It's amazing what a fine chart Richard Nixon has regarding his character. As a Capricorn, he is a good hard worker. His only drawback is that he has Neptune in his seventh house, which means he can't come across in as fine shape as he is—i.e., he is good, his image is bad." Now we know what caused Watergate—that nasty Neptune.

"For those who can see them, the course of Jackie Onassis' marriage, more riots in France, something very peculiar for President-elect Nixon and a plummeting stock market all are reflectied in the sky," Ed Wilcox revealed in a full-page article, "It's in the Stars," for the Dec. 29, 1968 issue of *This Week.* It is vagueness of this sort that enables soothsayers to claim after something happens that they forecast it.

When the first lottery in a generation was held for selective service, *Chicago Today* made an astrological breakdown of the first 100 birthdates selected. Under the boxed head "Stars Frown on Scorpios," Dec. 2, 1969 the paper reported:

> It was a bad day for Scorpios as 13 of their birthdays were in the first 100.
>
> The Scorpios' horoscope for Monday warned they had "better be slow and not give vent to hasty word or act. Brighten the dull spots."
>
> Following the Scorpios on the popularity poll were the Sagittarians who had 11 birthdays in the top 100.
>
> Luckiest of all were Pisces.
>
> Only three were in the top category.
>
> "Don't waste time on unworkable projects" is what they were told on Monday, and they probably didn't have to be told twice.

"What Astrology is to Alexandra Mark," according to Otile McManus in the *Boston Globe* for Oct. 3, 1970, "isn't the occult. . . . or fortune telling . . . or predestination. It's a science, the connection between the natural clock and an individual's biological clock." She was encouraged by her husband, chief of neurosurgery at Boston City Hospital.

Chicago Today used a half-page April 4, 1971 to introduce Sybil Leek, self-acclaimed British witch, as author of a weekly column to deal with "specific topics such as creativity, beauty and finances." Of Virgo that day she wrote: "There is rarely enough warmth in your nature to draw people to you easily, but this can be an advantage for you are not likely to go thru life cluttered with people who call themselves friends but are actually only acquaintances."

Not many authors of any kind get the free space in newspapers that those subscribing to the Newhouse News Service gave Paula Dranov's plug for Julia and Derek Parker, co-authors of *The Compleat Astrologer*. In the Jan. 18, 1971 release the Parkers were credited with harboring heretical ideas among fellow stargazers. They belittled the importance of daily horoscopes and insisted that astrology "tells the truth about people . . . because it relies entirely on those factors which make the personality."

When employers and others ceased being reluctant to admit their interest in astrology their public utterances became newsworthy. June 10, 1973 the *Austin* (Tex.) *Statesman* reported that a Fort Worth mechanical engineer, C. R. Apitz, told the Texas Sign Manufacturers Association that astrology can be used to place employees in proper positions. March 25, 1973, the same newspaper quoted Dr. Zipporah Dobyns as telling the Astrologers Guild of Austin that psychologists are increasingly referring patients to astrologers for treatment.

The 1974 Psychic Expo in Chicago's McCormick Place was billed as a "complete learning experience" in the psychic sciences. Frank Zahour revealed in the *Chicago Tribune* for April 8, 1974 that it also was haunted by the demon of commercialism. Jon Miller, the Expo's 31-year-old promoter, told the reporter he got a cut of $2.50 for every person passing through the gate, about as good as the astrological dating service he operated.

A student of astrology seeking information regarding employment possibilities was advised by Joyce Lain Kennedy in the *Chicago Sun-Times* of July 14, 1975 to join the American Federation of Astrologers, whose certification tests it should be possible to pass after five years. "Sooner than you think people will begin asking for readings," said Kennedy.

The right of the now-defunct *Chicago Daily News* to be considered the journalistic leader in covering news of the supernatural was challenged only by the *Suburban Week,* supplement to the *News'* sister publication, the *Sun-Times.* During the years 1975 to 1978 especially, hardly an issue appeared without a page 1 feature, mostly written by Mark Fineman, concerning some clairvoyant, haunted house or astrological prediction. On Oct. 15 & 16, 1975, the headline was "Psychics Foresee Acceptance," over a roundup of optimistic opinions by a dozen or so parapsychologists in the Chicago area, which is "probably more active for psychic happenings than anywhere in the country—even more so than California," according to David Techter, associate editor of *Fate* magazine, published since 1948 in Highland Park to tell "stories of people who make contact with the dead through seances, do experiments in psychic photography, predict the future through clairvoyance and report many other examples of psychic experiences." Another article, "A Magazine That's Out of This World," by Gary Wisby appeared in his Suburban Scene column in the *Sun-Times* for Dec. 14, 1978, based on an interview with Mary Margaret Fuller, *Fate's* editor. Grant Pick wrote "Fate Is in Their Hands," about both Fullers, for *Parade,* March 23, 1982.

Half of Page 1 of the May 26–27, 1976, *Suburban Week* section was devoted to a cabalistic zodiac with Gerald Ford's portrait in the center. The outline was "Astrological data in President Ford's star chart translates into political trouble ahead, according to an Oak Lawn astrologer." The story proper was headlined, "A Ford in your future? Not likely, seer says."

Aug. 4–5, 1976 Ken Swoyer Jr., wrote "Scientists Support Creation," with the overline, "Bible Story True?" Swoyer was quoted as saying, "We accept the Creation account as described in the first two Chapters of Genesis."

"Among psychics and bookies, Ford edges Reagan," according to the streamer headline over Roger Flaherty's story in the Aug. 8, 1976 *Chicago Sun-Times.* A poll of local astrologers and bookies indicated that Ford "just may beat out Ronald Reagan for the Republican presidential nomination." The president drew greater numerically but Reagan produced better vibrations. The nominating conventions over, Mark Fineman reported in the Sept. 8 & 9, 1976 issue, "Astrologer says stars favor Carter." The Oak Lawn authority, Grace K. Morris, was quoted as declaring that a solar eclipse expected Oct. 23 would mean a shift in the popular national issue to Ford's disadvantage.

In the Nov. 3–4, 1976 issue Steve Ginsburg told about Carolle Bailey, one of the first suburban psychics who explained the power she discovered she had at the age of eight: "I concentrate, touch a person's hands and pick up psychic impulses about a person's past and future."

Oct. 15–16, 1977, as related by Deidre Offen, Gloria Petell, a real estate saleswoman, uses astrology and handwriting to advise customers regarding purchases and interior decorating. She says that Leo, Aries and Sagittarius customers are seldom attracted to a conventional house; but Taurus, Virgo and Capricorn persons are very conventional.

For the Dec. 7, 1977 *Suburban Week* Manuel P. Galvan visited the third annual Psychic Fair in suburban Bolingbrook. A sampling of the approximately 100 psychics revealed strong optimism that their beliefs soon would become orthodox. After attending the same fair Bob Greene explained in his column for Dec. 5, 1977 what those beliefs are. Five leading prognosticators accepted his invitation to contribute lists, the most important aspects of which Greene summarized thus: "A huge airliner will crash around Dec. 20 of this year, Idi Amin will be murdered before 1978 is over. Prince Charles of Great Britain will have a sex change. The Leaning Tower of Pisa will collapse. Saboteurs will blow up the Alaska Pipeline." Greene commented: "Yeah, I know, looney tunes. I don't believe it either. But polls show that millions of Americans do believe in psychics and ESP and psychic phenomena."

The idea of a traveling psychic fair was that of Shirley Ann Tabatreck, an advertising executive of Fairfield, N.J. Mark Crane revealed how they work in an Associated Press story Aug. 23, 1981 from Paramus, N.J. A fair is a big money maker for shopping malls where shoppers can patronize clairvoyants, tarot card readers and other seers, with the proceeds shared between the merchants, psychics and Shirley.

Some journalists have written of personal experiences with stargazers. In *Chicago Today* for May 16, 1969 Dorothy Storck told of a luncheon with her friend Michelle Carleton, who explained that Dorothy's being late was not because of the loss of a button from her dress and the jamming of the drawer of the desk that contained her purse. Rather the friendly seer explained, "It's that retrograde Mars. It's in your seventh house." The rest of the column-long piece was a labeling of all the men in the Wrigley restaurant! "Very Gemini." Not an iconoclastic word from Storck but plenty of chuckles for the cynic from the straightforward account.

In the Jan. 15, 1970 *Chicago Daily News,* Miriam Perrone told of having lunch with her college roommate, whom she hadn't seen for twenty years. The old friend, now a professional astrologer, interpreted every word or deed as determined by the stars. In his Jan. 8, 1970 column Mike Royko related an annoying experience of reading the restaurant placemat with generalized horoscopes. A Virgo, he read: "You have a logical analytical and precise mind, which causes you to hate disorder. You must guard against being cold, unemotional and fault finding." Mike insisted that he is really muddy, sloppy, sweet tempered, compassionate, gentle and kind and lamented the fact he was not born a few weeks earlier so as to be a "born leader, bold, energetic, proud and ambitious." The rest of the column was a satire on himself. In his Jan 22, 1970 column Royko condemned the growing practice of personnel managers' using standard horoscopes when considering job applicants.

The forecasts for 1971 of Sybil Leek, the British "witch" who authored a monthly column in the *Ladies Home Journal,* and Linda Goodman, author of *Sun-Signs,* were presented at length by Sally Quinn in the *Washington Post* for Jan. 3, 1971. Highlights of their prophecies follow:

President Nixon will be involved in a major scandal in October that will take him out of the running in 1972.

George Wallace will be the dark horse in the presidential race.

Ramsey Clark, siding with youth on the drug issue, will be the sacrificial lamb politically next year.

Mrs. Onassis will raise eyebrows with flamboyant behavior.

Sen. Edward Kennedy will be betrayed by friends connected with drugs and alcohol during the first part of the year.

Spiro Agnew's power will increase in the next eight years.

Editors say they give the public what it wants by using such news.

Here are some of the forecasts for 1980 that Gary Wayne, Palatine stargazer, made for Larry Weintraub who wrote a long feature for the *Chicago Sun-Times* of Dec. 31, 1979:

Generally mild winter but with lots of snow and cold about Feb. 16; inflation to hit 17 or 18 per cent; unleaded gasoline to $2.35 a gallon by August; Carter to be reelected, his popularity restored by his handling of the Iran situation; Kennedy to withdraw in June or July for health reasons; political violence to occur often, in New Hampshire, Illinois and probably Oregon or Washington state; Khomeini's reign in Iran to end in August, probably by assassination.

Not adverse to consulting psychics to aid political reporters, the *Chicago Tribune* gave a half-page Aug. 25, 1974 to "What do the stars have in store for President Ford—and for us?"

In his *Tribune* column for Sept. 18, 1980 Jack Mabley reported one of the craziest scenarios of that presidential election year. Ruth Montgomery, he reported, foresaw Robert C. Byrd, majority leader of the Senate, as the next president with Walter Mondale as vice-president, after independent candidate John Anderson forced the decision into the House of Representatives.

The election over, Dec. 30, 1980 Mabley wrote: "Ted Kennedy is not the president-elect, much to the surprise of seven psychics, or Supermarket

Seers. The *National Enquirer* has ten psychics in its stable. Its major competitor, the *Star,* relies on Jeane Dixon." Then came Jack's analysis of the forecasts and results. He counted 62 predictions in the *Enquirer* and "not one was on the mark unless Lassie has been kidnapped and we haven't heard about it yet."

In his Dec. 12, 1975 column Mabley had sarcastically written that he wanted to know the 1976 predictions of Dr. Gil E. Gilly of Phoenix who had forecast there would be a suicide in the White House during 1975, Margaret Chase Smith would be appointed to the Supreme Court and Patty Hearst was a dope addict.

The same paper carried Dear Abby's answer April 19, 1982 to a reader who wanted to know "when and where astrology originated and who keeps this nonsense going?" The reader was tired of being asked, "What's your sign?" and of a friend who dropped her because one was a Libra, the other a Scorpio. Abby traced the origin of the "nonsense" from before 2000 B.C. in Babylonia to the present. Horoscopes began appearing in English newspapers in the 1930s and soon spread around the journalistic world. Scientists, she wrote, consider astrology hogwash but many people take it seriously or as good fun. It's harmless unless believers and nonbelievers come to blows over it.

Not all columnists are so brave. Ann Landers, for instance, told a reader who inquired about the validity of astrology Oct. 30, 1973: "Several readers have written to say, 'A plague on all your houses,' but I am not so quick to pass judgment on a subject that has so many supporters. Thanks for writing."

When Lawrence E. Jerome's book, *Astrology Disproved,* was published in 1977, most reviewers merely summarized its contents—briefly. Carol Olsen in the Phoenix *Arizona Republic* wrote, "Astrologers and their followers will now have even more reason to consider Jerome their 'chief enemy.' " But Robert Allen ended his column in *Science News:* "We have personally believed that astrology and all of its accoutrements represent one of the most insidious rip-offs to which modern man is subject."

To offset such news of failure the press avidly plays up success stories. For example, *Chicago Today* ran Ellen Holstein's story of a Skokie astrologer, Eileen Appleton, who successfully predicted that Ellen's son would take a trip. Sure enough, the boy's aunt sent him a round-trip ticket to visit her in California.

The *Chicago Daily News'* News Lady for the day, Lucille Ernst, a Hoffman Estates housewife, confessed to greater peace of mind after embracing astrology to learn about herself. She cited several friends who had similar experiences, including a "regular guy" who became silent and easily hurt after learning he was a Pisces.

How an astrologer helped select the jury to try Joan Little on a charge of murdering a prison guard she said raped her, was told by Joyce Wadler, in the *New York Post* for Aug. 1, 1975. The stargazer, Richard Wolf, felt that a venirewoman's attitude suggested her husband was playing around and probably caused her to blame younger women as seducers. The voir dire disclosed that she was prejudiced against the defendant who was subsequently acquitted.

Feb. 19, 1976 the *Chicago Sun-Times* published an astrological guide to the presidental candidates that year. It amounted to no more than listing the zodiac sign for the candidates. Frank Lombardi went further when he reported "How it stacks up for the astrological vote" for mayor in the *New York Daily News* for July 28, 1977. Among the seven Democrats and two Republican contenders there were three Sagittarians, for instance, who "in their emotional makeups are supposed to be aggressive, adventurous, jealous, unconventional and not too loyal" and so on for all the hopefuls. Nothing about their records or stands on issues.

In an interview with the *Chicago Daily News* fashion editor, Patricia Shelton, for publication in the issue of June 29, 1976, Joyce Jillson, astrological forecaster on the "A.M. Los Angeles" television show, advised stuffing fat men with love to cause them to lose weight. The nearly-a-full-page article is mostly advice for men according to the zodiac influence, as Aries men should join exercise clubs, Taurus men should eat big mostly when they have financial good luck, etc.

From Miami the *New York Times* reported July 26, 1976 on the first annual conference on science and parapsychology sponsored by the University of Miami School of Continuing Studies. One of the main purposes was said to be "to separate the genuine from the quackery." The University of Miami already had courses in parapsychology.

A way to beat the stars was explained in the *New York Village Voice* for March 14, 1977. "Even if you were born under a bad sign, now you can remove yourself to a place where things are going to be quite different," says Jim Lewis, inventor of Astro-Carto-Graphy, which provides people with maps of astrological power zones, "lucky cities, states or regions as determined from the position of the planets in relation to the geography of the earth at the exact moment of birth."

Kathy Megan interviewed local astrologer Scott Andrick for what was tantamount to a lesson in elementary astrology in the *Charleston* (W.Va.) *Gazette* for Feb. 6, 1980. Using the date and time of birth and birthplace of a person or nation, Andrick computes a series of trigonometric calculations based on the angles among the planets. From there the study diverges from science because every astrologer will interpret these calculations differently. Andrick would not say that the Russian invasion of Afghanistan in 1979 was in the stars but he did say the alignment of planets reflected a tendency among Russians for such a strategy.

It apparently is not a matter of deciding what should be done; rather, individuals and nations should merely ask astrologers to tell them what they're going to do anyway.

Feb. 12, 1982 Ron Hutchison updated the Scott Andrick story in the

Charleston Daily Mail, with emphasis upon his use of planetary charting as a counseling indicator. Andrick obtains the basic data about place and exact time of birth before he meets a client, and so makes early progress in diagnosing his needs. Frederick Hufford, director of outpatient service for Shawnee Hills Community Mental Health–Mental Retardation Center, said the charts "are nothing we use here."

Dec. 28, 1980 Bill Plunkett reproduced the predictions of Kathy Minier for 1981. The closest guess was that the hostages would be home from Iran in February, a matter already negotiated before her stargazing. Contrary to Minier's forecasts DeBartolo did not buy the White Sox baseball team, Richard Nixon did not play an important role in American relations with China and John Lennon's accused killer did not commit suicide.

There is no rational disproof of astrology, Nick Lawrence told Laurence Eighner, reporter for the *Daily Texan,* student newspaper of the University of Texas. Lawrence made no predictions but said, "We do not know exactly why it works, but astrology cannot be disproved on a statistical basis." No attempt was made by the student editors to find someone on their faculty who might disagree. Instead, the undergraduates acted as professional journalists in treating astrology as a sure thing, hardly controversial, at least not in the press.

In a eulogistic piece in her *New York Daily News* column Dec. 16, 1981, Suzy quoted friends of Richard M. Nixon as saying that the former president has "the marvelous mind of a true Capricorn survivor."

"The greatest gathering of astrologers the world has ever known," about 2,700 in all, met for a week in San Francisco with John Peterson covering it for the *National Observer* of Aug. 24, 1974. He noted the effort of soothsayers to improve their reputation by avoiding far-out predictions and "hocus pocus interpretations of life and death," but then he enumerated some of the prophecies at the convention such as that Saturn was to blame for droughts, floods, poor crops, and tornadoes that worsened the United States' economic condition. Membership in the American Federation of Astrologers was announced as about 12,000.

The activities and predictions of foreign astrologers and their gullible devotees are considered newsworthy by many American editors. When William Tucker, president of the Federation of British Astrologers, predicted that Princess Margaret would marry in 1960, the Associated Press cabled the news to America Jan. 6, 1959.

A decade later, Dec. 16, 1969, the *Chicago Daily News* used a dispatch from its correspondent, Milt Freudenheim, in Paris that French soothsayers predicted that Jackie and Aristotle Onassis would divorce, British Prince Charles would have a serious love affair and Pope Paul VI would permit some priests to marry.

For 1970 French astrologers wrongly predicted that Brigitte Bardot would be kidnapped, Jackie Onassis would have both a baby girl and a divorce and Elizabeth II would abdicate. For 1971 their prophecies included a 100-carat diamond for Jackie, victory in an important fight for Muhammad Ali, who, however, would be exiled from America to Africa, and a shift of attention by Bardot from young to older men.

Elizabeth II's abdication also was forecast by British astrologer Maurice Woodruff, the Canadian Press reported Feb. 20, 1973. Woodruff also saw an engagement for Princess Anne and royal family concern over one of its elderly members.

The *Chicago Daily News* devoted almost one-third of a page July 21, 1973, to an interview its correspondent Georgie Anne Geyer obtained with Egypt's most famous astrologer, Youssef El Meniawy, who predicted that Nixon would not fill out his term but mysteriously added, "But it will not be because he resigns." The seer, who is consulted by dignitaries throughout the Mideast, predicted that followers of exiled King Constantine would overthrow the Greek government, General Francisco Franco would relinquish leadership of his country, and the Suez Canal would be reopened.

Another Egyptian was written up by Michael S. Barret of the UPI from Cairo Sept. 22, 1974. He was Hussein Climy, known as the Erudite Astrologer. He presumably forecast Nixon's resignation, the deaths of Presidents Nasser of Egypt and DeGaulle of France and the dates and outcomes of two Israeli-Arab wars. Now he was predicting a third war with nuclear weapons. He also predicted that in March or April of 1975 Vice-President Nelson Rockefeller would take over the White House and Northern Ireland would become a separate state when the British left before 1980.

From Beirut, Lebanon Oct. 26, 1974 Georgie Anne Geyer had a second interview with Meniawy, who this time predicted another Arab-Israeli war before the end of 1975.

Two of France's best-known mystics were not surprised when they were charged with nonpayment of $56,000 in taxes. Reuters reported Jan. 14, 1976 from Paris that Mrs. Germaine Sobell said she was "expecting difficulties because Cancer will be under the bad influence of Saturn until the spring."

The predictions in the 280th edition of *Old Moore's Almanack* were reported from London by UPI Dec. 26, 1976." Queen Elizabeth II will step down and her son will succeed her; floods, earthquakes, bank crashes and political and military turmoil just about everywhere."

In the *Chicago Sun-Times* for Oct. 29, 1978 Judith Morgan told of visiting the in-house astrologer, R. Ramakishna Sarathy, at the Ashoka Hotel in New Delhi. She concluded: "This astro-palmist was startlingly accurate about my past. Of the future, who knows? But if he is right, romance is assured, my doctors won't have much business and, six months from now, I may or may not be writing this column. Maybe I should get a second reading from my editor."

Although Ronald Reagan was starting his presidency, the year 1981 was to be the year of British Prime Minister Margaret Thatcher, according to *Old Moore's Almanack* for 1981, the UPI reported Dec. 28, 1980 from

London. The venerable publication, founded in the 1680s, explained that seldom does one man or woman shape the destiny of the world in any one year, but Mrs. Thatcher's prowess derives from the "epochal conjunction of Jupiter and Saturn in Libra at the start of the year coinciding with Mrs. Thatcher's Mars in Libra."

From Prague Aug. 24, 1974 the AP reported that an amateur astrologer was sentenced to three years in prison and fined $900 for "illicit undertakings and parasitism," meaning he made about $5,000 preparing horoscopes.

In the United States the Internal Revenue Service for Manhattan announced in October 1979 that the National Astrological Society would be tax exempt because it announced a racially nondiscriminatory policy on admissions.

The *Sun-Times* Action Time for Jan. 22, 1975 answered a reader's inquiry concerning the Chinese belief in the inheritance of the good qualities of animals in years named for them. From Oct. 17 to 29, 1974 the *Sun-Times* ran a series on "Chinese Chance." A typical paragraph was the following which pertained to the years of the Rat—1960, 1972, 1984, and so on, every 12 years: "Rats are seductive, energetic, of good counsel, charming, meticulous, social, jolly, persistent, humorous, intellectual, lovable, sentimental, generous and honest."

After Suzanne White's *Chinese Chance* was published in 1976, the *Chicago Daily News'* Michael Dixon gave it a quarter-page review. He explained: "The theory is that over every 12 year period there is a recurring cycle of financial boom, recession, famine, drought, etc. Each year is endowed with certain characteristics as to the kind of events that will take place, and the character of the people born."

The twelve animals are those that visited the dying Buddha. Jan. 1, 1982, in the Year of the Dog, the *Chicago Sun-Times* facetiously editorialized to hope it would be a Sophia Loren Year instead of a Charles Bronson Year, especially since the following year would be that of the boar and "the dreaded Orwellian 1984 comes after that as the Year of the Rat."

When a Chinese dies his burial may not take place for weeks or months until an astrologer has determined the exact moment the spirit will, visibly, leave the corpse. The calculations are intricate, requiring an expert, and his divining rod is called a *feng shui,* a kind of astrological compass. In the *New York Times* for Sept. 22, 1974, there was a lengthy article by David Saltman telling of his search on several continents for a *feng shui* for his collection. His quest failed, but he finally saw one in the Lewis Museum of Anthropology in Berkeley, Calif.

The item "Lucky Dick" led off the "Parade's Special" column edited by Lloyd Shearer, in *Parade* for Feb. 6, 1972. It read: "When President Nixon arrives in Peking on Feb. 21, his planned arrival date, he should meet with good luck. According to Chinese tradition, the omens for a successful mission are excellent. Feb. 21 falls on the seventh and most auspicious day of the 10-day Chinese New Year season."

To usher in the Year of the Dog, the AP reported on Dec. 29, 1981, from Tokyo, that Japanese temple bells would ring 188 times, one for each of the passionate sins of mankind. To be born during the year means to have a deep sense of duty and loyalty but too often it means fault-finding and stubbornness. In addition to Sophia Loren the list of celebrities born in a Year of the Dog include Jack Anderson, Shelley Winters, Van Cliburn, Hank Aaron and Norman Vincent Peale.

When Louise Brown, the first test-tube baby, was born in London, the UPI reported July 28, 1978, the assurance of Katina, the *Evening Standard's* stargazer, that the baby's lifetime prospects were good. The stars showed that she had been impatient to be born and indicated she is a strong willed, self-confident individual well able to make success out of life.

Two days later Christine Adrienne, an astrologer, explained that the child was born under the astrological sign of Leo and therefore "will tend to be magnanimous, fun-loving and often the center of attention." The first of five more paragraphs that the *Chicago Sun-Times* used July 30, 1978, read: "The moon, which represents one's personality, was in the exciting sign of Aries at Louise's birth, indicating she will have a decidedly optimistic and uninhibited temperament."

"Signs are There: Marriage May Truly be Heaven-Sent" was the headline the *Chicago Tribune* gave Dec. 21, 1980 to a half-page article from London by the paper's correspondent there, William Mullen. The story's content related to the findings by Beverly Steffert after a three-year study for the London Institute of Psychiatry that showed marriages are happiest when the partners have the same astrological signs. The research was conducted in Scotland, where hours of birth are given on birth certificates and in southern England where such is not the case. More than 500 couples cooperated by rating their marriages. Steffert said she changed from a skeptic to a believer in astrology as a predictor of personality.

Publication of *Nostradamus: Historian and Prophet,* with updated interpretations by Jean Charles de Fontbrune was a sensation, the Associated Press reported from Paris Aug. 23, 1981. After citing a number of historical events that the 16th-century astrologer supposedly forecast, the new scholar unraveled the seer's thoughts on the late 20th century to mean: there will be a Soviet-Arab invasion of Western Europe, then a major conflict with China followed by a "golden age."

When an obscure astrologer in India forecast that Prime Minister Indira Gandhi would be assassinated or killed in an automobile accident, he was taken into custody by police. In Parliament he was charged with being part of a conspiracy to create anarchy and confusion in a country where prophecies are taken seriously. Stuart Auierback sent a long story on the situation to his newspaper, the *Washington Post,* which published it Dec. 23, 1981.

Regardless of what some high officials think, what the *New York Times* correspondent William Stevens concluded to be the situation was summarized in the headline the paper gave to his account Jan. 4, 1983, "In the Computer Age, India Still Consults the Stars."

A potential setback to the growth of the army of astrology believers was an article in *Christianity Today* by J. A. Sargent, pastor of the English Worthing Tabernacle. According to the *Chicago Sun-Times* for Feb. 4, 1983 Sargent wrote that the Bible "sternly forbids" Christians to dabble in astrology. Such is so because astrology is basically polytheistic and "a prostitution of revealed religion [and] reduces man to the level of a pawn."

2

Astrologers

There probably is not a city, town, village or hamlet without its astrologer. Since there is no registration, certification or licensing required, anyone can call him/herself an astrologer, tell fortunes and participate in what is estimated to be a multi-million dollar business.

Some seers enjoy fame outside their own communities. This is especially true of the handful whose prognostications are syndicated and appear in scores or hundreds of newspapers and magazines. Some of them are as much celebrities as the movie stars and other public figures about whom they make forecasts.

Patriarch of the Hollywood colony of stargazers is Carroll Righter, a onetime Philadelphia lawyer who began to study astrology to debunk it but became converted to belief in it instead. In 1938 he moved to the motion picture capital because his horoscope indicated the climate would be better for his injured back. Within a year he had a long list of actors and actresses that included Marlene Dietrich, Zsa Zsa Gabor, Jackie Gleason, Robert Cummings, Faye Dunaway, Susan Hayward, Steve McQueen, Peter Lawford, Lana Turner, Joan Fontaine, Dick Powell, Arlene Dahl and many others. For years Righter gave lavish parties for hundreds to welcome each new sign of the zodiac. He calls himself "the gregarious Aquarian" and says, "The answer to any question can be found in the stars," according to Diane Monk's story about him in the *Chicago Daily News* for Oct. 30, 1969. That paper was one of approximately 300 that used his daily horoscope.

Righter receives an estimated 10,000 phone calls a year, according to Joe Hyams' article, "Why Is Hollywood Horoscope Happy?" in *This Week* for April 22, 1962. His clients call at all hours of the day and night to ask advice on what days and/or hours would be best to sign a contract, undergo an operation, take a trip or engage in many other types of activity. Iconoclastically, Mort Weisinger recalled in his article "Is Astrology a $100-million Hoax?" in *Parade* for June 3, 1973, that Righter failed to warn any of his film colony luminaries about a forthcoming earthquake and that his predictions of marital bliss failed to materialize in the cases of the Zsa Zsa Gabor–George Sanders and Linda Christian–Tyrone Power marriages.

In a comprehensive story on the extent of the astrology fad in Hollywood July 28, 1968 the Associated Press revealed that Righter and some other prominent stargazers served only celebrities. Aspiring actors and actresses generally patronized the Astrological Metaphysics Institute, which provides horoscopes for $30 apiece.

Diane Monk revealed in her piece about Righter that "he forgets a name but never a sign," explaining that the seer addresses people by their zodiac signs rather than their names. Righter also made a 12-record album, "Astromusical Houses," one record for each of the 12 signs of the zodiac so all could select a record "to suit the mood." Following another interview with Righter, Monk wrote a lengthy feature April 23, 1969 on "Mr. Daley, a 'Bull,' " the horoscope of Chicago's Mayor Richard J. Daley, a Taurus. She thought the seer's description of Daley resembled what was generally thought about him, but Righter denied he was influenced by anything but the stars.

In a profile of Righter in the *Los Angeles Times* for January 15, 1975, David Larson quoted his subject as believing, "even if the planets have no effect, the fact that so many people believe that they do is influence in itself."

Typical of the advice Righter concocts daily is the following for June 21, 1969, for Virgoans: "Don't get involved in your new interest without more study or you won't be able to handle problems that arise. This is a good day to investigate thoroughly much that is vital to your welfare." The same day, on the same page, another Hollywood soothsayer, Sidney Omarr, told Virgoans: "There is more social activity than you expected. More distractions. Leave details for another day. Ride with the tide. Be sociable—enjoy yourself. Friends make fine gesture."

At least it can be said that few if any are likely to be injured by either of these forecasts.

In announcing its adoption of the Omarr daily column Aug. 9, 1970 the *Chicago Sun-Times* said that its six months' experiment with computerized horoscopes had not been satisfactory. When it announced its adoption of Astrodata editorially March 3, 1970 the paper hailed it as the first change in thousands of years in the methods by which horoscopes are made. Strangely, a decade later than the Omarr acquisition, Sept. 2, 1980, the paper published an Associated Press story from Danvers, Mass., under the three-column headline, "Computer Edges Out Crystal Ball." The story told that astrologers had just discovered the new way of doing things and had introduced it at the annual conference of the National Astrological Society.

Nevertheless, the *Sun-Times* has stuck with Omarr. A showman, as is Righter, Sidney Omarr insists that "people confuse astrology with fortune telling." "You don't have to be psychic to be an astrologer though intuition helps," he said. "But you do have to be a writer, historian and mathematician. The public doesn't realize this."

Omarr has many Hollywood stars as clients, but he declines to name them, saying that psychiatrists don't tell who their patients are either.

In addition to Righter, the *Sun-Times* also uses the horoscopes of its home talent, Irene Hughes, in its *Suburban Week*. It also relies on her for periodic comments on current events; and it and its sister paper, the now-defunct *Daily News*, were generous with free publicity. It headlined Lois Wille's half-page profile June 22, 1968, "She sees the future—sometime" with an underline, "Irene Hughes, blending luck and psychology, prospers on others' faith in her powers of extrasensory perception." Wille cited Hughes' Jan. 3, 1967, forecast of a terrible blizzard, which occurred three weeks later. On the other hand Hughes forecast that Michigan Gov. George Romney would be elected president in 1968.

Later that year Hughes made the second prophecy, which, with the blizzard forecast, is always cited to prove her prowess. That was her prediction that Lyndon B. Johnson would not run for reelection in 1968. Those were her two major successes. Her most persistent predictions have been that the Chicago Cubs will win the National League baseball pennant and that a major earthquake will devastate California, especially the San Francisco Bay area. Both of these forecasts were made in speeches that Diane Monk covered for the *Daily News* March 25, 1969.

In his Feb. 8, 1967 column in the *Chicago American,* the usually skeptical Jack Mabley gave Hughes credit for correctly forecasting the big blizzard in the Jan. 18 edition of a suburban paper. He reported that she got messages or images of future events and also has periods of quiet contemplation during which the same happens. Mabley did add that she has had her share of bloopers, many of which he cited.

June 28, 1967 the *American* reported on a meeting of the Illinois Society for Psychic Research, at which Hughes stated that Lee Harvey Oswald was under complete mental control by the Russians when President Kennedy was assassinated.

In its magazine for Dec. 10, 1967 the *Chicago American* used a series of Hughes predictions concerning prominent Chicago and Illinois residents as a sidebar to a feature by Glenda Daniel entitled, "The Supernatural Finds New Believers."

Somewhat offsetting the generous quantity of favorable publicity given her by the press was an article by a leading banker and radio performer, Norman Ross, in the *Chicago Daily News* for March 20, 1968. It began, "Anyone anxious to peer into the future would be wise not to heed the predictions of Chicago Heights clairvoyant Irene Hughes." Thereafter he enumerated several of Hughes's worst mistakes.

The journalistic pendulum swung back in her favor, however, when Basil Talbot wrote in the *Chicago American* for April 1, 1968: "Two of the three local mystics who engage in predictions of major happenings today were saying 'I told you so.' " The reason was President Johnson's announcement that he would not seek reelection. Hughes and Clifford M. Royce had guessed correctly on that one. Joseph deLouise had been wrong.

Indicative of the prestige Irene Hughes nevertheless attained was the half-page feature that Don DeBat wrote for the *Daily News* Sept. 20, 1968, "Buy Home in '69, Says Psychic," with advice on what to buy and/or sell in real estate.

Hughes was featured in the *Sun-Times Midwest Magazine* Dec. 22, 1968 with the only important prediction being that there would be no moon-landing in 1969. Also identified were a half-dozen other local soothsayers, one of whom, Prof. Henry Y. Dutton, shared Hughes's optimistic belief that the Cubs would win the league pennant and possibly the World Series. Dutton began his contribution to the symposium on what 1969 would bring, "I would predict that Richard M. Nixon will be a dynamic president."

The Publicity Club of Chicago was treated to "The Medium With a Message," to quote the headline over Ron Powers's article in the *Sun-Times* for Jan. 15, 1970. Parts of the message follow: talk to your plants, they understand; once some live shrimp were dropped into boiling water and nearby plants recoiled in horror; the Russians have trained dogs by telepathy and the Germans have photographed spirits. In its report of the same speech *Chicago Today* emphasized Hughes' predictions that miniskirts were on the way out, Adlai Stevenson would be elected senator, and Mayor Daley would never again run for public office.

In a speech at Northern Illinois University in DeKalb, according to Bob Herguth's column in the *Chicago Daily News* for July 18, 1971, Hughes predicted that Nixon would serve only one term, the next Apollo mission would "get off to a bad start," America would never be socialist, violence on campuses would end in 1973, and World War III could start this month or next in Rumania.

Hughes' reputation received a boost from the story James H. Bowman, religion editor, wrote for the *Daily News* of May 19, 1973. She correctly spelled the name of Bowman's mother—Kathryn—and foretold that Bowman planned a trip to Vancouver, Canada.

Her prestige was deflated, however, by Anita Clark's article, "Prophet Sharing in Her Style," in the *Chicago Tribune* for Aug. 16, 1974. It began: "One of the most popular predictions by Irene Hughes was destroyed when President Nixon resigned. Hughes, a Chicago psychic and astrologer, had said many times that Nixon would serve his full term of office. The failure confirmed the view of skeptics who believe Hughes is a clever businesswoman and a good entertainer but not a talented psychic." The *Trib* poured it on by citing other occasions on which the stars doublecrossed Hughes. She had predicted that Chicago's Mayor Daley would be reelected and that when he decided to give up his office his successor would be a young Republican lawyer. Actually Mayor Daley dropped dead in 1977 and was succeeded by a councilman, Michael Bilandic, to fill out his term. Jane Byrne defeated him for the full four-year term in 1979. Hughes had said that Pope Paul would resign between the end of November 1974 and June 1975 and that his successor would have fewer powers. Pope Paul died in 1978 and his successors, Popes John Paul I and II, seem to be exercising more power than any other pontiffs during this century.

Two months later, Oct. 25, 1974 the friendly *Daily News* cited some of Hughes' most important successful predictions in an article by David Israel: "In late 1963 she predicted Jackie Kennedy would remarry 'an older man—a father figure.' In 1965 she said Lyndon Johnson wouldn't seek reelection in 1968. She predicted there would be a major earthquake in Iran last spring and there was. She predicted the exact dates of the blizzard of 1967 here." All and this and more means, she claims, 90 percent correct forecasts.

Hughes has had good luck getting one-liners or their equivalent in the gossip columns. Maggie Daly reported in her *Chicago Today* column for Feb. 9, 1972: "Hughes, the ESP lady, told us this about the Northern Ireland question: 'I have the feeling of gloom . . . a terrible war involving other nations . . . don't see an end to it.' " In her Sept. 12, 1971 space Daly wrote: "Irene Hughes, the ESP lady, who is currently touring Italy, Greece and Egypt will hold a spiritual retreat aimed at increasing spiritual awareness Oct. 8–10 near Elgin, Ill."

Chicago Today's Action Line answered queries about Hughes. March 11, 1972 it told someone who wanted the seer's address to look in the telephone directory. When a reader asked, "why you gave someone like that free publicity," the column replied, "If we can help people in some of the nutty requests we get, we don't see too much harm in passing along Irene Hughes' phone number." Then, however, the editor added that a reporter was assigned to have a session with the seer. After several other wrong guesses, Hughes said the reporter was finishing a book. He concluded his comment, "I'm afraid she didn't make me enough of a believer to write one about her, and I don't see myself writing any other."

In his June 4, 1973, column in the *Chicago Daily News,* Bob Herguth reported: "Irene Hughes (ESP) will hostess special VIP lunches each Tuesday at La Margarita del Norte (first guest this week is Pat O. Block of civil defense who'll discuss quakes and floods)."

Aug. 30, 1973 Mort Edelstein was a bit irreverent in his column when he wrote: "Clairvoyant Irene Hughes interviewed two men at the President's Restaurant in the First National Plaza Wednesday but failed to predict that an hour later they would be held up at gunpoint in their Old Town apartment. Better wash your crystal ball, Irene."

More complimentary were Aaron Gold's remarks in his *Chicago Tribune* column for Oct. 12, 1973: "If you watched ABC's Kennedy & Co. July 16 and Kennedy at Night on July 17, you would have heard Irene Hughes tell the Kennedys that Vice-President Spiro Agnew would resign in November. Her dates were wrong but not her facts. Score 20 points for Miss Hughes."

The followup was in Kup's Column in the *Sun-Times* for Oct. 12, 1973: "We've been flooded with calls from seers who now claim they predicted Agnew's resignation. One who did is Irene Hughes (on the Ch. 7 Bob Kennedy show of July 17)."

The *Chicago Sun-Times,* which uses Hughes' guesses, gave her and family three pages in its magazine for Oct. 29, 1978. About the only new facts that Jane Gregory gave pertained to Hughes' country home and her four children and six grandchildren surrounded by pets.

Usually in its *Suburban Week* supplement the *Sun-Times* annually devotes a page or two to Irene's guesses for the future. Some of them in recent years follow: 1975—a team of respected scientists will investigate a ghost in the White House and conclude it is a genuine example of the paranormal. 1976—high officials of the American, Soviet and Chinese governments will die; Ronald Reagan will cause chaos at the Republican convention and Nelson Rockefeller "just may be the next president." 1977—Quebec will split from Canada; the governments of West Germany and Taiwan will fall; Denver will ban auto traffic; Carter will establish wage-price controls. 1978—UFOs are coming closer and probably will land in 1978 or 1979; the pyramids will give up new treasures; there will be breakthroughs in discovering the causes of cancer and arthritis; someone will be brought back from the dead through massive injections of a newly discovered medication. 1979—Mayor Bilandic will be reelected; Liz Taylor won't like being a senator's wife and will return to a former husband; Jackie Onassis will find her true love; there'll be a new sports stadium near Comiskey Park. Jan. 1, 1979 the *Sun-Times* streamer-headlined "What 3 psychics see in '79; it's mostly woe." The three seers were Hughes, David Hoy and Sydney Omarr and among their predictions were these: President Carter would be reelected in 1980, the Equal Rights Amendment would be passed by three more states and become the law and Soviet missiles would be discovered a few miles from Alaska.

Hughes made news in the *Suburban News* July 7, 1976 when she predicted that the Regional Transportation Authority would be reorganized, thus hopefully ending the political hassle regarding it in the Illinois General Assembly. It was wishful thinking and the RTA continued to be a political football.

Nov. 3, 1976 Irene received a brief press notice for congratulating Gov. James Thompson while reminding him she had forecast his election victory. Jan. 14, 1979 George Lazarus covered the Super Market Institute in Miami at which Hughes said there would be a sharp decline in the stock market in March and no upward trend in the market could be expected before August 1980. The delegates, all considered experts, were there to learn from her.

Hughes' most startling predictions for 1980 included the following: Ed Asner to quit show business to edit a newspaper he would buy in Canada; Barbara Walters to be fired by ABC for slanting a news program to favor Fidel Castro; Suzanne Somers to be kidnapped in May and held for $1 million ransom. However, FBI agents would capture the kidnappers and release Somers after she spent three days in a log cabin in northern California.

Hughes lost some devoted believers when she filed a $50,000 personal injury law suit against American Airlines because an overhead light reflector came loose and hit her on the head as she was boarding a plane from Chicago to Phoenix. The stars had failed to warn her. She recovered, however, to make her year-end forecasts for 1982. They were published Dec. 18, 1981 and forecast that there would be a mild epidemic (unnamed) but that ways to cure it will be known; the Soviet Union will make another military move; the stock market will edge up now and around Dec. 26 but then it will go into mild tantrums; the weather will be bad and welfare cuts will make news again.

When Hughes was fired from her morning fortune-telling program after many years, Gary Deeb took pleasure in writing in his *Sun-Times* column for April 7, 1982, that it was because an audience-research survey showed that many listeners disliked her intensely.

The astrologer-prophet considered by most to be the nation's best undoubtedly is Jeane Dixon whose most important prediction presumably was the assassination of President John F. Kennedy. The claim derives from a statement she made to the author of an article in *Parade* in 1956, that "a blue-eyed Democratic president elected in 1960 would die in office" as all preceding presidents elected in years divisible by 20 had done since Millard Fillmore. Although some friends say she was more definite in private conversation, in 1960 she publicly predicted that Richard M. Nixon would be elected.

Another oft-repeated boast is that Dixon predicted the great power-failure of 1965 in New York and New England. The basis for this claim was a vision that a Russian satellite would pass over the United States and cause the lights to go out. Ruth Montgomery, who had been associated with Dixon for years, helping to prepare her annual New Year's predictions, wrote *A Gift of Prophecy* and it was the prodigious sale of that book that gave Dixon her biggest boost to fame. Thereafter when Dixon said any sooth, whether in a syndicated article for which newspapers paid or publicly, it was news. An example was a small box on Page 1 of the *Chicago Daily News* for May 24, 1967. Captioned "Crisis Prophecy," it read:

Prophetess Jean Dixon, according to Clayton Fritchey in the current edition of *Harper's,* said in January predictions for 1967:

"For Lyndon Johnson she sees nothing but trouble ahead. He will soon face the most momentous decision of his life (revolving around a new crisis in the Middle East) but the President must be alert to avoid being doublecrossed by State Department efforts to neutralize his decision."

In his article "Gullibility in Marketing" in the June 1967 *Harper's* Fritchey ascribed Dixon's popularity over scores of other crystal gazers to the fact that she was the first to headquarter in Washington and specialize in political forecasts. He also pointed out some of Dixon's misses: World War III will break out in 1958; Red China will be admitted to the United Nations in 1959; Walter Reuther will be the Democratic nominee for president in 1964; Richard Nixon will be the Republican candidate that year; war will break out over Quemoy and Matsu in 1958; Britain's Conservative Party will win the election in 1964.

When Dixon addressed the Chicago Executives Club, David Anderson covered the meeting for the *Chicago Sun-Times* of Dec. 16, 1967. The green-eyed prophetess, as he described her, predicted an uneasy peace in Vietnam in 1968 at a cost of "either $30 billion or $60 billion." Reparations would come from the World Bank, "McNamara's bank," she said.

Disregarding the evidence of Dixon's fallibility, Jan. 28, 1968, the *Chicago Tribune* used a half-page to invite readers to "Meet Jeane Dixon: She'll Read the Stars For You" beginning the next day. To the author of the partial biography of the seer her eyes were blue, not green as they had seemed to Anderson. Her birthplace was given as Medford, Wis. where a gypsy fortune teller told her when she was eight that she had psychic powers. Some of her predictions for 1969 were: Russia is on the verge of using magnetism or magnetic fields for space travel; leaders high in the Kremlin will face some important changes; Dean Rusk will resign as secretary of state; UFOs are missiles that the USA and USSR are testing; Fidel Castro will be removed from office and not by a natural death; in the near future labor unions will cease to exist as we know them.

Fred Bauer found Jeane Dixon "youthful and attractive" when he interviewed her for the April 5, 1968 *Fort Worth* (Tex.) *Star-Telegram*. She told him of her God-given ability: "I think He has given me a number of visions because He knows I'll tell others about them. I'm a little girl who can't keep a secret."

After using Dixon's column for six months, in its June 23, 1968 issue, the *Chicago Tribune* devoted an entire page to text and pictures, "Jeane Dixon Predicts . . ." She first explained the difference between the assassinations of John F. and Robert Kennedy. Her prediction of the president's murder was a revelation, she explained, "A vision is a revelation; a revelation is a word of God and cannot be changed." Her vibrations concerning Robert Kennedy, however, were obtained through mental telepathy. "It was not God's will that Robert Kennedy die, but the will of humanity."

"Steamroller tactics will be used to get Edward Kennedy on the Democratic ticket in either first or second place," Dixon wrote. LBJ will not stand for reelection, she correctly forecast after LBJ already had announced his withdrawal from the race following the New Hampshire primary. Student and worker strikes were "controlled, financed and instigated by the Communists. European worker strikes are being masterminded by a man whose name begins with D." And so on and so on.

Dixon's prophecy regarding Ted Kennedy seemed to have been correct according to Betty Beale in the *Chicago Daily News* for June 17, 1968. An old acquaintance of the stargazer, Beale advised Kennedy to listen to Dixon rather than to those who were urging him to run for president.

Just about every prophecy by Dixon receives headlines, in papers that subscribe to her horoscopes and those that don't. May 22, 1969 the *Denver Post* used a special piece she wrote for *Newsday*—the horoscopes of the three Apollo 10 astronauts, Thomas Stafford, John Young, and Eugene Cernan, who she said were "a perfect balance." The Apollo 11 trio, the first to land on the moon July 20, 1969, were Neil Armstrong, Edwin S. Aldrin Jr., and Michael Collins.

Believing that animals are affected by the stars as well as humans, Dixon wrote the book *Horoscopes for Dogs,* James Warren wrote in the *Sun-Times* Public Eye column for June 17, 1969. When her book *My Life and Prophecies* appeared she was the subject of Marcia Seligson's half-page feature in the Oct. 19, 1969 *New York Times.* Dixon talked about her visions and accused Communists of the murder of Dr. Martin Luther King and other atrocities. Seligson called much of the book "ludicrous" and added "Jeane Dixon has down pat the occultnik technique of excusing error with mumbo jumbo."

Incidentally, Sarvat Hasan beat Dixon to it with *Dog Days: Does the Sun Sign on Your Canine?* which the *New York Post* publicized on November 19, 1982, with a six-column headline, "Doggone! Your Pooch Has a Horoscope, too."

Helen Thomas, UPI White House correspondent, began her column-long dispatch July 6, 1970: "What does seeress Jeane Dixon do when she wants her own fortune told?" The answer: She consults a fellow seer, Hal Gould, who "is making a name for himself on the Washington party circuit with his political and romantic predictions."

When a reader wrote to the *Chicago Today* Action Line to inquire if Jeane Dixon predicted an earthquake that did not occur in Iran, an aide to the seer was quoted in the March 21, 1971, column as saying that Dixon "never predicts specific catastrophes." She had predicted a disaster would occur somewhere in 1971. "But," the column's editors commented, "we wouldn't worry about it." In 1969 this column reviewed her 1968 predictions. She saw Lyndon Johnson being reelected, Jackie Kennedy not getting married and the enemy being offered $30 billion reparation in Vietnam, a fact that would lead this nation into bankruptcy."

The *Tribune* disregarded the skepticism of the editors of *Today,* owned by the *Tribune* at the time. Beginning Jan. 25, 1971 the Dixon column was being syndicated to about 300 papers by the *Chicago Tribune–New York Daily News* Syndicate.

The *New York Post* devoted a full page Jan. 8, 1972 to "Jeane Dixon looks at '72 and Sees." Among other things she saw President Nixon needing tight security on his trip to Peking. Democratic presidential candidate channels "flowed" in this order: Kennedy, Jackson, Humphrey and Muskie, with no mention of McGovern who won the nomination. Both the India–Pakistan and Israeli–Egyptian confrontations are "part and parcel" of the Communists' Plan.

One of the few, perhaps the only, attempt to probe into Dixon's past was conducted by Daniel St. Albin Greene, investigative reporter for the *National Observer* of Oct. 27, 1973. He wrote that records in Medford, Wis. reveal that Frank and Emma Pinckert produced, not seven as Jeane said, but ten children, none named Jeane. It was not possible to trace Lydia, born in 1904. Greene suspects that Jeane is Lydia which would make her eight years older than she admits to being. More important, Greene was puzzled by a 15-year gap in Dixon's life history. According to a marriage certificate on file in Santa Ana, Calif. Jeane A. Pinckert married Charles Zuercher, a Swiss immigrant, in January 1922. Jeane's age was given as 22 when it probably was 18. A death certificate in November 1940 for Zuercher identified him as divorced.

Greene could find no proof that Dixon ever was a guest of Franklin D. Roosevelt in the White House. Some former associates of the seer doubted the income from the Children to Children Foundation, a Dixon operation, was used in accordance with the avowed purpose: to finance travel and schooling for deserving youngsters. James Dixon, whom she married in 1932, is an automobile distributor and real estate man in Washington.

Letters commenting on Greene's article occupied about a half-page of the *National Observer's* Nov. 17, 1973 issue. There were more congratulatory than denunciatory communications. Perhaps the most amusing was the one suggesting that Dixon dropped Lydia as her name because it was associated with Lydia Pinkham's vegetable compound.

One of the few psychic watchers to downgrade Dixon is Wally Phillips, a *Chicago Sun-Times* columnist. His Nov. 19, 1972 column was headlined, "Better polish crystal ball, Jeane." He recalled her warning that Nixon would be in danger on his trip to Peking, especially upon his arrival. Wally taunted, "Sorry Jeane, but the only unusual thing that happened to Mr. Nixon in China was that he got kissed by a passionate panda." He also cited the fact that her early 1972 forecast of who the leading candidates for president were had made no mention of George McGovern. A typical paragraph from Phillips' column of Jan. 5, 1974 was, "Three years ago Jeane Dixon predicted that Angela Davis would 'pay the price for faulty judgment.' Oops, Angela was acquitted. Also in 1971 she predicted that

Jane Fonda 'is headed for tragedy.' Oops. Jane that year won an Academy award."

March 23, 1973 Daniel St. Albin Greene reported for the *National Observer* that a jury of six in a federal court had awarded a ghost writer, Adele Fletcher, 5 percent of the royalties from Dixon's book *Jeane Dixon, My Life and Prophecies* that the plaintiff proved Dixon had promised her for doing the job. By the end of 1972 the book's royalties totaled $184,440.

It took more than bad publicity to dim Dixon's reputation. Typically, 800 students of Harper College attended her lecture during which she said that a momentous event would occur before the end of the century. "Jews," she said, "will call it the coming of the Messiah. Christians will call it the second coming of Christ." Nancy North covered the speech for the *Arlington Heights* (Ill.) *Herald* of July 12, 1974.

After interviewing Hans Holzer, the prominent parapsychologist, Philip Nobile considered him "a more credible source than the publicity-seeking he mentions but the whole business of prognostication is still a lot of hocus pocus to me." Of Dixon's "awful whoppers—for example, her prediction that the Russians would be the first to put a man on the moon," Holzer remarked, "She's entitled to some whoppers if she comes up with an occasional true prediction." Nobile's article, "Checking Up on the Prophets" appeared, among other places, in the Jan. 14, 1973 *Midwest Magazine* of the *Chicago Sun-Times*.

Chicago Today's Action Line took another crack at Dixon Aug. 21, 1972 after a reader asked what the seer's mid-year predictions were. The *Washington Star-News* published them Aug. 6, 1972 and they included the forecast that Sen. Thomas Eagleton's political future might include the presidency due to the boost Sen. George McGovern gave him. Dixon also forecast that Chicago's Mayor Richard J. Daley would seek and obtain higher office and become friendly with President Nixon. Action Line reminded the reader of several Dixon failures.

Jack Mabley, who retired in 1982 from the *Chicago Tribune*, the last of at least four papers for which he was a columnist, was fond of goading soothsayers. Feb. 4, 1975 he recalled that Jeane Dixon had insisted President Nixon had committed no indictable offense and would remain in the White House while Irene Hughes predicted in 1969 that Mayor Daley would not run again in 1971.

"Reading a year's headlines in the stars" was the streamer headline the *Chicago Tribune* gave "Jeane Dixon on 1976" in a half-page of its Jan. 11, 1976 issue. Among her predictions: it would be revealed that a foreign influence was back of the Watergate burglaries; a hidden power will be revealed within the American government, the source of many major mistakes by the last several presidents; we soon will be able to communicate with unborn children and both Mao Tse-tung and Leonid Brezhnev will leave office this year.

Inauguration of a new service, Horoscopes-by-Phone, was heralded by the *New York Times* Oct. 6, 1976 with a three-column headline, "Age of Aquarius, Leo. etc. Dawns for Ma Bell." The article by Richard J. Meislin began: "The telephone company and private enterprise have joined forces to give New Yorkers one more way—along with the weather forecast—to decide whether to get out of bed in the morning." The recorded messages were by Jeane Dixon and the commercial took only fifteen seconds.

In an effort to deflate Dixon the *Madison* (Wisc.) *Press Connection* on Dec. 31, 1979 published her noteworthy forecasts for the future and then satirized them with a list of its own. Dixon predicted that Jimmy Carter would suffer a church-related assassination attempt in 1980; spies would be discovered in high government jobs in 1980; there would be a war over energy in 1981 and revolutionaries would seize a television station in 1982. Satirized the newspaper: Bob Hope will be named U.S. ambassador to China; Frank Sinatra will be miraculously cured of vascular disease at Lourdes and Arab-financed mercenaries will attack Fort Knox.

In her column Dixon forecast that a religious fanatic would attempt to kill President Carter, whose health would be bad often during the year. She said Jimmy would postpone seeking reelection because of scandals in his administration that would result in the resignations of Hamilton Jordan and Jody Powell.

Jeane was sure that Ted Kennedy would postpone announcing his candidacy until Carter took himself out of the race. The two men would declare a temporary peace because of a murder that would touch off an international crisis to bring the United States to the brink of war.

For 1982 Dixon predicted that the economy was entering an almost unprecedented gain, a cure for baldness would be discovered, the Iran army would be purged of dissenters and Princess Diane would give birth to a girl.

Neither the psychics who fail to predict the future correctly nor the newspapers that record their failures become discouraged. This is illustrated by the case of Joseph deLouise whose selections of winners in the 18th Illinois lottery was heralded by the *Daily News* with a two-column headline Dec. 11, 1974: "Psychic Has $300,000 Vibrations." DeLouise was sure a Grafton woman would win the $300,000 prize. Instead, a St. Louis man did so. Second prize went to a Moline man rather than to a Centralia man as deLouise forecast. The winner, a shoe company employee, explained that he knew he was going to win as he "said a Hail Mary whenever any number came up." The *Chicago Tribune* for Dec. 1974 headlined the story, "Seer fooled; 'outsider' wins lottery."

DeLouise, until recently a Chicago Loop hairdresser, was catapulted into the public eye (to use Jerome Watson's terminology in a full-page feature in the *Sun-Times* for Jan. 8, 1968) Nov. 25, 1967 when he predicted over a Gary, Ind. radio station that before the year's end, "a bridge—not as large as the Brooklyn or Golden Gate but a large one—will collapse causing a great number of deaths and making newspaper headlines." Dec. 15, 1967 the newspapers had the story of the disaster of the "silver bridge" across the Ohio River at Mount Pleasant. The *Chicago Daily News* for Dec. 18, 1967 said that deLouise's claim to having made the forecast was proved because what he said was on tape.

In his feature story Watson related deLouise's account of digging up $3,000 on command from the apparition of a dead uncle in southern Italy when he was five years old. The bonanza paid the family's way to the United States. DeLouise did some predicting for 1968: President Johnson will be reelected but not with Hubert Humphrey as a running mate; Sen. Charles Percy will be the Republican candidate; Richard B. Ogilvie will win the Illinois governorship from Sargent Shriver; neither the USSR nor the USA will send a man to the moon; France will make a big "breakthrough" in developing a major non-nuclear weapon, and so on.

For the "1969" special section in the *Chicago Sun-Times Midwest Magazine* for Dec. 29, 1968, deLouise contributed quite a few prophecies, including the following: President Nixon will have difficulty forming a cabinet; the stock market will face its greatest difficulties since the depression; the Cubs will win the pennant but lose the World Series; the Bears will win the world championship; the Black Hawks will wind up in first place; the horse with the shortest name will win the Kentucky Derby; and neither Russia nor the United States will put a man on the moon before 1972.

As deLouise's predictions came more and more to relate to economic affairs, Dan Dorfman wrote in the *Wall Street Journal* for March 23, 1973: "Chicago hairdresser Joe deLouise never has read a stock analyst's report, knows nothing about stock charts and rarely reads newspaper business pages, but he isn't at all bashful in handing out investment advice." Dorfman continued at length to cite instances in which deLouise didn't know what he was talking about.

March 20, 1975 the *Wall Street Journal* quoted deLouise as saying that his clients now worry about their jobs more than about stocks and bonds. He predicted the Dow Jones industrial average would dip below 500. In the same column the paper took cracks at Irene Hughes and Katherine deJersey, Chicago seers, and Ann Armstrong of Sacramento.

DeLouise's change of occupation and his methods were described by Tim Metz in the *Wall Street Journal* of Feb. 17, 1981: "Mr. deLouise is the analyst who divines the course of the stock market by relaxing, closing his eyes and waiting for an image to form. In this pursuit of financial knowledge through mysticism, he has left behind his former professional calling. He used to be a hair dresser." He told Metz he once looked "way up into the eye of the mind." There he spotted the client "rowing out too far in a boat and getting lost." The client had overcommitted on corn. DeLouise publishes a newsletter, *Prophet-Sharing*, full of advice and predictions, distributed free.

A five-column headline, "Economic psychic predicts a bitter year" in the *Chicago Sun-Times* for Jan. 6, 1974 drew attention to deLouise's prophecies: unemployment would reach 11 million and the Dow Jones index would decline to 720. He said that ill health would cause Nixon to resign in April or May. During the "highly vulnerable time" to follow, deLouise declared: "I see the military becoming very involved in the government during this time. There will be censorship of the press, economic controls, possibly the use of troops to quell problems. It will be a military or close-to-military government operating this country for a while."

DeLouise made virtually the same predictions at the Midwest Psychic Fair, Monroe Anderson reported in the *Chicago Tribune* for Sept. 15, 1974. He said President Ford would resign when conditions worsened, with banks closed, the stock market crashed, 10 million unemployed and the National Guard in charge.

To fathom the outcome of the forthcoming Republican national convention, Roger Flaherty interviewed a number of psychics for a *Chicago Sun-Times* story, "Among psychics and bookies, Ford edges Reagan," in the issue of Aug. 3, 1976. DeLouise was quoted as saying the initial "R" made the difference. DeLouise told Flaherty, "It was always my feeling that the next president's initial will be R and Reagan is the only one right now. Up to now we haven't heard a peep from Rockefeller so the only other one is Reagan."

In his Dec. 5, 1977 *Sun-Times* roundup, "Superstars gaze at '78," Bob Greene listed deLouise's prophecies: the second of two attempts to assassinate Egyptian Anwar Sadat will succeed; guerrilla war in the Philippines; Michael Daley will run for mayor and win; Chicago is two years away from a major league baseball championship; Richard Nixon will be accepted by the public again, and so on.

Another loyal publicist for Joseph deLouise is Robert J. Herguth, whose "Herguth's People" column in the *Chicago Daily News* became "Public Eye" in the *Sun-Times*. In his Nov. 7, 1972 column Herguth quoted deLouise as saying he predicted an Illinois Central wreck June 27 on radio station WVON. May 17, 1973 Herguth quoted Joe again saying that Watergate was good for his business: "In one week I received more than 50 calls from politicians and government officials in Washington. They were worried." Joe's pacifying prediction at the time was: "Nixon will survive . . . Watergate as the most observed president in American history."

In his April 9, 1975 column Herguth offered "a sneak view" of deLouise's predictions: Mayor Daley will resign by the end of '75 and President Ford will resign before his term is over; Jackie Onassis will re-wed before Sept. 15 and Patty Hearst is on an island off the continent.

Even more popular with Herguth than deLouise is Milton Kramer of Skokie about whom H. R. Whitaker wrote in the *Chicago Tribune Magazine* Oct. 19, 1969: "His predictions of impending misfortune so far have been steadfastly ignored by almost everybody." The article's title was a Kramer quotation: "I see disaster coming, honest." Whitaker found Kramer, a Palmer House bellhop, to be publicity mad, begging to have his picture taken.

Herguth either didn't read Whitaker's article or was unimpressed by it. He frequently refers to Kramer as his favorite psychic. Some of the free publicity items Herguth has given Kramer in "Public Eye" include the following:

June 19, 1972—Nixon will beat McGovern; the Sox will win the pennant, and the Cubs will do well next year.

Nov. 20, 1972—Sen. Charles Percy will be president of the United States in 1976; Repr. Philip Crane will be vice-president in 1980; the Cubs will have a tremendous 1973 season.

March 26, 1973—Mayor Daley won't run again; first place for the Sox and second for the Cubs; Percy will run for president in 1976.

May 2, 1973—Nixon is not involved in Watergate and will serve out his term; Percy will run for president in 1976; the Black Hawks will win the Stanley cup.

Aug. 14, 1973—A complete white Christmas; Nixon will be cleared; "I wrote him not to worry; couldn't see anything for Agnew, spiritually. It was solid and no response; I still hope to get on a large network in New York and make big money. Meanwhile, I put power on people and they thank me; they are able to handle their husbands and boyfriends. Goodbye."

Sept. 13, 1973—"I was confused when I predicted a revolt in Algeria I meant Chile . . . I'm on a jet stream from O'Hare so I can't concentrate sometimes."

Dec. 3, 1973—There will be a cold war by the end of 1974 near the Philippines; a tornado next June in the southwest suburbs; another Mideast war will break out in 1978; Israel should finish the war now for lasting peace in the future; the Bears will stick with Bobby Douglass.

Herguth doesn't ignore the local favorites. July 12, 1971 he quoted Irene Hughes that Mayor Daley's lakefront stadium will be built; President Nixon will serve only one term; America never will be a socialist nation; World War III could be triggered this month or next by uprisings in Romania.

Nov. 11, 1977 Herguth reported the New York Center for the Strange's survey of the predictions of 280 American witches which included: Carter will establish full diplomatic relations with Cuba; Castro will visit the United States and reject a razor blade company's offer of $100,000 to shave off his beard for a TV commercial; New York will have another blackout; there'll be a nationwide shortage of Beluga caviar, earmuffs, bagels, and auto dipsticks.

Sept. 18, 1980 Herguth reported that Jeane Dixon predicted Alan Dixon would be elected to the U.S. Senate, as did everyone else.

The prophecies allegedly made by the Irish St. Malachy who died in 1148 were cited by Herguth Aug. 15, 1978: the Second Coming is set for the year 2000; the last pope will reign during a time of "persecution and great tribulation" followed by the destruction of Rome and the Last Judgment; two of the last four popes will be anti-popes who try to destroy religion rather than preserve it.

Feb. 5, 1980 Herguth mentioned astrologer Joyce Jillson's prediction that Dustin Hoffman would win an Oscar because he is a Leo whereas other nominees, Peter Sellers and Roy Scheider, are both Virgo, thus cancelling each other out.

Aug. 13, 1980 he quoted Israeli astrologer Ilan Pecker as saying that Kennedy would obtain the Democratic Party nomination.

March 17, 1981 Herguth quoted the astrologer Zolar that Ronald Reagan "is destined to be a truly great president. His sun in Aquarius is needed to lead into the coming Aquarius Age which promises global peace and prosperity. The last Aquarian president we had was FDR who pulled us out of the depression."

Chicago psychic Fred Rosen, a school principal, notified Vail, Colo. that one of its gondolas was due for an accident, so safety checks on equipment were intensified, Herguth reported Dec. 13, 1981.

In a class by herself was Svetlana Godillo, whom Mary Alice Kellogg called "the astrological Ann Landers of the nation's capital" in a profile in the *New York Times Magazine* for Jan. 16, 1977. Since the late '50s Svetlana built a large clientele, about 25 percent politicians who did not hide their association with her. Wrote Kellogg: "What devotion there is to Godillo in high and low Washington circles stems not only from her record of accuracy but also from a personal mixture of unshakable enthusiasm, impeccable discretion and charms." A wartime refugee, once imprisoned by the Russians, Svetlana had what she described as "a horrible childhood." According to Henry Allen's sketch of her life in the *Washington Post* for Sept. 10, 1978, when she looked at her own astrological chart, she saw "a person incredibly tough. There is a great deal of afflictions with a certain amount of luck."

Letters commenting on the Kellogg article appeared in the *Times* for Feb. 6, 1977. One mentioned Godillo's close acquaintance with celebrities and concluded: "I would guess her accurate predictions are made not with the help of the stars but with the information accumulated in her 'gray, three-foot-square safe.'"

June 14, 1979 the *Washington Post* gave a page to an article by Sally Quinn who solicited Svetlana's opinion regarding the leading aspirants for the presidency. Quinn began her page-long article: "A lot of people don't believe in astrology. They think it's a lot of trash. They can't understand how any intelligent person could possibly see anything to it at all. If you are one of those, then stop reading."

In retrospect that was very good advice, considering what the stars presumably told this seer. Example, "One candidate who looks politically strong is Baker." Her shortest comment of all was on Ronald Reagan. "It doesn't look to me at all like he's got anything. He has a very weak chart. No aspects."

Dec. 23, 1979 in a column devoted entirely to Reagan she wrote, "Neither of his charts—including his natal chart cast for the moment of his announcement—looks promising." Reason: he announced his candidacy under Mercury retrograde and "it is axiomatic in astrology that one should never begin anything during such a period because, for some unknown reason, the end result never seems to be the one intended."

By the time Ronald Reagan had doublecrossed the stars and was in the White House, Svetlana Godillo was doing a daily column for the *Washington Post.*

There she has commented on virtually every native or foreign celebrity. There was not a situation, no matter how knotty, that she could not explain, probably to have a greater effect on readers than any sage comments on the editorial page. When, for instance, the Columbia Broadcasting System named Dan Rather instead of Roger Mudd to succeed Walter Cronkite, the stargazer provided this explanation in her column for Feb. 24, 1980:

> Usually an astrologer can easily answer such a question (Why Dan Rather instead of Roger Mudd) provided he can obtain the charts of the contenders and of their present employer. The contender whose chart is the most closely and congenially tied to that of an employer will have the winning edge. If all of the contenders' charts are tied to the employer equally well, then the contender whose chart is aspected the strongest will forge ahead.
>
> In this case the power figure is William Paley. He was born Sept. 21, 1901 and has his sun in Virgo. Roger Mudd was born Feb. 9, 1928 and has his sun in Aquarius. Dan Rather, in addition to his sun in Scorpio, has also Venus and Mercury in that sign. His Mercury is karmically tied to Paley's chart. Their charts are also connected by other aspects that are both strong and benevolent.
>
> Mudd's chart has no exact connections with Paley's chart and the few close aspects it has are restrictive rather than productive . . . .

Svetlana used the heavens to explain the eccentricities and idiosyncrasies of about everyone prominent in the Reagan administration and the Reagan family. July 18, 1981 she emphasized that similarities between Jerry Falwell and Phyllis Schlafly are because their birthdays are respectively Aug. 11 and Aug. 15. Incidentally, my granddaughter, born Aug. 17, fortunately does not resemble either Falwell or Schlafly.

While American Secretary of State Alexander Haig and Soviet Foreign Minister Andrei Gromyko got along together surprisingly well, Svetlana explained Jan. 31, 1982, "even their opposite ideologies cannot interfere with a basic compatibility between their planets. In short, they are indeed diplomatic as well as astrological counterparts."

Because Nancy Reagan's birth year is in dispute, she saying it was 1923 but school records saying 1921, casting her horoscope is difficult, Svetlana confessed Dec. 13, 1981 but she managed to make the commendable traits of the first lady seem to outweigh her shortcomings.

Svetlana stirred up a controversy in Herguth's column after he quoted her prediction that absentee ballots or a recount might change the declared winner in the Illinois gubernatorial race between incumbent Gov. James Thompson and the Democratic challenger, former Sen. Adlai Stevenson. A Thompson aide informed Herguth that Big Jim was born a Taurus on May 8 and that Omarr forecast: "This can be your power play day . . . you'll win."

Sunday, Dec. 26, 1982 the *Post* devoted most of its Magazine to Svetlana's predictions for 1983. Five days later she was found dead in her apartment. Chuck Conconi, her editor on the paper, saw Svetlana the day before she died and says that the stars apparently had not given her any warning of what was in her own future.

Although most astrologers are versatile in their ability to forecast future events in numerous areas of human activity, some develop specialties. One such is Laurie Brady who was hired by Charles Finley, the eccentric owner of the Oakland Athletics, as the team's official astrologer. The *Chicago Sun-Times* heralded her appointment April 15, 1976 with a streamer, "Baseball's Astrologer; She Knows Her Stars" over a story by Tom Greer. He revealed that Brady had predicted three straight championships for the team; when it lost the American League title to the Boston Red Sox in 1975 Finley added Brady to his staff. June 25, 1976 Tim Weigel reported in the *Chicago Daily News* that Finley had challenged the authority of Baseball Commissioner Bowie Kuhn to invalidate Finley's sale of three players. Weigel reported that Brady had advised Finley to be smug, that his horoscope revealed that his "style, methods, statements, impress one in role of authority. Recognize advantage and press forward." Ultimately Kuhn won.

Brady was known already to sports figures, reporters and readers. The March 6–7, 1971 *Chicago Daily News* carried a story by her predicting that Joe Frazier would defeat Muhammad Ali. Despite the correctness of this prediction, contrary to what most other dopesters said, in their short-lived column in the *Chicago Daily News* for May 16, 1971, Jon and Abra Anderson bestowed a "dubious prediction award" on Brady for picking the Blackhawks to defeat the Montreal Canadiens in the end-of-the-season game. In his "In the Wake of the News" column in the *Chicago Tribune* for Sept. 3, 1978, David Condon publicized a Brady forecast under the streamer headline "Stargazer sees Payton in eclipse until third game," because of a sore shoulder. Sometimes sport writers value the diagnoses and prognoses of soothsayers more highly than those of medical authorities.

The strength of the confidence all concerned have in soothsayers was evidenced in Brady's case when her Lake Point Tower apartment was burglarized and jewels worth $250,000 were taken. To newsmen who reported the crime Sept. 26 and 27, 1970 she insisted that she had foreseen the disaster; that, in fact, she had purchased a safe deposit box. Unfortunately, however, she never got around to using it.

Joe Cappo, *Chicago Daily News* columnist on marketing, noted that an astrologer wanted to make predictions on the stock market. His comments provoked a letter from Laurie Brady which appeared in his Nov. 23, 1974 column. She asserted she had been making such predictions for years with considerable accuracy. She said a financial editor had considered her a crackpot until her prediction came true. Cappo remarked that he agreed she was a crackpot but she shouldn't feel badly because he thought the same of most economists.

Herguth gave publicity July 15, 1981 to Brady's prediction that "the very earliest" the baseball players strike would end would be July 17. Actually it continued until Aug. 1.

Other soothsayers occasionally take a whirl at sports forecasting. The *Chicago Daily News* used Irene Hughes' picture and a two-column head, "Irene Hughes: Cubs to win." That was her guess April 4, 1969 at the beginning of a season during which the Cubs led most of the way but flopped in September to be passed by the New York Mets who beat the Baltimore Orioles four games to one in the World Series.

A United Press International story datelined New York, June 20, 1970 reported that an extraordinary number of high-scoring major league baseball games were caused by the fact that 45 percent of the leading hitters were born under the sign of Leo the Lion, Cancer the Crab or Taurus the Bull.

According to a story with a New York dateline Oct 9, 1970, the Associated Press consulted Astroflash, a blinking monster that combines the ancient art of astrology with the modern computer. As a result the AP predicted the Cincinnati Reds would win the first game, with Gary Nolan the losing pitcher. However, the AP prophesied that the Reds would go on to win the Series. The guess regarding the first game was correct but the Orioles won the Series, four games to one.

Called "the Irene Hughes of hockey" Joe (Scoop) Morang got a streamer headline in the *Chicago Sunday Tribune* for June 3, 1973: "Computer predicts Wilbur to win 52." Wilbur Wood was a White Sox left-handed pitcher who Morang said would win 52 games while losing 12, as the Sox would win 104 while losing 58. Actually the White Sox won 72 and lost 85 to finish fifth in their division. Wood won 24 and lost 20.

Herguth identified Joe Gergen, an astrological spoofer, but reported his prediction that the Cubs will play Detroit in the World Series. Detroit will win by a forfeit when a riot breaks out as darkness descends just as Dave Kingman is at bat with the score tied and the bases loaded in the sixth inning.

An indication of the effect the astrologers have on sports writers was the lead to a *New York Times* piece June 19, 1974. Wrote James Tuite:

> Joe Frazier who turned 30 last January is a Capricorn.
> Jerry Quarry became 30 in May and that makes him a Taurus.
> And as every card-carrying astrologer will explain at the drop of a horoscope, Capricorn and Taurus are most compatible with each other in companionship and business.
> Their compatability will be put to a 12-round test tomorrow night at Madison Square Garden.

To compete with the *National Enquirer* and its competitors who devote pages and pages to year-end predictions annually, the sober everyday press uses the forecasts of its own syndicated seers and an occasional roundup by a staff member. It is interesting and usually potentially devastating to the reputation of the soothsayers to consult the files. For instance, the syndicated newspaper supplement, *This Week,* published "The Stars Look Ahead" by Leslie Lieber Sept. 12, 1964. According to Pauline Messina, "Barry Goldwater, a Capricorn from Arizona, after a rough-and-tumble campaign, will lose the presidential election by a razor-thin edge to Lyndon Johnson." On the other hand, Mrs. Ernest A. Grant, a fellow of the American Federation of Astrologers, said, "I think Goldwater has a good chance of winning." Johnson won 486 electoral votes to 52 for Goldwater; the popular votes were approximately 42 million to 27 million.

Because of their bad showing, Messina prophesied, the Mets would fire Casey Stengel as manager. After all, she recalled, when he won nine pennants in ten years (1949 to 1960), he had Jupiter in his corner.

Lieber commented that Ol' Case also had Mickey Mantle in center field and Phil Rizzuto at short.

With much less subtlety Herbert Strentz recalled what the prophets had forecast for 1981 in the *Des Moines Register* for Dec. 25, 1981. Strentz, in fact, added up the forecasts that one *National Enquirer*'s "10 Leading Psychics" had made for the years 1978 to 1981 inclusive. The score: 0 correct guesses out of 260. Among the incorrect forecasts: Paul Newman did not run for governor of Connecticut; Robert Redford did not run for governor of Utah; Elizabeth Taylor was not appointed to an ambassadorship nor was Frank Sinatra appointed ambassador to the Vatican; Larry Hagman and Dick Van Patten did not quit television to become evangelists, nor did many other of the predicted startling events occur.

"How can the psychics be so wrong?" Strentz asked. "Their striving for the Guiness world record for incompetence cries out for understanding. Part of the psychic's problem is bad timing; part of it stems from a fixation on Debby Boone, Liz Taylor and a handful of other celebrities; part of it is an understandable fascination with voices from the dead; part is wishful thinking; and part of it is trying to strike it rich with one accurate prediction so off the wall that lifetime recognition as a seer is guaranteed."

Dr. Strentz, dean of the School of Journalism of Drake University; wrote previous analyses of the leading physics for the *Des Moines Tribune* Dec. 20, 1978, Dec. 27, 1979 and Jan. 1, 1981. In the last of those three pieces he wrote, "The psychics make predictions because—just as in the Dark Ages—we're fascinated by the thought that the future can be foretold."

Despite exposés of this sort, the annual forecasts of the "grocery store tabloids" are considered newsworthy.

Charles A. Jayne does it every Jan. 1 for the *New York Daily News*. Jan. 1, 1981 the *Washington Post* devoted almost a full page to a summary of what the sensational weeklies were predicting followed by a series of satirical prophecies by Tony Kornheiser, a typical one being this: "A singing elephant will be discovered in Bhutan, flown to Hollywood and booked on all the talk shows. During a 'Love Will Keep Us Together' duet with Toni Tennille, it will suddenly swoon, squashing and killing the Captain."

After one's hysterical laughter subsides one can balance the effect of such an approach against Philip Nobile's question-and-answer interview with Dr. Gil E. Gilly of Phoenix in the *Chicago Sun-Times Midwest Magazine* for Feb. 2, 1975. Nobile explained that "prophets are honored because they are usually wrong. I am amused by soothsayers of every stripe. Although I disbelieve in their future telling talents I make it my business to interview one card-carrying prophet annually." All the rest of the article was serious answers to serious questions, as "Q—How do you make your prophecies? Do you have any particular method? A—First I relax and go into the vortex of my mind and then the ideas, thoughts and pictures necessary for projecting a future event are attracted to it."

In the *Chicago Sun-Times* for Jan. 3, 1982 Herb Gould summarized the prognostications of the seers in the *National Enquirer, Star, Globe* and *Weekly World News*. A typical paragraph was that devoted to *Di's baby boom.* "Princess Diana will suffer a near miscarriage" (*Globe*), or "Di will probably have a little girl" (*Star*), or "she will give birth to a beautiful baby boy" (*Weekly World News*), or "Princess Di will have quads" (same *Globe,* different psychic). Meanwhile "Unrest in Ireland will keep Prince Charles in danger all of 1982" (*Star*). But Charles "will bring peace in northern Ireland (*Globe*).

"Lady Di's Horoscope promised she'd find her Prince Charming and bear England a King," was a three-column headline the *New York Post* gave to a lengthy feature article by Tom Kennedy in its Jan. 3, 1983 issue. Two days earlier, New Year's Day, in her column in the same paper, Cindy Adams reported that astrologist Frederick Davies phoned from London that Prince Andrew will announce his engagement to Koo Stark, a car will be named "The Greatest" for Muhammad Ali and Lauren Bacall will marry Harry Guardino.

An outstanding exception to the journalistic policy of relying on syndicated experts for year-end forecasts was the page the *Washington Post* gave Jan. 1, 1982 to the opinions of five seers (one astrologer and four parapsychologists) by reporters Sandra R. Gregg and Leah Y. Latimer. There was little agreement on the future of the Washington Redskins, the possible pregnancy of the zoo's panda, Ling-Ling, or the outcome of the city's mayoral election. All were agreed, however, that Reagan's economic policies will fail.

One *Chicago Sun-Times* article that could not be mistaken for anything except an attempt to belittle professional prophets, especially Irene Hughes, was an interview by Tom Fitzpatrick of Dr. Benjamin Burack of Roosevelt University that the paper published Jan. 11, 1971.

"There is a certain amount of quackery and dishonesty about them all," Dr. Burack declared. He has placed a challenge on the psychology department's bulletin board offering to pay $1,000 to anyone who can demonstrate a genuine ESP to him. Dr. Burack has written a three-word sentence and put it in a sealed envelope in safe keeping. The test is for Irene Hughes, Jeane Dixon or anyone else to state the message. To date the $1,000 has been unclaimed.

As Lee Kottke reported in the *Chicago Daily News* for May 15, 1972, "Being psychic isn't easy but it's a living." That was the opinion of Daniel Logan, author of *Your Eastern Star* and *The Reluctant Prophet*. He conducts classes in meditation and teaching in Hazelton, Pa. He believes that everyone has a sixth sense to be developed.

Of a different opinion is Neil Marbell, subject of an "Openers" feature in the *Chicago Tribune Magazine* for Oct. 13, 1974. He says, "With your birth chart I can tell you more about yourself in an hour than a qualified psychiatrist can tell you after two years of therapy." He runs Chicago's Old Astrologer's Shop.

3

Prophecy

It was a startling experience for a venerable university professor who was participating in a two-hour radio talk-show to have a garrulous caller insist that stories and pictures of astronauts landing on the moon were a gigantic hoax concocted by Mobil Corporation, no explanation given.

That skeptical woman has company—at least 1,500 members of the International Flat Earth Society, headquartered in London where it was founded in 1800. The society was unimpressed by the astronauts' feat. In Dover, England July 25, 1969, the society's secretary, Samuel Shenton, told Robert C. Toth of the *Los Angeles Times* that the moon is less than 2,700 miles away and is only 32 miles across. Shenton accused NASA and its contractors and mapmakers of conspiring because of their vested interest in perpetuating the globite teaching.

According to the *Chicago Sun-Times* Action Time in answering a reader's inquiry July 8, 1976 the society's president, Charles Johnson, argues that if the world were round the water would fall off and Australia's population would do likewise. The earth, he says, is a flat disk with the North Pole the magnetic center. Antarctica is explained as an ice ring that encircles the edge of the land masses somewhere in between, and nobody has ever crossed the ridge.

"We are the oldest continuous society in existence," Johnson told David Larsen, who reported his words for the *Los Angeles Times* of May 15, 1978. "Adam was our first member." Others are following the first man's example, he insisted.

Don Bishoff, columnist for the *Eugene* (Ore.) *Register-Guard,* did not depend on his own background knowledge to challenge Bill Kaysing, author of the book *We Never Went to the Moon.* Instead, Bishoff interviewed E. G. Ebbighausen, professor emeritus of physics and astronomy at the University of Oregon, concerning Kaysing's arguments. One by one the scholar knocked them down. Typically he explained why there was no dust stirred up when the astronauts landed: because the topsoil of the moon has the characteristics of damp beach sand. "This fellow is really ignorant," Ebbighausen said. The lengthy column was published May 22, 1977.

Some of the leading astronomical misconceptions that have endured for centuries relate to the direct influence of the moon on human behavior. In fact, meteorpsychiatry is a branch of science that seeks to understand how the lunar cycle, barometric pressure, winds, electricity and other meteorological variations affect human behavior, according to Sidney Katz, who wrote "Moon Madness 'Myth' Under Serious Study" for the *Toronto Star* of Nov. 25, 1972.

Katz quoted several police authorities, health and mental hygiene workers and others who believe crimes and other antisocial acts increase when there is a full moon. Dr. Arnold Lieber, University of Miami psychiatrist, analyzed 1,959 murders that occurred in Greater Miami between 1956 and 1970 and concluded that a higher number of homicides had occurred during full moon and new moon.

In another *Toronto Star* article, "When the Moon is Full" June 2, 1973, Sandra Peredo cited numerous cases of people who became weird, fell apart, became fearful or acted in deviant ways. Various theories have been advanced, including the "sea within" hypothesis, that the moon is influential because the human body consists of a considerable amount of water. Very little skepticism was expressed by any of the interviewees except perhaps by a Sydney, Nova Scotia psychiatrist who said statistics can be used to prove anything and someone had correlated the flight of storks with childbirths in different places.

Not even that much doubt was cast on the statement, "The moon's influence cannot be denied though it is unexplainable," which is what Collie Small wrote in a lengthy article, "Full Moon Leaving Us More Than Just Spellbound?" in the *Chicago Tribune* for Nov. 7, 1978.

The author cited several studies to indicate that certain worms always turn to the left during a full moon; sexual desires are heightened; mental hospitals take extra precautions, homicide rates increase, people are restless and apt to become addled and suicides increase.

"I doubt if anyone can prove it statistically," Police Chief Lt. Ken Johnson of Chicago Heights, Ill. told Jim Ritter, who wrote the article "Full Moon: Night Light to Crime" in the *Chicago Sun-Times Suburban Week* for March 9, 1979. "But I have been a policeman for 15 years and I know there is a definite change in the nature of things that happen under a full moon." Psychic Irene Hughes explained that a full moon upsets a person's fluid balance just as it upsets an ocean's tides," usually with a negative effect.

Another favorite Chicago astrologer, Laurie Brady, wrote to Bob Herguth March 17, 1981, for use in his Public Eye column in the *Chicago Sun-Times* of March 31, 1981: "The full moon on March 20 is the first time this has ever coincided with the vernal equinox, the first day of spring during the entire century." She warned of another interesting planetary alignment to occur April 4 when a stellium of planets in Aries opposes three planes in Libra, "pointing for a dramatic and possible dangerous chain of events." Two days earlier March 29, 1981, the *Sun-Times* had editorialized satirically on a similar warning from six astrologers. Titled, "Don't say we didn't warn you," the editorial concluded, "And as for next Saturday we've decided that discretion is the better part of valor. We'll stay in bed and unplug the phone."

The March 20 vernal equinox of which Brady wrote was called "probably the most important of your personal life in this century," the UPI quoted Richard Alan Miller, a former occult shop owner, as saying in a story March 14, 1981, from Seattle. Miller, a doctor of philosophy in physics, said: "Friday the 13th is a superstition that doesn't have any major energy to it. Seasonal changes are much more significant."

When the moon is full people tend to act things out in a more bizarre fashion. And it's not only mental patients, a hospital nurse told reporter Ann Pepper, who wrote, "Does Full Moon Inspire Bizarre Acts?" for the *Petaluma* (Calif.) *Argus-Carrier* for July 16, 1981. "The whole town goes nuts when the moon is full," a police sergeant said.

A reader whose inability to control her temper when the moon is full was told by Abigail "Dear Abby" VanBuren in her column for Jan. 4, 1982, "Although there is no scientific evidence to support this age-old theory, those who are convinced it's true can be physically affected to the point of looniness." She explained that "loony" is slang for "lunatics," which translates into "made crazy by the moon," the Latin word for which is "luna."

In the belief that during a full moon is the best time for meditation and spiritual rejuvenation, in 1956 a New York metaphysicist, Florence Garrigue, and six others founded Meditation Group, which now has 8,000 members in the United States. It maintains a $1 million Tibetan structure on Meditation Mount, Calif. where Garrigue, now 95, lives. When the moon is full adherents gather there. Charles Hillinger wrote about one meeting in the *Los Angeles Times* for Jan. 10, 1982.

Because they believed a mythical monster was devouring the moon during an eclipse, Cambodian soldiers wasted so much ammunition the army's supply became dangerously low, the Associated Press reported Feb. 8, 1972 from Phnom Penh.

The book of a Boston journalist, Paul Katzeff, *Full Moon: Facts and Fantasy About the Lunar Influence,* inspired a full-page review and comment by Kathleen Ennis in the *Washington Post* for Oct. 1, 1982. It described the supposed moon-caused erratic behavior of birds, animals, fish and humans.

Not only the moon but all other heavenly bodies have been objects of awe, veneration, and fear throughout the centuries, from caveman days up to and including the present. In 1948, the date of a scheduled United Nations plebiscite in South Korea was changed after a University of

Chicago astronomer, Dr. George Van Bissbroack, pointed out that it coincided with an expected eclipse of the sun, Gerry Robinchaud and Carleton Kent revealed in their *Chicago Sun-Times* column for July 13, 1950. The paper's Action Time told a reader that Japanese girls born in 1936 were supposed to be ill natured, poor wives, and eventually fatal to their husbands. There were a half-million abortions in 1965 for fear of having daughters born in 1966, supposedly another unlucky year, as will be 2026. Ernest Weatherall told *Chicago Daily News* readers on May 30, 1970, that "Stars hold Indians under mystic spell." Astrologers are consulted before pregnancies, financial ventures, trips and other occurrences.

The coronation of Nepal's King Birendra Bir Bikram Shah Dev was set for Feb. 24, 1975 by a committee of royal astrologers who consulted the monarch's horoscope and the lunar calendar to determine the most auspicious time, the UPI reported Feb. 16, 1975 from Katmandu.

The *Chicago Tribune's* Action Express quieted the fears of a reader who had been advised not to marry in May. Officials at the marriage license bureau said that, although more marriages occur in June than in May, there is no evidence that May marriages are jinxed. Last year 5,075 were married in Cook County in May; 6,467 in June.

As the maverick comet Kohoutek approached Earth for its 1973 visit, not to be repeated for 75,000 years, people reacted in many different ways. Typical of a great deal of the journalism of the time was the Jan. 1, 1974, Associated Press story from San Francisco that began:

> To devotees of the comet Kohoutek, the dazzling visitor from outer space heralds the end of the world, a new beginning and a businessman's galaxy of telescopes and T-shirts.
>
> Star-struck astrologers, cultists and self-described "comet freaks" call the fiery phenomenon a portent of war, peace, natural disasters, the energy crisis and further Watergate revelations.
>
> "The Great Comet warning: Forty days and Ninevah shall be destroyed" proclaim the pamphlets distributed by the Children of God fundamentalist sect roving Market Street here.
>
> They call the comet a "Christmas monster" warning of "the total downfall of America" as it approaches its celestial rendezvous with the sun.

Typical of some stories that appeared in papers in other parts of the country was what Dan L. Thrapp, religion editor, wrote for the *Los Angeles Times* of Dec. 3, 1973 after he interviewed a Jesuit, the Rev. John J. Dahlheimer.

> I'd like to think that this crossing of man's messenger, Pioneer 10, and the messenger of God, Kohoutek, is almost as though we'd slipped our hand into God's and He's given it a warm squeeze of reassurance. . . . "Pioneer 10 and Kohoutek! God knows. God cares. God gives us a sign. And He gives it to us at Christmastime."

In another long article, Dec. 22, 1973 Thrapp cited all biblical passages that might be interpreted as referring to comets, including the Star of Bethlehem.

Another *Los Angeles Times* backgrounder by Steve Harvey was published Nov. 25, 1973. It compared the calmness with which it said people in general regarded Kohoutek in comparison with the near panics that were widespread in 1910 when Halley's comet neared Earth. There were many gloomy predictions, some by otherwise reputable scientists, that the comet might engulf the planet in poisonous gas or at least a deluge of water. One rumor was that the world would be enveloped with laughing gas, which inspired an editorial comment that there certainly were those whom it would kill if they had to laugh. Anti-comet pills were on sale and an Australian advertised for someone to share the expense of an oxygen-filled room.

By contrast, in 1973 one of the few commercial scams was that of a Madison, Wis. lawyer, Edward "Crazy Eddie" Ben Elson, who sold tickets for a ride on Kohoutek. Dec. 24, 1981 he was quoted in the article "My Most Memorable Christmas" by Sunny Schubet in the Madison *Wisconsin State Journal:* "That Christmas Day it suddenly dawned on me that if any one of the thousand people who were waiting on their roofs for the intergalactic Comet Kohoutek to pick them up and transport them to salvation, were to fall off, my malpractice insurance would not have been sufficient to cover my liability."

At about the same time Elson was quoted by Bob Schenet in the *Chicago Daily News* for Dec. 19, 1973 as saying Kohoutek was really not a comet but a spaceship. UFOs would pick up 143,000 people to be saved, plus 1,000 others to be selected by Elson. He said he had ten baskets in his basement filled with minimized human beings, each about an inch long. Dec. 20, 1973 the UPI reported from Milwaukee that it had been revealed that the 143,000 were delivered by a ten-foot-tall visitor. Christmas Day, he said, Earth would drown in a sea of petroleum oil. Dec. 26 *Chicago Today* reported that Elson waited on the roof of his house until after midnight but the astral escalator never arrived. On the back of the tickets he sold was printed: "No refunds allowed. Paid for on faith—whether or not you get off the ground, whether or not you are carried away." To reporters Elson confessed, "I never hit the nail on the head with any of my prophecies. I even prophesied that George McGovern would win the last election."

Apparently despondent because of the death of two sons from Sudden Infant Death Syndrome, Feb. 8, 1983 Elson committed suicide by carbon monoxide poisoning after he left the motor of his auto running in a locked garage. Editorially the *Madison Capital-Times* for Feb. 10, 1983 called Elson an "inspired zany" who "elevated unconventionality to an art form." Many recalled some of Elson's stunts: announcing his candidacy for district attorney from a theater platform in the nude; running for state superintendent of schools on a platform urging abolition of public schools; defending the messy pet dog of Attorney General Bronson LaFollette by insisting the animal should be tried by a jury of its peers.

One of the best attempts to give perspective to the Kohoutek phenomenon was Michael T. Malloy's article, "So You Think Comets Influence Us, Eh? Well, the Truth Is . . ." in the *National Observer* for Dec. 29, 1973. The article is a cursory account of the historical effect comets have had on politics, philosophy and literature. Poets from Homer to Shakespeare paid homage to comets. A typical paragraph from Malloy's article follows:

> A comet welcomed Attila the Hun to Western Europe in 452 A.D. Another was seen in London a year before the Great Plague of 1965. Mark Twain was born during the 1835 visit of Halley's Comet, always said he would die when it came back and died on schedule when it reappeared in 1910. A comet also named the death of the Roman Emperor Macrinus in A.D. 218, but this was not strictly speaking disaster; actually Macrinus was a lousy emperor.

The rest of the article was jampacked with similar anecdotes. Currently, however, Kohoutek is considered by many as a good rather than a bad omen. Al H. Morrison, secretary of the Congress of Astrological Organizations, believed Kohoutek would more likely bring a religious revival than the usual wars and plagues, Timothy Leary's psychedelic followers thought it would cause the impeachment of Nixon and Leary's release from prison and followers of the teen-age Guru Maharaj Ji saw the comet as more evidence that he is ushering in a thousand years of peace.

That many continued to have the jitters even as Kohoutek moved away was evidenced by an article in the *Houston Chronicle* for Jan. 20, 1974. The comet added to the uneasiness of the citizenry, but a local astrologer, John Woodsmall, said the celestial visitor signaled a time of upheaval and inner conflicts that would result in a change for the better.

This was the same paper that ran the story of an interview its reporter Mary Lu Zuber had with Carroll Righter whose daily horoscopes appeared in that paper. The comet Kohoutek would have a beneficial effect, he said, "The comet will put conditions on Earth on a more solid and secure structure . . . its good effect will last for years."

According to Jim Scovel in *Newsday* for Jan. 10, 1974 Kohoutek was "a coast-to-coast bust." In the *New York Times* for Jan. 15, 1974 Russell Baker elaborated on the same idea: "Kohoutek has failed its promoters. It is a nothing act. It is the biggest flopperoo since 'Kelly' hit Broadway at a cost of $700,000 and folded on the first night. It is the Edsel of the firmament."

The next day the *New York Times'* science editor, Walter Sullivan, explained: "Because of its searing loop around the sun Dec. 28 the comet Kohoutek, now fading from view to the unaided eye, has become enveloped in a cloud of hydrogen dust three million miles wide."

Quite independent of the furor over Kohoutek the First Assembly of God in North Hollywood, Calif. changed its by-laws to provide continued leadership if its officers were suddenly taken to heaven, the *New York Times* reported April 1, 1973. Justification for the action was cited in I Thessalonians 4:17, "Then we who are alive who are left shall be caught up together with them in the clouds to meet the Lord in the air and so we shall always be with the Lord."

Dec. 30, 1973 George Alexander wrote in the *Los Angeles Times* about a Duluth, Minn. group calling itself Stop the Comet Citizens' Action Group. It urged that a nuclear-tipped Saturn 5 rocket be used to blast the comet out of the heavens. The last time Kohoutek came this way it destroyed the protective Van Allen radiation belt and the dinosaurs all died from cosmic ray bombardment, the group said.

Fear that light pollution will make it difficult for scientists and spectators to enjoy the sight of Halley's comet in 1986 was expressed by Joan Beck in her column in the *Chicago Tribune* for May 11, 1982. She advertised the attempt of Fred Schaff, a columnist for *Astronomy* magazine, that cities dim their lights for hours or longer on designated days so that the phenomenon can be enjoyed. On the other hand she argued that robbers and burglars work better in the dark.

For 50 years none of many theories advanced by scientists and pseudo-scientists, science-fiction writers and others seemed to be adequate to explain the colossal midair explosion that rocked a remote area of Siberia June 30, 1908. Among the hypotheses were visitors from outer space, an atomic blast of natural origin, the fall of antimatter, and an encounter between the planet and a black hole.

The *New York Post* gave a column to an AP dispatch from Moscow Oct. 23, 1978, reporting the surmise by a reputable scientist, Felix Figel, of the Moscow Aviation Institute, that the "Tunguska Mystery," as it was known, was caused by a UFO. Feb. 12, 1980, Theodore Shabad reported in the *New York Times* that Soviet scientific publications had revealed the discovery of tiny diamondlike grains of the type that would be generated by carbon from an extreme shock. Thus it was finally concluded that the disaster was caused by a meteorite.

Another mystery involving a meteor was declared a hoax in 1964, just 100 years after it was committed. During that time the meteor fragment had been protected in a sealed jar in a French museum. University of Chicago scientists discovered seeds and other material in the specimen to be found in the area in France where the alleged meteor shower occurred. Both the *Washington Post* and *New York Times* had lengthy accounts of the hoax in their issues of Nov. 28, 1964. Still another meteor anecdote was finally proved a hoax by William Hines in the *Chicago Sun-Times* for Sept. 9, 1979. The gist of it was that a Fountain County, Ind. farmer named Leonidas Grover was killed in his bed by a meteor. Painstaking research involving a half-dozen or more century-old newspapers traced the origin to the *Indianapolis Journal* of Jan. 12, 1879. It probably originated as a joke by a printer's devil on a wire editor. The story was printed and reprinted for a century and doubtless will never die as students or scholars encounter it who have never seen the exposé.

In an article by Adrian Berry that American newspapers reprinted March 24, 1982 from the *London Daily Telegraph,* the one-in-a-million chance that the comet Swift-Tuttle will crash into Earth during 1982 is evaluated. The result would be "the worst disaster since the extinction of the dinosaurs," causing a crater 12 miles wide and total destruction over a radius of 200 miles. The article repeats the "fact" of the strike in Siberia in 1908.

Aug. 10, 1981 in a story from New York the Associated Press quoted Kenneth Franklin, astronomer of the American Museum of Natural History's Hayden Planetarium, "Comets are great celestial litterbugs." Every August stargazers look for the Perseid meteor shower as the Earth crosses the orbit of a comet and the debris scattered along its path is destroyed in Earth's atmosphere. Meteors have been the cause of much fear on the part of the ignorant in centuries past but today most newspapers know better than to report them as threats to humans on this planet.

The threats that scientists do recognize are faults in the earth's surface that lead to earthquakes, volcanoes, floods resulting from deforestation and the like. The most "far-out" fear that some scientists have is that the ice at either pole will avalanche and cause huge tidal waves or that there may be some unforeseen cosmic collision.

The *Wall Street Journal* for April 22, 1969 had a comprehensive article by Drew Fetherston on these and similar fears.

Since the San Francisco earthquake and fire that took 453 lives and caused $350 million property damage April 19, 1906, the prophets of disaster have been warning that California is in imminent danger of an even worse catastrophe. Several scares have received nationwide publicity. That of 1969 was the most serious, lasting from mid-1968 until the end of 1969, when all of the definite dates forecast for the disaster had passed and been uneventful.

Among the first warnings to attract widespread attention was that of Billy Ray McCollum, a member of a religious sect that was fleeing to Atlanta because, he explained: "God told us to come here. He sent a vision of the destruction of California and told us to flee to Atlanta." To which John Estes, another sect member, added that California is doomed because "it's full of sin. Especially in Hollywood and Beverly Hills where the movie stars live."

Religious fanatics, however, were not the only ones who contributed to the anxiety of California. In an attempt to calm readers' fears and counteract hysterical talk and acts, the *Los Angeles Times* ran a long comprehensive account of the situation by Linda Mathews in its issue of March 1,

1969. Headlined "Doomsday in April? Experts Ridicule Mystics' Warnings," it began:

> California, in case you haven't heard, will be shaken in April by an earthquake so devastating that the land mass west of the San Andreas fault will shudder, split off from the rest of the continent and crash into the sea.
>
> Los Angeles, Santa Barbara and San Diego will simply no longer exist, except as a modern-day Atlantis; San Francisco will be shaken into ruins and inundated and the Imperial and San Joaquin valleys will be flooded with salt water.
>
> And more than 15 million people—three-quarters of the country's most populous state—will lose their lives.
>
> Inconceivable?
>
> The most knowledgeable scientists say not only inconceivable but ridiculous.

The article included the statement issued by the California Institute of Technology that, epitomized, said: "Wild prophecies of disastrous earthquakes are not supported by scientific evidence and are frightening many Californians needlessly."

"But," Mathews wrote, "Why trust seismologists and geophysicists when a growing band of mystics including a 6,000-year-old society of telepaths, astrologers, cultists, fundamentalist preachers, hippies and kooks here for months have been predicting doom for us all?"

The lengthy piece includes specific references to pop-songs, the most popular being "Day After Day"; a Mama Cass record, "California Earthquake"; a book, *The Last Days of the Late, Great State of California* by Curt Gentry; a 1941 prediction by Edgar Cayce that Los Angeles, San Francisco and New York would be destroyed sometime between 1958 and 1998 and forecasts by several other seers; and counterstatements by Dr. Charles Richter, inventor of the scale by which to measure earthquakes, and others.

In a different category from the crackpot prognostications was that of Max Wyss, 29, a geophysics student at the California Institute of Technology, who forecast earth movements to occur in April 1969 near Parkfield, Calif. He was reported in the *World Book Encyclopedia* Science Service as having made two correct similar forecasts in the past, basing his predictions on measurements of rock strain, changes in tilt and level of the earth, part movements along the fault and the characteristics of the rock.

Such a prophecy quite obviously was more reliable than one based on some religious nut's visions. In reporting it the *Chicago Daily News* April 1, 1969 distinguished between an earthquake and a creep which is a land-mass shift of only an inch or two. The newspaper account contrasted Wyss' scientific study with the hysterical warnings that were rampant at the time.

Under the heading "Warning! California Will Fall into the Ocean in April" Steven V. Roberts wrote for the *New York Times Magazine* of April 6, 1969 very much the same kind of article that Linda Mathews wrote for the *Los Angeles Times*. He told of the stir caused in the San Francisco City Hall when the Fellowship of the Ancient Mind, a Druidic order that traces its lineage back 6,000 years, applied for a salvage permit to allow it to rescue great works of art when the disaster occurred.

Came April 4, 1969 and April 5 the *New York Times* ran a story by Steven V. Roberts from Los Angeles that began: "California did not fall into the sea today," followed by a rehash of the six months' hysteria.

Linda Mathews' story in the *Los Angeles Times* that day was similar, beginning: "If you can read this, chances are that California didn't shake, shudder and crash into the sea at 3:13 P.M. Friday." She quoted an official of the U.S. Geological Survey: "People like to scare themselves." And the *San Francisco Examiner* wrote, "If you are reading these lines we did not have an earthquake today. If you aren't reading them. . . ."

Even more to the point humorist Art Buchwald wrote in his column for April 10, 1969, entitled "Farewell to California": ". . . this is now a nation that believes its astrologers before it believes its scientists."

Making fun of the whole situation, the Associated Press reported April 11, 1969 that San Francisco's Mayor Joseph Alioto announced a pre-dawn party April 18 to celebrate the 63rd anniversary of the city's great fire.

On the other hand Irv Kupcinet in Hollywood began his daily column in the *Chicago Sun-Times,* "Geologists here aren't pooh-poohing the clairvoyants' predictions of a major earthquake in California." Because such is quite possible, a Stanford scientist said the big scare served the purpose of awakening citizens to the ever-present danger.

Since many of the predictions had merely mentioned April, not a specific date, the uneasiness continued. And, when a slight tremor was felt near the Salton Sea in Southern California, the Associated Press sent a story from Indio that received prominent positions in many papers April 29, 1969.

As Leslie Lieber put it in *This Week* for Nov. 1, 1969, "The swamis lost by a landslide." Most of the article, "Can Anyone Predict the Future?" was a compilation of the bad misses of Maurice Woodruff, Jeane Dixon and several other stargazers.

Despite the happy ending the earthquake scare influenced many motion picture stars to become interested in astrology, Dorothy Manners reported in her syndicated column from Hollywood for Feb. 23, 1971.

And Dec. 31, 1972 the self-named "psychic cynic" Wally Phillips, columnist for the *Chicago Sun-Times* and WGN commentator, chided Irene Hughes for her prediction of a San Francisco earthquake between Jan. 2 and 9, 1973. Phillips said he'd be much more impressed with ESP if its adherents could tell the whereabouts of a number of persons whom he named who had disappeared mysteriously. He also said nobody had won the prize he offered for the identity of the living person whose name Wally sealed in an envelope in the Custody of WGN. Feb. 24, 1982 Phillips revealed that the name was that of Jean Rogers, now in her mid 60s who, as Dale Arden, starred with Buster Crabbe in early Flash Gordon movies. Phillips had to hire a private detective to find her after the Chicago Public Library had said she was dead. Because nobody had guessed her identity, after six years, at $1 per day, Phillips was able to donate $3,900 to his Christmas Children's Fund. The solution of the mystery received brief notices in the Kup, Inc. and Herguth columns.

And, sure enough, Don Bishoff's column in the *Eugene Register-Guard* for Dec. 19, 1978, was entitled "Here It Is LA, Right from Witch Mouth." A member of the Eugene occult, whose request for anonymity Bishoff respected, warned Californians that the long-awaited earthquake was due within a week.

Earlier the same year, June 14, 1978, the *San Antonio News* ran a story by Mike Ullman from Corpus Christi. It began: "This city of 300,000 has at most 37 days to live, a psychic predicts. Another clairvoyant says that Houston and the entire South Texas gulf coast will be hit by a hurricane in a matter of days."

What doubtless was a familiar magician's trick caused the Associated Press to send a story from Durham, N.C. March 31, 1977 that Lee Fried, a Duke University freshman, resolved to make no more prophecies after his success in forecasting a major airplane disaster that took 577 lives in the Canary Islands as well as the headline in the day's paper giving the outcome of a basketball game between Marquette University and the University of North Carolina. His predictions had supposedly been placed in a sealed envelope in the president's office a week earlier. In its special story the *New York Daily News* reported that the student admitted he was an amateur magician. President Sanford congratulated him for a good trick.

The ever-skeptical Jack Mabley, who delighted in exposing astrologers and other fortune tellers, was befuddled by Fried. When Jack asked him on a long distance telephone call if it was a trick, Fried replied, "I don't see how I could have tampered with them" and avoided a yes-or-no reply.

Wrote Mabley in his *Chicago Tribune* column for April 12, 1977: "The classic question to ask people like Fried is 'If you can predict the future why aren't you rich?' How do we know there aren't a lot of people with Fried's talent who have become rich and are darned well keeping the secret?"

Take a tip from an ex-magician: anyone with a modicum of experience in performing tricks can do it. Furthermore, they do do it. Stories like the one from Durham get on the wires periodically from all parts of the country. A typical example was a lengthy UPI story from Pittsburgh to which the *Columbus Citizen* gave almost a column June 20, 1947. The papers were the *Pittsburgh Sun-Telegraph* and the *Pittsburgh Press,* and the magician was Robert Nelson of Columbus.

If the stories of all involved were correct, three days before an American Airlines DC-10 crashed in Chicago killing 274, the office manager of a car rental agency called airline officials and the Federal Aviation Authority offices in Cincinnati to say that for ten nights he had had dreams during which he witnessed a disaster. Most of the details of the actual crash were identical to those David Booth related, the *Cincinnati Enquirer* reported and papers in other cities rewrote June 1, 1979.

Before citing the achievements of three forecasters, in his *New York Daily News* column for Feb. 12, 1982, Hans Holzer said that "even 50 per cent accuracy is astounding for psychics." Then he cited Yolanda Lassaw, who foresaw a building collapsing two weeks before a huge scaffolding on a Fifth Avenue apartment did just that. Johanna Sherman predicted a political assassination in the Middle East sometime before the murder of Egyptian President Anwar Sadat. Taken to the Amityville haunted house blindfolded, Ethel Johnson Meyers knew she was in a house where a murder had been committed. None of the predictions were too definite.

The U.S. Army Corps of Engineers and the police and public officials of Niagara Falls, N.Y. and Niagara Falls, Canada were put to considerable trouble and expense by what Alan Richman of the *New York Times* called "the single greatest disaster that never happened at Niagara Falls."

The scare that caused the season's largest crowd to gather Sunday, July 22, 1979 began when Mrs. Pat St. John of Bridgewater, Conn. announced on a Canadian radio talk-show July 4 that she had learned during a seance on June 9 that a retaining wall above the falls would give way at 4:56 P.M., E.D.T., July 22, drowning a boatload of deaf children on a vacation tour.

July 7 the Associated Press reported that the Army engineers had inspected the area and said there was no reason for alarm. July 15, however, the AP reported that a seismic alarm on Friday the 13th had revealed that seeping water and new cracks had been spotted at the bottom of Terrapin Point, an observation station overlooking Horseshoe Falls. July 22 it was reported by both AP and UPI that the rock shift was only one-fourth of an inch and not dangerous. It also was revealed that Mrs. Martha Ramsey of Skaneateles, N.Y. told a Syracuse newspaper that she had a vision of falling rocks.

Came Doomsday and the largest crowd of the season was on hand. The mayors of the twin cities were aboard the yacht *Maid of the Mist* as was Paul Kurtz, chairman of the Committee for the Scientific Investigation of Claims of the Paranormal and his 12-year-old son. Some Ohio tourists complained that they traveled a long distance and nothing happened. In Bridgewater Mrs. St. John said she had erred only on the date; she insisted that some day there would be a calamity at 4:56 P.M.

Aug. 4, 1979 the *New York Times's* editorial, "A Limit on Prophets?" contended that if a disaster had occurred 13 superstitious days later than the prediction, "the world would consider the prediction a pretty good one." If a soothsayer says "sometime this summer" she might be absolved but when one cites an exact time and place, judgment should be by the same "time of the essence" principle that prevails as a generally accepted accounting practice.

More cynically, Henry Mitchell began the Any Day column of the New York *Village Voice* for March 23, 1980 with a number of improbable and/or silly predictions and then explained, "I did it the same way all the other idiots do it. I let my brain go into neutral and jotted down whatever popped into my head. Then I dished it up as likely to happen. It is sheer bunk, of course, like all the other claptrap dished out by seers and which I, at least, have the grace to blush at a little."

Not so sarcastic but just as cynical was Janet Cook's "Confessions of a Zodiac Junkie," in the *Chicago Tribune* for Feb. 24, 1982. After the journey her horoscope said she would take turned out to be a $38.50 tow for a broken down car, she decided to change her sign. So every week she read the horoscope of a different astral house. But "I was still the one who had troubled waters ahead; watch your step!"

Despite the errors of the prophets they continue to receive plentiful attention from the press. At year's end it's not only the best-known professionals whose forecasts are considered newsworthy. Lesser talent, mostly hometown, is sought for opinions. A prime example was the long piece Larry Weintraub wrote for the *Chicago Sun-Times* of Dec. 31, 1979 after interviewing Gary Wayne of suburban Palatine. Among his guesses that the editors considered of importance to readers: Carter will be reelected; the Bears will be first in the division; inflation will hit 16 or 18 percent and there'll be political violence in New Hampshire, Illinois and probably Washington State or Oregon. Batting average: zero.

So, attention shifts back to Los Angeles where, the UPI reported April 7, 1981, Joseph Granville, noted stock-market analyst, announced that the city would be devastated by an earthquake April 10. Government geologists called the prediction nonsense and irresponsible. Those terms were mild by comparison with what was said four months later when the Blue Monday crash on the stock market Granville predicted did not materialize. As Herb Gould reported in the *Chicago Sun-Times* for Tuesday, Sept. 20, 1981, ticker watchers "described Granville in phrases that were universally unkind and often unprintable."

Joseph W. Granville is the son of an astrologer mother and of a father who was wiped out in the stock-market collapse of 1929. Dedicated to recouping the family fortune, he headquarters in Holly Hill, Fla. and publishes a weekly newsletter for about 13,000 subscribers. He also is in demand as a lecturer. When he spoke in Charleston, W.Va., he was interviewed by Edward Peeks, business-labor editor of the *Charleston Gazette*. He said the stock market does not follow events; it predicts them. The *Wall Street Journal,* he asserted, is wrong about 90 percent of the time in its predictions; and he, Granville, hopes to get a Nobel prize for his economic wizardry.

After Granville made his forecast that Los Angeles would be struck by an earthquake at 5:50 A.M. April 10, 1981, Peeks recalled Granville's lecture in an article, "On Quakes or Blue Chips, People Listen to Joseph Granville," in the *Gazette* for Jan. 15, 1981. By that time Granville had been blamed for a 23.8 point drop in the Dow Jones industrial index Jan. 7 because so many took his advice and sold short. In the *Wall Street Journal* for Feb. 27, 1981 Alan Bayless reported on a speech Granville delivered in Vancouver, where he told 1,800 that the index would drop another 16 points. That didn't occur.

Sunday, Sept. 27, 1981, the day before Blue Monday, Granville was reported to be in London advising: "Don't just sell, sell short," and predicted a big plunge in the London stock-market that did occur. He prophesied that the Dow Jones index would fall to 550 or 650 by the end of 1982.

Instead of plummeting, as Granville predicted, the New York Stock Exchange closed 18 points higher Monday, Sept. 28, 1981 but only after a shaky start caused by stockholders who followed Granville's advice to "sell everything." Financial writers called Granville "the guru of gloom" who almost succeeded. Gerald M. Connors reported, "Joe Granville's dancing bear act flopped on Wall Street" in the *Chicago Sun-Times* for Sept. 29, 1981 under a streamer headline, "Joe's 'Blue Monday' Turns Rosy."

The havoc caused by a Granville "sell everything" message to holders of his A list was reported April 1, 1982 by the *Wall Street Journal*. Real estate holdings were put up for sale and social activities were disrupted.

Wild as Granville's prognosticating now seems to insiders, if not to many gullible investors, he is not the first, perhaps not even the worst financial analyst to be guided in part by mysticism. For many decades Chicago's leading authority on economic trends was Phil S. Hanna. In the *Chicago Daily News* for July 25, 1949 Hanna declared that the reason for a rise in stocks was the disappearance of sun spots. On the other hand in the *Sun-Times* for June 24, 1976, Carol Mathews answered a reader's inquiry regarding what credence to give the prediction of a Canadian psychic that the Dow Jones industrial average would drop more than 70 points to fall below the 800 level. Mathews advised: "About as much value as that of anyone else these days. Economic forecasters have not been very accurate in recent years." As early as March 17, 1947, Arthur J. Snider, *Daily News* science writer, quoted Dr. Roy A. Doty, who warned the Chicago Production Conference against such "pseudo-sciences as astrology and numerology." And Edwin Darby, the *Sun-Times* financial editor, wrote March 23, 1977:

> People are always doing irrational things. Take the hundreds of thousands of newspaper readers who always turn first to the astrology column. Astrology was developed centuries ago and anyone who has ever taken a serious look at it since has found that there's no validity to it. Out of all the great things in civilization from Christ to Freud astrology is the thing they

pick to hold onto because they are terrified of the future. Astrology is booming among young people. You have to be bemused by the kids. They keep telling us where we are wrong, and lord knows, that's not hard to do. But when it comes to answers, they offer astrology and marijuana, both irrational.

To counteract Darby's sane comments is the dismal fact that, by and large, professional economists have been wrong in just about all of their predictions for as far back as anyone can recall. A good summary of recent failures of the nonastrological prophets to know what was happening was an article, "Gloomy Economists—Right or Wrong" by Donald C. Bauder of the Copley News Service, one use of it being in the *Columbus Ohio Dispatch* for Jan. 19, 1975.

Granville isn't the only economic analyst who relies, in part at least, on astrological knowledge. There also is Augie Alonzo of Northbrook, Ill. about whom Lynn Voedisch wrote in the Pioneer Press papers for Sept. 26, 1980. An ascetic, he sleeps under a pyramid in a small coachhouse and explains, "I'm not a psychic. Everything I do is strictly mathematical. What I do essentially is find certain times that are favorable for clients to elect to do certain activities. I let them know when it will be easiest to schedule a business meeting or look into a new investment."

And there also is Arch Crawford, whom Granville has praised in his own newsletter. Dan Dorfman told of Crawford's remarkable successes in an article that the *Washington Post* used Jan. 15, 1981. At the moment Crawford was warning that the fact Saturn and Jupiter were together, as they are every 20 years, meant a slumping stock market and a sliding economy. Crawford has tracked planetary cycles to correlate with the gyration of the Dow Jones index since 1897 and claims about 78 percent correctness in the forecasts he has made.

USA Today from the start considered Arch Crawford newsworthy. Dec. 22, 1982 it reported his successful forecast of a 25-point gain in the Dow Jones industrial average because, he said, he obtained signals from the positions of the planets. Dec. 27, 1982 the same newspaper featured Crawford in an article by Charles Koshetz, "Starry-eyed look into market future." Other offbeat methods of forecasting mentioned were the full-moon theory, sunspot theory, necktie indicator, Super Bowl indicator and the presidential cycle theory.

In a similar article in the *Chicago Sun-Times* for Aug. 27, 1982, Stephen Z. Ryvkiewicz described ticker-tape astrology as practiced by Grace Morris of Oak Lawn, Ill. Of the '80s Morris says: "We're going through the same cycle we were going through in the '30s." She cited the positions of the planets to illustrate her point.

That the *Wall Street Journal* has not soured on all astrologers was shown by an article from Dallas Aug. 22, 1980, which read, "The price of Recognition Equipment Inc. stock has soared heavenward in recent days and it may have been drawn there by the stars and planets." Specifically many investors followed the advice of Florida astrologer Jack Gillen, who said the stock would "skyrocket" to $83 a share because "Saturn is moving into Libra." "Even if the predictions come true," the newspaper said, "investors in these companies shouldn't feel too smug. Mr. Gillen makes 1,000 other predictions for 1980 including the approach of a new ice age, mounting assassinations, racial violence, revolutions and 'sheer panic in many areas.'"

In his daily column for Jan. 3, 1982, in the *Chicago Tribune,* Jack Mabley distinguished two major types of publicized predictions. One, the frivolous, is harmless nonsense, "the junk that sell millions of copies of the *Enquirer* and *Star*—from 1976 through 1980 *Enquirer's* ten psychics had four correct predictions in 422 tries." The other type of prediction, the financial, is not much better. "Innocent and gullible people can get burned by taking some of these 'experts' seriously," Mabley wrote. He listed a half-dozen forecasts by governmental and private authorities and made his own prediction that come Jan. 1, 1983 not one would have been proved correct.

That Wall Street investors nevertheless still place reliance on the mystics was evidenced by an article by the skeptic Carol Mathews in the *New York Post* for May 22, 1978. It advertised the talents of Maha Yogi Nayarana, who collected $2,000 a page for any report and charges a minimum of $10,000 for a retainer. He has clients in the United States and abroad. Many were directed to him by their wives. Mathews hinted that his record of successful predictions was no better than average. That, the *Wall Street Journal* suggested March 13, 1975, is not very high. A study by R. H. Bruskin Associates of New Brunswick, N.J. showed that adults give high grades for accuracy in forecasts to sport writers, sports announcers and weathermen. The lowest ratings go to economists, stockbrokers and people who prepare horoscopes.

In the *New York Post* for Nov. 2, 1978 Carol Mathews quoted Narayana as explaining he makes his predictions based on his personal understanding of the unseen forces of nature.

Embarrassed by their bad record the previous year, economic forecasters took New Year's resolutions to do better according to the *Los Angeles Times* for Jan. 6, 1982. Otto Eckstein, who was President Johnson's top economic advisor, now president of Data Resources, said, "Our forecasts were all backwards" to which Michael K. Evans, president of Evans Economics, added "We got it all mixed up."

Just how badly they erred was reported in the *Chicago Tribune* for April 10, 1982 by William Gruber who extended the effort of looking up what most of the leading "economic seers," as he called them, predicted. Even the supposed best made big mistakes. That means Nobel prize winner Milton Friedman, Walter W. Heller, John Kenneth Galbraith, Alfred Kahn and David Stockman.

So take your pick: astrologers who talk to the stars or economists who talk to themselves.

Jack Mabley rubbed it in again when he pointed out in his April 3, 1981 column that not one had come anywhere close to predicting the attempted assassination of President Reagan March 30. Then, however, he proved as gullible as the rest of us when he summarized the Associated Press story of April 2, that a psychic, Tamara Rand, had predicted the shooting Jan. 6 on Dick Maurice's talk-show over Atlanta radio station WTBS.

To the *Madison* (Wis.) *Capital-Times* for April 2 Rand was a hometown girl who made good. It was in Madison that she founded her institute in 1970 before moving it to Los Angeles several years later.

Her story about her supposed forecast was dramatic: that she had predicted Reagan would experience a thud in the chest during the last few days of March, with some fair-haired man named Jack Humbley and there would be shots "all over the place." When she heard of the attack by John Hinckley she was "shocked but not surprised."

Immediately after the supposed Jan. 6 broadcast was rebroadcast April 2, skepticism mushroomed. The general manager of the Las Vegas station where the recording was made said, "We have reason to believe the interview was taped on March 31, the day after the assassination attempt." Other associates at the station corroborated the charge that Rand made tapes March 31 and their testimony drowned out the denials of Rand and Maurice. So April 5 newspapers had the news that the latter had confessed. In a copyrighted story in the *Las Vegas Sun*, Maurice wrote, "My interview with Tamara Rand in which she predicted the assassination attempt on President Ronald Reagan is a lie."

Thereupon Rand apologized for taking "literary license" with a "re-inactment" of a prediction. She persisted in declaring she had forecast the assassination attempt several times before it happened. And all three major networks plus Cable News Network, on which the hoax originated, made apologies. Appearing on separate segments of the "Today" show Sunday, April 5, Rand and Maurice denounced each other as the major culprit, Kup revealed in his April 7 column. Three days earlier, before the confession, Kup had written, "Psychics around the nation are coming out of the woodwork with self-serving statements that they predicted the assassination attempt on President Reagan. Take it with a grain of salt. Too many psychics have 20/20 vision after the fact."

To Art Petacque and Hugh Hough, who conduct an OutFront column in the *Chicago Sun-Times*, Rand insisted April 12 that it wasn't a hoax but a "screwup" in a TV taping because she'd frequently made such a prediction. Commented the columnists: "Rand, who has either unlimited chutzpah or extraordinary psychic powers, also maintained that she once predicted she would become nationally famous 'because of a screwup.' "

Some of the best scolding of the broadcasters and the press came from within journalism. In a scorching column in the *Chicago Tribune* for April 8, Ron Alridge wrote, "A few years ago few respectable newspapers would even print paid advertisements for fortune tellers and the like. Today the media, electronic and printed, are chuck full of 'news' that gives a back door kind of credibility to self-proclaimed soothsayers . . . Journalism has started taking this supernatural business seriously, casting professional standards and responsibilities to the wind."

Even more caustic was the syndicated columnist Andy Rooney, who wrote April 9: "I am not inclined to laugh this off . . . There's nothing funny about the readiness of so many Americans to believe in this sort of thing and nothing funny at all about other people's readiness to take advantage of them. The people who believe in psychics are the same people who read their horoscopes every day just as if their lives depended on something other than themselves."

Six months after the hoax an unrepentant Tamara Rand announced that she had filed a $10 million lawsuit against Dick Maurice, the talk-show host since fired by the show, and producer Gary Greco, also fired. She told Steve Harvey of the *Los Angeles Times* that if she were guilty of anything it was gullibility. The paper ran the account Oct. 1, 1981 without comment.

About the same time Jack Mabley, the veteran *Chicago Tribune* columnist, asked, "Did any seer foresee Sadat's assassination?" He found nothing in the lists of forecasts by Jeane Dixon, the *National Enquirer*, the *Star*, or others. However, June 3 the Rev. Louise Helene of Calumet Park wrote in a suburban paper: "Anwar Sadat will fall victim to an assassin's bullet in the near future." Enough to make Helene an international authority on the supernatural. However, Mabley wrote that it also should be realized that Hellene predicted Menachem Begin would be out of office in 1981, Castro would die of cancer, Ronald Reagan's daughter would pose for *Playboy*, and Chicago's Mayor Byrne would separate from Jay McMullen and eventually divorce him.

The *Washington Post's* Svetlana probably had a better claim as regards Sadat's murder. Oct. 11, 1981 she listed the seven occasions between Sept. 9, 1979 and Sept. 20, 1981 on which she had warned the Egyptian leader. It is quite likely that there were others who made no claim to supernatural powers who also would not have placed heavy bets on Sadat's chances for survival after he signed the Camp David accord.

Between Aug. 28 and Oct. 16, 1982 the *Post* ran a number of letters from readers condemning and defending Svetlana's column and the soothsayer's comments therein. Aug. 8 the same paper had a four-column picture of Sandra Pullano, a professional psychological astrologer, sketching a star chart for two followers. An accompanying half-page article was headlined, "Astrology Buffs Share Conviction That Stars Shape Their Behavior."

In Chicago the convention of the American Federation of Astrologers received full-page treatment from the *Sun-Times* Sept. 1 and the *Tribune* Sept. 2, 1982. However, articles tending to downplay astrology appeared in San Francisco newspapers. June 21, 1982 Bill Mandel analyzed the current apocalyptic thinking in the *Examiner* for June 21, 1982 and Michael Robertson wrote a full-page piece, "The Skeptics Who Debunk Pseudo Science," in the *Chronicle* for July 22, 1982. The former was inspired by an article by William Martin in the *Atlantic Monthly* on believers in an imminent second coming by Jesus Christ. The latter reported the iconoclastic activities of the Bay Area Skeptics.

4

Doomsday

Despite the glowing terms with which religious leaders have described the afterlife throughout history, prophecies that Doomsday is imminent have caused millions or billions to become terrified with fear. Even the faithful, generally confident they will be saved on Doomsday, have been apprehensive.

Early Christians believed that the Second Coming of Jesus would occur in their time and for centuries signs and portents were misinterpreted as heralding the advent. One of the first end-of-the-world scares to be caused by fear of astronomical accidents occurred in 1179 when John of Toledo warned that in 1188 there would be a conjunction of the planets, meaning they would all seem to be in the same place, under the stormy sign of Libra. Earthquakes and storms were certain to occur, the astrologer declared; some feared the worst.

Today's resurgence of interest in the imminence of Doomsday dates from the early part of the 19th century, when quite a few evangelical preachers thought that some biblical prophecies were coming true. Foremost among them was William Miller (1782-1849), who interpreted Daniel 8:13-14 to mean that the world would end "about the year 1843" with the coming of Jesus. The definite date he predicted was March 21, 1844, later changed to Oct. 2, 1844. When that Day of Great Disappointment came, about half of Miller's followers, estimated at 50,000 to 100,000, dropped out. Adventism, however, did not do so and in 1863 the Seventh Day Adventists were organized. Today they number about 1.5 million worldwide. April 7, 1948 the Overseas News Agency distributed a story from London that the church there believes the end of the world is imminent but will not reveal the day. Australian church members, the story said, have been advised to desert all the cities that presumably will be the first victims when the finish comes. Undaunted, the British said, "God will warn us when it is time to leave." June 24, 1949 the *Washington Post* reported that the president of the Potomac Conference of the Adventists had declared that the current "enormous" increase in crime, murder and lawlessness is part of a direct fulfillment of the "last days" as prophesied in the Bible.

As might be expected today, consistent with the recrudescence of interest in the supernatural, the words of the champion prognosticator of all times are being recalled. He was Nostradamus, court astrologer to King Henry II of France and his queen, Catherine de Medicis. As has always been the custom of those in his profession, his prophecies were "replete with code meanings, symbols and word plays," to quote from Allen Spraggett's article, "Nostradamus And the End of the World," in the *Pittsburgh Press* for Sept. 8, 1974. Further, he wrote, "Skeptics retort that Nostradamus wrote in puzzles and each reader finds in the cryptic prophecies exactly what he wants to find."

Because so many of the 16th-century seer's forecasts have been interpreted to apply to some historical events, today there are many who expect the world to end in 2000 to fulfill a supposed prophecy that an Arab-Israeli war to begin in 1973 would be the beginning of the apocalyptic conflict to lead to the biblical Battle of Armageddon.

Certain that Jesus' second coming was imminent and that he would live with the Lord for 1,000 years, Will Nicholson spent nine years building a house of stone, marble and concrete that would last that long, the UPI reported Nov. 2, 1959 from Alcoa, Tenn. Five years after the work was completed, Mrs. Nicholson, who had helped in its construction, died. According to her husband, "Her faith just wasn't strong enough."

Throughout history the faithful have gathered on mountaintops to be taken to heaven by their god's emissaries. Others have liquidated all their assets to spend their supposed last days having a riotous good time. Generally newspapers everywhere play upon the superstitious and the repercussions of their behavior.

For example, an Associated Press photograph Jan. 30, 1960 showed a 17-year-old Filipino shoeshiner, who was dubbed Seer Sampaloe for his prediction that the world would end Jan. 23, 1960. When the planet kept on spinning his $4,000 bank account was impounded and he faced charges of obstructing traffic, disturbing the peace, swindling and collecting contributions for charity without a permit.

The next year the entire world's attention was centered upon India, where Jan. 20, 1961, dispatches revealed, some 740 Hindu priests held a 16-day prayer vigil to avert the end of the world Feb. 4, 1961. The calamity would result from a conjunction of several planets and other celestial bodies bound, the astrologers said, to touch off thunderstorms, earthquakes, tornadoes, floods and fire. The *Chicago Daily News* for Jan. 31, 1962 provided background as follows:

> According to Hindu history, the last time the planets lined up this way was 3,000 years ago and India was swept by war, fire and flood. The event has created such a stir that India's Prime Minister Nehru issued a public denunciation of such superstition.

There's no doubt that much of the Far East takes astrology seriously. In Burma the proclamation of independence in 1948 came at the unlikely hour of 4:20 a.m. because the stars were more propitious then. The crown prince of Sikkim, in the Himalayas, postponed his wedding because 1962 looked bad to the stargazers. Hindu priests are working with Mammy Yorkum's own zeal right now to head off whatever disaster awaits this weekend.

Leads of Associated Press dispatches as they appeared in the *Chicago Sun-Times,* were:

Saturday, Feb. 3, 1962—"D Day Hysteria Mounts"; New Delhi—"With the chiming of the midnight hour, temple bells began tolling in many cities of India Saturday while the voices of millions were raised in prayers to save humanity from doomsday."

With newspapers of all languages splashing astrological forebodings that "the next three days will see the earth bathed in blood of thousands of kings," a near-panic situation was reported from many areas of India and Nepal.

Sunday, Feb. 4, under a streamer headline, "Doom Fear Lingers in India"—"Millions of frightened Indians bathed in sacred rivers and prayed to the goddess of destruction and fire Saturday but the first day of Doomsday Weekend passed with nothing more spectacular than the bright red sun setting behind the Indian Ocean."

Monday, Feb. 5, under a streamer headline on page 3, "Doom Prophecy Comes to Nought"—"The dreaded serpent Rahu slithered across the heavens early Monday and swallowed the sun—and lo the world is still with us."

For all the soothsayers' blood-chilling predictions of universal calamities the eclipse of the sun went off over the Pacific somewhat uneventfully.

Many smug Americans, of course, smiled at the gullibility of the non-Christians on the other side of the world. Of others, however, William Braden wrote in the *Sun-Times* for Feb. 4, 1962:

> Twenty centuries ago three wise men from the East saw a sign in the heavens that led them to the birthplace of a Savior. Some men believe the same thing will happen again Sunday.
>
> In effect they are expecting a second star of Bethlehem to appear and herald the coming of a new redeemer.
>
> Ironically, other men are expecting the world to end.

Braden explained what a sketch in the Saturday paper had illustrated, an almost straight lineup of the planets and a total eclipse of the earth by the sun, not visible in Chicago.

Braden's article was headlined, "A 2nd Star of Bethlehem Sunday?" The Monday *Sun-Times* followup appeared under a streamer, "2,200 Pay 'Doomsday' Visit to Planetarium." This attendance was double normal.

Robert I. Johnson, planetarium director, answered queries from anxious persons:

> We at the Adler Planetarium plan to be in business next month. Our rent is paid. And some of our staff, the younger ones, will be looking at the next configuration of the eight heavenly bodies May 2, 2500. That's when they will catch up with each other again.
>
> Also, before you get worried about any collisions, consider the fact that they are tens of millions miles apart. They won't even scrape fenders.

This was one of the few constructive statements to appear in any Chicago paper during the past quarter-century. The space given scientists and other iconoclasts is meager by comparison with that devoted to the views and acts of the ignorant, superstitious and gullible.

Failure of their fears to be realized did not make disbelievers out of many Indians if Ernest Weatherall's article in the *Chicago Daily News* for May 20, 1970 is authentic. The headline, "Stars Hold Indians Under Mystic Spell," epitomizes the article, "Nothing," Weatherall wrote, "succeeds in India like astrology. It is one of the country's biggest industries."

And the same seems to be true of much of the rest of the world. July 10, 1971 the UPI reported from Rio de Janeiro that police had to rescue Madalena Rosa Cavalcante from neighbors because she falsely prophesied that the world would end the previous day.

Because workers quit work and hundreds of families took to the hills, Australian Premier Don Dunstan had to appeal by radio for calm after a clairvoyant in Adelaide predicted an earthquake and tidal wave were imminent.

A warning that human fears and hysterical behavior will increase as the year 2000 comes closer was sounded by Prof. Roy Peter Clark of Auburn University in the *New York Times*. He cited several examples of irrationality today and traced the history of millenarianism with special reference to the decade before the year 1000.

When a total eclipse of the sun swept across central Africa and the Indian Ocean the government of Tanzania campaigned vigorously on radio and television and in newspapers to assure natives there was no danger from plague, famine and death as the superstitious believed, the UPI reported Oct. 25, 1976 from Dar-Es-Salaam.

"Despite the fact that Mars, Saturn and Uranus were in 'bad aspect,' in relation to each other for the first time in 25 years, the end did not come yesterday, and astrologers seemed miffed," was the consoling news Fred Ferretti reported in the *New York Times* for Feb. 25, 1977. Ferretti rewrote dispatches from all over the world, a typical paragraph being this: "Over in London the stargazer Charles Harvey was prepared for vast outbreaks of tension and anger. Another, Peter Clark, had told businessmen to postpone meetings because he expected a bad day for decisions. June Penn had warned of earthquakes, accidents and, at the very least, nasty weather." Similar paragraphs were based on reports from other countries.

Self-appointed prophets also continued to command valuable newspaper space. An example was a half-page in the *Chicago Daily News* Oct. 30, 1976 devoted to an interview by James Bowman, religion editor, with a born-again former boat captain who takes the Bible seriously and writes best-selling books, including *The Late Great Planet Earth*. He is Hal Lindsey, whose viewpoint was summarized by the headline, "To Him, the end of the world is in sight."

Lindsey's book is mentioned in a column report on "Bible Scholars to Discuss Doomsday" by Jack Houston, religion editor, in the *Chicago Tribune* for Jan. 29, 1978. Because so many events suggest fulfillment of biblical prophecies, the Moody Bible Institute will devote the school's annual Founders' Week conference to the study of Bible prophecies. Born-again Christians, Moody authorities believe, will be removed from Earth before the period of worldwide devastation and Jesus will return to rule for 1,000 years.

Contrasts between the old and new were described by Michael T. Kaufman in a columnlong article from Kuruksshetra, India in the *New York Times* for Feb. 17, 1980. Over one million pilgrims witnessed an eclipse of the sun by the moon. Stores were closed, no marriages were performed, pregnant women stayed indoors and hundreds bathed in ancient holy pools. All had come for "moksha," the Hindu concept of salvation by which mortals are released from the cycle of rebirth. Kaufman described it and other ceremonies but made no mention of fear such as gripped the country in 1962.

The failure of previous Doomsday prophecies to come true has not discouraged others from making similar warnings. In Public Eye for March 30, 1980, Michelle Stevens publicized the prediction of the Rev. Willie Day Smith of Dallas that April 1, 1980 would be the Day of Rapture mentioned in the Bible. That day all true Christians were to be changed to immortal bodies, swept up and transported to heaven leaving the earth to nonbelievers and sinners.

Seventy-five astrologers from around the world weren't so definite when they held an international conference in New Delhi, the *Baltimore Sun* reported Jan. 5, 1981. They did believe the end of the world during the '80s was likely, although a few said 75 to 80 percent of the world's people will perish in a natural calamity in 1995.

That year is just short of the Doomsday that Charles Berlitz predicts for the end in his book *Doomsday 1999 A.D.* Counteracting the generous publicity it has given to Berlitz's earlier theories about the Bermuda Triangle and similar matters, the *Chicago Sun-Times* March 1, 1981 printed a strongly critical review by James Randi, the iconoclastic magician. The review concludes, "Those of us who live to see the arrival of the next millenium will be going about our business as usual while Berlitz and his white-robed apostles gaze skyward from mountain-tops awaiting The End. If it were not so genuinely sad, that picture would be funny."

"It's Heyday for Prophets of Doomsday" is just what Russell Chandler's full-page article in the *Los Angeles Times* for April 8, 1981 was about. The author summarized the views of Hal Lindsey, Jim McKeever, Jerry Falwell and others and gave their answers to "Why apocalypse now?" It is that, by contrast with the situations when earlier prophecies did not come true, never before have all the elements described in the Bible's signs of the last times been present. Wrote Chandler:

> For those who seek them, portents of catastrophe are not hard to find. Fascination with finitude is spreading.
> Fundamentalist Bible believers who take the end time prophecies literally number in the tens of millions according to polls.
> And there are signs the public at large is detecting ominous omens.

Most prophets today hesitate to predict exact dates and times for "rapture," the division of the saved from the sinners. Most seem to believe the premillennialism period will end before the 21st century begins. At least one, however, impatiently prepared for it June 28, 1981. He is Bill Maupin of Tucson, founder and president of the Lighthouse Gospel Tract Foundation. June 16, 1981 Charles Hillinger quoted him in the *Los Angeles Times,* "All of us on earth who have accepted the Lord will slowly rise from the ground in our bodies and drift into the clouds. Millions of people will ascend into heaven . . ." Then, Maupin said, Satan will take over the world for seven years and behead a billion people. May 14, 1988, one day before the 40th anniversary of the establishment of the state of Israel, Christ will return to earth with all those who went to heaven with him June 28, 1981 and will reign for 1,000 years.

When the ascension day came and went about 40 or 50 of the faithful who had quit jobs, sold homes or spent their bankrolls and besieged Maupin for an explanation he couldn't give, the press associations reported June 29 from Tucson. Hillinger in his June 29 article in the *Los Angeles Times,* however, quoted several of the faithful about how exhilarating the expectation had been for months. Maupin told his handful of disciples that he had made a slight miscalculation and set a new date, Aug. 7, 1981. The lead of the United Press International's story from Tucson that day was:

> Members of a Bible prophecy sect expect to cause a unique air traffic control situation as they ascend to heaven to avoid the Satanic legions preparing to take power on earth.

Examples of the press' handling of news related to astrology in this and the three preceding chapters have not been selective. Rather, they are a 100 percent sampling of what was contained in the author's reading material in recent years. With few exceptions the handling of the news has been strictly objective except for some feature articles and some jibes by a few columnists. Overwhelmingly astrologers are treated with respect; their claims and prophecies are published without adverse comments.

But not always. Tom O'Connor was not-so-subtly satirical when he covered the convention of the American Federation of Astrologers for the *New York Compass* of Nov. 22, 1949. After listening to speeches and interviewing the convention's chairman, he still was unable to translate the jargon. However, he came away with the knowledge that he had a stomachache because he was a Leo.

Another comical and thought-provoking article was "Meet the Man Called Prophet" in *Parade* for June 7, 1981. The author was Morris West, who explained coincidences between the fictional events in *The Shoes of the Fisherman* and actual events, in that case the election of a non-Italian to the papacy. Also he was credited with magical powers when the outcome of the Vietnam war seemed to resemble the plot of his novel, *The Ambassador*. Regarding his book *The Tower of Babel,* he wrote: "There is no doubt now about the dangers of assuming a prophet's mantle. The book was banned in certain South American countries. I provided my publisher with guarantees of funds and press support . . . It was made clear to me . . . I could travel only at grave personal risk."

Some anti-superstition remarks sometimes are included in letters to the editor. The *Chicago Tribune* for Aug. 9, 1981 had a satirical piece by Bob Casey, who said of horoscopes, "I'll bet anybody could write them— even me." He then proceeded to compose horoscopes for all 12 zodiac signs. An example: "Virgo (Aug. 24–Sept. 23)—You will become active in political affairs. You will be assigned to put bumper stickers on cars. The cars will be moving. You will quit."

A Chicago lawyer, John H. Shurtleff, became so annoyed with the "insane" column conducted by Bette Peters in the *Suburban Life Citizen* that he attacked not only the value of astrology but also the poor answers Peters gave to readers, with "absolutely no imagination or style." He cited the answer the seer gave to a 69-year-old mother worried about her 38-year-old son's beer drinking and bachelorhood. Peters had counseled: "Your son will cut down on drinking this spring. There is marriage in the picture for him toward the end of 1981." The paper ran Shurtleff's letter Dec. 17, 1980, including his suggestion that the paper give constructive advice if any, such as "I see you telling your son to join Alcoholics Anonymous or else move out of your home."

On a few occasions the *Chicago Sun-Times* Action Time has done what Shurtleff advocated. May 2, 1975 it replied to a woman who regretted not being able to talk to Irene Hughes on a radio talk-show to ask if she would get a job. The newspaper's expertise read in part: "too bad we missed Irene Hughes . . . One of our staff members, if he had had advance warning, would have liked you to ask her what happened to his promised trip to either the Hawaiian or Virgin Islands, which Ms. Hughes saw in his future years ago."

March 27, 1978 Action Time answered a reader who asked information about Nostradamus' prophecies, ". . . remember, many of Nostradamus' prophecies are suspect . . ." The editors pointed out that the 16th-century stargazer saw World War II ending in 1951, with a long period of peace to follow. Some translators say he saw World War III breaking out in Greece in 1949. New York also was supposed to have a civil war that year with atom bombs bursting all over, with dire events to follow.

Checking on the accuracy of prophecies is easy but doesn't seem to reduce the confidence followers have in their favorite fortune tellers. The ease with which present-day astrologers "get away" with fantastic failures was cited by H. R. Whitaker in a *Chicago Tribune Magazine* article Oct. 19, 1969. He wrote:

> The amazing thing to me is the nonchalance with which today's astrologists view their recurrent lapses in prophecy. In olden times, if you made a horoscopic error, you suffered for it. For failing to predict an eclipse that caused pandemonium in the realm, the court astrologers of ancient China, named Hi and Ho, were put to death. For darkening the birthday of a prince by forecasting evil that failed to materialize, an Egyptian seer was exiled.

By contrast, Whitaker continued:

> Such retribution need no longer be feared, mainly because the fans won't permit it. Today's Jeane Dixons and Catherine deJerseys command support that is not only numerous but irrationally loyal. They can fire eight blanks in a row, but if the ninth is on target—or even near it—the rafters will vibrate to the cheers of the faithful . . . Russ Burgess seemingly cooked his professional goose by predicting in close succession that Sen. Charles Percy will be elected vice president . . . Jacqueline Kennedy will not remarry . . . the Viet Nam war will end in the fall of 1966. Burgess has remained alive and kicking chiefly because, along with the three eggs he laid, he was prescient enough to add that Sen. Robert Kennedy will never be president—the only one of his four major predictions Burgess' hosts can now recall when they introduce him to an audience.

Most of the Whitaker article entitled "I Can See Disaster Coming, Honest" is favorable to psychics Milton Kramer and Dr. Gilbert N. Holloway.

In an article, "Did They 'See' Tomorrow?" in *This Week* for Jan. 14, 1968, T. F. James balanced the right and wrong forecasts of three outstanding prophets, Michel Nostradamus, Edgar Cayce and Jeane Dixon. Cayce was right in predicting earthquakes in California, hurricanes in Cuba and an increase in Norfolk harbor traffic. He was wrong in predicting that New York City would disappear, China would become a new "cradle" of Christianity and the lost continent of Atlantis would reappear. Take your pick.

In an interview Feb. 12, 1978 with a UPI reporter, Mike Feinsilber in Washington, Paul Dicksin, author of *The Future File,* said a prophecy of disaster may be good if it causes a change of behavior as was the case after Rachel Carson's *Silent Spring* gave a boost to conservation efforts. A 1976 analysis by the General Electric Research and Development Center showed that of 1,556 predictions by American inventors, industrialists and writers between 1890 and 1940 fewer than half were fulfilled. Example: Adm. William Leahy to President Harry Truman: "The bomb will never go off and I speak as an expert on explosives." No stargazer claimed credit for having forecast the opposite.

Jack Smith analyzed the paperback *Predictions for 1976* for the *Los Angeles Times* of Nov. 14, 1980 with "power that all those seers lacked— the power of hindsight." He found that ". . . a great many vague predictions that might have been worked out by anyone who reads a newspaper; predictions that didn't come about at all; and long shot guesses that have little chance of fulfillment but make good reading even now . . . Most of the seers predicted such inevitable disasters as a flood, fire, famine and accident, though usually they were careful not to mention specific places, and there were the inevitable predictions that Jackie Onassis would find happiness or would not; the same for Elizabeth Taylor."

Ten Harvard undergraduates, cooperating in a test of psychic powers to forecast the future, did slightly better than ten nationally prominent psychics whose predictions appeared in the *National Enquirer,* Boyce Rensberger reported in the *New York Times* for Dec. 31, 1976. The tests were described in the magazine *Zetetic.* They dealt with the year 1973. Dr. Gary Alan Fine, University of Minnesota sociologist, was quoted as believing psychic forecasts may have some value. He said, "People have a desire to reduce the uncertainty in their lives. By making the future somewhat more predictable and less problematic anxiety about the unknown is reduced."

In the *New York Times* for Dec. 25, 1980 Christopher Lehmann-Haupt devoted a full column to mere recitation of scores of the forecasts in the *Prediction* book without any comment, critical or otherwise.

After chiding some seers who only pretend to see the future, Clarence Petersen cleverly satirized the whole business of soothsaying in the *Chicago Tribune* for Jan. 5, 1981. First he pointed out that the least inaccurate *National Enquirer* soothsayer did so by getting one right out of 25 predictions, then he invented a new 100 percent accurate forecaster and wound up with a hilarious list of predictions, as "The biggest [movie] hit of 1981 will be 'Rocky III meets Jaws II starring Sugar Ray Leonard and the Rev. Jesse Jackson' and 'A band of Thomasinas will be apprehended in Miami after one of them, a 36-year-old mother of five, is stopped as she seeks entrance to the Dolphins locker room with a counterfeit press card and turns state's evidence.' "

Throughout the quarter-century of accelerating popular interest in the occult, most serious scientists remained aloof. They had more important things to do than take part in controversies that were settled centuries earlier. The claims of the astrologers especially were thoroughly ridiculous to anyone with a modicum of knowledge of astronomy and related fields such as geology, anthropology, paleontology and others. As the clamor augmented, however, with books and magazines devoted to the unseen skyrocketing and organized ignoramuses bringing pressure to bear on schools and universities to modify their science teaching methods, real scholars could not persist in ignoring the nitwit age; it would not go away as a result of their silence. So gradually the scientific society had to forget its dignity and recognize the need for some form of organized resistance. To avoid Doomsday for science they want a Doomsday for superstition.

One of the first inklings of what was to come was a piece by John Dart in the *Los Angeles Times* for Nov. 10, 1974 headlined, "Scholars Taking Potshots at Sky Chariots, Sentient Plants." The *Chicago Tribune* reprinted it Nov. 24 with the headline, "Science Assumes Debunking Mood." Dart wrote that an increasing number of scientists had become alarmed over the "widespread popular interest in theories that mix the supernatural with 'science' providing contrived explanations for alleged mysteries of science. The trend most disturbing to scientists is the broad appeal for public rejection of hard-nosed standards of scientific investigation and verification." Scientists are "suspicious of work tied to mystical or supernatural explanations and not subjected to vigorous scientific procedure" and are increasingly abandoning the defeatist attitude usually expressed thus: "You never convince a true believer so why waste time trying? Under urging from *Science* magazine and others they attack specific ideas or books such as *Chariots of The Gods* and *The Secret Life of Plants* but mostly avoid engaging in public debates."

Dart quoted Paul Saltman of the University of California at San Diego, "I see today, as never before, an intense and polarizing struggle for man's mind between the forces of faith and mysticism and science and reason."

And then came Sept. 4, 1975 and a UPI story from Buffalo that began, "Astrology is just a lot of Taurus—or bull—according to a group of prominent scientists." The scientists numbered 186, including 18 Nobel Prize winners. Their statement appeared in the September-October 1975 issue of *The Humanist*, publication of the American Humanist Association edited by Dr. Paul Kurtz, professor of philosophy at the State University of New York at Buffalo. It expressed concern over "the continued uncritical dissemination of astrological charts by otherwise reputable newspapers, magazines and book publishers. This can only contribute to the growth of irrationalism and obscurantism. The time has come to challenge directly, and forcefully, the pretentious claims of astrological charlatans. It should be apparent that those individuals who continue to have faith in astrology do so in spite of the fact that there is no verified scientific basis for their beliefs and indeed that there is strong evidence to the contrary."

The group's attitude was expressed in part as follows:

> Those who wish to believe in astrology should realize that there is no scientific foundation for its tenets. In ancient times people believed in the predictions and advice of astrologers because astrology was part and parcel of their magical world view. They looked upon celestial objects as abodes or omens of the gods and thus intimately connected with events here on earth; they had no concept of the vast distances from the earth to the planets and stars. It is simply a mistake to imagine that the forces exerted by stars and planets at the moment of birth can in any way shape our futures.
>
> Why do people believe in astrology? In these uncertain times many long for the comfort of having guidance in making decisions. They would like to believe in destiny predetermined by astral forces beyond their control . . . One would imagine in this day of widespread enlightenment that it would be unnecessary to debunk beliefs based on magic and superstition.

The magazine contained two articles devastating to astrological belief: "A Critical Look at Astrology," by Bart J. Bok, professor emeritus of astronomy, University of Arizona, and "Astrology, Magic or Science" by Lawrence E. Jerome, science writer. Several additional articles on the subject appeared in subsequent issues.

One of the 186 signers, George O. Abell, professor of astronomy at the University of California in Los Angeles, wrote an article for the *Los Angeles Times* of Sept. 14, 1975. The paper headlined it "The Occult Might Be a Hindrance," with the subhead, "Belief in Astrology Can Foster Irrational Thinking." The *Austin American-Statesman* used about half of the piece Oct. 1, 1975, calling it "Astrology: Sham or Science?" Whatever called, the article was an explanation of the alarm that caused the scientists to forget their dignity and join a crusade against the growing acceptance of astrology. In a subsequent piece in the *L.A. Times* Abell wrote Oct. 1, 1975: "Astronomy and astrology are totally different subjects and there is no 'debate' over which is correct. Astronomy is that science that deals with the study of the universe; astrology is an ancient religion."

News of the statement by the 186 scientists was not considered to be as important as a movie star's broken leg or a promise to balance the budget by a presidential candidate would have been. The *Austin American-Statesman* gave 12 inches to the Associated Press story from New York Sept. 3, 1975. The *Denver Rocky Mountain News* gave 5 inches to the same story, most of which was direct quotation from the statement.

Under the heading, "All the Stars That Are Fit to Read" with the hanger head, "astrology defended against 186 mean old scientists," the *New York Times* Sept. 20 devoted one column to text by Vivienne Killingsworth and two more to facetious pictures. Of the 186 she wrote from Princeton, N.J., "If their purpose was to deter horoscope readers, they would have done better to tell us that astrology is based on sound scientific evidence. For the appeal of the occult is that it is irrational, fantastic and does not attempt to confuse its devotees with mere facts."

The rest of the article was a recitation of the benefits of a belief in astrology. The editor's note identified the author as one "who works in public relations, admits to a vested interest in fantasy." The *Minneapolis Tribune* reprinted the article Sept. 23.

Jake McCarthy's personal opinion column in the *St. Louis Post-Dispatch* for Sept. 22, 1975 was just as destructive. Under the heading, "Just an Astrology Buff," he wrote, "I was sorry to see a group of scientists stomp down hard on astrology as they did not long ago. Astrology seems like a lot of fun to me." And so on, supposedly being clever but disregarding the opportunity to contribute to public enlightenment and sanity.

The first Chicago newspaper readers knew of the unprecedented declaration by 186 scientists was Sept. 27 when the *Sun-Times* used a two-column picture on page one of a "small but, uh, spirited group of astrology buffs [who] held a rally in the Civic Center Plaza to protest what they said was an irresponsible attitude toward them by scientists."

The *Philadelphia Bulletin* Oct. 9, 1975 devoted almost a page to a large map of the zodiac and an article, "Astrology Makes Money and Enemies" by Doris B. Wiley. One-third was devoted to a sketchy history of astrology, one-third to quotations from the *Humanist* declaration and one-third to adverse comments by local stargazers. Most important, the soothsayers insisted that a properly calculated horoscope describes personality "inclinations" but does not interfere with free will.

Beginning a full-page article on "Astrology: It's a matter of faith to followers but fiction to doubters," in the *Detroit News* for Oct. 12, 1975 Joan Walter wrote, "Either you have faith in astrology or you don't" and then went on to describe the number and identities of famous persons throughout history who had at least been open-minded on the subject. Walter quoted Dr. Andrew Laurent, a mathematics professor at Wayne State University, as considering the scientists' petition "totally irrelevant as a disclaimer of astrology . . . since there are a lot of things that are true—that don't have a scientific basis." To answer a rhetorical question, "Why do people believe in astrology?" Walter wrote, "Probably because they find in it what they seek."

Quick as ever to take advantage of a current issue, Oct. 19, 1975 George Gallup reported from Princeton for the American Institute of Public Opinion that some 32 million Americans believe in astrology and think their lives are governed by the position of the stars. One in four adults—and nearly one in three women—reads an astrology column regularly and, Gallup surmised, were unaffected by the protest of the 186 scientists.

Perhaps the first strong statement on the subject was that with which Philip Nobile began his syndicated column for Nov. 2, 1975: "Astrology is the new opiate of the people . . . a fraud and astrologers are quacks." The rest of the two-column article, however, was a question and answer interview with Marsha Kaplan, editor of *Astrology Guide Magazine,* asking questions that gave her the opportunity to boost the cause of astrology without rebuttal.

A brief summary of the *Humanist* statement plus some comments by Paul Kurtz on the need for an attack on ignorance and gullibility were counteracted by comments by E. Donald Paplon, a professional astrologer and director of the Academy of Mystic Arts, and a few others in a full-page article by David W. Hacker in the *National Observer* for May 15, 1976. A balanced piece but not very informing on any of the important issues.

Organization of the Committee for the Scientific Investigation of Claims of the Paranormal was announced in the May–June 1976 issue of the *Humanist.* Co-chairman were Paul Kurtz and Marcello Truzzi, Eastern Michigan University sociologist who became editor of *Zetetic* (Greek for skeptical), which began as a semi-annual in fall 1976 but became a quarterly in the fall of 1978. By then the editor was Kendrick Frazier, formerly editor of *Science News,* and the name had been changed to the *Skeptical Inquirer.* The changes followed the resignation of Truzzi from the editorship and membership in the committee. He publicly charged his former colleagues with condemning paranormal phenomena without sufficient investigation. The *New York Times* for June 25, 1978 devoted a full column to Truzzi's condemnation of the committee. Boyce Rensberger quoted Truzzi as believing the works of J. Allen Hynek, who is interested in UFOs, J. B. Rhine, an experimenter with ESP, and Michel Gauquelin, a French astrologer, deserved study. Truzzi's rival magazine is called *Zetetic Scholar.* In late 1980 Paul Kurtz became editor of another new publication, *Free Inquiry,* published by the Council for Democratic and Secular Humanism. It takes on Jerry Falwell's Moral Majority and other right-wing organizations and publications. The *Skeptical Inquirer* specializes in debunking psychics, astrology, biorhythm, ESP, Uri Geller and other topics related to the supernatural.

As the committee's influence grew so did the attacks on it. In his column for June 29, 1976, syndicated by Universal Press Syndicate, the Rev. Andrew Greeley sarcastically wrote, "I couldn't figure out last year what they thought they were going to accomplish. Predictably the astrological enthusiasts responded with protest, anger and outrage. But it turns out that the busybodies actually enjoyed the reaction. They really don't expect to make converts, but they feel great when they can smugly shake their heads in dismay over the ignorance of the great unwashed who take astrology seriously."

Aug. 10, 1977 Paul Kurtz called what was presumably a committee news conference in New York to announce filing a complaint with the FCC against the National Broadcasting Company for "quasi-documentaries" and films in prime time on Bigfoot, the Outer Space Connection and demonic possession.

"The Great Randi broke a metal spoon that someone else was holding, Philip J. Klass predicted a wave of flying saucer sightings before the end of the year, Dennis Rawlins said that even professional astrologers think many newspaper horoscopes are nonsense and Marcello Truzzi denied that witchcraft and demonic possession exist." That was the lead to Edward Edelson's article in the *New York Daily News* for Aug. 10, 1977.

In his coverage of the same conference for the *New York Times* Boyce Rensberger stressed Kurtz's plea to the journalistic media to stop contributing to public gullibility toward "pernicious" doctrines and "virulent programs of dangerous sects." He said "NBC's treatment in 'documentaries' of such subjects as 'The Bermuda Triangle,' 'In Search of Noah's Ark' and 'The UFO Incident' constitutes in scientific terms a scandal . . ." George Hoover, an NBC spokesman, defended the programs, saying, "They are done as entertainment, not as news."

The Associated Press' story from New York Aug. 11, 1977 was what some would call "a bit snotty." Belief in some "cults of unreason" could harm or kill you, the story represents the view of the committee to be. The committee's definition of paranormal, according to the AP, is "unproven or mystic phenomenon." The *Chicago Sun-Times* used about 8 inches of the Associated Press account. The next day the Madison *Wisconsin State Journal* used more than twice as much.

Editorially the *New York Times* Aug. 13, 1977 adversely criticized the committee for its program. "In its effort to reverse the trend and to reestablish the worship of science the committee goes too far too fast. The strategy, it seems to us, should not be to badger the media—or even the candle-lit gurus and zodiac scholars. The first goal should be to get the fakery out of the college catalogues, the second to revive the vigorous training of all students in the scientific method."

In his Aug. 24, 1977 column in the *Christian Science Monitor,* Robert C. Cowen chastised scientists who, he said, for decades have "undermined their own credibility by being needlessly hostile to 'silly' subjects that cause public interest or less than candid in dealing with public issues." He accused scientists of ridiculing individuals as well as ideas.

Support for the committee's work came from Carl Sagan, noted Cornell University astronomer, the UPI reported Aug. 28, 1977 from Cambridge, Mass. He charged the media and scientists have been a "disastrous failure" in allowing the public interest in borderline science. Regarding the astrologers' claim that the position of the planets at the moment of a child's birth affects the child's future, he said, "At the moment of birth the gravitational influence of the obstetrician is greater than that of Mars."

Sept. 2, 1977 in the *New York Times* Boyce Rensberger reviewed the two-year history of the Committee for the Scientific Investigation of the

Claims of the Paranormal. To explain the apparent slow growth of the movement, Rensberger wrote: "The anti-pseudoscience movement does not have the support of all scientists. Some feel it unnecessarily dignifies the various cults and cliques to frame formal responses to them. Others believe that no matter what scientists say, the true believers have already closed their minds. Still others could not care less; they see the various cults as harmless and the followers as quite unimportant to science."

Philip Nobile used the same question and answer technique as when he interviewed Marsha Kaplan when he gave Paul Kurtz an opportunity to reply to critics in an article that the *Chicago Sun-Times* used Feb. 5, 1978. In answer to Nobile's question, "But where's the harm? Is believing in the Bermuda Triangle and astral projection any more dangerous than belief in heaven and angels, which is intellectually acceptable?" Kurtz said: "It's a value judgment. Truth is better than falsehood. When a society begins to abandon critical judgment I see horrible consequences in the long run. There is no guarantee that a society so infected by unreason will be resistant to even the most virulent programs of dangerous sects."

Finally the committee received a writeup that depicted it as not primarily interested in shooting Santa Claus. It was "God's Chariot! Science Looks at the New Occult" by Michael Kernan in the *Washington Post* for June 11, 1978.

Kernan wrote, "There is a multi-million-dollar business built around people who believe their lives are in the most literal sense ruled by medieval lore about stars and planets." He quoted Paul Kurtz, "It's just amazing this reversion to primitive credulity in the world's most technologically advanced country."

The committee's skeptical attitude toward many phenomena was detailed, Bermuda Triangle, Loch Ness monster, biorhythm, Uri Geller, UFOs, early visitors from another planet, ESP and more.

In reporting on the committee's third annual convention in New York AP reporter Kevin McKean took a sly dig Dec. 17, 1979 when he wrote, "Although they didn't produce any scientific evidence to prove it, several committee members said there is a trend away from scientific thinking." Kurtz said studies showed 80 percent of college students believe ESP is true or at least likely, 60 percent believe in UFOs and smaller proportions accept astrology, possession and even human vampirism.

About the most severe condemnation of the committee appeared in the *Washington Post* for Aug. 22, 1979. In a half-page article Ted Rockwell, a nuclear engineer in private practice and an associate member of the Parapsychological Association, wrote:

> Despite statements to the contrary, the committee demonstrates that its purpose is not scientific but persecution of heretics. It harasses magazines, TV stations, universities and research labs, trying to stop investigation or discussion of ideas its members consider heretical . . . This sampling of

events in the science world shows scientists behaving more like religious inquisitors than cool-headed rationalists.

Rockwell vilified John A. Wheeler, noted physicist, who wants the American Association for the Advancement of Science to "excommunicate parapsychology from their ranks." He said Wheeler does not evaluate the research being done into psi, some of it being "at least interesting."

Despite her confession that she falsely claimed to have broadcast a prediction that President Reagan would be shot, Tamara Rand appeared on KTTV's "PM Magazine" in Los Angeles. As a result Howard Rosenberg wrote in the *Los Angeles Times* for April 29, 1981 that it was no wonder Paul Kurtz believed the Rand hoax was "the consequence of an age gone mad and overwhelmed with fiction." Rosenberg quoted Kurtz further, "The paranormal is no longer merely a novelty. They're accepted in the electronic media and also in newspapers. Astrology, UFOs and psychic phenomena are deep in America."

Kurtz told Rosenberg, "The media are extremely unbalanced in their treatment of psychics because they never present a dissenting point of view."

If Kurtz had seen the *Chicago Tribune* for June 2, 1981 he would have noted at least one exception. Jeff Lyon was given a half-page in which to trace the origin of Kurtz's organization, its purposes and activities, as well as the views of several prominent members regarding the current state of public gullibility. He reviewed the contents of the then-current issue of the *Skeptical Inquirer* and anti-superstition books published by Prometheus Books. The dissident Truzzi was quoted and his viewpoint answered by Martin Gardner and others who explained: "Marcello withdrew because the rest of us wanted a periodical that would take sides and would present arguments against pseudoscience. Marcello wanted to provide a forum for equal times for both sides."

One of the best journalistic attempts to explain the recrudescence of interest in the supernatural was written by Russell Chandler, religion writer for the Feb. 14, 1972 *Los Angeles Times*. His interpretative piece, "In Troubled Times, 'Messiahs' Abound," with the subtitle "Human Search for Eternal Hero Finds Many to Answer the Call" had as its news peg the court challenge of the will of Ernest Digweed of Portsmouth, England, who left $56,700 to provide for Jesus after his return to Earth. Chandler wrote, "There is no dearth of current messiahs and their advance men." He quoted Clinton McLemore, associate professor of psychology at the Fuller Graduate School of Psychology in Pasadena, that in times of political unrest and socioeconomic hardship people are much more likely to look for a charismatic leader for direction and to make sense out of things.

Chandler told anecdotes of a dozen or so messianic candidates, many of them humorous. One example was the bearded young man who visited the

Times office trying to see Chandler. He told a messenger sent to get rid of him, "This may come as quite a surprise to you. I am the messiah." To which the quick-witted young woman replied, "Well, this may come as quite a surprise to YOU, but you're the third messiah we've had here today."

One of the most successful modern John the Baptists is Benjamin Creme of London. He insisted that Jesus was alive on Earth and would proclaim himself during 1982.

A clue as to what chance a charismatic messiah might have may be found in the gullibility that was exhibited worldwide for about a month before March 10, 1982, a much-advertised Doomsday. During that period the press associations and large city newspapers were, without exception, skeptical and outspoken in their analyses of the argument that Earth would be destroyed on that date. The evidence was that contained in a book by two Cambridge scientists, John Gribbin and Stephen Plagemann, authors of *The Jupiter Effect,* published in 1974. Its thesis was that on Doomsday all of the planets would be on the same side of the sun. "This would affect the Earth's magnetic field, inducing a torque that would alter the motions of the planets that form the planet's surface or would change global wind patterns, increasing friction between air and the Earth," to quote from Walter Sullivan's article in the *New York Times* for Feb. 14, 1982.

In the weeks that followed all of the media quoted authorities that planets would not be in a straight line but would be spread out in a 96-degree arc and that such a syzygy had occurred countless times in the past, every 179 years in fact, the last occasion being 1803 and the next due in 2237.

The Kitt Peak National Observatory in Arizona issued several statements to indicate that if there were any gravitational pull it would be insignificant. It also said, "Religious tracts have notified millions around the world of this day by relating it to biblical prophecy and the current fashion to predict the imminent end of the world." Robert Cooke used the quote in his article in the *Boston Globe* for Feb. 22, that began: "This may be disappointing but the so-called Jupiter Effect probably will flop."

A reader asked the *Chicago Sun-Times'* Action Time, "In your personal opinion, will the phenomenon trigger any action in Chicago?" He was reassured Feb. 11, 1982: "Action Time adheres to scientific theory that believes the planet configuration which has occurred before with no negative side effects will again happen with no negative reactions."

Unusually consoling was the lead to Dennis Byrne's story in the *Chicago Sun-Times* for March 4: "The world won't come to an end on March 10." He repeated the reasons why the catastrophe was unlikely but revealed that the Adler Planetarium was receiving 40 calls daily by worried people. In a lighter mood but also iconoclastic, the brief in the paper's Public Eye column March 4 telling of an End-of-the-World party being given by two television personalities said, "We're having the party so we all can go out in style."

March 7 the AP national story that the *New York Daily News* used was the first to reveal that a beneficial by-product of the scare was increased attendances at planetariums everywhere. The same day in a worldwide roundup the UPI reported that the Chinese government had launched a gigantic publicity campaign to stop fears generated by some papers that predicted earthquakes and floods. The *China Youth Daily* also called the fears groundless. In a separate story from Peking, Paul Loong quoted from Chinese newspapers that attempted to assuage fears.

In India, however, the *Sunday Herald* voiced the fears, saying the event would cause "labor unrest and death of a prominent labor leader" and "a strange epidemic affecting the abdomen will stalk India and there'd be earthquakes and communal unrest."

The New York Center for the Strange, a private group that issues annual Halloween predictions of 285 witches, took a poll and announced the lineup would trigger "nationwide shortages of sparkling wine, hockey pucks, gerbil cages and soy sauce." A Norfolk, Va. astrologer, K. K. Skinner, said, "Earthquake sensitive spots will get a shaking up" and there will be "some social unrest and a deepening of the recession."

A UPI sidebar the same day was a first-person reminiscence by Patricia Walsh which began, "I always knew I was living on borrowed time. I had a perfect childhood." She anticipated her 26th birthday March 10 with mixed emotions.

Ronald Kotulak, science editor, began his article in the *Chicago Tribune* for March 8: "Good news: the world will not end two days from now." The theory is "pure poppycock," but he added, "It is especially unfortunate because the theory has been used to generate fear among the unsuspecting unscientific community."

Allan R. Bruce began the UPI roundup March 9: "A respected if erratic Indian astrologer predicts Los Angeles will be destroyed Wednesday, and the Pacific Ocean will swallow up some islands. Peruvian cosmosbiologists say hungry animals will stalk the earth, a tidal wave will sweep the Caribbean and Peru will be hit with torrential rains." Lower in the 800-word story he reported that the San Francisco planetarium was besieged with calls and a New Orleans professor got calls from persons who said there were cracks in the walls of their houses.

In a separate report from New Delhi the Indian astrologer was revealed to be B. V. Raman. The prestigious *Times of India,* however, belittled the scare. In Calcutta Brahmin priests presided at ceremonies to invoke the assistance of the fire gods.

The same day the AP roundup repeated the history of the controversy and reported that two small earthquakes in California threw a scare into many, whom the seismologists tried to pacify by declaring the tremors had nothing to do with Jupiter.

Also March 9 the *Wall Street Journal* ran a detailed piece by Jonathan Twitny citing experts who believe the planets do have some effect on the weather. The article cited studies by Chinese scholars that, he wrote, should be good news for Gribbin and Plagemann.

Come Doomsday, March 10, and the morning papers waxed courageous and reassuring. "Despite widespread rumors, the world is unlikely to end today as a result of an unusual alignment of the sun, the planets and the moon, known as a syzygy," Walter Sullivan wrote in the *New York Times*. On the same paper's editorial page Russell Baker, writing much more soberly than usual, reviewed the situation. He claimed not to be contemptuous of the frightened people, "expecting catastrophe is very sound policy," he wrote, "expect the worst and you'll be happy to settle for the humdrum."

Writing bravely, Henry Allen began his long resumé in the *Washington Post*, "If you've got any guts at all you'll march outside today to rant scorn at the heavens. You'll dare the cosmos to swallow you with an earthquake, drown you with a tidal wave, hit you with its best shot. . . ."

From Nashville David Graham wrote for the Gannett News Service: "Will the world end today?" followed by a recital of the Jupiter Effect theory.

Editorially the *Chicago Tribune* asked why worry; if the world ends there'll be no more mortgage payments due, there won't be any jobs to lose or worry about, no Form 1040 and so on until near the end, a call back to reality. "All the familiar problems you worried about yesterday will still be there to worry about tomorrow."

Both press associations had to lead off with an account of tragedy. In Miami at a Doomsday Dawn beach party, sponsored in part by John Keasler, *Miami News* columnist, four teenagers were taken to hospitals with stab wounds inflicted by another youth who escaped in the crowd. Police said some of the young people were dissatisfied because there was no music; they were raucous but not violent.

The UPI roundup story written by William C. Trott began: "If you were disillusioned by the Kohoutek comet, today's Jupiter Effect planet alignment may be a letdown. The only people taking it seriously were an Indian astrologer, some insurance executives concerned about end-of-the-world claims and the extremely gullible." An amusing sidebar was a story from Augusta, Kan., where a sheriff's sergeant asked if he could get his paycheck early so as to spend it before the world ceased to be. He also wondered if the world was coming to an end would he be called out to handle it.

Later in the day the reports took on an "I told you so" attitude. "If you are reading this, there is a good possibility you are not dead," Don Hayner wrote in the *Chicago Tribune*. "The world did not end today—a fact that made liars out of assorted astrologers and soothsayers who saw a day of doom in a rare alignment of the earth and its neighbors in the solar system," said the *New York Daily News*. "If California is still in one piece and a tidal wave hasn't consumed the Caribbean by the time this day is over, then Alexander Graham Bell's place in history will be secure," Kathleen Kerr wrote in *Newsday*. The headline suggesting the tone of the *Philadelphia Daily News'* editing of the UPI account was: "Nine in a Line. 'Jupiter Effect' Bunk? Tune in Tomorrow."

From Los Angeles the Associated Press' Laurinda Keys reported, "If you're reading this, the world probably didn't come to an end today." In another piece she wrote from Los Angeles, "No increased solar activity bombarded the earth on Wednesday, the day of the so-called 'Jupiter Effect' and no large earthquakes split California off from the rest of the continent." She mentioned the worried who pestered astronomers with questions and cited a Filipino Christian sect that continued to wear padded clothing, believing the date should be March 26.

Both press associations had updates on the Miami stabbings. The *New York Daily News* wrote its own story from combined dispatches, to emphasize the determination of the co-sponsor, John Keasler, never to attempt anything of the sort again.

The UPI roundup written by Peter Costa, began: "The tide in Brazil may have risen 0.04 millimeters higher than normal and suspected drug traffickers in Puerto Rico were indeed arrested while gazing at the dawn sky but planet Earth revolved quietly in its orbit Wednesday—utterly unmoved by the so-called Jupiter Effect," Stewart Russell wrote from Miami for Reuters: "The Jupiter Effect did not bring earthquakes, eruptions and the end of the world as some had predicted—just a few stabbings, 30 arrests and a near riot at Miami's Doomsday party." It quoted Keasler as saying, "The creeps won again."

Having exhausted themselves with tricky leads and anecdotes, the newspapers had few journalistic post mortems. The headline, "Doomsayers Just Aren't What They Used to Be" suggests the tone of the March 11 article by Kevin Donovan in the *Daily Oklahoman* of Oklahoma City.

In the *New York Times* the same day Ben A. Franklin wrote from Baltimore about an all-night party in a bookstore and bar sponsored by the Greater Baltimore Committee in expectation of the arrival of a "visitor from the future" who somehow got waylaid.

There was only rehash in the UPI's followup story by William C. Trott that began, "The planets aligned but the earth did not move. Fans of the Jupiter Effect will have to wait until 2357 for another chance to see if the rare celestial configuration can destroy the world."

"Doomsday rumors worried a lot of Chicagoans. We even had our Friday night bingo on Tuesday evening," said Hercules Mulligan in Bob Herguth's Public Eye column.

And, according to Gerald M. Connors in the *New York Daily News*, "The stock market, perhaps inspired by the planetary Jupiter Effect made a mighty effort at a rally yesterday but failed."

The danger past, a reader asked *Chicago Tribune* Action Line to explain what it was her brother recalled from his childhood about 1920 when there was wine flowing in the streets amid hilarity. "Was it a national concern or strictly a community thing?" A lengthy reply March 27, 1982 concluded with the supposition that the writer's Italian neighbors were having a last fling before prohibition went into effect Jan. 19, 1920.

In its Sunday, March 14, 1982 week's roundup, the *New York Times* reported: "The word is out. The world did not end last week . . ." followed by a brief resume of the scare. The headline was "It's All Right to Come Out Now."

March 30 the *Times* ran a letter from John Gribbin in Brighton, England to correct an error in the paper's March 9 editorial. "The book," he wrote, "has had no adverse effect on my academic career, or on my work as an author, and at no time has anyone put any pressure on me to retract in order to get other work published. The scientific community has always dealt with the hypothesis outlined in the book fairly and I retracted it because it was proved wrong and for no other reason."

5

Fortune Telling

Not all fortune tellers and prophets rely entirely on the stars. Many look into crystal balls, examine tea leaves, handwriting, head shapes, facial characteristics and other bodily features, read palms, study tarot or plain ordinary playing cards, translate signs and dreams in their efforts to make a living.

In May 1943 the *Chicago Sun* published a series of four short articles to expose the extent to which the fortune-telling market was flourishing as a result of anxieties engendered by World War II. A reporter posing as the fiancée or wife of a soldier patronized the practitioners who mulcted war-weary and anxious Chicagoans "by means of crystal balls, cards, palm readings, camera minds and piercing eyes," to quote from the May 17 installment. Some of what was learned from those who said they knew included:

1. Your soldier husband or fiancé is safe and will continue to be safe (for an extra fee).
2. You will have lots of children, maybe five or six.
3. The war will end in (a) 1943, (b) 1944, (c) 1945 or (d) 1946.
4. Lemon and oil will cure a cold.
5. Carrot juice will fix up that falling hair.

Thereafter, for about a quarter-century, as was true of virtually every other Amerian newspaper, the *Sun* paid only slight attention to the sooth-sayers.

That fortune telling can be a dangerous occupation was indicated by a story the *Baltimore Sun* used Aug. 10, 1949. It told of the murder of a crystal gazer and the speculation of the merchant who supplied her with magic dust and herbs that the killer was someone about whom the dead seer had seen too much in her crystal ball.

The patron also must beware, Dr. George Crane emphasized in his "Case Records of a Psychologist" for Feb. 14, 1936. Dr. Crane told of a businessman whose wife became unreasonably jealous of him because a fortune teller had told her the husband was interested in a blonde girl. The distressed businessman happened to have a blonde secretary in whom, however, he had only a professional interest. Wrote Dr. Crane: "Because so many people place absolute trust in what fortune tellers say, a great deal of harm can be done in society."

The misery of one who becomes addicted to fortune seeking was explained in a full-page piece, "Seer Sucker," in the *Every Week Magazine,* a syndicated newspaper feature supplement for Dec. 18, 1943. The dilemma in which the subject finds himself when he tries to evaluate what a soothsayer has told him goes this way: "Human nature being what it is, if you do take a trip you will remember it was amazingly prophesied by this remarkable fellow. If you don't take the trip you will remember he also said you might not."

As Clinton R. Wilkinson explained in the *Sun-Times* for Feb. 24, 1963, the golden age of the fortune teller appeared to have ended as a result of state and city laws. Both the Better Business Bureau and police reported a drastic decline in complaints against gypsies and others who formerly advertised and operated openly. In a two-column article, "Fortune Tellers Gaze Into Future—For Them It's An Ill-Omened One," Wilkinson revealed that "many a muddied crystal ball stands ready in a tiny store. Many a fortune teller gazes downward from a dingy upper flat, looking for business in the street below. The last seer will disappear at about the time the last policy runner turns to more conventional pursuits."

Despite the law that makes predicting the future a crime, there were at least 1,000 gypsy "reader-advisers" in New York City, Leslie Maitland reported in a half-page article, "For Those Who Dare Seek the Future, No Lack of Soothsayers," in the *New York Times* for Jan. 31, 1975. The New York Code of Criminal Procedure states that the purpose of penalizing fortune tellers is "to prevent the ignorant and the gullible as well as the curious from being ensnared by the guiles and fantasies of those who profess to be able to 'crystal gaze' as to the course of human events." Nevertheless, Maitland visited the establishments of several of the most successful soothsayers. Esther Massimilla told him, "Readers here read with the intent of helping people. We're the poor man's psychiatrists. They come in with things on their mind. In our own little way we try to help people solve them." Others spoke similarly.

Another *Times* reporter, Jerry M. Flint, received similar explanations when he covered the First American Aquarian Festival of Astrology and Occult Sciences in Minneapolis for a story in his paper's Sept. 10, 1971 edition. Carl Weschicke, who runs an occult publishing house in Minneapolis, said that the removal of mystery and ritual from church services leads people to turn to the occult. Many said that some of the interest has come from a revolt against this technological age that promised much but delivered no inner peace.

To learn what effect the booming field of the occult has on reading habits Martha MacGregor interviewed Donald Weiser, with the largest store in the field. In the *New York Post* for Jan. 18, 1972 she reported that books on astrology had been best-sellers for seven or eight years, followed by books on witchcraft and tarot cards. The most popular authors were Jess Stearn, Hans Holzer, Suzy Smith and Ruth Montgomery.

In Chicago Roy Larson reported in the *Sun-Times* for Sept. 24, 1972 that the number of specialty shops had increased from 2 to 12 in just a few years. In addition there are standard bookstores, drug stores and other outlets for occult literature. Larson received the stock explanations of the rise in interest but said that what seemed to sum it all up was a poster: "On sale here, the Occult Gazette. Solves the Mysteries of the Ages."

One skeptical recipient of advertising solicitations was Jack Mabley who ridiculed the whole business in his column in the *Tribune* for Dec. 28, 1976. He cited Free Enterprise, whose publishers sent "15 Surprising Predictions for 1977–1979." Of such forecasts, Mabley wrote, "Their predictions are more fun to read a year later than the week they are issued."

Michael Goodwin also was skeptical after surveying the New York fortune-telling business for the *New York Times* of Jan. 23, 1978. The police told him the "seers" had increased in number 30 percent in five years and victims were paying to have curses removed. Most of the fortune tellers are gypsy women, descendants of tribes that left India in the 14th and 15th centuries to roam and steal their way through Europe.

Typical of the disdain with which most journalists held soothsaying was the reply Ann Landers gave in her column for Aug. 15, 1968 to a reader who complained because Ann had belittled fortune tellers in an earlier column. The correspondent wrote that a tea-leaf reader had prolonged her life by warning her to avoid planes, helicopters and motorcycles, which had taken the lives of several relatives and friends. Ann's response was to ask if the tea-leaf reader had warned against taking a bath since thousands are injured getting in or out of a tub.

Newspaper exposés of fortune tellers usually are conducted by sending a reporter to several so as to compare the readings. One of the first and best such stories was by Hyman Goldberg in the *New York PM* for Nov. 16, 1942. The two sages who examined his future agreed that he was going to make money but on not much else. Many other reporters have had similar experiences.

Beginning April 29, 1947 the *Chicago Daily News* published a series of five articles by reporter Lois Thrasher, who visited self-advertised "psychologists" for "advice on problems common to the day." Typical of all the articles was the following extract:

> In the guise of "Louise Taylor" a *Daily News* reporter spent four days with the prophets only to learn that she is an introvert, an extrovert, a definite psychiatric case, a well-rounded personality, a social washout, full of come-hither for the boys, about to marry and about to die.

Louise got a message from her grandfather, who has been dead 13 years; learned that she can retrieve her nonexistent husband's affections by magnetizing a handkerchief and discovered that her equally nonexistent mother-in-law is plotting against her.

All this for less than $50 and the ability to keep a straight face.

To the editors' liking are news stories like the one the *Chicago Sun* used Nov. 1, 1946 that an 82-year-old woman was found dead two days after she told a neighbor that the cards indicated a death was imminent. Also to the paper's liking was an Associated Press dispatch Aug. 7, 1965 from London about a woman who died as a fortune teller had predicted she would when she became 45 years old.

Journalistic attention to practitioners of the occult began to accelerate in the '70s. After the murder in Santa Cruz, Calif. of five persons the *Daily News* Oct. 22, 1970 explained the significance of the signatures on a note left by the murderers who signed themselves Knight of Wands, Knight of Cups, Knight of Pentacles and Knight of Swords. The names are those of the four suits of the tarot deck that is used for divination and fortune telling. The *News* consulted a local occultist for an explanation of the four suits, which symbolize the four elements—earth, water, air and fire. The next day, Oct. 23, 1970, the *New York Times* reported that a warrant had been issued for a suspect in the case. In a separate article Michael T. Kaufman wrote that bookstores at Harvard and Berkeley and many other universities reported a large increase in the sale of tarot cards and of books explaining their ancient origin and meaning.

One of the few articles in which journalists paid attention to tarot cards was "You Pays Your Money and Takes Your Card," by Cynthia Stevens in the *Washington Post* for March 25, 1979. The article also included mention of the many manifestations of interest in the occult. Tarot cards also are mentioned several times on the four pages the *New York Daily News* devoted June 17, 1979 to "Setting Your Sights on Planning Ahead." Included were articles by psychics, astrologers, palmists and others, together with forecasts of what is in store for the world.

Similarly, May 7, 1972 the *Minneapolis Tribune* drew upon a *Saturday Review* article to report, "In America trying to predict the future by way of visions, crystal balls and zodiacal signs has become a burgeoning commercial enterprise . . . Sales of old fashioned ouija boards have tripled in the past few years." The "timeless" appeal of psychic prophecy, it said, is a "way out" in troubled times. The popularity of the Ouija board was recognized by the UPI, which distributed a picture of Martha Mitchell, wife of the attorney general, consulting a board with a woman friend. The *Milwaukee Journal* used the photograph in two columns Dec. 4, 1970.

Of surefire interest was an Associated Press dispatch from New York Oct. 7, 1972. It told of a Czech immigrant who bought a fortune card for a penny from an organ grinder in 1914. At 77, after the lifetime of hard work and illnesses the fortune predicted, he was the winner, with his wife, of a $1 million state lottery.

Things began to pick up journalistically for the soothsayers when eating establishments added them as fringe benefits for hungry customers. Michael A. Pollock updated the situation in a half-page article, "It's dealer's choice at the fortune teller's" in *Chicago Today* for March 14, 1974. The first few paragraphs were:

Using ordinary playing cards, Irene can deal happiness or despair.

She reads cards and tea leaves in Kay's Reader Club, 32 N. State St. For $2, you get a cookie, a cup of tea, and a hint of things to come.

But no promises.

Fortune tellers who made that mistake have been prosecuted under state and city fraud laws.

The laws forbid fortune tellers to take money in return for predictions of a million-dollar inheritance or a trip to Europe. They can't promise what they can't deliver.

But such laws haven't made it difficult to find a professional seer in Chicago.

Bulletin boards at occult shops are plastered with their business cards. Palmists, spiritualists, and ESP advisers abound. Astrologers even are listed in the Yellow Pages.

One of the first full-length sympathetic writeups of a local seer was written by William Braden for the *Chicago Sun-Times* Jan. 23, 1967 after an interview with self-styled Prof. Henry Y. Dutton, whose office on Skid Row was frequented mostly by "poor people and rich people, many of them desperate; whites and Negroes . . . Mexicans and Puerto Ricans . . . and from time to time perhaps a major league baseball player whose batting average has suffered a mysterious slump." For all of them the elderly Negro spiritual advisor provided palm reading, numerology, lucky charms, candles, perfumes and other objects with supposed potency for good or evil.

Another evidence of the skyrocketing interest in things occult was the full page devoted by the *Chicago Tribune* June 21, 1974 to a detailed account of a visit Anita Clark made to the divine reader and adviser, Miss Sara, near the Golf Mill shopping center. Miss Sara explained that she is "strictly a prophet of the Lord. Most of my work is secret, just between me and God." The "three witches cards" she uses are merely to amuse patrons. Her prophecies were routine: the man in your life has moved but will come back.

Once the newsworthiness of psychics became recognized the attention paid to them increased, slowly at first but steadily until it snowballed. For the March 7, 1973 *Chicago Daily News* Margo interviewed Jess Stearn, author of books on psychic phenomena. He related the circumstances of his life that made him a believer and commented on several contemporaries in the business.

The *Sun-Times Midwest Magazine* for Jan. 5, 1975 advertised Ruth Revzen who did readings in R. J. Grunts restaurant and also had her own body-scent corporation and a rock band and did consultative work for radio stations WLS in Chicago and WKRS in Waukegan. She said, "The human body sends out energy forces. Different colors mean different emotions. I ask God to see the white light which shows me the past, present and future. It's called an aura and is somewhat like a spectrum which forms around the body."

"Color Preferences May Hold Key to Psychic Investigations" headlined a story by Bill Boshears in the *Cincinnati Enquirer* for May 4, 1975. Drawing on numerous scholarly books and articles, Boshears wrote, "Colors can tell us a lot about ourselves." According to a test devised by a Swiss psychologist, Dr. Max Luscher, "Gray as a first choice indicates a desire to wall everything off, to remain uncommitted, and uninvolved and shields oneself from outside influences or stimulus. Blue . . . shows a need for either emotional tranquility, peace, harmony and contentment or physiological need for rest, relaxation and recuperation." And so on, but no explanation of how the scholars know what they're talking about.

In the *Sun-Times* for May 30, 1977 Paul Galloway told of accompanying Abe Black on a visit to psychic Gary Wayne, who uses a tape recorder and cassette instead of a crystal ball so one can replay his prophecies. To avoid interference from the vibrations of customers down below Wayne operates in a deserted room above a Morton Grove restaurant.

The techniques of the women soothsayers in South Vietnam, Della Denman wrote in the *New York Times* for Aug. 3, 1973, "range from the exotic, such as communing with an embalmed head and reading flowers, to the more mundane, such as palmistry, cards, horoscopes and coins. Some give advice for the following day; others tell a story spanning birth to death." Buddhism, as well as many esoteric religious cults in Vietnam, is closely tied to the occult. Prominent politicians and military leaders are among the fortune tellers' clients.

For the *Chicago Daily News* of Jan. 11–12, 1975 the peregrinating Georgie Anne Geyer wrote a balanced account of the importance of fortune telling in the Middle East and the charlatans who thrive on tourists. Her lead anecdote was a recollection by Gehen Sadat that a soothsayer had predicted years earlier that she would become Egypt's first lady.

As for Hong Kong, "Fortune-telling is a way of life," according to the headline over Margaret McEachem's page-length feature in the *Chicago Sunday Tribune* for Nov. 10, 1974. According to the Hong Kong Tourist Association the Chinese are the world's greatest believers in fortune telling, so McEachem recommends that when in Hong Kong do as the natives do. She did, consulting one of the 2,000 unlicensed but legal soothsayers, and she writes like a convert about the history and nature of the practice.

Many foreign psychics have international interests. For instance the *Chicago Tribune* for Nov. 19, 1973 reported that Yolande Sultana Halahi, of Santiago, Chile predicted that Henry Kissinger would marry a very attractive and well-known woman. The seer also predicted a scandal in the British royal family.

From Kinshana, Zaire, Rick Talley reported in the *Chicago Tribune* for Oct. 26, 1974. Dr. Ng'Ombe, self-proclaimed "Greatest Fortune Teller, Healer and Seer" in Africa, said that George Foreman would clobber Muhammad Ali and he had even written Ali to call off the heavyweight championship fight. Actually Ali won by a knockout in the eighth round.

"Belief in the supernatural—in spirits, seances, signs and magic—remains important for millions of Indonesians, even for some intellectuals and politicians like Suharto, who have a reputation for pragmatism . . . The influence of mysticism is strong in Indonesia, even though 90 percent of the people are Moslems," wrote Bob Sector from Jogjakarta, Indonesia for the *Los Angeles Times* of May 27, 1982. Most of the long article consists of anecdotes of how religion affects life.

Most successful fortune tellers today are versatile. The big money is in astrology which had benefited from the public interest in space explorations and the respectability of regular newspaper horoscopes supposedly derived from a study of the stars. Nevertheless, ancient methods of character reading and forecasting persist. And the journalistic treatment is generally sympathetic.

In a two-column article in the *Chicago Sun* for Aug. 5, 1946 Charles Leavelle cited some of the highlights of 10,000 years of chiromancy, now called palmistry. Raphael, who operated in a north-side supper club, told the reporter the meaning of the lines, signs, symbols and signatures that the palmist interprets. He correctly declared that the person of whose palm he was shown a photograph had murderous tendencies, but his warning of a sudden death did not materialize. The print was that of William Heirens, notorious child murderer.

In the United States palm reading became associated with peregrinating gypsies who were suspected of taking more than their fees. A factual but obviously satirical account of how one gypsy ran afoul of the law appeared in the *Chicago Daily News* for Feb. 19, 1968:

> The gypsy palmist had everything very clear when it came to the customer's life line, but the focus became a little fuzzy later on.
> The palmist convinced a client that the cause of his stomach distress was his obsession with money—something that distressed the spirits.
> The gypsy told him that if he washed his hands of the filthy lucre his illness would go away. He apparently did a good job scrubbing.
> Well, the money somehow was spirited into the hands of the palmist's daughter, who apparently was not bothered by the spirits.
> From this point on things were out of focus.
> The gypsy's tax return failed to show the "spirit" cash. The tax court did

not believe the plea that it was a gift from the client to the daughter, in spite of earnest testimony.

The tax court gave the Internal Revenue Service the right to look at the gypsy's palm. The IRS decided it indeed, had been crossed. The crystal ball cleared up and the gypsy anted up.

The Commerce Clearing House, in reporting the case, never did say if the stomach distress disappeared.

Because they read palms and told fortunes by means of a crystal ball a mother and daughter were banished from the Rockwood Baptist Church of Independence, Mo. according to an Associated Press story from there Dec. 26, 1979. In her May 30, 1981 column Ann Landers told a reader: "Palmistry is neither a science nor an art. It can, however, be a fairly good source of income for convincing talkers who need to make a few dollars. As Barnum said, 'There's a sucker born every minute' . . . and two to take him." The reader had been uneasy because her husband's life line was short, which made her wonder if they should have a second child if he would not be alive to help rear it. But, Ann, Barnum never said what you say he said. His famous aphorism was that people like to be fooled. (See my book *Hoaxes*, page 139.)

One of the most successful restaurant entertainers in the Chicago area was Carolle Bailey, known as Miss Carolle. Many customers in several eating places had her touch their hands and ask their favorite color before she answered their questions, usually related to family life, romantic involvements or business. Steve Ginsburg wrote her up for the Nov. 3, 1976 *Suburban Week*. For him she also made a few prophecies for 1977: Jackie Kennedy Onassis will marry a man with the initials J. S.; Caroline Kennedy will be kidnapped; Sonny and Cher will remarry, etc.

Already enough doctors take account of palm lines to give a name to the attempts to link some diseases to them—dermatoglyphics. Marilyn Goldstein told about it in her article, "The Science of Occult," in the *Chicago Sun-Times Midwest Magazine* for Sept. 5, 1971. She also told of the growing interest in astrology by stockholders and brokers and extolled the work of Mazine Fiel, expert hand-analyst able to tell personality and character traits.

"Chiromancy—the ancient art of palm reading—has come off the street into the classroom where businessmen are learning how palmistry and a related art—physiognomy—can help," according to a six-page article in the *Midwest Magazine* of the *Chicago Sun-Times* for May 3, 1970. The piece is an anonymous plug for Milan Bulovic, who classifies facial types as jupiterian, appollarian, venusian, lunarian, martian, mercurian and saturnian. The article is illustrated by pictures of important examples of each classification. For instance, Truman Capote, Harry Houdini and Sammy Davis, Jr. are all Mercurians, which means "Sleek and quick in judgments; excels in medicine, the law, sales and politics. The Mercurian can grasp complex problems and assimilate information quickly. His peering eyes seem to slant upward and his ears are pointed. His hair is short and curly and the shape of his head gives him a small upturned chin. He is a good family man and chess player" and quite a bit more similar nonsense.

Like Raphael whom the *Sun* advertised more than 30 years earlier, Ilona Haizmann was a follower of Cheiro (real name Count Louis Hamon), an Englishman who based his system on the fact that every portion of the brain is in contact with the nerves in the hand. Ilona received full-page treatment Feb. 5, 1977 in the Tempo section of the *Tribune*.

Similar is foot reflexology, which Mark Fineman wrote in the *Suburban Sun-Times* for April 7–8, 1976 is the relatively unknown art of pinpointing and relieving bodily ailments and stresses through massaging critical reflex points in the feet. In good-sized outlines of feet the bodily areas affected are marked (big toe—pituitary, next toe—eye; other toes—ear, and so forth) to cure insomnia, poor circulation, tension, menstrual cramps, kidney and bladder problems, certain muscular pains, some types of headaches, prostate difficulties and spastic areas in the colon.

Charts of iridology and foot reflexology dominated a full-page feature on "One doc's RX: heart and sole," by Kitty Hanson in the *New York Daily News* for Dec. 5, 1980. Imaging is a form of visualization in which patients "observe" the body's immune system destroying cancer cells and tumors. It is popular with believers in a holistic approach to good health. Iridology involves studying the fibers of the iris that radiate from the pupil. These correspond to organs and other areas of the body. Those who espouse foot reflexology believe that areas of the sole of the foot reflect areas of the body.

This rigmarole was reminiscent of what the *Chicago Sun* related in the fourth of its May 1943 series. A prosperous soothsayer named Anna required every client to surrender his/her left shoe, upon examining which Anna told its owner much about the past, present and future, most of it wrong, the newspaper's representatives discovered.

A performance that makes most others seem amateurish is that put on by Gay Darlene Bidart, if one can believe the two pages the *New York Daily News* used Jan. 24, 1982 to describe the methodology of "The Witch with a Yale Degree." Wrote Cynthia Raymond: "For Bidart, bones don't lie. The bumps on your head, the shape of your feet, the curl of your hair, and even the rumble from your stomach can tell her a lot about you and your future."

In the belief that a total body reading is needed for an accurate forecast, Bidart tells her customers, "I'm here to make you strip," which she does enough to examine armpits, navels, birthmarks and bodily features from tip to toe. All this she does while wearing a diaphanous black gown.

With facial charts and photographs of 11 living celebrities, Marilyn Bender explained Hawley Turner's "face analysis." In her article "What's In Your Face?" in *Parade* for Aug. 16, 1959, she quoted Turner: "You can judge a man by the shape of his nose, the quiver of his lip or the jut of his chin—no matter how stiff-lipped or iron-jawed he pretends to be."

Timothy Mar, a native Chinese, believes "the face is a road map of life, a veritable Rand McNally atlas that charts tragedy, hope and destiny," according to Rudy Maxa in a Front Page People feature in the *Washington Post Magazine* for Dec. 2, 1979. Mar believes that Ronald Reagan "has the best balanced and most proportionate face of all candidates. His inner energy is strong and enduring and he may be regarded as the most able person in the political arena today regardless of his views."

In the *New York Daily News* for Sept. 3, 1980 Tish Jeff wrote about "Beyond Face Value. The wrinkles, twinkles and crinkles that give away our innermost secrets." He defined physiognomy as "the art of determining temperature and character by studying facial features" and advised anyone can do it. Just consider the three stations: from hairline to brows, brows to the tip of the nose and nose to chin. The general rule is that when they're in balance, life is balanced. "For example, if the forehead is longer there is great potential, but if the second station is too short that potential might never be reached. The person might be a dreamer instead of a doer." Ying, the mother, is the right side of the face; Yang, the father, is the left.

One's faith in the possibility of reading character in faces would have been shaken by Bob Greene's Sept. 3, 1973 column in the *Chicago Sun-Times*. The famous Chinese face-reader, Grace Lee, told Bob she could give him a general overlook from viewing photographs of subjects. So Greene gave her six unidentified pictures. Of the notorious criminal, John Dillinger, she said: ". . . a charming man, a lover of life. He would never willingly cause pain to anyone or hurt another person." Joseph Paul Goebbels was "very kind," Al Capone, "a policeman" and so on, all completely wrong.

Despite such demonstrations in their own offices, newspapers persist in publicizing quacks. July 26–27, 1975, for instance, the *Chicago Daily News* used a three-column picture of Toni Lockhart, formerly a San Diego legal secretary, who, using the professional name of Gypsy Rose Knee, has read the knees of about 2,000 persons.

Despite what scientists and journalists can say, however, there are some businesses that have been relying on unorthodox criteria to select employees and keep them at maximum efficiency. Dr. George Crane told an employer who asked his advice regarding phrenology and physiognomy that reputable psychologists consider neither as valid. In his March 4, 1936 "Case Records of a Psychologist" he answered an employer's question as to whether character can be "determined by feeling the bumps on the skull or measuring the thickness of the lips" with an emphatic "no."

Crane doubtless would have responded similarly to any query concerning the full page the *Chicago Tribune* gave May 13, 1981 to Dr. Leopold Bellak's book, *Reading Faces*. A four-column-wide colored portrait of Dr. Bellak's face accompanied Eric Zorn's article. The doctor's zone system means to separate the face into four sections in the belief that the contours of the face—from furrowed brows to fleshy lips and jutting chins—are the results of the temperament of the individual. Regarding the upper left quarter of his own face Bellak believes it shows "right eye—baleful, dubious: tightly closed, skeptical." He also points to his "pretty firm chin showing determination if not assertiveness and at times aggressiveness."

"It's all very simple," Zorn said Bellak growls. "All you have to do is look closely. Most people never even really look at each other."

In the *Suburban Week* for Aug. 11–12, 1976 Mark Fineman asserted, "You can be more successful, socially and in your family life, if you learn to interpret body language," the authority on which is Cody Sweet, head of Mount Prospect based Non-Verbal Communications.

"The bumpy road to the phrenologist" was a humorous piece by the *Daily News'* news lady Susan F. Fine of Park Forest. It related the experiences of the writer and her mother at an Occult Fair. Typical episode was the insistence of the spiritual advisor that he never was wrong, even when he incorrectly declared the subject owned a home or rented an apartment when actually she rented a house. Offsetting the value of the iconoclastic piece was "Reading between the lines in the faces of the famous" in the July 14, 1975 Everyday section of the *Daily News*. It illustrated what Robert Whiteside, exponent of personology, said the photographs indicated. For example, the face of Thomas E. Keane, convicted felon and former alderman, meant this to Whiteside: "That's a thinker. Keen, analytical mind. Very authoritative, competitive, won't back down. Sort of a bulldog jaw, pugnacious. Soft eyes mean he's interested in the higher values, not just in the grosser side of life. Pleasant laugh lines, has a sense of humor. Very conscious of details, very observant, thinks things out. A head like a lion. Strong. Thorough. He likes to outfox other people. A very interesting man."

There have been many attempts to correlate mental with physical traits. The best known, coming from otherwise reputable scientists, were those of Ernst Kreschmer in 1925 and William Sheldon in 1940. The former, a German psychologist, cited three leading types and described their personality traits: (1) asthenic—long and thin, given to melancholia; (2) athletic—well-rounded physically, and well adjusted psychologically; (3) pyknic—round and ruddy in appearance, jolly in disposition, overcompensated extrovert. Sheldon described the (1) endomorphic—fat, good family men; (2) mesomorphic—athletic, risk takers, most uninhibited; (3) ectomorphic—cerebral, alert, introverted. Overwhelmingly, attempts of other scholars to verify these conclusions have been negative. Many experiments have proved students, newspaper readers and others cannot pick criminals, scholars or others from photographs.

Three days after the *News'* story, the *Sun-Times* gave Whiteside an entire page. The headline, "On the face of it, almost anyone can size you up at a glance," suggests the slant the interview writeup took. According to Whiteside the eyes are "the window" to the soul. So, eyes that slant down mean a person is quick to notice flaws, a nagger who's quick in criticism. An upward tilt indicates just the opposite. Luminous sparkling eyes indicate an alert nature. A large amount showing beneath the iris is the tipoff to a gloomy, melancholy disposition and much more of the same.

No paper ever has devoted anywhere near so much space to a refutation of charlatanism. At least, however, they no longer call in phrenologists and handwriting experts whenever a criminal is at large and his identity unknown. Characteristically March 30, 1936 the *Chicago Herald and Examiner* had a full-page spread with the headshots of four youths accused of murder. The headlines read: "Bestiality Marks Faces of Killers" and "Boys' Ruthlessness Shown by Features." Arrows pointed to the facial features that supposedly showed such characteristics as: "decides moderately fast, good capacity for facts, little imagination, somewhat secretive, little curiosity and so on"—ten for each youth. The accompanying article was by C. A. Bonniwell, whom the paper called a "noted character analyst." He was impressed by the similarities among the four: ears, eyes and other features, almost all alike. Regarding them he wrote: "Selfish, petty people never consider any but themselves and their own interests." In 1961, one of the four, Emil Reck, was released from the Illinois penitentiary where he had spent 25 years for the $20 robbery murder of Dr. Silbar B. Peacock. The United States Supreme Court found that his confession had been beaten out of him by Illinois police. The state did not attempt to retry him.

In December 1945 the unknown murderer of Frances Brown, former WAVE, wrote in lipstick on the wall of her hotel room: "For heavens sake catch me before I kill more. I cannot control myself." On its front page Dec. 11, 1945 the *Daily News* ran a three-column facsimile of the message and a two-column artist's sketch of what the murderer looked like based on analysis of his handwriting. Its article, by Jack Mabley, began:

> The killer of Frances Brown is a short, swarthy man whose instincts are guided by gluttony and self love.
> This is what "the handwriting on the wall" tells Leon York, noted Chicago graphologist, who had spent 35 years judging persons from their handwriting.
> "I visualize this man as about 36 years old, about 5 feet 4 inches tall and weighing 174 pounds," York told the Daily News today.

The *Chicago Times* converted the case into a contest between newspaper experts. "Acting on exclusive information provided by the *Times,* police today were searching for a musician as a crazed killer of a pretty 95 pound ex-WAVE found shot and stabbed in her apartment," the paper's lead story began Dec. 11, 1945. The exclusive information came from Dr. Martin Grassman, who the paper said was a "widely known Chicago psychiatrist." He pointed out that the letter "r" as written by the maniac resembled a musical symbol. In a separate article headed "Murdered to music?" the letters "f" and "k" were also said to resemble musical symbols. To the testimony of Grassman was added that of Mary Frances Mears, alleged handwriting expert known in newspaper offices as a prolific free-lance and letter writer.

The actual murderer was a frail 17-year-old University of Chicago student, William Heirens, who bore no resemblance whatever to either the artist's sketch or the description when he was picked up for burglary more than six months later. Today he's serving a life sentence in a penitentiary.

One might think that the experience would have soured the paper's editors on handwriting analysts. Not so. Rather, in March 1949 the paper, by then the *Sun-Times,* began giving away $1,500 every week to readers who sent in samples of their penmanship expressing wishes. Amy Grant, the paper's graphologist, decided the winners and composed such gibberish as: "Let's make an analysis of Whittingham's handwriting and see what it reveals to me. Notice the U-shaped 'm's and 'n's with small vowels. It showed he knows how to handle people and has a strong sense of responsibility."

And the ever-gullible *Daily News* headlined a UPI story from New York Sept. 20, 1968 "Moody? Gay? Jealous? Handwriting tells all." The article, by Patricia McCormack, eulogized Charlotte Ronda who worked the cocktail terrace of the Commodore Hotel. "Handwriting can indicate a mild or bad temper, reveals one's sex and state of mind, as a moody person tends to slant down," she said.

When Mrs. Carolyn Lamb was certified by the International Graphoanalysis Society, the *Sunday Oklahoman* of Oklahoma City devoted about a half-page Nov. 23, 1969 to a discussion of the history and practice of graphology. Illustrations of handwriting samples and what they revealed were included. Cutlines on one read: "Loops on 'd' show sensitivity to criticism. Loops on circle letter such as 'a' and 'o' indicates secretiveness. Proportion of 'f' loops shows organizationability."

Several years ago, how it happened I don't know, but I was invited to be the banquet speaker at the annual convention of the society. When I inquired how they knew the meanings of different samples, I was told, "Dr. Bunker said so." A huge portrait of Dr. Milton Newman Bunker hung on the wall as an icon. Sharon Calhoun in her *Oklahoman* article quoted an unnamed member of the state's law enforcement agency in the forgery division for some 12 years who considered graphology "about like reading the zodiac. I don't put much stock in it."

After *Parade* published a letter from Martha Mitchell, some readers asked that her handwriting be examined. So *Parade* submitted a sample to two handwriting experts who, of course, did not know the identity of the writer. One considered Mrs. Mitchell's "outstanding quality" to be "almost overemphasized" extroversion, an acquired characteristic. Strong vitality, drive until collapsing, unable to "calm down easily." The other expert was impressed by the subject's fantastic imagination. Careless, with a quick temper, compulsive, aggressive, domineering. The analyses appeared in *Parade* for Dec. 3, 1972.

After an auction of autographs of famous persons—royalty, statesmen, musicians and other celebrities from the 12th century to the present brought $131,590 at Parke-Bernet Galleries in the nation's capital, the *Washington Post* hired a famous graphologist, Dorothy Sara, to analyze the handwriting. She did so, making some startling discoveries as regards the characters and personalities of Louis XIV, Catherine the Great, Martin Luther, George Washington, John Hancock and others. In its issue of April 29, 1973 the *Post* gave a half-page to Nancy L. Ross' article and a list of 25 quiz questions and meanings. Example: If writing slants forward to the right it means the person is friendly, affectionate.

"Want a Job? Watch Your p's and q's," was the title of an article in the *Texas Magazine* section of the *Houston Chronicle* for Jan. 2, 1974. The story, by Connie Lunnen, told how Arthur A. Surette, a Dallas salesman with a hobby, instructed a small class of businessmen and employees in how to understand another's abilities by his handwriting. One example was a printer whose carelessness with details was shown by his failure to dot his i's, enabling both him and his boss to get along better.

Similarly headlined, "Job Applications Are Trickier Than Ever: Mind Your P's and Q's," the *Wall Street Journal* used a story June 20, 1974 by David M. Elsner. He led off with the example of an applicant who lost a job because his a's, e's and m's were much too small—a sure sign of unsalesmanlike self-doubt and uncertainty according to his prospective employer, Howard MacKenzie, president of Standard Manifold Co. of Chicago.

There are believed to be about 1,000 employers who rely on handwriting analyses in selecting employees. Most scientists pooh-pooh the practice and there have been few, if any, valid studies made of its efficiency. Nicholas R. Burczyk, a Lansing, Ill. graphologist, says, "The way a person writes represents his reactions to life, his past experiences, his impressions and attitudes." He says he can distinguish 40 separate personality traits, including ability to overcome obstacles, sales aptitude, profit orientation, initiative and ability to make use of time.

About the same time, the *Houston Chronicle* Feb. 21, 1974 used an article by Donald Thornton, a UPI staffman in Sacramento, about Sherwood Morrill, who recently ended 39 years with the California Identification and Investigative Bureau, during which time he appeared in court as an expert witness in more than 3,300 cases. His work was mostly to discover forgeries or the identity of ransom note writers and the like without apparently attempting to describe character or personality traits.

Among the handwriting experts is Jeanne Drew, director of Drew Associates in Wheaton, Ill. During the political campaign of 1974 between Rep. Samuel Young (R) and Abner Mikva (D) for congressman from the 10th Illinois District, the *Evanston Review* submitted samples of the handwriting of the opponents to Drew for analysis. The results in the publication for Aug. 8, 1974 included Drew's conclusion that she would

vote for Young because he wrote on yellow lined paper rather than on a 3 ×
5 card as did Mikva. Nevertheless, Mikva won the election and a few years
later was appointed by President Carter to be an associate judge on the
U.S. Appellate Court for the District of Columbia.

" 'Sinking' Nixon seen in scrawl" was the headline over an AP story
from New York that the *Chicago Sun-Times* featured Aug. 14, 1974 with
facsimiles of the former president's signature in 1969, just before he took
office, and two others after disgrace hit him. Graphologist Felix Lehman
was quoted as saying that the disintegrating signatures were evidence of
"a person sinking within himself."

The respect with which handwriting experts often are held was demonstrated by a half-page article, "Handwriting can be revealing," in the
Austin American-Statesman for Oct. 5, 1975. Mary Dudley wrote the piece
about Arthur Surette, a Dallas salesman for a company that specializes in
decorative accessories. Surette says he can learn about a person's personality elements and characteristics, the emotional foundation, goal orientation, driving capacity, learning perception and other factors, all valuable
considerations for any employer.

When the International Congress and Institute of Graphoanalysis met
in Chicago, Henry Hanson of the *Chicago Daily News* asked Joel G. Kent of
the Kennedy Space Center to analyze the handwriting of the three Apollo
astronauts then in space. The reply, published in the paper July 23, 1975,
indicated that their personalities differed as much as their handwriting.

A short time later, when the Para Dimensional Conference met in
Chicago, Jack Mabley, *Tribune* columnist, asked Mrs. Alexandria East to
analyze his handwriting. He gave her a sample omitting the letter "P"
because she says she can describe one's sex life by the way one writes "P".
The seer also said neat handwriting is not necessarily good. Anyone who
imitates fine penmanship examples gets little from life and may be a bore.
Mabley's writing slants up and down, which means he uses judgment, he
wrote Aug. 31, 1975.

Mary Thompson, 72, a veteran Manhattan palm reader, was shown a
blown-up picture of a man's right hand without being told his identity. She
said, "his health is not very good and he's not a very contented man . . .
He will be happy in the future." That was the fortune of Gen. Leopoldo
Galtieri, leader of the Argentine junta, whose print was given Thompson
by the *New York Post,* which ran the story and picture May 27, 1982.

The *Chicago Daily News'* Beeline for Sept. 8, 1976 gave a lengthy
answer to a correspondent who wanted to know where to get doodles
analyzed. The answer, based on information provided by the International
Graphoanalysis Society, was illustrated by doodles by John F. Kennedy
and discussed the doodling habits of several presidents.

Similarly, Bob Greene used facsimiles of his doodles in his *Sun-Times*
column for July 31, 1970 and related what Bernard Stoltie, a delegate to

the graphologists' convention, thought of his reporter's notes, generally undecipherable by anyone but their author. The expert, however, was able to discover complimentary things to tell Bob about himself.

After John Wayne's death the UPI interviewed Bill Burke, a handwriting expert in Easton, Pa. and obtained the surprising news that for years before his death from cancer the movie star clearly drew the picture of a human lung every time he signed his name. Illustrations of the signature were included in the article and the anonymous author concluded, "It's a point that no one but Bill Burke would notice." The article released Dec. 21, 1980 contained many other examples of persons whose health status was reflected in their handwriting.

Feb. 3, 1981 the Inquiring Reporter for the *New York Daily News* asked six persons, "A number of companies use handwriting analysis as part of the job-screening process. What could they tell about you from your handwriting?" One answered she would be found to be neat and efficient, a second said his writing is clear and so the thoughts expressed are logical and a third confessed that her handwriting is sloppy but she isn't, so an employer would have to meet her to know her.

President Reagan's handwriting is "very American" but shows he has a more complex personality than he outwardly seems to have. He gives the impression of being more extroverted than he is, at least according to Dr. James Bruno, a UCLA professor of education, whose analysis appeared in *Parade* for Feb. 22, 1981.

"Home town girl makes good" was the theme of a long piece by Martha Gardner in the *Milwaukee Journal* for April 16, 1981. Subject was Beverlee Dean, who grew up in Milwaukee but makes her living as a psychic in Hollywood. For three years, 1978 to 1980, she was employed by the American Broadcasting Company to forecast the success or failure of the network's shows. More recently she has specialized in handwriting analysis. She commented, "I can't explain it. I just see these different things. But I have now accepted this as a God-given gift. For me it was my life saver."

Obviously most newspaper accounts involving handwriting are objective or neutral. Over the years, however, some syndicated columnists have made iconoclastic remarks that subscribing editors have used. Among the first was Prof. Joseph Jastrow of the University of Wisconsin, author of a half dozen or so debunking books. His Nov. 14, 1927 column was entitled, "What You Cannot Tell From One's Handwriting" in which he called both palmistry and graphology "foolish and vain." He related the results of a test among students at Madison whose ratings of one another were different from what the handwriting experts proclaimed.

Much more recently another skeptical comment regarding graphology appeared in Ann Landers' column for April 27, 1969. A correspondent had written Ann that her sister-in-law, a student of handwriting analysis, told her: "Your handwriting shows that you are very dishonest. You have a tendency to steal and lie. Also you are lazy and disorganized and petty."

Ann's reply included: "Your sister-in-law is vicious, destructive, cruel and malicious, and I didn't need to see her handwriting to make THIS analysis."

Not many years later Ann's daughter, who used the name Margo for a column in the *Chicago Daily News,* lauded Nicholas Burczyk, who developed his own system of graphology, noting there are four basic kinds of handwriting: thread, garland, angle and arcade. Threads are real or potential geniuses. They should marry garlands—the Debbie Reynolds type. Angles are self-aggressive and arcades are introspective and distant.

With the purest of reportorial motives Daniel P. Hanley, Jr. made the rounds of delegates to the convention of the International Graphoanalysis Society in Milwaukee for a report in the *Milwaukee Journal* for April 20, 1975. "You can become unduly hurt by criticism," one told him. "Can handle criticism," said another. Most of the rest of the long, drawn-out article was in the same vein.

Despite the condemnations by scientists and the growing skepticism of journalists, the free advertising and puffery for all manner of psychics persists in the press. A. Don Hayner made his visit to a Rumanian-born fortune teller in Skokie, Ill. seem exciting in his account of it in the *Chicago Tribune* for April 24, 1981. There was suspense even in the account of the woman's brewing coffee so as to have grounds in which to read her visitor's future. And the reader of the article experienced vicarious fright when Hayner learned that a visitor he was to meet fit the description given by the psychic.

Comprehensive trend articles began to appear in the press from coast to coast and local papers began paying respectful attention to conferences and fairs.

Earl King wrote a two-page article, "Mind Reading for the Millions," for the *New York Sunday News* of Feb. 12, 1967. The article's subhead was, "The occult arts are 'in' again—neatly packaged to bring out the Gypsy in you," and just about every attention-getting specialty was described: voodoo, ESP, tarot cards, I Ching, palmistry, tea leaves, crystal balls, X-ray glasses, Kreskin's ESP game and others. The popularity of one and all led King to write, "It proves that fads may come and fads may go, but fortune telling goes on forever."

An extensive account of a psychic conference was that written by Carole Getzoff for the New York *Village Voice* March 22, 1973. She was given more than a half-page to describe the Second Western Hemisphere Conference on Acupuncture, Kirlian Photography and the Human Aura. A morning session was devoted to the photographic successes of the Russian Semyon Kirlian. With his camera, allegedly human auras can be photographed. They are light emanations by which changes in human and physiological conditions can be measured. Pictures were shown of psychic surgery and of Russian experiments in levitation and much more.

Because "We're sick of being thought of as a collection of freaks and rip-off artists," Martin Ciani, leading psychic, underwrote a conference in Chicago that Joel Weisman covered for the *Washington Post* of Sept. 14, 1975. At issue was how to designate competence without coming under either governmental or professional inspection. Some sort of official sanctioning for persons engaged in paranormal fields was supported by several of the leaders, "not like licensing or traditional regulatory agencies but something that will attest to a person's actual ability to perform the practice he holds himself out to perform."

Weisman conjectured that the declaration by the 186 scientists accelerated the movement to demystify and reduce "pretentious claims that can only contribute to the growth of irrationalism and obscurantism."

The respectability that the psychics craved came closer to attainment when they induced the anthropologist Margaret Mead and the astronaut Edgar Mitchell to serve on the panel of judges of 100 films dealing with ESP, parapsychology and other aspects of the psychic world. Occasion was the New York–Montreal Psychic Film Festival that Steve Cuozzo covered for the *New York Post,* Oct. 3, 1975. The producer, Howard Kirp Parker, told the reporter that there's a scientific explanation for everything.

In its story about the first annual conference on science and parapsychology, sponsored by the University of Miami School of Continuing Studies, the *New York Times* reported July 26, 1976 that psychics and psychic phenomena are regarded as promising subjects for serious scientific inquiry.

A weeklong New Age Festival was summarized by Leonard Levitt in *Newsday* for July 31, 1976. Founder was Anthony J. Fisichella, a businessman who says a psychic restored him to good health. Teacher was Frank Baranowski, who described himself as "an authority on pre-natal regression and researcher in reincarnation."

After the Foundation Faith of the Millenium had its regular weekly healing service, during which five healers attended 70 patients, there was a psychic fair that Laurie Johnston covered for the *New York Times* of Jan. 1, 1977. She kibitzed while at $5 per 15 minutes 22 psychic readers revealed what they had learned from tarot cards, personal auras, palms, handwriting, astrological and numerological data.

The extent to which the occult business has developed into a major commercial enterprise was related by the Associated Press in a comprehensive story Aug. 23, 1981 from Paramus, N.J. Participating in a traveling Psychic Fair are "clairvoyants, tarot card readers and seers from every sign of the zodiac," a "traveling sideshow of the mind," a "big money maker for shopping malls. Shoppers can choose between specialists in palmistry, numerology, astrology and psychics." The typical customer is an upper-income intellectual who "goes for the fun of it but deepdown is hoping the reader will provide some insight to life. These people have had it with the aggravation of the rat race."

Is it any wonder that psychiatrists and leaders of the mental health movement have a tough time combatting such superstitions as that brunettes are more untrustworthy than blondes, red hair indicates a quick temper; a recessive chin means a weak will, a square jaw is a sign of courage; smart people are physically weak; hair on the chest is a sign of virility; heavy hair is a sign of strength (remember Samson and Delilah?); brains and beauty do not go together; a "lean and hungry look" is a sign of deceitfulness as are also shifty eyes. In his June 4, 1947 column, Sydney J. Harris, declared, "Superstitions die hard. Science has conclusively proved that you can't tell anything about a person's character from his look—but most people go on judging others by childish standards." Among the incidents he mentioned was the University of Kansas experiment asking students to select the criminals among 75 men whose pictures were distributed. Over half picked J. Edgar Hoover, FBI head, and not one picked "Baby Face" Nelson, notorious bandit.

One of the best journalistic investigations of fortune telling was one of the first reported by Leslie Lieber in the article "I Went to 24 Fortune Tellers" in *This Week* for Jan. 7, 1950. The hanger began: "You guessed it—he got 24 sets of predictions." More specifically he wrote, "All the methods of divination ever practiced here or in the Orient were used on me: periscope eyes perused my palm, scrutinized my tea leaves, scanned my stars, and watched the events of the next three decades kaleidoscope in my coffee grounds."

One tea-leaf reader in Pennsylvania predicted Lieber would fall off a fishing sloop and drown next year. The same day, however, a New York clairvoyant looked into a crystal ball and saw him making contributions to the Atomic Commission in 1960.

The article is full of howlers and the reader wonders with the author, "The surprising thing to me was that none of the 24 mediums detected the fact that I planned to write a magazine article on their powers of divination."

One form of fortune telling is premonition—the person foreseeing some disaster, perhaps his own death. It is not uncommon for reporters to ask survivors of important deceased persons if there was any indication the departed had an expectation of death.

While their parents were obeying a premonition to move them to a safer place, "two children were crushed to death under a landslide," the UP reported Feb. 3, 1947 from Seattle. Shortly thereafter, Jan. 26, 1947, the AP reported from New York that singer Grace Moore had told a reporter in Copenhagen: "It is wonderful to live and sing." Nevertheless, "apparently without premonition of tragedy" a few days later she was killed in a commercial aviation accident. Another woman, the AP reported from Detroit, acted on a premonition and wrote a will before taking a flight that ended in her death. And the UP wrote Jan. 31, 1948 from New Delhi that

Mohandas Gandhi apparently had a premonition of death when he insisted on signing some paper because "Tomorrow may never be."

Columbia Broadcasting System suppressed a segment of its "Celebrity Cooks" show already taped for use July 10, 1978 because actor Bob Crane had made an "inordinate number" of death jokes in it. Crane was murdered a few days earlier and associates said he might have had a premonition, Bob Herguth reported in the *Chicago Sun-Times* for July 4, 1978.

After her nine-year-old son Todd collapsed and died while playing football his mother, Jacqueline Bunn, told the *Tribune's* Steve Kerch, "He had begun to have a sense of God." The story was published Aug. 10, 1982.

The widow of an FBI agent killed in an air crash near Cincinnati told Thomas Powers of the *Chicago Tribune* that she had a revelation and knew her husband was going to die, Powers wrote in his paper for Dec. 21, 1982.

Under the headline "Good Vibrations" March 27, 1983 the *New York Daily News* told of Al Weinstein, a 69-year-old former cab driver who said he had a feeling (premonition) two days before he won the weekly $5,000 Sunday Bonus Zingo.

In *McCall's* magazine for December 1969, as reported by Marie Smith of the *Washington Post* Nov. 20, 1968, Dr. Janet Travell, the White House physician, was certain that President John F. Kennedy had such a premonition. Three times, she wrote, she saw "the shadow of death in the president's eyes."

May 15, 1972 the Knight-Ridder News Service distributed a story that Gov. George Wallace of Alabama had a premonition he would be shot while campaigning for the presidency, as he was May 15 at Laurel, Md. According to the news story, one day in late April Wallace interrupted lunch with his wife and State Repr. Thomas W. Gloor to say, "Somebody's going to get killed before this presidential primary's over and I hope it's not me."

A more startling case was reported by Robert Nelson, founder and director of the Central Premonition Registry in New York. He told Rona Cherry, who reported it in the *Wall Street Journal* for Aug. 22, 1972, that in May 1968 an American psychic, Alan Vaughan, wrote him from Germany that Sen. Robert Kennedy would be assassinated, which he was the following month.

Nelson, a *New York Times* circulation executive, founded the registry in 1968. During the first four years of its existence it received 3,500 premonitions, only 1 percent of which he said were hits. In her article Cherry recalled that in 1898 Morgan Robertson wrote a novel, *The Titan*, about the sinking of a steamship by that name after it hit an iceberg, an uncanny premonition (?) of the disaster that befell the *Titanic* April 15, 1912.

Dec. 13, 1972 the Associated Press reported from Baltimore that, when Alan C. Ray had a dream that the branch bank of which he was manager was to be robbed, he notified police. Despite the heavy police guard that was placed, someone held up a teller for $1,500 and escaped. When Ray had a similar premonition ten months earlier the robber made off with $4,500.

On the other hand, Emmett Stovall owed his life, he said, to a premonition he had about a converted B-25 bomber that crashed on Chicago's southwest side, killing three persons. Stovall was supposed to be on the plane but refused to board it when he heard the engine being warmed up, Peggy Constantine reported in the *Chicago Sun-Times* for Aug. 8, 1976.

After the murders, April 9, 1969, of Sharon Tate and her friends by the so-called Manson Family, the National Enterprise Association distributed an article by Dick Kleiner, its West Coast correspondent. Three years earlier, Kleiner recalled, Sharon had been prone to tell stories of murderers and ghosts.

There are many anecdotes about famous persons having predicted their own deaths. In June and July 1972 the *Chicago Daily News* ran a series of articles relating what has been surmised about Abraham Lincoln, Rudyard Kipling, Robert Browning, Johann Wolfgang von Goethe, Thomas Edison and a number of lesser figures. For several years employees of the *News* had premonitions that the paper would fold, as it did March 4, 1978.

Shirley MacLaine told Tom Buckley what he wrote in the *New York Times* for Oct. 31, 1980 about her eerie experience when Peter Sellers died. She was in California when she suddenly told friends, "Something's happened to Peter Sellers." What happened was his death in England. MacLaine then related that, while they were working together on a picture, Sellers told her after the doctors proclaimed him medically dead following a heart attack he hovered over the operating table and saw his open chest cavity. In July 1983 she announced her belief in reincarnation.

Following the death of John Belushi the *New York Post* March 6, 1982 had a short sidebar, "Chilling Premonition." The story said that three months earlier Belushi told someone, "I'm going to die at a very young age here in New York." He was a dope addict, according to some.

To help people find reputable psychics, Carol and Mary Cocciardi, sisters, have produced *The Psychic Yellow Pages* for northern California. Bill Martin reported for the Associated Press from San Francisco June 11, 1978 that the paperback has listings for psychics, palm readers, graphologists, numerologists, tarot readers, astrologers, holistic health practitioners and researchers.

When E.S.P. Productions was forced to cancel a weekend psychic fair, it announced it would sue the village of Schaumberg, Ill. asserting that the village ordinance forbidding fortune telling is unconstitutional. Gary Wisby quoted the law in the *Chicago Sun-Times* for May 27, 1982 as stating it is illegal to advertise fortune telling or ". . . promise to find or locate oil wells, gold or silver, to restore lost love, friendship or affection, to reunite or procure lovers, husbands, wives, lost relatives or friends, or to give advice in business affairs . . . by means of occult or psychic powers, faculties or forces, clairvoyance, psychology, psychometry, spirits, mediumship, seership, prophecy, astrology, palmistry, necromancy or like crafty science, cards, talismans, charms, potions, magnetism, Oriental mysteries or magic."

And that, folks, is about all there is.

6

Spiritualism

At 12:30 P.M. every March 13, usually with reporters and photographers present, a small group led by Arthur Weinberg gathers on the Clarence Darrow Bridge behind the Museum of Science and Industry to eulogize the famous Chicago lawyer whose ashes were thrown into the stream after his death March 13, 1938.

According to Weinberg, Darrow's biographer, the purpose is to keep alive the ideas and ideals of the great criminal lawyer and philosopher.

In the '40s and '50s similar services were conducted by a Detroit businessman, Claude Noble, who had made a pact with Darrow and the magician Howard Thurston that the last survivor would test the possibility of communication between the living and the dead. On one knee Noble would declare, "Clarence Darrow, I am here in fulfillment of our pact and if you can manifest yourself, do it now." The script, as agreed upon by the three friends, was that a book, usually one by or about Darrow, would be wrenched from Noble's hands. It never was, nor did anything unusual occur either in Chicago or when Noble repeated the ceremony in Columbus, Ohio, where Thurston died April 13, 1938.

In addition to the Darrow, Thurston and Noble pact, the Great Blackstone, master magician, and Harry Houdini (real name Erik Weiss) promised to contact the living if possible after their deaths.

As the *Chicago Tribune* Action Express told a reader Nov. 17, 1972, at a Halloween seance conducted by Joseph DeLouise, hopes that Houdini would communicate were raised when a tinkle of a bell was heard. It turned out to be caused by an ornament on one of 20 guests. Commented DeLouise: "You may attend 100 seances and something might happen at only three or four."

Better luck attended the seance conducted by Mrs. Anne Fisher, self-proclaimed psychic medium, Halloween night in Niagara Falls, Martin Gershen reported in the *Chicago Sun-Times* for Nov. 2, 1974. Attendance was limited to 12, one a UPI reporter, with an empty 13th chair for Harry Houdini. Mrs. Fisher asked Houdini to make himself known, a flower pot on a shelf behind her chair fell to the floor, as did a book about Houdini's life, opening to a page with a picture of a poster advertising the magician's performances. Then, it was reported, the chair moved slightly.

According to the *Chicago Daily News* for Oct. 31, 1976, Warren Freiberg, a self-styled ghost hunter, put his wife into a trance during a radio show on WCGO-AM. Using her voice, Houdini, dead since 1926, explained one of his tricks. The headline on the page 1 story was "Houdini 'surfaces' for radio." There was a picture of Houdini.

Quite the contrary had been the reports of the Olde Towne House in New York that has never endorsed any claim by a medium to the $10,000 standing offer by Joseph Rinn, one of Houdini's close friends. On Oct. 31, 1979, the 53rd anniversary of Houdini's death, the UPI reported from New York that Walter Gibson, biographer, recalled that the great magician considered all mediums fakes. He left a sealed message and code with a friend and promised to communicate if such were possible, which he didn't think was the case.

All of these are discounted by the fact that Houdini told his wife the signs that would indicate a contact if one occurred. The pact was to last ten years, at the end of which the Associated Press reported Oct. 31, 1936 from Hollywood, Calif. that a small group would attend the widow. She said that if there was no contact "either personal survival after death is a falsehood or there is no hope for any of us to contact someone who has gone on."

Until his death March 9, 1975 Joseph Dunninger, "last of the great name magicians," constantly goaded psychics to translate the coded messages entrusted to him by Houdini. Dunninger also offered $10,000 to any medium able to produce by psychic or supernatural means any physical phenomenon that could not be duplicated by trickery or explained away naturally or scientifically. The *New York Times* ran Dunninger's obituary March 11, 1975.

After Thomas Edison died in 1931 a medium claimed to have received a spirit message from the great inventor that he had hidden a "momentous message in a fountain pen." This was recalled in a United Press story from West Orange, N.J. Feb. 9, 1947. It was reported that uranium nitrate, used in manufacturing atom bombs, was found in Edison's desk. Three fountain pens, however, were empty.

Parade for June 13, 1982 revived the story that Edison wanted to try to create a machine for communicating with the dead. Despite the fact that he mentioned the matter in a *Scientific American* article in 1920 and in an interview with *American Magazine,* officials at the Edison National Historic Site in West Orange, N.J. do not believe he was serious.

Jan. 19, 1933 the *Chicago Tribune* ran a column-long story from Paris to the effect that Dr. Miller Reese Hutchison, who was Edison's chief engineer for ten years, "was inclined to believe he had talked to Edison through a medium about a year ago."

The credence that newspapapers give to stories of successful seances was demonstrated by a Reuters dispatch July 20, 1960 from London. It told of the discovery of a diary kept by the Rev. W. R. Packenham-Walsh, recently deceased. In it he related conversations for 30 years with the restless spirit of Henry VIII, who died in 1547 but refused to believe he was dead. Through the prayers of Anne Boleyn, Henry's second wife, whom he had beheaded, and the diary's author, Henry's soul was finally redeemed, and there was a document allegedly signed by Henry's ghost.

The amazing story of a suburban London housewife who takes dictation from the spirits of several great musical composers was worth about a half-page in the *Chicago Daily News* for Aug. 8, 1969. The woman, Rosemary Brown, says that Franz Liszt appeared to her when she was 7 and later gave her a composition schedule. By daily work she turned out more than 400 compositions in the styles of such masters as Beethoven, Schubert, Grieg, Bach, Chopin and Liszt. Some critics say they are definitely in the styles of the dead composers. Mary Firth released a record of piano pieces by several of them.

Similarly, Nov. 22, 1976 the *Sun-Times* devoted a column to a story by Jane Gregory, the nature of which can be derived from the 4-col. headline, "A flutist says Bach told her to do it." What Bach told her was to go ahead with the recording of all of the great composer's sonatas for flute and harpsichord. The flutist, Paula Robison, was frying liver when the master materialized and ordered, "Play it. Play it and enjoy it."

Perhaps the weirdest research project ever was announced Oct. 25, 1979 in Liberty, Mo., where, the Associated Press reported, the Clay County Parks Department advertised for a "gifted" psychic to make contact with the area's most infamous ancestor, Jesse James, dead 97 years. The hope was that the bandit would reveal lore if the seance were conducted near the cabin—now in a county-owned park—where he was born in 1847.

Under the headline, "Spirit Hand Guides Mrs. Bush at Easel," the *New York Times* Feb. 7, 1935 devoted a full column to telling of the startling "spirit paintings" on exhibit in a prominent art gallery by Mrs. Irving T. Bush, wife of a prominent financier. Ever since her mother died 11 years previously, the painter had turned out unconventional compositions that she believed were not her own work but those of long-dead masters. She considered herself merely an automaton working under spirit control. The *Times* did nothing to contradict that judgment.

When a 60-year-old spiritualist was strangled to death in her home, the *Baltimore Sun* for Aug. 9, 1949 covered the murder with about 1½ columns devoted to details of the police investigation and almost as much to a separate story based on interviews with other spiritualists on plans to make contact with the murdered woman, how and when. The United Press reported that a close friend of the deceased would attempt to contact her through a medium even though other spiritualists said it was too soon to attempt a seance. The UPI reported that a seance attended by the dead woman's friends failed to produce a clue. Police, however, found a prescription bottle with the paper doll figure of a man upside down, a familiar signature of a voodoo murderer.

Questions of afterlife, communication with spirits and the like have commanded the attention of scholars of many different kinds for centuries. Journalistic interest has developed during the past half-century with the proliferation of scholarly attempts to find answers scientifically. So important were exclusive stories considered that they were often copyrighted, as was the story G. B. Lal wrote for the Universal Service and the *Boston Advertiser* used Feb. 15, 1937. It pertained to the announcement of Prof. John F. Thomas of Duke University that his research indicated the existence of ghosts and their ability to send messages.

Worldwide spiritualism has an untold number of believers. A little known Asian religion founded on spiritualism is Coadaism, prevalent in what used to be called Indochina. The *Milwaukee Journal* reprinted an article by Jean Dorsenne from the French publication *Grinoire*, in its issue of May 4, 1935. More recently the AP reported from Sao Paulo, Brazil that the Sao Paulo Spiritist Federation is thriving, in part because its seances are free.

Much of the literature supporting spiritualism consists of anecdotes. Dr. Gardner Murphy's article, "Can We Communicate With the Dead?" in *This Week* for March 3, 1957 was about "authentic cases that will baffle any skeptic—and an astounding scientific theory that may explain them."

In an article in the *National Observer* for Dec. 4, 1967, "The Occult: Do Mediums Have a Message?" Daniel St. Albin Greene gave what the subtitle suggested: "A Measured Look at Seances and Sensitives." He began the more than a pagelong piece with anecdotes, notably about the Rev. Ernst Schoenfeld, medium, and his control, Krueger, who had been in life a German preacher and schoolteacher. When Schoenfeld goes into a trance Krueger uses his vocal chords to deliver messages from other dead people to the living. The article included a succinct history of the development of psychic mediumship, now more popular than physical mediumship, which is characterized by darkened rooms, holding hands, trumpets, flying objects and the like, since the invention of infrared photography not too difficult to expose. Greene also described the views and activities of the Rev. Arthur Ford, who was thought by many to be the world's leading medium until his death in January 1971.

What made Greene's article significant was his focus on ideologies and scientific facts rather than on seemingly miraculous occurrences. More typical was a four-page feature in the *Kansas City Star* for May 3, 1975, "Juanita Teske Asks: Was I Dreaming, or Did My Friend's Children Appear to Me After Their Death?" by a reader. It was a first-person chronological account of how she attended meetings and classes of psychics and then had several apparitions.

Most newsworthy, of course, are messages from celebrities. That was exactly what Ruth Montgomery said she had from Arthur Ford. Victor Wilson reviewed her book on the subject, *A World Beyond,* for the Newhouse News Service Nov. 12, 1971. After describing what death is like, Ford's spirit predicted Castro had about had it in Cuba, California and Manhattan will both break away from the continent before 2000 and the world will shift on its axis so "those in the north will live in a tropical climate and vice versa."

July 14, 1963 the UPI reported that a British medium, Marjorie Staves, had learned that Lex Barker, recently deceased actor who played Tarzan in the movies, was "happy and alive in another world."

A fulsome account of the Staves seance appeared in the *New York Post* for June 12, 1972. It took place in New York's Waldorf-Astoria Hotel. Among those present were the actor's fifth wife, his 26-year-old son, the astrologer Carroll Righter, Mrs. Maude Uchitel, a real-estate man's wife, and the actress Joan Fontaine. Of primary interest was the secret message that Barker wrote, along with Robert Cummings, Arlene Dahl and Rhonda Fleming, to be guarded by the *National Enquirer.* The best Staves could do was utter a four-line verse that caused reporter Jan Hodenfield to end her two-column article "Barker was not, apparently, giving away all his secrets."

June 20, 1963 the *Chicago Daily News* used a picture of Barker's widow and reported that she considered the seance "satisfactory."

Even more so presumably was the seance Marilyn Monroe's private psychic, Kenny Kingston, had on the tenth anniversary of the actress' death. One of the 17 "ordinary" people that Marilyn wanted present was James Bacon, who wrote about the experience in the *Pensacola Journal* for Aug. 21, 1972. After a fountain in the patio suddenly spouted water, Marilyn appeared in white on the arm of Clifton Webb. She said she would be alive if she had stayed married to Joe DiMaggio, but said she did not kill herself. Errol Flynn, she said, had already been reincarnated in Monte Carlo and Otto Preminger would win two Oscars. And more of the same.

In his Public Eye column in the *Chicago Sun-Times* for Feb. 25, 1981 Bob Herguth reported that Kingston claimed that Monroe has been reborn on the Isle of Capri and her name is Luigi. Nov. 22, 1981 Herguth quoted Kingston that Humphrey Bogart materialized to tell him he would be reborn in February in Boston. In his Nov. 7, 1982 column Herguth reported that Kenny Kingston claims Mae West materialized and told him she isn't speaking to Jayne Mansfield up there.

Not too unusual are stories of what some person saw, asleep or awake, in a vision. Such a story, written by Tom O'Connor, was published in the *New York Compass* for Feb. 12, 1950. It told of a woman who said her dead mother appeared to her in a dream and told her to reveal the secret she had kept 17 years, that her father raped and murdered her 5-year-old daughter.

From Oakland, Calif. the UPI reported June 2, 1974 that the estranged husband of the late Nancy Ling Perry had appeared to her in a dream to tell her the Symbionese Liberation Army never would capitulate.

With a spiritualist's moral support Mrs. Charlene Lucas finally met her grandparents after her father confessed he had murdered his wife (Mrs. Lucas' mother) when Mrs. Lucas was a child.

Reports of persons once declared dead but later resuscitated are always fascinating. In its issue of Oct. 9, 1976 the *Chicago Daily News* began printing excerpts from a book, *Life After Life*, by Dr. Raymond A. Moody, Jr., who studied 150 such cases. Readers were invited daily for a fortnight to send in accounts of such incidents, either experienced personally or by others; the result was more than satisfactory to the circulation department. "In general," the paper declared Oct. 18, "the readers believe they truly died—and found a tremendous sense of power."

Even more sensational was the story beneath the page-one streamer headline, "Doctor tells of visit from dead," in the *Chicago Tribune* for Nov. 7, 1976. Written by James Pearre to fill space approximating a full page, it related the career of Dr. Elisabeth Kubler-Ross in studying terminally ill patients. It began nine years earlier, when a long dead patient visited her to persuade her not to abandon her pioneering work. The handwriting on a note the doctor had the specter write was the same as that of the dead woman. The article contained many anecdotes of alleged contacts with other deceased persons and out-of-body experiences. Kubler-Ross says the terminally ill go through five psychological stages: denial, anger, bargaining, depression and acceptance.

The veteran syndicated columnist Max Lerner was obviously flabbergasted when he wrote his June 8, 1977 column. In it he reported the audience's impression of Elisabeth Kubler-Ross' speech on dying at a meeting of the Association for Humanistic Psychology. Especially dumfounded was Lerner at her tale of a spook who materializes at sessions she holds regularly with a large therapy group. The being talks, sings, answers questions and dematerializes. She also says she has a spirit guide who shows up on occasions when she needs advice. Lerner said he was emulating Coleridge, who advocated a "willing suspension of disbelief."

The crude methods traditionally used at seances to communicate with the spirits—trumpets, rappings, and the like—will become obsolete if the Metascience Foundation at Franklin, N.C. succeeds in perfecting SPIRICOM, a radio by which to carry on conversations with the Other Side. Inventor is George Meek, a retired engineer who pioneered an air conditioning system for Carrier Corporation and served on the technical staff of U.S. Ambassador Averell Harriman during the war. He insists that he carries on radio conversations with George Jeffries Mueller, a Cornell University physicist who died in 1967. *The Red and Black* undergraduate newspaper at the University of Georgia gave his story more than a full page May 25, 1982.

The *New York Post* Oct. 1, 1977 headlined a full-page article by Steve

Dunleavy, "Science begins to believe that there is life after life." It told of the work of three doctors—Kubler-Ross, Moody and George Ritchie, all authors of books on out-of-body experiences. He wrote: "The most constant experience from the thousands of subjects they have interviewed have been this: A strong warm light, an encompassing feeling of well-being, the sound of a loud bell ringing, feeling one's physical being floating through a long dark tunnel and the ability to see one's own life form and leaving it behind." Dunleavy commented: "their research has produced a compelling picture that cannot be dismissed by the most cynical of minds."

A few months earlier the *Tribune* reported the results of a survey of 399 randomly selected residents in the six-county metropolitan Chicago area to determine the extent and nature of psychic astral projection or out-of-body-experience (OOBE). In the paper's Jan. 12, 1977 edition, Peter Gomer and James Robison summarized the findings of "mystical-ecstatic experience." Most common was "a feeling of deep and profound peace" experienced by 55, followed by "a certainty that all things would work out for the good" (48 participants), "a sense of my own need to contribute to others" (43) and 14 other categorical responses. A typical anecdote was that of a George Williams, a Henrotin hospital patient, who suddenly floated to the ceiling, light as a feather, from which place he watched doctors and nurses frantically giving his body shots.

After advertising for subjects a team of Evergreen State College students interviewed 30 Puget Sound residents who had been declared clinically dead or who felt they had died and returned to life. As reported from Olympia, Wash. March 25, 1981 by the UPI they mostly described a tunnel, a bright light, a feeling of separation from the body, and, finally an encounter with other beings.

The same day the *Los Angeles Times* distributed a story from San Diego about a clinical psychologist who said it is possible to remember one's own birth, complete with details of what doctors and nurses said and how your mother reacted to the delivery. About 100 such cases were to be summarized in a book, *Birth and Before: What People Say About It In Hypnosis,* by David Chamberlain.

Dec. 24, 1981 the *Chicago Sun-Times* used a large picture of Owen Thomas and his mother over a story with a New York headline: "A man stabbed through the heart and clinically dead for 10 minutes said Wednesday he had a vision that his dead brother pushed him back onto the operating table and told him to go back to life."

Two feature stories on the near-death phenomenon were "Back From Death," by Susan Seliger, in the *National Observer* for May 15, 1976 and "Life After Death," by William M. Kutik, in the *New York Daily News* for Dec. 2, 1981. The former drew heavily on Moody's book and studies of 104 cases by Dr. Russell Noyes, professor of psychiatry at the University of Iowa. Fascinating summaries of cases cited by them and several others occupied a half-page of the paper. Kutik featured the case of John Migliacci, who was declared clinically dead from drowning but recovered and told of floating in the air peacefully while looking at himself swimming. Kutik cited the five stages Moody noted common to those who have the experience: (1) viewing their own body from a distance; (2) being overcome with feelings of great peace and joy; (3) moving through a dark tunnel; (4) seeing a brilliant golden light; (5) entering the light.

Because the Rev. Arthur Ford was considered America's leading psychic, his two articles on "Life Beyond Death" in the *New York News* for Jan. 19 and 20, 1972 were significant. Ford told of "a brief visit to paradise, then back to earth again." He described his deathbed scene, hearing the doctor tell a nurse to give him the needle to relieve his suffering; then he floated to the ceiling and away into a green valley with mountains on all sides, meeting old friends and relatives. He philosophized on the meaning of life and of death, grief, sorrow and related matters and wound up grateful for overcoming fear and getting a glimpse of the glory beyond.

Drs. Moody, Kubler-Ross, Ford and others were anticipated by almost a half-century by the Nobel Prize-winning Dr. Alexis Carrel. The Associated Press' science editor, Howard Blakeslee, reported the great scientist's views in a syndicated article that the *Chicago Tribune* used Dec. 15, 1935. After studying spirit experiments Carrel declared, "It is far from being unreasonable to believe that some part of human personality may escape death."

In the same newspaper for Aug. 3, 1982 columnist Joan Beck told of the work of Dr. Michael B. Sabom of Emery University. About half of the 116 cases he studied told of floating above their bodies and observing medical efforts to resuscitate them. They recounted a sense of blackness with a light showing at the end of a tunnel.

When Dr. Sabom's book, *Recollections of Death,* appeared the UPI distributed a lengthy review of it by Cathy Reim for use Nov. 7, 1982 or thereafter. The review epitomized several of Dr. Sabom's cases, of which he wrote there are three kinds: autoscopic, in which the consciousness is separated from the body and looks down on it; transcendental, the consciousness leaving the body and entering a dark region, and a combination of the two.

Another epochal *New York News* article was "Feel of Flying," by Robert Zintl, in the issue of May 4, 1978. It was an eyewitness account of watching Alex Tanous have an out-of-body experience at the American Society for Psychical Research where Karlis Osis was research director. Tanous says he has been able to create a second version of himself, usually in the form of a tiny spot of light that he can send anywhere, since he was five years old. Two electrically sensitive boxes in separate booths recorded his presence while Zintl looked on.

Chris Roberts of the Associated Press wrote from Philadelphia March 19, 1980 that Joan Dinerstein claims she began having such experiences when she was four years old. The article related some of her weird experiences.

Despite many reports like the foregoing, according to the *New York Times* for June 16, 1975 the American Society for Psychical Research told the Probate Court it had spent $175,455 from the estate of James Kidd, an Arizona hermit miner, without proving the existence of a soul by photographing it as it left the body.

Selection of the society to receive the grant had been reported at length in the *New York Times* for July 29, 1971. Originally an Arizona Superior Court had selected the Neurological Sciences Foundation. On appeal, however, the New York group was chosen because the Arizona Supreme Court felt Kidd thought of the soul as a "separate entity" not as a part of the nervous system. Among the disappointed applicants were some mediums who said they already had been in contact with Kidd's spirit. Israel Shenker reported the story.

A group of social and medical scientists have formed the association for the Scientific Study of Near-Death Phenomena, which publishes a newsletter, *Anabiosis* (Greek for "return to life").

Sooner or later every newspaper assigns a reporter to attend seances and meetings of different spiritualist groups. The *Washington Post* did so when the first Psychic Fair was held on the American University campus. In the paper's issue of May 5, 1975 reporter Emily Fisher concluded: "It turned out to be less a lesson in parapsychology than a form of spiritualism." She quoted one of the 3,000 who attended as saying that it was a coming-out of "Washington's weirdo underground." Beneficiary was the National Spiritual Science Center, a group of 100 who study psychic phenomena as gauges of the inner self.

Clay Gowran began a series in the Jan. 23, 1950 *Chicago Tribune*. The editors were careful to announce in a box that it was "in no way meant as an attack" and declared that many if not most groups and mediums are not affiliated with the National Spiritualist Association, which it described as a religious body founded in 1893, with 10,000 members in 30 states.

Gowran fairly reported his experiences in the Friendly Spiritual Church, a converted store where he was encouraged to purchase 15 candles of different colors that once lit under no circumstances were to be blown out. Gowran was given a spirit message that "things will turn out all right," his father was treated for a nonexistent ailment and he held hands with a middleaged lady to exchange what she called "tinglings."

In the Sept. 18, 1966 *Chicago Sun-Times* Sarah Boyken described her visit to the Spiritual Frontier Fellowship where the Rev. Arthur Ford told of three paratroopers who survived an ambush in Vietnam. They saw the soul of one of their dead buddies arise and survey them. About ten minutes later they were rescued by a helicopter whose pilot said he was drawn to the spot by some strange impulse.

As might be expected the *Chicago Daily News* gave the most fulsome treatment with a two-column article by Roberta Billings in its issue of Aug. 28, 1970. The reporter attended a seance conducted by Zelda, a faith healer, and a Rev. John who warned everyone not to be alarmed if someone were touched by any object in the dark. The article contained much dialogue and messages from the spirit world.

The *Chicago Tribune's* religion editor, James Robison, covered the Free Spirit Festival at the College of Du Page in Glen Ellyn, Ill. April 12, 1975 he quoted Ann Kahalas, psychology instructor and coordinator of the festival, "The needs behind traditional religion are the same ones that are encouraging people to investigate Eastern philosophies, mind control and transcendental meditation."

The *Tribune's* Action Express for July 25, 1974 had disappointing news for a reader who objected to use of the mails to tout the book *Invisible Powers*, which purports to do all sorts of miraculous things. It cited a miracle that got $20,000 for one reader; also a husband for another. The bad news was what the postal authorities advised: the First Amendment protects the publisher.

In the *News-Sun-Times Suburban Week* for April 14–15, 1976 Lorelei Czarnecki burlesqued the forthcoming 1976 Free Spirit Festival, noting the barkers for awareness and consciousness raising, reincarnation, Kundaliin yoga and a number of other weird movements. In a dream she tried to rescue a woman being jumped on by a man but was dissuaded by being told it was a rolfing treatment.

For the July 8, 1976 issue of the same publication, Mark Fineman reported on a seance conducted by a minister of the U & Universal Understanding Church, featured by a spirit message that someone's father was keeping her alive against her will.

Also in the suburban supplement for Jan. 12, 1979 Jim Wisuri told of a performance in Arlington Heights by Phyllis Allen of Chicago's ESP Productions and Enterprises for the benefit of the Arlington Heights Woman's Club. Two hypnotized mediums received spirit messages for several members of the audience.

The popularity of spiritualism skyrocketed during World War I. Almost every home had a Ouija board that answered questions regarding the safety of menfolk in the service. Two famous men, Dr. Arthur Conan Doyle, author of Sherlock Holmes mysteries, and Sir Oliver Lodge, eminent British scientist, lost sons in the war. Both wrote books detailing the nature of seances in which they insisted they conversed with dead soldiers.

The *Milwaukee Journal* for Oct. 18, 1925 ran a Consolidated Press Association interview with Sir Conan Doyle in which he insisted on the reality of the spirit world, every planet having its own heaven. He said: "Oh, of course I've shaken hands with spirits—often. I've seen them, heard them, touched them, talked with them. They've been interviewed, photographed and fingerprinted." He displayed some fingerprints.

Ectoplasmic fingerprints presumably made by spirits during a seance were exposed by the Boston Society for Psychic Research to be those of a living man, the *New York Times* reported March 21, 1933. The true owner of the prints, whose identity was protected, confessed that he gave a set of his prints in wax to the notorious medium Margery, most of whose tricks had been exposed by Houdini.

In his syndicated "Human Riddles" column for June 4, 1936, Vincent Towne told how Mrs. Leanore Piper of Boston impressed the great philosopher William James. To test the woman James persuaded James H. Hystop, professor of logic and ethics at Columbia University, to mask and, under an assumed name, visit Mrs. Piper. Hystop became a convert to the possibility of communication with spirits. Mrs. Piper went to London where she was tested and entertained by Sir Oliver Lodge.

What Theon Wright called "a ghost war" in a UP story Nov. 11, 1938 from New York was the virtual abduction of a 12-year-old "ghost girl," Alice Bell Kirby, who arrived in New York from Catahoula County, La. to demonstrate her spiritualistic powers for the Universal Council for Psychical Research. Instead, she was spirited off the plane by a believing group. Joseph Dunninger, the council's president, said the offer of $10,000 still stands for anyone who can use supernatural powers to do anything he cannot do by magical trickery.

As for the Ouija board, its popularity ebbs and flows. July 30, 1968 the *Provo* (Utah) *Herald* editorialized openmindedly about a test to be conducted to determine whether a computer or Ouija board is more reliable in predicting the outcome of sports events.

In his syndicated column, "Pitching Horseshoes" in 1950, Billy Rose posed "The Riddle of Patience Worth," correctly calling hers "the strangest literary collaboration in the history of psychic phenomena." For 15 years, 1913 to 1928, Mrs. John Curran of St. Louis, who lacked even a high school education, wrote four full-length novels and almost 2,500 poems that she said had been dictated to her by Patience Worth who was born in 1694 in Dorchestershire, England, migrated to the New World and was killed during an Indian attack during King Philip's War. The novels were well reviewed and five Patience Worth poems were included in Braithwaite's *Anthology of Poetry for 1917,* more than ones by Vachel Lindsay, Amy Lowell and Edgar Lee Masters. Patience, Mrs. Curran said, first made contact with her through the Ouija board one letter at a time; later she got words and sentences at a time.

"Recalling the interest in spiritualism stimulated by the last war, a reporter went around to the LaSalle hotel where the Illinois State Spiritualists Assn. is in session today to learn what effect this war was having on the membership," wrote Hazel MacDonald in the *Chicago Times* for April 29, 1943.

Although the organization grew steadily there was no boom and the leaders said their main worry was the "racketeers, fortune tellers, astrologers, numerologists, people of that sort—who are taking advantage of people's worries in wartime."

One of the earliest journalistic boosts for spiritualism was a series of seven articles by Austen Lake in the *Boston Evening American* and *Sunday Advertiser,* between Aug. 22 and 29, 1937. Amply illustrated with photographs by the paper's photographer, Bill Jones,the full-page articles related Lake's experience during a week at Lily Dale, N.Y., where hundreds of mediums come, mostly during the summer, for classes, lectures and especially seances.

The principal building is the cottage in which Margaret and Catharine Fox lived when they discovered the spirit of the peddler, Charles E. Rosman, who had been murdered there. The sisters worked out a vocabulary of rappings to converse with the spirit and in 1847 founded the spiritualism movement in America. They took their show on the road and impressed such prominent members of their audiences as William Cullen Bryant, Horace Greeley, James Fenimore Cooper and Thomas Carlyle. The cottage was moved from Hydesville, N.Y. to its present site in 1916 and Lily Dale has been the mecca for believers in spiritualism ever since.

Lake reported objectively what occurred during the seances in which he participated: table thumping, trumpets, trances, spirit messages using media and so on. He did not, however, relate that in 1888 the sisters confessed publicly that the rappings were made by their cracking of toes and fingers. For some time they returned to the stage to expose themselves; then, impecunious, they recanted their confessions and the future of the church they founded was assured.

Nor did the reporter who visited Lily Dale for New York's *PM* of Sept. 1, 1940 report anything iconoclastic. The three-page article is mostly pictures. Eight years later, however, a *PM* reporter, Louise Levitas, accompanied Rose Mackenberg, a "ghost detective" and onetime assistant to the great magician and exposer of spiritualistic frauds, Harry Houdini. The three-page story was a detailed account of visits to many mediums and attendance at numerous seances, together with explanations of how some of the trickery was performed and the ways in which the visitors tricked the practitioners.

"As they have for each of the last 103 Independence Days, hundreds of members of the Lily Dale Spiritual Assembly convened there this holiday weekend and proved they could outdo almost any other group of Americans in independence and spirit." That was the lead paragraph of Richard D. Lyons' column-long story from Lily Dale, N.Y. in the *New York Times* for July 6, 1982.

Whereas there are many types of psychics in the assemblage, according to Lyons they all "feel that a human personality is a passing manifestation of an ongoing spirit" that goes through many transformations and is a little divine. Thus death is a transformation back to the original spirit, not the end of the experience.

To the *New York Daily Compass'* Richard Carter, ghost-hunter Mackenberg revealed that though she never married she had "dressed herself in mourning and spoken to 1,500 nonexistent husbands and 3,000 offspring at seances." Carter quoted her in his June 6, 1950 story as believing all mediums are fakes.

That's what two police sergeants accompanied by a reporter concluded after attending a "church service" at which a husband and wife got messages from the spirit world and gave health advice. The illustrated story appeared in the *St. Louis Star-Times* for April 2, 1936.

When John C. Given of the Associated Press visited Lily Dale for an Oct. 2, 1981 story he found the population depleted and consisting mostly of elderly people. The 86 year-round families were augmented during the summer but there is no private land ownership and to lease a lot one must have belonged to the National Spiritualist Association for at least a year.

Nancy Lee Browning was ordered off the premises of the Spiritualist Camp at Chesterfield, Ind. but not before she had obtained enough material for a three-part series in the *Chicago Sunday Tribune Magazine* for Jan. 6, 13 and 20, 1957. The privately owned camp calls itself "The Hub of World Spiritualism, Largest Phenomenal Center in the World," not affiliated with the National Spiritualist Association of Churches. Commented Browning: "Tho not precisely spiritual, it is certainly phenomenal, for here, at $3 a sitting, you can unburden your problems on the ectoplasmic remains of Great-Grandpa Moses, Uncle Ned, Cousin Horace and all kinds of long-gone kinfolk you never knew you had and whose advice you wouldn't have paid two bits for anyhow, when they were alive. In the astral world they become omnipotent, especially in a pitch-black seance room with a medium who has a complete dossier on you."

Browning described the seances she attended, complete with Indian spirit guides, ectoplasm (foggy vaporous stuff that allegedly comes out of a medium's mouth, clothes of the spirit), trumpets, cabinets, hymns and all. Her third article was devoted to the mail-order factory operated in Columbus, Ohio by Robert A. Nelson who says, "The world wishes to be deceived so I deceive it." Nelson, Browning wrote, "is probably the world's finest expert on ghosts and the only one who makes a business of haunting houses and seance rooms. Nelson's made-to-order ghosts, gimmicks and black magic are shipped all over the world. The famous fakirs of India are among his best customers."

The press pays attention when the *Scientific American* or some other prestigious source announces the results of surveys tending to discredit belief in spiritualism. This happened when the magazine's editor opened 284 letters purporting to describe what Dr. J. Allen Gilbert of Portland, Ore. placed in a safe years earlier. Of 284 attempts to translate the message, 284 were wrong and none anywhere near correct.

In reply to a reader's query "How can I attend a seance?" Aug. 29, 1972, the *Chicago Daily News'* Beeline recommended a forthcoming retreat in Chicago and added this advice: "Do you have some interesting questions for Mrs. (Irene) Hughes to transmit to spirits? Things you always wanted to know about some long gone greats but never had a chance to ask? Or maybe why spirits move and tip tables so much and make things fly around rooms? Think of this so you will be prepared for one rap session to which this term can be applied more than just figuratively?"

Progress of the spiritualist movement anywhere in the world is as newsworthy as the purchase of an American business by a foreigner or vice versa. So Gavin Young reported June 14, 1972 for the *New York Post* from Phnom Penh that the Cambodian spirit world was backing Low Mol's government. In a column-long story he told of the growing group helping to put soldiers in the right mood. One captain, a Buddhist monk for 25 years, told Young, "I am now instructing soldiers in the use of magic and spells."

The same newspaper ran a full page March 16, 1974 on three English spiritualists scheduled to lecture at Hunter College and to seek publicity throughout the New York area. Barbara Trecker, the reporter, was interested in how they became psychics. Carol Polge said she was first aware of her power when at 8 or 9 she followed a hunch and warned her sister to get off a piano bench just before the ceiling fell in. Kathleen St. George became a convert when she talked to her dead father during a seance. She now talks to plants and explains, "It's not psychic at all. I just read the marks on the flowers." Doris Collins professed to be talking with Trecker's grandmother but most of the information was faulty.

William Hines' tone was skeptical-cynical when he reported on what a National Press Club press conference in Washington was told was "the greatest breakthrough in 2,000 years." According to his story, to which the *Chicago Sun-Times* gave a streamer headline April 7, 1982, agents of Metascience Foundation of Franklin, N.J. said they had invented a device to make possible two-way communication between living and dead. Unfortunately the machine was temporarily out of commission but reporters were given cassettes of the voices of Ellen Terry, English Shakespearean actress, and William Randolph Hearst, American newspaper publisher, both long-since dead. Hines commented: "Terry did not discuss her long relationship with Sir Henry Irving, nor Hearst his with Marion Davies."

Beginning in 1901 mediums in many parts of the world began receiving messages with references to Latin, Greek and English literature that three deceased Oxford scholars presumably agreed to transmit from the spirit world. Known as the cross-correspondence the messages have never been studied in their entirety, nor do parapsychologists agree regarding the meaning of those that have been published. Oct. 3, 1982 the UPI reported at length from London about the presidential address of Prof. Arthur Ellison at the Society of Psychical Research convention in which he asserted the cross-correspondence contains proof of life after death.

The most celebrated post-World War II case was that of Episcopal Bishop James A. Pike. An Associated Press story from New York Sept. 13,

1967 told of the dropping of charges of heresy, brought by some of his fellow bishops after publication of Pike's book *If This Be Heresy,* in which the author expressed some doubt about the divinity of Jesus, the existence of the Trinity and resurrection after death. Pike, however, declared that psychic research had proved "personal survival after death is a fact."

Associated Press stories Sept. 25, 1967 from New York and Sept. 27, 1967 from Seattle gave details of a seance taped Sept. 3 in Toronto for broadcasting Sept. 17 over a Canadian television station. The Rev. Arthur Ford, of the Disciples of Christ, a prominent medium, was pictured blind-folded in a trance. Through his spirit control, Fletcher, he received messages from Bishop Pike's son who had shot himself to death Feb. 3, 1967.

Further details of Bishop Pike's seances in which he said he spoke directly to his dead son, who exonerated his father of any responsibility for his death, were included in a *Chicago Sun-Times* story from New York Sept. 29, 1967. By that time affiliated with the Center for the Study of Democratic Institutions at Santa Barbara, Pike said the spirit of his predecessor as Episcopal bishop for northern California, Bishop Carl Block, who died in 1958, also assured him that his son was happy. In the *Chicago Daily News* for Sept. 30, 1967 David Meade, religion editor, wrote an account of Pike's allegedly heretical views, "Pike Cast in Doubting Thomas Role." William Stringfellow and Anthony Town wrote a book, *The Bishop Pike Affair,* to refute the bishop's critics.

In a lengthy feature, "The Other Side of Bishop Pike," in the *Chicago Daily News* for Jan. 8, 1968, Phyllis Battelle revealed that Bishop Pike had had 12 talks with his deceased son which Jess Stearn elaborated upon in *This Week* for Jan. 28, 1968 in an article headlined, "Bishop Pike's Strange Seances." The first presumably occurred three weeks after the suicide which the young man said he regretted through the English medium Ena Twigg, whom the bishop consulted after a number of poltergeist tricks, including books and other objects being mysteriously moved. The bishop also received messages through Arthur Ford and the Rev. George Daisley, a Santa Barbara medium.

The third marriage of the twice-divorced Pike, 55, was predicted in the *Chicago Daily News* for Dec. 17, 1968 and reported in the same paper for Dec. 21, 1968. The bride was Diana Kennedy, 31, who collaborated with her future husband on a book, *The Other Side.* Eight months later the two rented a car and ventured into the Judean desert to study the conditions that Jesus endured for 40 days in the wilderness, about which the couple contemplated writing a book. However, the car broke down and Mrs. Pike went in search of help. Four days later the bishop's dead body was found at the bottom of a cliff. In the meantime Sept. 5, 1969 the *Chicago Daily News* ran a story by Jay Bushinsky headlined, "Pike Alive, Vision Tells Wife." The vision was that of the Rev. Arthur Ford who told Mrs. Pike's parents in California that the missing bishop was alive in a cave.

The finding of Bishop Pike's body was reported by the UPI from

Jerusalem Sept. 8, 1969. The same day Jay Bushinsky reported from Bethlehem, "Exhaustion Called Pike Death Cause." In his *Sun-Times* column for Sept. 11, 1969, Kup wrote, "Clairvoyants and ESP experts who relayed messages on where to find Bishop James Pike during his recent disappearance suffered a tremendous loss of face. None came close to revealing where the body of the bishop finally was found."

Nevertheless, the Associated Press reported from Augusta, Ga. Feb. 6, 1970 that the widow said she continued to have frequent contacts with her dead husband. Sept. 18, 1971 the AP reported from Santa Barbara that Mrs. Pike had sold her house and planned to establish a "free university of the spirit." May 2, 1972 the *Chicago Daily News* ran a lengthy article by Sandra Pesmen, "Still in touch with bishop." The widow was in Chicago to promote a book, *The Wilderness Revolt,* written from Pike's notes with her brother, R. Scott Kennedy.

A startling revelation regarding the Pike case was reported by Eleanor Blau in the *New York Times* for March 11, 1973. She revealed that Allen Spraggett and the Rev. Canon William V. Rauscher, while researching for their biography of Ford, came across evidence that he cheated in the celebrated Toronto seance. Much of the supposedly secret information the dead told Ford was contained in a *New York Times* story Sept. 21, 1958. The biographers said that Ford collected obituaries, had a prodigious memory and was reported to have admitted faking during the darkest days of his alcoholism.

Another tactic that might accelerate communication with the dead didn't impress Mike Royko who commented in his April 18, 1982 column about an advertisement that read, "Send a message to a departed one with a Heavens Union messenger. Messengers are terminally ill rendering a final service." Royko confirmed the existence of the service, which costs $40 of which $10 goes to the valetudinarian. One messenger, however, may receive as many as 125 messages for delivery in the Great Beyond. Royko's reporting was in his best cynical style.

It has been centuries since testimony allegedly obtained from supernatural sources has been admissible in an Anglo-American court. In January 1979, however, the credibility of a witness who claimed to have been an unwilling medium for a murder victim was a factor in a case before Illinois Cook County Criminal Court Judge Frank W. Sarbaro. Result: a mistrial.

The defendant was Allan Showery. Dr. Jose Chua told police that his wife, Remibias, had gone into a trance and spoke in the voice of the murdered Teresita Basa who accused Showery of the crime. The *Chicago Sun-Times* March 5, 1978 used a page 3 streamer headline, "Slaying tip in voice from the grave." Later headlines in the same paper included "Plot thickens in 'voice from the dead' murder trial" (Sept. 10, 1978) and "Possessed spirit named murder suspect, court told" (Aug. 31, 1978), when the judge and the jurors both declared themselves baffled, the two-column headline Jan. 27, 1979 was "Mistrial called in 'spirit' talk trial."

Other papers and the press associations also covered the story. The *Evanston* (Ill.) *Review* for March 9, 1978 told of the reluctance of the Evanston police to inform Chicago police of the alleged spirit message. The Associated Press Sept. 3, 1978 raised the issue of the validity of the arrest warrant naming Showery without sufficient evidence.

The story was the page 1 feature in the *Miami Herald* for March 6, 1978. The streamer headline was "Beyond the Grave—Did Dead Woman's Voice Name Her Killer?" A half-page was devoted to the *Chicago Tribune* Service story by John O'Brien and Edward Baumann, a comprehensive summary of the entire case.

If the courts ever become convinced of the reality of spiritualism, the voices from the grave may be introduced into evidence by means of tape recordings. According to a half-page story, "Voices from dead on tape recorder?" by Mary Travers in the *Chicago Daily News* for Nov. 30, 1973, a Latvian engineer, Konstantin Raudive, already has made such recordings about which he wrote in a book, *Breakthrough: An Amazing Experiment in Electronic Communication With the Dead.*

Just as seriously the widow of a murdered man insisted that he would resurrect and found "a worldwide government of God." The *Clearwater* (Fla.) *Sun* gave the entire page 1, column 1 to the story May 29, 1982.

What *Newsweek* for Jan. 9, 1956 called "probably the first mass-distributed, electronically-captured evidence of the spirit world" was a book consisting of transcripts of wire recordings of what a Pueblo, Colo. housewife under hypnosis recalled of a previous life 150 years earlier.

If valid *The Search for Bridey Murphy* revealed that Mrs. Virginia Tighe, called Ruth Simmons in the book, was born in 1798 near Cork, Ireland, as Bridget Murphy, daughter of Duncan and Kathleen Murphy. Speaking often in Irish brogue, always under hypnosis, she described the neighborhood in which she spent her childhood and recalled incidents dating from the time she was 4. At 20 she married Brian McCarthy and the couple moved to Belfast. There, in 1864 at 66, she died after a fall and observed doctors trying to restore her to life. She even described her tombstone. After 56 years in the spirit world during which time she met relatives and old friends, she was reborn in 1923 as Ruth Mills.

The book, whose author was Morey Bernstein, a prominent Colorado and New York businessman and amateur hypnotist, became a best-seller and was serialized by newspapers throughout the land. The *Chicago Daily News* published 11 installments beginning Jan. 6, 1956. It also assigned several of its crack reporters to seek verification of the "facts" concerning Bridey Murphy's life. Friends and relatives of both Bernstein and Tighe were interviewed; the history and nature of hypnotism were detailed and the opinions of psychiatrists, hypnotists and readers solicited.

For more than a month the Bridey Murphy story had top priority, getting more than a whole page several days. The paper asked, "Could YOU too, Have Lived a Previous Life?" but the hanger revealed the difficulty the paper had in obtaining corroborative expert opinion: "Some doctors here and even hypnotists skeptical."

Another headline was "A Previous Life Possible? Many Experts Say It Is." The experts, however, were mostly L. Ron Hubbard, originator of dianetics, now called Scientology, and faith-healer Edgar Cayce, whose successes caused his biographer Thomas Surgue to suggest Cayce must have been a physician in a previous incarnation. The *News* headlined a speculative piece by Miller Davis, "Was Hillbilly Wizard Doctor in Earlier Life?" The same reporter wrote, "What It's Like When You Are Hypnotized." Readers who flooded the paper with letters had been asked who they would have liked to have been in a previous life. Just about every noted historical figure was mentioned by someone, among the favorites being Plato, Cleopatra, St. Paul, Leonardo da Vinci and Thomas Jefferson.

The story began to wind down when reporters could find no records in Ireland to validate names, places and incidents mentioned by the hypnotized Ruth Simmons. Ernie Hill, one of the *Chicago News'* leading foreign correspondents, could find no record of Bridey Murphy's birth, marriage or death, leading the paper to declare in a Jan. 18, 1956 headline, "Our Own Search for Bridey or Kin Fails in Ireland." Another journalist whose quest ended in discouragement was William J. Barker of the *Denver Post* whose wife had been hypnotized by Bernstein and said she also recalled events of a previous life. The *News* ran his stories.

Finally April 25, 1956 the *News* reported the theater performance of an entertainer, "The Great Morton," who demonstrated how a Bridey Murphy could be created. First he hypnotized a member of the audience and told him he was Sir Thomas Tightpants, discoverer of the New World in 1494 after Christopher Columbus got lost in 1492. When hypnotized a second time the subject identified himself as Sir Thomas Tightpants and related what the hypnotist had told him during the first session.

"Teresa Wright, back in the movies after a two-year absence in television, has chosen the most difficult role of her career for her comeback— Bridey Murphy," the UPI reported June 15, 1956 from Hollywood. Wright was quoted: "I wouldn't have accepted the part if I didn't feel sure that Ruth Simmons actually regressed to a former life as Bridey."

Persons claiming to have lived before cropped up all over the country and received diminishing journalistic attention. In Shawnee, Okla. a 19-year-old news carrier committed suicide, leaving a note that he was curious about Bridey Murphy and was going to investigate. A Milwaukee husband filed an alienation of affections suit against a hypnotist who had convinced his wife they had been married in a previous incarnation.

The Bridey Murphy story blew up journalistically when the *News'* rival, the Hearstian *Chicago's American,* explained the origin of Virginia Tighe's supposed Irish anecdotes and, most important, found the real Bridey Murphy whose picture, with grandchildren, it ran. The journalistic triumph was related by Bob Smith, *Chicago's American* reporter and author of most of the paper's articles to win the newspaper war with the rival *News.* His memorandum, dated July 24, 1968, prepared for the author of this account follows:

Chicago's American learned that Virginia Tighe, the Colorado woman who claimed to be Bridey Murphy in a previous life, was a former Chicagoan whose relatives still lived here. Wesley Hartzell, who was then city editor, learned this from a friend, the Rev. Wally White. Mrs. Tighe's aunt was a member of Rev. White's congregation.

We played a recording made by hypnotist Morey Bernstein of a session in which he took Mrs. Tighe back to her life as Bridey Murphy, for the aunt. The aunt recognized several things Mrs. Tighe said as having happened to Virginia as a child in Chicago.

With this *The American* launched an investigation, talking to merchants who had stores near Virginia's girlhood home, looking up names in old phone books and generally trying to track down piece by piece everything Bernstein had written in his book about Bridey.

We were able to find many points of similarity between incidents that supposedly happened to Bridey in her previous life and those that actually occurred to Virginia in Chicago.

We talked to the parents of Virginia's husband, or former husband (I can't recall which), and literally retraced the steps Virginia had taken as a girl in her neighborhood. We learned that shop owners, long out of business, had displayed high shoes and other articles Bridey remembered seeing in stores in "Ireland."

We talked to psychiatrists who helped us explain some of the fuzzy details that could be attributed only to "Bridey's" imagination.

However, we were not able to find anyone named Bridey Murphy, and so closed our series.

A few days after the articles ended, I received a phone call from a woman who asked what we were trying to hide. When I said I didn't know what she was talking about, she explained that Bridey Murphy was really the mother of one of the *American's* editorial employees.

I interviewed this woman later and we were able to come up with the final explanation; we were able to introduce the real Bridey Murphy and even publish a photo of her.

Bridey Murphy was the maiden name of the mother of an *American* employee who had lived across the street from Virginia Tighe. For one reason or another, he had elected to say nothing of this to any of us assigned to the investigation. To shield his identity, and also to keep the *Daily News* from saying it was a put up job, we did not mention this in our final article.

The secret of Bridey Murphy was in our office all the time—but we didn't know it.

Fifteen years later Mrs. Tighe was interviewed by David Lamb of the *Los Angeles Times*. The *Sun-Times* ran the story June 1, 1971. Mrs. Tighe recalled the events leading up to her trances, said she was tired of the attention she attracted. Especially she was distressed by a letter from the mother of the boy who committed suicide. "I hope you're happy now." Dec. 18, 1971 the *News'* Beeline answered a query by saying that Virginia lived with her second husband in Colorado and is not convinced of the reality of reincarnation. In newspaper interviews, however, Bernstein professed strong belief. He called the *Chicago's American* series "a shoddy, superficial and totally unfounded hatchet job."

In "Bridey Murphy Revisited," in the *Chicago Tribune Magazine* for Nov. 28, 1971, Olga Curtis rehashed the whole Bridey Murphy story. The only new facts possibly were that Virginia Tighe began hypnosis to try to end her sneezing and that she and her husband separated in 1964 and were divorced in 1968 for reasons having nothing to do with Bridey Murphy. In May 1971 she married Richard Morrow, a Denver businessman.

The debunking of Bridey Murphy by no means put an end to the widespread belief in reincarnation, nor to journalistic reports of such matters. In *This Week* for July 20, 1968 Jess Stearn told of "My Search for the Girl with the Blue Eyes." Subject was a 14-year-old Canadian girl, Jeanne MacIver, who, under hypnosis by her father, became Susan Ganier, presumably born in 1832 in Canada's north country. At 17 she married Thomas Morrow who died in a barn accident after a few years. Susan Ganier Morrow lived until 1903, so there were persons alive when Stearn conducted his research who were alive then. Stearn was astounded at the accuracy of Jeanne MacIver's knowledge of geography. Recalling the Bridey Murphy fiasco, however, he refrained from expressing all-out conversion.

When 500 followers of the late Edgar Cayce met in Chicago the *Sun-Times'* Tom Fitzpatrick covered the event Aug. 20, 1969. He quoted Mrs. Alice Platt of Arlington Heights that Cayce's prediction that the lost continent of Atlantis would rise from the sea in 1968 or 1969 had come true in three feet of water off the coast of Bimini. She insisted she knows at least two persons who lived in Atlantis 1,000 years ago and are reincarnated today. One is her husband who "must have come from the civilization in Atlantis because he is so brilliant."

Atlantis also figured in Daniel St. Albin Greene's feature in the *National Observer* for Oct. 30, 1976. It was really a review of Ruth Montgomery's book, *The World Before* and a sketch of the seer's career. The cosmological narrators of the book are named Lily, Art and the Group, who contend that there are discarnate spirits who regularly communicate with Montgomery in automatic writing. Their Transmigration File reveals that many present-day celebrities once lived on Atlantis, including Richard M. Nixon, Jackie Onassis, Gerald Ford, Barbara Walters, Merv Griffin, Elizabeth Taylor and Richard Burton, the last two lovers even then.

Montgomery herself spent most of her time on Atlantis in a temple of free love where pious women improved the race by selective motherhood.

Chicago Daily News' Beeline received a letter from Harris Asher saying that ten years earlier he had been hypnotized and taken back to a previous life. He wished to be hypnotized again to determine if the things he recalled can be verified. Aug. 9, 1968 the *News* published the results of the hypnotic session it arranged. Its story began: "Carry Janocz, Colorado trapper wounded in an Indian raid Oct. 17, 1887, died Wednesday in a hypnotist's chair. He was 57. Death was attributed to an arrow in the chest."

The *Miami Herald* gave five pages Sept. 19, 1971 in its supplement, *Tropic,* to Nancy Beth Jackson's article, "Dr. Stratos and Miami's Bridey Murphy." This was a story about Maria Marin who "is convinced she has come in all shapes and sizes, colors and religions, classes and characters, learning and suffering with each life and carrying the lessons and the guilt from one existence to another."

Dr. Stratos is a chiropractor whom Maria recognized as her master in Egypt 4,000 years ago. He put her under hypnosis and she recalled events through several generations of lives to make fascinating reading for anyone who wants to believe fiction is real.

Ostensibly to advertise the motion picture *Let's Scare Jessica to Death,* Psychic Dimensions staged a seance that Michael Putney attended for a nearly half-page article in the *National Observer* for Sept. 18, 1971. The medium, called Oceana for the occasion, told many of the reporters present that they had lived previous lives. The score included a violin maker, movie star of the '20s, pearl diver in the South Seas and the victim of a great injustice that affects his disposition in his current reincarnation.

Tom Valentine answered a reader in his Aquarian Age column in the *Flagstaff* (Ariz.) *Sun* Dec. 8, 1971 with a recitation about Bridey Murphy. The reader who signed himself "Good Memory" wrote that for 45 years "pictures of what I believe are of a previous life experience have flashed in my mind." He wanted to know if these impressions proved reincarnation.

A pathetic case was reported by the Associated Press March 13, 1978 from Reeds Spring, Mo. It was the story of an evangelist, Daniel Aaron Rogers, who placed his dead mother's body in a freezer and, assisted by three other preachers, prayed for more than two hours for her resurrection. Then he sorrowfully told members of his congregation who were praying in the mortuary, "We have tried everything Jesus told us to do and we don't know what is wrong. She has not risen from the dead."

March 27, 1978 the UPI reported that Rogers had been ordered by health officials to raise his mother from the dead by March 29 or prepare her body for burial. Rogers said the prayers of him and his parishioners might bring about the miracle.

The risks that both buyer and seller take in this area were demonstrated when Prof. Albert Hyma of the University of Michigan was permitted by the Michigan Supreme Court to bring suit against Lillian Lee, pastor of the Church of Christ, for giving him spiritualistic advice that led to losses of $10,480, the UPI reported from Ann Arbor.

In March 1982 book reviewers cited the anecdote in Rodney Duggers' *The Politician* alleging that Lyndon B. Johnson thought the Holy Spirit visited him in the White House in early morning hours.

Ann Landers answered a toughie in her column for March 25, 1982. A reader hesitated to will the gold crowns in her mouth to anyone because she was convinced she would need them on Resurrection Day. Ann advised her "keep them in your mouth and out of your will. The decision is sure to take a load off your mind."

"Psychics, Schmychics, Says Randi; It's All Fake" was the headline March 14, 1982 in the *New York Daily News* over a short summary of the views and activities of the magician James Randi who offers $10,000 to anyone able to perform a trick with psychic powers that he can't reproduce. "If people—kids—believe this stuff about pyramid power, flying saucers, it changes their philosophy of life and they lose control over it," he said.

After confessing that she believes in a flat earth, extraterrestrial life and reincarnation, Beverly Friend nevertheless said she just could not believe, in Jess Stearn's book, *The Search for a Soul,* an attempt (à la Bridey Murphy) to take author Taylor Caldwell back through several previous lives. She told why not in her review in the Jan. 20, 1973 *Chicago Daily News.*

In the *Chicago Tribune* and *New York Daily News* for May 2, 1972, Carol Jouzaitis wrote about psychologist Helen Wambach, "a master of the mental journey." "She has taken hundreds of people back in time thousands of years, guiding them into eras when there was no car, no electricity, even no written languages." She began her experience with hypnotism as an intern in a veterans' hostpial in Gulfport, Miss. during the Korean War. In an accompanying article another *Tribune* reporter, Margaret Kriz, told of participating in Wambach's performance and imagining she was a Roman boy about 100 A.D.

"A couple hundred years in a Hillside motel one night," was the way Jon Hahn began his report in the *Chicago Daily News* for Feb. 4–5, 1978 as one of 50 who attended a hypnotic session conducted by Dr. Helen Wambach. Hahn learned that he had been a 32-year-old Swedish sailor with a rather attractive farm wife. He needed almost a half-page to describe the session and give Wambach's background.

Wambach also was the subject of a piece in the New York *Village Voice* for May 15, 1978. She said 90 percent of her hypnosis patients recall incidents of previous lives. She argued, "My subjects know too many minute details that check out historically with the period of time and place they claim to have previously lived in. For this reason I am convinced the time has come to study rigorously the possibility of reincarnation."

Still another reporter not only interviewed Wambach but also let her help him through hypnosis to recall several of his own prior lives, including that as a girl killed by a spear about 500 B.C. In the interview Wambach said she had the idea she once was 18th-century Quaker leader John Woolman considering it pretty hilarious" for him "to return as a fat middle-aged lady from California." Knight-Ridder syndicated the story May 4, 1979.

James S. Sweeny wrote "I was the Bishop of York. Who Were You?" for the *Chicago Sun-Times Midwest Magazine* March 24, 1974. It is a long recitation about a boy Mark who was six years old in 1650 in Cornwall, England. In his introduction Sweeny listed as believers in reincarnation Plato, Buddha, Pythagoras, the Essenes, Henry David Thoreau, Walt Whitman and Henry Ford.

Aug. 4, 1974 the *New York Daily News* began a series by Alton Slagle on "Reincarnation: Fantasy or Fact?" The series was based on the files of Dr. Ian Stevenson, professor of psychiatry and director of the Division of Parapsychology at the University of Virginia Medical School. Typical anecdote was the girl who recognized her previous parents when she was a boy. It is reasonable to speculate that after death a person would be exposed to guilty memories as well as pleasant ones, Stevenson believes. He said: "Thus we would be punished by our sins rather than for them. Some philosophers have said that a fear of death is really a fear of another unpleasant review of one's misconduct. It follows that as a man cultivates goodness, he loses his fear of death until, as Socrates taught, a truly good man has no fear of it at all."

Another article telling what Stevenson's 1,700 case files contain was written by Sari Staver. Entitled "Survival After Death; Search for Proof," it appeared in the *Chicago Sun-Times* for March 3, 1980. Stevenson was quoted: "Reincarnation has not yet been proved and may never be. Nevertheless, reincarnation is no more illogical than the assumption that each life is encompassed by a single birth and death."

Even more effusive was the full page the *Washington Post* gave Nov. 14, 1978 to an intensive interview of Stevenson by Tom Zito to whom Stevenson said, "The thing you look for in a good case is richness of obscure details." Among the "good" cases, he cited that of Bridey Murphy.

A minister's wife in Elkton, Va. got a half-page in the *Washington Post* for Jan. 20, 1975 after it was revealed that under hypnosis she became an illiterate German girl. Although in her present incarnation as Mrs. Dolores Jay she speaks no German, as Gretchen Gottlieb she told of her murder in Bismarck's Germany when she was 16. Dr. Ian Stevenson was investigating, among other things to determine which of several towns named Elberswaldes might have been her home. The UPI broadcast the story Jan. 21, 1975.

In Cairo, Egypt a *Los Angeles Times* reporter, Don A. Schanche, encountered Dorothy Louise Eady, who supplied him with enough reminiscences of a former life to fill a half-page of his paper Nov. 2, 1977. The septuagenarian said she was a contemporary of Seti I and his son Rameses II, both of whose mummies are in the National Museum in Cairo. Eady described the buildings and monuments of that era and said she has been helpful in telling archeologists where to dig to excavate valuable ruins and artifacts.

The *Sun-Times* for Dec. 2, 1979 devoted a full page to an interview by Marian Christ with Ruth Montgomery who believes she has been reincarnated several times, once as the sister of Lazarus of biblical fame. She said a ghost who signs himself Lily communicates with her by automatic writing on the typewriter.

Jan. 30, 1980 the *Sun-Times* reported that singer Loretta Lynn thinks she was King George II's girlfriend and was murdered by the king's best friend after his death.

For $15 one can get a past-life reading from a pagan priestess, Christa Heiden, who operates out of the Evanston Unitarian church. Heiden and her congregation of 24 follow Epiphanes, a pagan religion meaning "manifestation of god." By hypnosis she relaxes her customers to reach the "eternal now" from which they travel to childhood and earlier. Johnny Heller wrote a half-page article about it for the Feb. 29, 1980 Suburban *Sun-Times*.

Many problems people experience are traceable to experiences in previous lives, Sylvia Schwartz, as "Past Life Counselor," believes. David Markus covered one of her meetings in New York for the UPI March 1, 1980. Schwartz said her own compulsive eating derived from the fact she was a 19th-century Indian who was tied to a tree and allowed to starve to death.

Another admirer of Ian Stevenson is Dr. Gina Cerminara who told Barbara Somerville for the article "Past-Life Therapy: A New Way to Study Reincarnation" in the *West Palm Beach Post* for Feb. 15, 1982: "I don't believe one lifetime of 60 odd years is enough to learn the lessons we need to learn to become perfect as Jesus suggested we do."

Cerminara, also a follower of Edgar Cayce, blames *Life* magazine for destroying public belief in Bridey Murphy. She was a speaker at the 1980 Association of Past Life Therapy. She says that inherent to the belief in reincarnation is the concept of karma—the law of cause and effect that says everything you do and think has an effect for which you are responsible, during this life or another.

In Los Angeles Elizabeth Long had a come-as-you-once-were party, the AP reported April 17, 1971. The hostess says she was Queen Isabella of Spain and remembers sending Christopher Columbus off on his journey in 1492.

7

Ghosts

The spirits with whom those who attend a seance converse through a medium are not the ghosts that the same people fear and do their best to avoid. Spirits are at peace, happily adjusted to their new environment. They have to be summoned by the medium's spiritual contact and often resent being disturbed. Ghosts, on the other hand, may not realize that they are dead. Often they want to attend to some unfinished business. They search for loved ones, sometimes for enemies, so they frequent houses and other landmarks. They are unhappy, often wailing in despair.

According to a well-researched historical sketch that Lloyd G. Carter wrote for United Press International for Halloween 1977, the common misconception that ghosts wear white sheets probably can be traced to earlier times when the dead were buried in sheetlike shrouds. In reality, according to Carter, Halloween apparitions are usually seen dressed as they were in life. Mark Turck, psychic researcher who founded the International Ghost Registry in Santa Cruz, Calif., says the chain-dragging ghost was memorialized by Charles Dickens in his account of Ebenezer Scrooge's encounter with the ghost of Jacob Marley.

Journalistic authors of Halloween feature stories and cartoonists perpetuate the sheet and chain myths and most newspapermen probably believe in ghosts and maybe also in goblins, fairies, banshees, leprechauns, trolls, devils, demons, angels and other supernatural beings as well.

Presumably ghosts haunt a house or some other place at least occasionally on the anniversary of their earthly birth or death date, the latter especially if they were murdered. Persons who report apparitions or other evidence of ghostly presences attempt to identify their visitors by researching the history of the spot or date. Belief in the reality of ghosts is many centuries old and there probably is no human group of any kind that is not credulous.

In modern times the English are supposed to have the most haunted houses. However, the United States is catching up, thanks in considerable part to journalistic support. A streamer headline in the *Chicago Sunday*

137

Tribune for Oct. 28, 1979 was "Here's a Guide to Haunted Houses and Spooky Spirits in the US." The author was Stephen Bimbaum, a radio man. His random sampling of the "earliest and most goose-pimple inspiring" houses, all open to the public, included Madame Lalurie's Mansion, French Quarter, New Orleans; The Cottage, near Baton Rouge, La.; Parlange Plantation, near New Roads; La.; Robert E. Lee's boyhood home in Alexandria, Va.; Oaklawn Manor, Franklin, La.; Shirley Plantation, Westover, Va.; Haw Branch Plantation, Amelia County, Va.; Winchestor Mystery House, San Jose, Calif.; Governor's Mansion, Dover, Del.; and the town of Wiscasset, Me.

Five of these places also were listed in an article by Sabin Robbins IV, "You can tour America's haunted historic houses," in the *Chicago Sun-Times* for Oct. 28, 1973. In addition the author devoted about a half-page to ghostly myths that included the White House; New York City's Morris-Jumel and Edgecombe mansions; the Loudoun Mansion in Philadelphia; Fielding Lewis' estate in Fredericksburg, Va.; the Wyth House in Williamsburg, Va.; Old Brit Bailey near Houston, Texas and Chicago's St. Rita, where not one but six ghosts hang out.

More than 20 ghosts in eight states and 29 cities are listed in an eight-page foldout guide issued by the United States Travel Service. Entitled "The Supernatural-Haunted Houses and Legendary Ghosts," the guide was dubbed *Who's Whoooo in America,* Robert J. Dunphy wrote in the *New York Times* for July 17, 1977. He also gave the numbers of the free telephone service network. The New York *Village Voice* for April 3, 1978 briefly reviewed another similar guidebook, *Weird America,* by Jim Brandon, which listed Superstition Mountain, Arizona among other entries in what the paper said could be called *Five Shudders A Day.*

The *New York Times* for Jan. 15, 1978 mentioned several spots not included in either, the Bimbaum or Robbins article, among them St. Maurice, La.; Fort Monroe, Hampton, Va. and aboard the *U.S.S. Constellation* at Baltimore where a sailor's ghost presumably is a haunt.

Also mentioned is the Decatur House in Washington, "haunted by the spirit of its first owner, Stephen Decatur, a naval hero who died in a tragic duel."

Sarah Booth Conroy included Decatur House in her lengthy feature, "The Haunts of Washington," in the *Washington Post* for Nov. 1, 1981. She said the window before which Decatur stood on the eve of his duel has been boarded up because so many people say they saw the long-dead admiral still gazing through it. The Conroy article included tales of the house owned by Robert Gray that burned down shortly after the Reagan inauguration, of which Gray was co-chairman of arrangements; also the Woodrow Wilson house; the Octagon House once owned by George Washington's friend, Col. Benjamin Tayloe; the Smithsonian Castle and the White House.

Other straight news accounts of Washington, D.C. ghosts appeared in the *Chicago Daily News* May 14, 1957 and Oct. 31, 1975. The first was a United Press story headlined, "What? Spooks in White House?" and reported what James Hagerty, press secretary of President Eisenhower, said were familiar tales: that Queen Wilhelmina of The Netherlands fainted when Abraham Lincoln's ghost appeared and that Mrs. Lincoln heard the ghosts of Andrew Jackson swearing and Thomas Jefferson playing the violin.

In his article, "Mr. Ghost Goes to Washington," Robert Signer of the *News'* Washington staff, cited several other anecdotes included in a new book, *Ghosts: Washington's Most Famous Ghost Stories,* by a radio broadcaster, John Alexander. Lincoln's ghost presumably has been the most active, being sighted by Theodore Roosevelt and Eleanor Roosevelt, among others. In an interview with the Associated Press that the *New York Times* published Nov. 6, 1975, Alexander said that until the 1920s there were many empty houses in Washington because they presumably were haunted and nobody wanted to live in them. Many subsequently were razed. Among the most active Washington ghosts was John Quincy Adams whose spirit supposedly is seen on the spot in the capitol where he suffered his fatal stroke.

Unable to explain how locked doors became unlocked and lights turned off and came on unexpectedly, the National Park Service changed locks at the Lincoln Memorial and guides on night tours work in pairs, Paul Hodge reported in the *Washington Post* for Dec. 12, 1981.

Lincoln's ghost can be heard and felt though not seen in Ford's Theater, where John Wilkes Booth shot the president. Actors forget their lines, especially when they walk across the stage in the same way the assassin did. Hal Holbrook and Jack Aronson are among those who said they felt chills, the UPI reported from Washington Dec. 17, 1972.

Visitors to Lincoln's home in Springfield, Ill., now a museum, also report "the feel of Lincoln's presence," John Bonnan reported in the *Chicago Daily News* for March 6, 1976.

When an Associated Press photographer printed a negative he made in Washington's St. John's Episcopal Church, he discovered that he had not only a picture of the pew occupied by FDR but, superimposed, a fuzzy face that might seem to some to be that of the president himself, AP Wirephoto distributed the picture March 6, 1942 so newspaper readers could make up their own minds.

Probably the most historical haunted house in the nation's capital is Prospect House, originally owned by a Revolutionary War hero, General James Maccubbin Lingan. Throughout the 19th century it had several owners, most of whom preserved the 18th-century features of the 22-room mansion. During the Truman Administration it was used as a guest house while the White House was being renovated. Patricia Firestone Chatham purchased the house from Mrs. James Forrestal. When she put it up for sale the *Washington Post* had a two-page historical feature Sept. 10, 1967.

The author Winzola McLendon made several references to the ghost, allegedly seen and heard by some guests and about which most of the others heard stories.

New York has been the site for many first-class ghost stories. One of them was concluded by Asa Bordages in the *World Telegram* for Nov. 29, 1938. Ever since 1870 it had been believed that the shrouded ghost of Alexander Hamilton frightened a longshoreman named Kelly when it accosted him as he passed near Hamilton's grave in Trinity Church cemetery. As a result of the experience Kelly, it is said, joined the Temperance and Benevolent Society. Sixty-eight years later, Mike and Billy Fitzpatrick, then 75 and 73 years old, confessed to the reporter that it was they and their sister Emma who masqueraded to scare the inebriated Mr. Kelly and start a legend.

Another legend of comparatively recent origin was created at nearby West Point Military Academy when two plebes reported they were disturbed by a handlebar-mustached ghost, a cavalryman of the early 19th century, carrying a musket. After cadet officers could find nothing amiss the students were given new quarters and the incident provided news for the AP and the UPI Nov. 15 and the *New York Times* for Nov. 21, 1972. Moise Sandoval authored a feature in the *National Observer* for Nov. 25, 1972. In it he told of Molly, Irish cook of the 1820s, whose ghost occasionally played tricks, the cavalryman of the 1830s and the good luck presumably attached to the statues of several old war heroes. Carol Kramer updated the story in the *Chicago Tribune* for March 11, 1973. In so doing she ignored an AP story from Annapolis Nov. 29, 1972 that a Naval Academy midshipman confessed the ghost was a hoax he and some others perpetrated before the Army-Navy football game.

Probably the most famous Manhattan haunted house is the 125-year-old building at 11 Bank Street where the ashes of Elizabeth Bullock, cremated Jan. 26, 1931, were discovered in 1954 when the house was renovated. According to Joyce Wadler's story in the *Washington Post* for Nov. 1, 1980, Elizabeth's ghost likes parties and cheap perfume and is a neighborhood favorite.

Included in a three-page feature, "Haunted Houses. True Ghost Stories from Gotham" in the *New York Daily News* for Oct. 29, 1980 were the Governor Clinton mansion, now a rundown apartment building in Hell's Kitchen; the Staten Island Dutch mansion now maintained by the Staten Island Historical Society and an apartment in Brooklyn.

Herguth reported in his *Chicago Sun-Times* Public Eye column that Chicago's Warren Freiberg was investigating haunted houses in Greenwich Village by conducting seances in six houses said to be haunted, including one where Edgar Allan Poe once lived.

As a guide for souvenirs the *New York Times* for Oct. 29, 1976 ran a feature, "Inside Occult New York," that listed several stores, including Magickal Childe, Mason's Bookstore, Astrology Center and Mekaneesas.

The *New York Post* reported June 27, 1977 that "two ardent psychics" from Chicago, researching a book on American ghosts, would conduct seances at a half-dozen spots in Greenwich Village. Among them: 12 Gay Street where Jimmy Walker once lived; the Changes bar on Mercer Street and the Phi Upsilon fraternity house at NYU, former home of Edgar Allan Poe.

The Bullock House was one of a half-dozen haunted houses whose backgrounds were sketched by the ghost-hunter Hans Holzer in the *New York Daily News* for Oct. 30, 1981. Others were: 226 Fifth Avenue, haunted by General George Edward McGowan, Civil War hero; Clinton Court, 420 W. 46th Street, haunted by numerous spirits since Governor Clinton's time; 12 Gay Street, the puppet theater of the late Frank Paris, where a number of pathetic female ghosts are observed floating around; Morris-Jumel Mansion, Edgecombe Avenue and 160th Street, where George Washington headquartered during the Battle of Long Island, haunted by the onetime wife of Aaron Burr and 228 W. 44th Street, June Havoc's onetime home haunted by Lucy Ryan who starved to death in 1792.

Presumably a British psychic persuaded the ghost of an Annette Williamson to leave the Hadaway House, a restaurant near Stony Brook on Long Island. As Jean Schindler told the story in *Newsday* for Nov. 1, 1979 Annette was hanged for being pro-British during the Revolutionary War after being incarcerated in what was then a stagecoach stop. Sure enough, the name Williamson was found on a tombstone in an old graveyard nearby.

The indifferent attitude that most journalists have toward the ghostly phenomenon probably was stated by John Wilcock in his column, "The Village Square" in the New York *Village Voice* for June 18, 1958:

Why do so few Americans believe in ghosts? Are the others skeptical because they don't want to admit the existence of things they don't fully understand? In Europe, where there is less skepticism, apparitions are more common. But some inexplicable spirits have been sighted here too—inexplicable, that is, unless you accept that ghosts might be merely disembodied versions of people who have been here before.

In a full-page illustrated feature that *American Weekly* syndicated in 1936, an anonymous author explained "Why We Are Afraid of Dead People." Mostly the article is a collection of historical anecdotes to describe but hardly explain the phenomenon. Wearing black, it was explained, originated in an attempt to hide the identities of survivors, to protect them against the deceased.

A series of bizarre events caused Arch Oboler of Studio City, Calif. to ask, "Was it Satan at work?" He told his story in the *National Observer* for Aug. 28, 1976. Events included doors that were held shut though nobody was there, door knobs that turned by themselves, dogs that bristled at unseen objects, rattlesnakes that didn't strike and more "coincidences." All of this followed publication of his first novel, "a tongue-in-cheek tale about an ordinary family cursed by a grandmother in league with the devil."

Almost every city in the United States has, or could have, some spot associated with the spirit of some departed personage, or the site of some ghastly newsworthy occurrence. In Philadelphia, for instance, there is the mirror in which Peggy Murphy and some sorority sisters say the face of Marie Rourke, a year dead, appears when observed from the right angle. The United Press reported the crowds that gathered July 30, 1936.

Philadelphia also was the site of an eerie experience that befell Dr. Herman Hilprecht, a professor of Oriental studies at the University of Pennsylvania, about which Doane R. Hoag wrote in his "Random Time Machine" column, which the *Columbus* (Ohio) *Dispatch* used Sept. 20, 1979. As the story goes the scholar was guided by a midnight apparition through his study wall into a room the ghost told him was the Temple of Bell in Nappur. There he obtained the missing part of a ring with an ancient Assyrian inscription, made, his guide told him, for King Kurigaizu.

What may be New England's last haunted house is the Ocean-Born Mary House near Henniker, N.H. Donald Wayne told the fascinating story in *Parade* for April 30, 1950. In 1720 pirates captured a boatload of Irish settlers but Captain Pedro saved their lives on a promise that a baby girl being born to one of them would be named Mary for his mother. When years later Mary was widowed with four children, the old pirate moved in with her and shared his pirate's wealth. In 1938, when the area was struck by a hurricane the Ocean-Born Mary House was occupied by Gus Roy and his mother, the mother saw a tall woman protect her son and help him prop up the house's wall. Gus never saw her. Gus says he's not psychic but "there's a presence there. Everyone feels it right away."

In nearby Cuttingsville, Vt. the Haunted Mansion is a strong tourist attraction. The elaborate 21-room edifice and an elaborate mausoleum were built by John P. Bowman where he believed he would be united with his wife, whom he married in 1849, and their two daughters whose deaths he refused to accept. His will left $50,000 to maintain the properties and specified that the table be set every evening in case the spirits were able to use it. When the $50,000 ran out in 1953 the furniture was sold at auction and about that time "strange things started happening." Paintings fell from walls, there were sounds of a baby crying, nighttime apparitions were noted, lights went on and off and more of the same. The present renters of the place, Clint and Lucille Fiske, maintain a book shop, specializing in out-of-print books, but they do not use the third floor. The fascinating story, with illustrations, was told by Frederick John in the *National Observer* for Oct. 27, 1974.

Bucksport, Me. was named for Judge Jonathan Buck, who once sent a man to the gallows as the murderer of a woman whose body was found with one leg missing. After the judge died the granite tombstone over his grave was stained with marks resembling a woman's leg. Attempts to obliterate it failed and today it is a tourists' attraction about which Mary Bolte wrote in the *Chicago Daily News* for June 17, 1972. The article also included a list of other haunted spots in New England.

A short detour will take the haunted-house hunter to restored Smithville, N.J., where the Garrison house is shrouded in mystery. Cornelius Garrison, according to the legend, rescued and married a shipwrecked Swedish princess. The *New York Daily News* had the story Nov. 12, 1978.

A bit farther south is the Ghost Museum in the Trapezium House in Petersburg, Va. The building's peculiar shape is said to have been the result of the advice of a West Indian servant who told Charles O'Hara, the owner, that ghosts and other unearthly denizens prefer right-angled corners in which to hide. The *New York Times* had the story Aug. 20, 1980.

After he heard footsteps and pictures fell from the wall, Gov. Linwood Holton of Virginia announced that the executive mansion in Richmond is haunted, the *New York Times* reported July 26, 1973. Aides said former governors had reported there were ghosts in the house.

The sorrowful tale of the Curse or Mother-in-Law Tree was related by James T. Yenckel in a page-long story in the *Washington Post* for Oct. 31, 1982. Two 17th-century lovers are buried beneath it but over the years the tree has separated them. That was something the girl's parents were unable to do when 17-year-old Sarah Harrison married 37-year-old James Blair, a founder of William & Mary College. Tourists visit the site on the Jamestown Island settlement.

About the most romantic haunted building in Virginia is the 132-year-old Barter Theater in Abingdon. According to the UPI June 7, 1982 the theater, in earlier years a church, a temperance hall and a town hall with jail, has two ghosts, one friendly and the other evil. The benevolent spirit is believed to be that of Robert Porterfield who founded the theater group in 1933, when actors and actresses performed for their dinners during the depression. Today the theater is the longest-running professional company in the United States.

According to Tom Maier in the *Chicago Sun-Times* Public Eye column, a ghost who works the night shift in a North Carolina furniture factory shocked enough employees to cause production to drop 30 percent. The factory owner says the phantom, wearing a checkered workshirt and khaki pants, is the best watchdog the place could have. The AP had the story April 1, 1982 from Thomasville, N.C.

The 57-room Bethany Colony Mansion in Pennsylvania's Wayne County, built in 1911 by Norm Gauthier, is a popular resort, to which it was converted after a half-century as a private dwelling. Tourists seem to like the eerie footsteps, opening and closing of doors and windows and other phenomena, the UPI reported Aug. 1, 1982.

Another popular home for ghosts supposedly is Franklin Castle in Cleveland. It was built in 1881 by a German immigrant, Hans Tiedemann, one of the city's first bankers. In addition to its 20 bedrooms it has some secret passageways, which tourists are charged to examine by the present owner, Sam Muscatello. A nonbeliever, Sam set about making another secret stairway, when he found a pile of human bones that caused him to wonder whether what the neighbors had said for years might be true. The United Press International distributed a story of the coroner's opinion; the *Pittsburgh Press* used it Jan. 19, 1975.

In nearby Toledo a carload of *Toledo Blade* reporters exploded the belief in the existence of a ghostly motorcyclist on a stretch of country road. The legend grew that the single light that went on and off was the ghost of a motorcyclist whose head was severed in an accident. Actually, on the undulating road at a distance two automobile headlights were seen as one. Kenneth Clawson wrote a long account of the journalistic detective work for the *Toledo Blade* of Jan. 11, 1964.

The extent and intensity of public fright was reported Sept. 14, 1981 from Norfolk, Neb. With no timely news peg, the report told of two vacant houses that nobody would rent because nine persons met tragic deaths in them within 15 months. Some neighbors moved away because sightseers became a nuisance.

A quilt that straightened itself out on a bed, tugged for possession from anyone sleeping under it and was capable of moving around a room was under investigation by a committee of women in Poy Sippi, Wis., the UPI reported Oct. 18, 1963. One young man said while the quilt was acting up a man with dry clothes and no face came in out of a rainstorm.

For its Halloween feature the *Eau Claire* (Wis.) *Country Today* Oct. 27, 1982 reviewed the book *Haunted Wisconsin* by Beth Scott and Michael Norman and devoted an entire page to an excerpt telling of a Neillsville woman who was visited by the apparition of a former boyfriend who evidently wanted her to console his mother when her husband died and her mortgage was foreclosed.

For its 1982 Halloween feature *Parade* used a piece by Dean Faulkner Wells concerning the family ghost Judith, about whom her famous uncle, William Faulkner, told tales in Oxford, Miss.

Another UPI spook story originated in Los Angeles, where two women, sisters-in-law, saw the face of a dead man in their window daily at 9:25 P.M. Lights flashed on and off, a smell of gardenias flooded the room, although there were no gardenias growing in the area. As usual this story was related as straight and important news.

A description of how and why "Spirits and ghosts are plentiful in Hawaii" was included in a story by Charles Hillinger from Kapaa, Hawaii in the *Toronto Star* for Aug. 3, 1973. The three-times mayor of Lihue blamed his defeat for reelection on a ghost in his attic. Other equally bizarre anecdotes are plentiful.

"Nobody knows who the ghost is or why the old Hively place is haunted. They just know something is there," Sandy Wells wrote from Rock Creek, W.Va. for the *Charleston* (W.Va.) *Gazette* Oct. 30, 1981. "Practically everybody on Rock Creek has heard things or seen things . . . Or they know somebody who did."

Mostly the witnesses tell of doors that don't exist slamming on windless days, of frightened dogs and of a headless man. The house has been abandoned for years but it attracts tourists.

The *Sun-Times' Midwest Magazine* for March 13, 1973 devoted two pages to a feature by Albert M. Gallegos on "La Llorona, the wailing ghost of los Latinos." La Llorona presumably is the Mexican and Mexican-American version of the Irish banshee, a young woman who was buried in her wedding gown and who warns of deaths in the family on both sides of the Rio Grande.

Mrs. Katinka Park of Denver says she has a ghost in her house, according to Donald Yalwish in the Newsmakers column in the *Chicago Tribune* for Sept. 18, 1973. Her neighbors tell her it's only bad plumbing but she says that, in addition to being noisy, the unwelcomed guest has pushed her down the stairs. Evidently he didn't like it when she papered her bedroom wall with red.

A much weirder case was resurrected by the AP from an article in a 1916 edition of *Institute Quarterly,* an organ of Illinois' charity services. The AP story July 14, 1974 from Bartonville, Ill. told of an old man who forgot his name and was called A Bookbinder because of his occupation. Hundreds allegedly were witnesses when the man's coffin flew into the air as it was being lowered into its grave, and the dead man's apparition was seen weeping and wailing.

During the past two decades Chicago papers have done a competent objective job of informing readers of the whereabouts and backgrounds of ghostly habitations in the area. As might be expected the *Daily News* set the pace. June 29, 1970 it began a three-part series by Susan Root on "Chicago's Haunted Houses." Early in the series she wrote, "Lawyers, stockbrokers, college professors, interior decorators, actors and even a cynical ex-newspaper editor will confide that they live in 'haunted' houses." Root related the eerie experience that caused several persons whose sleep was interrupted by wailings to become converts to a belief in ghosts. Carol Broman, Palatine psychic, helped Ruth Kovac, a west suburban housewife, to understand the sounds of wailing and children playing that disturbed her rest. The English witch, Sybil Leek, did the same for Sara Gold of Hyde Park. Other psychics explained that ghosts are the traumatized, trapped spirits of people who died sudden deaths or deaths they could not accept.

"If a person is filled with guilt or feelings of intense hostility or has any kind of strong emotional bond with a place or the people in it they refuse to leave when they die," according to Carol Broman, "They will stay until the conflict is resolved. A ghost is just like you and me only they've lost their bodies. They still have a soul and spirit."

Most press accounts of ghostly phenomena do not include comments by psychiatrists, other scientists, religious leaders or iconoclasts. The phenomena of the spiritual world as stated by the psychics—many of whom are complete frauds when it comes to prophecies—are accepted as serious fact, not to be questioned.

A couple of *Chicago Daily News* Beeline answers illustrate this point. Sept. 16, 1974 a reader was told the Haunted House in Melrose Park is staffed by volunteers of the St. Paul Lutheran Church, which shares in the proceeds from the admission fees. Oct. 30, 1975 Beeline advised a newcomer desirous of seeing a ghost on Halloween to go to (1) Bachelor's Grove cemetery near Midlothian, although most authorities agree that disembodied spirits do not haunt cemeteries but rather places important to them during their lifetimes; (2) Holy Family Church, which survived the great Chicago fire; (3) the entrance to Resurrection Cemetery, where a murdered Polish girl, known as Resurrection Mary, allegedly often appears and (4) the site of the St. Valentine's Day massacre of gangsters in 1929.

Several other ghostly sites were included in a page-and-a-half spread, "A Ghostly Guide to Chicago," in *Everyweek, Daily News* supplement, for April 7–8, 1973. A large colored map indicated the location of 11 of the most famous haunts. Still more sites were included in "A Spook Haunter's Guide to Chicago" by Steve Marshall in the *Daily News* for Oct. 29, 1974. This article was a description of what is included in the five-hour, 100-mile Chicago Ghost Tour conducted weekends by Richard T. Crowe. Crowe also received considerable free publicity from the *Sun-Times,* chiefly a feature article by Joe Ziomek, "A dark night . . . a lonely road . . . just right for ghost hunting," in the Sept. 11, 1974 issue and Patricia Smith's "Tour With Chance of a Ghost" in the *Suburban Week* supplement Oct. 27–28, 1978. This despite a story by Bill Granger, "Haunted Houses Spooked by Price," in the Oct. 28, 1973 issue relating to the profit-making activities of the operators of the sites, including the Lombard Jaycees, Wheaton Youth for Christ, Mundelein Jaycees and the Melrose Park Lutheran Church.

The Associated Press put a lengthy story about Crowe, written by Charles Chamberlin, on its wires from Chicago Oct. 31, 1974. On All Souls Day Crowe planned to conduct 60 persons to a 100-foot-high landmark in Starved Rock Park near Ottawa. It was there in 1704 that the Potawatomi and Kickapoo Indians nearly wiped out the Illinois tribe. Over the years many persons have reported hearing screams emanating from the spot.

Crowe received his biggest publicity bonanza in the *Sun-Times* for Oct. 31, 1980, in a page and a half feature by Connie Fletcher, "13 Ghosts You Can Meet." Crowe is quoted as saying, "Chicago's No. 1 in my opinion.

Chicago has such a rich variety of ethnic groups and blends, so Chicago ghosts represent every culture and every walk of life. The best of the world's ghosts are represented in Chicago. We've got Polish, Irish, Italian and Jewish ghosts and all the ghosts have the unique Chicago flavor."

Typical of the paper's descriptions of the 13 sites is that for Holy Sepulchre Cemetery; "Mary Alice Quinn who died in 1935 at the age of 14 is thought to have performed many miraculous cures since her death, curing everything from cancer to infertility, with special interest in terminal illnesses, according to Crowe. Quinn vowed to her parents that she would someday help suffering people and reportedly said, 'I will shower roses on the world.' An overwhelming scent of roses in the dead of winter—a 'phantom scent'—often is reported at Quinn's gravesite, says Crowe."

Except for a few punch taglines, as "Maybe it's just another jogger," after relating the habit of the Calvary Cemetery ghost who crossed Sheridan Road after supposedly having drowned, there is nothing to distract from the value of the advertising for Crowe's business.

It was a refreshing surprise to note the *Tribune's* Action Line answer Oct. 27, 1974 to a reader asking what haunted houses there were in the Chicago area and how one could visit them. The reply in part was: "If you're speaking of 'honest-to-goodness' haunted houses, the answer is 'none.' However, if you're asking about a scare house set up with props for the Halloween season, we know of just the place. You can visit one sponsored by Campus Life, a collegiate Christian group that yearly sets up a haunted house for the spook season . . ."

The *Sun-Times* Action Time squelched one ghost scare when it persuaded a furnace repair company to make one more visit to the residence of a customer who was given no rest from whining, knocking and howling emanating from the heating unit. Having been assured there was nothing wrong mechanically she had become convinced she had a ghostly tenant.

Anita Gold added a few more haunted houses to other people's lists in the *Chicago Tribune* for May 7, 1982. One is Victorian House Antiques, 806 W. Belmont Avenue, where a woman presumably was murdered when the house was new and where four persons died in an attic fire. Another is on Cherry Valley Road near Crystal Lake, a house once used for seances. It has been known as Witches House and Spirits House, where lots of spooky sounds and sights abound.

"Old Haunts," subtitled "A do-it-yourself tour of real haunted houses," by Ronald Pazola filled two pages of the *Sun-Times* for Oct. 29, 1982. Dale Kaczmarck, a ghost hunter, and Joseph DeLouise, psychic, were quoted for background. DeLouise explained, "A ghost is the surviving emotional memory of a person who has died under tragic conditions. It cannot leave the spot where the tragedy occurred. It is tied to the spot. It keeps reliving those final moments of agony, usually unaware that it has passed on and that it is what we commonly call a ghost." Among the haunts listed were

Hull House, Luetgert House, Stickney Mansion, Lexington Hotel, Glessner House, Irish Castle, Victorian House Antiques and Schuttler Mansion. In the same issue the paper listed Halloween activities, including "tales of terror that frightened early Illinois settlers," to be told at the Chicago Historical Society; a parade at Brookfield Zoo; a Horror Film Fair; "scary films for the kids" at The Public Library Cultural Center and enough other events to fill a news page.

When a reader complained that officials would not help her research Bachelor's Grove Cemetery, the *Sun-Times* Action Time Oct. 29, 1982 explained that the resting place of south suburban pioneers "has been desecrated by vandals . . . by droves of teenagers who dot the landscape with beer cans, overturning and stealing markers, shrouding the place with tasteless graffiti and even digging up tombs."

Chicago's Archer Street was the subject of a full-page *Chicago Tribune* feature Oct. 29, 1982. One of the many legends is that a driverless hearse terrifies onlookers as it dashes between the Resurrection and St. James Sag cemeteries. Author Kenan Heise quoted some who claim to have witnessed this and other ghastly phenomena.

For its 1982 Halloween feature the *Chicago Tribune* used a feature story by Bill Stokes about a house haunted by the memories of its last inhabitant, an elderly Daisy Fish. Amid the creaks and squeaks Stokes found a letter written in 1910 to Daisy by a friend, to tell of her youthful romances.

When John Phelan inserted an advertisement in the *Sun-Times* for May 2, 1969 the paper made an illustrated news story of the reasons he spent money on "Haunted house owners, Adventurous Foursome Wish to Challenge spirits in house of their dwelling." Phelan said he did it "just for fun" and there was no followup as to what he got for his money.

Once in a while but not often a haunted house is mentioned legitimately in a straight news story. For example, in the *Chicago Times* for Oct. 26, 1946, Marvin Quinn wrote of the discovery of the decomposed body of an old man in a house that neighborhood children shunned because they said it was haunted. For the May 28, 1947 *Sun* Herman Kogan wrote of whining sounds in a Leyden bar, which customers insisted was a baby ghost despite the owner's insistence it was a missing kitten that evaded all efforts to rescue it.

Although several of the guides mention sites in nearby suburbs, more fulsome treatment of the thrills to be encountered outside the city limits appeared in the *Sun-Times* and *Daily News Suburban Week*. Especially Irene Piraino's "Suburbia's Haunted Houses" in the issue of Oct. 23–25, 1973 and Pat Krochmal's "Ghost Story: Meet suburbia's ghosts—and some of their haunts" in the issue of Oct. 29–30, 1976. The former article told of the attempts of Penny South, president of Berwyn's Society of Psychic Awareness, to exorcise seven Chicago-area haunted houses. She succeeded in only one instance. The latter article drew on Crowe's expertise to try to

explain the noises and lights in Bachelor's Grove Cemetery. Piraino mentioned the weird sounds and apparitions in the Woodstock Opera House
which was the subject of a lengthy article by Gary Wisby in the *Sun-Times*
for Nov. 1, 1979. The paper even ran a three-column artist's conception of
what the phantom looks like when seated in Seat DD113, reserved for her
by a group of teen-agers.

When renovation of the 96-year-old Beverly, Ill. Unitarian Church
began, the *Chicago Tribune* gave about a half page April 10, 1983 to an
article by Mark Brown regarding the rumors connected with the edifice
popularly known as the Irish Castle. Typical was speculation as to what
effect the hammering would have on a small Irish girl in a long white dress
whose ghost supposedly dwells in the building.

A scantily clad young woman was sighted by several autoists near
Byron, Ill. Because no human presumably could survive without additional protection and because she always disappeared when anyone
showed an interest in her, she became known as the Phantom of Kennedy
Hill Road. In a column-long article in the *Chicago Tribune* for Jan. 22,
1981 Mary Elson reported that cars were bumper-to-bumper as sightseers
became ghost hunters. Neither city policemen nor sheriff's deputies, however, could find any clues to solve the mystery.

In November, 1943 *Times* reporter Eddie Throm slept three nights in a
Sterling, Ill. house believed to be haunted because of an orange hand that
wrote every night on an inside wall to the terror of residents of the small
downstate Illinois city. The answer to the mystery: Mayor Shawger's
grocery was directly across the street from the afflicted house. A sign in the
window, advertising bread, had blue and red bulbs. When an auto turned
into the street from the right its headlights picked up these cardinal colors
and changed them into a bright orange that skittered across the wall of the
haunted house's living room staircase in the shape of a menacing hand. It
took lengthy stories Nov. 9, 10 and 11, 1943 to debunk the explanations
that superstitious and gullible townsmen were circulating.

What spectators called "a miracle of God's" was explained by glaziers as
merely a refraction through an inexpensive frosted glass called "fracto-
lite." Nevertheless, crowds continued to gather to view the lighted crosses
in the bathroom windows of several apartments in the Bronx, the *New
York Post* reported Jan. 21, 1972. Roman Catholic priests said that if the
crosses "are a reminder of the people's religion and God then they're good."
A psychiatrist called the phenomenon a "mass psychosis." According to a
policeman, "It's just a goddamn nuisance."

In his "On the Sun Beam" column in the *Sun-Times* for June 7, 1943, W.
A. S. Douglas complained that the only World War II ghost stories were
adaptations of ones circulated in earlier wars. Among them was the uni-
formed soldier who walked up to and through you and the patrolling of the
Rogers and Clark bridge at Vincennes by soldiers wearing uniforms of the
days of the explorers. Substituting for the vacationing Douglas Sept. 27,

1946, Walter F. Morse lamented the dearth of haunted houses, poltergeists and other kinds of ghosts. More than a decade later Dick Griffin wrote "Being a Ghost Here is Tough" for the Jan. 17, 1959 *News*. He did, however, tell an old one about the glamorous dance partner who gave her escort her address which turned out to be a cemetery.

A receptive audience is being kept alive by horror movies and other programs on television, about which Norman Mark wrote a comprehensive piece for *Panorama,* the *News* and *Sun-Times* supplement for Feb. 5–6, 1972.

In the *New York Times* for Jan. 9, 1972 Raymond Ericson praised Benjamin Britten's new opera, *Owen Wingrave,* based on a short story by Henry James. He said the symbolism is obvious when the principal character challenges a supposed curse on a bedroom where murder was committed and is found dead in the morning.

Despite the fame or notoriety that numerous American ghosts have attained, their Mother Country is still believed to be England. Newspapers carry few if any accounts of ghastly phenomena from other parts of the world but every few months there is an account of some supernatural occurrence in the land from whence came the Pilgrims and the Puritans almost 500 years ago.

Sept. 28, 1947 the UPI reported from London that a tax assessor and a medium investigated a 12-room mansion whose owner asked for a lowering of the tax assessment because the place has been haunted ever since a wall was removed. Supposedly 300 years ago the then owner sealed his daughter and her lover behind it.

What the Society for Psychical Research called "the best documented ghost story of our time" was related by the United Press International in a story from London Oct. 1, 1948. Subject was a transparent nun walking around Borley Rectory, appearing deliberately and lingeringly to at least 200 persons, 40 of them professional people selected to investigate the phenomenon.

After Mrs. Irene Bradshaw told the press about Ignatius the ghost, she was harassed by psychics, would-be suitors, hooligans and just curious people. Ignatius also was very annoyed by the publicity but he continued to toll the church bell whenever a death was imminent, although only Mrs. Bradshaw heard it or ever saw him. All this was news for the UPI July 11, 1949.

Another UPI story Sept. 10, 1958 was that an amateur photographer thought he was taking a picture of empty choir stalls but the developed film showed people sitting in the stalls of London's Winchester Cathedral.

Many aspects of how the law relates to ghosts were reviewed in a UPI article by Robert Musel in London Feb. 20, 1968. The reporter drew on the *Law Society Journal* that the law pertains to humans only and ghosts have no legal protection against being exorcised from a building. Usually a court is interested only in whether a litigant is a believer in spirits. "There are, however," the magazine said, "occasions on which it may be necessary for the court to descend into the psychic arena and find as a fact whether a spirit or spectre actually existed." Already a writer and an artist have convinced courts that they have close relationships with ghosts.

Still another UPI story June 2, 1972 told of the engagement of a medium to quiet a ghost that disrupted construction work on a factory in Stoke-on-Trent. The *Chicago Tribune* also had a story about this June 11, 1972.

The Canadian Press carried a story from Chertsey, England Aug. 29, 1972 that workers at a printing factory in Surrey banned overtime until the management banished Henry, a ghost who, they said, opened and closed locker doors.

Associated Press stories included the following:

Nov. 30, 1946, a vicar reported seeing a procession of brown-robed monks marching down the aisle of St. Dunstans Church in West London.

Dec. 4, 1946 the British Society for Psychical Research said it would "send a man around" to investigate the stories of the Buckland family that hazy apparitions appear at their bedsides and there are rappings and footsteps and other ghostly happenings in the 800-year-old house into which they moved recently.

Feb. 19, 1971, in Chicago on a visit, the Irish author and actor Richard Harris told AP reporter Vivian Brown about the eight-year-old-boy ghost who disturbed him and guests in his 120-year-old London house.

An expert on traditional beliefs told the British Association for the Advancement of Science that Scottish Highlanders still report seeing three-foot-high fairies and an 80-year-old witch, the AP reported Sept. 2, 1958 from Glasgow.

A Cork, Eire woman, supported by neighbors, went to court to protest renewal of a license to a ballroom because of the noise by patrons who said they were hunting leprechauns "because, as everyone knows, they carry crocks full of gold," the AP reported April 1, 1971 from Cork.

A similar story Oct. 19, 1958 from Limerick had told of the difficulty in extending the runways at Shannon International Airport because the government insisted that a fairy fort on Trade's Hill not be disturbed.

A Ouija board's report of the exorcism of a ghost named David was related at length by Alexander Ross in the *Toronto Star* for Feb. 2, 1972. Until his banishment David caused several tenants in the Village Corner Club to move. He had manifested himself by making sounds like shoveling coal when the building had no coal-burning furnace as, however, it once did. Also David gave people a creepy feeling.

From a faraway part of a British Commonwealth, Sydney, Australia, the AP reported Nov. 4, 1975 that the Sydney Opera House was investigating "ghostly drum raps" that interrupted concerts.

A yarn suitable for a session during which those attending try to frighten the others was datelined London in the *Milwaukee Journal* for

Jan. 13, 1936. It told of a doctor who was directed in a fog to a house where his timely services saved a woman's life. The stranger directed him to tell Flo it was Basil. Flo was the woman's name and Basil was her brother who was killed at Grasfontein.

"Whether you believe in wraiths or not, we trust you will find this article entertaining—with a dash of wit and whimsy" was the editor's note to introduce a 2½-column roundup of English haunted houses by Dennis Bardens in the *Chicago Daily News* for Nov. 29, 1958. "As Samuel Johnson once said, there has been no country in which the existence of ghosts has not been taken for granted," the British journalist wrote. Among the conclusions to which he came after several years of study were: "One hears of apparitions in cavalier costume but never in bathing trunks; castles are more in favor as the scene of haunting than, say, a pre-fab—although I have heard of a pre-fab that is haunted . . . Ghosts certainly have much in common. Usually they are not more than several hundred years old. They are normally transparent; they can pass through solid objects, such as doors and walls."

Early in the '70s travel bureaus and airlines began competing with each other for tourists to take their special trips specializing in "ghosts and gurus," as the *New York Times* put it July 30, 1972. Pan-American World Airways had a series of London tours called The Psychic Scene and another to India, The Mystic Scene. Pan-American's Psychic Scene included seances, meetings with mystics, experts in tarot cards and crystal balls and lectures by spiritualists. Pan-Am also had a Mystic Scene to India. Swissair offered Legendary Castle Tours.

July 2, 1971 the *National Observer* announced a Pan-American Airways two-weeks psychic tour of London led by an internationally known clairvoyant named Deziah. July 16, the *New York Times* reported that Dezia (*sic*) also had put together a four-hour Psychic Cruise on a rented Staten Island ferry in the company of 50 clairvoyants, astrologers, palmists and other psychics, mostly English.

Officially there are 236 apparition spots listed in *Gazetter of British Ghosts,* edited by Peter Underwood, Nino Lo Bdellow wrote in the *Chicago Tribune* for Oct. 26, 1975. At the time the London Ghost Club was 110 years old with membership restricted to 4,000, mostly professional people.

Among the many other books on the subject, *The Ghost's Who's Who* by Jack Hallam is outstanding, Roy Reed wrote from London for the *New York Times* of Nov. 24, 1977. It lists about 500 apparitions ranging in age from a Bronze Age man to a jail matron who died in 1970 and in prominence from Henry VIII to a nameless man in a bowler hat who haunts the No. 1 runway at Heathrow Airport.

The UPI had reported the Heathrow ghost in a dispatch from London Nov. 22, 1974. An investigation followed the complaint of a cleaner that a ghost grabbed him and held him down.

Aug. 5, 1979 the *New York Times* advertised "Psychic Tour of Britain" with the cooperation of the Spiritualist Association of Britain.

Launching of a worldwide scientific investigation of apparitions and hallucinations was announced by the Institute of Psychophysical Research, Reuters reported from Oxford, England April 10, 1974. Especially desired are incidents in which two or more persons observed the same phenomenon, as when a man and wife awakened to observe a nunlike figure in their bedroom, putting out a night-light on a mantel.

In June, 1937 the *American Weekly,* a Sunday supplement mostly for Hearst newspapers, began serializing *Lord Halifax's Ghost Book,* "a collection of astonishing real-life stories of spooks, dreams, premonitions and eerie happenings authenticated in each case by some eminent personage." Publisher of the book was the Rt. Hon. Vincent Halifax, British public servant, who obtained it as a legacy from his father, Lord Halifax, who collected the stories throughout his lifetime. The titles of some of the "complete and perfect short stories" were: "Apparition of the Murdered Man With the Bag of Money," "The Ghost Pilot Who Jammed the Controls and Wrecked Three Airplanes" and "A Warning Cry From the Coffin That the Remains of the Dead Man Were in Danger."

A more recent guidebook that includes "collections of gossip, legends and old wives' tales with no serious attempt to separate fact from fiction or the well-documented from the rumored," is *A Guide to Occult Britain* by journalist John Wilcock, who subtitles his book, *The Quest for Magic Britain.* It has 300 pages of highway directions to and photographs of the spots in England, Scotland, Wales and Ireland with pagan or mystical associations. Reuters distributed a review by Lloyd Timerlake that the *Los Angeles Times* used May 9, 1976.

Leading British ghost hunter has been Harry Price who received a two-page writeup by Keith Kerman in the *St. Louis Post-Dispatch* Sunday magazine for Jan. 17, 1937. In *Confessions of a Ghost Hunter* and other books Price recalled spending nights in haunted houses where he was unable to obtain photographs. He organized the National Laboratory of Psychical Research and for 30 years investigated haunted houses, mediums, poltergeists, seances, mind readers, fire walkers, "spirit" photography, the Indian rope trick and other psychic phenomena. "Some of the marvels came from normal, natural causes, some were brought about by trickery. Some he was unable to explain and it is evident he believed there are forces in the world and physical and psychological principles which human beings have not yet learned about," Kerman wrote. "He admits that some of the mysteries that have stumped him could be explained if the spiritualist theory were accepted that the spirits of the dead can return to earth and manifest themselves in ways perceptible to living beings. But he has never been able to find scientific proof of such survival."

Other ghost hunters have had similar experiences. The UPI reported Aug. 14, 1958 from Palmi, Italy that a landlord closed a house when the hunters failed to account for the apparitions and other manifestations that caused tenants to move. In Baltimore a committee overseeing restoration of the frigate *Constellation,* the U.S. Navy's first fighting ship, refused permission for 20 ghost hunters to spend a night on the ship in the attempt to contact the spirits of those who were killed in 1799 and 1800 battles.

When more than 50 people visited the Bradford, Pa. cemetery after midnight looking for a ghost named Luke, Police Chief William Neatrour objected to the damage to roads and lots and declared, "All I've got to say is that if I've got to chase ghosts, then they better raise my pay," Joe Krovisky wrote in the *Harrisburg* (Pa.) *News* for Nov. 5, 1968.

The first American to win a reputation as a ghost hunter was Dr. Henry C. McComas, Johns Hopkins psychologist, whose many books included *Ghosts I Have Talked With.* He led the attack on the notorious medium Margery. He was profiled by P. Stewart Macauley in the *Baltimore Sun.* The *Milwaukee Journal* reprinted the article Feb. 29, 1936.

After the death of Harry Houdini in 1926 the leading American ghost hunter and debunker of supernatural manifestations was the professional mind reader Joseph Dunninger. July 12, 1936 the *New York Times* reported that Dunninger offered a $10,000 prize to anyone who could point to a haunted house that couldn't be proved to be "either a hoax, a myth or some natural or scientific manifestation." July 30, 1936 the *New York World-Telegram* reported on the futile search by 50 persons led by Dunninger, chairman of the Universal Council for Psychic Research. According to the story's author, H. Allen Smith, a noted writer, with 1,000 persons outside the Dunninger group congregated in a bedroom where a husband murdered a wife 20 years earlier. It was "the greatest ghost hunt in the history of New York City," Smith wrote.

The next day, July 31, 1936, the *Milwaukee Journal* ran an account of the foray by Laura Lou Brookman, whom the paper labeled "Green Sheet Ghost Writer." She reiterated Dunninger's skeptical remarks and his facetious explanation that maybe the ghost operated on standard rather than Daylight-Savings Time. Anyway, Dunninger still had his $10,000.

Foremost among academic believers in ghosts is Dr. Hans Holzer a parapsychologist at New York Institute whom John R. Thomson wrote about in the *Chicago Tribune* for March 13, 1972. Holzer defined a ghost as "a surviving emotional memory of someone who has died traumatically and usually tragically but is unaware of his death." Most ghosts, he said, don't know they're dead and those that are aware of it "are confused as to where they are or why they feel not quite as they used to feel."

Clarence Peterson interviewed Holzer for the *Chicago Tribune* of April 17, 1972 at a National Association of Broadcasters convention. He was there in the interest of his then unproduced television series called "Haunted." Holzer called "The Sixth Sense" and some other shows "pure hokum." He said he encountered difficulty because of the broadcasters' code that forbids "fostering belief" in the supernatural. In his Aug. 2, 1972 column in the *New York Post,* Leonard Lyons related a passage in Holzer's forthcoming book, *Haunted Hollywood.* It was about the revelations of Sybil Leek who went into a trance at a party in Clifton Webb's home.

Another parapsychologist devoted to chasing ghosts is William Roll, director of the Psychical Research Foundation at Durham, N.C. He said his interest was not proving that ghostly phenomena exist but *why.* In 20 years, he said, he has found only one haunting and six poltergeist cases to be authentic. The article by A. R. Kleinfiels in the *Wall Street Journal* for Jan. 7, 1974 described the nature of those cases. The lengthy article contained details about all of the cases. At that time Roll also was interested in out-of-the-body experiences. One significant experience involved a subject's cat that meowed 37 times when the subject was miles away but was silent when he presumably was there in invisible form.

In a full-column report of a meeting of the Spiritual Frontiers Fellowship in Durham, N.C. the *New York Times* for Aug. 26, 1973 quoted Dr. Roll that there is as yet no scientific evidence concerning survival after death. Other speakers told of messages from the spirit world.

True believers Ed and Lorraine Warren, of Monroe, Conn., spoke at the University of Illinois in Urbana. Jeff Drumtra covered the affair for the *Daily Illini* of Oct. 30, 1975. The Warrens described ghosts very much the same as did Holzer. They said that demonic possession of humans occurs as the demon's supreme insult to God. Apparently the performance went over with the audience of 300; at least that was true of the reporter.

Several ghosts, including those of Peter Stuyvesant and a Lady in White, are said to haunt St. Mark's in the Bowery Episcopal Church. In the *New York Daily News* for Oct. 27, 1979 Don Gentile reported on the effort of ghost hunter Eric Maple to capture a spirit in a "witch bottle," into which a spirit can be lured by whistling and the bottle corked and thrown into a river to float to the Red Sea, where the spirit will stay. Maple's venture was a failure.

That the profession seems attractive to some was indicated by an item in the Jon and Abra column Sept. 25, 1971 in the *Chicago Tribune.* It stated that Alex Drier, who played an ESP expert on the ABC-TV movie *Sweet, Sweet Rachel,* wanted to star in a TV series as a professional ghost hunter.

The case for ghosts will be much stronger if the infrared photography of Phyllis Schlemmer, an Orlando, Fla. medium, lives up to expectations. In an interview with James H. Bowman published in the *Chicago Daily News* of May 2, 1973 she said she was made aware of her psychic powers by a Roman Catholic priest in Peckville, Pa. Via telephone he told Bowman, "She's crazy. She's a liar. She's cracked. I knew her when she was in grade school. She didn't even know how to blow her nose."

By a vote of 17 to 9, a class of fourth-grade students expressed a disbelief in ghosts, according to a survey made by Steven Pratt for the

Chicago Tribune of Oct. 31, 1973. A similar result was reported Oct. 10, 1979 by the UPI from Kansas City, where only 21 percent of seven-year-olds believed, by contrast with 57 percent of an adult group and half the high school seniors questioned by the Hallmark Cards Company.

Perhaps the answer to how to control spooks was reported Feb. 4, 1980 by Ronald Yates for the *New York Daily News* and *Chicago Tribune* from Sonoma, Calif. For a fee Sande Marsolan will arrange for the adoption of a spirit, including those of some of history's greatest figures. She prefers to call the spirits "entities," but attracts customers with a business named Ghost Adoption Agency "only because people can identify better with ghosts than with entities." One satisfied customer was the operator of a beauty salon who adopted the infamous Marquis de Sade "to liven up the place a bit."

Another way to court ghostly friends was reported June 9, 1982 by the Associated Press from Union, N.J. There the ghost of a woman shot to death by a British soldier during the Revolutionary War was formally invited to attend an open house on the Fourth of July at the house that she, Hannah Ogden Caldwell, supposedly has haunted ever since.

Not so desirous of being friendly are the staff of the Community Development Corporation of Brownsville, Texas, according to the UPI June 13, 1982. The weird sound of organ music, vibrating furniture and flashing lights have made work there unpleasant, especially since the landlord says there is no organ within hearing distance.

Possibly inspired by public-relations counsel several newspaper feature stories were printed about persons involved in motion pictures related to the supernatural. For example, Aug. 13, 1982 the *Chicago Sun-Times* used a story by Richard Friedman from New York about Thelma Moss, whose career as a spook hunter inspired the role of Dr. Lesh in *Poltergeist*. She was quoted as saying that most ghosts are "friendly and a lot of fun to have around." Her old schoolmate, Beatrice Straight, plays Dr. Lesh in the film.

A free-lance makeup artist, Leonard Engleman, had just completed work on *The Amityville Horror* when he was written up by Ruth Ryon for the Aug. 29, 1982 *Los Angeles Times*. Engleman had purchased a house that its previous owners said was haunted by the ghost of a young man who had committed suicide therein. The Englemans were not disturbed, and their association with the movie was good publicity.

The famous ghost hunters Ed and Lorraine Warren were the subjects of a full-page feature in the *Chicago Tribune* for Sept. 23, 1982. The story was headlined, "Demonologists hell bent on selling 'Amityville II.' " The entire story of the first picture and the subsequent controversy regarding it was rehashed.

Typical of the help some newspapers give readers who think their houses are haunted was the advice "Spooked" received Dec. 21, 1982 in the *New York Post*'s Dear Meg column. It was to consult town hall records to learn the house's history or seek newspaper publicity to stimulate the interest of old-timers able to recall past events. In the same column Feb. 1, 1983 were two letters. One said the writer's fears were quieted upon learning the history of the house the writer inhabited. The other advised advertising for a witch to exorcise the ghost. Meg commented: "It's been said that old houses don't belong to people; people belong to them."

And typical of the way the press continues to perpetuate belief in the supernatural was the item in Bob Herguth's *Chicago Sun-Times* column for July 26, 1983 that John Wayne's ghost haunts *The Wild Goose,* according to the current owner of the yacht.

8

Poltergeists and Exorcism

One type of ghost that doesn't cause living beings to be paralyzed with fear is the fun-loving poltergeist. Their tricks can be annoying and even frightening but they are generally regarded as more of a nuisance than a menace. The headline the *Minneapolis Tribune* gave to an Associated Press story from San Jose, Calif. Jan. 10, 1937 suggests the majority attitude: " 'Ghosts' Scare Tenants a Little." The story was of footsteps, voices and creaking doors that bothered the caretakers of the Winchester Ghost House, a fantastic place on which the owner spent many millions because a psychic told her as long as the place was being built she would not die. By the time Mrs. Sarah Pardee Winchester did die in 1922, at 82, the house contained 160 rooms, 17 fireplaces, 40 stairways and countless doors, windows and other features, all of which tourists paid to view.

A more recent writeup of what is now California's Historical Landmark No. 868 was written by Pamela Lansden for the *Chicago Sun-Times* of Dec. 8, 1973. She updated some of the statistics: there were 10,000 windows, 467 doorways, a maze of stairs, a labyrinth of passages, six safes, 47 fireplaces and four elevators.

A still more recent story of the house "where there's enough of the unexplained to go around" was written by William Schiffmann for the Associated Press Aug. 15, 1981. It explained, as had Lansden, that the 38 years of construction was due to the Boston mystic's telling Mrs. Winchester that the spirits of thousands who had been killed by the repeating rifle, "the gun that won the west," invented by her father-in-law, could be appeased only by the additions to the house.

In a full-page article in the *American Weekly* for March 3, 1944, Dr. Thomas L. Garrett, president of the Garrett Foundation for Psychological Research, gave a good description of how playful ghosts work, at least in the home of Louis Hilchie in Halifax, Nova Scotia. Beginning Dec. 24, 1943, among the eerie happenings were unaided movements by a washing machine, scissors, alarm clock, a kettle of boiling water, pillows, soap flakes, eggs that jumped into a frying pan and mattresses that refused to be still. Dr. Garrett said it was one of the first cases of telekinesis manifestation to attract attention.

Another early case that attracted journalistic attention occurred at the Lively Grove, Ill. home of Mr. and Mrs. Tony Greten and their ten children. Beginning May 29, 1949 the spirit attached itself to the youngest child, 11-year-old Jerome, and used crayon to produce unintelligible writing. The *Chicago Sun-Times* used a column-long story on the situation June 27, 1949 and devoted 1½ pages to pictures of it July 1, 1949, five days after the press learned of the incident. That was when the Rev. Edward Dahmus reported to the Roman Catholic bishop of Belleville that he had witnessed weird knockings, hammerings and spirit writing. Father Dahmus, pastor of St. Liberius Catholic Church, suggested that the Greten family might have been chosen "to awaken the world to the fact that not all things are material things." Nobody else came up with a better theory. The *Chicago Daily News* editorialized July 6 on the spirit's refusal to answer "Are you a good or an evil spirit?" by remarking that "If such rudeness doesn't prove an evil spirit, it at least indicates a fellow traveler. Our advice is to dust it with DDT before it starts plowing the pigs under."

A month later, Aug. 10, 1949, an equally weird case was reported from Washington by the AP and newspaper bureaus. On the authority of Richard C. Doarnall, president of the Society for Parapsychology, the newspapers reported a 14-year-old boy whose bed shook too wildly for him to sleep in it; he also was thrown out of a rocking chair and left without covers under a bed. An unnamed clergyman was said to have witnessed the phenomena in his own home as well as in that of the boy.

A happy ending to another spook story was reported Aug. 27, 1950 by the AP from Muscatine, Iowa where a rocking chair stopped rocking after five months when the family moved.

It was the United Press International that reported Aug. 28, 1950 from West Plains, Mo. that a barrel on a farm refilled itself every night, dusk to dawn, causing William Cox, associate of the American Society for Psychical Research, to declare, "Forces other than natural are responsible . . . a genuine supernatural happening."

Sept. 24, 1950 the AP reported from Paradis, La. on a phantom whistler who terrorized a bride-to-be. Because deputies posted around the house heard no sounds, the sheriff concluded that it was "an inside job." A suspect was a jilted former suitor.

One case was solved after five days during which hundreds of curious neighbors, police and journalists overran the farmhouse of Henry Thatcher in Fern Creek, Ky. when an 11-year-old girl boarder confessed she had been seeking fun and attention. Regarding the many eyewitness accounts of objects flying around the house, the girl said, "I threw a lot of those things but I didn't move everything in the house. The rest of it was their imagination." According to the United Press Jan. 3, 1952 Dr. Charles H.

Shaw, Ohio State University physics professor, said, "There is no scientific explanation whatsoever." University of Kentucky and University of Louisville scholars who investigated were not quoted. The *Chicago Tribune's* Jan. 4 headline was "Spook Keeps Things Alive in Farmhouse." The episode's ending was headlined by the *Sun-Times,* Jan. 4, " 'Spooking' Just Girl's Spoofing."

The seriousness with which clergymen, scientists, police and journalists all regarded the incident proved that they all believed the phenomenon could have been supernatural, so deeply are superstitious beliefs ingrained despite centuries of scientific discoveries.

From South Laguna, Cal. the AP reported Jan. 20, 1957 that flashing lights in Hanover House were believed to be caused by the ghost of Richard Halliburton, famous adventurer, who built the house shortly before he was lost at sea.

A typical example of a newspaper's failure to follow up on a sensational story was that which the *Chicago Sun-Times* provided Aug. 7, 1957 on page 1 with a streamer headline, "A Spooky Spoof or Spoofy Spook?" The story told of the misery suffered by Mr. and Mrs. James Mikulecky and their 13-year-old granddaughter of Rest Haven in Will County, Ill. The family had no peace from strange rappings, whistling and bed-shakings. A shoehorn mysteriously clattered to the floor, pencils skidded across a table, a tapemeasure fell from a sewing machine and many other similar events occurred, even after the family moved in with neighbors. Reported Deputy Sheriff Chester Moberly: "No evidence of a ghost. Could be some of the immediate family playing tricks but no evidence of that yet. It's August, the silly season." And that's all.

It is not often that a newspaper fails to follow up its major story of the day, for all kinds of news except the supernatural.

Much the same kind of story first came to the attention of the United Press Feb. 21, 1958 when it reported from Seaford, N.Y. that a mysterious outbreak of bottle popping, flying figures and a sailing sugar bowl caused Mr. and Mrs. James Herrmann and their son Jimmy, 12, and daughter Lucille, 13, to move out of their six-room ranch house. Detective Joseph Tozzi presumably witnessed some of the performance. The next day, Feb. 22, the *Chicago Sun-Times* quoted Tozzi as saying it would have been impossible for any human hand to have touched the flying sugar bowl. Scientists from the Brookhaven National Laboratory and the Long Island Lighting Co. suggested poltergeists, but the paper reported, "Poltergeists have been unavailable for comment."

In his column in the *Sun-Times* for the same day Herb Graffis commented on the report that "perfume, paint, turpentine, cough medicine, ammonia and holy water . . . all seemed bitten by an invisible bug as they skitted crazily from their places, popped their tops and spilled," all of which reminded Graffis of prohibition days when bottles containing home brew exploded, tumbling to the pantry and kitchen floors so "a little thing like the bottles that jiggled, steamed and burst open in Seaford would have been too mild to notice."

After a 10-pound portable phonograph reportedly flew ten feet through the air, radio experts tested the frequency of radio waves in the area without finding any interference. The *New York Times* story Feb. 27, 1958 was illustrated by pictures of rooms and objects in the house and stated that Dr. J. Gaither Pratt, assistant director of the Parapsychology Laboratory at Durham, N.C., would investigate. March 7 the *Times* ran a UP story from Durham quoting Dr. Pratt that during the four days he spent in Seaford he observed no untoward happenings. He said the trouble might be due to unconscious psychokinesis by 12-year-old Jimmy. Children are said to have this mental power more than adults and poltergeists usually attach themselves to children.

John T. Shanley called the Seaford story "one of the most baffling news stories in years" in an article he wrote for the *New York Times* of Oct. 30, 1958. He reviewed the telecast "The House of Flying Objects," in which the mysterious events were reconstructed by actors, after which members of the family involved participated in the program.

By then on the faculty of the University of Virginia Medical School, Pratt stuck to this theory when furniture began to move and household objects to fall in Pearisburg, Va. As a result of his diagnosis that a 9-year-old boy released psychic energy causing things to move, the child's foster mother returned him to the state's welfare department although the sheriff remained skeptical. The *Washington Post* covered the events with a story by Ken Ringle Jan. 3, 1977 and another by Athelia Night Jan. 5, 1977.

Although composed in a whimsical way, Emery Hutchison's piece in the *Chicago Daily News* for Oct. 31, 1950, Halloween, entitled, "Here are some tips. Are You Ready to be a Ghost?" mentioned several cases of presumed activity by poltergeists. "These are only a few suggestions for possible activities if you should ever find yourself in the role of a ghost," Hutchison wrote.

About 100 persons, including scholars from the University of Iowa with geiger counters and other scientific instruments, had to be dispersed, the *Chicago Daily News* reported from Millville, Iowa Jan. 9, 1960 when no ghostly phenomena occurred, such as flower pots spinning across the room a heavy refrigerator suddenly tipping over and cracker boxes tumbling from the shelves, about which a farmer and his wife had complained to authorities.

As a followup of a news story from Indianapolis about how a disembodied "Henry" had made life miserable for a family, the *Chicago Daily News* for March 15, 1962 used a four-column article by Henry. M. Hansen who gave a resume of a half-dozen Chicago poltergeists, together with an artist's map to show where the eerie visitors operated, under the headline, "Ghost Revived Spooky Past."

One of the very few occasions on which any Chicago newspaper reported iconoclastic comments regarding poltergeist activities was in a special *Sun-Times* article from Osceola, Ind. Oct. 12, 1966, "Flying Furniture And Leaping Food; Poltergeist? Hogwash, It's Just . . ." The skeptic was the man of one of two families involved, a representative for a brewery workers' union. Both Mr. and Mrs. David Cobert disavowed any belief in the supernatural, calling such talk hogwash. They went about seeking the reason for the unusual happenings by asking representatives of the electric company and the gas company and the fire department to inspect. Samples of rock and ore found lying around the house were sent to the University of Notre Dame for examination.

Sonia Masello, the *News'* July 19, 1971 News Lady, asked, "Did you ever smell a ghost?" and answered that she had had the delightful experience on several occasions.

In "Downstate 'ghost' comes to account," the *Chicago Daily News* for Aug. 28, 1974 reported that Edwardsville, Ill. had an unusual visitor—a ghost—someone no one had seen but who made his presence known by causing large metal filing cabinets and heavy coat racks to crash to the floor.

In Bridgeport, Conn. police accepted the confession of an 11-year-old girl who had read a number of books on religion and culta that she caused furniture in her foster parents' home to move about so to attract hundreds of spectators and photographs. A Roman Catholic priest, however, insisted that the girl could not have been responsible for all of the phenomena. The *Chicago Sun-Times'* account headlined a UP story, "Family's furniture takes to leaping," in its Nov. 26, 1974 edition. By afternoon, however, the *Chicago Daily News* had a UPI story, " 'Jumping' furniture a hoax by girl: police."

The next day the UP quoted the police chief as saying "There are no ghosts in Bridgeport." Dissenting were the priest, who was teaching a college course in the occult, and a team of researchers from Duke University.

The definitive article on the Bridgeport incident was "Is the Devil at Work on Lindley Street?" by Daniel St. Albin Greene in the *National Observer* for Jan. 25, 1975. When Marcia, the Canadian Five Nation Indian girl Gerald and Laura Gedin adopted after their eight-year-old son died, confessed causing the "strange occurrences" and using ventriloquism to make the cat, Sam, speak, the police reported that the parents "felt relieved and said that they had not actually seen any of the unusual happenings."

No similar confessions came from police and others who had reported seeing furniture and other objects in motion. The report of one policeman mentioned "seeing the refrigerator actually leave the floor approximately six to eight inches and move towards me . . . a TV slowly make a 90 degree turn . . . a bureau bounce on the floor a couple of times . . . a crucifix vibrate and pull itself off the wall . . . three reclining chairs bouncing around . . ."

Greene observed: "It didn't take long to notice how faulty eye-witness testimony can be. Father Charbonneau, for instance, had told me that the chest of drawers that had fallen in Marcia's bedroom was so big and heavy that he could hardly budge it. But after pulling out the heavily loaded top drawers a bit officer McDonough demonstrated that the wobbly old chest could almost tip over without a nudge. Contrary to some accounts the recliner chairs in the front room could be slid across the bare wood floor with little effort."

The last chapter to this story, unless somebody has written more on it since Greene retired from the scene, was a repudiation of Marcia's confession by her parents, who said the girl did what she did while under the hypnotic influence of a psychic couple who also gave the girl "drugged candy."

The closest any Chicago paper ever came to a scientific examination of poltergeists was an interview Betty Washington had with Dr. Gary Jay, a resident physician in neurology at the North Side Veterans Hospital. It ran in the *News* Oct. 29–30, 1977 headed, "MD not easy to spook." The authority said there is a theory that poltergeists often develop from a force born in the unconscious, a progression of aggression, tension, resentment and frustrations, frequently experienced by adolescents.

Which is well to remember when reading, "Expert tails 'ghost,' " in the *News-Sun-Times Suburban Week* for Sept. 29–30, 1976. It told of a suburban policeman called in to investigate noises that had bothered a family for two years. It so happens that I was in on the investigation too. Two adolescent boys took us individually to the basement of their house and turned off the lights, after which things happened. Upstairs I answered the parents' questions, "First your son showered me with bobby pins and then the two threw flashlight batteries across the room to smash against the wall." My reply was greeted with violent resentment. My statement "Your son is just trying to have a little fun with you" was greeted with "I'm very sorry we invited you." So I left proclaiming that those parents were making it impossible for the children to confess. According to the *Suburban Week* story the boys were undergoing psychiatric care which would have done the parents more good.

What came to be called the Great Columbus Ghost Hunt ended when the disturbances that caused Mrs. Charles Hunsinger to call the police just died down. Nothing was solved despite the attention the phenomena created nationwide, with letters, phone calls and visits from strangers, most of whom had suggestions. One policeman claimed he saw a refrigerator leave the floor and other furniture shift; the occurrences seemed to follow the 13-year-old daughter, Beth. After the experience Mrs. Hunsinger resolved never to summon police again. The UPI wrote up the story from Columbus, Ohio March 24, 1977.

In Newport, Ark., the UPI reported Aug. 26, 1982, Charles and Sharon Johnson filed a $1-million suit against developers who sold them a house knowing that underneath was an old graveyard. Strange occurrences, such as doors opening and shutting, fire alarms going off, children crying and the like made the place uninhabitable, the suit said.

Sept. 12, 1977 Robert Kirsch began a book review in the *Los Angeles Times:*

> Jay Anson's *The Amityville Horror* (Prentice-Hall: $7.95; Illustrated) is quite simply the scariest true story I have read in years. I won't ask Pilate's question about it, but at least most of it is verified and witnessed by reliable people and it is written in a factual and convincing style.

Other equally ecstatic reviewers helped make the book an all-time best-seller. Few if any questioned the account of the 28 days George and Kathleen Lutz spent in a Long Island house they bought a year after Ronald DeFoe had murdered his mother, father and two brothers in their sleep. During the month the Lutzes lived in the house there were the usual voices and rappings but, in addition, windows slammed, furniture moved, Mrs. Lutz levitated a foot above her bed, hundreds of buzzing flies harassed them in dead winter and other harrowing events transpired.

Feb. 28, 1978 Bob Greene used his half-page column in the *Chicago Sun-Times* for a recitation of "Strange encounters of a horrifying kind." The next day, Feb. 29, he continued his review under the heading, "Amityville house story a haunted hoax?" The iconoclastic piece was based on an interview with James and Barbara Cromarty who moved into the house after the Lutz family vacated it. They categorically denied that any of the supposed untoward events had occurred and called the entire book a hoax. Nevertheless, the book was made into a motion picture that broke New York box-office records and was equally successful almost everywhere else. In his full-page review of it in the *Chicago Sun-Times* for Aug. 2, 1979 Roger Ebert quoted Frank Burch, occupant of the house during the preceding eight months, as agreeing with the Cromartys that the Lutz story was a fabrication. July 27, 1979 the Associated Press wrote from Amityville that William Weber, the lawyer who had represented the killer, Ronald DeFoe, said that parts of the best-seller were invented "over many bottles of wine."

That such confessions have little effect on the millions who want to believe was made clear by Ed Lowe, columnist for the Long Island newspaper, *Newsday.* His feature, "The Relentless Horror of the Amityville Tourists," appeared in the *Chicago Tribune* for March 2, 1980 and the *Milwaukee Journal* for March 30, 1980. A typical anecdote of the exasperation citizens of the town felt with tourists follows: a middle-aged couple accosted Lowe in front of the house they were photographing, which they thought was the horror house.

"It's true, isn't it?" the man asked.

"No," Lowe replied, "it isn't true at all."

"Come on," he said incredulously.

"Come on?" Lowe asked, his voice rising. "How can you say 'Come on' to me? Don't you hear yourself talking? I'm telling you that there is no red-eyed flying pig, no green slime, no disembodied voice, no invisible 50-piece marching band in the living room of that house in the middle of the night and no ghosts. And you are saying, 'Come on' to that, as if I'm trying to put one over on you? How come you don't say 'Come on' when someone tells you that there is a flying piggie and there are flies and there is slime and there are ghosts? Where's your 'Come on' then?"

The man startled. His wife had stopped shaking and stared at me indignantly.

You want something to 'Come on' about? "I'll give you something to 'Come on' about. You've just taken 24 pictures of the wrong house."

For its PhotOpinion feature May 10, 1979 the *Chicago Sun-Times* asked four persons, "So you believe in ghosts?" One said "yes" because she remembered the stories her mother told of living near a cemetery and hearing howling at night. A second believer said one night she was crying and heard her deceased father tell her to stop it which comforted her. A disbeliever wasn't sure because one day when her grandmother was sick, kitchen utensils started rattling and moving around. The fourth interviewee replied, "I don't dare. I'm from Egypt where they believe that ghosts appear where a murdered person's blood is shed. If I believed that I'd be surrounded by ghosts in Chicago. There are so many killings here."

The first account of the Tau Kappa Epsilon fraternity house at Alma College's being haunted appeared at Halloween time in the campus student newspaper. A bit later it was rewritten by a local weekly paper and then by a local daily. Finally it was rewritten again by the United Press International whose story received almost a column space in the *Grand Rapids* (Mich.) *Press* for Dec. 19, 1979. Present students told of a ghost wearing a T-shirt roaming the corridors, making noises and playing practical jokes since 1975. Several recent graduates told of having encountered eerie figures.

An inquiry regarding the affair resulted in a reply from Gordon D. Beld, director of news service, who gave his personal opinion that the ghost "is a product of the imaginations of fraternity members, probably intended to get them attention" (which it certainly did).

In Raleigh, N.C. two brothers who had lived in the same house for 38 years suddenly were annoyed by heavy furniture mysteriously crashing to the floor and spinning around without apparent cause, the UPI reported Dec. 25, 1980. Building inspectors and other municipal officials could find nothing wrong and the parapsychologist who visited the site returned to Durham before he could be questioned.

When it publishes objective accounts of haunted houses or places or bewitched persons, a newspaper disregards what modern science has discovered regarding the eccentricities of human behavior and is true to the tradition of the ancients. That means acceptance of the concept of demonology. Believing that Earth was flat and the sun and stars alive, it was understandable that early man conceived of Earth as a battleground between unseen forces of good and evil.

Equally understandable was the development of rites and ceremonies to obtain the protection of friendly spirits and defend against evil demons. There is evidence of such widespread practices in ancient Egypt and Babylonia, Persia and India, Greece and Rome.

The New Testament contains anecdotes of Jesus casting out devils, especially the Mark 5:8 account of curing a possessed man by causing demons to enter a herd of swine; and in Mark 6:17 Jesus told his apostles to cast out devils in his name. So, during the first two centuries of the Christian era, it was believed that the power could be used by any believer. About 250, however, a special class of the lower clergy, called exorcists, was created to perform the rites. An exorcism also came to be performed before any baptism to remove impediments to grace as a result of the effects of original sin and the power that Satan and his fallen angels wielded.

For more than 1,000 years there were few exorcisms, and in 1014 the Catholic church issued the *Rituale Romanum,* detailing how a priest, with the permission of his bishop, should conduct an exorcism. The last major periods of supposed demonic possession were in the 1630s, when the nuns in a French convent went through a series of possessions that lasted a dozen years and spread to the townspeople and, just before 1700, to Salem, Mass., according to the Rev. Richard Woods of Loyola University in Chicago, whom Joe Ziomek interviewed for a story in the *Chicago Sun-Times* for Feb. 8, 1974. By that time the press could not avoid taking cognizance of the widespread interest in William Peter Blatty's book, *The Exorcist,* and the terrifying movie based upon it. Father Woods deplored the public's "near hysteria" as a result of the picture. Skeptical regarding any claims of possession, Father Woods declared that suggestible people find it comfortable to blame someone or something, the devil for example, for personal failings, especially in a time of "national pass-the-buck."

The *Chicago Tribune* for Feb. 18, 1974 contained a long interview with Father Woods by Jim Szantor. Father Woods said, "So to indicate us to sin is the devil's main work and it can involve an individual or an entire group . . . But the main experience of evil in our lives is sin, and we shouldn't worry about being overtaken by cosmic bogeymen or goblins that go around grabbing 12-year-old girls. We have to worry about the evil we do, not the evil that happens to us."

Prior to the flurry of journalistic interest following that picture and a few others, *Rosemary's Baby, Amityville Horror* and *Omen,* about the only

American case of exorcism to attract the press' interest occurred in Earl-
ing, Iowa in 1928 and came to public attention eight years later when the
exorcist published a 48-page pamphlet, *Begone Satan,* subtitled, *A Soul
Stirring Account of Diabolical Possession in Iowa.* It is a detailed account of
a 23 days' battle after which the devil left the body of a 40-year-old woman.
The exorcist was the Rev. Theophilus Riesinger, a member of the minor
order of Capuchins of Marathon, Wis. who wrote that his prayers and
exhortations rid the woman of "billions and billions of devils," including
Beelzebub, Judas Iscariot and the woman's own father.

The most fulsome newspaper account of Father Theophilus' career,
which included 22 exorcisms, appeared in the *Milwaukee Journal* for
March 1, 1936 in a half-page article. Frances Stover reported that the
victim was said to have flown through the air and to hang on the wall.

During the following 35 years most news stories of exorcism in the
American press originated in England or other places abroad. Nov. 2, 1951
the *Chicago Tribune's* correspondent reported from Lambourne, England
that a service of exorcism was led by a vicar of the Church of England to
rid a racehorse trainer's house of ghosts whose apparitions and footsteps
annoyed family members and friends. June 12, 1958 the Associated Press
reported from London that a Church of England commission concluded
that illness caused by demons was possible. It doubted that either
spiritualists, faith healers or Christian Scientists could help, but reaf-
firmed the fact that exorcism still is practiced by the church.

What William Stoneman reported in the *Chicago Daily News* Nov. 16,
1963 from London was the official opening of "a long hard winter of spook
stories from Merrye Olde Englande" with the announcement that the
bishop of Exeter had formally exorcised a ghost in the village of Ab-
botskerswell, Devonshire.

In a half-page article by Loren Lind May 31, 1968 the *Toronto Star* told
how "Anglican body says ex-leader of exorcism cult should submit to
mental test," all about the ideological split in the Diocese of Toronto partly
involving interpretation of exorcist prayers in the Anglican Prayer Book.

From Zurich, Switzerland came the UPI report Feb. 5, 1969 that two
German members of the International Community for the Promotion of
Peace were sentenced to ten years in prison for having killed a 17-year-old
girl in the attempt to drive the devil out of her.

Frank H. Woyke apparently had much the same in mind when he
bludgeoned to death his mother and grandmother in an Oak Park, Ill.
hotel. They and the elder Woyke, associate secretary of the Baptist World
Alliance, had come from their Maryland home because of anxiety over
their son's health. The young man's roommate said he had been reading
the Bible incessantly, underlining passages referring to an afterlife. He
also claimed to see the devil in the faces of people. He told police that he
killed the women because he had seen a vision of the devil. The *Chicago
Sun-Times* had a full account by Richard Foster Oct. 23, 1969.

While scenes for the motion picture *The Exorcist* were being shot on the Georgetown University campus, a prominent member of the faculty, the Rev. Juan B. Cortes, predicted an outbreak of supposed demonic possession upon the film's release. He told William Hines for publication in the *Chicago Sun-Times* of Nov. 24, 1973 that the ancient ritual of casting out demons is worse than useless and should be abolished by the Roman Catholic church. Not only are there no demons, Father Cortes said, but the picture is likely to have a bad effect on the emotionally disturbed.

Summarizing and commenting upon Father Cortes' remarks in his column in the *Chicago Daily News,* William J. Cromie quoted Cortes as denying the New Testament has any reports of possession by the devil, only by undefined demons. In biblical days sufferers from epilepsy, deafness, muteness or psychoses were described as "afflicted by demons"; today a psychiatrist might diagnose organic brain disorder.

Not quite so vehement was the Rev. H. Douglas Stewart of St. Andrew's Presbyterian Church of Toronto. He told his congregation, according to the *Toronto Star* for Jan. 21, 1974, that the motion picture had a "significant religious message, . . . a profound struggle between good and evil." However, Stewart would not recommend the film to everyone. "I would particularly caution the impressionable," he said.

A Toronto believer is Dr. George Owen, director of the New Horizons Research Foundation, profiled by Allen Spraggett in the *Toronto Sunday Sun* for Sept. 23, 1973. His conversion to a belief in poltergeists came in 1960, when an 11-year-old girl, Virginia Campbell, who had recently moved to Scotland from Ireland, was the focus of an outbreak of thumping and objects flying around the house. Owen figured the outbreak was triggered by the girl's emotional upset by moving from her childhood home.

Owen also believes that thought waves can be measured by electroencephalogram as are physical symptoms.

The controversy aroused by *The Exorcist,* book and movie, heightened when the Associated Press reported Jan. 1, 1974 that a Lutheran minister and a Jesuit priest confirmed that many of the things depicted actually occurred, not to a daughter of a motion picture star in Georgetown but in 1949 to a 14-year-old boy in Mt. Rainier, Md. The minister, who remained anonymous, verified many of the book's incidents but was bothered by other aspects of the real case. His suspicions were especially aroused when it was revealed the writing, "Go to St. Louis" on the boy's chest was written upside down as he would have done it from his position in bed. The Jesuit priest's report on the experience is on file at Georgetown University.

Feb. 6, 1974 papers subscribing to the service of the North American Newspaper Alliance began a series of articles on "True-Story Behind 'The Exorcist' " by Louis Antosh. It was essentially the same account that the AP had reported. The Rev. Eugene H. Gallagher, a Jesuit in Philadelphia, made public part of a document prepared 25 years earlier about the case of the 14-year-old Mt. Rainier boy. Blatty had been a student of Gallagher at Georgetown in 1950. The *Philadelphia Bulletin* also contacted some St. Louis priests familiar with the case that Blatty plagiarized.

How deep the differences among members of the Georgetown faculty were was suggested by William J. Cromie in the *Chicago Daily News* for May 15, 1974 in which two researchers concluded several years' study, including the case on which *The Exorcist* was based, by saying, "Clear-cut cases of possession by the devil have never taken place . . . Exorcism in the Catholic Church should be abolished because they are useless and potentially harmful."

Because of what the president said were "irreconcilable differences," the Rev. Edmund G. Ryan was fired by Georgetown University, the UPI reported April 16, 1974. Father Ryan was the school's resident authority on exorcism and had a walk-on part in the film *The Exorcist*.

With exorcism suddenly a newsworthy subject papers and press associations sought to exploit it not only by keeping alive the debate over the merits of the motion picture but also by a variety of sidebars. To buttress belief in the possibility of exorcism the Rev. Miles O'Brien Riley, director of the San Francisco Archdiocese Communication Center, told the Associated Press of an exorcism that "has a happy ending. And what makes it all the better is that it is not fiction, that it is all true." A team of 15 priests prayed for 15 days to free an entire family of demonic possession. A physician testified to the success of the exorcism.

From London the *Chicago Tribune's* correspondent Robert Merry wrote an article to which the paper gave almost a half-page Jan. 20, 1974 about the career of the Rev. Christopher Neil-Smith, a Church of England vicar who had performed 2,000 exorcisms. He told Merry that one in 20 of those who think they are possessed are imagining. Father Neil-Smith and about 20 other Anglican priests to exorcise raise their hands and pray, "I command you, every evil spirit, in the name of God the Father Almighty, in the name of Jesus Christ his only Son, and in the name of the Holy Spirit that harming no one, you depart from this creature of God and return to the place appointed you, there to remain forever."

As the motion picture became an immediate success reporters turned their attention to the behavior of crowds waiting in line for tickets. Michael Porney reported for the *National Observer* Jan. 26, 1974 that during its first week the picture grossed $1.8 million. In 22 cities people waited hours to see the film in the 24 theaters in which it was shown. Porney wrote:

In the Los Angeles suburb of Westwood hundreds wait in the rain for hours outside the National movie theater just to buy a ticket. In Boston they stamp their feet to ward off the cold in the blocks-long line at the Carver, many clutching dog-eared paperback copies of the novel. In Washington, D.C. where evening performances at the Cinema are sold out less than an hour after the box office opens at midday scalpers do a brisk business. But 50 movie goers are still turned away most evenings and at every weekend showing.

In New York Judy Klemedrud wrote a similar story for the *Times* of Jan. 27. The paper gave a page and a half to her eyewitness account of crowd behavior and the opinions of theatergoers. Of the audience, she wrote: "It seemed that the largest group after the 'I-read-the-book' people were the 'I-must-be-crazy-to-be here' people. 'We're here because we're nuts and because we wanted to be part of the madness.'" The reporter called Dr. David Riesman, the Harvard professor who wrote *The Lonely Crowd,* for an opinion, which he gave: "Standing in a movie line doesn't commit you to have a motive. It's a relationship that doesn't ask too much." The *Times'* coverage also included lengthy interviews with Mercedes McCambridge, the voice of the devil in the movie, and Linda Blair, who played the role of the possessed.

One to-be-anticipated by-product of the interest in the movie was an increase in requests for exorcism, few if any of which were granted, according to Clarence Page's article in the *Chicago Tribune* for Jan. 27, 1974. A priest in the Chicago Catholic chancery office said, "An exorcism is a very serious process which involves much more than just making a phone call to order an exorcist."

The various pastoral and theological problems that Roman Catholic clergymen had to grapple with were enumerated by Edward B. Fiske in the *New York Times* for Jan. 28, 1974. Terrified teen-agers and persons think- ing they were possessed appealed for help. Theater managers reported that it was a rare performance during which nobody fainted or vomited.

Another reporter, who went to the show after it had run a month to see "What's pulling Them in?" was Donald M. Schwartz who told what he learned in an article under that title in the *Chicago Sun-Times* for Feb. 12, 1974.

Despite the supposed current interest in the occult, the signs outside the theater read "Terrifying Deeds! Bloodchilling Horror!" The answers the reporter got as to why patrons were there were mostly to see if it was as scary as their friends told them it was or out of curiosity because of the controversy regarding the picture.

Sandra Saperstine had about the same experience, she reported in the *Chicago Daily News* for Feb. 15. She was amazed that 300 persons got in line at dawn to be sure of admission.

In his column in the *New York Times* for Feb. 17 Russell Baker wrote that on the advice of a friend he changed plans to review *The Joy Of Sex* because, the friend said, "sex was done for with the public. The new thing was the supernatural." So then he told a ghost story from his boyhood. The column, however, was illustrated with a scene from *The Exorcist.*

All that a reviewer from the Soviet newspaper *Izvestia* could find to praise after seeing the film was the popcorn, *Variety* reported Feb. 20. The picture itself was called "a scandalous, horrifying film that mixes pornography and sadism."

According to Allen Estrin who reviewed the film for *The Illini* Feb. 22, *The Exorcist* "is a hoax; it is bogus in every sense of the word. It stands as a remarkable example not of how low movie makers can go but of what a good public relations firm with the help of media hungry for sensationalism can do." From all parts of the country anecdotes were related of parishioners seeking help. Most frequently quoted were Fathers Woods of Chicago and Cortes of Georgetown University. The former does not believe in the devil and the latter, though believing, finds no biblical reference to possession.

Roy Meacham answered the headline in the *New York Times* for Feb. 3: "How did 'The Exorcist' Escape an X Rating?" The R rating that it was given by the Motion Picture Association of America permits 17-year-olds to attend with adults. The board's explanation was that the standards for an R rating had been met: no nudity or overt sexuality. Still, most critics said it was not a picture for children.

In the letters column of the *Chicago Daily News* for Feb. 9 Father Woods wrote: "There is no doubt, in my mind, that the film (no less than the book) is theologically inaccurate—worse, misleading. It is also a gross misrepresentation of the Catholic Church's position and distorts factual evidence to a point of total unrecognizability . . . merely another indication of the moral bankruptcy of the times—a rank inability to tell good from evil."

Six weeks after the premier of the picture, the *Chicago Tribune's* movie critic, Gene Siskel, saw it again "and what I saw outside the theater frequently was more disturbing than the film itself. People still were being carried out in a faint." Like several other reporters Siskel remarked on the disproportionately large number of blacks in the audience.

A University of Chicago graduate student in literature, Marsha Kean Dewell, wrote a half-page article for the *Chicago Tribune* of Feb. 12, 1974 that began: "A 14th century audience would have loved *The Exorcist*. To them the devil was a mean old bastard who caused sin and suffering universally, although he was especially fond of torturing the faithful and the young." The rest of the article related incidents in literature utilizing the same theme, with the good God always conquering the evil Devil.

Once the newsworthiness of exorcism was recognized in newsrooms as good copy, a variety of reportorial efforts began to occur. Feb. 13 the *Champaign-Urbana* (Ill.) *Courier's* Gary Benson wrote that, whereas *The Exorcist* was fiction, the Watseka Wonder was real in 1877. That was when she (real name Mary Lurancy Vennum) was captured by the spirit of one Mary Roff, a girl 12 years dead. After spending four months in the Roff home, she told the family Mary Roff was leaving for heaven; so she became Mary Lurancy again and had no memory of the episode. Dr. E. W. Stevens of Janesville, Wis. wrote a book about the incident of 1879, titled *The*

Watseka Wonder. The Associated Press had a story from Watseka March 30, 1974.

From Hong Kong the Associated Press reported March 1 that 70 Buddhist priests had performed a lengthy exorcism ritual to rid a new government building of "troublesome guests." Presumably the trouble was traceable to World War II when the Japanese used the spot for public executions.

Because of his slow recovery from an unnamed illness, a Malaysian merchant hired 30 Chinese exorcists to "ferret out the spirits, fight them and place them in bottles which they would throw in the sea," the AP reported Oct. 13, 1974 from Kuala Lumpur. The six carloads of exorcists just about wrecked their patient's house and furniture but at the end he said he felt better.

The results of a national survey conducted by the Center for Policy Research before *The Exorcist* appeared were revealed by George Cornell, religion editor of Associated Press, April 4. They showed that belief in the devil had increased in nine years from 37 to 48 percent, whereas belief in a god had declined from 77 to 69 percent. Dr. Clyde Z. Nunn accredited the growing belief in Satan to "a mood of uncertainty and stress when things seem to be falling apart and resources seem limited for coping with it." In such circumstances people look for scapegoats and the devil is a natural.

One pleasant aftermath of the hysteria was reported by Larry Weintraub in the *Sun-Times* for May 2, 1974: "A theater manager and a woman he assisted when she fainted during the showing of *The Exorcist* were married. Asked if he thought the devil was making him do it, he replied, "I'm not sure. Ask me again in about five years."

Between Feb. 6 and 13, 1974 papers subscribing to the North American Newspaper Alliance syndicate service had a series of articles with a many-sided discussion of what was stated in the editor's note introducing the series:

> Good vs evil. It's an age-old struggle. Stories abound about people being "possessed" by evil spirits. But is the problem really good vs evil in the religious God vs devil belief or is it medical, with the malfunction of one of the body's systems? William Peter Blatty's *The Exorcist* has renewed interest in the religious side of the question. But there are other Demon Hunters, those who probe the causes of human evil—brain researchers, archeologists and psychologists. Warren Shore talks with these people whose findings are far removed from magic and any connection with satanism.

The articles were replete with accounts of successful brain surgery, archeological evidence of such surgery centuries ago and social and economic conditions causing erratic behavior. Also, details of successful exorcisms, including details of that performed on the 14-year-old boy in St. Louis.

Because he believed "the whole thing is getting too serious. We need some comic relief," Barry R. Steiner, a Skokie accountant, created the Herman Garbonzo Fatty Home Exorcist's Kit, a do-it-yourself demon repellent that contains an airplane motion-sickness bag, a little candle, a balloon and a candy pacifier. The *Chicago Sun-Times* gave it a story Feb. 26, 1974.

And Albin Krebs reported in the *New York Times* for March 5, 1974 that Canon John Pearce-Higgins, a professional exorcist, called for a ban on showing the picture in England because "You may become crazy or become possessed by evil spirits if you sit through it . . ."

Roger Ebert, *Chicago Sun-Times* motion picture reviewer, also belittled the movement by a satirical feature, "The Son of Exorcist," in the March 17, 1974 issue of his paper. He concocted several fanciful plots using the exorcist theme, as the baseball pitcher who sold himself to the devil in exchange for one more season of winning 20 games. A team-mate, a Jesuit, battled for the pitcher's soul with mixed results.

In his *Chicago Daily News* column for May 15, 1974 William J. Cromie quoted several Jesuits and other Catholics who believe exorcism should be abolished.

Entertainers, journalists and others made rich use of the squabble. A Chicago Cubs player in a batting slump said he was going to take his bat with him to the movie and hold it up whenever the exorcist came onto the stage "to see what he can do to it," Joe Goddard reported on the sports pages of the *Chicago Sun-Times* for May 2, 1974.

The *Chicago Tribune Magazine* for June 10, 1974 had a long article by the eminent psychologist Albert Ellis. Under the title, "Occult Follies," he said the motion picture *The Exorcist* was permeated with "arrant hogwash." He also wrote: "When a person rigidly believes anything outlandish, highly improbable and deliberately stated in an untestable way, we can easily suspect that he or she has important psychological reasons for inventing or accepting this kind of twaddle. These reasons or hangups are usually as follows: the need for certainty . . . the need for dependency . . . grandiosity and ego-raising . . . unwilling to accept human restrictions . . ."

Eugene C. Kennedy, a Maryknoll priest and professor of psychology at Loyola University in Chicago, wrote an analytical article on the film for the *New York Times* of Aug. 4, 1974. Pertinent parts follow:

In truth *The Exorcist* rates high on the list of phenomena not to be taken seriously; it should be filed under "Midwinter Madness" and forgotten as soon as possible by all literate and mature people. Discussing the movie seriously gives it an importance that, of itself, it does not deserve . . . The best thing about *The Exorcist* was its timing, arriving as it did in a winter of discontent when people were aching to find somebody to blame for our national frustrations, and the devil has served admirably as a scapegoat throughout history.

The first case to receive maximum newspaper coverage after public interest was aroused by *The Exorcist* was made public five months after its occurrence in August 1973 in Daly City, Calif. Both the AP and UPI dispatched stories Jan. 19, 1974 about the successful rite performed by the Rev. Karl Pazelt, Jesuit priest. A family of husband, wife and small son had suffered the sensation of being choked by a force strong enough to make them scream. There also were objects, including a knife, thrown around the room. This, Father Pazelt explained, was a case of "obsession," an attack from without, rather than one of "possession," as in *The Exorcist,* in which a victim is allegedly taken over by the devil. The AP reported that the *San Francisco Chronicle* said the son seemed to be the main focus of the evil spirits' attention. Lacey Fosburgh wrote a column-long story for the *New York Times* of Jan. 25, 1974.

Special UPI-AP stories from San Francisco in the *Toronto Sun* and the *Toronto Star* for Jan. 21, 1974 quoted Father Pazelt at length regarding the physical injuries the family received, as the devil seemed "to have a whole army of demons with him . . . The activity would start all over the house at the same time." The *San Francisco Examiner,* in a copyrighted story, quoted the couple as saying, "The devil revealed himself by knocking both of us down. Often he would knock one of us almost unconscious . . ." Jan. 22 the Toronto papers had UPI-AP specials quoting several Catholic leaders as being skeptical and lamenting the fact that many parishioners were seeking help for what they insisted was demonic possession.

Because they believed they could cast out the devils by exorcism, Lawrence and Alice Parker refused to obtain medical aid for their 11-year-old son who died a painful death from diabetes, the UPI reported June 14, 1974 from San Bernardino, Calif.

The headline, "Controversy on Exorcism Grows as Practice Spreads," over a *New York Times* story from Newton, Mass. Nov. 29, 1974 summed up the nationwide situation. The half-page story began with an anecdote of a woman's being relieved of demons by a Presbyterian minister and was illustrated by a picture of a woman receiving prayerful assistance at a charismatic service in the Trinity Assembly Church in San Antonio, Texas. The article was replete with anecdotes and quotations of clergymen and psychologists. The anonymous author of the article wrote:

> The widespread revival of exorcism among Christians also seems to be a direct counter to the occult movement—an evangelical response to what is perceived as an alarming spread of satanism—which has touched every city and major university in the nation. At the same time it has become an integral part of the renewed interest among many Christians of all denominations in the supernatural aspects of Christianity.

"In England Ritual of Exorcism Now Is an Everyday Affair," headlined the *Wall Street Journal* Dec. 10, 1974. The subhead to Richard F. Janssen's story was "Anglican Church Enforcement of Rite Is Spur to Those Claiming to Be 'Possessed.' " A pertinent paragraph from the account, datelined London, follows:

> What underlies the spread of exorcism here, observers believe, is a good deal more than *The Exorcist*. Among adherents and skeptics alike there is a rough concensus that the times have been ripened for the ritual's renewed vogue by the mental distresses endemic in urbanized society, by the search by many people for something too individual to be computerized, and by a longing for a spark of mystery in a Christianity that has largely drained of angels and hell fire.

The exorcism revival movement received a setback in the United States with the widespread dissemination of a dossier by Dr. William Storey, a University of Notre Dame theologian, who charged that unauthorized exorcisms were performed by True House, a local community of the Catholic Pentacostal movement. The exorcisms allegedly were conducted by lay leaders to climax long midnight interrogations of members to persuade them to confess all of their lifetime sins. The *New York Times* had a fulsome report Aug. 10, 1975.

A case that attracted attention internationally was that of Anneliese Michel, a 22-year-old West German teacher-student who died of dehydration and undernourishment after extensive exorcism administered with the approval of the Roman Catholic bishop. The *New York Times* carried a story by Craig. R. Whitney from Bonn Aug. 8, 1976 that the district attorney of Aschaffenburg was investigating four criminal complaints against Dr. Joseph Stangle, Catholic bishop of the diocese involved. The sessions of the exorcists were recorded on 43 cassettes and when some of them were played over the radio the public became aroused.

The *Chicago Tribune* had its own reporter cover the case. The paper's page 1 streamer headline Sept. 5, 1976 over Alice Sigert's story from Klingenberg, Germany was "Exorcists battle devil, and girl dies." The girl's agonizing screams were heard by radio and the six evil spirits were named: Hitler, Nero, Lucifer, Judas, Cain and Fleischmann, a defrocked priest.

March 31, 1978 the Associated Press reported on the trial underway in Aschaffenburg. The woman's father, also on trial, said he always knew no doctor could cure his daughter so "We laid her into the hands of God." He said he was being persecuted for his "faith in God."

April 24, 1978 the Associated Press reported the guilty verdicts for the mother, father and two priests for negligent homicide by starvation. The court ordered, and then suspended, six-month jail sentences for the four.

A similar outcome of a trial was reported Nov. 20, 1976 from Yakima, Wash. by the UPI. A Bible cult leader and four women were found guilty of beating a 3-year-old boy to death, "blinded by a bizarre unrealistic belief in the Bible," as the judge put it. Dec. 9, 1976 the UPI reported the sentencing of the five, ranging from 5 to 20 years.

The public controversy about exorcism caused some people to take personal inventory, as evidenced by a question that Billy Graham answered in his syndicated column for Aug. 17, 1976. It was: "The Devil is trying to make me think that I am the 'beast' spoken of in the Bible. I know I'm not. I am a Christian who slid backward but nothing more. Could you give me some reassurance?" In reply the noted evangelist did not question the reality of the devil's bewildering the writer. Instead, he wrote:

In Revelation, particularly chapter 13, there is the symbolic picture of two beasts. Both are represented as the arch-opponents of the Christian.

Let me give you two reasons why you are not the beast of Revelation 13 and 17. First, if you have any anxiety about being that evil person, you are definitely not the one. The beast is the totality of evil and does not question his identity. Second, you would need to have such power and position that all the earth would worship you (Revelation 13:8). And that is not the case.

Satan does tempt us with fantasies of all kinds. Perhaps a counselor could help you. Beyond that, live in an atmosphere of prayerful dependence on God's support and protection.

During a press conference two years earlier Graham said that after reading *The Exorcist* he tore the book into shreds and threw it down the toilet. He resolved not to see the movie "because of the effect it may have on me and my ministry," David Satter reported in the *Chicago Tribune* for March 3, 1974. "True Christians cannot be possessed," Graham said.

"We might pause to wonder why Satan is such big business and why he seems to have preempted the more conventional means of inducing horror and titilation," Desmond Ryan wrote in the *Chicago Tribune* movie review column for Aug. 25, 1976. The answer in essence: "Science keeps answering things today. When I was a kid the moon and Mars were frightening and mysterious things. Now they're not unknown . . . People are instead turning to the devil they don't know . . ."

In an attempt to exorcise demons she believed were causing her nightmares and evil visions, Elaine Marciel Barbosa, 16, had herself strapped to a 44-lb. crucifix for three days, the UPI reported Feb. 14, 1978 from Rosário Do Sul, Brazil. A photograph showed part of the crowd of 5,000 that gathered in hope of witnessing a miracle.

A student's letter in *The Phoenix,* student publication at Chicago's Loyola University, was intended to simplify the act of exorcism. In the paper's issue of April 14, 1978, David Mulchrone, a member of The Way, Biblical Research and Teaching Ministry, merely quoted Mark 16:17 to indicate that anyone who is a believer has the God-given ability to cast out evil spirits.

In Hackensack, N.J. a self-proclaimed psychic was indicted on charges of extorting $13,770 from four clients who thought they were paying to be purged of the devil, the *New York Times* reported Dec. 12, 1978.

"A sudden wave of superstitious activity that has swept China in defiance of an official ban from Peking" was blamed for the torture deaths of two small children by a self-proclaimed witch and her male accomplice, the *Los Angeles Times* learned in a dispatch from Hong Kong April 29, 1979. One boy she accused of being possessed by the spirit of a drowned man. The *New China Daily* reported that a large crowd watched the exorcism in a public place and nobody interceded.

A similar story of religious fanaticism appeared Jan. 3, 1980 in the *Chicago Sun-Times*. A mother scalded her baby boy with boiling water and then put him in a heated oven in an attempt to drive the devil out of him. A photograph of the distraught father who had not been present, accompanied the article.

Two women and a priest were accused of a bogus exorcism scheme that really was one of extortion, the AP reported March 14, 1981 from Rome, Italy. The victims were young women whose bodies were covered with ice while prayers were recited for them.

There was nothing bogus about the rash of defenses in murder trials attempting to shift the guilt from the defendant to demons. One of the first was what James Warren and Brian J. Kelly called "far-from-traditional" in the *Chicago Sun-Times* for Aug. 19, 1980. Instead of pleading insanity, Roland Kashney contended that the devil made him commit two murders. A onetime barber, Kashney said he abandoned his wife and child after "receiving a call from God asking him to become a messenger." A year later, he testified, he was visited by the devil and forced to be a murderer.

May 15, 1981 the newspapers reported Kashney's conviction for one of the murders. He said he confessed because he saw that the police were believed. A witness for him was the Rev. John J. Nicola, a Roman Catholic priest who had been a technical advisor for the motion picture *The Exorcist,* who proved, the defense attorneys contended, that one can believe in devils and be terrified by them. Nevertheless, the papers reported June 6, 1981, Kashney was sentenced to 30 to 60 years in prison.

Later in the year a case in Danbury, Conn. attracted so much journalistic and other attention that it has been erroneously referred to since as the first in which the "devil made me do it" defense was used. From March 10, 1981 when the Associated Press began its coverage of the case until Oct. 29 when the United Press International reported, "A judge threw the devil out of court," most leading newspapers told and retold the details of the murder and the plans of defense attorney Martin Minnella. The highlights of the case were these: Arne Cheyenne Johnson, 19, stabbed and killed his employer, Alan Bono, during an argument. His defense was that he was possessed by demons who had been tormenting David Glotzel, 11, brother of his fiance, Deborah. Five Roman Catholic priests conducted mini exorcism rites and there were tape recordings of the ordeals. Johnson was heard more than once demanding that the demons leave the boy and enter him. The prominent demonologists Edward and Lorraine Warren who had worked on *The Amityville Horror* case were involved. About the most thorough resumé of the careers of the Warrens was written by Vernon Scott, UPI Hollywood reporter, and distributed for use Sept. 26, 1982. The story described several of the 42 exorcisms of houses and individuals in which Ed had a part and some of the frightening experiences the couple had while ghost hunting.

Among the most detailed backgrounders on the case were "The Devil in Connecticut," by Tony Burton in the *New York Daily News* for April 20, 1981 with two sidebars concerning a trial and acquittal of two witches for murder in Dimmit, Texas, written by Alton Slagl and "What the devil the argument is all about," a history and summary of Roman Catholic procedures; "Murder—Did Devil Make Him Do It?" by Michael Coakley in the *Chicago Sunday Tribune* for Aug. 9, 1981 and "New Plea: Devil Made Him Do It," by Russell Chandler in the *Los Angeles Times* for Aug. 16, 1981.

On the eve of the trial Oct. 26, 1981, Minnella declared his first task was to convince the jury that there is such a thing as the devil and demonic possession which he hoped to do by the testimony of priests and the Warrens. Then he would have to prove that young Johnson was possessed. He told Scott Kraft, AP reporter, that he would seek jurors who were Catholic, female, between 40 and 65 years old, preferably mothers who had children Johnson's age, and believers in the existence of both God and the devil.

Minnella never had the chance to get such a jury. As James V. Healton, UPI reporter, put it, "A judge threw the devil out of court." He did so before the first potential juror could answer the second question put to him, "Do you believe in the existence of a demonic force?" Superior Court Judge Robert J. Callahan interrupted to say, "I'm not going to allow the defense of demonic possession. It is simply not relevant."

Whereupon the press lost interest. Dec. 19 the *New York Post* had a 1½-inch piece, "Teen Killer Gets Max," to the effect that Judge Callahan sentenced Johnson to 10 to 20 years in prison, the maximum, noting that Johnson had shown no remorse for the stabbing.

A failure of exorcism was reported by the AP from Bournemouth, England Aug. 18–21, 1981. Charles Burden, 62, and wife Catherine, 56, said their house was a shambles after furniture, a heater, crockery and other belongings smashed after flying around the rooms. At their invitation a retired Church of England priest, Frederick C. Oliver, 95, conducted the rite of exorcism. Mediums advised the Burdens to send away their adopted 8-year-old retarded son. They did so and Mrs. Burden left town. The *New York Daily News* had a first story Aug. 18, the *Chicago Tribune* used a followup Aug. 20 and the *Chicago Sun-Times* did so Aug. 21, 1981.

By contrast, a priest, name withheld, was credited with making it possible for Mr. and Mrs. Lui G. Passetto, Jr. and their two children to move back into their house in Lee, Mass. after a month. Driven out by flying furniture, upset refrigerators, smashed crucifixes and other poltergeist pranks, they consulted Edward and Lorraine Warren, lecturers on exorcism, to help; the Warrens obtained the services of the priest. The afflicted family described the offending spirits as a small boy dressed in white and a tall, evil-looking hooded "thing."

In a motion for a new hearing as to the mental competency of Mark David Chapman, his lawyers said their client believes he "summoned demons" that made him shoot John Lennon, the former Beatle. Chapman experienced hallucinations in which he heard the voices of God and the devil, the UPI reported Aug. 10, 1981 from New York.

An occult "princess" testified that she murdered a shopkeeper stabbing him 63 times, to rid herself of three demons—lust, suicide and murder—and so was not responsible. It took a jury only a half-hour, however, to find her guilty of murder, the UPI reported July 16, 1982 from Dodgeville, Wis.

To one competent to speak with authority the devil no longer is the most horrifying of film monsters, the UPI reported Feb. 15, 1982 from Tucson, Ariz. The authority was Vincent Price, veteran actor famous for playing villain parts, who said the film *Jaws* was the turning point. "The devil was the hottest box office attraction around, at least until that darn shark came along," he said.

In his column in the *Chicago Tribune* for Dec. 11, 1972 Clarence Peterson wrote, "Television's affair with the supernatural is turning out to be nothing but flirtation." He was encouraged by the cancellation of such series as "The Sixth Sense" and "Night Gallery." How wrong he was anyone can test by merely turning the dial during prime time.

And the same for those who did not believe the success of the motion pictures *Rosemary's Baby, The Exorcist* and others would encourage Hollywood to stretch its luck. Peterson had written, "The failure of the horror series is understandable. They could not be truly horrifying without bringing down the wrath of the public." When the movie *The Poltergeist* was released, Roger Ebert called it "an effective thriller" in the *Chicago Sun-Times* for June 4, 1982. On the same day, however, Gene Siskel wrote in the *Tribune* that the film "is without thrills, terror or entertainment value . . ." Some people scare easy, others not at all.

To try to find out how far physical laws can be adapted or extended to explain psychokinetic phenomena, the Institute of Psychophysical Research of Oxford, England wants anyone who observes any inanimate object moving by itself to make a report.

9

Luck, Good and Bad

When a woman became alarmed because her husband did not say "God bless you" whenever she sneezed, she wrote to Ann Landers. In her May 11, 1968 column the journalist-counselor advised the woman to continue the custom she learned as a child and not worry because her spouse had a different upbringing.

By comparison with their ancestors, all the way back to the caves, modern men and women put less faith in omens and supernatural beings to be feared or courted, cajoled or importuned for help. Most people are no longer terrified by the thoughts of banshees, gnomes, imps, warlocks, goblins, hobgoblins, phantoms, vampires, fiends, wraiths, trolls or demons. Nor do we believe our fates are determined by a whole mountainful of supernatural helpers for every occasion: angels, fairies, leprechauns, elves, pixies and sylphs.

Abandonment of belief in such unseen influences, for which no chemical or physical explanations are possible, has come about without much help from the press. More than a quarter-century before Ann Landers' equivocal reply to a reader, in the same newspaper for Aug. 13, 1946, W. A. S. Douglas wrote, "Generally speaking the man or woman who makes a point of saying he or she is not superstitious is the most superstitious person in the assembly—be it large or small." Douglas' column was entitled, "Waft a Sneeze Upon the Air And Good Fortune May Appear," which indicates he gave historical evidence that the sneeze, with or without a blessing, has been considered good as well as bad luck at different times. He also cited the persistence of the belief that a howling dog portends death and that dropping a dish towel means there will be unexpected guests for dinner.

A favorite newspaper feature is a recital of superstitions in either an area of interest or in some place, with or without historical background. Advice to maidens on how to evaluate their chances of marriage was given by Mary Durham in the *Chicago Sun-Times* for March 25, 1962. One clue is to count the number of times the bird answers the supplication, "Cuckoo,

cuckoo, tell me true when shall I be married?" Or the young woman can write the letters of the alphabet on different pieces of paper put to soak in water overnight; by morning the first letter of the future husband's name should have turned over. And so on. The *Chicago Tribune's* Almanack, edited by Janet Murray, had a reminder Jan. 18, 1981 that Jan. 28 was St. Agnes Eve, a time when a girl could learn who her future husband would be. She could do so in any of several ways. One to ensure that he would appear in her dreams was to pluck a row of pins to stick in her sleeve while singing the *Pater Noster*.

As a prelude to *A Dictionary of American Beliefs and Superstitions* by Wayland H. Hand, the Associated Press June 10, 1967 distributed a long feature article citing "tidbits of folklore" included among the 400,000 collected by Professor Hand over 20 years. The AP account led off with "Hanging a horse's halter on your bed will cure nightmare." Superstitions, he found, are strongest among those in hazardous occupations: seamen, miners, steeplejacks and steel riggers, but strangely, despite Paul Bunyan, not among lumberjacks. "Folk beliefs," Hand said, "are a part of the inherited mental baggage that people of all countries carry. Thus, much material here is centuries old."

On the edge of the Ozarks, the *Branson* (Mo.) *Beacon* began a feature story March 23, 1972 as follows:

> Did you ever wish on a falling star? Or try to avoid bad luck by knocking on wood? If you have don't feel alone because practically everyone you know caters to at least one pet superstition.

Because she believes everyone is beset with idiosyncracies or quirks they think are sick, Judy Reiser, a social worker, interviewed more than 600 persons, among them those who always put coins face up, take vitamin pills in alphabetical order, insist on being paid in crisp new bills or engage in other forms of compulsive behavior. She then wrote a book, *And I Thought I Was Crazy*. In reviewing it in his column in the *Chicago Tribune* Nov. 4, 1980 Bob Greene began:

> When you get home from work at night, do you have an uncontrollable habit of putting all your coins face up on the nightstand? When you go to bed do your shoes have to be on the floor facing in precisely the same direction? When you get into the shower do you have to say, "budda-budda-budda" before stepping under the water?

There followed the summaries of 20 cases in Reiser's book, upon finishing which Greene facetiously said he was going home as soon as he touched the space bar on his typewriter seven times.

Herb Daniels devoted his *Chicago Tribune Magazine* column for May 17, 1981 to "350 million two-dollar bills floating over us like a green cloud of bad luck," followed by the history of the bill and the belief that tearing off a corner would neutralize the bad luck.

Most welcome are accounts of the superstitions of people in other parts of the world. Readers got smug satisfaction, for instance, from the "High Road to Superstition" article in the *Christian Science Monitor* for June 29, 1938. It detailed the difficulties encountered by road builders in Hawaii where native workers refused to help because they believe the lava rocks were protected by the goddess Pele who would punish any intruders.

Asking "Are You Superstitious?" in the *Chicago Tribune Magazine* for Feb. 8, 1959, Carol Douglas answered, "Of course you are." She then cited the Scandinavian belief that no woman will grow old if she carries an acorn in her pocket and the firing by the Duke of Wellington of a servant who absently put his master's boots on a table.

For the same paper Feb. 27, 1965, Robert Merry reported from London that superstitious spinsters in Warwickshire were putting bowls of purple spring flowers on their window ledges in hope of catching rich husbands. And from the same base Gail Borden reported June 8, 1937 for the *Chicago Times* that an English woman who poured tea from the same pot as another woman already had done would become pregnant according to one of a columnful of similar Mother Country beliefs.

Some who are in the business of satisfying the public's need, or at least desire, for supernatural assistance are considered newsworthy. For example, Queen Dora Mathews, to whom Chicago southside Negroes turn "from the depths of misery in which they exist," to quote Austin O'Malley and Carleton Kent in the *Chicago Times* for April 27, 1939. The article was illustrated by pictures of High John roots, herbs and other ingredients of various charms and potions. The paper headlined the piece, "Lady Luck's Charms Cost Plenty Here."

That the situation has remained unchanged except for the addition of members of the Hispanic community to the list of customers was indicated by John Adam Moreau's article, "Successful Smell of Superstition" in the *Chicago Sun-Times* for Nov. 10, 1969. Mostly the piece was about Senora Visanti, owner of Botanica Briases Michoacan where can be obtained lotions, liquids, herbs, amulets, statuary, perfumes, candles and dolls "whose purpose is to do good or evil."

The anonymous winner of the *Chicago Daily News'* daily News Lady article for Oct. 31, 1977 described the activities of two superstitious acquaintances. One kept files to make certain she never wrote to a person twice on the same kind of paper and with the same pen. The other protected her baby from seeing herself in a mirror, and did not allow peacock feathers, with their evil eyes, to be in a sickroom and obeyed other superstitious rules. Said the News Lady: "Giving in to a pack of idle superstitions makes life so unnecessarily complicated.

And that certainly has been true throughout history of many famous persons. W. A. S. Douglas reminded his readers of the following: Voltaire had an abject fear of such omens as cockeyed horses, blind dogs, hair-lipped women, three-fingered men, bow-legged boys and one-legged girls.

Napoleon Bonaparte always saw a star, invisible to others, shining in the sky. When it failed to shine the night before the Battle of Waterloo the emperor told Brigadier Girard he knew he was doomed. On the other hand Oliver Cromwell never doubted he would become ruler of England because a 7-foot woman awakened him when he was a boy to tell him so and then disappeared.

In an article concerning the disposition of the estate of Pablo Picasso, dead at 91, the UPI reported from Moulins, France April 11, 1973 that the great artist never made a will "as a way of avoiding death, one might say," according to his lawyer.

Several writers have been able to prepare features enumerating the superstitions of actors and actresses without borrowing material from each other. In a Newsreel Featurette in *Parade* for Aug. 14, 1948, Hy Gardner, under the title "This Superstitious World" revealed that Jimmy Durante never would start an engagement, picture or radio program on a Friday, Ted Lewis canceled an engagement because his lucky silk topper was lost en route, Bill "Bojangles" Robinson had a tiny rabbit's foot strung to his jeweled .38-caliber pistol and many other similar anecdotes.

In "Superstitions of the Stars" in the *Pittsburgh Press* for Sept. 2, 1974, Alan D. Haas revealed that Zsa Zsa Gabor always wears a child's ring given her by her grandmother; Arlene Francis tries not to be without a heart-shaped diamond pendant given her by her husband, Martin Gabel; Bette Davis has a charm bracelet she is never without; Tony Perkins thinks an untied shoelace is bad luck; Tony Curtis avoids white (not black) cats and so on for many more.

In their "Glad You Asked That" column in the *Rocky Mountain News* for Aug. 21, 1973, Hy and Martha Gardner reported that Zero Mostel kept all his shoes in a basket under his bed; Woody Allen won't take off his shoes until he gets into bed; Red Skelton won't talk on the telephone and many other foibles of the cinematic great.

In a full-page illustrated feature, "Circus Superstitions" the *Chicago Times* for May 2, 1943 revealed that peacocks are taboo in a circus but nobody knows why, a girl about to be shot out of a cannon spits on the muzzle for luck, trapeze artists kiss before beginning their act, and so forth.

The extent to which radio entertainers joined the ranks of the jittery was reported by Dora Albert in an article, "Jinxes and Jitters of the Air" in the *Milwaukee Journal* for June 28, 1936. She noted how many radio artists walked twice around a microphone before broadcasting, probably in imitation of poker players who think walking around the table brings luck. She cited the pet fears of some of the early celebrities: Graham McNamee wore a rabbit's foot in his lower vest pocket; Floyd Gibbons carried a magic stone given to him by a witch doctor in Africa; Ed Wynn, possibly the most superstitious entertainer of all times, would not broadcast unless he had the dilapidated shoes he had worn in every theatrical production for a quarter-century, and so on for many more.

Among the most superstitious always have been athletes. In the March 17, 1947 *Chicago Times* Jerry Holtzman reported that Tony Maffia, basketball coach at Chicago's South Shore high school, deliberately defied tradition by taking 13 players to the Illinois state tournament in an attempt to break the jinx that seemingly affected every Chicago-area team.

Four Chicago professional baseball players answered the question, "What is your special jinx?" for publication in the *Sun-Times* Talkies column as follows: Bob Chipman, Cubs pitcher: "I always throw my glove face up; if it lands face down, it's a bad omen"; "Rube" Walker, Cubs catcher: "I never did like to change my uniform during a winning streak"; Dave Philley, White Sox fielder: "When I come in from right field I always touch two bases—second and third. It makes me feel sort of uneasy if I don't"; Luke Appling, White Sox short stop: "If I have any superstitions it's news to me . . . But I'll admit I pick up lady's hairpins; they bring me base hits."

When the Chicago White Sox had a winning streak, according to the paper for May 29, 1951, the behavior of many of the players was motivated by superstitious beliefs. For instance, the same ball was used for infield practice and only Eddie Robinson was allowed to throw the ball into the dugout at the end of practice; Nelson Fox, second baseman, always touched third base going on and off the diamond, and so forth.

Similarly, when the Chicago Cubs were winning Jerry Holtzman wrote March 18, 1971 that Manager Leo Durocher continued to wear the same orange sweater. Because Durocher had a deep-seated superstition about team photographs, none were taken during his managerial years, 1965 to 1971. The first to break the taboo appeared in *Chicago Today* for Sept. 19, 1972.

When the Cubs broke a 13-game losing streak Ray Sons wrote in the *Sun-Times* for June 15, 1982 that it must have been St. Jude, patron of lost, hopeless causes, who did it in relief so the team eked out a 12–11 victory over the Phillies. Eddie Gold recalled that in 1944 when the Cubs also had a 13-game losing streak a fan sent Manager Charlie Grimm a four-leaf clover which the pitcher Eddie Hanyzewski put in his cap and won the game 5–3 over the Phillies.

In the *Chicago News* for Sept. 2–3, 1972 James H. Bowman, religion editor, accredited the batting prowess of Dodger Willie Davis to his chanting mystical Buddhist words to make him "peaceful, confident, unworried about his performance, more aware of others, wiser, enlightened, in love with life and convinced that the best things in life are free." This recalled the fact that Yankee star Joe DiMaggio, during a 56-game hitting streak, had the same breakfast daily: bacon, eggs and grapefruit. Also, Babe Ruth used to pick up hairpins and whenever he found one supposedly hit a home run.

The superstitions of many other baseball players were reported by Bill Shirley in the *Sun-Times* TopLine for Aug. 2, 1974. The streamer contained the gist: "Players pin hopes on baseball voodoo." The Atlanta Braves Ivan Morrell of Costa Rica said of Latin American players, "All wear beads and chains around their necks with medals or charms. A lot of guys say they don't believe in witchcraft and voodoo but they still wear the medals." Morrell accredited a triple cross he wore around his neck with having brought an end to a series of injuries.

It took almost a column for Martin Gershen to tell the story, "Gamblin' man reunited with his Lady Luck," in the *Sun-Times* for Jan. 20, 1975. The plot involved the search of a Chicago gambler to find a woman who allegedly brought him good luck at the dice tables in Las Vegas. A Detroit television show led to a reunion between the two whose luck hopefully continued.

In his Sept. 2, 1974 *Pittsburgh Press* article Haas revealed the superstitions of several other athletes. Among them were these: Ralph Branca, star Brooklyn Dodgers pitcher, always wore No. 13 until New York Giant Bobby Thomson hit his famous home run off him. The next year Branca shifted to No. 27 and whenever Ron Bryant pitched for the San Francisco Giants, there was a stuffed teddy bear dressed in a Giant uniform on the team's bench.

Suggesting that baseball players are superstitious all the year round, not just on Friday the 13th, the Associated Press enumerated some of the stars' foibles in an article Aug. 13, 1976. Mike Cuellar, Baltimore Oriole pitcher, was called "the king of quirks," among which was his belief that it is bad luck to warm up between innings with anyone but the team's catcher, the baseball must be sitting on the mound and not handed to him by the umpire or anyone else. Sparky Anderson, "probably the most superstitious manager in baseball," ordered "don't anybody move" during a rally.

"You don't become the best basketball team in Minnesota on ability alone . . . A little superstition helps," wrote Jim Wells in the *St. Paul Pioneer Press* for March 24, 1975. He elaborated on the fact that Coach Bauman of the Little Falls Fliers had worn the same suit for every winning game and that a star player never failed to take a shower before as well as after a game. The only time the team lost the superstitions had been disregarded.

When ex-Cub Jose Cardenal got into the 1980 World Series with the Kansas City Royals, the *Chicago Tribune* for Oct. 16, 1980 called it "a 'blessed' event" because he had emulated Bake McBride, Philadelphia Phillies opponent, in getting himself blessed by a Philadelphia priest. McBride hit a three-run homer to put his team ahead to stay. Unfortunately Cardenal went hitless.

The Associated Press distributed a picture of Seipo Spink, St. Louis Cardinal, receiving a haircut from teammate Orlando Pena, explaining, "I do this every time I want to change my luck." The AP also reported from Austin, Texas that although mostly bald, University of Texas football coach D. X. Bible gets a haircut of what he has left before an important game, apparently with good results most of the time.

Bill White's article, "Superstitions abound on Friday the 13th," in the *Clearwater* (Fla.) *Sun* for Aug. 13, 1982 dealt mostly with the superstitions of athletes, mostly members of the local baseball team, the Bombers. Just about everyone shunned the number 13, on uniform, locker or anywhere else.

Possibly because they're a captive audience for researchers and also should be expected to be smarter than their less educated peers, college students are objects of interest, certainly to scholars interested in superstitions. Most of the findings go into learned articles in professional magazines. June 7, 1947, however, the *Chicago Daily News* devoted four rotogravure pages to "Students at Northwestern University [who] dust off their books and good luck charms for final examinations." Pictured were a sorority girl wearing old blue jeans because they bring her luck; roommates rubbing each others' shoulders in emulation of Jeanette MacDonald who always rubbed an extra's shoulder; a student who keeps her fingers crossed the entire time in the examination room; a coed asleep with her text and notes under her pillow the night before exams; a man student, who always wears dungarees to an exam; another who gets his luck from a battered hat; still another who gets comfort from chewing a twig and a boy who worried whether his girlfriend will approve of his not having shaved during examination week.

Thirty percent of a nationwide sample of 671 teen-agers admitted to being superstitious according to an article, "Young Moderns Are Superstitious" by Eugene Gilbert in the *Chicago Sun-Times* for July 24, 1959. Fifty-four percent said their mothers were superstitious whereas only 24 percent said their fathers were. About half the young people said they do not walk under ladders, almost twice as many girls as boys preferring to walk around them. Black cats that crossed their paths were avoided by only 15 percent. The teen-agers said their friends are more superstitious about three on a match, the ladder, black cats and four-leaf clovers. Mother, they said, does a lot of knocking on wood and believes that tragedies happen in threes. Dad is especially careful not to open an umbrella in the house.

After many years of studying the problem Dr. Sander S. Feldman of the Rochester School of Medicine concluded that luck is "a person's own appraisal of reality." In the *Chicago Sun-Times* for July 21, 1963, Judith Brown quoted him as saying:

Most people say they are not superstitious but many believe that "bad luck" dogs their steps. Typical is the "everything happens to me" fellow. Whenever he wears a new suit he spills something on it; whenever he drives a new car he scrapes a fender.

The truth is that the mishaps he gripes about do happen to him—but happen infrequently. And he ignores the fact that they also happen to others.

Dr. Feldman has devised a 13-question true-false test. Typical statement considered true is: "If you really wait for a 'lucky break' your chances of success are decreased." Considered false is: "If you believe in good luck you're more realistic than those who believe in bad luck."

No area in the United States, perhaps in the world, has been studied more often to determine its superstitions than the Ozarks of Missouri and Arkansas. The findings are to be found mostly in learned magazines and books. Typical of the articles that appear occasionally in newspapers was "Fresh From the Hills" by Marc of Sunrise Mountain Farm in the *Chicago Tribune* for Sept. 24, 1944. It began with the anecdote of the author's being prevented from leaving a house by a different door than that by which she entered. "Down here in the Ozarks," she wrote, "superstitions are taken seriously. And there are literally hundreds of them. In fact there are so many superstitions that a sensitive person might get plumb discouraged." The article went a long way toward including most of them, as "If your dog habitually runs away, you can fix that . . . just snip a little hair from his tail and put it under the doorstep."

To explain "Ozark Leap Year Superstitions," the *St. Louis Globe-Democrat* devoted a doubletruck of pictures March 2, 1952. The illustrations supported the means by which would-be brides could influence suitors: slip a few shavings of ladyslipper root into his coffee; pin a small bag of peach pits to the petticoat; put chicken bones under his buggy seat and other ways.

In two pages in the *Chicago Tribune Magazine* for Aug. 7, 1954 Margo Lyon answered the title, "Are You Superstitious?" for Ozarkians, who, she wrote, deny that they are. Still, if they see a cardinal they make a wish, to remove a wart they rub a potato over it and then feed the potato to the hogs and to avoid bad luck, if they get a garment on wrong-side out they kiss it before reversing it, and so forth.

Such feature stories serve an iconoclastic purpose only if the reader considers what they report absurd. The same is true of spot news related to superstitions. Newspapers play them objectively without evaluation or editorial comment. Some typical stories over the years included the following:

When Capt. Lord Mountbatten left to take command of the British aircraft carrier *Illustrious,* his wife insisted that he wear a St. Christopher medal as he had done when he escaped injury after his ship was mined, torpedoed and sunk, the Associated Press reported Aug. 28, 1941 from Washington.

After a University of Washington professor shot a rare specimen of white albatross for a museum the U.S. Fish and Wildlife Service's vessel experienced several calamities: the net cables fouled up three times; the net caught in the sea bottom and was ripped to shreds; the main shaft snapped and it took 5½ hours to reel in the 1,700 feet of cable, the Associated Press reported Sept. 15, 1951 from Port Angeles, Wash. Editors naturally recalled S. T. Coleridge's *Rime of the Ancient Mariner,* inspiring such headlines as "Shades of the Ancient Mariner."

When band leader Xavier Cugat threw a coin in Rome's Trevi Fountain honoring a legend that such an act ensures a safe return, a crowd gathered, crushing Cugat's automobile and ending in a riot, the Associated Press reported July 14, 1968 from Rome.

An ecumenical service for children and their pets was announced by the *Toronto Star* Oct. 2, 1970. At similar services the preceding two years, all pets—cats, dogs, raccoons, birds, rabbits, ducks and mice—sat "quietly and there is almost supernatural harmony among them" as they awaited their turn to be blessed.

Holding a horseshoe which he thanked for his winning a special New York lottery for $1 million, Charles Klotz was shown with a nurse in a photograph distributed Jan. 29, 1971 by the Associated Press.

When Nigerians began driving on the right side of the road, bus drivers slaughtered a dog and splattered the blood on their vehicles to assure the approval of the god Ogun who presumably controls all things metal, the wire services reported April 3, 1972 from Lagos.

Janet P. Bonnema, a woman supervisor, walked into a tunnel being dug through the Rocky Mountains to defy a superstition that women underground are bad luck. She had been hired by mail in the belief she was a man. Although nothing happened 60 male diggers walked out, the UPI reported Nov. 10, 1972 from Georgetown, Colo. According to a *New York Times* report by Anthony Ripley from Silver Plume, Colo. the project already had had its bad luck. It was costing double the original estimate and was running two years late.

To accompany an AP story from Paris about the resumption of talks tending to end the fighting in Vietnam, the *Daily Texan* for Dec. 5, 1972 used a large UPI picture of a black cat climbing on the windshield of presidential advisor Henry Kissinger's automobile, under the caption, "Bad Luck?"

When Edith Russell died at 98, the AP, in a news story from London April 6, 1975, recalled an interview she had given three years earlier. She said that she was one of the 711 survivors of the Titanic which sank April 14, 1912 because a stuffed pig with a built-in music box, given to her after she survived an automobile accident in France, had saved her life again.

Although she devoted a half-column to declaring herself possessed by no superstitious belief, Carol Kleiman admitted in an Observer piece in the *Chicago Tribune* for May 29, 1982 that she carries a small straw figure of a woman that a friend brought her from Africa. She took it with her on a trip and concludes: "There's not one doubt in my mind that all good things would have happened anyway, but I know if I didn't use my good luck charm my friend's feelings would be terribly hurt."

Another 20 or so who "played it safe" were recipients of a prayer chain-letter containing an admonition to send 20 copies of the enclosed prayer to others to be lucky within four days. The *Hartford Times* interviewed the professional and business men involved and in its Feb. 15, 1980 issue revealed that most of them denied being superstitious but the Xerox machine made compliance easy. Typical explanations were "It looked harmless," "Prayer doesn't hurt anyone," "It can't hurt," "It seemed little trouble," "felt like a victim," "wanted to be a good Samaritan" and more of the same.

Herb Gould gave a word picture of the more than 100 dogs and cats who "wiggled in their owners' arms or tugged nervously on leashes" at rogation services in Chicago's St. Chrysostom's Episcopal Church. In his story in the *Sun-Times* for May 12, 1980 he explained that the ceremony is an urban adaptation of a traditional church ceremony in which the fields and animals of rural communities were blessed.

Especially in recent years there have been almost no iconoclastic articles concerning superstitions in most American newspapers. More than a generation ago, Nov. 24, 1935 the *Philadelphia Record Weekly Magazine* used an *Every Week Magazine* article by Helen Welshimer about the debunking career of Claudia de Lys. Miss de Lys was born with a cap of skin called a caul. Because a caul was considered lucky, especially by seamen, she sailed with her sailor grandfather and once was kidnapped by other sailors to safeguard their voyage. Those early experiences caused her interest that led to debunking 8,000 superstitions. The articles included anecdotes of some celebrities, including Sarah Bernhardt's dread of death which she thought she could avoid by having her casket with her at all times.

Welshimer epitomized de Lys' views:

It began when people, being quite human, started to transfer power to an object. If something good happened several times under certain circumstances, the faith in the object was established. Such an action is a psychological one, due to lack of spiritual development . . . There is no superstitious belief or practice of any kind that knowledge, coupled with scientific training, cannot cure.

Dr. George W. Crane devoted his "Case Records of a Psychologist" for Dec. 28, 1935 to the fetish worship of professional athletes. A baseball player told him of a teammate who carried a pair of his baby's shoes in his pocket when he went to bat, even though the baby was then a teen-ager.

Other players use only the same bat or carry rabbits' feet, and good luck pieces of various sorts. Commented Dr. Crane:

> Belief in magic was prevalent among us when we were children. It is present among primitive races who believe that trees have spirits and that good or evil beings dwell in the fire or earth or water . . . Belief is a powerful thing and can lead to great good if harnessed to intelligent thinking. On the contrary it can lead to lynchings and witch burning and other marks of human degradation when unsupported by analytical thinking.

An article in the Feb. 1, 1948 issue of *Parade* concerned the cynical attitude of Dr. Bergen Evans, professor of English at Northwestern University and author of *The Natural History of Nonsense*. Epitomized were Evans' views on astrology, numerology, prenatal influence, telepathy and a few other "illogical beliefs that would have brought tears from a reasonably bright caveman."

An Episcopal clergyman chided Navy rocketeers for seeking "divine guidance" by means of a religious medal in the rocket that put the Vanguard satellite into orbit. He was Dr. Charles D. Kean, rector of Epiphany Church, and, the UPI reported from Washington March 24, 1958, he said using a St. Christopher medal as a good-luck charm was "blatantly superstitious."

According to a United Airlines official, a St. Christopher medal is good only up to 60 miles an hour. "After that you're on your own," Wade Franklin quoted the man in the *Chicago Sun-Times* for April 17, 1960.

Early in 1961 the Roman Catholic church declared that St. Philomena, the virgin martyr, "was only a figment of the imagination." Nevertheless, the UPI reported Aug. 14, 1961, the village of Mugnano del Cardinale, Italy defiantly continued to celebrate the feast day of its patron saint in whose name, it was believed, several miracles had been performed. Her remains had been in the church since their discovery in Rome's catacombs in 1802.

Eight years later, May 9, 1969 the church dropped St. Christopher and 40 other saints from its liturgical calendar and made optional the commemoration of 90 others. All were dropped because of doubt they ever existed. April 17, 1960 in the *Chicago Sun-Times* Wade Franklin had identified St. Christopher as a Christian martyr circa 250 A.D. who became the patron saint of ferrymen because he carried wayfarers over bridgeless rivers. By contrast the accounts of the saint's demotion said the legend was that he once carried the infant Jesus across a river. In any case countless travelers relied on his medals for protection.

Although not a Catholic, Art Buchwald regretted St. Christopher's dropping in his syndicated column of May 15, 1969. Wrote Buchwald:

The decision couldn't have come at a worse time. With all forms of travel escalating, with 400-passenger air buses coming off the production line, with rail travel coming back into its own and auto sales going up and up, it seems to me that not only should the Vatican have saved St. Christopher but it should have assigned another saint to help him.

One instance of a newspaper's checking was revealed in the *Chicago Tribune's* Action Express column April 21, 1974. A young woman had been advised not to marry in May so as not to be jinxed. The paper interviewed the county marriage license bureau's superiors who said there is no evidence that the thousands of May marriages were jinxed any more than those solemnized in any other month.

Eleven years after St. Christopher's demotion his medals, keys and statues continued to sell in the millions, Grant Harden reported in the *Chicago Tribune* for Nov. 15, 1980. The article was based on an interview with the Rev. Edward McShane of the University of Santa Clara who distinguished between legendary and mythical persons and asserted the church was attempting to separate the real from the fictitious.

Perhaps the most instructive piece in this field of interest was "A word to the wise: What you 'know' can hurt you too," by Edward Barry in the *Tribune* for Dec. 20, 1980. Barry disabused those who believe it is best to remain in an automobile during a tornado or to control bleeding by applying a tourniquet or that hunters should wear red for visibility or that a cold should be fed and a fever starved and many other wrong ideas that are widely held.

Indubitably the net effect of the press' handling of news regarding luck, good and bad, is to help perpetuate rather than diminish ignorance and superstition.

Some people today don't want to help themselves to the last cookie on a plate. They refrain from walking on cracks in the sidewalk, don't throw hats on beds, spit whenever they see a certain animal, until recently the horse, avoid walking on one side of an obstacle when a companion takes the other side and much more of the same.

To increase the possibility of success of a questionable venture some still knock on wood and to escape the consequences of any prevarication they cross their fingers.

The superstitious person seeks to guard himself against harm from evil spirits by avoiding behavior that might offend the unseen forces, by cajoling them and by behaving so as to please them.

Following a ceremony at the tomb of Abraham Lincoln in Springfield, Ill. on his birthday Feb. 12, 1981, Illinois Governor James Thompson rubbed the nose of the Great Emancipator's statue, an act presumed to bring good luck. The UPI took a picture of the governor in the act.

Another attention-getting picture was one the AP took March 18,1981 in Clovis, Cal. of ten-year-old Shawn Buffer peering over a pile of "lucky horseshoes for sale." Inflation's effect was shown by the alteration of the advertising sign to raise the price from 20 to 30 cents.

Superstitious people avoid doing anything that presumably would displease the evil spirits surrounding them. They are especially fearful of acts that automatically cause mishaps. The list of such actions throughout history and in all parts of the world runs into thousands.

There are as many theories as there are experts expounding them to explain how 13 came to be regarded as an unlucky number and Friday a day on which to be wary. Regardless of how either or both superstitions originated, triskaidekaphobia (fear of Friday the 13th) has been epidemic since ancient times. For their one, two or three features on the phenomenon annually, journalists have, of course, consulted the writing of the scholarly researchers, but their stories contain discrepancies because they obviously did not all use the same reference books.

Chuck Dilday asked "Unlucky for Whom?" in the *Appleton* (Wis.) *Post-Crescent* for Sept. 13, 1968 and answered that there are 13 letters in his name which also was true of Richard Wagner who was born in 1813 and composed 13 operas. Woodrow Wilson favored the number and regularly entertained at lunch and dinner with 13 guests. Also, Dilday wrote: "On the great seal of the United States there are 13 stars and 13 bars, an eagle with 13 tail feathers holding 13 darts; there are 13 olives and the motto—E Pluribus Unum—has 13 letters. And don't forget, there were 13 original colonies."

Nevertheless, Dilday reported, in northern Wisconsin there are many who will not begin a new task on Friday the 13th and who believe a journey begun on that day will end disastrously. In Europe, he wrote, some believe it bad to be born or married on Friday the 13th and housewives refrain from making beds on such days. French Link, Ind. has an ordinance requiring black cats to wear bells on such days.

"Today," the *Quincy* (Ill.) *Herald-Whig* editorialized May 12, 1966, "a Friday the 13th is largely a matter of kidding . . . Many of our ancestors simply accepted the fact that a Friday the 13th was an ill-omened day. They did not ask why. And even today, in our enlightened era, there would be no clear answer to the question. There are answers, of course, but not that quite satisfy our present sense of reality."

Nevertheless, the editorial went on to cite some of the answers: that it was on a Friday that Eve succumbed to the wiles of the serpent; there were 13 at the Last Supper and Jesus was crucified on a Friday. One celebrity who obeyed the taboo was Winston Churchill who refused to travel on a Friday.

To these explanations the *Lincoln* (Neb.) *Journal* for Sept. 13, 1968 added in an article, "Precautions Revealed For Witches' Sabbath" by

Glenda Peterson, that in the 17th century public hangings were held on Fridays and the hangman received 13 pence. Friday is named for Freyja, the Norse goddess of love. The myth has it that 12 gods were having a banquet in Valhalla when a 13th arrived; there was a fight in which there was one fatality. The day became known as the witches' sabbath when 12 witches met with a 13th, the devil. The article was illustrated by the photograph of an owl, generally considered an omen of disaster.

Believers in the occult regard Friday the 13th as a festive occasion, Kit Bauman reported in the *Dallas Times-Herald* for Aug. 13, 1973. In Dallas they celebrate at a dinner as guests of the Black Magic Woman, proprietor of a psychic occult shop. Leader of the group said, "The number 13 symbolizes death but death to an occultist means a new beginning." The article recalled that the first trial of a witch in Salem, Mass. was held on a Friday the 13th in 1630.

"Friday the 13th Fog Eclipses Astronomical Phenomenon," was the headline over Paul Malloy's article in the *Chicago Sun-Times* for Dec. 14, 1974. He told readers "Relax and stick around because there will be other Friday the 13th eclipses. The next one, for example, will occur on July 13, 2018."

Malloy made the Norse legend more comprehensive, saying it was Loki who crashed the party and Tobar who was killed.

According to Michelle Pemberton in the *Daily Texan* for June 13, 1975, thirteen originally got its bad name when practitioners of black magic following ancient books evoked 13 demons. The uninitiated came to believe the number had an evil significance of its own. Modern manifestation of the fear, she wrote, is the absence of 13th floors in hotels and other buildings. In Berlin the number is omitted from streets and Italy does not include 13 in its lotteries. Pemberton wrote it was Baldur, not Tobar, who was killed in Valhalla.

Chaucer in his *Canterbury Tales,* recalled gloomily in Old English, "And on Friday fell all the meschaunce." Today it is wise to avoid cutting one's fingernails or to wash on a Friday. It has long been a mystic number associated with King Arthur and his 12 knights of the roundtable, Jacob and his 12 sons and the 12 other parts of Osiris' body.

"Superstitious? Stay Home Today," was the headline over Don Brannan's story in the *Arlington Heights* (Ill.) *Herald* for Feb. 12, 1979. After quoting the opinions of several townsmen he pointed out that sailors often refuse to leave port on the 13th, that the Egyptians considered it a lucky number and the taboo of 13 began when man learned to count and could go no further than ten fingers and two feet. "Beyond that was the unknown or the supernatural," Brannan wrote. The term Black Friday commemorates disastrous results that occurred on Fridays, such as the financial panic of May 11, 1866 in London and those in New York Sept. 24, 1869 and Sept. 19, 1873.

Robert E. Dallos explained the headline, "It's No Day to Ask How Business Is" in the *Los Angeles Times* for April 13, 1979. He wrote:

It is a fact that more workers play hookey on Friday the 13th, some travelers refuse to board planes or ships, some businessmen won't close a deal, some people won't eat in a restaurant, some won't go shopping. There are couples who won't get married that day and some who won't buy a house or a car.

In about two columns more Dallos quoted figures regarding automobile and other sales comparing the voodoo days with others. He cited several of the legends included in other reporters' accounts and added the fact that there is no gate 13 at the Dallas International Airport. To prove Friday the 13th has not always been an unlucky day, he wrote:

Columbus, it is said, first set foot on the North American continent on Friday, June 13, 1498. On Friday, Oct. 13, 1792 construction began on the White House. On Friday, Sept. 13, 1814 *The Star Spangled Banner* was written. On other Fridays the Mayflower passengers disembarked at Plymouth Rock, Bunker Hill was fought for, the British surrendered Saratoga and the Declaration of Independence was read to the Continental Congress.

"Friday the 13th Based on Deep Fears" headlined Carla McClain's article in the *Tucson Citizen* for Nov. 13, 1981. She revealed that President Franklin D. Roosevelt is said to have been so suspicious of the number that he would make his secretary attend a function if the guest list added up to 13. Most of the article summarized the views of a number of psychologists, most of whom believed that the sufferers from triskaidekaphobia had some experience in early life to create an attitude of fear.

In his "Reporter at Large" column for Jan. 30, 1981 in the *Harrisburg* (Pa.) *Evening News,* Paul B. Beers wrote:

George Washington took command of the Continental Army on Friday the 13th and led 13 disorganized colonies to victory. Subsequently, construction of the White House was begun on a Friday the 13th. Some of our most illustrious were born on that day: former Commissioner Charley Hoy, jazzman Jack Snavely, caveman Ed Swartz, conservationist Maurice K. Goddard and this left-handed slightly imperfect columnist.

The feature for Nov. 13, 1981 of the Associated Press contained the following:

For the superstitious the combination of Friday and 13 is a double whammy—a day for avoiding ladders, black cats and broken mirrors and an equally good day for carrying four-leaf clovers, horseshoes and tossing salt over the left shoulder. In its catalogue of things to avoid, the AP listed the following:

—Wearing a peacock feather which on the surface seems to be a truer indicator of bad luck for the peacock with the plucked plummage.

—Searching for a one-legged chicken which, for reasons lost in time, is supposed to be a bearer of bad tidings.

—Stepping on a crack which, according to the children's sidewalk song, is a guarantee your mother will be hospitalized with a broken back in the near future.

In his column for March 11, 1964 Sydney J. Harris told how difficult it was to explain to his young daughter why there was no 13th floor in a hotel. He told her the Norse, Christian and other legends. He also recalled that when Gen. Emilio Mola was killed in an airplane crash he was in his stocking feet because some Gypsy fortune teller had told him he'd die with his boots on. Harris also spoke of the Quatorziennes, French persons who were available to accept invitations to a dinner where otherwise there'd be only 13 at the table.

Adaptation of the French custom by American hotels was reported in a full-page article in the *American Weekly* for June 9, 1949. A dummy in full dress known as Louis XIV is available to be placed at a table, often to be served food the same as the other guests. A hotel proprietor told the article's anonymous author that some guests are squeamish about paying a $13 bill, either paying a nickel more or asking that the bill be reduced by that amount. Other superstitions of some guests forbid throwing a hat on a bed and not being able to get out of bed on the right-hand side. Pigeons alighting on a window sill are thought to be bad luck by some, as is an interruption while someone is dealing cards.

The architect for the five skyscrapers rising along the Detroit River in the Renaissance Center told William A. Clark of the *Detroit Sunday News* for use Sept. 14, 1974 that not one of the guest rooms in the Detroit Plaza will have a room numbered 13, nor will any of the hotels have 13th floors. "Hotels do not think that 13th-floor rooms are marketable," he explained.

"What Not to Wear Friday the 13th" was the heading the *Chicago Daily News* gave an article by Carl DeStefano Sept. 4, 1968. It contained the omens cited by Bob Connors and others at Hart, Schaffner & Marx. The list of "don'ts" included the following: button a coat wrong; change clothes originally put on wrong-side out; pick up a glove, or for that matter, to drop one; walk with only one shoe or slipper. It is also supposed to be unlucky to put both the stocking and shoe on one foot before putting on the second stocking and about 20 more similar taboos.

Black cats are associated with witches and bad luck. Sept. 13, 1968 the *Lewiston* (Mont.) *Daily News* used a two-column headshot with these cutlines:

It's a shame to lay the blame on an adorable black kitten like Bippidy but the fact remains that ever since his picture was taken as the Friday the 13th cat, bad luck has plagued the *Daily News* employees. It got off to an early start

Thursday evening when a *Daily News* photographer had the misfortune to break the news camera. Friday morning, for the first time in five years she has worked here, the editor found she was locked out of the building because she had left her keys inside. Later in the morning she went out to "cover her beat" and ran out of gas. And another member of the news staff followed suit running out of gas on the way to work. Could be coincidences but—on Friday the 13th?

The same day the *Pittsburg* (Kan.) *Headlight-Sun,* page one'd a picture of a strolling black cat with cutlines: "Bad Day for Superstitions—This black cat posing unknowingly for the photographer is symbolic of the special significance attached to this day, which is Friday the 13th—the first such day in 1968."

March 13, 1981 the *Harrisburg Evening News* headlined "Beware of 13th For Once Again It's on a Friday." The story by Barker Howland was illustrated by a drawing of a humpbacked cat on a fence. After reciting most superstitions and numerology he quoted Christopher Potter, professor of psychology at Harrisburg Area Community College: "People are afraid not to believe in these superstitious ideas. If you ask them seriously if they believe these ideas or not they will chuckle and deny them but underneath they still believe in the superstitions. . . The fears we have of the environment and the world are carryover from years ago."

A similar statement by the editors had top column 1 position in the *News-Tribune* which serves LaSalle-Peru-Oglesby-Spring Valley, Ill. for Nov. 13, 1981, namely: "Even in a day when objective evidence is valued highly, there are few people who, if pressed, would not admit to cherishing secretly one or two irrational beliefs." Across the top of the page were four shots of a black cat in flight. Black cats, the note read, are symbols of superstition.

A reader who signed herself Crossed Fingers wrote to Ann Landers to ask if she was "a little nuts" because she avoided black cats and ladders, became upset when she broke a mirror and refused to get married on Friday the 13th. Ann's reassuring reply follows: "Many intelligent people are superstitious. These precautions against bad luck are emotional, not rational. Such behavior is the result of early training and once the patterns are established they are virtually impossible to break. So long as they don't interfere with your daily routine go ahead and enjoy the comfort you derive from doing little things to ward off bad luck. Nobody is 100 per cent sane."

What newspapers do is exploit the Friday the 13th angle if they can. Jan. 13, 1957, for instance, the *Chicago Daily News* used a half-page picture of a raging fire in New York's Queens Borough. The large caption was "It Happened on Friday the 13th." Has anyone ever seen a caption, "It Happened on Thursday the 12th?"

Enumerating coincidences involving the number 13 is a favorite pastime for some reporters. Sept. 14, 1946 the *Chicago Sun* had a feature about a defendant with 13 letters in his name doing business at 1313 W. Randolph Street, accompanied by his son on the boy's 13th birthday, charged on line 13 of the court sheet with speeding 13 miles over the limit. The prosecutor, with 13 letters in his name, agreed to a postponement until the 13th of the next month, and the judge was happy that he had only 12 letters in his name.

Morris A. Hall reminded readers of *Parade* for Dec. 8, 1957 that a Friday the 13th was imminent. He asked, "Are *you* superstitious?" and then gave thumbnail sketches of 15 persons who had either good or bad luck associated with 13. Example: the mayor of a small town in the state of Washington missed being re-elected by two votes, demanded a recount, lost by 13.

Sept. 13, 1968 the *Kalispell* (Mont.) *Daily Inter Lake* ran a story, "Friday the 13th Jinx Plagues Local Driver." The news was that a driver swerved to avoid hitting a dog and rammed another car. What the date had to do with it was not explained.

The same could be asked of the Eureka (Calif.) *Humboldt-Times Standard,* which had a story the same day, "Bad Luck True to Form." The story was that an automobile ran off the road resulting in slight injuries to two men.

From Houston came a feature April 14, 1970 enumerating coincidences in connection with the flight of Apollo 13: it blasted off at 13:13, the power failure that crippled the command ship occurred April 13 and, with the moon landing canceled, the splashdown was set for 11:13. Rather far fetched, but news for the *Chicago Daily News.*

Aug. 19, 1978 the UPI reported from Baguio, Philippines that Viktori Korchnoi had asked for a postponement of the 13th game of his championship chess match with Anatoly Karpov until Sunday.

When about 1,000 riders on the Chicago subway were forced out of their cars because of a minor fire, a passenger took a picture showing smoke. The *Sun-Times* used it March 14, 1981 with the caption, "L track fire—it happened on Friday the 13th."

Good luck on Friday the 13th also is newsworthy. When Elsa Hahn completed 50 years as an employee of the *Milwaukee Journal* the paper ran her picture and a story of her career and reminiscences Sept. 13, 1968. June 11, 1969 the paper did the same for Sharon and H. Mitchell Allen, operators of The Owl's Nest art gallery for a half-century.

Feb. 13, 1971 the *Chicago Sun-Times* ran a picture of a retired police sergeant who had patrolman's star No. 13 and sergeant's star No. 213. His state auto license is MP1300, his city vehicle sticker 1313 and his Illinois Police Association number 1313. The same paper reported the safe return of a gold coin worth $240 that a passenger accidently deposited in a bus coin-box on Friday the 13th. And the UPI reported Nov. 19, 1981 from

New York that a maintenance man from Brooklyn won the world's biggest lottery jackpot—$5 million—by picking the lucky numbers on Friday the 13th.

Nov. 14, 1946 the *Portland Oregonian* recognized the birthdays the day before, Friday the 13th, of former Circuit Judge Clarence H. Gilbert and Mrs. Dela B. Howard. The former said 13 has always been his lucky number. The latter said she had a party for 13 guests.

In 1968 the Newspaper Division of the Association for Education in Journalism asked its members who represented all parts of the country to monitor what newspapers in their areas did in recognition of Friday, Sept. 13. Among other things the informal research showed that by far the most popular kind of feature story is an interview with someone whose birthday occurs that day. The *Columbia Missourian* used a picture of 13-year-old Tony Richie seated under a ladder with a broken mirror and a black cat as props. He was quoted as not being superstitious although he once fell and cut his head on his birthday. The *Great Falls* (Mont.) *Leader* had a three-column picture of 17-year-old Susan Kerin hanging onto the under side of a ladder propped against the house. The *Buffalo Evening News* used a three-column picture of 13-year-old Tina Fricano holding an opened umbrella under an indoor stepladder. The story by Jack Balysek told of her party plans. Still another 13-year-old, Debra Pollard, got a full-page picture peering out from under a ladder with large numbers 13 in her arms in the Pocatello *Idaho State Journal*. The *Helena* (Mont.) *Independent* used the AP wirephoto from Westbrook, Me. showing 3-year-old triplets on a ladder. The *Rock Hill* (S.C.) *Evening Herald* used a picture of a black cat. After sketching the history of the fear, the paper said, "Superstition belongs to the ages, not to us moderns. Or does it?" The *Muncie* (Ind.) *Evening Press* used only a UPI short from Cincinnati about a 48-year-old man who was the 13th of 16 children. The figures in his age, 58, his house number 904 and the letters in his name all totaled 13. The most elaborate feature of the day was the Associated Press' article by Rob Wood, a Friday the 13th baby, who wrote a long review of hard-luck escapades "all accounts due, of course, to the curse of the day." Typical example: when in first grade mistakenly wandering into the girl's restroom, breaking the lock and spending the entire day in a cubicle, ashamed to emerge. And another: dashing 98 yards in a tied high school football game only to drop the ball two yards short of the goal line. The feature was used at least in the *Charleston* (S.C.) *News and Courier*, *Columbia* (S.C.) *State* and *Spartanburg* (S.C.) *Herald*.

"The bad luck associated with Friday the 13th doesn't seem to faze the Rollog family," the AP reported Sept. 15, 1968 from Ketchikan, Alaska. Jerry Rollog celebrated his 31st birthday. He was born on Friday the 13th, as were his father and his son. The same day the *Fort Collins* (Colo.) *Coloradan* made a survey of delivery rooms in Fort Collins and Loveland.

The result was expressed in the headline: "Proud New Parents Could Care Less About Friday the 13th."

Among the other examples of Sept. 13, 1968 coverage were the following:

Ed Erlandson reminded readers of his "Hell Gate Breezes" column in the *Missoula* (Mont.) *Missoulian* what day it was and advised, "So stay in bed all day, if you shy away from ladders and black cats and such." Then he related some bad luck he had experienced recently, chiefly the burning out of a light in a microfilm.

The Butte *Montana Standard* used a stunt picture of someone reading a newspapaper with backward headline type. The cutlines: "We're not superstitious . . . but . . ."

"Stumbling into Friday the 13th" was the cutline-caption on a series of five pictures in the *Chicago Tribune*. The pictures showed a man taking a fall and being aided by the American Red Cross who supplied the actors.

The *St. Paul* (Minn.) *Dispatch* had two short news items. One said it was good Harry L. Donovan of Cincinnati was not superstitious because he was born Sept. 13, 1910, the 13th of 16 children. On his 58th birthday the figures of his age added up to 13 as did his street number, 904, and the letters in his name. The second short piece said that Miss New Jersey made her 13th appearance since, as number 13 in the lineup, she won the state beauty contest July 13.

The Akron (Ohio) *Beacon Journal* had a short bottom-of-the page brightener about an epidemic worldwide of triskaidekaphobia, the principal symptom being "a generally skittish attitude throughout the day."

The *Champaign* (Ill.) *News-Gazette* had no story but used a Pogo comic strip in which Pogo tells Churchy one day is like another and then, in the last frame, slips away saying, "Yeoup, y'mean they is all Friday the 13th?"

"13 Not Unlucky for Widow Who Turns 100 on Friday" the *Chicago Daily News* reported Dec. 12, 1968. "We'll treat it just like any other day," said Mrs. Bernice Olson, widow of a long-time chief justic of the Chicago Municipal Court. She was shown in a picture with her great-grandson.

Feb. 14, 1981 the Associated Press distributed a picture of Jim Schleck of Madison, Wis. who, the cutlines said, "likes the number 13. That's how old he is, how many goals he's scored for his high school hockey team and his black cat was born Feb. 13, 1976.

Seeking a new angle for a Friday the 13th feature taxes the ingenuity of editors so that a majority of the papers examined by the professors had no such stories. A few samples from over the years show the strain involved in producing them. For example, for the *New York Star* of Aug. 14, 1948 reporter Powers Moulton wrote a rambling piece to create the impression of being deprived of some of his senses as he visited the Museum of Natural History.

Aug. 14, 1968 the *Chicago Sun-Times* had a seven-line story headed "It

Wasn't Cubs' Lucky Day." Among the items: Milwaukee beat the Cubs, getting 13 hits, Denny Lemaster (his name has 13 letters) struck out 13 and was the winning pitcher over Bob Buhl who was seeking his 13th victory for the Cubs, and Gene Oliver slugged his 13th (and 14th) homer for the Braves.

The Associated Press reported Sept. 14, 1968 from Pottstown, Pa. that the Pottstown police patrol car No. 13 was damaged in a two-car collision Friday the 13th. The patrolman driving it had 13 letters in his name and escaped injury.

The annual Wisconsin State Fair opened Sept. 13, 1971 with a voodoo good fortune performance to ward off bad luck, the *Chicago Daily News* reported.

When a partial eclipse of the sun occurs on a Friday the 13th, "all sorts of omens may be divined by the superstitions," the *Los Angeles Times* reported Dec. 12, 1973. The article, however, told only how, when and where to observe the phenomenon.

Although the *Sun-Times* headlined a UPI story from Vancouver June 11, 1980, "Will Friday the 13th Be Bad Luck Day for Mt. St. Helens?" the story quoted only scientists who belittled the effect the moon's being unusually close to Earth on that day would have.

The Friday the 13th stories most liked by iconoclasts are those that stress defiance of the superstition. Some examples follow:

The *Chicago Daily News* for Dec. 13, 1946 had a picture of two women from the Uptown Solidarity working under a ladder with a black cat as mascot as they prepared Christmas baskets for the needy.

New York's *PM* for June 13, 1947 had a picture of three bathing-suit models lighting three cigarets on one match under a ladder. A news story by John S. Wilson announced the first anniversary (after 13 months) of the National Committee of 13 Against Superstition and Fear.

Three 4-year-olds and one 3-year-old were pictured at the Children's Aid Society James Center with the usual black cat, umbrella and ladders. The *New York Compass* published the picture Jan. 13, 1950.

Aug. 14, 1965 the chief clerk of the Cook County, Ill. marriage license bureau told the *Sun-Times* that 161 couples had applied for licenses the preceding day. "It's not like the old days," he said. "People aren't superstitious any more." An iron-worker told a reporter he walked under ladders all day long and had number 13 on his jersey when he played football in high school. Said his fiance, "At least he won't forget our anniversary."

Two women hammering on mirrors and two men crouching under a ladder on which a third is climbing were used Sept. 13, 1968 by the *Pittsburgh Press*. In an accompanying story Ralph Miller quoted several persons who scoffed at superstition.

The same day the *Muncie* (Ind.) *Evening Press* used a two-column picture of a woman who accidentally put on her dress backwards smashing a mirror.

A 79-year-old man and an 83-year-old woman are shown kissing as they obtain a marriage license to "Defy 13th Bugaboo" as the *Chicago Sun-Times* put it Aug. 14, 1971.

It is apparent from all of the foregoing that the press covers Friday the 13th with a skeptical tongue-in-cheek attitude. By merely mentioning the superstitious trivia—black cats, mirrors, ladders and the like—newspapers shake readers' faith in the ridiculous. Blatant iconoclastic attacks supposedly are not necessary. The spirit of good fun is similar to that with which Santa Claus, the Easter Bunny and tooth fairy are treated.

Not always, of course. Not taking a chance that people will not be gullible, some journalists have been slam bang in their handling of Friday the 13th news. An editorial in the *Evanston* (Ill.) *Daily News-Index* for March 13, 1936 contained the following typical observations: "It's all nonsense, of course, as any sensible person knows . . . For every instance of a misfortune that occurs on a Friday the 13th there could be related thousands of instances of good fortune . . . Belief in the mystic qualities of any number, either for good or bad, presupposes an anthropomorphic idea of the unseen universe, with some evil spirit capable and desirous of shaping destinies according to malicious whim."

Marvin Quinn tried satire in the *Chicago Times* for Dec. 13, 1946. Under the headline, "Know what day it is?" he began, "This is the day newspapers write about. But on this occasion we refuse to mention it" and he ended with, "Without looking at the calendar, what day is it? Thirteen guesses." In between he had a dozen potential items that he swore not to mention. Among them: "In New York 13 models will join the National Committee of 13 Against Superstition and Fear. They will give 13 rabbits' feet back to the rabbits provided 13 rabbits can be found to accept them." "Chicago's Anti-Superstition society will meet at 6:13 P.M. in the Drake Hotel. Unable to obtain room 13 it will have to settle for Parlor D."

After stating that superstition is not an antiquated funny notion, in his column for Feb. 13, 1948 Sydney J. Harris wrote, "Our modern superstitions are strangling society without our even knowing it." He cited them as chauvinism, racism and science-worship. His most specific swipe was, "A good many large sized American cities have Anti-Superstition societies. I don't know exactly what their members do, except that you see their pictures in the papers every Friday the 13th, usually in some corny stunt like walking under a ladder. Instead of frittering away their time the silly asses ought to latch on some superstitions that really threaten our survival as a free people."

Marc Grogin was more facetious than bitter when he wrote "Friday the 13th—On Your Own" to tell of his library search for prayers and incantations to ward off evil. The only ones in English were some sure-fire Assyro-Babylonian. "I was going to write them down for you," he wrote, "when it occurred to me that if they were such good protection for Assyro-

Babylonians, how come there aren't any Assyro-Babylonians any more?"

In fine literary fettle Nov. 13, 1970 Mike Royko wrote of a Friday the 13th in the life of his creation, Slats Grobnik. One time Slats was afraid to go outside so he went to sleep in a closet. Alarmed at his snoring Mrs. Grobnik summoned police who rapped the resting Slats on the head giving it a normal shape for the first time, whereupon Slats philosophized, "You can't hide from bad luck."

Oct. 13, 1972 Robert J. Herguth burlesqued the occasion in the *Chicago Daily News*. The day, he cautioned, "can mean bad luck for a lot of people." Among them would be "any Chicagoan who has 1313 unpaid parking tickets." And "if 113 people try to stand under 13 umbrellas on a rainy Friday the 13th some of them get wet," and so on for a half-column of laughs.

To make the day a little less frightening Steve Renefrow analyzed the reasons for fright in the *Daily Texan* for Oct. 13, 1972, explaining that the uneasiness, nervousness and panic caused by superstition become progressively worse. This he demonstrated by the deterioration of his typing and wound up 11 paragraphs later, ". . . you don't know what to do but give up and go back to bed before you start drooling and someone pulls the typewriter away from uoy esuaceb tahw reve uoy od smees ot emoc tuo sdrawkcab."

Ridgely Hunt debunked the Friday the 13th bugaboo in the *Chicago Tribune* for Oct. 13, 1972. In part he argued: "Pearl Harbor was bombed on a Sunday the 7th, and the *Titanic* sank on a Monday the 15th and the *Hindenburg* burned on a Thursday the 6th, but all of them were safe as safe could be on Friday the 13th."

The silly asses (as Sydney J. Harris calls them) who belong to anti-superstition societies get a good press. The Chicago society was founded in 1930 and incorporated in 1953 by Nathaniel Leverone, president of a coin-in-the-slot vending machine company. At an early meeting, which Leverone called to order by heaving a horseshoe through a mirror, a resolution was passed, "whereas fear and particularly superstition, which are the outward expression of fear of the unknown, dominates the mind and directs the actions of millions of people . . ." and the society pledged itself "by word and action to banish all forms of fear of the unknown from the public mind and to eliminate from public thought all superstition and to discredit and urge the destruction of all good luck pieces, amulets and talismen."

A full-page profile of Leverone, then 84, was written by David Anderson for the *Sun-Times* of Sept. 12, 1968. He related the anecdote Leverone liked to tell of Mayor Edward J. Kelly's refusal to enter Leverone's No. 13 office in the Merchandise Mart. Meetings of the society always start at 13 minutes after the hour, with members paying $13.13 for tickets and usually donating a similar amount to some charity. Members crawl under ladders with 13 rungs, trample on four-leaf clovers, smash mirrors with horseshoes, spill salt, sit at tables set for 13, pet 13 black kittens and if they smoke wait until two others are available to share the same match.

Reporters assigned to cover society meetings try to uncover a new fact or angle to avoid monotony. The *Daily News* for Sept. 13, 1968 broadened the scope of its coverage by quoting Dr. Edwin G. Boring of Harvard, who said superstitious people are afraid to face life. He said: "They feel more secure if they can explain that they got hit on the head by a flower pot after walking under a ladder. So they blame it on bad luck." The next day the *Sun* quoted Leverone as saying women were excluded from the society because some were caught slipping rabbits' feet into their purses before attending meetings. As a shirttail the paper also reported that the marriage license bureau had more business than usual on Friday the 13th. One woman said she got out of a sickbed so as to get her license on the voodoo day. Then she confessed that she did so on the advice of an astrologer.

Sen. Everett Dirksen presided with Judge Abraham Marovitz at his side at a society meeting in the '50s. The picture illustrated a story by Sarah Boyden in the *Sun-Times* for Nov. 8, 1959. The story covered the origin of the society and of many of the most widespread superstitions.

The first organization of its kind was New York's 13 Club, founded and chartered in 1882. It survived until the outbreak of World War I. March 13, 1936 the United Press distributed an article by J. Arthur Lehman, the only surviving member. The hijinks he described were the same as those performed by the Chicago club.

A disappearance of the number 13 superstition may be indicated by what Robert J. Herguth reported in the *Daily News* for Jan. 13, 1967. Mrs. DeWitt H. Montgomery revealed that her husband, who was working in the secretary of state's office, took auto license No. 13 because nobody else would have it. "Now, everybody wants it," she said.

"Today is Friday the 13th, a day of bad luck for the superstitious and for newspaper reporters assigned to write about Friday the 13th," is the way Donald Zochert began his story in the *News* for Sept. 13, 1968. He noted that George Halas, owner of the Chicago Bears, would be guest of honor at that day's society meeting.

The *News'* Beeline's Friday the 13th guest on the VIP line, Les Lear, society secretary, confessed that as a boy he had a lucky penny but he reached the "age of enlightenment" and put it in a peanut vending machine. He answered numerous questions advising one person to play with the black cat in the backyard and another to preserve salt rather than throwing it over either shoulder.

Aug. 13, 1971 Tom Seibel reported for the *News,* the Man of the Day would be Wally Phillips of WGN, who has 13 letters in his name. Five years later, Aug. 13, 1976, Lloyd Green quoted Lear in the *Sun-Times* as saying none of the society's 313 members had ever suffered any bad luck either during or immediately after a session. Lear died in 1983 and the society died with him.

10

Curses and Cures

Even though he is reelected in 1984 Ronald Reagan will die in office, according to those who believe every president elected in a year ending in a zero is doomed. Basis for this belief is a legend that the brother of Indian Chief Tecumseh placed the curse on William Henry Harrison and every president elected at subsequent 20-year intervals. So far, as *Parade* pointed out Sept. 28, 1980, the faithful insist that the Indians' Revenge has been responsible for the deaths in office of William Henry Harrison, Abraham Lincoln, James A. Garfield, William McKinley, Warren G. Harding, Franklin D. Roosevelt and John F. Kennedy. Oct. 27, 1980 UPI retold the story with details of Harrison's war and of the other presidential deaths.

A counterargument to indicate there can be an end to coincidence is the fact that the National League entry, Philadelphia, won the 1980 World Series. Previously it was pointed out that whenever the American League entry won the series the Republican candidate that year won the presidency; when the National League team won so did the Democrats. The record shows these winners: 1952—New York Yankees (A) and Eisenhower (R); 1956—New York Yankees (A) and Eisenhower (R); 1960—Pittsburgh Pirates (N) and Kennedy (D); 1964—St. Louis Cardinals (N) and Johnson (D); 1968—Detroit Tigers (A) and Nixon (R); 1972—Oakland Athletics (A) and Nixon (R); 1976—Cincinnati Reds (N) and Carter (D). And then in 1980 an American team, Kansas City, lost but a Republican, Reagan, won anyway. So maybe he can circumvent the 20-year morbid jinx.

In an amusing editorial on the phenomenon, entitled "Baseball and Crystal Ball," Oct. 15, 1980, the *Chicago Sun-Times* pointed out that the World Series victories had gone American, American, National, National, American, American, National, then question marks that were answered when National won again.

Disenchantment also resulted when the supposed inevitable didn't continue to be inevitable. Supposedly the political pendulum would swing from legislator to governor to nonelective candidates, as it had since Abraham Lincoln. Categorizing the public service for which every winner was best known indicates how the electorate considered its interests would best be represented. (See chart.)

Congressman	Governor	Nonelective
Lincoln		
	Johnson	
		Grant
	Hayes	
Garfield		
	Cleveland	
		Harrison
	Cleveland	
McKinley		
	Roosevelt	
		Taft
	Wilson	
Harding		
	Coolidge	
		Hoover
	Roosevelt	
Truman		

And then the pendulum went wild and, instead of Governor Stevenson, General Eisenhower became president. There followed another skip and three senators: Kennedy, Johnson and Nixon. With the election of Carter the pendulum resumed its "normal" course but then another governor, Reagan, upset the sequence. In this tabulation Arthur and Ford are omitted, as neither was chosen at the polls.

The curses that have received the most attention journalistically for many years have been those associated with the Hope diamond and the tomb of Egyptian King Tutankhamen, followed rather closely by the so-called Bermuda Triangle and the pyramids. Also, despite the postal laws, almost every American at one time or another has received a chain letter containing a prayer or plea for financial or other assistance that the recipient must give to avoid misfortune.

It is not possible to read what the papers have published during the past quarter-century and be confident one knows the facts about the 44½-carat Hope diamond, now in the Smithsonian Institution in Washington which received it Nov. 11, 1958 (1959 if you believe Robert L. Rose in the March 24, 1975 *Chicago Daily News*) as a gift from a New York jeweler, Henry Winston, who purchased it from the estate of Mrs. Evalyn Walsh McLean,

Washington society leader, who died April 26, 1947 of pneumonia at the age of 60. According to Mrs. McLean's will the gem was to be guarded for 20 years by four trustees until the three oldest of her seven grandchildren became 25. However, the sale was necessary to settle the estate according to a United Press dispatch for May 1, 1947. However, Diane Monk wrote in the Dec. 15, 1967 *Chicago Daily News* that Mrs. McLean's possessions, including the diamond, were to be kept in storage until her fifth grandchild and namesake became 25. The Monk article followed the death Dec. 12, 1967 of the namesake in Plano, Texas. It contained a summary of the gem's ownership as did the AP story Dec. 14, 1967 from Plano.

All of the diamond's biographers trace its western peregrinations when it was brought to Paris by a diamond merchant, Jean-Baptiste Tavernier, in 1642, according to Emery Hutchison in the *Chicago Daily News* for Nov. 29, 1958, or in 1645, according to Rose in the same paper's March 24, 1975 issue. Rose wrote that what came to be known as the Hope diamond was part of a 112½-carat diamond stolen from the eye of an Indian idol, Ramn Sita. Hutchison suggests it may have been a Buddhist idol, a Burmese god or a decoration in a Hindu temple, or maybe it was bought and paid for at the kollur diamond mines in India. Anyway, Tavernier sold the gem to France's King Louis XIV and the Buddhist, Burmese or Hindu curse began to work as Tavernier was killed by a pack of dogs. The Marquise de Montespan, to whom the king gave the jewel, fell from favor after being accused of Satanism, according to Rose, or of infidelity according to an Associated Press dispatch from Washington April 28, 1947. At any rate Louis XIV got the diamond back and his son, Louis XV, kept it locked up throughout his reign (one of the few facts on which all writers agree). Louis XVI, however, gave it to his queen, Marie Antoinette, and they both went to the guillotine. Princess de Lamballe, whom Marie Antoinette had permitted to wear the diamond, was killed by a revolutionary mob.

In the April 27, 1947 account of Mrs. McLean's death, the United Press declared the diamond once was part of the French crown jewels. Four days later, the UP said the "fabulous bauble" had been owned by Catherine the Great of Russia as well as by Marie Antoinette.

Hutchison reported that the diamond, which everyone agrees disappeared during the French Revolution, in 1792 came into the possession of Wilhelm Fals, a Dutch diamond cutter. He died a ruined man after his son Henrik stole the gem. Henrik committed suicide in London in 1830. That same year, the AP reported, the stone appeared on the French market, cut down from 66 (all others say 112) carats. A French broker, Francois Beaulieu, who said he got it from a nameless suicide, sold the diamond to an English broker, Daniel Eliason, and died the next day. Eliason sold it to an Irish banker, Thomas Henry Hope.

Hope gave the diamond to his daughter, the Duchess of Newcastle, who left it to her son, Lord Francis Pelham Clinton (Clinton-Hope, according to Hutchison). He gave it to his music hall bride, May Yohe, who left him and ended her life as a scrubwoman. Clinton-Hope also died penniless. Thereafter, according to Hutchison, a succession of ten owners all suffered misfortune, such as bankruptcy, murder and suicide. Eventually the famous French jeweler, Pierre Cartier, came into possession, and in 1908 or 1911 (Hutchison) it was purchased by Edward M. McLean, son of the former owner of the *Cincinnati Enquirer* and *Washington Post*. Their son was killed by an automobile and a daughter, Evalyn McLean Reynolds, fifth wife of Sen. Robert Reynolds (Dem., N.C.), 60, died at 24 of an overdose of sleeping pills Sept. 20, 1946, less than a year before her mother, who died April 26, 1947, aged 60. Edward McLean died in a mental hospital.

The UP ended its obituary of Mrs. Reynolds, Sept. 21, 1946, "There is a popular belief that the gem is a jinx, but members of the family have belittled the idea." The next day, Sept. 22, 1946, the AP distributed a story by Gardner L. Bridge from Washington that read, "A vague aura of mystery tonight surrounded the death," although the coroner said death resulted from "acute congestive heart failure."

When Mrs. McLean died the UP used a box with its main story April 27, 1947, to declare, "The Hope diamond has a long reputation as a 'jinxed' stone whose ownership carries with it a cloud of tragedy." Mrs. McLean died of pneumonia after being under oxygen treatment for 24 hours. The next day, April 28, 1947, the AP began its story from Washington, "What is to become of the fabulous Hope diamond with its reputed curse was the question that engrossed capital society today . . ."

May 1, 1947 the UP began its story of the contents of Mrs. McLean's will, "The tragedy-haunted Hope diamond, whose supposed jinx followed Society Leader Evalyn Walsh McLean to her deathbed last Saturday was removed from circulation today—perhaps forever."

Study of the complete history of the fabulous jewel reveals that at least half of those who owned or used it seemingly were not affected by any curse. How unusual is it for about half of the members of any family to experience bad luck? For almost a quarter-century the Smithsonian Institution has not suffered from fire, theft or death as a result of its famous possession. Because of the prominence of many of the diamond's owners the press has kept alive the myth of a curse, translating every untoward occurrence to fit the pattern.

Dec. 29, 1968 the AP reported from New Delhi a diamond necklace, said to have once been worn by Marie Antoinette, got no bidders at an auction because it was thought to have been cursed. From Washington the AP also reported that James G. Todd, who delivered a registered mail package containing the diamond to the Smithsonian Institution, asserts he is not superstitious "and never will be." However, his leg has been crushed by a truck, and his wife, mother of four, died from a heart attack while he was recuperating. Todd also was thrown from a car in an accident; his dog jumped through a basement window and was strangled to death and four second-story rooms in his house were wrecked by fire.

In Burbank, Calif. to assist in filming a CBS special, "The Legendary Curse of the Hope Diamond," the curator of gems at the Smithsonian Institution told Robert L. Rose for the *Chicago Daily News* of March 24, 1975, "The Hope may have been a curse to others but it has been good for the Smithsonian." Oct. 22, 1970, however, columnist Art Buchwald wrote that "the mess" the country was in could be traced to the gem's arrival at the Smithsonian. As a solution the humorist suggested giving it to the Soviet Union, China or the widow of Mao Tse-tung.

The myth of the Tutankhamen curse was created and nurtured by sensational journalists. Someone falsely reported that the expedition that discovered the tomb of the Egyptian pharaoh in 1922 hesitated to open the innermost room because of an inscription, "Death shall come on swift wings to him that touches the tomb of Pharaoh." Actually, the delay in completing the excavation was to give Lord Carnarvon time to return from England.

There was no such warning, as those who participated in the removal of the mummy of the 18-year-old king who ruled 3,300 years earlier have stated, but whenever anyone dies the nonexistent curse is mentioned as a possible cause.

What provoked the hoax was the death of Lord Carnarvon, co-leader of the expedition, five months after the inner wall of the tomb was opened. News accounts suggested mystery; actually, Lord Carnarvon died from double pneumonia complicated by erysipelas caused by a mosquito bite. Howard Carter, co-leader who broke the seals on the inner doors, died in 1939 at the age of 66. Chicago's James Henry Breasted was 70 when he died in 1935. Prof. Douglas E. Derry, who unwrapped and dissected King Tut's mummy, was 75 in 1950 according to an Associated Press story from Washington Jan. 8, 1950.

That iconoclastic article was typical of many that were written even after the fact that most of those who participated in desecrating the tomb were unaffected by any curse. Henry Hanson interviewed Prof. John A. Wilson of the University of Chicago Oriental Institute who vigorously debunked the curse myth. The account appeared in the *Chicago Daily News* for Nov. 12, 1956. Nevertheless, reporters persist in quizzing principals. When an exhibit of some of the King Tut treasures couldn't be unlocked at the Chicago Natural History Museum because the key was unavailable, it was news on which to capitalize. So Lois Wille revealed in her story for the June 5, 1962 *News* that she asked if the notorious curse was to blame. A museum official replied, "I don't think so. All I know is we feel pretty foolish."

More important, a long account of the X-raying of Tut's body, which led experts to believe he met a violent death, included a statement by the University of Liverpool professor who made the X-rays at Luxor that he hoped the body would not have to be disturbed again. Thereupon the author of an AP story Oct. 26, 1969, wrote: "If that wish is fulfilled maybe the ancient curse which has haunted so many of those associated with discovery of his tomb will finally be laid to rest."

Probably it won't be, not as long as there are some who think they can profit by keeping it alive and irresponsible journalists to contribute to the myth.

In a letter to the *Toronto Star* for Oct. 9, 1975, Edmund S. Meltzer said other newspapers started the curse rumor because they were angry when Lord Carnarvon gave the *London Times* exclusive rights to the story. He also said archeologists are fulfilling the hope of the ancient Egyptians that they and their works be remembered.

Jan. 13, 1982 the UPI reported from San Francisco that a police officer who guarded some of the Tut treasures on display there in 1979 had filed a suit for $18,000 disability pay from the city Retirement Board, charging the curse was responsible for a stroke he suffered.

Articles in trashy magazines and books likewise keep alive the myth of the Bermuda Triangle, an area formed by drawing a line from Miami southeast to Puerto Rico, north to Bermuda and back to Miami. The bible for believers is *The Bermuda Triangle* by Charles Berlitz, who claims that an inordinate number of ships and planes mysteriously disappear in the area. A point-by-point rebuttal is included in *The Bermuda Triangle Mystery—Solved* by Lawrence David Kusche, an Arizona State University research librarian. Richard R. Lingmen wrote in the *New York Times Book Review* for Feb. 14, 1975, "Although the zany success of Charles Berlitz's book, which now has over 215,000 copies in print, may be dismissed as simply a mutation of popular taste, students of the delusion of crowds might want to mount it in their specimen trays." Of Kusche's scholarship he said, "He demonstrates that those incidents on which reliable information exists are plausibly explainable by natural causes or human error—or didn't occur in the Bermuda Triangle at all."

Three months later, May 11, 1975, the *Times* reported that total sales had reached 350,000 copies and the book had been on the best-seller list for 26 weeks, the last 15 in first place. Another book, originally a pamphlet by the same name, had sold 175,000, the author being Adi-Kent Thomas Jeffrey.

Entitled, "Solved: the Bermuda Triangle 'hoax,' " Philip Nobile's Q and A interview with Kusche got a full page in the *Chicago Sun-Times* for March 4, 1975. The researcher revealed that the myth really began in 1965 when Vincent Gaddis published *Invisible Horizons,* with a chapter on the so-called triangle, after which a number of pulp magazines had sensational articles. Historically, Kusche found about twice as many disappearances between New York/Boston and Europe. After obtaining Kusche's answers to other questions, Nobile concluded: "If I were Berlitz or any other believer in the Triangle I'd be awfully ashamed."

John J. O'Connor concluded his review of public television's "Nova" program on the Triangle thus: "The tracing by 'Nova' is painstaking and as detail is piled on detail the case for debunking becomes extremely convincing." On the other hand the full-page color illustrated advertisement for John Coleman's weeklong program on WLS-TV cites many of the unproved Berlitz charges.

There was circumstantial evidence that astrologers and other psychics believe their own prophecies when 75 of them canceled a Caribbean cruise that would have taken them into the mythical Bermuda Triangle. Jean Boyd of Silver Spring, Md., who planned the excursion, heard from Irene Hughes that she had "very negative vibrations about the cruise." An Ohio psychic saw seven crosses in a dream, which caused her to cancel, and others responded similarly. Noel Epstein reported the news July 28, 1975 for the *Washington Post*.

Finally the Federal Aviation Administration in its magazine *FAA World* scoffed at the existence of any supernatural explanation for any accidents in the area called the Bermuda Triangle. Nov. 16, 1975 the *Chicago Sun-Times* reprinted a *Los Angeles Times* special summarizing the agency's report.

In its World Digest column Jan. 17, 1977 the Chicago *Daily News* reported that a Soviet mathematical physicist had warned the Bermuda Triangle would be especially dangerous the next day because the sun, moon and earth would be in the same positions then as during previously recorded disasters where more than 100 ships and a score of airplanes have disappeared since 1945.

The interest of the Soviets was explained in a lengthy article reprinted from *Oceans,* the magazine of the Oceanic Society, submitted by the Soviet press agency. The *Chicago Tribune* ran it Oct. 8, 1977. As a result of experiences encountered aboard a Russian icebreaker in the Arctic, the Soviet researchers concluded that weak infrasounds cause seasickness and may lead to digestive disorders and emotional upsets. Other theories held by Russian scientists and cosmonauts are mentioned.

Oct. 10, 1977 the AP reported from Moscow that a Soviet research team had returned from a study of the Bermuda Triangle and had concluded that "nothing supernatural" is responsible for any disasters there, and "there were no unexplainable phenomena—either mental or environmental."

This followed a new shocker from Berlitz that the Agence France-Presse reported April 6, 1977 from Mexico City. The author's claim is that he has discovered a pyramid on the sea's bottom larger than the famous Cheops pyramid in Egypt. This, Berlitz said, could be the key to proving the existence of the mythical civilization of Atlantis. Thus was rekindled hope that had ebbed four years earlier when an expedition of about 79 American scholars, students and others, with financing from Mrs. Maxine Asher of Pepperdine University, who had been searching for 12 years for the legendary continent that vanished beneath the sea 11,000 years before Plato wrote of it in the fourth century B.C.

When the beginning of the expedition, which had the Gulf of Cadiz as its objective, was reported in the *New York Times* for July 5, 1973, Mrs. Asher said: "I simply know we will find it because I am psychic. Oh God, how strong the vibrations are these days, and I know that the highly civilized people of Atlantis also were very psychic."

Aug. 8, 1973 the Associated Press reported from Cadiz, Spain that the 50 students, who paid $3,000 each to be a part of the expedition to earn college credits, had abandoned the quest. At the same time Mrs. Asher said scuba divers had photographed "man-made roads and columns" on the sea bottom.

The failure of one venture never discourages those who seek another. In *The Great Lakes Triangle,* Jay Gourley postulated that the Great Lakes and the Bermuda Triangle are on the same "agonic line," a line of zero magnetic deviation where true north and the magnetic north are the same. Gourley suggests that interplanetery visitors might like to use that route. John Camper concluded in his review of the book in the *Chicago Daily News* for Aug. 6, 1977 that the events described probably were caused by "giant birds [that] swooped down and took the planes and ships to the North Pole where a big white bear ate them." Nobody spoke up to contradict this theory.

Basing their hypothesis on "mysterious structures" seen in 460 photographs of sunken Ampere Mountain, Soviet oceanographers said they may have found Atlantis about 450 miles west of Gibraltar, Bryan Brumley reported for the Associated Press from Moscow April 5, 1981. The positions and regular shapes of blocks suggest artificial origin, the Soviets reported. This was hardly fresh news. The *New York Times* had the same story, written by Craig R. Whitney, May 21, 1979. Prof. Andrei Arkadyevich Aksyonov said he had photographic evidence, 11 stones that bear the mark of human handiwork.

A detailed examination of the Berlitz claims, beginning with the 1945 disappearance of five Navy Avenger aircraft, is to be found in *Flim-Flam!* a debunking book by a foremost magician, James Randi. A majority of the disasters supposed to have occurred in the triangle actually occurred outside it. Randi includes a map on which the sites are marked. According to him, "The media are largely to blame for the Bermuda Triangle deception." He also blames book publishers for uncritical acceptance of trashy manuscripts. He summarizes the phenomenon: "It is the product of mass exposure, repeated lies, large profits from book sales, irresponsible publishers, a gullible public and the current taste for the ridiculous."

Another not-so-well-known lost continent was Mu, whose believers say was seven times as large as North America, covering most of the South Pacific. The facts about it presumably were revealed in 1936 to Dr. Robert D. Stelle, a Chicago homeopathic doctor. Today the Lemurian Fellowship he founded has a very modern headquarters on a mountaintop in San Diego County, California. Since Stelle's death in 1952 the president has been Reynolds G. Dennis, who was quoted by Charles Hillinger in the *Los*

Angeles Times for July 31, 1977: "We believe everyone living on Earth today is a descendant of the world's original civilization. We believe each and every human being alive today has walked the face of the earth for thousands of years in a succession of different bodies. We have all lived on earth since the beginning."

To their credit standard newspapers have not gone all-out to perpetuate the Bermuda Triangle myth. They, in fact, now play down to a few short paragraphs such accounts as the one the AP sent from New York March 11, 1981 that the Coast Guard was searching shark-infested waters in the Bermuda Triangle for 12 men missing since an Israeli freighter sank a day earlier. After enjoying a deep-sea fishing trip in the area, Irving Kupcinet wrote May 18, 1975 from Club Cay, Bermuda that he sided with Kusche rather than Berlitz. Kup's column originates in the *Chicago Sun-Times*.

When a reader asked help in finding accounts of the Philadelphia Experiment mentioned in a movie and some paperbacks, the *Chicago Sun-Times'* Action Time replied that Berlitz says in 1943 the Navy rendered the destroyer escort *U.S.S. Eldridge* invisible and then teleported the craft from Philadelphia to Norfolk and back. The Navy denies the story, which is included in a book by Berlitz and William Moore.

Oct. 17, 1981 the UPI dispatched a 1,000-word story from Charleston, S.C. saying the Coast Guard could not determine the cause of the sinking a year earlier of *Brecks & Joy* near the Bermuda Triangle. Probable cause was the fouling of the propeller, but it was difficult to understand why the boat did not alter its course, as other craft did when bad weather harassed them.

During the past century and longer there have been an abundance of crackpot theories concerning the pyramids in Egypt, Mexico and other places. Since the space explorations began the lunatic fringe has been titillated by fictional accounts of invaders from other worlds visiting Earth long enough to build the pyramids, Stonehenge, airfields in Peru, sculptures on Easter Island and other contemporary tourist attractions. Science fiction, trash magazines and television have contributed much more to public ignorance than has the press.

Almost since the ancient Egyptian civilization ended 3,000 or so years ago there have been scores, hundreds of attempts in research papers, articles and books to explain the supposed mysteries of the Giza complex of pyramids in the desert just 11 or so miles south of Cairo. Without modern machinery and engineering knowhow, how were 2.3 million blocks of stone, weighing from 2 to 70 tons each, lifted to build something as high as a 40-story building, large enough to enclose 30 Empire State Buildings?

Judging by the account in the *New York Times* for Aug. 16, 1971 the true answer to the riddle of the Great Pyramid may be in Peter Tompkins' book, *Secrets of the Great Pyramid*. Whoever built it as a megalithic calendar by which the length of the year, including the awkward .2422 fraction of a day, was measured, the article said, knew the precise circumstance of the planet and the length of the year to several decimals—data which were not discovered till the 17th century.

A more detailed description of the Cheops pyramid, the largest, was given by Edwin Newman in the article "O great Cheops, what hath thy offspring wrought?" in the *New York Times Magazine* for Aug. 29, 1976. The "parent of pyramid power may be a Frenchman named Antoine Bovis," he wrote and explained that Bovis discovered a room one-third of the way up in the Cheops pyramid. In it he made the startling discovery of garbage cans filled with dead cats and other small animals that had been mummified. The story is told in more detail in *Psychic Discoveries Behind the Iron Curtain*, by Sheila Ostrander and Lynn Schroeder, who, along with other writers, surmised some sort of mysterious energy generated within a pyramid with the same relative proportions as Cheops. In 1959 a Czech electronics engineer named Karl Drbal received a patent for a small cardboard pyramid in which, he claimed, a razor blade remained sharp for 200 shaves. Since then belief in pyramid power has spread worldwide. Newman explained as follows:

> Pyramid power is based on the belief that the shape of the great Cheops pyramid near Cairo, when reproduced to scale, focuses energy in a psychic or mystical way that produces surprising and beneficial results. No negative effects have yet been reported. The belief, among some scientists and many more would-be scientists, is that the pyramid design creates an environment that somehow serves as a resonator altering the quality of whatever falls within its aura.

A good summary of what contemporary addicts believe was given by Cindy Rose in the *Chicago Sun-Times* for Feb. 22, 1977, in which she wrote: "According to a widening circle of devotees pyramids provide new power for the people. They can sharpen razor blades, sweeten wine, cure sick plants, lessen pain, improve sex life and boost psychic energy." She cited specific examples of persons who bought or built pyramids to overcome any weakness. She estimated that 100,000 persons had purchased six-foot pyramids at $89.95 retail and many times that number had bought smaller pyramids during the preceding five years.

Rose's article was objective. To many it was comical that the Toronto Maple Leafs lost the Stanley Cup hockey playoffs despite their placing pyramids under their bench and at other strategic places. Others were impressed by the fact that, when Ted Sizemore forgot his pyramid, his team, the Los Angeles Dodgers, lost a road trip.

Numerous examples of persons who claimed they benefited from pyramid powers were included in the first of a series of articles by Marilynn Preston, "The Pyramid Mystique," in the *Chicago Tribune* for April 17, 1977. Example: a withered cactus revived, milk turned to creamy white yogurt while another glass soured, and so on. Also there was a sidebar of diagrams and directions for how to build one's own pyramid. The negative views of several scholars were cited, but Dr. Michael Kosok of Fairleigh Dickinson University declared, "There's no question, no question whatsoever, that something happens under the pyramid."

In the second of her series, April 18, 1977, Preston reported on 25 experiments conducted by the Mankind Research Foundation with some startling and some not-so-startling results. Dr. Ted Horner was reluctant to discuss the matter, but admitted the most scientifically significant results involved the meat decay experiments. Hamburger under the pyramid registered 2.3, whereas uncovered meat was 4.6 and had decayed. Dr. Kosok was quoted at length as to both his experiments and opinions, almost all favorable to the theory of pyramid power.

The third day Preston told the story of Rosemary Clark, "professional astrologer, teacher, lecturer on the occult sciences and the founder of what may well be the country's only serious temple dedicated to the rites and rituals of the ancient Egyptians, the Temple of Ra-Heru-Khuti."

The 15 members meet twice monthly to study the wonders of Egyptian life and knowledge, such as how they were able to make such precise mathematical calculations. One authority says the Great Pyramid stands in the exact center of the Earth's land mass. Also, it now seems the ancients must have known the exact circumference of the Earth and the length of the year to several decimals, data presumably not known until the 17th century.

The interest in pyramid power stimulated by the American tour of treasures from King Tut's tomb was reflected in the commercial fashion world. Eugenia Sheppard wrote about how manufacturers catered to the interest in things Egyptian in an article, "Pyramid Power in the Marketplace," in the *New York Post* for June 2, 1977.

In the feature "Power to the Pyramids," to which the *Chicago Daily News* gave two full pages July 7, 1977, John Petrie related some personal failures in trying to take advantage of pyramid power. Most of his article, however, was devoted to the history of pyramidology, which he says began with the publication of *The Great Pyramid: Why Was It Built and Who Built It?* by John Taylor in 1959. Taylor thought some Old Testament character, probably Noah, built the Great Pyramid of Giza in Egypt. He contributed to the King Tut mystery by stating that at the moment of Lord Carnarvon's death Cairo experienced a five-minute blackout, still unexplained. And three years later, other explorers discovered a mosquito-like wound on the neck of King Tut's remains.

A bewildering contribution to the controversy was made by Don Hayner in the *Suburban Trib* for May 6, 1981. Subject matter was the efforts of Jim Onan to build a pyramid, 54 feet high with an 85-square-foot base, near Gurnee, Ill. Four people who worked on it died, and there were many mishaps: plywood delaminated and fell apart, as did window caulking. Most baffling was the water that flooded the structure and the differences chemical analyses discovered between sealed bottles of water inside the edifice and those outside.

July 6, 1982 the *Chicago Tribune* ran a picture of the Gurnee pyramid together with a story describing the structure. Onan's purpose was given as: "to test the alleged mystical powers of structures of that shape."

Athletes not only have confidence in good luck charms and omens; they also are notorious for their faith in evil eyes and curses to weaken opponents. Especially superstitious in this regard are baseball players. In 1945, for instance, Philip Wrigley, Chicago Cubs owner, refused to admit a goat to the World Series between the Cubs and the Tigers. Five years later, according to the *Sun-Times* for Sept. 22, 1950, Wrigley wrote an apology to the goat's owner, William "Billy Goat" Sianis, proprietor of Billy Goat Inn, a hangout for journalists as well as sportsmen. In part the letter read: "Will you please extend to him (Murphy the goat) my most sincere and abject apologies . . . and ask him not only to remove the 'hex' but to reverse the flow and start pulling for wins." Opening day 1982 was highlighted by a parade of a goat as the team's mascot. This was obviously a sports department publicity stunt, but other stories related seriously the superstitions of many players, especially those of Cubs manager Leo Durocher, who refused to discard a dirty sweater during a winning streak or to permit a team picture, as related in the preceding chapter.

Beginning Sunday July 4 through the first two innings of the Thursday, July 8, 1976 game, Cubs pitchers held the opponents scoreless for 31 straight innings. In his pre-game story on the latter day, Joe Goddard reported in the *Sun-Times* that a radio station had hired a self-proclaimed witch, Ruth Revzen, to cast an evil eye on Randy Jones, San Diego Padres star pitcher, and at the same time bless all Cub hitters during batting practice. After the Cubs lost, 6 to 3, the next day's headline was "So much for good luck charms." Bill Madlock, who, with José Cardenal, refused the blessing, declared, "It wasn't Randy Jones who beat us. It was that bleeping witch." The witch, Goddard reported, "dabbed potion lotion (juices of magnolia, cypress and cinnamon) on the foreheads and hands of a number of players, including starting pitcher Bill Bonham. The clubhouse smelled like the perfume counter at Marshall Field's with the odor just falling short of Chanel No. 5."

Among the firsts scored by Charlie Finley, eccentric owner of the Oakland Athletics, an American league baseball team, was hiring astrologer Laurie Brady to be the team's official astrologer. Her duties consisted of preparing horoscopes and forecasts rather than casting spells on opponents. Professional boxing by contrast, has had Benjamin "Evil-Eye" Finkel, who put the hex on fighters for a fee from their opponents' managers. His operations were described by Robert C. Ruark in his syndicated column for Aug. 8, 1949 on the occasion of the imminent heavyweight championship contest between Ezzard Charles, the title holder, and Augustus Lesnevich. "Things being equal, I cannot see how Mr. Charles can possibly avert some horrid tragedy for Mr. Finkel is a very proud fellow and possessed of tremendous vindictive powers," Ruark wrote. Charles won the fight.

In his column in the April 3, 1973 *Sun-Times* Irving Kupcinet recalled Finkel and Jimmy Grippo, a nightclub hypnotist who cast spells to benefit former light-heavyweight champion Melio Bettina. Both men, Kup wrote, "were good for laughs and a box office hypo." Kup's immediate interest was the belief held by some that a hypnotist, Michael Dean, helped Ken Norton win the heavyweight championship from Muhammad Ali. That the generally objective Kup has his secret beliefs was indicated in his column for Sept. 15, 1982, when he wrote, "And once again a trilogy of death—Henry Fonda, Ingrid Bergman and now Princess Grace." July 31, 1983 Kup wrote, "Once again celebrity deaths come in 'threes'—David Niven, Lynn Fontanne and Raymond Massey.

The story " 'Evil-Eye' Still Casting Spell on Life in Italy" was related in a Reuters dispatch from Rome Dec. 14, 1975. To break a spell one woman dipped her finger into a spoon containing olive oil, and, muttering an incantation, allowed seven drops to fall in a plate of water. When the oil sank and dissolved into a shapeless cloud, the performer of the ancient rite confirmed the existence of a spell. On the third test the drops of oil remained as round, compact globules floating on top of the water—an indication that the spell was broken.

Millions of Italians still believe in the evil eye. Even the president clenched his fists and projected the first and fourth fingers of each hand to ward off a curse.

In the *Wall Street Journal* Sept. 8, 1981, Edmund Fuller gave "A Provocative History of the 'Dreaded Evil Eye,' " based mostly on Lawrence DiStasi's book, *Mal Occhio (Evil Eye): The Underside of Vision*. It included:

> All the countries around the Mediterranean, and others, share the dread of the blighting eye. In Turkey one sees horses, donkeys, even taxicabs decked out with blue ceramic beads that repel the evil eye as garlic repels vampires.

The principal targets of *Mal Occhio* are "the valued, vulnerable ones, children, pregnant women, crops and farm animals, particularly dairy animals. The source of the evil, whether consciously or unconsciously, was envy." A jettatore is one with eyes that damage whatever they see, without malicious intent. Some thought Pope Paul IX was one.

One of the most fascinating accounts of how a fan can use his psychic influence was composed by one of Chicago's all-time journalistic greats, Lloyd Lewis, at various times book editor, managing editor and sports editor of the *News*, as well as author of several books involving Chicago and Illinois history. In the *Chicago Sun* for Oct. 27, 1946 Lewis described how he and his two dogs listened to radio broadcasts of the World Series in which the St. Louis Cardinals, whom Lewis favored, won a close victory

over the Boston Red Sox. Neither humans nor animals were allowed to
change positions or engage in extraneous activities lest what happened on
the ballfield a thousand miles away might be affected. Lewis' masterpiece
described the anguish of a loyal fan and his frustration at not being able to
assist his heroes.

A more recent insight into the sports fan's mind was the *Sun-Times*
satirical editorial, "The Devil Made Them Do It?" Aug. 11, 1980. It was
inspired by the action of 200 fans in Richmond, Mich. who petitioned the
school trustees to require the public school sports teams to change their
"satanic" nicknames: Blue Devils at the high school; Demons at the middle
school and Red Devils at elementary grades. The objectors charged that
"the devil is the father of lies, and the instigator of all evil . . . The name
is synonymous with snakes, scorpions, darkness, filthiness, injustice,
unholiness, sorcery, witchcraft, idolatry and every other evil imaginable."
The *Sun-Times* recalled that the students picked the names themselves in
1947 to honor the World War II Air Corps unit known as the Blue Devils.

In recommending that the nicknames not be changed Superintendent
Wayne F. Case said, "I do not agree that the Blue Devil of Richmond is a
symbol of evil. All schools have nicknames or mascots and the Blue Devil is
the Richmond mascot. A Blue Devil is a representative of the school; there
is much pride associated with being part of the school. Many people have
represented our school; they are proud to be called Richmondites or Blue
Devils. There is no connotation toward evil." The board voted 6 to 1 to
uphold the recommendation but suggested that consideration be given to
moving from the evil face to a comic one for the devil and requested the
student council to consider community feelings when ordering things for
sale and perhaps ordering so people could have a choice of buying something with a devil on it or without a devil.

A similar protest was reported to have occurred in Vernon, N.Y. the
Associated Press reported June 13, 1981. There a grandmother, shocked
when her grandson proudly told her he was a Red Devil, organized God's
Concerned Citizens to try to persuade the school board that the devil must
go. Superintendent Albert Kouba commented, "If they could come to me
and show me that the mascot makes our kids different in any adverse ways,
then we'd consider changing the thing." So the mat outside the school door
continues to read, "Welcome to the home of the Red Devils," a sign in the
basketball gym reads "Satan's Pit," the newspaper is called the *Devil's
Advocate* and the devil's head is painted on gym floors and on souvenir
mugs, pencils and class rings. March 12, 1982 Kouba wrote, "the issue has
died down without any change to our school mascot."

Dave of Park Ridge wanted to know "How did DePaul get the name
'Blue Demons' and what's so blue about a demon?" The *Chicago Sun-Times*
Action Time informed him March 16, 1981 that the nickname derived from
the blue D's on the sweaters of lettermen who came to be called D men; the

transition to demons was easy in 1924. Nobody, Action Time said, can be positive about the color of demons.

Just as 13 generally is shunned as unlucky, so other numbers are believed to be lucky. One such number is 7. Although he declared he was not superstitious Jim Crowley, coach of the Chicago Rockets football team, pointed out that "perhaps the number 7 might hold something favorable in store for the boys," according to Will Anderson in the *Chicago Times* for Oct. 10, 1947. Anderson commented that 7 entered the picture in a definitely negative way: the Rockets would be trying to avoid a seventh straight defeat in their forthcoming game with the San Francisco 49ers.

After he was robbed of his wallet, Paul of Skokie, a reader, was distressed because the Illinois secretary of state's office would not issue him a new driver's license dated the same day as the original. That date was July 7, 1977, a 7-7-77 combination that will not appear again for a century. Paul tried unsuccessfully to obtain the help of the Action Time, the *Sun-Times* reported Jan. 21, 1981.

July 7, 1977 had received journalistic notice. The *News* used a five-column headline, "Lucky day? 7th day of 7th month—it could be magic" over a United Press International story which began:

> Seventh son of a seventh son . . . roll a seven to win . . . on the seventh day God rested . . . seven virtues and seven deadly sins . . . seven years of bad luck for a broken mirror . . . seven wonders of the world.

The article said "no number is more suspicious—for good or evil." Betters, it reported, favored the seventh horse in the seventh race on July 7, 1977, although at least one oddsmaker told them the horse probably would come in seventh. At Florida's Hialeah racetrack there were no odds and no payoff for the seventh race that day. Parachutist Ken Wallace of Harrisburg, Ill. planned to make seven jumps in seven states within a period of seven hours, seven minutes and with a seven-second free fall on every jump.

The next day, July 8, 1977 a followup UPI story reported that most betters failed to win except at Hollywood Park in Inglewood, Calif., where those who bet on the 7-7 combination in the daily double got $17.20 on a $2 bet. The rest of the article reported a 100-year-old Virginia woman who was born on the seventh hour of the seventh day of the seventh month in 1877, on a Saturday, the seventh day of the week. Also mentioned was an Australian baby born seven days late.

In his June 14, 1961 column Sydney J. Harris enumerated the apparent influence of the number 40 in myths, legends and customs. Moses was 40 days on the mount; Elijah was fed by ravens for 40 days; the rain of the flood fell for 40 days and it was another 40 days before Noah left the ark; Jesus fasted for 40 days in the desert and was seen 40 days after his resurrection. In medieval times a widow was allowed to remain in her husband's home for 40 days; the privilege of sanctuary was for 40 days; tenants gave their knight landlords 40 days of labor.

And so on, throughout recorded history. No explanation, however, as to why, or of how any supernatural forces played a part and, if so, why? The same questions can be asked about 7 or any other number, especially regarding lucky numbers that individuals seem to have, or say they do. As Bob Herguth quoted Eva K. Edwards of Manhattan in his Jan. 22, 1981 column, the number 4 was important for the hostages when being held in Iran: they were captured Nov. 4, were in captivity 444 days, or 14 months; they were released during the inauguration of the 40th president. Eight men were killed trying to rescue 52; subtracting 8 from 52 you get 44. And Iran is a four-letter word.

Hank Aaron's lucky number also seems to be 4, according to Kup's column for April 11, 1974. Bernie Kriss is quoted as noticing that Aaron wore No. 4, hit his record-breaking 715th home run off Al Downing, whose number was 44, in the fourth inning of the fourth month at the age of 40.

In an earlier column Dec. 16, 1968 Kup reported that numerologists were having a field day with the forthcoming space flight a few days before Christmas. It was the Apollo 8 flight and Santa Claus has eight reindeer. The three spacemen also were being compared with the biblical three wise men.

All of this may seem far-fetched to laymen but not to numerology addicts. They make predictions based on their studies. In its Nov. 25, 1942 issue the *Sun* ran a prediction of a numerologist who signed himself Jamac of Evanston. To him it seemed likely that World War II would end Sept. 3, 1944, because the dates by which American wars are identified—1776, 1812, 1898, 1917 and 1941—added up to 9344.

The prediction of a Vietnamese numerologist that the war there with the United States would end in 1972 was belittled by the *Sun-Times* editorially March 24, 1969. The numerologist had pointed out that most major wars ended in years of which the last two digits added up to nine: World War I in 1918, World War II in 1945, the Geneva accord on Vietnam in 1954. The *Sun-Times* pointed out that both the French-Indian War and the Seven Years War ended in 1763. However, there was as much reason to predict 1971 because so many other conflicts ended in years of which the last two digits added up to eight: Korean War, 1953; Franco-Prussian War, 1871 and the Hundred Year War, 1453. Using 11 the Vietnam war should end in 1974, the following wars having concluded in years whose last two digits added up to 11: Civil, 1865; Revolutionary, 1783; Crimean, 1856.

Numerologists obviously consider coincidences significant. The *Chicago Daily News* for Oct. 30, 1952 carried an Associated Press story from Summit, N.J. of a prediction by the Human Engineering Foundation that Dwight D. Eisenhower would be elected because his last name had ten letters whereas there were only nine in Stevenson. In 98 percent of the presidential elections of the preceding 60 years the candidate with the longer name won, the foundation pointed out.

During World War II several numerological predictions made the rounds. About the silliest was reported by Dale Harrison in his column in the *Sun* for Jan. 20, 1944. For any important figure, set down the year of birth, the year of attaining power, length of time in office and age. Add the four figures and divide by two. Invariably the outcome would be the current year. Many of the gullible were unable to figure out why such was the case.

Many actors and other entertainers have changed their names or use professional names while retaining their original names in their private lives. Often the change is to Anglicize a foreign name; so David Daniel Kominsky becomes Danny Kaye and Frederick Asterlitz becomes Fred Astaire which has the added advantage of being short enough to fit on most theater marquees. Others, especially at the beginning of their careers, consult numerologists, who recommend changes. The *Sun-Times* for Nov. 12, 1956 featured a UP story from Hollywood telling of how actress Jil Jarmyn changed her name four times on the advice of a numerologist who worked in a restaurant. In their Oct. 21, 1971 column in the *News,* Jon and Abra reported that on the advice of her numerologist model Marcia Metzger Binzer changed her name to Marcha, pronounced Marka. There were no followups to record the effect on the performer's fortunes.

There have not been many attempts by the press to explain the so-called science of numerology. One was an article, "The Numerology of Dr. Matrix," by Martin Gardner in the *Chicago Daily News* Panorama section for March 30, 1968. Dr. Irving Joshua Matrix claimed to be the reincarnation of Pythagoras. Gardner is on the editorial board of the *Skeptical Inquirer,* publication of the Committee for the Scientific Investigation of the Paranormal. The examples that Matrix gave Gardner were almost impossible to comprehend. For example, Matrix said numerologists are certain that William Shakespeare worked secretly on the King James Version of the Bible. They derive their idea from the fact that the 46th word in Psalm 46 is "shake" and the 46th word from the end of the Psalm is "spear" and when the translation was completed in 1610 Shakespeare was 46 years old. The best-known Psalm is the 23rd; 23 is half of 46. Case proved!

David Clarkson Swarm failed to convince Philip Nobile of his credibility, Nobile related in his Q and A interview with the numerologist that the Universal Press Syndicate distributed March 11, 1973. Explained Nobile, "Numerology, if you don't already know it, is a 'science' on a par with astrology which explains human affairs through the interpretation of names and numbers. Give Swarm your first name and birth date and he'll tell you all about yourself."

Numerology began with Pythagoras, a Greek philosopher who taught that numbers are the basis of all things, including human personality.

Nobile chided Swarm for his inability to prove cause and effect relationships, mistaking cause and coincidence. Swarm provided an example of the powers inherent in names: "For instance, persons whose first names begin with a vowel and have no protective consonant will tend to have their emotions closer to the surface than persons whose first names begin with a protective consonant."

As a result of a protest by a Carol Stream-based evangelical group the Internal Revenue Service consented to abandon the numbers 666 for one of its forms. The religionists quoted Revelation 13:18: "Let those who are able to interpret this code: The numerical value of the letters in his [the Antichrist's] name add to 666." William Harms wrote the story for the June 24, 1981 *Chicago Tribune*.

During rehearsals for a New York ballet production of *The Dybbuk*, Leonard Bernstein, the conductor, talked to Richard F. Sheppard for a story in the *New York Times* for May 9, 1974. It is a classic story that has much to do with cabala, traditional Jewish mysticism, and the plot is about a disembodied spirit of a dead person that has entered the body of a live one, with tragic consequences. Bernstein said, "Every note in the ballet was arrived at by cabalistic or mystical manipulation of numbers."

The powerful influence that belief in numerology has in some other parts of the world was described by Peter R. Kann in the *Wall Street Journal* for March 20, 1969. The article was written in Saigon and dealt mainly with South Vietnam. Kann wrote: "Fortune telling here is a respected art that influences much more than the private lives of Vietnamese. Indeed, it is inextricably part of the fabric of politics and the affairs of state."

The number of articles in the South Vietnamese constitution is said to have been dictated by a numerologist, according to Kann. The date of the inauguration of President Nguyen Van Thieu was set and then changed on advice of an astrologer.

Kann's article is jampacked with other examples of how the destinies of millions of people are determined by what the stars or the numbers advise.

Even more esoteric is an offshoot, biorhythm, which is predicated on the concept of three cycles that occur from the moment of birth, as astrological forces presumably also do. A 23-day cycle for men and a 28-day feminine cycle were graphed by two Viennese numerologists, Hermann Swoboda and Wilhelm Fliess, and a third, an intellectual cycle was discovered later by an engineer named Alfred Teltscher. So now there are charts showing curves of physical, emotional and intellectual cycles. By using the charts giving birth year, month and day one can determine his permanent biorhythms. Newspapers that run such a feature publish the physical, emotional and intellectual numbers so any reader can determine what the day holds for him. For instance, on a day that I exerted myself to make a difficult trip (difficult because of transportation) to Milwaukee for a day of strenuous interviewing, my prospects were: physical—overexertion not for you; emotional—easy to get along with; intellectual—avoid decision-making. James Randi ends his chapter in *Flim-Flam!* on biorhythms: "The so-called science of biorhythm is nothing more than glorified numerology that, on the basis of a simple birth date and some supposed research, generates infantile emotions about predetermined cycles that govern human existence. It is one of the purist—and simplest—forms of idiocy to assume the mantle of logic and science."

A *Discover* feature that papers used Jan. 24, 1982 reviewed an article in the September 1981 issue of *American Journal of Psychiatry* reporting the findings of researchers at the Veterans Administration Center in New Orleans that led them to conclude: "The biorhythm theory is much too simplistic to account for the complexities of everyday life." The doctors had examined the biorhythm charts of 600 psychiatric patients. Scientists at Oak Ridge National Laboratory and others have come to similar conclusions.

Despite the danger of perpetuating ignorance newspapers persist in considering items about presumed curses. Especially in their headlines, they avoid displaying any skepticism. For example, the *Chicago Times* Aug. 10, 1949 ran an AP story from Baltimore under the headline, "Find a voodoo curse in spiritualist slaying." The story concerned the discovery of a flask with the paper doll figure of a man suspended head down, near the body of a murdered medium. Similarly the *Chicago Sun-Times* for Nov. 1, 1949 headlined an AP story from Oliver, Ga., "Curse's Lone Survivor Dies." The story told of the curse placed on Jacksonboro by a hunchbacked itinerant minister. A map accompanied the account of the disasters, which led to the death of the town, once a flourishing county seat and coach stop, halfway between Atlanta and Savannah.

In neither of these stories was there any hint that there might be reason to question the veracity of the report. Nor was there in the story that Paul Ghali sent from Paris for the *Chicago Daily News* of Feb. 19, 1955. It pertained to the shooting up of a chapel in Vietnam by a Communist soldier who then suffered a heart attack, presumably as a heavenly punishment.

The *Sun-Times* ran an AP story from Genoa, Nev. March 27, 1977 of "The Hangman's Tree," illustrated by a pen drawing of a lynching. All sorts of misfortunes befell members of the party that hanged a man in 1897. The *Sun-Times* also ran a story Oct. 10, 1980 by Sarah Snyder, "New Tragedy Strikes Family: Is It Jinxed?" telling of the hesitancy of Diane Wilk, 23, to set a third wedding date after a brother was drowned on the first date she set and her mother was killed by a hit-and-run driver on the second. The story also listed other deaths in the family. Because she believes the family is jinxed she hardly lets her son, 7, out of her sight.

Perhaps the *Sun-Times'* worst offense against common sense occurred when a freighter, caught in a hurricane squall, crashed into the Sunshine Highway bridge over Tampa Bay. Jeff Klinenberg of the *St. Petersburg*

Times wrote a story that the *Sun-Times* published May 10, 1980 under the headline, "Most Recent Span Disaster Recalls Curse." Supposedly, when the bridge was being built, a construction worker was buried in some wet concrete and was never rescued. Several natives who believed in the curse were quoted but the *Times* never was able to confirm the incident.

Forty years earlier, the *Springfield* (Ill.) *Register* had advertised a long-existent curse. In its issue of Jan. 28, 1940 it ran an INS story from Hollywood on the Curse of Cahuenga. Occasion was the death of the ninth person who had sought the $250,000 worth of gold and jewels buried by the Mexican Gen. Benito Juarez near the Hollywood Bowl.

An up-to-date curse was reported from Knoxville, Tenn. July 30, 1982 by the UPI when an Indian leader called down the curse of "valley fever" on scientists who wanted to unwrap a 1,000-year-old Indian mummy.

Persons who escape the evil effects of a curse are newsworthy no matter how they did so. Typical were the following accounts:

March 7, 1947, a United Press dispatch from London, "British Relax Bread Ration to Avert an Ancient Curse," told that the food ministry granted Sir Anthony Doughty-Tichborne 14,000 bread units to hold off an 800-year curse that required his family to give flour to every resident of Alresford in Aylshire every March 25.

March 7, 1949, the Associated Press reported from Altoona, Pa., "Open grave to end hex on GI's widow." The uniform in which the soldier was buried was removed and burned and salt was sprinkled on the corpse to prevent the "restless spirit" from tormenting his widow.

From London Jan. 29, 1950 the AP reported that, as the *New York Compass* headlined it, "Nobody Dead After Playing Tchaikowsky's Haunted 6th," "The Pathetique" or "Haunted Symphony" is believed by many musicians to be peopled with demons who murder musicians who play it. The AP story mentioned a few players who had suffered harm. The next day the *Chicago Daily News* jubilantly declared that the piece had been performed at least 50 times by the Chicago Symphony Orchestra without mishap.

Bob Herguth revealed Dec. 4, 1970 that George Tesar, new president of C. D. Peacock jewelers, broke a five-generation family superstition of about 133 years by showing an opal, supposedly a bad-luck gem, and offering to sell the rare $5,000 black stone encircled with diamonds.

An AP story Jan. 23, 1961 from Glasgow was headlined, "Boy to Tell Clan Secret Foiling Scholars 200 Years." The secret, handed down for two centuries, was the name of the murderer of Colin Campbell, the "Red Fox" of Glenure.

Hans Holzer, professional psychic, is writing a book on the Hapsburg curse that affected the rulers of Austria for centuries, believed to have begun in the 12th century, according to Leonard Lyons in his *New York Post* column for June 27, 1972.

Aug. 19, 1977 Mike Royko devoted his column to the story of a woman who was swindled by a psychic who took money to rid the victim of a curse, a not unusual swindle to police, informed Royko. The details of the racket should be helpful to gullible readers.

A UPI story from London Aug. 8, 1980 told that Princess Margaret tried to persuade actor Peter O'Toole to overcome his fear of ever uttering the name "Macbeth," substituting "Mr. Lauder" instead.

Sometimes, as already illustrated, curses or their effects, are newsworthy and may be treated as routine news. Some miscellaneous examples follow:

The *New York Times* correspondent in Beirut reported that Syrians believe that the Evil One is responsible for the hot weather that caused wells to dry up and farm crops to spoil. A committee of sheiks blamed the yo-yo, recently introduced from Europe.

The Associated Press reported from Rochester, England that a 12th-century record book of the Rochester Cathedral had been found. It contains details of "the curse of Bishop Ernulf" by which anyone excommunicated from the church could be cursed "to the fingernails."

The supposed curse befalling anyone whose picture appeared on the cover of *Time* magazine struck again, New York's *PM* reported May 3, 1946 when Mrs. Elizabeth Arden Graham lost $800,000 worth of race horses by fire near Arlington Park, Ill. Her picture appeared in the issue of the magazine dated May 5.

After a survey by the Japanese Ministry of Education revealed that 70 percent of the people of Japan were superstitious, the government appointed a committee to investigate. Among the detrimental taboos, it was reported, are those obeyed by fishermen not to put to sea on the 7th, 17th or 27th day of a month and never return on a 5th, 15th or 25th, according to an AP story from Tokyo Jan. 20, 1948.

With no ifs, ands or buts, the *Chicago Sun-Times* reported Aug. 29, 1950 that "for 14 years a strange and tragic jinx has plagued the Camobruzzi family of Joliet." Specifically, 15 years earlier one was knocked into a river while on a construction job and drowned; six years later a distant relative was killed while working on another construction job, and at the time of the story a 21-year-old son fell off a truck and died of a broken neck.

The widespread instance of belief in hexing was investigated by Karl Kohrs who wrote about how "modern science wrestles an age-old problem." The article consisted mostly of anecdotes of North Carolinians who said they had been hexed and had paid others to unhex them. Dr. Kintross-Wright of Duke University was quoted as saying "the patients try to escape deep feelings of guilt by putting the blame outside themselves."

During the Vietnam war Georgie Anne Geyer reported Aug. 11, 1968 from Chau Doc, South Vietnam that native soldiers feared to invade Superstition Mountain which they believe is a terrifying place filled with curses for anyone who dares to climb it. Skeptical American allies thought it more likely the fear was of living Vietcong soldiers.

A controversy among scientists resulted when the Royal Ontario Museum of Archeology placed an Egyptian mummy on display in a Toronto subway station. Dr. Janice Preston, a metaphysician who practices witchcraft, insisted that there was danger because the 3,200-years-dead boy probably had a curse on him. She declared her belief in such curses and the *Toronto Sun* for Oct. 11, 1975 filled a page with her misstatements about the fate of those who had a part in discovery of the tomb of Tutankhamen. Nobody qualified to rebut her statements was interviewed although some were quoted as saying they disbelieved in curses.

When the broadcast commercial campaign for the motion picture *The Devil Within Her* began in Chicago Bob Greene expressed disgust and alarm in his *Chicago Sun-Times* column for Feb. 20, 1976. The advertisements featured the horrid screams of the devil-possessed baby and the evil effect on other characters. Greene blamed the death of an infant who was hurled from a window in a housing project on the picture and quoted American Medical Association officials on the dangerous effects of such pictures on children.

The UPI reported from London Oct. 7, 1980 that the magazine *New Musical Express* said the mysterious death of rock musician John Bonham and others connected with the Led Zeppelin group might be linked to black magic.

One kind of curse may be entirely fictional. Certainly many novelists, poets, movie makers, actors and playwrights have made good livings off of vampires, all the consequences of an 1897 book, *Dracula,* by Bram Stoker. Today there is a Count Dracula Society, described by Daniel St. Albin Greene in the *National Observer* for June 1, 1974 as "an association of chic literature and cinema buffs." There is also a Vampire Research Center of American headquartered in Elmhurst, Ill. and other groups interested in the gruesome vampire business.

Greene's article was an excellent history of the development of the fascination with vampires. There was a real Count Dracula who ruled Wallachia, a principality bordering Transylvania, now part of Romania, from 1448 to 1476. He was brutal; it is estimated he caused the deaths of 100,000 persons, some of them personal enemies whom he impaled. There is no historical evidence, however, that he was nourished by human blood that he sucked from his victims. Nevertheless, that is what vampires have been doing in literature ever since, and tourist companies have special excursions to Dracula Country. Greene summarized the cases of ten contemporary vampires. The ghost hunters, Ed and Lorraine Warren, tried in vain to exorcise whatever possessed one of them. Greene quoted Dr. Devendra Varma of Dalhousie University in Halifax, Nova Scotia: "Dracula stands as the symbol and essence of all philosophies of the East and West. He presents the message of resurrection, transmigration, rebirth, renewal and immortality."

In six months the Count Dracula Society of Toronto attracted more than 100 persons, the AP reported from Toronto Nov. 20, 1974. The society plans to promote serious study of the legend, Dracula movies and plays and Gothic literature.

A tour that Pan-American advertised vacationers "will enjoy sinking their teeth into," was the airline's Dracula tour, described by Richard C. Balough in the *Chicago Daily News* for June 19, 1972. It began with several Dracula motion pictures and concentrated on Transylvania where the real Count Dracula lived. Visits were paid to his home town and grave as well as to spots presumably referred to by Stoker.

Obviously not all credence in the generally unbelievable and impossible has disappeared. In his Sept. 23, 1980 *Chicago Tribune* column, Bob Greene summarized the findings of a vampire census conducted by the Vampire Research Center in Elmhurst. Its director, Dr. Stephen Kaplan, defines a vampire as "a creature who must drink blood to sustain himself," and says there are at least 22 true vampires in North America.

In a full-page article in the *New York Daily News* for June 22, 1979 Annette Bonus and Tom Cherwin quoted Kaplan that 20,000 to 30,000 Americans not only believe vampires exist but actively engage in some form of vampirism. Kaplan said he takes self-professed vampires seriously if they meet four qualifications that all bloodsuckers possess—charisma, dominance, sexual magnetism and longevity. The average vampire is male, 25 to 35 years old, with some college education.

Kaplan destroyed some myths regarding vampires, especially that they do not see their reflection in mirrors because they possess no souls. Garlic is the best way to repel a vampire, he advised.

July 4, 1981 the *Chicago Sun-Times* had a brief item about a mental patient who killed his grandfather by driving a wooden stake into his heart because he believed he was a vampire having escaped from a St. Louis hospital.

Beginning Oct. 28, 1981 the Associated Press covered a trial in Brockton, Mass. of a 24-year-old man charged with shooting his grandmother to death with gold-tipped bullets and then trying to drink blood from her wounds. He said he had been ordered to perform the murder by "the vampires." Despite the testimony of psychiatrists that he was irresponsible, he was found guilty and received a life-imprisonment sentence, the Oct. 31, 1981 story related.

Prince Dracula may have been suffering from an allergy, Dr. Thomas McDevitt, formerly a researcher at Idaho State University, announced. His views were contained in an article in *Diagnosis,* a medical magazine, the UPI reported June 15, 1982 from Pocatello.

An even wilder court case was reported by Ann Landers May 16, 1982. To answer a reader's inquiry she verified the fact that William T. Hardison, Jr. is suing Elizabeth Ann Honig in Nashville, charging that she placed a curse on his sex life 20 years earlier as revenge for his having dangled her naked out of a second-story window as "a sort of a joke."

June 18, 1982 Ann Landers told a reader who wanted reassurance there is no such thing as a hex, "No matter how many times I say it, the True Believers will be unconvinced." The reader had been puzzled by the fact that a girl whose boyfriend supposedly hexed her had a miscarriage, was mugged, fell down and broke her wrist and was laid off at the plant where she worked. According to Landers the name for odd coincidences is "fear psychology." For instance, tell a kid, "Be careful with that pitcher" and sure enough the kid will drop it.

11

Animals and Plants

City dwellers patronize pet shops for their domesticated dogs, cats, canaries, parakeets, goldfish and guppies. Parents and teachers escort children to zoos, circuses and aquariums. Picture books and television cartoons create sympathy for creatures to whom are ascribed human characteristics—Bugs Bunny, Mickey Mouse, Donald Duck, Yogi Bear, the three little pigs, big bad wolves and others.

As a result of the decline of firsthand acquaintance with most varieties of wildlife, myths concerning animals, birds and fish are much less prevalent now than in grandmother's day. Nevertheless, regardless of how much thought they had given the matter, a majority probably would indicate in a true-false test that an earthworm cut in two does not die but becomes two worms, warts come from handling toads and can be cured by grasshopper's "tobacco spit," beheaded turtles and snakes remain alive until sundown, dragon flies (darning needles) will sew one's lips together if one goes to sleep with an open mouth, horse hairs turn into water snakes, powdered rhinoceros horns are an aphrodisiac, wolves travel in packs, sharks swallow human victims whole as in *Jaws,* black cats are unlucky, a howling dog portends death, ostriches hide their heads in the sand, goats eat tin cans, giraffes, although possessed of no vocal chords, utter death cries, opossums steal shoelaces to use in their nests, owls are especially wise, cannot see in the daytime and relish the taste of human ears, bats are blind and like to roost in human hair, elephants never forget and are afraid of mice lest they climb up their trunks, camels' wounds won't heal, the age of rattlesnakes can be determined by the number of rattles and these reptiles will not crawl over horsehair ropes, most snakes can hypnotize birds, swallow their young when danger is near and, if captured, commit suicide with their own venom, ants are overly wise and some squirrels use their tails for sails in crossing water on chips of bark.

To the press' credit it has not attempted to keep alive any of these superstitions except for an occasional cartoon showing some ostrichlike public official burying his head or a Republican elephant frightened by a

229

mouse representing some small minority political group. As regards one popular belief that certain animals can forecast the weather, the journalistic handling has been iconoclastic. In his column in the *Chicago Daily News* for April 15, 1946, Lloyd Lewis debunked the idea that katydids make reliable weather forecasters and that crickets make good thermometers. Lewis explained that around the beginning of August katydids like to rub their legs together, which amusement lasts six or more weeks until about the time of the year's first frost, thus giving rise to the fallacy that katydids can predict the arrival of cold weather. As for the cricket, Lewis said scientists know that heat causes it to work faster whereas cold causes it to work slower. Lewis also belittled the claim of woodsmen that squirrels grow heavier pelts in anticipation of a cold winter.

Crickets are valuable if you lack a thermometer and want to know the temperature, according to Carl Strang, naturalist for the DuPage County, Ill. Forest Preserve District. As Gary Wisby reported in the *Chicago Sun-Times* for July 20, 1982 the number of chirps per minute of the snowy tree cricket equals 4.7 times the temperature in degrees Fahrenheit, minus 143. So if the cricket sounds off 92 times a minute the temperature is 50.

The *New York Times* in its issue of Aug. 13, 1961 disparaged the katydid-as-weather-prophet myth. By August the katydid reaches the winged state and the male begins to make himself heard. The *Times* editorial stated, "Sometimes it frosts six weeks after the first katydid is heard, but more often it doesn't in this area. Our katydids miss the mark by at least two weeks." Nevertheless, Sept. 3, 1979 the *Times* ran a long article illustrated by Nelson Bryant that counterbalanced much of the journalistic iconoclastic writings. Recalling several rhymes he learned as a child, he confirms that the weather affects a person's health, that spiders do work best as fair weather approaches, wolves, pigs and other animals howl, grunt and groan when bad weather is imminent and so forth for about a half-page of fascinating folklore.

In his "On the Sun Beam" column in the *Chicago Sun* for Aug. 31, 1946 W. A. S. Douglas debunked "some weird beliefs" that children have about the animal kingdom: angleworms and toads are rained down; a lion or bull can be tamed by a fierce stare straight in the eyes; the stings of wasps and bees will not hurt if one holds his breath while being stung; lizards crawl down the throats of persons who sleep with their mouths open; cats can kill babies by sucking their breath; if a cat touches a human's extracted tooth, that person's next tooth will be a cat's and false teeth will not fit again if a cat touches them.

In her syndicated column that the Oklahoma City *Sunday Oklahoman* used March 15, 1981, Ann Landers answered Graying who was afraid a friend's pampered and jealous cats might smother another friend's baby: "It's amazing how myths persist even though they have no validity whatever," Landers wrote, "This cat story has been kicking around since I was in rompers—and that's at least 60 years. So stop worrying and get a good night's sleep."

In four columns, Nov. 20 and 25 and Dec. 1 and 11, 1974, in the *Los Angeles Times,* Jack Smith analyzed reports that animals, at least domesticated dogs, cats and horses, can forecast earthquakes. Seismologists, including Charles Richter, were consulted and the consensus was that earthquakes often are preceded by small foreshocks that sensitive pets may feel and their masters do not. At best, however, the animals can give only a few moments warning.

The behavior of a number of animals is watched for clues as to what the weather is to be. David Anderson described many of these efforts in the article, "By Fish, Bear! Bad Winter Seen," in the *Chicago Sun-Times* for Nov. 5, 1974. He quoted Willie Smith, 74, of Murphysboro, Ill. as preparing to go south for the winter because he observed the caterpillars were black rather than brown. A Chicago restaurant owner agreed it would be a hard winter because fat on black bears was thicker than usual. A Vermont agency said woolly bears had shaggier fur coats than usual. A fisherman watched the perch in Lake Michigan; the deeper they went the colder the weather was likely to be.

The prediction of Jim Janek, proprietor of the Cafe Bohemia, that the winter would be cold based on his observation of bear fat was reported by Will Leonard in his *Chicago Tribune* column for Feb. 1, 1975.

Both the caterpillar and bear yardsticks for amateur weather forecasting were included by Bayard Webster in a feature in the *New York Times* and Dec. 21, 1976. The article also included the clue that geese flying south earlier than usual provides; also activity of squirrels in storing acorns, the thickness of the skin on apples and other fruits and other signals.

Sept. 20, 1981 for instance, the UPI reported from Crab Orchard, Tenn. that Helen Lane took stock of spider webs and woolly worms on Crab Orchard Mountain and predicted the coming winter may be tough.

Although *Old Farmer's Almanac* does not take animal behavior into account, its editor, Judson Hale, told Isabel Abrams of the *Chicago Tribune,* "I do believe the answer is in nature if we were wise enough to spot it." In her Oct. 10, 1981 article Abrams suggested counting the number of walnuts falling from a tree, see if there are any skunks in the barn and listen to the grunts of restless pigs.

The same newspaper devoted almost a half-page Jan. 31, 1982 to a story from San Jose, Calif. about Jim Berkland who knows an earthquake is coming if the advertisements for lost cats increase in number. He keeps a Cat-a-log and says he's been 75 percent right in his predictions since 1974. Marsha McNutt, a seismologist for the U.S. Geological Survey, says much of what Berkland says makes sense but he's been lucky and his method of forecasting is not scientific.

In his column, "The Unexplained," in the *Toronto Sun* for Oct. 11, 1972, Allen Spraggett told of "The grieving foxes of Germantown." On the authority of a former Duke philosopher, a Roman Catholic abbot noted the strange behavior of a yardful of foxes when he attended the funeral of Lord Gurmanstown in Ireland. Another guest told him: "This is a very ancient family; whenever a head of house dies, beginning several hours before the death and until the body is in the ground, all the foxes in the vicinity come to the manor and surround the house."

The one animal weather-prophet that is newsworthy is the groundhog, also known as a woodchuck, scientifically as either a marmota monax or arctomys monax. According to a tradition that apparently was imported from Germany, Candlemas was celebrated Feb. 2 when a hedgehog or badger played the part of prophet by arousing itself from hibernation. If it saw its shadow it returned to bed as a harbinger of cold winter weather for six more weeks. Since there were no hedgehogs in North America, the groundhog came to be the weathervane.

In several communities there are Feb. 2 ceremonies. An Associated Press story from Lancaster, Pa. in 1968 reported that in the east on the Octobara Creek at nearby Quarryville the famous furry weather animal poked its head out at a gray, rainy dawn and stayed above ground. In the west, however, at Gobbler's Knob, 400 soaked followers observed the little animal see its shadow before ducking back into his burrow.

Exactly six weeks after the groundhog's alleged appearance, the *Kansas City Star* for March 16, 1949 published the diagnosis of J. R. Lloyd, chief weather forecaster for the district, that the little animal was "somewhat off the beam this time," and Lloyd had records to prove it. In 1966 the *Chicago Daily News* quoted the U.S. Weather Bureau that during the preceding 40 years predictions based on the groundhog's behavior were incorrect 22 times. Still, editors persist in believing that their readers expect coverage of the event every Feb. 2. On most newspapers the assignment is passed around among the most imaginative writers year after year. Always officials of the Weather Service, zoo officials and scientists are interviewed and photographers try to get unique shots of the little animal or of his human followers.

Punxsutawney, Pa. calls itself the weather capital of the world and annually an official proclamation by Punxsutawney Phil is issued at Gobbler's Knob. With a brief explanation it was inserted in the *Congressional Record* for Feb. 2, 1981 by Rep. John P. Murtha of Pennsylvania. In July there is a weeklong festival honoring Phil with a parade of floats and bands.

According to Walter Masson in the *New York Times* for Feb. 2, 1975 the Slumbering Groundhog Lodge was organized in Quarryville, Pa. in 1907. And at Inman, Kan. more than 1,000 persons attended a Groundhog Day supper at the Evangelical and Reformed Church. The *Chicago Daily News* Feb. 2, 1954 devoted almost a half-page of pictures to the event and explained that the meat course was ground (or roasted) hog.

Feb. 2, 1982 the *Washington Post* had a long article by Donna Jacobs, a

Canadian syndicated columnist, who said a 20-year test indicated the groundhog accurately forecast the weather eight times, waffled five times and was wrong seven times. She traced the history of Groundhog Day and described the behavior of the animal, apparently an aggressive creature.

The *Chicago Sun-Times* Action Time answered a reader's query with an epitomized history that included Candelmas candles symbolize Simeon's words to Mary that Jesus would be "a light to lighten the Gentiles and the glory of thy people Israel."

In an editorial, "Candles and Groundhogs," Feb. 2, 1975 the *New York Times* remarked, "Why was this day chosen as the day for prophecy is not clear, but since all of February was a time for atonement and correction it probably was as good a day as any. Nobody expected much of February, which was merely the bridge between January and March. Nobody expected spring in February, no matter what happened on Groundhog Day."

Although Groundhog Day is not much more than the occasion for some journalistic tomfoolery, another nonhuman prophet is taken seriously. It is the cicada, or 17-year locust, called the "war prophet." According to a *Chicago Sun-Times* story June 1, 1961 Robert Mann, a forest preserve naturalist, researched the maturity appearances of the insect, separated by 17-year spans, back to 1752. He found that only one cicada year of the preceding 12 cycles failed to be followed by the outbreak of a war. His charts showed the following:

> 1752—Seven Years' War, four years later.
> 1769—Boston Massacre, one year later.
> 1786—French Revolution, three years later.
> 1803—Napoleonic War, same year.
> 1820—Greek War of Independence, year later.
> 1837—Cherokee and Creek Indian Wars, same year.
> 1854—Crimean War, same year.
> 1871—Franco-Prussian War, same year.
> 1888—Britain-Tibet War, same year.
> 1905—Russo-Japanese War, same year.
> 1922—No war.
> 1939—World War II, same year.

In 1956 the Suez crisis occurred, when the Israelis, French and British attacked Egypt. In 1973 the Vietnam war ended. The cicada had nothing to do with the start of either the Korean or Vietnam wars, or the India-Pakistan war or the Iran-Iraq conflict.

Although the groundhog and cicada may be lovable frauds as weather prophets, editors believe that readers enjoy accounts of precocious or unusual animals, birds, fish or reptiles. The eagerness of gullible readers to believe some outlandish hoaxes supports this editorial judgment. Preeminent in his ability to concoct animal tall tales was Louis T. Stone, editor of the *Winsted* (Conn.) *Evening Citizen,* who became known as the Winsted liar because of his inventions which press associations distributed and newspapers published all over the world with no hints as to their spuriousness. Among the best of Stone's creations were a hen that laid a red, white and blue egg on July 4; a squirrel that brushed its master's shoes with its tail; a bald man who painted a spider on his head to keep the flies away; a tree on which baked apples grew and many, many more of a similar character.

The accounts of numerous other animal hoaxes are included in my *Hoaxes,* now a Dover paperback.

The late Elmo Scott Watson conducted a Tall Tales column in *Publishers' Auxiliary,* of which he was editor. A typical story was that of a rattlesnake that a farmer rescued from a steel trap. The snake became a pet and rewarded its owner by keeping burglars at bay until police arrived.

The United Press distributed a story from Salem, Ore. about a man who lost his voice as the result of an infantile paralysis attack. After he opened his mouth and slipped a live frog down to the vicinity of his larynx, he regained his speech with a froggy accent. The reader might suspect ventriloquism, but the story did not hint at it.

Nor did the Associated Press suggest any skepticism regarding its Nov. 2, 1945 story from New York about Sabine, a talking dog who startled a pokey Bronx elevator operator by demanding "come on." Ethel Daccardo, the reporter, wrote that she witnessed the canine following commands by its mistress and others. Nine years later, Daccardo wrote an article for the *Chicago Daily News* of March 10, 1955 about another talking dog, Kid, who performed many of the same tricks as had Sabine.

Unless those who report the occurrences are liars, it is difficult to explain accounts of animals, usually dogs, who travel hundreds of miles to find a master who has moved or in some other way become separated. Several such stories were digested by Felicia Ames in an article in *Family Weekly* for Feb. 18, 1973. Most amazing was that about which Charles Alexander wrote in *Bobbie: A Great Collie of Oregon,* the story of a dog who followed his family from Indiana to Oregon.

Similar cases had been related by Richard T. Stock in the *Chicago Daily News* for June 20, 1962. It was based on reports of experiments by Dr. J. B. Rhine, director of the Parapsychology Laboratory at Duke University. "Psi-trailing" cats and pigeons also were studied.

Throughout history there have been instances of even scholars being fooled by animals with apparently great intelligence. Ultimately someone experienced in the tricks of professional magicians exposes the deception, accomplished by means of subtle signals to which the animal has been trained carefully to respond.

The performance of a German shepherd named Fellow before a Columbia University psychology class was reported in the Oct. 11, 1927 *New York Times.* Prof. Carl J. Warden concluded that the animal, owned by Jacob Herbert of Detroit, responded to vocal clues rather than words, sensing the proper objects and commands. Fellow amazed the students by obeying commands spoken by his owner through a keyhole.

Today it is not difficult to obtain journalistic recognition for a smart pet. Jan. 16, 1975 the *Chicago Daily News* used a two-column picture of Ralph Dadd, a Redmond, Wash. horse farmer who contends that animals, like the one shown peeking over his shoulder, have ESP and can sense what humans are thinking.

Perhaps the most celebrated of the allegedly clairvoyant horses was Lady Wonder, owned by Mrs. Claudia D. Fonda of Richmond, Va. She became nationally famous in 1951 when, aged 24, she directed searchers to a quarry where they found the body of a 4-year-old Pittsfield, Mass. boy. Lady Wonder spelled her answer on a mechanical device. The *Chicago Daily News* for Feb. 9, 1953 ran her picture with a story of a Naperville mother whose 3-year-old son and his 6-year-old playmate were found drowned in the DuPage River after Lady Wonder spelled R-I-V-E-R when Mrs. Geraldine Rosenstiel went from Naperville to Richmond to consult her. A sketch of the mare's career, illustrated with a picture of her tombstone, appeared in *Rural Living* for February 1973.

Certain to gladden an editor's day are stories of the discovery of a previously unknown species of mammal or the survival of a living species believed to be extinct or a previously unknown form of life. Care must be exercised to avoid being taken in by hoaxers. Even the experts are not immune, as Prof. Byron Patterson proved in 1967 when he composed and mailed a number of letters from Kenya and nearby African countries to his former colleagues at the Field Museum of Natural History in Chicago. The spurious correspondence was published in *Saturday Review* for June 1, 1968 under the title, "The Dancing Worm of Turkana, a 'Very Dangerous Animal.' "

Geologists and biologists were thrown into an academic spin, according to a United Press story Sept. 25, 1946 from Artesia, N.M. The cause was the discovery of a frog when a cellar was being dug. It was found tightly embedded in a calcium formation seven feet below the earth's surface. Scholarly opinion differed as to whether the small creature, who lived for two days had been in a state of suspended animation since the geological formation of the calcium bed perhaps two million years ago.

"Some sloppy scientific investigation" was blamed for the story that a 4-inch-long amphibious salamander known as a triton had been revived after lying frozen 5,000 years in Siberian soil. From Moscow Feb. 28, 1963 the United Press International quoted Prof. Lev Losino-Losinsky, head of the cosmic biology laboratory at Leningrad's Institute of Cytology, as saying that the perpetrator of the false report should be punished.

A *Washington Post* article which the *Milwaukee Journal, Chicago*

Sun-Times and doubtless many other papers used March 27, 1969 related the refusal of Frank D. Hansen of Rollingstone, Minn. to permit Smithsonian Institution scientists to examine the Silberskoye Creature he was exhibiting at fairs and carnivals. The hairy creature was frozen in a block of ice and could be viewed through glass. The scientific world became interested after an eminent Belgian scientist, Bernard Heuvelmans, viewed it and expressed belief that it was a member of a still living race of subspecies of modern man.

Heuvelmans had been introduced to Hansen by Ivan T. Sanderson, a science writer for *Argosy*. The *Milwaukee Journal* for Dec. 27, 1968 quoted the Belgian scholar as having said in Waupaca that he believed stories of an abominable snowman living in the area. Footprints he measured could not have been made by an ordinary human, he said. Heuvelmans is the author of *On the Track of Unknown Animals* while Sanderson is director of the Society for the Investigation of the Unexplained. According to Loran Frazier, Waupaca county undersheriff, the tale originated when a man masquerading in a coonskin outfit jokingly told some girls in a tavern that he was an abominable snowman. One of the repercussions of what started as a harmless joke was the construction of a huge cage into which some Fremont residents hoped to lure the yeti. The *Journal* used a photograph of it.

Hansen said he had obtained the creature in Hong Kong where it had been received from fishermen who found it in the icy waters of the Bering sea. It had bullet holes in an arm and eye. Hansen declared he didn't want to know more and continued to advertise it as a complete mystery. Whatever it was or is it was still on exhibition seven years later according to a column by John L. Perry in the *Kingsport* (Tenn.) *News*. The price of admission had been reduced from 35 to 25 cents but Hansen was still adamant in his refusal to allow scientists to examine the source of his income. He told Perry: "If it's proved to be the missing link that would upset a lot of religious beliefs so the information never should be revealed. If it's really a fabrication it would lose its exhibition value. So I won't let it be examined scientifically. Best to keep it a mystery and let people believe what they want to believe."

As Phineas Barnum, the great showman and inventor of numerous fakes, knew, people like to be fooled, so the task of the hoaxer is not difficult. It is so easy that many have had to confess to stop panicky behavior by believers. Such was the case regarding two animal fakes that originated in Australia in the '60s. In one case a Mangrove Mountain farmer's boast that his area was infested by huge rabbits was published and magnified. In England the story was enlarged to make the monster rabbits so tall they damaged orange trees while eating the bark off them. The Australian Pastures Protection Board set traps and citizens overran the area armed with guns to eliminate the menace. The *Chicago Tribune* reported from Sydney March 17, 1968 that for five years the story traveled around the world, despite denials from natives.

Four years later the United Press International reported from Perth, Australia that the Nullabor Nymph, a "naked-breasted young blonde nature woman" galloping with kangaroos, was merely a joke, especially the pictures which showed a farmer's daughter chasing four kangaroos that had just been let loose. The *Wall Street Journal* used the story May 14, 1972.

What doubtless was another tall tale was reported from Malmoe, Sweden by United Press International for use in the *Chicago Sun-Times* of Aug. 25, 1969. It told of a Korean sailor who had fallen off his ship and had ridden on the back of a huge turtle for 15 hours before being rescued by a Swedish ship. There was no confirmation of the story by the Liberian ship *Pedelara* from which the sailor said he had fallen about 113 miles off the coast of Nicaragua.

How hard it is to stop a hoax once it's in circulation was revealed by the *Chicago Today* Action Line Jan. 6, 1971. A reader wanted the address of Roy Tutt, an Englishman who successfully crossed a dog and a cat. Unfortunately for the correspondent who wanted to buy one of the litter, Tutt already had confessed that his "dogats" were "nothing more than mongrel puppies which cost me five shillings each." By spending $1.20 Tutt befuddled British animal experts and "earned a few pounds," personal appearance interviews and photographs. If the past is any guide some researcher, possibly a student preparing to write a paper, will run across the original story but not the sequel and start the tall tale on its way again.

How such happens was suggested by a story in the *Chicago Daily News* for June 5, 1938. It pertained to a story that research workers for the Federal Writers Project uncovered. Years ago, it was related, all pigs in Beaucoup Township, Washington County, Illinois were of a long-haired species. The day came when one porker was too large to be dipped in the scalding barrel. Blankets were dipped in boiling water and used to soften the hair. When the task was about half-completed the pig bolted and disappeared in the forest. There he shed the rest of his hair as he ran and ever after pigs were born short haired.

It is vain to expect readers to be wary of such spoofs. In its issue of April 1967, *Natural History* magazine of the prestigious American Museum of Natural History, ran an article on "The Snouters" by the late Harald Stumpke, curator of the Darwin Institute of the Hi-yi-yi Archipelago. Illustrated by line drawings, the article described the discovery of the elongated-snouted animals that preferred to stand on their tails rather than on their noses and were able to mate only when the wind blew strongly. An epilogue related the sad news that the Hi-yi-yi Archipelago had disappeared during tests of secret atomic explosives.

The *New York Times* reported May 17, 1967 that, instead of enjoying a hearty laugh, more than 100 readers wrote or wired seeking further information. One was a Washington University student preparing for her examinations; another was a California civil servant who wanted to protest the government's annihilation of the archipelago.

The *Times* exposed another hoax Feb. 27, 1972 in an article from Denver by Anthony Ripley. The news was that Big Mac, the 1972 Grand Champion Steer of the National Stock Show, was not, as entered, an Angus but a black-dyed white Charolais named Jeep that had been exhibited at several other shows with proper classification.

The refusal of victims of a hoax to accept the truth when it is revealed was stressed by Melvin Maddocks in a *Christian Science Monitor* feature that the *Minneapolis Tribune* reprinted March 25, 1975. Just for fun Bogart F. Thompson of Montclair, N.J. constructed plywood overshoes that left footprints resembling those of a huge sea gull parading on the beach. In vain he repeated his stunt in daylight before witnesses, many of whom he cornered to confess. True believers tried to persuade police to fence off the area and appealed to the Audubon Society and other naturalist groups to do something to capture and/or protect the strange unknown bird. Maddocks speculated; "If every hoax—and its response—makes a comment on the age what does this sensational non-response say about us? Are we so distracted by following the footprints of the economy that we have no time for anything else? Or after Watergate are we so skeptical that we don't believe even in little bird-tracks?"

Another example of the refusal of the gullible to be cured was reported Aug. 9, 1977 by Tom Metz in the *Wall Street Journal* and Nov. 27, 1977 by the *New York Times*. Armies of tourists don't want to be told that there is no such thing as a jackalope of which signs warn them to "watch out" and of which there is an eight-foot-high statue in the middle of the town of Douglas, Wyo. The unreal animal has a jackrabbit's body and the antlers of a deer. Natives long have known that the hoax was perpetrated in 1934 by two brother taxidermists. As the joke took root signs indicating the town limits cautioned tourists to beware of the jackalope. Licenses to hunt the animal from 12 midnight to 2 A.M. on June 31 are available as are numerous souvenirs. Said Ralph Herrick, one of the taxidermists, "People get real mad if you tell them there's no such thing as a jackalope. They take it very seriously. And why make people mad?"

One characteristic that the gullible and the skeptic have in common in such situations is lack of fear. Such is decidedly not the case, however, on many other occasions. Entire communities have been disrupted by reports that monsters have been sighted. Law enforcement officials have difficulty restraining posses searching for the usually nonexistent animals. The testimony of children and hysterical adults is often given credence over reports and opinions of trained investigators and scholarly authorities.

Withal, the press has considered it its duty to be objective in reporting when anyone says he has seen some strange monster. In his book *Little*

Adventures in Newspaperdom, Fred W. Allport told of the fright that citizens of Blanco, Ark. experienced in 1897 until a posse tracked a gowrow to its cave and killed it. The monster had been reported as having slaughtered cattle, horses, hogs, dogs and cats. There were numerous witnesses who said the creature uttered a cry that sounded like "gowrow," hence the name. It was described as 20 feet in length with a ponderous head, two enormous tusks, with short legs terminating in webbed feet with vicious claws. The body was covered with green scales and its back bristled with short horns. The bones presumably were sent to the Smithsonian Institution for analysis but somehow never arrived there. According to Allport it was "a great fake." Elmo Scott Watson added in his "Dear Ed" column in *Publishers' Auxiliary* that it was probably in the same genus as the hodag, a synthetic fearsome beast discovered (or manufactured) in the Wisconsin woods near Rhinelander by a group that included the father of Walter J. Lemke, head of the department of journalism at the nearby University of Arkansas.

Newspapers often create reader interest with first accounts of a wild animal or monster at large and then fail to satisfy the curiosity they have aroused. Probably in most such cases the mystery is solved quickly, leaving some people feeling foolish. Such doubtless was true in the cases of Montie the Monster of Pottstown, Pa. and the Beast of Momence, Ill. According to the United Press Nov. 14, 1945 Montie screamed like a panther, wailed like a banshee, barked like a dog and laughed like a hyena. After a thorough search the game warden dismissed Montie as the figment of the imagination of a handful of witnesses who disagreed in their descriptions of it. While the search was on a 17-year-old girl was shot when a gun went off in an automobile filled with monster hunters, two others in the search were injured when their car went over an embankment and a 17-year-old boy was shot in the thigh by a trigger-happy member of the posse.

In Momence the son of the postmaster displayed scratches on his hand inflicted, he said, by an animal 7 feet long and two feet high who was peeking at him through the kitchen window. Other townspeople said they had noticed mysterious animals in the vicinity and police cautioned all citizens to be on the alert. Sept. 29, 1946 the *Chicago Times* reported that the people of Momence still believed in the marauding animal, probably a lynx, cougar or puma. Police still received calls whereupon they go "rifles in hand prepared to fight to the death to protect their community against the ferocious beast. Instead they usually end up by gazing into the innocent eyes of a small pup just minding its own business, burying a hard-to-get bone."

Two months later a Lowell, Ind. farm woman called the sheriff to protect her from a creature she said resembled the Momence monster, with "a head like a cat, a body like a dog and big red eyes." Sheriff Fred Stults got the horsemen members of the Lake County Fox Hunters Association to stage a fox hunt with bloodhounds. The result: the what-is-it was not a fox. Nor were the dogs trained to follow the scent of a werewolf which someone suggested be done.

To their credit the Chicago papers didn't take too seriously reports from Evanston about a monster, which the *Sun* for Oct. 11, 1946 reported, "looks something like a bear, can jump a high hedge, is hairy and snarls like a dog." Evanston police concluded: (1) it isn't a pink elephant; (2) it's an early halloween stunt; or (3) it has something to do with a Northwestern University fraternity. The tabloid *Times* had the most fun with the story. Oct. 20, 1946 it published a cartoon showing a startled policeman staring at a white blob. Readers were invited to draw in their own conceptions of what the monster looked like with a $5 prize for the best entry. A week later two entries that tied for first place were published. Everyone got a good laugh and the story disappeared from all Chicago papers.

By contrast the entire population of Lebanon, Ind. took very seriously a monster that cried like a baby, carried away a 500-lb. calf and killed dogs, cats and chickens. Yielding to pressure from several farmers who had suffered losses, the mayor hired a veteran big-game hunter, Harry McClain, 64, to capture the marauder. Judson Chrisney of the United Press Aug. 24, 1946 wrote a first-person account of the dull fruitless night he spent with McClain. Four days later the *Chicago Daily News* printed the first of three articles by the masterful reporter and writer Bob Casey. He quoted McClain as believing he could have caught his prey had he not been befuddled by fireflies "who were making a kindly but mistaken effort to light up the surrounding landscape."

As a result McClain set a trap that, Casey wrote, "looks something like a guillotine, cattle chute and Noah's ark . . ." The next day, Aug. 29, 1946, Casey reported: "If you build a better mousetrap the world may beat a path to your door, but in the resulting jamboree you aren't likely to catch many mice." In other words the crowd of hundreds were sufficient to explain why the monster stayed away. Casey went home after his third article which began, "The Lebanon beast business, like other American industries, is suffering at the moment from plenty of buyer demand and a depleted inventory."

Four days later, Sept. 4, 1946, the United Press reported from Lebanon that the monster, "definitely a black panther" according to McClain, had been shot and killed but the carcass could not be recovered from the muddy creek into which it fell from an overhanging tree. Anyway, reports of casualties among the neighborhood livestock ceased. Other reports, however, continued to come from midwestern towns and cities. The *Chicago Sun-Times* published a special dispatch from Bethalto, Ill. Aug. 9, 1949 that 150 farmers were recruited by the mayor to track down a bear that killed a 7-month-old bull, mangling its body and eating its head. Two days later, the *Sun-Times* reported that the Canadian Fur Corporation of New York offered $350 for the pelt of the Indian Creek monster provided it was not a bear, moose, elk or some other common animal. Aug. 13, 1949 the United Press reported from Gooseville, Ill. that a farmer thought he had wounded an animal 4 feet long and 2½ feet high with a .22 caliber rifle. Footprints that resembled those of a bear were sent to Alton for study. And that's where the story ended.

It was an Alton citizen who, a year earlier, reported he saw a bird large enough to cast a shadow the size of a Piper Cub airplane. Milburn P. Akers, onetime administrative assistant to Illinois Gov. Henry Horner, who died in his arms, and later editor of the *Chicago Sun-Times,* wrote a piece for the Aug. 26, 1948 edition of his paper to recall the legend of a thunderbird that the Illini Indians worshiped and memorialized by a weird petroglyph, while became known as the Piza bird. It was seen by the explorer Father Marquette near the confluence of the Mississippi and Illinois rivers.

The iconoclastic Jack Mabley, who wrote his irreverent column at one time or another for every Chicago newspaper for a half century, until his retirement in 1982, asked "Have you been wondering what's happened to this year's crop of monsters?" in the *Chicago Daily News* for May 24, 1948. He mentioned the Lebanon, Evanston and other scares and said the last monster was reported by fishermen near South Haven, Mich. to be "a horned sea monster with a long tail thrashing around off shore." Mabley finished the account: "Unfortunately that monster swam to shore, said 'Moo' and walked to its barn to be milked."

As Mabley was writing his piece a United Press story was received from Omak, Wash. about the failure of a posse to capture or kill a large grizzly bear that had killed $22,000 worth of cattle.

Aug. 10, 1949 the Associated Press reported from Crisfield, Md. that the eastern shore was being "spooked" by some large creature variously called a gorilla, mountain lion or wildcat capable of blood-curdling screams. Police and posses could find nothing.

The discovery of large tracks, probably made by owls and rabbits, inspired John Kolesar of the Trenton bureau of the Associated Press to recall the legend of the Jersey Devil in an article that the *Passaic Herald News* used Oct. 28, 1960. Kolesar drew on my book *Hoaxes* to recall the statewide fright caused by a clever publicity stunt by Norman Jefferies, press agent for the C. A. Brandenburg's Arch Street Museum in Philadelphia in 1906. The beast was a live kangaroo painted green and white and harnessed with bronze wings. When the curtain of its cage was removed, projected by a small boy with a stick, the beast leaped forward causing the crowd to vanish. For years people in all parts of the east reported seeing the devil, presumably the bewitched child of a mother who placed a curse on it. Nobody has ever claimed the $10,000 reward offered by Camden's Broadway Improvement Corporation for the devil captured alive. According to the American Guide series, "There is a tradition that each appearance of the devil is an omen of war."

In the first of two articles on "Consider the (gasp) American Monster," in the *New York Daily News* for Jan. 2, 1978, Barbara Rehm mentioned the Jefferies hoax but gave more space to the persistence of belief in the Jersey Devil. She also mentioned a Grey Monster sighted in Bear Swamp near Lake Owassa, N.J. and the Skunk Ape in Big Cypress Swamp in the Everglades in 1971 and a number of other better-known frightful creatures.

Douglas Martin traced the entire history of the Jersey Devil and the theories concerning it in a two-column article in the *Wall Street Journal* for Oct. 31, 1979. From Double Trouble, N.J., he wrote, "For 244 years, the hideous Jersey Devil—appointed New Jersey's 'official state demon' in 1939—is said to have prowled the Pine Barrens, a dark 1,500 square mile wilderness infested with rattlesnakes, black widow spiders and incongruously wedged between Camden's boarded-up slums and the seashore's sunny boardwalks. Verily the Barrens are a land befitting Beelzebub."

Under the sponsorship of the Monmouth County Parks Department, 46 persons were to spend a weekend in Shark River Park hunting the Jersey Devil, the UPI reported Nov. 7, 1982. During the preceding three years the department took 400 people on devil hunts, many of them going just for the lark but many seriously dedicated.

Under a two-line streamer headline, "Playing Peek-A-Boo With the Jersey Devil," the *New York Post* for Nov. 8, 1982 reported that a posse of 46 searched the New Jersey woods for a weekend in a vain attempt to capture, or at least see, the Jersey Devil. The same day the *San Francisco Chronicle* devoted a half-page to a United Press story and picture from Neptune, N.J.

After at least 15 persons reported being frightened at intervals during a two-month period by a huge "thing," about 1,000 persons caused mammoth traffic jams as they came to help observe sheriff deputies and police search the environs of Monroe, Mich. The UPI quoted Christine Van Acker that the beast weighed more than 400 lb., smelled moldy, growled like a dog and disliked automobiles. She said it attacked her while she was driving her mother home. The *Chicago Sun-Times* used the story Aug. 17, 1965, also noting that 15 other persons sighted the beast during the preceding two months, and that other sightings were reported from nearby Frenchtown and Ashe counties. According to an Associated Press report Aug. 18, 1965 scratches that a boy, 17, and a girl, 18, displayed were dismissed as having been self-inflicted.

Quidnuncs also crowded the yard of a farmer's home near Foueke, Ark. from where the Associated Press reported the incident May 7, 1971. The huge black animal, who stuck its arm through a farmhouse window, was too fast to be a bear, the farmer and his wife reported. Authorities believe the creature, a panther or wolf probably, had made its den under the house where the family had lived only five days.

When farmers near Orleans, Ind. reported seeing a reddish-brown animal that screamed, roared and howled, the United Press rather sarcastically commented, "It was the first strange beast Indiana has turned up this summer." The *Chicago Daily News* used the story Sept. 3, 1954.

An AP story from nearby Benton, Ill. Sept. 8, 1958 reported that "eight responsible citizens" of West City saw an 8-foot tall man with arms that hung below his knees, dressed in a long white coat. Commented Police Chief John Smothers: "Everyone is breaking out their shotguns. If it's a plug for a movie I can't guarantee the monster's safety."

The UPI reported Nov. 17, 1966 that two Mt. Pleasant, W. Va. couples were followed by a "birdlike creature" 6 to 7 feet tall with red eyes and a 10-foot wing span. The "thing" supposedly glided along above the couples' automobile into and out of town. Police could find nothing but some townspeople said the "thing" must live in an abandoned boiler of a power plant.

"Reports of Oklahoma's Abominable Chicken Man have feathers flying from coast to coast," the Associated Press reported from Oklahoma City in a dispatch that the *Stillwater, (Okla.) News-Press* used March 9, 1971.

Evidence of some unusual marauder was handprints on the door of a chicken coop ripped off its hinges in El Paso, Okla. Only three animals in the area could make tracks that size: bears, mountain lions and man. Zoo authorities conjectured a manlike creature. When the matter was publicized letters poured in from all parts of the country. A Springdale, Ark. man gave details of sighting three strong, hairy, six-foot men one of whom pushed over a tree. Several citizens of Lawton, Okla, observed a seven-foot hairy creature in pants several sizes too small able to jump 15 feet straight up. Later some youths confessed to a Halloween prank. One was 6 feet 1 inch tall but not hairy or an especially good jumper. Commented Oklahoma City Zoo Director Lawrence Curtis: "It does indicate how people exaggerate what they see."

During the mid-'70s monster scares reached almost epidemic proportions in the Midwest. One that aroused widespread attention was Momo (for Mississippi Monster) first seen July 21, 1972 about ten days before it received its first press by an 8-year-old boy and his 15-year-old sister, son and daughter of Edgar Harrison of Louisiana, Mo. As others reported catching a glimpse of the monster its size grew from 6 to more than 12 feet. All agreed that it emitted a terrible stink and was black and hairy, with only three toes on at least one foot. A few days after the first publicity Hayden C. Hewes of Oklahoma City, director of the International Bureau for Unidentified Flying Objects, joined the search. He said the descriptions of the visitor were similar to those reported a year earlier from the Florida Everglades and Vader, Wash. No beasts ever were caught but they fit the UFO believers' category of Giant Hairy Biped from outer space. So did Momo, with a large pumpkin-shaped head, glowing orange eyes and an apelike growth of hair. It was strong, too, as several reports had Momo carrying a dog across the street. The *Chicago Daily News* and the *New York Post* had stories daily June 20 to 27, 1972.

Strength also was suggested when the United Press International reported that Momo had been sighted in Creve Coeur, Mo. and 120 miles south of Louisiana which believers were convinced he reached by swimming. A posse of 100 failed in its search for the creature in Creve Coeur as others had failed in Louisiana, and as more would fail in East Peoria, where the *Chicago Daily News* for July 27, 1972 also reported Momo was being hunted by a posse of 100. East Peoria is about 560 miles northeast of Louisiana. The paper also reported that a similar creature was seen standing at the Ohio River levee near Cairo, Ill. about 230 miles to the southeast. Cairo's police chief was quoted as saying that anyone reporting other monsters would be required to first submit to a breath test to determine its alcohol content.

After the excitement died down a bit Dick Brass wrote in the *Wall Street Journal* for Sept. 25, 1972, "Seeming catastrophes can work out nicely for small towns." He recalled the extent to which Momo upset the residents of Louisiana, Mo. and commented: "That was in July and at the time the good people of Louisiana were inclined to pound a stake through the monster's heart. But, now if Momo were ever really to show up, they'd more likely elect him president of the local Chamber of Commerce."

When some teenagers said they saw a monster emerging from the water and running for cover in the woods, "making horrible noises," a posse of from 40 to 100 persons scoured the area for the Hairy Monster of Pasquale's Sandwich. The police finally announced the scare was occasioned by a shy recluse who avoids companionship, the *Philadelphia Inquirer* reported July 30, 1972 from Vineland, N.J.

According to the Associated Press Nov. 30, 1972 an Ironton, Ohio sheriff's deputy said, "Personally I think it's just someone who hasn't got over their Thanksgiving hangover." That was after a cab driver reported his taxi was shaken by a "large, ape-like, white hairy monster with blood stains on his arms, dragging a dog or a deer." Fur found on nearby bushes was proved to be synthetic.

After the story died down, journalistically speaking, I wrote Ralph Otwell, editor of the *Chicago Sun-Times,* on Aug. 24, 1972: "Is it fair to excite your subscribers and then leave us quivering?" He answered: "When the mysterious beast is captured we will report it."

How the effect of a community scare persists was revealed in an Associated Press story from Flatwoods, W. Va. that the *New York Times* ran April 28, 1973. Twenty years later there was interest in the Braxton County Monster that was 8–10 feet tall, had a red face, bright-green robe-like clothing and a black hood shaped like the ace of spades. Mrs. Kathleen Lemon May, who was the only adult among the seven who saw the creature, said: "I get sick of it. Never a week goes by that someone doesn't contact me about it, either by phone or letter." The Braxton County Jaycees sell monster replicas made from an artist's drawing.

True to form other monsters—300 during the past decade according to Harlan Sorkin of St. Paul, an expert on the subject—are seen by a growing number of persons; frightful in appearance, the creatures then disappear and, despite strenuous efforts by police and posses, never are captured. Their memory lingers and generations to come believe their legends. The Murphysboro (Ill.) Monster followed that formula. In the *Chicago Tribune* for June 29, 1972 Donald Yabush reported that it had been seen for the third time that year by two teenagers and "folks don't think it's a phony any more." It was described as a creature seven or eight feet tall with light hair (an unusual feature), covered with mud and weighing 300 to 350 pounds. So impressive was it that the *New York Times* sent Andrew H. Malcolm to do an article that took up almost a full page in the issue of Nov. 1, 1973. After several reports the police authorities imported an 80-pound shepherd dog noted for his tracking ability. The dog led a posse to an abandoned barn that it refused to enter. Fourteen area police cars answered a summons for help. When the door was forcibly opened the barn was found to be empty. When, ten days later, some carnival ponies bolted and onlookers reached several hundred, Riverside Park was closed. Three carnival workers said they saw the monster watching the animals with obvious curiosity but, as almost always happens, it wasn't there when its would-be captors arrived.

Something new in monsters was reported April 27, 1973 by the Associated Press from Enfield, Ill. What Henry McDaniel, a 50-year-old antique-dealer, said he shot on his front porch had three legs, a short body, two little short arms and two pink eyes as big as flashlights. It stood 4½ to 5 feet high and was grayish-colored. Its footprints were like those of a dog except it had six toes. One trooper among those called to inspect and protect said that McDaniel seemed rational and sober.

Also different was the reaction of the citizenry of Enfield. The *Springfield* (Ill.) *Journal Register* devoted two full pages May 10, 1973 to an article by Chris Dettro based mainly on the skeptical answers he received when he interviewed townspeople. When would-be game hunters and television crews arrived, Sheriff Roy Poshard, Jr. made some arrests of unlicensed hunters and ordered every stranger out of town.

Still more original was the shrieking what-is-it that ran rampant in Arlington, Va. for at least a month, killing scores of dogs, cats and rabbits but not devouring them, according to June 22, 1974 stories in both the *Washington Star-News* and *Washington Post*. Authorities were certain that the tracks were not those of a raccoon, opossum or badger. Possibly it was a bobcat, although none were known to be in the area, or an exotic pet brought into the country illegally. It was recalled that a year earlier there had been a monster scare at nearby Sakesville, Md. where it was guessed by some to be a dwayyo, snallygaster or sasquatch. The Arlington marauder was described as thin, hairless, with no tail but with big teeth, about 3 feet long and very smelly. Police authorities refused to permit posses with firearms to conduct a hunt since the area is residential.

A terrifying puzzler, mostly for Texans, were mysterious blobs first described by the *Dallas Times-Herald* May 29, 1973 as pulsating, multiplying organisms with black mucous inside and thick reddish bubbles on top. One was reported to have multiplied 16 times within a week. A scientist who sent specimens to Colorado for testing postulated that the blobs were bacteria that have tremendous growth potential. June 8 the UPI reported a blob was discovered in Warren, Mich., where a Michigan State University expert said it probably was a member of the family Fuligo septica, the largest slime mold in existence.

And that was the correct analysis, the UPI reported June 22, 1973 from Garland, Tex., where a University of Texas scientist translated the term as just plain fungus. This was a disappointment to some citizens who were convinced the blobs were visitors from outer space.

Other strange objects have been controversial and newsworthy. April 6, 1974 F. K. Plous reported in the *Chicago Sun-Times* that plans to send a stainless steel sphere the size of a bowling ball to Evanston for examination by Prof. J. Allen Hynek, UFO expert, were abandoned on advice of the Aerial Phenomenon Organization in Tucson. The ball was found on the property of Antoine Betz, Fort Georges Island near Jacksonville, Fla. and was believed by the Arizona scholars to be similar to objects that exploded over the Atlantic Ocean and in Brazil, probably of some military use.

Two purple gooey blobs in Frisco, Texas were found not to be from outer space but part of the refuse behind a plant that recycles batteries, the UPI reported Sept. 10, 1981.

An illustrated story in the *Star-News* for July 11, 1974 told of the capture by police of an Oriental civet, hardly the huge monster that caused so much trouble. Harold Egoscue, a curator at the National Zoological Park, said he did not believe the Arlington beast was a civet, noting that the animal had a collar mark and was in good condition which suggested it ate regularly and probably was someone's pet that had escaped.

Dave Schneidman in the *Chicago Tribune* for Aug. 30, 1974 recalled the Murphysboro Monster when he reported what Bob Calusinski of suburban Carol Stream told police. One Monday while "playing around with some friends" in a cornfield, Bob heard heavy breathing. Tuesday he and some friends returned to the scene and threw corn playfully at each other. That angered the monster who hit Bob in the shoulder. Bob did not wait to become acquainted but Wednesday he got a complete look before running away. What he saw was a six-foot seven-inch hairy monster with glowing eyes the size of softballs, fuzzy hands and considerable body hair. Schneidman said the only difference between the Murphysboro and Carol Stream monsters was that the former ate tree bark instead of corn. Sept. 2, 1974 Monroe Anderson reported in the *Chicago Tribune,* "The west suburban beast has fled." Richard Crowe, ghost hunter and consultant for the International Fortean Society, said the footprints were those of Bigfoot of whom more in the next chapter. In his *Chicago Daily News* column for Oct. 8, 1974 Robert Herguth quoted a Carol Stream policeman as saying, "I interpret it as a joke that may be blown out of proportions."

In a lengthy piece in the *Chicago Tribune* for Oct. 6, 1974, Schneidman quoted Gordon Prescott, head of the Yeti Research Society with head-quarters in St. Petersburg, Fla. regarding the nature and habits of the yeti. Prescott advised Carol Stream citizens not to panic because yeti mean no harm. The society became convinced that a yeti was roaming the country-side according to an answer to a reader's inquiry in the *Chicago Tribune's* Action Line column for Dec. 22, 1980.

That editors were tiring a bit trying to keep up with monsters was indicated by the small (1½ in.) play the *Chicago Sun-Times* gave a July 9, 1975 Associated Press story from Murphysboro that police failed to find footprints or other evidence of a "white and shaggy haired creature about 7 feet tall" that one citizen reported he saw.

Few wild animal scare stories ever received more international atten-tion than Chicago's kangaroo hunt. The first publicity came Oct. 18, 1974 when two policemen reported that while they tried to handcuff a kangaroo it kicked its way to safety. The animal was said to be four or five feet tall, brownish gray in color, probably weighing 100 to 120 pounds. When the first news story appeared in the *Chicago Daily News* for Oct. 18, 1974 two newsboys said they had seen a kangaroo a week earlier. There were followup stories almost daily for more than a month. They contributed to readers' general knowledge by citing the World Book and other reference works. Oct. 26 the *News* summarized all the previous kangaroo scares about which the paper's morgue had information. Seeking a new approach Alan Merridew ghostwrote a letter from the elusive Curl to Blue, his mate in Australia. There was a glossary of Australian terms accompanying the story which the *Chicago Tribune* ran Oct. 27.

Fascinated by the fact that the Chicago police had tried to handcuff a kangaroo, the Australian press asked the Associated Press to fill it in on all the details. Soon, as might be expected, reports of sightings in other places were received. According to the *Daily News* for Nov. 4 the animal was seen in Plano, Ill. about 40 miles southwest of Chicago. More attention-getting were the reports from Rensselaer, Ind. about 90 miles south of Chicago. Great fun was made of the comment by campaigning President Gerald Ford that the Chicago Bears football team could use the kangaroo as a fast-getaway runner. The Bears train on the campus of St. Joseph College in Rennselaer.

Five days later when a sighting was reported from Carmel, Ill. 400 miles to the south, Saul Kitchener, assistant director of Chicago's Lincoln Park Zoo, publicly scoffed at the idea a kangaroo was on the loose. He said: "I'm just waiting for someone to report seeing a kangaroo riding a flying saucer. Then I'll believe it." Other scientists said no kangaroo could hop the distances involved in such a short time.

The *St. Paul Sunday Pioneer Press* for Nov. 17, 1974 told of a woman who noticed a furry creature on the doorstep of her home and both she and the police who responded to her call thought it might be a kangaroo. It turned out to be a squirrel monkey.

March 31, 1975 the *Chicago Sun-Times* lamented the fact that the kangaroo had not been seen since Jan. 27. Publicity was given letters from two New York schoolgirls who suggested building a cage or a hole covered with paper as a trap. Then May 15, 1975 Bob Herguth announced "Weather's right—Kangaroo back!" in his *Daily News* column. The authority was Patrolman Leonard Ciangi, one of the two policemen who failed to capture the animal more than a half-year earlier. This time, however, he and his companion, Patrolman Michael Byrne, didn't get close enough for a good look. A while later, July 15, 1975 to be exact, the *Daily News* related from Dalton City, Ill. 170 miles south of Chicago that a St. Elmo woman had seen the beast. "I was cold sober and wide awake," she told police. As always the search was futile. Once again Herguth wrote, in his July 27, 1975 column, "Calling All Cars; the Kangaroo's Back." This time his information was obtained in a phone call from a citizen. So famous had the peregrinating beast become by now that the Australian consulate in Chicago sent 50 kangaroo pins to be worn by policemen as a sort of combat medal. And the Chicago 16th District policemen's softball team called itself the Wallabies, a wallaby being a small kangaroo.

From 1975 to 1980 between 7,000 and 10,000 instances of mutilated cattle were reported to various government authorities according to a *New York Times* story from Sante Fe, N.M. April 16, 1980. Kenneth N. Rommel, who investigated for the state and the Federal Law Enforcement Assistance Administration, said the deaths resulted from natural predators, scavengers and decomposition and were not caused by religious cultists, UFOs, vampire bats or government experiments.

Among the first stories about cattle mutilations were those originating in Carrollton, Ill. where a dead cow was found with its left ear apparently skillfully cut off and the left eye and part of the tongue removed. In the opinion of Sheriff Ben Picou, "It's all just a bunch of bull," the Associated Press reported April 9, 1975.

Nov. 1, 1980 the AP reported from Dallas that Tommy Blann, a research associate for UFO Studies, said cult activities and government experiments are more likely explanations for the cattle mutilations than UFOs. He was trying to determine if an aircraft was involved as he had observed markings on the ground near the dead animals.

That it is possible for a wild animal to elude pursuers even in well-inhabited places was indicated by an AP dispatch from Zumbroto, Minn. that the *Austin* (Tex.) *Statesman* ran Oct. 20, 1975. It was the story of a wallaby that escaped while on exhibit at the Goodhue County fair, where it was on loan from the Como zoo in St. Paul. A housewife caught the animal in her dog pen but not before embarrassed Zumbroto businessmen had spent $1,000 for two new wallabies. They tried unsuccessfully to convince the police that one of the animals was the missing link. The search over the Como zoo had three instead of only one wallaby.

The persistence of monsters to elude police and citizen posses is matched only by that of editors who persevere in the attempt to chronicle the frustrations and fears of the gullible. One of the most outstanding examples of a newspaper's attempt to solve a longstanding mystery was a 22-page tabloid supplement to the *Washington Post* for Oct. 10, 1976. It was entitled, "The Grand Bicentennial Washington Post Potomac Expedition to Darkest Maryland in Search of the Monstrous Snallygaster." The six-person expedition included a former *Life* photographer and a filmmaker. Gordon Chaplin wrote the play-by-play account of the quest for the elusive snallygaster that Marylanders had reported seeing for three-quarters of a century. It is described by *Webster's Third International Dictionary* and the Federal Writers' Project as part reptile and part bird although some who claimed to have seen it recently said it resembled the sasquatch or Bigfoot of the Northwest.

In an article, "On the Benevolent Necessity of Belief in Monsters Now More Than Ever," in the *Post's* special section, Henry Allen pointed out that *The Reader's Guide to Periodical Literature* showed virtually no nonfiction monster entries 30 years ago but scores during the past ten years. Monster sightings, Allen wrote, have traditionally been linked with cataclysms. Needless to say, the *Post's* searching party searched in vain for anything except persons who claimed to have been disturbed.

Despite the dismal record of monster seekers, newspapers continue to give good space to reports of horrendous creatures. Both Chicago papers did so when an 18-year-old farmhand in nearby McHenry County reported having been attacked by a huge beast that also damaged barn doors. After a posse of 50 failed to find the creature, the farmhand admitted his story was a hoax. The *Chicago Tribune* and *Chicago Sun-Times* both reported the end of the scare May 23, 1980.

A strong factor to explain the susceptibility of witnesses to exaggerate and sincerely believe their own stories is the believability of the monsters they think they saw. All resembled human beings or familiar animals. None looked like the fabulous fantastic creatures that early explorers reported they encountered. Nothing like the devils belching fire from mountaintops, or men with heads like bears or birds able to carry an elephant in their claws and other horrendous phenomena reported by the 14th-century English explorer Sir John Mandeville, "the father of English prose." When few people had ventured far from home those who did, as Benjamin of Tudela, Captain John Smith, George Psalmanazar and, most recently, Trader Horn and Richard Halliburton, were able to concoct real whoppers. No unicorns, griffins, dragons, hippogriffs, gorgons, mermaids or other mythical monsters have been seen for centuries. Instead, the objects of contemporary fear and/or fascination are believed to be atavisms, mutations or regressions, and a tremendous amount of time, effort and expense has gone into the search for them. Those who hunt the elusive terrors are armed and their object usually is to kill the unknown. They are prepared to shoot on sight regardless of the nature of the beast or the extent of its hostility.

Some people talk to images, idols, other objects, pets and themselves. And today, since 1968, there has been a developing cult of those who converse with plants and flowers.

Originator of the belief that plants possess something closely akin to feelings or emotions is Cleve Backster, a polygraph (lie detector) expert who wondered how long it would take water he gave a tall droopy-leafed dracena plant to travel from the roots to the leaves. So he connected a pair of polygraph electrodes to a leaf and was surprised when he got an immediate polygraph reaction pattern similar to a human's if his safety were threatened. Experiments followed with eggs, fruits and vegetables, human blood and mold cultures. The one most cited by writers who have publicized Backster's experiments involved dumping cups of small brine shrimp into boiling water with plants reacting immediately.

One of the first newspaper features on the phenomenon was by Richard Martin in the *Wall Street Journal* for Feb. 2, 1972. The first book inspired by it was *The Secret Life of Plants* by Peter Tompkins and Christopher Bird. Reviewing it for the *New York Times* of Dec. 31, 1973, Elsa First called it "the funniest unintentional funny book of the year." She warned, "Zeitgeist-watchers should take note. This is the first in a new genre mid-cult occult. The New Occult was an alliance formed in the mid-60s between the old credulousness and popular superstition and the new openness of expanded counter-culture minds." The entire review is extremely uncomplimentary to not only plant experiments but also to many other parapsychological activities.

Clarence Petersen was much more generous when he reviewed the paperback edition of the book in the *Chicago Tribune* for Oct. 13, 1974. In fact, he wrote: "The authors have built a mountain of evidence that plants not only have emotions but also can diagnose disease, communicate by ESP, in fact, respond to just about everything with more sensitivity than humans."

As might be expected popular entertainers became amateur experimenters. Interviewed by Peggy Constantine for the *Chicago Sun-Times* of Nov. 16, 1973, singer-composer Dory Previn related how a friend told her that her plants didn't grow because they were insane, psychotic and did not know which way to grow. Said Previn: "Now that my head is straightened out a little more, my plants are doing better. I talk, sing and entertain them. They're like friends. If you approve of them they approve of you. If you ignore them, they ignore you."

In a half-page article, illustrated by artists' drawings, in the *New York Times* for Jan. 14, 1974, Georgia Dullea summarized the effects of "Backster's effect." After she reported that plants "fear, love, hate, worry about dogs—who knows—may possess the power to read people's minds," people "immediately began being nice to their plants to make up for those years they sat bored and lonely in the windowbox."

Dullea cited George Milstein's *Music to Grow Plants.* The music's sonic hum causes plants' pores to widen and grow longer so carbon dioxide and water vapor are absorbed faster. Also cited was the Rev. Franklin Loehr's *The Power of Prayer on Plants,* which tells of experiments in which prayed-over plants did better than others.

In an accompanying article Nadine Brozan quoted the skeptical Dr. Henry McCathey, chief of the U.S. Department of Agriculture's ornamentals laboratory at Beltsville, Md., who said, "The only definite claim you can make about plants is that they need abundant light and correct temperature and humidity." He and Carlton B. Lees agreed that if a person hovers over plants he exhales more carbon dioxide than usual. Several other authorities were either noncommital or said it was absurd.

From Newark the Associated Press reported April 26, 1974 that a florist, Sonny Purcell, sings to flowers and plants in his store for an hour every day. The response was similar to that of his daughters to whom he sang when they were ill; the plants and flowers improved in color and appearance.

When a portion of a field that had been played over yielded a better crop of soybeans, Dr. Gus Alexander of the University of Dayton said, "Somehow God's creative energy of growth can be channeled through us, even to plants," the *Chicago Tribune* reported Dec. 14, 1974.

Headlines that told the story included "Stop whispering—the philodendrons aren't listening" (*Chicago Tribune*); "Your Plant Isn't Sorry for You" (*Chicago Sun-Times*) and "Scientists Rebut Theory That Plants Can Emote" (*New York Times*) all from editions of Jan. 30, 1975 and all related to the views of five of six panelists at a session of the American Association for the Advancement of Science in New York. The dissenting panelist was Backster who chastised the professors for not duplicating his experimental methods exactly. He said that he now has proof that yogurt has emotions too.

Dr. Arthur W. Galston of Yale University said that he tried to duplicate Backster's experiments after a poll of his students revealed that half of them talked to their plants and one-fourth believed it had an effect. Nevertheless, Dr. Galston said that plants do not respond to human thoughts and emotions even though they do show altered electrical responses to light, chemical agents and disease. The four other experts in the field agreed with him.

One group that decided to conduct experiments of its own despite what the scholars said consisted of the editorial staff of the Tempo section of the *Chicago Tribune*. The outcome was reported in the paper's issue of Feb. 25, 1975. Three groups of three plants of the same varieties were subjected to exactly the same environment and care. The instructions were these: only nice things should be said to Group 1; only nasty things were to be said to Group 2; Group 3 was to be ignored. Pictures were taken of the subjects Nov. 22 and Dec. 2, 1974 and Jan. 19, 1975. Gradually, Elaine Markoutsas wrote, "Those verbally stroked with tender loving care became perky. Those plants which had been ignored kind of sulked, shriveled up, turned yellow around the edges and dropped their leaves. Those cursed out turned mushy, became comatose and perished."

In its Books End section for April 20, 1975 the *New York Times* reviewed the action of the convention panel, about the only new fact being that Backster had written an article for *Chronicles of Higher Education* in which he made a passionate appeal for "the end of the slaughter of innocent little brine shrimp in college labs all over the country."

Aug. 5, 1975 the *Wall Street Journal* reported that new experiments using Backster's methodology had been conducted at Cornell University with negative results.

12

Monsters

For at least three centuries the Sherpas of Nepal have believed that their mountainous country in the Himalayan range between India and Tibet is also inhabited by yetis, shy, wild creatures that some westerners thought might be the missing link in the Darwinian evolutionary chronology between ape and man. According to natives who either caught a glimpse of the strange being or who knew someone who knew someone who did so, the elusive stranger was a large bipedal anthropoid ape, from 5 to 8 feet tall, with thick brownish fur, a cone-shaped skull, large feet with a prominent big toe. Supposedly a few yetis had been captured and/or killed but the only bits of evidence were a few tufts of hair, droppings and tracks in snow and/or mud.

So firmly did the Nepalese believe in the existence of the yeti that the government forebade killing them or removing any of the bits of evidence from the country. Nevertheless, during the past half-century there have been numerous expeditions by foreigners to obtain photographic or other proof of the existence of what they called Abominable Snowmen.

Typical of the frequent reports by press associations was an AP story from London April 30, 1959 that Chinese peasants had captured a yeti which they domesticated and trained to work before killing it. Unfortunately there was no followup and so the account obtained no more credibility than the UPI story July 12, 1958 from Moscow that Soviet scientists had discovered Neanderthal-type humans in the deserts of Mongolia. The *Chicago Daily News* gave good space to both stories and also to a picture of a shaggy-headed man with closed eyes that the cutlines in its Dec. 16, 1958 edition said was taken by Father Franz Eichlinger, a Roman Catholic priest of Frankfort, Germany who, on his return from Tibet, said the Abominable Snowmen are "saint-like recluses who devote their lives to healing."

Father Eichlinger scoffed at the idea yetis are shaggy giant cannibals. Similarly adversely critical of efforts to track down a yeti was an article in a Soviet scientific publication by Dr. N. Kislyakov, eminent Russian ethnographer. The *Chicago Tribune* devoted a column Oct. 14, 1959 to a Reuters dispatch from Moscow about the reports of Prof. Boris Pershnev from Nepal. Dr. Kislyakov accused Pershnev of confusing facts with folklore.

What should have ended the legend was the report of a four months' expedition in the winter of 1960–61. Announcement of the project was made Dec. 20, 1959 by Dailey K. Howard, president of the Field Enterprises *World Book Encyclopedia,* which appropriated $200,000 for what Howard said doubtless was the first venture of its kind financed by an encyclopedia.

Heading the expedition was Sir Edmund Hillary, the New Zealand beekeeper who was the first man to scale the world's highest mountain, Mt. Everest, 29,141 feet high. Other members of the group of 14 included the noted British explorer Eric Shipton and R. Marlin Perkins, then director of Chicago's Lincoln Park zoo. Their everyday activities were reported by Desmond Doig representing the *Chicago Daily News,* another Field publication.

In addition to seeking yeti, the *Sun-Times* reported Dec. 22, 1959, Hillary also would attempt to climb the 27,790-foot Mt. Makalu without using oxygen, to determine the maximum height at which men can live for long periods without deterioration. Among the earlier searches for the Abominable Snowman, as summarized by John Masters in *Harper's* for January 1959 were a Colonel Waddell in 1887; H. J. Elwes in 1906; and Colonel Howard-Bury in 1921.

In a lengthy interview in the *Chicago Daily News* for Dec. 22, 1959 and in an article he wrote for the *New York Times Magazine* of Jan. 24, 1960, Hillary related many rumors he had heard during previous visits to Nepal. He said he hoped to capture a yeti alive, if necessary by means of a "capture gun" with a range of 100 yards, loaded with a tranquilizer.

Interest in the project was enhanced when Ringling Brothers–Barnum and Bailey circus announced it was sending a big game hunter, McCormick Steele, to the Himalayas to trap an Abominable Snowman. John Ringling North, the circus' president, said if Steele captured a Snowman it would become the biggest circus attraction since Jumbo, the giant elephant that the great showman P. T. Barnum imported in the 1880s. There was no followup of the *Chicago Tribune's* account of the announcement March 30, 1960. Possibly the Nepalese government's edict against killing or exporting a yeti was the reason.

Support for the Hillary expedition was announced by the *Chicago Daily News* May 21, 1960. It came from a Texas millionaire explorer, Tom Slick, who after three trips to Nepal believed in the yeti's existence. He said it might be the missing link between man and ape and "If it's what we think it is, its finding will be the greatest natural history discovery of all time."

In early November 1960 in Nepal, Doig interviewed natives and foreigners from whom he obtained a score or more stories of past encounters with yeti. The only tangible evidence, however, was a withered scalp, which was preserved, it was said, for 240 years in the Pangbioche Monastery and sacred to the people of Khumjung. Although it had been photographed many times it never had been removed to be examined by scientific experts. Dec. 2, 1960 Doig announced that the Nepalese government had given permission for Hillary to borrow the scalp for one month in exchange for a promise to provide funds to renovate the monastery and give the village of Khumjung its first school. One of the three village elders accompanied the precious relic on its round-the-world trip.

A week later, Dec. 9, the *Chicago Sun-Times* published an Associated Press story from Katmandu, Nepal of a press conference at which Hillary showed journalists the scalp. According to the story, "it had a high peaked conical skin with a ridge running over the top. The top is nearly bald but bristly red and brown hair covers the lower portions. It is 8 inches deep, 7 inches across, 9 inches long and 27 inches around the base."

Another press conference held in Chicago was described as "uproarious" by D. J. R. Bruckner in the *Sun-Times* for Dec. 14, 1960. The scalp was examined by experts at the Museum of Natural History and the Lincoln Park zoo. Afterward it was taken to London and Paris for additional independent studies. An Associated Press story from Katmandu, which the *Chicago Daily News* ran Jan. 6, 1961, reported the safe return of the scalp while thousands of Sherpas cheered and prayed.

Back in Chicago Sir Edmund released his final report which stated that, according to all the expert opinion, the scalp was not a scalp at all but a skull cap manufactured from the skin of a serow, a form of goat-antelope. An article Hillary wrote for *Life* was summarized by the *Daily News* of Jan. 11, 1961. Perkins was quoted in the *Daily News* for Jan. 16, 1961 as saying that the imitations of the yeti howl the natives gave him suggested the original howler was a snow leopard. The *News* devoted a full page to pictures of the marks in the snow incorrectly believed to be footprints of the illusive beast, and to other supposed clues—all explainable. In the *Sun-Times* for Jan. 17 in an article by D. J. R. Bruckner, Perkins elaborated on the findings, "The Sherpa stories are not as exaggerated as many European reports, and I feel much of the distortion is the work of careless explorers and reporters."

The Abominable Snowman is only a legend and its cries are the howls of a snow leopard, Marlin Perkins said in Tokyo from where the AP reported his words June 10, 1961. Thereafter journalistic interest in yetis subsided until Jan. 11, 1973 when the AP reported from Katmandu that an American expedition camped at 12,500 feet in the Himalayas discovered apelike footprints that Sherpa guides identified as those of the Abominable Snowman. Among the papers giving the story good play were the *Austin* (Tex.) *Statesman,* the Springfield *Illinois State Journal* and the *Champaign* (Ill.) *Courier.* The next day the *New York Times* used a short piece by Reuters.

April 26, 1973 the UPI reported from Katmandu that a Japanese expedition had photographed similar footprints. From Hiroshima the AP reported Oct. 27, 1974 that two Japanese geologists had photographed what they believed were footprints of an aboriginal snowman in the Himalayas. A Polish mountaineer and a Sherpa guide also claimed to have seen yeti footprints, the AP reported Nov. 8, 1974 from Katmandu. And Oct. 20, 1975, under a Boston dateline, the AP summarized an article to appear in the November 1975 *Atlantic Monthly*. The author, Edward W. Cronin, Jr., a geologist, told of footprints he saw in December 1972. Also mentioned was the assertion of a teenaged girl that a yeti knocked her unconscious in July 1974 and killed five yaks she was guarding. Also mentioned was the report of a Polish mountaineer who saw tracks in October 1974. Hillary concluded that all of the footprints were made by wild dogs or leopards and then were enlarged and distorted by melting snow.

Evidently in the belief that any animal mystery is important, the *New York Post* gave a column Jan. 9, 1976 to the identity of an "apelike creature that walks upright" for which Michael Miller, a lawyer, paid $8,000. Henry Trefflich, an animal importer, needed only a glance at a picture of the creature to say "it's a chimpanzee."

Advice on how to behave in the presence of an Abominable Snowman was given by Bhola Rana in a UPI story Oct. 12, 1976 from Katmandu. The *Milwaukee Journal* gave almost a column to such instructions as "Don't try to photograph the yeti, especially with a flash."

A century-old mystery regarding the Wild Men of Yakutsk, USSR was believed solved when I. E. Grovich reported on a half-century of research that indicated the shaggy-haired, shrill-voiced creatures were Chuchuna (outcasts), tragic victims of a tribal custom. Nikki Finke reported for the Associated Press April 9, 1979 that the outcasts were fishermen who survived shipwreck but were thought by their fellow tribesmen to be evil spirits and were driven away.

Another account of a Russian expedition was made by Douglas Stanglin Sept. 8, 1979 for the United Press International from Moscow. Home from a summer in the Pamira Mountains the 160 searchers had a plaster cast of a footprint 14 inches long and 6 inches wide at the toes. They also were told natives had seen huge hairy creatures. The AP reported the same news from Moscow Sept. 9, 1979. Reuters Nov. 12, 1979 and Agence France-Presse Nov. 19 had reported that the expedition's leader said he actually saw an Abominable Snowman. Sept. 9, 1979 American newspapers had a picture of a member of the Soviet expedition displaying a plaster cast 14 inches long and 6 inches wide that was found in the Pamira Mountains.

On the 50th anniversary of the discovery of the Peking Man, an important anthropological find, Zhou Gouxing of the Peking Museum of Natural History reported on an eight months expedition in the mountainous Shennongjia region where in 1976 a large creature with reddish hair was sighted. The *New York Times* had a story Jan. 5, 1980 that said the accidental shooting of a gun frightened the creature away before pictures could be taken. There were, however, large footprints.

No matter how many expeditions led by reliable scientists report there is no Abominable Snowman in the Himalayas, others will continue to search. One such quest was led by John Edwards, a squadron leader in the British Royal Air Force. Nikki Finke reported from London Dec. 24, 1979 for the Associated Press that the group heard terrifying screams and brought back photographs of huge footprints in the snow. Nobody saw a yeti but some believe one was nearby all the time.

Footprints also were seen by a Polish expedition climbing Mt. Everest, the AP reported March 9, 1980 from New Delhi, India.

Early in 1982 an Indian army expedition reported it had seen naked cave men and women in the Himalayan Mountains eating raw meat because they had not learned about fire. In reporting the discovery from New Delhi Jan. 25, 1982 the UPI quoted Gerald Berreman, a University of California anthropologist, as surmising the army might have seen yetis, not human beings. He and other scientists doubted that any descendants of people who had existed for the past 200,000 years could not know the use of fire and cooking.

Any news hole created by a diminution of Abominable Snowman reports from the Himalayas was more than filled by the acceleration of sightings of sasquatchs in the American Pacific Northwest. In an editorial that the *Chicago Sun-Times* reprinted Nov. 28, 1959, the *Kansas City (Mo.) Star* congratulated the people of Kamloops, British Columbia for "the acquisition of a fine fullgrown monster" by use of a hitherto unheard of Indian legend that "certainly won't hurt the tourist business in Kamloops."

In addition to the "fierce-eyed, 8 feet tall, fur covered" full-grown monster sighted in the Canadian province, enormous human footprints, 16 inches long and 6 inches wide, were found four times on a mountain logging road, according to a UPI dispatch Jan. 6, 1958 from Witchpec, Calif. The *Laramie* (Wyo.) *Boomerang* reported Feb. 14, 1968 that a huge creature heaved head-sized rocks at three rabbit hunters.

The *San Francisco Chronicle* devoted about one-third of Page 1 of its Dec. 6, 1965 issue to an artist's drawing of a "man-animal" compiled by reports based on numerous eyewitness sightings of strange mountain creatures, nearly ten feet tall, hairy, standing erect. Some who did not actually see the creature heard its screams and smelled its vile odor. On an inside page the newspaper ran a map showing where 15 reports of sightings or discovery of tracks occurred in the states of Washington, Oregon and California.

Inspired by an alleged 480 similar sightings during the preceding half-century, a wealthy Washington hostess, Mrs. Allen Rosse, financed an expedition to search for what the north Pacific Indians called sasquatch and whites called Bigfoot. To head the search she hired Peter Byrne, founder of the International Wildlife Conservation Society, who led two unsuccessful expeditions to find an Abominable Snowman in Nepal. In the *Chicago Daily News* for Aug. 16, 1971, Betty Beale quoted Byrne as saying he was convinced of the American yeti's existence because of a short motion picture of an erect black, hairy creature. That picture, the only one ever claimed to be of a sasquatch, has been controversial ever since it was taken Oct. 20, 1965 in North California by Roger Patterson, a rodeo performer. Scientists are virtually unanimous in saying it is the photograph of a man in a fur suit, but true believers in monsters scoff at such cynicism. *Newsweek* published the picture Oct. 9, 1972. The *New York Times* did so Jan. 20, 1975.

That the skepticism was shared by a section of the press was indicated by a July 1972 editorial in the *Portland Oregonian*.

> Big Foot still alive
> We'd wondered what had happened to Sasquatch, alias Big Foot, the hairy monster who left its giant tracks in various parts of the Pacific Northwest and which had been seen by some and photographed by at least one person.
> It has been several months since reports of sighting the beast have appeared in the press. Not since Ray L. Pickens, a Colcille, Wash. bricklayer, said he had made some of the tracks by attaching foot-shaped plywood cutouts to his boots had Big Foot been reported.
> The Sasquatch appeared to have disappeared like the hairy ape men of Mt. St. Helens who terrorized some miners in 1924 and whose existence was questioned by a young Oregonian reporter named L. H. Gregory. Gregory pointed out that all the tracks the ape men made were right-footed and later some jokers admitted they had made them.
> Well, we're glad to hear that Big Foot is not dead. Maybe he was only offended by the doubts expressed in these parts about his being real. In any event he has shown up in the hills of Missouri and so frightened the family of a man named Edgar Harrison that they departed for safer life in the town of Louisiana. Mr. Harrison stayed home, however, to fend off the monster, and said he found its tracks up in the hollow near his place.
> The description of the beast given by two Harrison children, who saw it, is very close to that of our Big Foot. But our Sasquatch had five toes, according to plaster casts made of his tracks. The Missouri monster had five toes on one foot, but only four on the other. Maybe Big Foot lost a toe crossing the Rockies last winter.

To offset journalistic cynicism there are a number of prestigious believers in Bigfoot. One, Grover Krantz, associate professor of anthropology at Washington State University in Pullman, Wash., told *Chicago Today's* Action Express editors, "I've examined evidence that can't be explained any other way," according to that column for Aug. 25, 1974. In *Newsweek* the professor was quoted as saying, "Either the animals are real or the footprints were faked by an anatomy expert." He believes in the authenticity of the Patterson picture and that the failure of researchers to find skeletal or other remains is because any hunter who kills a sasquatch is ashamed to confess it, according to an article "Stalking the Sasquatch" by David C. Anderson in the *New York Times Magazine* for Jan. 20, 1974. That article gave the pro and con of many incidents, perhaps the most fascinating of which was the revelation in 1957 by Albert Ostman, a lumberman, that he had been kidnapped in 1924 by a family of four sasquatches.

A shorter objective, comprehensive account of the phenomenon was "Is that 8-foot apeman for real?" by Larry S. Finley in the *Chicago Daily News* for July 29–30, 1972.

Months after the monster scare in Murphysboro, Ill. the *Kansas City Star* financed a five-man expedition to capture or at least photograph the supposed 8-foot erect creature weighing about 1,000 lbs. with dirty white matted hair, an obnoxious odor and a terrifying scream. Instead, they found some trees uprooted and some with the bark scraped off. They heard of Reb, "the meanest dog in southern Illinois," who cringed when thrown into a barn where the monster was supposed to be.

The Kansas City newspaper's interest was aroused because of the similarities between the monsters reported in Illinois and in the Pacific Northwest where the much-sought stranger is called Bigfoot. Dec. 23, 1973 the UPI reported from Atlanta that Jeoffrey Bourne, director of the Yerkes Regional Primate Center, thinks that both the Abominable Snowman and Bigfoot may exist, being Gigantopithecus, a humanoid form that lived three-quarters of a million years ago. Bourne was shown in a picture studying an alleged plaster cast of Bigfoot's footprint.

Remembering the Cardiff Giant hoax that fooled many reputable scientists in 1889, and the Jersey Devil, the *Wall Street Journal* wondered editorially Jan. 24, 1974 how "any reputable scientist would confess to even the slightest doubt" that there is no Bigfoot.

In his review of Marian T. Place's book, *On the Track of Bigfoot,* David C. Anderson wrote in the *New York Times* for May 3, 1974: "The larger point to be made about Bigfoot is that it reveals the interesting, if not bizarre, ways civilized men can behave when they have to cope with the unexplained."

With a $50,000 grant from the National Wildlife Federation and the Academy of Applied Sciences of Boston and $20,000 from the family of Louise Carpenter of Fort Lauderdale, Fla. an eight-man expedition led by Peter Byrne began hunting Bigfoot, the AP reported July 22, 1974 from The Dalles, Ore.

When several youths in Carol Stream, Ill. reported seeing a beast, 7 feet tall and weighing about 500 pounds, Dave Schneidman wrote in the *Chicago Tribune* for Oct. 6, 1974 what he learned about yetis from the Yeti Research Society headquartered in St. Petersburg, Fla. The advice was not to panic because yetis, though curious, mean no harm.

Believers received a boost when the Army Corps of Engineers officially recognized the existence of sasquatch in its *Washington Environmental Atlas*. As reported from Spokane by the Associated Press July 5, 1975, the animal is "reported to feed on vegetation and some meat and is covered with long hair, except for the face and hands and is of distinctly humanlike form."

Lengthy sympathetic accounts of the Bigfoot Information Center operated by Peter Byrne in The Dalles, Ore. appeared in several papers. One of the first was by David P. Johnson in the *National Observer* for Aug. 24, 1974. He reviewed the work of Byrne who had followed up 80 reports in four years but nobody had claimed the $1,000 reward for leading the investigative team to discover a sasquatch. Johnson talked to Wayne Jones who was leader of a camping party of 30 who say they saw a huge erect creature on the shore of Harrison Lake. Also there was the report of Mr. and Mrs. Richard Brown who refrained from shooting the creature they encountered because they were not certain it wasn't human. Old Indians told of stories they heard of sasquatch traveling in groups of 18 or 20.

June 10, 1976 the *New York Times* had a story by Boyce Rensberger to whom several persons related encounters with a strange creature. Nov. 11, 1975 the *Chicago Tribune* had a sizable story from Bellingham, Wash. telling of six new sightings of Bigfoot, or sasquatch, as the Indians called it. An Indian reservation police sergeant said he flashed his light on a 7½-foot-tall creature with a furry body and no neck with steam coming from its body. Also three bear-hunters hastily abandoned their camp near Yakima, Wash. when a large creature growled at them. Peter Byrne said there had been 340 sightings since the early 1800s. Byrne was shown in an AP photograph examining plaster casts of footprints.

Nov. 20, 1975 Joe Frazier wrote an article for the Associated Press from The Dalles. Much of it was verbatim from the *Tribune's* story with a few extra details. The *Milwaukee Journal* accompanied the article with a 3-column reproduction of the picture taken in 1967 in Del Norte County, Calif. by Roger Patterson.

May 24, 1976 the AP reported from Eureka, Calif. that Cherie Darvell, 22, of Redding, had been abducted by "a large hairy animal" according to four of her companions. Two days later the AP reported the young woman had shown up screaming outside a rural resort but sheriff's department officials didn't believe her story, especially after she and her friends refused to take polygraph tests. A sheriff's posse had conducted an all-night search and suspected a hoax.

In an editorial, "Nessie, Yeti and Bigfoot," July 2, 1976 the *Washington Star* gently ridiculed the *New York Times* for its interest in mythical beings. The heft of a confirmed sighting, the editorial said, would ensure the presence of a dozen National Football League scouts. "With that heft," the editorial concluded, "Sasquatch could make the wildest middle linebacker in the history of the NFL. We'll keep you posted."

And yet Aug. 1, 1976 the same *Washington Star* gave a full page to an article from Portland, Ore. by Thomas Love: "I'd Heard About Bigfoot. There He Was, Watching Me." It related the experience of someone named Al, a camper, who was watched quietly for 45 minutes by Bigfoot who then was frightened by a flashbulb and ran away. Unfortunately, apparently the photograph didn't turn out well. The article continued with an exhaustive rehash of all that other reporters had written about sightings, past and present, and the activities of the Byrne expedition.

A sobering note was added to the controversy by Anabel Parshall of Old Greenwich, Conn. in a letter to the *New York Times* for July 1, 1976:

> Why are the alleged observers of Big Foot so anxious to stone and kill him? It seems the Big Foot, who quietly retreats, is the more civilized animal. We need to be alerted to the rights of all other animals.

One newspaper columnist who followed Bigfoot's peregrinations was Don Bishoff of the *Eugene* (Ore.) *Register-Guard*. His July 11, 1976 column was headed, "Hot on the Trail of Big Foot Once Again." It recounted the optimism of Ron Olson, founder and head man of North American Wildlife Research, in the search being conducted in northern British Columbia by his colleague Roy Lack. Olson said that if Bigfoot were captured scientists would be flown in and after their examination Bigfoot would be turned loose.

June 12, 1977 Bishoff told of the finding of a case of Canadian Club near Mt. St. Helens by Tom Dalton, a Portland auto-repair-shop owner who recognized the spot in pictures used by the advertising concern promoting the stunt of hiding cases in remote spots all over the world. The Dalton find had been advertised as in Bigfoot's feeding ground. The column's heading was "Big Foot'll have No Booze With Brunch."

"For Big Foot Fans, Four-Toed Tracks" was the title of the Sept. 8, 1977 column telling of the discovery of some large tracks in the mud near Eugene. All agreed that they weren't made by a bear or a human, but the mystery remained.

Ten days later, Sept. 18, 1977 Bishoff reported that Ron Olson said he didn't believe they were Bigfoot's tracks. Gordon Kliewer, another sasquatch hunter, took a cast of the impression and insisted it was Bigfoot's footprint. Bishoff entitled his column, "Some Say Phooey to Big Foot's Foot," and apparently so did the columnist.

The avidity of widely separated places to obtain publicity and of the press to accommodate them was demonstrated by a UPI story from Goldsboro, N.C. Sept. 14, 1976 that dogs had howled and tree branches were crunched during a night when there was no thunderstorm. A mental therapist said he had been puzzled for six years by 18-inch, three-toed footprints, and a farmer declared that he once saw a figure seven or eight feet tall with "black fur, sort of hunched over and looking at me."

Back in the Northwest UPI reported May 16, 1977 from Mission, B.C. that a large furry creature standing 7 feet and leaving 14-inch footprints crossed the path of a bus in sight of the bus driver and six passengers. May 18 the AP released the facts, stressed the creature's "horrible smell" and reported that many people believed it was Bigfoot. May 22 the *Chicago Tribune* gave a half-page to an article, "Bigfoot sightings keep Canadians on their toes," by its correspondent Michael Coakley, writing from Mission, B.C. Pat Lindquist, the bus driver, explained how he swerved to avoid what he thought was a man in a monkey suit. Lindquist said that he chased the creature into the woods where they confronted each other silently for some time. The six passengers at first corroborated Lindquist's account but later two repudiated their first statements. John Green, author of several books on sasquatch, examined the footprints and called them authentic. He described the beast's supposed habits and recalled several other sightings of recent years. The *Vancouver Province* assigned a reporter-photographer team to scout the area, which it did, causing their city editor to declare they had disproved an old Indian legend that sasquatch are attracted by large quantities of beer.

This "good practical joke," as they called it, was solved when three young men went to a radio talk-show and confessed that one of them, Ken Ticehurt of Port Coquitlam, staged the incident. Ken, 6 feet 3 inches tall, had rented a gorilla suit for $200 and the resin-cast footprints were patterned on instructions in a book by Don Hunter, a reporter, and Rene Dahinden. Hunter refused to accept the hoax confession but Dahinden said it seemed authentic. One of the conspirators had been a passenger on the bus instructed to stir up the others which he did. The Associated Press reported the story May 27, 1977 from Vancouver, Canada.

Among those who must have been disillusioned by this solution of the mystery that had excited them for days were readers of the May 22 story in the *Chicago Sun-Times* by Bruce Ingersoll who interviewed the intrepid Peter Byrne at his Bigfoot Information Center at Hood River, Ore. Byrne, who had spent six years seeking Bigfoot after his original backing by socialite Mrs. Allen Rosse, said the Mission sighting was "quite creditable" and not a hoax because the passenger-witnesses were strangers to each other.

Real or myth, Bigfoot was offered protection in a resolution passed by the Committee on Environment of the Oregon House of Representatives, the UPI reported July 6, 1977 from Salem, Ore. Originally its introducer did so "with tongue in cheek," but the nationwide interest it aroused convinced him that there should be a serious law to protect the creature from harassment and possible extinction should it be found. The resolution also asked school and public authorities to be on the alert for Bigfoot.

Explaining "[I'm] not doing this for fun. I'm doing it for science and mankind," a Flint, Mich. automobile worker, Wayne King, established a Michigan Bigfoot Information Center in his home at Millington to seek and find a sasquatch in the neighborhood of Traverse City. The UPI announced the plans in a story from Flint May 6, 1977. It quoted King: "There are probably 12 Bigfoot in Benzie County alone. We'll be loaded for plaster castings, and immediate movie taking. We'll be looking for a nine foot giant who weighs between 800 and 1,200 pounds." July 11, 1977 the *Detroit Free Press* devoted almost a half-page to publicize King's venture. King never has seen one but he had a tape recording of its screeching. Unfortunately, as Steve Orr, the *Free Press* writer, put it, "someone did a Rose Mary Woods number on the tape," making it unavailable. A retired state policeman, Lt. Zane Gray, was examining some feces thought to be those of Bigfoot. Gray also discovered some 19-inch footprints. King hopes the Michigan legislature will enact a statute to protect what he says will be "the biggest find of mankind."

In the fall of 1977 there was a Bigfoot scare in South Dakota. The *Sioux Falls Argus Leader* and the *McLaughlin Messenger* reported that residents had seen an evil-smelling, hairy erect creature whose height was variously reported from 12 to 18 feet with footprints measuring from 16 to 18 inches.

Search party activities were directed from the Little Eagle Trading Post. Beginning Sept. 30, 1977 the Associated Press covered the story and the *Bismarck* (N.D.) *Tribune* reported developments until well after the New Year. Its issue of Nov. 26 contained a two-page well-illustrated spread, "Bigfoot Invasion Upsetting Life in Reservation Hamlet."

There also was coverage by the *New York Times* and the NBC Nightly News sent a crew to cover the story. Under the heading "Legends" *Newsweek* summarized the main features of the story in its Oct. 31, 1977 issue.

The excitement began to diminish when Pat McLaughlin, Standing Rock Sioux tribal chairman, and Shirley Plume, Bureau of Indian Affairs agent for the Standing Rock Agency, issued a joint appeal to people to stop using firearms in their search. McLaughlin said he had received phone calls from six reservations in a five-state area appealing for action to protect Bigfoot. They came from longtime believers in a Bigfoot or "Taku he" who feared that if the beast were injured harm would come to the Indian people.

Although the atmosphere became more peaceful, Bigfoot continued to be remembered—and occasionally seen. The *Bismarck Tribune* had the following accounts: Jan. 7, 1978, AP from Little Eagle, S.D.—Alexander saw two about 600 yards away; Jan. 29, 1978, AP from Washington citing authorities of the Fish and Wildlife Service that Bigfoot would be protected under the Endangered Species Act; April 14, 1979, an illustrated feature about Alexander's Trading Post where activities came to a virtual standstill after the Standing Rock Reservation Tribal Council placed a ban on Bigfoot hunts and even tried, unsuccessfully, to put a ban on talking about Bigfoot; Oct. 24, 1979 AP from Rauville, S.D.—a Little Foot, 4 or 5 feet tall, but otherwise resembling Bigfoot, was reported near Watertown but was not found as expected in an abandoned farmstead; Nov. 14, 1979, AP from

Werner, N.D.—two men in a truck were certain they saw Bigfoot by the roadside.

Dec. 27, 1977 the AP sent a little brightener from Sumter, S.C. about the theft of a six-foot, 160-pound stuffed animal called Bigfoot from outside a taxidermist's shop. It was worth $500.

In its lengthy news release Jan. 29, 1978 the U.S. Fish and Wildlife Service warned against hysterical crowds. After receiving 12 days temporary protection under the Endangered Species Act, Bigfoot "would undergo the humdrum processing for long-term safe-guarding."

When the motion picture "Sasquatch" was released Janet Maslin in the *New York Times* for Jan. 12, 1978 called it "the kind of pseudoscientific silliness that manages to discredit itself entirely, thanks to an approach that might best be labeled simulated-verite."

In his comment on the film in the *Washington Post* for Jan. 30, 1979 Gary Arnold wrote:

> Like the similarly cheapskate, slipshod, pseudoscientific exploitation movies about UFOs, the Bermuda Triangle, the Lincoln assassination or the end of the world, the Bigfoot sagas are a self-perpetuating con, aimed at a public of incorrigibly gullible adults and raucous chortling kids.

Feb. 18, 1979 the *Post* ran a long account that Kay Bartlett wrote for the Associated Press from Seattle. It explained the viewpoints, mostly the differences, of the leaders of the 200 or so Bigfoot hunters. Peter Byrne, the only one ever to receive any financial backing, runs the Bigfoot Information Center and Exhibition in Hood, Ore. He swore out a warrant against Rene Dahinden to keep him out of his territory. Dahinden's main rival, however, is Jon Beckjord of Seattle, who collects pictures, blood samples, hair, droppings and tape recordings and shows the Patterson film. Dr. Grover Krantz of Washington State says only capture of a sasquatch will satisfy skeptics. Dr. John Gillespie has offered $50,000 for one, dead or alive. John Green, former newspaper editor, converted Krantz to the cause when he showed him 1,000 footprints ascribed to Bigfoot.

"There are 245 legends about Bigfoot from 195 different tribes in Alaska, Canada and the United States. The creature has been spotted at least 750 times this century from Mexico to California to the Yukon," Barbara Rehm wrote in the *New York Daily News* for Jan. 3, 1978. Her full-page article included mention of several of the most important reports, dating from 1811 when the first footprints were reported by David Thomson. In 1928 an Indian reported he had been kidnapped but not harmed by 20 sasquatch near Vancouver. Rehm summarized the usual situation.

Curiously, in all the sightings, Bigfoot does nothing spectacular. It does not roar or charge or act ferocious in any way. In report after report the creature simply walks along or watches people until it senses that it has been seen and then walks away.

Refreshing was a story by Charles Hillinger in the *Los Angeles Times* for Jan. 2, 1980 about the course "Bigfoot, Myth or Reality" that Turhos Murad, anthropology professor, taught on the Chico campus of California State University. Murad prefaced his other remarks to the reporter by stating, "I'd better tell you, I don't believe in Bigfoot." After stressing the lack of any scientific evidence that there is a sasquatch, Professor Murad exclaimed, "The class on Bigfoot is designed to make students think for themselves."

Robert Gardiner of Columbus, Ohio, who has been searching for yeti for years, got 400 words from UPI Oct. 7, 1980 from McArthur, Ohio. Although he saw no sasquatch, Gardiner is convinced they surrounded him in a nearby ravine because footprints were visible where there had been none an hour earlier.

Although a committee of Chinese scientists found many footprints they believe were made by a human or ape 8½ feet tall and weighing 550 lb., they had no eyewitnesses until a country girl said she had encountered such a creature—and there were footprints to support her story. Michael Parks sent the *Los Angeles Times* a lengthy story for the paper's April 10, 1981 edition.

An anthropologist said the giant footprints discovered near Olympia, Wash. were those of a bear, not Bigfoot, the UPI reported May 28, 1981. That the elusive creature gets around, however, was reported in the *New York Post* for Aug. 26, 1981. An IBM computer analysis said there have been 94 sightings in the area of New York north of Poughkeepsie and south of Kingston.

The October 1980 issue of *Passages,* magazine of Northwest Orient Airlines, succinctly summarized the features of a Bigfoot scare. "The pattern is familiar, calls to authorities by startled witnesses, frantic hunts aided (or impeded in many cases) by excited CB-equipped, rifle-toting volunteers: then nothing. As likely as not, the reports recede in a few days, weeks or months, leaving police with the plaster cast of a footprint here, some alleged hair or feces sample there, and defensive, head-scratching observations that the witnesses seemed sincere."

Keeping track of Bigfoot has almost become a business to some. In addition to Peter Byrne's Bigfoot Information Center in Hood River, Ore. and Wayne King's Michigan Bigfoot Information Center in Millington, there also are Irwin Alpert's Sasquatch Research Group in Kansas City, Mo. and many more study and watchdog groups, some of them primarily interested in Unidentified Flying Objects. Among the books to date are *Bigfoot: The Yeti and the Sasquatch in Myth and Reality,* by Grover Krantz; *Startling Evidence of Other Forms of Life on Earth Now: Bigfoot,* by John Napier; *Bigfoot,* by Barbara Ann Slate and Alan Berry; *Sasquatch,* by Rene Dahinden and Don Hunter and *My Travels with Bigfoot* by Charles Edson.

"We have to end this mystery and the only way that can be done is to take a specimen," Wayne King said as he enlisted a trio of hunters to stake out the Culhan farm in rural Ingham County, Michigan where a grain shed was broken into and 50-pound bags of seed and salt were ripped to pieces. The AP reported Sept. 25, 1979 that the Culhans found an 11-inch-long handprint in the dew on the top of their pickup truck. There never was a followup telling of success.

Reports also continued to come in from all over the Midwest. According to the UPI for Nov. 23, 1981 two farm girls near Yale, Mich. encountered a furry creature in the darkness of their cattle barn.

The biggest blow to the true believers in the Northwest Bigfoot came in a copyrighted story in *The Columbian* of Vancouver for Sunday, April 11, 1982. It announced the confession of an 86-year-old retired logger that he was responsible for perpetrating the legend of the Bigfoot of Mt. St. Helens by stamping large footprints in the snow. A photograph of Rant Mullens holding the wooden feet accompanied the article.

Actually, Mullens said, the joke began in 1924 when he and his uncle rolled some rocks down a hill that caused three miners to tell rangers they had seen huge hairy creatures who hurled boulders at them. The Mt. St. Helens footprint hoax was executed in 1928 and helped further the legend.

Unfazed, Prof. Grover Krantz told reporters that Mullens' confession added credibility to the legend because the Mt. St. Helens story didn't mesh with other sightings.

In more than a full-page article June 4, 1982 the *Los Angeles Times'* William Overend explained "Bigfoot Legend Engenders a Feud." On one hand there was Mullens, whose story was given in great detail. Opposed to him was Ray Wallace pictured with eight sets of plaster casts he says he made. From Toledo, Wash. Overend reported: "Wallace originally had no quarrel about the existence of Bigfoot himself. Wallace was simply one of those who had managed to profit from the legend and Mullens wasn't. It was Mullens' view that Wallace had cheated him out of some money and Wallace made it known to all in town that he feared Mullens was eventually going to shoot him over the disputed debt." The rest of the story is a fascinating account of how the two old-timers contend with each other. June 3, 1982 the UPI reported from Walla Walla that a Forest Service employee sighted Bigfoot about 25 miles north of Walla Walla. Oct. 25 the *San Francisco Chronicle* used a United Press story from Vancouver, B.C. that Professor Krantz examined footprints and said they proved the existence of a sasquatch.

Although newspapers persist in printing such news, they show increasing skepticism when interviewing some of the professional investigators of the unknown. Such certainly was the case when they interviewed the leaders of two different expeditions to hunt for dinosaurs in darkest Africa, which used to be called the Belgian Congo and now is the independent nation of Zaire. June 6, 1981 Robert Locke of the Associated Press reported that Roy P. Mackal, a University of Chicago biologist, was returning to the area where a year earlier pygmies had told him of the existence of mokele-mbembe (meaning eats off tops of trees) described as brownish-gray with short thick legs, stretching 35 feet and weighing from nine to 15 tons. One presumably was killed by natives in 1959. June 11, 1981 Locke began his article, "It sounds like a Late Show movie but two scientist-adventurers say they're going to search uncharted African jungles for what may be a living species of dinosaur that somehow escaped extinction 60 million years ago." He quoted Mackal as saying, "I admit to having some romance in my soul." In the *New York Times* for Oct. 18, 1981 John Noble Wilford elaborated on Mackal's announcement, saying the natives called the atavism half-elephant, half-dragon. He disclosed that Mackal's financing came from the National Geographic Society, *Geo* Magazine and Jack Bryan, a Plano, Texas oilman. He also recalled that Mackal had spent years investigating the mythical Loch Ness monster and its supposed relative in Lake Champlain.

Satirically the *New York Daily News* editorialized Oct. 23, 1981 on "Preserve Our Myths." It quoted Mackal as saying that if his dinosaur quest were successful he would go after the dodo bird, extinct since 1681. The editorial concluded, "Move over, Don Quixote."

Dec. 10 Wilford reported in the *New York Times* that Mackal had returned with accounts of what might be a new species of snake and of strange footprints in the jungle but without success in finding the legendary mokele-mbembe. However, he said he was "more convinced now than ever" of the animal's existence. The next day the AP had a story quoting him similarly.

When he returned home Mackal was interviewed by a reporter for the *Chicago Sun-Times,* who quoted him Dec. 12, 1981 as having found footprints of a dinosaurlike creature. Although he believes dinosaurs may still exist he admitted the footprints could have been made by a lizard. In either case the creature would have a body the size of a hippopotamus or a small elephant, with a snakelike head and tail.

A week later the attention turned from Mackal to Herman Regusters an engineer at the Jet Propulsion Laboratory in Pasadena, and his wife, Kia, who returned from six weeks in the jungle to say they had sighted a dinosaurlike animal that looks like a small brontosaurus, presumably extinct for 65 million years. Dec. 16 the *Chicago Sun-Times* had a story based on a letter and telegram the explorers had sent their Los Angeles spokesman, John Sack.

Another week later, Dec. 23, both the UPI and AP had stories of a rather tumultuous press conference at which the Regusterses were unable to produce pictures or any other evidence to substantiate their claim to have found a dinosaur. They said the animal was seen several times but always mostly submerged in Lake Tele. Only one picture was taken and it was being developed.

Dec. 23 the UPI distributed a picture of Mr. and Mrs. Regusters pointing to the area they explored on a wall map. In an accompanying article Lee Dembart, science writer, quoted the couple as saying they would make available later a tape recording of the creature roaring. They said they spent $40,000 of their own money on the expedition.

In the *Washington Post* for Dec. 25 Henry Mitchell waxed satirical for about a half-page. He expressed great skepticism and was strongly suspicious of the dinosaur hunters because "They believed dinosaurs still existed. Then they set out to find them. Whenever men believe something exists, they have no trouble whatever finding it does exist. They have an ax to grind. Humans have been exploring the world more or less carefully for about 3,000 years, and it is odd that dinosaurs have not been met with in those centuries . . . One of the firmest principles of human behavior is that if you want something to be it is bound to be."

The *New York Daily World's* Dec. 19 headline "Scientists doubt dinosaur-like animal sighting" understated the situation, especially after the UPI reported Dec. 9 from Los Angeles that the photographs the Regusterses took turned out to be "severely underexposed" and hence of no help in verifying the claims that there still are dinosaurs in darkest Africa.

In a journalistic post mortem Barbara Varro considered "Why the study of dinosaurs still fills humans with awe" in the *Chicago Sun-Times* for Jan. 3, 1982. She wrote:

> Part of the reason for the universal appeal of dinosaurs is that they are not mythical beasts but very real reptiles that roamed Earth in the springtime of its existence as the dominant form of life on the planet for 140 million years, starting in the Mesozoic era that ended 63 million years ago.

In the same issue, capitalizing on the interest in the subject, the paper had an article by James Gorman, "Baby dinosaurs provide clues." It pertained to the archeological findings of John Horner, a Princeton University paleontologist. It was a *Discover* article.

Creation was announced of the International Society of Cryptozoology "to promote scientific inquiry, education and communication among people interested in animals of unexpected form or size or unexpected occurrences in time or space." Its symbol is the giraffelike okapi, thought extinct until discovered in 1900 in the Congo. John Noble Wilford wrote about it in the *New York Times* for Jan. 19, 1982. President of the society is Bernard Heuvelmans of France with Roy P. Mackal as vice-president.

Dr. Mackal was the subject of "Heath's Critique" in the *Oklahoma Publisher* by Dr. Harry Heath, director of the School of Journalism of Oklahoma State University. He noted Mackal's return from Africa and chided the journalistic shortcomings of its coverage.

> What the wire service doesn't say is that this is the same Dr. Mackal who spent a good chunk of money from a foundation sponsoring some of his early work. That was at Loch Ness in Scotland where he presumably expected to

find the mythical sea serpent Nessie whose drawing power has made the area a tourist attraction. What's my point? Just this. If writers don't do enough research in backgrounding the people in the news, the full significance of some stories goes unreported.

Describing "Top Denizens of the Myth Zoo," Josef Berger wrote in the *New York Times Magazine* for Nov. 27, 1960:

They are a hardy lot, those hairy giants and their kinfolk, the fearsome fauna of the borderland between nature and supernature. They come of a very old family. Some branches, like the dragons, go back thousands of years. And even today, strange tales, sending tingles up and down the human spine, are told, sworn to by perfectly sane, reliable eyewitnesses, often supported by tangible evidence, and lacking only the actual body involved.

May 28, 1983 the Associated Press reported from Pasadena repeating Regusters' claim of having seen a dinosaur in 1981 in the Congo. The *Stillwater News-Press* gave a full column to the story in which Regusters announced a new expedition planned for 1984.

13

Sea Serpents

Throughout history most prolific tellers of tall tales have been explorers, travelers, adventurers, pioneers, frontiersmen, landlubbers all but often outdone by mariners whose whoppers seldom were verifiable. A sailor's credibility was diminished by both his tendency to exaggerate and by obstacles preventing accurate observations.

Jerry E. Bishop reported in the *Wall Street Journal* for Feb. 11, 1981 that in its February 1981 issue the British magazine *Nature* two University of Manitoba scientists explained how certain atmospheric conditions preceding a storm can bend light waves so that low-lying objects are stretched to gigantic proportions. When a temperature inversion occurs over a body of water an observer at a distance actually sees objects over the horizon. Professors Waldemar H. Lehn and Irmgard Schroeder told of seeing a fearsome creature on the shore of Lake Winnipeg, armless with a huge bulbous head. Actually the monster was a distorted image of a foot-high boulder lying on the shore more than a half-mile away.

Such optical illusions as Lehn and Schroder wrote about could explain why Vikings 800 years ago reported seeing mermen as tall as water towers that foretold dangerous storms and mysterious hedges hemming them in at sea, the AP reported from New York Feb. 23, 1981. The story mentioned a book written in 1170 by a Norwegian who described a merman as "the largest wild beast but without head and tail," and a 13th-century book described a mermaid as possessing heavy hair, breasts, large webbed feet and a tail. Using computers the two Canadian scientists sketched how objects could be distorted and showed that the closer the observer is to the surface the greater the distortion. The decks of Viking ships were only a few feet above the waterline which explains why sightings of mermen and mermaids diminished as higher decked ships and elevated lookouts became common.

A report of an interview with Lehn written by Lois Sauer appeared in the *New York Times* for Aug. 14, 1979.

Most sightings of sea serpents are made just before dawn or just after dusk. This caused the *Boston Transcript* to speculate in an editorial Oct. 24, 1933 that the Great Western Sea Monster must be of the nyctipelagic order of marine creatures—those that rise to the surface of the ocean only at night to feed and gambol, seeing better in the dark like the felidae on land. "In all the *Transcript's* avid reading of sea serpent stories," the paper said, "never once has the creature appeared in broad daylight."

The same can be said of a majority of the denizens of the deep believed by their admirers to be plesiosaurus or other survivors from the prehistoric past.

According to a full-page feature in the *American Weekly* for Oct. 30, 1938, the legendary kraken is probably responsible for most of the sea serpents whose existence science is inclined to doubt. However, the subtitle of the article, "Fabled Kraken Super-Octopus Still Alive?" read "Dr. Julian Huxley, eminent scientist, explains why he thinks the monster, which ancient superstition gave supernatural powers may not be wholly myth after all." Huxley, among other things secretary of the London Zoological Society, based his belief on the discovery by the Prince of Monaco of the remains of a giant octopus in a whale's stomach.

Doubtless there are living things at depths in the oceans where men have not explored. Foremost seeker after their stories was Charles Fort (1874–1932) in whose honor the Fortean Society was established by some noted writers, including Theodore Dreiser, Booth Tarkington, Ben Hecht and Tiffany Thayer. The *Chicago Times* devoted a page Oct. 13, 1946 to an article by Louis Schaefle who speculated that the atom bomb tests at Bikini, in addition to killing millions of fish, would create a few new monsters. He buttressed his argument by recalling the after-effects of some earthquakes, volcanic eruptions and tidal waves of the past.

Schaefle recalled the Mobile Monster of 1938, which turned out to be an otter; the Sterling Monster which was a bobcat; and the beast that a Mr. Davy created after King Louis XIV expressed a wish for a new animal. Scientists differ as to whether it was a dog-boar hybrid or a hyena. Anyway, Schaefle concluded: "The self-respecting monster has had a hard time staying that way, because men's imaginations have always conjured up frightful rivals for the real thing. So the next time you hear a report of some fearsome creature stalking the land, don't be surprised if it's only a cow with a limp."

What doubtless will encourage a new rash of deep sea searches for new living species is the story the *Washington Post* had May 4, 1981 about a research ship off South America that reported the discovery of hot-water geysers on the bottom of the Pacific Ocean and new "unidentified and fascinating" creatures apparently never seen before, able to survive in the otherwise extremely cold ocean deep. The first "ocean vent community" was found in 1977 off the Galapagos Islands and the second sometime later in Mexico. The *Post* reported, "Together the finds are probably the greatest discovery of whole new animal communities in the history of biology."

Reports of a giant stingray measuring 50 feet across battling the freighter *Lewis Luckenbach* for two days in Mexican waters, of a 30-feet sea serpent with a flowing mane and dinner-plate eyes seen off the Scottish coast and of Mediterranean fishermen near Tripoli who escaped death when attacked by a monster with mooselike antlers and elephant ears inspired Marshall Sprague to recall the tall tales of other days for the *New York Times* of June 6, 1937.

Sprague began with Jonah's story in 750 B.C. of having been swallowed by a large fish. Aristotle was the first scientist to describe a monster that chased fat cows in the Libyan desert.

"Some historians," Sprague wrote, "claim that a huge sucker-fish, not Cleopatra, led to Antony's defeat at Actium in 31 B.C. The sucker-fish prevented Antony's flagship from going forward by clinging to the hull and swimming like mad in the opposite direction. The great Roman naturalist Pliny the Elder contributed to science by declaring in 70 A.D. that the Greeks rode between Crete and the mainland on the backs of trained dolphins."

Mermaids and mermen were seen frequently and in 1187 one was captured by Suffolk fishermen in the North Sea. Henry II honored it, as did many others, until a minstrel confessed it was only a seal. Although no sea serpent ever has been captured, reports of their sightings have been made incessantly in every century of our era; scientists may be skeptical but they are cautious.

Lehn and Schroeder are only two of hundreds of thousands of scientists who have been interested in sea serpents. Mostly the others have been members of searching parties or have examined the remains or fossils of creatures for identification purposes. At the International Congress of Zoology in 1955, with 500 attending, at Copenhagen, Denmark, Dr. Anton Bruun, the Congress' secretary-general, expressed his belief that sea serpents did and do exist. He based his opinion on examination of the discovery in 1930 of a six-foot fish identified as the pickled larval form of an eel. It had 450 vertebral plates whereas the largest known eels have only 150. Thus the full-grown eel would have been 70 to 90 feet long. A. J. Hotchner wrote about it in an article, "Are There Sea Serpents, Really?" in *This Week* for Aug. 14, 1955. In the Jan. 29, 1961 issue of the same publication, Dr. Robert J. Menzies, University of Southern California biologist, also declared himself a believer and was certain that a sea serpent broke his 1,200-foot fish line off the western coast of South America.

There is hardly a lake, river or other waterway that hasn't at some time or another been thought to be the abode of a sea serpent, the name used to describe any unidentified denizen of a watery area. Among the scares that have attracted journalistic attention in our times are the following:

The Canadian press reported June 3, 1938 that residents of a Wasaga Beach, Ont. summer resort were excited because of a lake monster that churned the water like an ocean liner at great speed.

The *Christian Science Monitor* reported July 28, 1938 that the skipper of an Italian fishing boat was frightened by a fish with wings instead of scales.

The *Chicago Sun* used a report from London Nov. 17, 1943 that a fish that collided with a submarine was either myopic or lovesick.

The *Boise* (Idaho) *Sunday Statesman* conjectured that Slimey Slim, a shy serpent that frightened vacationers at Payette Lake got there when Paul Bunyan's blue ox Babe twitched so violently when bitten by a horsefly that a sturgeon flew all the way from the Snake River to the lake. *Time* gave it good publicity in its issue of Aug. 21, 1944.

Both the AP and UPI reported Sept. 9, 1947 from Lynn, Mass. that the New England serpent was seen by a piano tuner and his two daughters for the first time in ten years and might be the Loch Ness monster fleeing British authority.

Officers of the Grace Line ship *Santa Clara* told a New York *PM* reporter of the boat's collision with a 45-foot monster. The story received almost a full page in the issue of Jan. 25, 1948.

The *Milwaukee Journal* reported July 24, 1955 that Green Bay sheriff's deputies and others sighted a 7- or 8-foot monster with humps.

A botanist, a geologist, a conservationist and 16 fishermen of Lyons Falls, N.Y. failed to net a monster supposedly 15 feet long with a round tapered body, according to the *Syracuse Herald-Journal* for June 15, 1951.

The *New York Herald Tribune* used a UPI story from Brisbane, Australia Jan. 30, 1960 that a creature with a head 2 feet long and 3 feet wide and no neck frightened boat riders by emerging to watch them.

With 16 scientists and divers aboard, a government research boat, *The Challenger,* hunted a jellyfish sighted by several off the New Jersey coast, the UPI reported Aug. 22, 1963.

A resident of Four Lake Village in Lisle, a Chicago suburb, said he saw "a strange black, shiny, moving monster," in a lake near his home. He blamed it for stealing bait off large steel hooks that were bent out of shape. The *Chicago Daily News* ran a photograph Robert Seeger took. It showed only two humps in some water.

The *Chicago Daily News* for April 29, 1972 also ran a lengthy piece by Harvey Duck speculating on the possibility of Lake Michigan's being the home of a piscatorial beast with a prehistoric shovel nose. Duck interviewed several old-time fishermen who told of the big fish they saw but that got away. There were statistics regarding the large sturgeons that were caught.

The UPI reported May 17, 1975 from Jacksonville, Fla. that five persons saw a pink monster with horns and dark slanted eyes in the St. Johns River.

In an editorial Feb. 3, 1975 the New York *Village Voice* wrote that since 1919 a 40-foot-long python had been seen at Broad Top, Pa. by a dozen persons. Supposedly it escaped during a circus wreck and has lived in coal shafts.

The Associated Press reported July 24, 1977 and the United Press International followed suit Aug. 21, 1977 after Japanese fishermen described the carcass of a 30-foot serpent that their nets unexpectedly hauled in off New Zealand. Because of its decomposing state the fishermen threw it into the water after taking photographs and measurements. Prof. Yoshinori Imatzumi, director general of animal research at the National Science Museum in Tokyo, said it might have been a plesiosaurus, a reptile thought to have been extinct for 100 million years.

"Was it a hoax? A deep-sea version of the Loch Ness monster? Or a prehistoric plesiosaurus?" asked John Saar in a story from Tokyo for the July 21, 1977 *Washington Post*. He added to the dead animal's description, saying it was about 32 feet long, with four flippers, a long neck and tail. The UPI added that it had batlike wings and weighed 2 tons. Both AP and UPI distributed pictures, none of much use in determining what the dead creature was.

When a reader asked what had become of the incident, the *Chicago Sun-Times* Action Time replied by restating what was previously reported except that it gave the date as April 25, 1977 and added, "The incident merely added fuel to the already raging fire over what, if anything, Nessie is."

Four students of Suffolk Community College received the assignment "Define and explain what you think is a powerful myth of our time" and decided to study many weird tales about Lake Ronkonkoma, N.Y., Frank Mooney reported in the *New York Daily News* for Nov. 13, 1977.

Whenever such a find is made journalists invariably surmise that other long-sought creatures are similar, especially the supposed denizens of Loch Ness in Scotland, the Soviet's Kol Kol, the Lac Pohenegamook monster in Quebec and British Columbia's Ogopogo in Okanagan Lake. There are long lists of sightings for all of them and of others like them, but no exhibits, dead or alive, or reliable photographs. Ogopogo was given a sympathetic writeup in the May 9, 1979 issue of *Read* magazine.

June 24, 1978 the UPI sent a story from Montauk, N.Y. that a harpooned 5,000-pound shark dragged a vessel more than 13 miles into the Atlantic Ocean before breaking free after a 13-hour battle. Two days later the UPI reported that the shark was sighted off Long Island but eluded capture by several boatloads of fishermen from the Montauk Marine Basin.

After 15 persons, most of them long-time residents, reported they had seen some strange creature in the Potomac River, the newspapers and press associations took notice. Aug. 18, 1978 the *Washington Post* reported the guesses of several witnesses who thought it probably was an otter, a porpoise, a ray or a snake. Two days later, Aug. 20, the Associated Press reported sightings from nearby Leonardtown, Md. Someone surmised that some reptiles had been stowaways on South American boats that had been left to rot in an estuary.

Sept. 10, 1978 the AP sent out the alleged complaint by a spokesman for the serpents, Patty McTavish, who said this kind had been there for 200 years, a distant cousin of the Loch Ness Monster. McTavish set about organizing S.O.S. (Save Our Serpents).

Nov. 19, 1978 the *New York Times* reported from Sting Ray Port, Va. that there had been 50 sightings of what had been nicknamed Chessie, in imitation of Nessie. The University of Maryland Marine Laboratory, however, said its vessels had had no reports in 50 years.

The *New York Post* used a headline, "Son-of-Nessie surfaces in Siberia" over an AP story from Ust-Nera, USSR April 19, 1979 that told of the sightings of a snake-headed, animal-eating creature in Lake Labinkir in the Siberian province of Yakutia. Antoly Pabkov mentioned it in his book, *The Oymyakobsky*.

Almost two years after the 1978 flurry, the *Washington Star* for June 20, 1980 reported that someone saw something 10 to 14 feet long, dark, with no fins and a head about the size of a man's hand. June 24 the *Star* editorialized on "National Capital Monster," reviewing the history of the sightings and the theories and then saying as follows: "The Potomac monster is a queer animal. It relies for sustenance on processed rhetoric and puffed platitudes, either partisan or bipartisan and has never suffered a day on short rations since moving here."

Giving much the same description as 30 persons had given in 1978, several Coles Point citizens reported sighting a strange creature, now nicknamed Chessie, in the Potomac River. The Associated Press' account was widespread, being used by papers as far away as the *Los Angeles Times* for June 27, 1980.

Chessie next became newsworthy July 11, 1982 and for a week thereafter there was speculation regarding videofilms taken Memorial Day weekend by Robert Frew of Love Point, Md. Karen Frew described the water animal as serpentine, about 30 feet long, dark brown in color. The *Washington Post* had daily stories of the examination by Smithsonian Institution experts who could not give an opinion but said other experts would view the material at some future time. Michael Frizzel of the Enigma Project was pleased the film was not dismissed as a hoax.

Rainbow Lake's Big Nax is as evasive as any or all other water monsters, Hugh A. Mulligan wrote from Ridgeville, Conn. in an Associated Press article that the *Milwaukee Journal* used April 24, 1979.

The *Southern Illinoisan* of Carbondale, Ill. told of a fantastic "thing" in New Crab Orchard Lake. After dragging a fishermen's boat for 45 minutes, it beached itself and climbed a tree. Just before the tree toppled under a timberman's ax, the mysterious creature flew off. Nobody was quoted as doubting the account.

Unfortunately, for science—or at least for fearful and/or gullible people—few monster scares end with the capture, dead or alive, of the object of terror. And when the disturber of the peace is felt as well as smelled, heard and seen, the storehouse of human knowledge usually is not increased much if at all.

In June 1891, an axolotl, a Mexican water reptile resembling a salamender, was captured alive in Peoria. About the same time two alligators were captured by New Boston, Ill. fishermen in the Mississippi River, according to researchers of the Illinois Writers Project, WPA.

"Alley," who terrified swimmers in Monocacy River for six months turned out to be a 40-pound, six-year-old alligator that had escaped from a pet shop, according to an AP story Dec. 29, 1938 from Frederick, Md. Somewhat similar was the story of Oscar, a seal that stole bait from Lake Michigan fishermen's lines. His identity was provided by a Chicago Shedd Aquarium employee who confessed to having disobeyed orders to kill the sickly seal and who instead allowed it to escape into the lake.

And when the monster that had been terrifying residents on Meyers Lake was captured alive it was identified as an alligator, according to UP story from Canton, Ohio Oct. 4, 1940.

The remains of a giant sea creature that washed ashore near Scituate, Mass. were identified as those of a basking shark, but only after several scientists admitted they were stumped, according to an AP story Nov. 16, 1970.

Sometimes the terror turns out to be a hoax. That was true when two dead snakes were found in Honolulu despite the belief that there were no reptiles in the Hawaiian Islands. The scare ended when an official of the Board of Agriculture and Forestry revealed that the snakes had been pickled in alcohol, the AP reported Dec. 12, 1938. And April 18, 1949 the mile-long sea serpent inhabiting a swamp near Lisbon, Me. was reported the work of pranksters.

One of the most successful hoaxes was the Lake George, N.Y. serpent, which an 80-year-old man confessed to having invented 30 years earlier. The story was distributed April 25, 1934 by the International News Service from New York. The octogenarian, Harry W. Watrous, confessed he fashioned the beast in 1904 from a ten-foot log. He anchored it beneath the surface of the lake and let it rise on occasion to terrorize the countryside by means of a rope and pulley controlled from the shore. Watrous called it a hippogriff and made it for the particular benefit of Col. William Mann, publisher of *Town Topics*.

The coast guard took possession of a 44-foot skeleton found on the beach near Provincetown, Mass. The *New York Times* for Jan. 19, 1939 said some old-timers believed it was part of the carcass of a 300-foot serpent sighted in 1886 by the town crier.

Proper identification of either living or dead objects of surprise and/or terror is not always easy and most newspapers fail to follow up their first stories to provide it. Such was the case when Cape May fishermen caught a

13-foot creature with characteristics of whale, shark and porpoise, according to the *Philadelphia Record* for May 3, 1939.

Other examples included the following:

The Oct. 3, 1944 story transmitted by Reuters from Machihanish, Scotland was of a fur-covered monster more than 20 feet long, with enormous eyes and feet, resembling neither whale nor shark, washed up by the Atlantic. Possibly it was killed during naval exercises or action at sea.

A Brooklyn captain landed a 4-foot long, 70-pound water denizen after killing it with a grappling hook, the UPI reported from New York Dec. 9, 1946.

A huge carcass more than 100 feet long and 15 feet wide that was washed up on the shore near Yakutat, Alaska did not fit the description of any known living creature or of any prehistoric beast, according to Bob Kedrick of the June *Daily Empire* who wrote a report that the AP distributed July 22, 1956.

What Dr. Vladimir Walters of the University of California at Los Angeles called "the find of a lifetime" was a dead oarfish that washed up on the beach at Malibu, Calif. according to Charles Hillinger of the *Los Angeles Times* Sept. 26, 1963. The ichthyologist said the eel-like animal was what a sailor's mistaken report said resembled a horse.

A legend of Canada's west coast supposedly died, the AP reported Dec. 9, 1947 from Vancouver, B.C., with the discovery of the remains of Cadhorosaurus, better known as Caddy. The very next day, however, the press association reported that the carcass was that of a giant shark.

Supposedly well-documented sightings of an 80-foot monster had been reported along the British Columbia coast since 1912. The AP sent a story from Seattle Oct. 23, 1933 of an expedition of newspeople, photographers, mariners and scientists bound for the Straits of Juan de Fuca where Captain W. N. Prengel of the Grace liner *Santa Lucia* allegedly observed a monster one dawn. The AP also reported Nov. 25, 1969 that two University of British Columbia scientists were searching for the serpent.

Searches for some of the most widely known sea serpents go on almost incessantly, even after decades or centuries. The accounts of both professional scientists and of amateurs are valued by the media. Often the report of a new sighting or of a vigil is supplemented by a review of previous attempts to capture, photograph or otherwise identify a local reptilian celebrity.

Such a story was used Sept. 2, 1970 by the *Sag Harbor-Shelter Island Pilot*. The news peg was the effort of two St. John's College youths who stood watch day and night with cameras and recorders. And, sad to relate, in vain. It took a full page, however, to tell the story of earlier attempts, beginning with the first sighting supposedly in 1689. Other important sightings occurred in 1784, 1862, 1925 and 1943.

True believers remain faithful and their ranks grow with new converts despite, possibly because of, the lack of reliable evidence. Hardly a sighting or discovery is ignored by the press and outsiders, including some reputable scientists attracted by the reports. One who gets around when a phenomenon becomes newsworthy is Hayden Hewes, director of the International Bureau for Unidentified Flying Objects with headquarters in Edmond, Okla. He received a half-page writeup in the *Memphis Commercial Appeal* for Sept. 11, 1971 after he went to Newport, Ark. to investigate the Great White River Monster or Whitey as inhabitants affectionately called it for 121 years if an Ozark historian can be believed. This, of course, was the same person who joined the search for the Mississippi Monster seen at Louisiana, Mo. and several other places. On both occasions Hewes said descriptions of the strange visitors fit that of the third type of alien beings whose ancestors were sent to Earth 121 years ago as experimental animals to test this planet's suitability. Though skeptical, John Opitz of Little Rock, executive director of the Ozark Regional Commission, told the newspaper he would try to interest some foundation to finance a study. Sept. 11, 1971 the *Commercial Appeal* used a picture of the White River Monster souvenir T-shirts complete with a paw print like ones the monster had left. After sightings were reported from Texarkana and Lake Conway the Arkansas Senate created the first known sea monster preserve, the White River Monster Sanctuary near Newport where no one is allowed to "molest, kill, trample or harm" the alleged creature.

By contrast merchants of St.-Eleuthère, Quebec refuse to commercialize Ponik, as the natives call the monster that supposedly has lived in Lake Pohenegamook for about a century. There's Ponik beer for sale but no sweatshirts or other souvenirs, according to a column-length feature story in the *Wall Street Journal* for Nov. 17, 1977. There still, however, are descendants of the first inhabitants who claimed to have seen the 35-foot black creature. The ardor of their belief is exceeded only by that of a Roman Catholic priest, Abbe Leopold Plante who hasn't changed the details of his sighting of the monster in 1958. A longer account of La Bête du Lac appeared in the *Chicago Tribune Magazine* for June 1, 1980, "Does a Monster Lurk Beneath These Waters?" by Stephen P. Monn.

Merchants of Port Henry, N.Y. emulate those of Newport, Ark. rather than those of St.-Eleuthère, Que. Champ, the supposed denizen of Lake Champlain, appears smiling on the stationery of the Chamber of Commerce which hopes to attract tourists to offset the economic blow the community suffered when nearby iron mines shut down. The *New York Times* devoted almost a full page of its Nov. 29, 1980 edition to an article by William T. Geist, "Village on Lake Champlain Seeking Its Fortune in Tale of Fabulous Sea Monster." Officials have declared the lake off limits to anyone who would harm or harass a sea serpent, one supposedly reported in 1609 by Samuel de Champlain, the explorer for whom the lake is named. Since 1819, it is said, there have been more than 100 sightings of a 20-to-30-foot-long dark creature with a horselike head.

Both the *Chicago Tribune* and *Chicago Sun-Times* Dec. 28, 1975 ran a lengthy UPI story from Burlington, Vt. reviewing the long history of sightings by prominent people, including the editor of *Vermont Life Magazine.* The belief of those who accept the accounts was strengthened in late 1980 with the revelation that a New Haven, Conn. couple had made available a photograph they took during a 1977 vacation trip. They copyrighted the picture before giving it to Prof. Roy Mackal, the University of Chicago zoologist whose hobby is searching worldwide for prehistoric animals. Mackal said the serpent probably was a zeuglodon, a long, serpentine whale thought to be extinct for 20 million years and identical to the fabulous Loch Ness monster near Inverness, Scotland.

Dr. Mackal sent the picture to J. Richard Greenwell of the University of Arizona's Arid Lands Committee. The Madison *Wisconsin State Journal* for March 20, 1981 used an AP story from Burlington, Vt. that Professor Greenwell had reported the snapshot was not a fake. Examination of the water pattern indicated the creature came from below the surface. March 24, 1981 the *Milwaukee Journal* used a UPI story from Tucson, also saying the snapshot was genuine. It showed a back, a long neck and a head about 150 to 180 feet off shore, which means the image was only a quarter of an inch by three-eights of an inch in size, not enough to convince many of the skeptical, but possibly sufficient to balance the village's budget.

Certainly the verdict on the photographs was enough to hype the promotion of Lake Champlain as a charming mystery and for vacationers. John Noble Wilford wrote a half-page article, "Is it Lake Champlain's Monster?" for the *New York Times* of June 30, 1981. It was illustrated by a three-column picture of some water with an object of some sort in the middle. It was supposed to be the "creature" that Sandra Mansi photographed July 5, 1977. Wilford elaborated on the techniques used by the Arizona experts to convince themselves the picture was genuine. He quoted Prof. Philip Reines of the State University College at Plattsburg, N.Y. as worried because Ms. Mansi could not recall where she took the picture and the negative is missing. Wilford also quoted skeptical Dr. W. H. Lehn and gullible Dr. Roy P. Mackal as saying what they would be expected to say.

July 1, 1981 the *Chicago Sun-Times* used the same picture and a story by Michael Anderson who rehashed the *Times* article and other oft-repeated facts. The same day the *New York Post* had a snide short piece, "Monster II." It stated that despite its embarrassment because of its fruitless expedition to discover the Loch Ness Monster, "the ever hopeful *New York Times* has gone after another aquatic mammal closer to home."

Also July 1 the *Los Angeles Times'* science writer, George Alexander, described the *New York Times* photograph which it also published. Wrote Alexander, "Scientists are not likely to be among the ranks of the true believers." He said the Arizona verdict that the picture was genuine "does not, however, establish that the emergent object in the picture is a living creature, let alone prove that it is a living descendant of a plesiosaurus or member of some other extinct dinosauria species."

"The sea monster of Lake Champlain is the summer's hot news all along this 125 mile inland sea," the Associated Press reported July 10, 1981 from Port Henry. "Nearly everyone in town claims or knows somebody who claims to have seen the monster." The town passed a resolution declaring the local part of the lake off limits to anyone who would harm, harass or destroy the Lake Champlain Sea Monster. July 12, 1981 the *New York Times* published Wilford's article again under the heading, "What the Camera Saw." July 19, the *Chicago Tribune* used the Wilford story and picture.

Since Samuel de Champlain reported seeing a strange beast in the lake in 1609 there have been 144 reported sightings, 109 of them during the 20th century, 300 persons were told at an all-day meeting sponsored by the Lake Champlain Committee. The UPI covered it at Shelburne, Vt. Aug. 30, 1981. Ms. Mansi described Champ, as he came to be known, as "majestic" although she had been terrified.

In its report of the same meeting Aug. 31, the *New York Times* said, "Current speculation holds that the creature, if real, may be a primitive whale or reptile and that others like it may inhabit other bodies of fresh water created by retreating glaciers in the last Ice Age." In its followup story Aug. 31 the UPI reported that the true believers were not deterred even though "Champ spurned his own party," not even providing a disturbance, ripple or wake to indicate his existence. The story was used by the *Chicago Sun-Times* with a cartoonist's sketch of a monster's protruding neck causing only a yawn from a man in a rowboat.

In its "Follow-Up on News" column for Oct. 4, 1981 the *New York Times* quoted Port Henry's mayor as saying Champ is "still going strong" and has seen more-out-of-state automobile license plates than ever before.

Other monster reports have come from New Delhi, India, where, the UPI reported June 30, 1982, a 5-ton beast with floppy ears was hauled out of the Bay of Bengal by 500 fishermen. And Reuters reported July 16, 1982 from Lake Utopia, Canada that a huge aquatic creature was seen by a fisherman.

How perspicacious newspaper editorial writers are can be discerned in an editorial in the *Kansas City Star* for March 14, 1949 as follows:

It Looks Like a Turtle, Anyway

A giant turtle variously described as "large as a dining room table," "thick as a sack of clover seed" and "too big to go through a door," is reported to have been sighted recently at a small lake near Churubusco, Ind. One "eyewitness" swore that the critter's head was the size of a man's.

These homey touches are in the American tradition of legendry. They keep the subject of the tale from being an obvious fantasy. In other lands, such as Scotland, the thing under description would be called a monster and embellished with such adjectives as "dragon-like" and "fire-breathing." But not so in the U.S.A. A mysterious object of fabulous proportions is dubbed a giant turtle and we let it go at that. For an enormous turtle, the biggest ever can be believed if not seen by all who would like to inspect it.

The Scots can have their Loch Ness monster. Our own mythological creatures are easier to visualize and therefore that much more enjoyable.

14

Loch Ness

Worldwide there are many bodies of water supposedly inhabited by exotic aquatic creatures. Among the best known, in addition to those already mentioned, are Flathead Lake, Mont.; Lake Walker, Nev.; Bear Lake, Utah; Lake Kussharo, Japan; Lake Kol-Kol, Soviet Union; the Baltic Sea's Knaken and Storsjo and Vaner, Sweden.

Most newsworthy on the European continent is the rose-colored sea monster with great horns and huge scales that causes fishermen in Italy's Lake Como to search with pitchforks and shotguns according to UPI dispatches of Nov. 20 and 22, 1946. Possibly it was a smuggler's submarine captured by customs officers carrying contraband between Italy and Switzerland.

The healthy skepticism with which some journalists see monster stories was reflected in the piece written in New York by the veteran columnist for the Associated Press, Hal Boyle, which included the following:

> Now if we can just get the five-cent glass of beer back we will all be ready to plunge again into that old happy daze where our only real worries were who could swallow the most live goldfish, how long can Joe Louis last, who killed Cock Robin and whether Jesse James is really dead or running a night club.

A similar skepticism characterized the first reports of the Loch Ness Monster, the most recent and certainly the most celebrated of the serpents of Scotland, which is as famous for them as England is for haunted houses. Other Scottish sea monsters allegedly abide in lochs Cauldcchields, Oich, Rennoch, Aire and Morar.

As true believers now tell it, Nessie was first sighted in 565 A.D. by St. Columba (521–597), the Irish missionary who established a monastery on the Scottish island of Iona and converted the Picts of Scotland to Christianity. As Tom Lambert of the *Los Angeles Times* wrote from London in a story the *Austin* (Tex.) *Statesman* printed Sept. 21, 1973, "that good man was crossing Loch Ness one day when he saw a monster bearing down on a swimmer." As told by Lambert and by Richard Lewis, in the *Chicago Sun-Times* for Sept. 11, 1967 St. Columba admonished the monster. "Think not to go further, nor touch thou that man. Quick, go back." Terrified, the monster did so.

In almost a full page feature in the *New York Times* for Feb. 3, 1974 Roy Bongartz elaborated on the anecdote, "All who were there; the heathen as well as the brethren, were stricken with very great terror and with his holy hand raised on high he formed the sign of the cross in the empty air, invoked the name of god and commanded the fierce monster." These quotations are from Book 2 Chapter 27 of St. Adamnan's *The Late Life of the Great St. Columba,* written in 565 A.D.

Another *New York Times* writer, William Touhy, changed the details somewhat in a long feature that the *Los Angeles Times* used Sept. 20, 1979: "On a journey from the isle of Iona about 565 A.D. to meet King Brude of the Picts, St. Columba was told about a monster which killed a man swimming in the River Ness. According to legend the saint frightened off the sea monster."

A still different variation of the legend was given by Robert Musel in a UPI dispatch from London that appeared in the *St. Paul Pioneer Press* for March 30, 1975: "The ancient chronicles say that when St. Columba visited King Brude of the northern Picts in 700 A.D., he came across the funeral of a man who had been savaged by a water beast out of Loch Ness. And ever since that day, one might say, eager observers have scanned Britain's largest, deepest and most mysterious fresh water lake for a sight of the Aquatilis Beastia that intrigued St. Columba 1,200 years ago."

All the journalists agree that there is no record of any Loch Ness monster ever actually injuring anyone although Lewis wrote in his 1967 article that according to archives in the monastery of St. Benedict of Fort Augustus, in 1527, "a terrible beast issued out of the water early one morning about midsummer and without straining himself overthrew huge oaks with his tail and therewith killed outright three men that hunted him, the rest of them saving themselves in the trees."

Lewis mentioned St. Adamnan as St. Columba's biographer. Other writers identify the author as the ninth abbot of Iona and the book's title as *The Later Life of the Great Columba* in volume 2 of which the Loch Ness anecdote allegedly appeared. The ancient book was edited in 1894 by J. T. Fowler, with an English translation in 1895 and confirmation in *The Sources for the Early History of Ireland* in 1924.

None of the St. Columba tale was included in any reports from Loch Ness until the mid-'60s. In an article in the Sheffield, England *Weekly Telegraph* that the *Milwaukee Journal* reprinted Aug. 14, 1947, J. Orton mentioned two sightings in 1871 and another in 1914, but neither apparently inspired hundreds of others to start seeing things. Such occurred in 1933, when either Alexander Campbell, a bailiff, or George Spicer, a

London businessman, was the first to incite widespread interest. Spicer and his wife described the "loathsome sight" to be a creature with a long neck thicker than an elephant's trunk with a small head, thick body and four sets of flippers, about 25 to 30 feet long.

From then to the present there has been no letup in the efforts of both amateurs and professionals to establish the identity of Nessie and their efforts have been considered newsworthy everywhere in the world. It is impossible to determine how much the press' avidity to make Loch Ness into a major matter of international concern has contributed to the perpetuation of the myth despite the uninterrupted series of failures to obtain any scientific evidence. And, although devoting an exorbitant amount of space to the phenomenon, until the St. Columba legend was resurrected in 1966, the press hardly took Nessie seriously. A few examples of the irreverence in which journalists reported follow:

—Orton ended his Sheffield *Weekly Telegraph* article thusly: "The Loch Ness monster incidentally, has proved of no little value to its locality. In fact it has become so great an attraction for tourists that the local authorities regard with anything but favor the latest attempt to capture it."

—Similarly Kermit Holt concluded an article in the *Chicago Tribune* for April 27, 1947: "Some unkind persons who failed to see the monster have pointed to the fact that there are several Scotch whiskey distilleries hereabouts."

—The *Chicago Daily News* editorialized July 15, 1961: "The monster was due this spring but it didn't show until June. Undoubtedly it is a patriotic sea serpent and waited patiently for the Festival of Britain."

—In a story from Drumnadrochit, Scotland March 12, 1957 the Associated Press reported: "This is early in the year for the monster, which is seldom sighted until the weather becomes warm enough for the tourist trade."

—Reporting several sightings, Richard C. Wald wrote from London in the *New York Herald Tribune* July 3, 1960: "One apparent consistency is that the reports always come thick and fast at the beginning of the Scottish tourist season."

—Similarly the Associated Press reported from Invemoriston, Scotland July 8, 1965: "Appearances of the monster, often at the outset of the tourist season, have been reported for decades."

—Two days later, July 10, 1965, the *Chicago Daily News* began an editorial, "Monster's Return: The Loch Ness monster has been sighted again—barely in time for the tourist season."

—Editorializing on "In Support of the Monsters" March 27, 1966, the *Kansas City Times* wrote: "It is that time of year again."

—Inspired by news that some scientists hoped to obtain a biopsy of monster flesh, the *Wichita Beacon* March 29, 1967 wrote: "It is time the monster left such inhospitable quarters. In the interest of his safety (and our tourist trade) we think Kansas should offer him a home. In Loch Cheney."

What caused the press to cease its expressions of disrespect was the multiplicity of sightings dating from the construction in 1933 of a highway along the 24-mile shoreline of Loch Ness, which made it possible to view the loch which is only one mile wide. That plus the publication of a photograph taken in April 1934 by Dr. Robert K. Wilson, a London surgeon (*New York Times,* Feb. 17, 1974) or Dr. Kenneth Wilson, a London physician (*New York Times,* June 5, 1956), or Dr. R. K. Wilson, a gynecologist (*Washington Post,* Aug. 1, 1976) or, in most other publications, by a London doctor who prefers to remain anonymous inasmuch as he was weekending with a woman not his wife.

What the picture showed was a body of water from which protruded a long neck resembling that of a giraffe tapering off to a small head like that of a kangaroo. It did not require any knowledge of photography to recognize that the original glossy prints distributed to the press were highly retouched. In fact, the entire picture seemed to be a painting rather than a photograph. So obvious was the fake that the Wide World Photo Service which distributed the photograph jokingly labeled it "an unretouched photo rushed here from London by radiograph."

To this day that is the only photograph resembling anything like a monster in Loch Ness and some critics of it have said it may have been an elephant's tail. After being retouched and reproduced many times for almost 50 years, today it cannot be evaluated properly; but it is the only supposed valid picture and is used over and over again to illustrate articles about the Loch Ness Monster.

Almost as useless are a couple of pictures showing long spots on water, probably logs or shadows.

Lack of any tangible evidence that there was anything unusual in the loch did not deter anyone from conjecturing as to what it would be if there were. In its *Sunday Magazine* for Jan. 28, 1934 the *St. Louis Post-Dispatch* summarized the excitement of the first six months after the celebrated 1973 sighting reports. During that period thousands either reported having seen a monster or volunteered their opinion regarding its nature. Lt. Com. R. T. Gould, a retired naval officer and author in *The Case for the Sea Serpent* analyzed the reports of 51 witnesses. *Time* for Jan. 15, 1934 reported Gould's conclusion as to the nature of the creature: about 50 feet long, not more than 5 feet thick, with long tapering neck and tail, a button head and rough skin with a ridge down the back. It had two appendages, possibly gills, and two or four propelling paddles or fins.

The *Times of London* received a roll of film from three operators who said motion pictures of the lake's denizen whatever it was—cephalopos, mobula, manta, polyp, squid, saurian, cuttlefish, kelpie, kraken, devilfish, catfish or sea serpent. The films revealed a long, black object similar to a tapering tree trunk but at the thick end a rapid and powerful splashing of water. Neither the paper's editors nor any specialist who examined them considered the films of any material value.

Whatever it was the Brighton Museum said it would pay $8,000 for it. According to *Time* for May 3, 1937 the Bronx zoo would buy it for $25,000. To protect the safety of the serpent and to prevent its removal from Scotland, under coaxing from Sir Murdoch MacDonald, M.P. for Inverness, local and national public officials became vigilant. The *New York Times* for Sept. 5, 1938 reproduced a letter from Sir Murdoch to the financial secretary of the treasury urging safety precautions. According to *Time* for Sept. 22, 1941 the House of Commons tabled a bill to erect hydroelectric plants in two scenic glens of Inverness. And, the *Chicago Tribune* reported May 3, 1950 that the House rejected a proposal to search the lake with underwater cameras.

This action, of course, did not prevent scores of private expeditions in search of Nessie. One of the first was organized by Captain D. J. Munro, a retired naval officer who set out to sell shares at one shilling each to raise $1,500 to establish three permanent stations on the broad lake, manned by naval officers and bluejackets. A fourth station would float on a barge. All would be equipped with telephoto cameras, range finders, binoculars and similar gear, the Associated Press reported in a dispatch from Glasgow that the *Christian Science Monitor* used Aug. 3, 1938.

The *Monitor* also ran a report from its London correspondent in its issue of May 31, 1938, recounting the reports of several recent sightings, including ones by Rear Admiral C. B. Prickett and seven other reports from Plymouth and other British cities during the preceding 18 months.

Among the many who announced an interest in forming a hunting expedition was the Right Rev. Sir David Oswald Hunter Blair, Bart. Eighty-three years old himself, Sir David said, "Nessie must be thousands of years old and belongs to the post-glacial period. He is so tame I expect little trouble in bringing him home. In fact I have invited the boys of St. Bede's Roman Catholic College in Manchester to join me in the monster hunt."

Time never followed up its announcement May 3, 1937 of Sir David's intention. Nor was the outcome of the search two men, K. Moorhouse and Charles Taylor, resolved to make after nobody claimed the $1,500 prize offered by Brighton Museum.

Eyewitnesses and scientists, according to *Time* of May 5, 1937 and June 20, 1938, surmised that Nessie was (1) an elephant seal that swam in from the North Sea via the Caledonian Canal; (2) a hippopotamus; (3) a 50-foot prehistoric reptile with a whiskery pinhead and eight scaly humps; (4) a giant squid; (5) an abomination with a three-arched neck; (6) a cruel fabrication.

During World War II understandably Scots had little time for serpent seeking. Come peace, however, new sightings accelerated. Among the stories, "Loch Ness Camera Fans Wait for Monster to Pose" because a picture was certain to bring at least $25,000 (*Chicago Daily News,* April 5, 1948); "Skeptic Reforms: He Sees Loch Ness 'Thing,' " an Associated Press account that the Lincoln, England town crier saw the monster June 27, 1947; "Hoot Monster! Loch Ness Back in News," an Associated Press story from Drumnadrochit (*Chicago American,* May 8, 1966); "Spot 'Sea Monster' in Scotland River" and a UPI story from Dundee (*Chicago Sun-Times,* July 29, 1958).

Theories regarding Nessie's identity also proliferated. During the war, it was revealed that Mussolini's newspaper, *Popolo d'Italia,* claimed that the monster had been blown to bits by a direct hit from a German bomber. From Inverness the AP distributed a cynical story that began: "Despite the shortage of Scotch whiskey, some people are reporting seeing the Loch Ness monster again (North Scotland's 1947 tourist season is just starting)." The Italian hoax was mentioned in the third paragraph with the insinuation that the Scots were acting in defiance of it. The *Chicago Daily News* for April 8, 1947 headlined, "Loch Ness Builds Up a Monster Season" with the overline "Thing Seen for Tourists."

Kermit Holt began his story from Inverness for the April 27, 1947 *Chicago Tribune:* "That talk you may have heard about the Loch Ness sea monster was a dastardly axis lie. The old fellow isn't dead at all."*American Weekly* reported that five sober Scotsmen had seen Nessie, including J. W. McKillop, town clerk of Inverness, and discounted the bombing story.

The faithful, however, received a jolt when torpedo and mining experts of the Royal Navy school at Plymouth declared that the controversial Loch Ness Monster was actually 40 monsters, all man-made—a string of dummy mines from World War I. They said 320 mines, joined together eight to a string, were moored at the bottom of the lake as an experiment in 1918 since when the strings have been popping up at intervals. The *Syracuse Herald-Journal* used the story Nov. 9, 1950.

Another theory that failed to diminish sightings was advanced in the prestigious London weekly *Economist.* A. W. Morrison of Glasgow suggested that the "humps" on Nessie's back are really "a series of huge bubbles of natural gas coming from a geological fault that passes under Loch Ness." This Reuters dispatch appeared in the *New York Post* for June 15, 1953.

Much more disturbing was an article in a Milan magazine that an Italian newsman, Francesco Gasparini, said he invented the story when he was a London correspondent in 1933. According to an AP account from Inverness that both the *Chicago Tribune* and *Chicago Sun-Times* used March 22, 1959, Gasparini said the yarn snowballed to such proportions that he just played along with it from then on. Several indignant Scotsmen condemned Gasparini but the AP quoted one elderly Scot as saying, "We don't care what folk say about the monster as long as they say something."

As more and more sightings were reported, many getting brief mention in American newspapers, plans for capturing or at least identifying Nessie by photography or otherwise also multiplied. The UPI reported that Neil McLean declared in the House of Commons that the plan of Peter O'Connor, a fireman, to kill Nessie was fantastic, according to the story in the *Chicago Daily News* for Oct. 12, 1959. Not long thereafter the House of Commons resolved not to attempt to identify Nessie. However, a number of Cambridge and Oxford university undergraduates announced plans to attempt to obtain pictures. A zoologist member of the group said the "most exciting and plausible theory" is that the monster is a plesiosaurus, supposedly extinct for 30 million years.

Evidently the picture-taking foray, about which Richard C. Wald reported from London for the *New York Herald Tribune* of July 3, 1960, failed. So also did the one-man attempt of James T. Duke, a Chicagoan who was an army specialist stationed in Pirmasens, Germany. The *Chicago Tribune* of April 8, 1962 devoted a column to his plans as told by his mother who said her son expected to camp by the lake until he got a picture.

The Oxford and Cambridge expeditions ended in disappointment. Only a single echo sounder was used and although some interesting echoes were obtained it was impossible to cover the entire loch. Also a live British Broadcasting Company search in 1958 detected nothing of value. The same could be said of many other amateur attempts. Nevertheless, books were beginning to appear. Most important were *More Than a Legend* by Constance Whyte, who had lived near Loch Ness for many years, and *Loch Ness Monster* by Tim Dinsdale whose motion picture film showing a moving object across the lake failed to convince many scientists. Especially after some large footprints on the shore were exposed as a hoax using a hippopotamus hoof, scientists were noncommittal about Nessie. Sir Arthur Keith, eminent anthropologist, was more outspoken than most when he said: "Strange to say, it is just the great number of witnesses and the discrepancy in their testimony that have convinced professional zoologists that the 'monster' is not a thing of flesh and blood. I have come to the conclusion that the existence or non-existence of the 'monster' is not a problem for zoologists but for psychologists."

Exception among scientists was Dr. Danys Tucker who inspired college students with his lectures. Also influenced by Professor Tucker was Lt. Col. H. G. "Blondie" Hasler, D.S.O., O.B.E., a war hero for his successful leadership of a canoe raid in 1942 on Bordeaux Harbour and celebrated for organizing the first single-handed transatlantic race from Plymouth to New York in 1960 in which he came in second in his unconventional 25-foot yacht *Jester*.

June 4, 1962 William H. Stoneman began a story from London that appeared in the *Chicago Daily News* for June 4, 1962: "The fate of Britain's legendary Loch Ness Monster is all but ended." The rest of the story was a summary of the announcement the day previous in the *London Observer* that it was sponsoring "the most exhaustive attempt yet made to solve the old and celebrated mystery of the Loch Ness monster." The first of two expeditions would be led by Hasler who, aided by volunteer crews, would undertake a continuous night-and-day patrol of the loch. His equipment would include cameras, underwater listening devices and tape recorders. A month later a second expedition would be led by two Cambridge research scientists, Peter Baker and Mark Westwood. For three weeks they and some fellow students would use motor launches equipped with electronic underwater detection apparatus. It was their hope to sweep the loch with a sonic curtain, with a better than 90 percent chance of discovering any large animal or object even if it were hundreds of feet down on the bottom.

At the end of eight weeks Hasler wrote in his diary, which was published in the *London Observer* for Aug. 19, 1962, "We came away having failed to achieve our primary object, and with a fresh respect for X's power of concealment." Because there were some clicking noises and some ripples in the water, Hasler still believed in Nessie and predicted that future expeditions could achieve success by stressing underwater observations. The following week, in the *Observer* for Aug. 26, 1962, Baker and Westwood likewise confessed failure in their 480-hour vigil. They elucidated the difficulties they encountered. Chief of them was the nature of the lake's bottom, making sonar soundings virtually impossible. "The sides and bottom of the lake are covered with peat and mud, with only occasional twigs and leaves. Mud from the bottom is perfectly fresh and, although it contains a few gas-producing bacteria, there is no evidence of substantial gas formation," they wrote.

Regarding the moving humps that witnesses reported, Baker and Westwood said, "There were two main sources of deception—wake effects and birds. Interference between the wakes of one or more boats, especially when viewed from loch level on calm sunny days, was occasionally very deceiving to the naked eye. A dark 'hump' would remain stationary for some time, then suddenly leap forward across the loch giving a strong impression of a bow wave and following wake. Very impressive 'monsters' with one, two or more humps were formed . . . Birds, in particular geese or black-throated divers swimming in line can also look very much like a series of humps, especially as size is difficult to estimate over water."

Baker and Westwood said that only 3 of 16 reported sightings remained unsolved. "To sum up after two expeditions to Loch Ness, we cannot say with conviction that the Loch Ness monster does not exist. Indeed, the small pieces of evidence we have obtained all suggest that there is an unusual animal in the loch. However, we consider that the 'monster' is much smaller than many people have claimed." They concluded their report with a hope that "the novel approach that Mr. David James, M.P. plans to employ this autumn using searchlights and radar to sweep the surface at night will prove successful."

As the *London Observer* was abandoning its attempt to solve the mystery, David James was organizing the Loch Ness Phenomena Investigation Bureau, having been inspired by Constance Whyte's 1957 book, *More Than a Legend,* in collaboration with Richard Fitter, Sir Peter Scott and Mrs. Whyte. Beginning in 1962 with two 6-inch cameras for a watch period of a fortnight, within five years the bureau had grown to a 5-month vigil every summer with 36-inch cameras manned by 150 volunteers from all parts of the world and visited by about 25,000 tourists annually.

Despite the unquestionable value of the tourist trade the Invernesshire planning committee denied the bureau's petition to develop its lochside headquarters. James wanted to have three or four caravans next to his camera platform and a workshop and a kiosk for selling books and postcards. The Inverness *Highland News* capitalized "NOT" in its April 8, 1966 account that the commission insisted the enterprise should be restricted to scientific and NOT commercial activities. James was ordered to remove as a safety hazard a sign advertising his presence.

The first important break that the bureau got was a report by the Joint Air Reconnaissance Intelligence Center that the film Tim Dinsdale took in 1959 probably showed an "animate object" nearly 100 feet long, not less than 6 feet wide and 5 feet high. Its speed was estimated to be 10 miles an hour. The Associated Press story from London May 14, 1966 quoted Dinsdale that he believed there is more than one monster. "In fact," he said, "I think there is a family of them."

This boost came after what James admitted in his booklet, *Loch Ness Investigation,* had been several lean years. Sightings declined from 42 in 1963 to 18 in 1964 and to 9 in 1965. After the report on the film journalists stopped ridiculing the monster hunts as publicity stunts to promote tourism and scientists became more open-minded. Typical of the respectful treatment the press now gave was a UPI story from Inverness Aug. 23, 1966 about the experience of a motor vessel. While the head lochkeeper who was piloting the *Phama* through the Caledonian Canal, which included Loch Ness, kept the creature on his radar screen the crew watched it through binoculars. "The monster seemed to be pacing the ship," the ship's engineer, Paddy Goodbody, said.

The most important scientist to be converted to the cause was Dr. Roy Mackal, associate professor of biochemistry at the University of Chicago, whose activities and opinions became newsworthy, especially in the Chicago area. The first significant story concerning him was sent by UPI from Inverness Sept. 21, 1966. It quoted him as believing Nessie was a giant sea slug and that at least six specimens of the so-called monster have been living in the lake at any one time over the past 14 centuries. Five days later the UPI reported that Mackal's sea slug theory was scoffed at by professional colleagues on both sides of the Atlantic. A spokesman for the Natural History Museum said sea slugs never exceeded 178 inches in length from nose to single foot. Mackal, identified as a co-director of James' organization, then declared there were living organisms in the lake "that cannot be explained by any ordinary hypothesis."

The next day, Sept. 27, 1966, the AP reported that Mackal had spotted the monster from a distance of 30 yards, his humps sticking 14 feet out of the water. It was too close for the bureau's high-speed cameras to be tilted low enough for a photograph.

Back in Chicago Mackal told the *Daily News'* Rob Warden Sept. 29, 1966 that the first sighting was in 565 whereas Curtis D. MacDougall, who also had visited Loch Ness that summer, declared the proper date was 1933. Mackal said thousands of persons had seen the monster but Mac-Dougall said nobody had done so. MacDougall called the photographs fakes and said that an expensive study Mackal advocated would be a waste of money.

The next day, Sept. 20, 1966, the *Chicago Sun-Times'* Lloyd Green quoted Mackal as saying he never caught sight of the monster during his 10-day visit to Loch Ness. He said that a specimen could be caught with heavy fishing tackle using live bait for about $75,000.

The *Daily News'* editorial, "Yes, Prof. There Is a Monster," Sept. 30, 1966, indicated that not all journalistic cynicism had disappeared.

> Prof. Curtis MacDougall, a professor of journalism at Northwestern when he is not poking holes in legends, is openly scornful of recent testimony that the Loch Ness monster has been seen again. MacDougall says that the only time the monster is sighted is when the Scottish tourist season needs a hypo, and that it has never had any substance outside the lively imagination of the Loch Ness publicity office.
>
> Fie, MacDougall. Everybody except spoilsports like you knows that the monster, or monstress, or a combination of them, has been in Loch Ness since 565 A.D.; that it is at least 100 feet long; that its four or five humps protrude from the water, sometimes five feet, sometimes 14; that it has a voice like a foghorn and fins like a shark. Oh, yes—and that it has some inherent pigmentation that renders it invisible to cameras, and sleeps away its winters in the bottom of the loch, whence it emerges, as if summoned by some subterranean alarm clock, when the weather ripens for the visitor season.
>
> No monster? Thank God he lives, MacDougall, and he lives forever—as long as there remains a spark of imagination to brighten the eye of the beholder, and a promotion-minded Scot to fan that spark.

Although Loch Ness never freezes over searches both for monsters and for news hibernated during the winter of 1966–67. Normalcy began to return when *Reader's Digest* ran a 4½-page article in its February 1967 issue and the AP distributed a lengthy article by Godfrey Anderson that the *New York World Journal Tribune* used March 12, 1967. Mackal was quoted in the third paragraph as believing the monster is an invertebrate transitional between a cephalopod (an octopus or squid) and a gastropod (a giant sea slug). Clem Liser Skelton, resident technician of James' bureau, claimed eight sightings himself and said the average is one sighting for every 350 man-hours of watching.

In a speech during a two-day symposium on energy and information transferring biological systems, Mackal told 80 scientists at the University of Chicago that Nessie might be a giant mollusk, according to Richard Lewis' story in the *Chicago Sun-Times* for March 21, 1967. Five days later, March 26, 1967, the *Chicago Tribune* had a story from Hugh Davidson, its correspondent in Glasgow, that began: "A silent deadly crossbow, used for sport in medieval days but outlawed by the Lateran council of Europe in 1130 as 'too murderous a weapon for Christians' may be used to shoot the elusive Loch Ness monster." The *News* source was David James who said the crossbow would be a "powerful modern version of the medieval weapon." Besides obtaining a fragment of skin, James thought it might be possible to implant a tiny transmitting device into the monster's body that, while the battery lasted, would help lochside observers to track its movements.

Although most of the field work was performed by volunteers who received no compensation, who in fact paid $12 for an annual or $240 for a life membership, money was needed for equipment. In 1967 the Highlands and Islands Development Board made a grant of $1,000 and then March 13, 1967 Field Enterprises Educational Corp. announced it was making a gift of $20,000 for photographic and related equipment for motion picture coverage of the loch during the summer months when daylight lasts as long as 18 hours. In Chicago James declared that he believed the creatures were trapped in the lake by geological processes that separated the body of water from the North Sea at least 5,000 years ago. The Adventurers Club of Chicago also gave $5,000.

These gifts enabled the bureau to increase the number of units from three to five and the coverage to about 70 percent of the loch.

The day after the *Chicago Daily News* broke the story, the other Field newspaper, the *Chicago Sun-Times*, ran a full-page interview with Mackal by Richard Lewis. In it Mackal ridiculed the idea that the creatures in the lochs of Scotland, Ireland, Canada and Siberia are remnants of some prehistoric beasts whose counterparts became extinct millions of years ago. In another press conference reported in the *Sun-Times* for May 20, 1967, Mackal revealed that he expected to use a one-man submarine and biopsy launcher. The sub, called "Viperfish," was built by Dan S. Taylor, Jr. of Atlanta of fiberglass and steel and able to withstand depths up to 1,000 feet. The average depth of Loch Ness is about 750 feet. Unfortunately a series of technical difficulties delayed the sub's debut as a monster chaser.

Once the Field Enterprises' $20,000 was put to work, the Field newspapers treated the search for Nessie almost as thoroughly as they did the astronauts' trip to the moon. Major interviews with Mackal, in Chicago by John Justin Smith Aug. 29, 1967 and by William Stoneman from Drumnadrochit Sept. 23 and Sept. 25, added little to what was already known. Mackal gave still another guess as to what he was looking for. "My judgment at the present is that a group of living creatures is the most probable explanation," he said. David James said he was a much stronger believer in the existence of living supercreatures, "probably because I have been coming here regularly for six years and have spoken to many responsible and serious people who have seen things which just about had to be living creatures."

Stoneman, one of the all-time great *News* foreign correspondents, wrote: "Now for a strictly inexpert verdict. After six days on and around the loch, equipped with a camera and high-powered binoculars and after talking to a large number of 'locals' who have lived on the shores of Loch Ness all their lives, our personal opinion is that Nessie exists only in the minds of some people."

Richard Lewis rehashed about everything he could find in the paper's morgue for use in a story of an interview with Mackal for the *Sun-Times* of Sept. 4, 1967. Then Lewis accompanied the professor to Loch Ness from where he sent daily stories for several days. His story Sept. 10 reviewed a debate between David McKay, a former provost (mayor) who disbelieved in Nessie, and Clem Lister-Skelton, the resident technician of the Loch Ness Phenomena Investigative Bureau. Lister-Skelton won a unanimous vote by a town hall audience when he asked it to decide whether it was easier to believe in Nessie than that 5,000 Highlanders were liars.

Lewis also interviewed Alexander M. Campbell, recently retired as Loch Ness bailiff (fish and game warden) after 47 years. Campbell was one of the first if not the first to report a sighting in 1934 and claimed to have seen Nessie at least 20 times since then. Lewis' Sept. 11 story was a rehash of Mackal's plans and a repetition of the St. Columba yarn. Sept. 12 Lewis interviewed longtime believer, the Rev. Andrew McKillip, a Benedictine monk in a monastery at Fort Augustus. Sept. 14 Lewis summarized the reports of a dozen or so witnesses and also quoted McKay as believing that Nessie is "an elaborate hoax."

Sept. 10, 1967 the *Pittsburgh Press* used a Lewis special digesting his reports. The paper may have obtained its facts from the World Book Encyclopedia Information Service, which produced a deluge of news releases on all aspects of the Field Enterprises' financed search for more than two years. Then, the director confessed, Nessie no longer had any promotional value for its sponsor. In what may have been its last release, it admitted failure. Key sentences from the report follow: "High-pitched or low, the noise inducers have had no apparent effect on Nessie . . . Underwater TV camera has probed beneath the surface in vain . . . A night-sight camera . . . has also been deployed without success . . . A helicopter . . . has buzzed its way the length and breadth of the loch—and sighted nothing unusual . . . Bait has been spread on the surface—and dangled below. But the creature has refused to be tempted."

As for young Taylor's yellow submarine, within an hour after it got into the water in July 1967 the hatch sprung a leak. Then the mobile crane to hoist *Viperfish* from the carrier dropped, its brake drums having failed.

Next there was a broken instrument panel, a leaky hatch and a burn-out of one of the brushes in the main motor. A sub used in the making of a scene for a motion picture, *The Private Life of Sherlock Holmes,* was able to descend to about 820 feet, whereas Taylor's homemade toy could go only 754 feet below the surface of the water.

The James–Mackal venture was not the only one to be disappointed that year. The British Plessy team carried out a horizontal sonar scan from a position in mid-loch. Coordinated with it a shore-based team from Birmingham University conducted a vertical scan. No luck for either or for an American diver, Robert Love, who was ready to assist Taylor and then resolved to make 20 complete traverses of the loch.

Despite the discouraging results the press, especially the Field newspapers, continued to provide full details. In the *Sun-Times* for Dec. 6, 1967 Jane Gregory previewed the appearance of C. Lister-Skelton, resident technician at Loch Ness, before the Chicago Adventurers Club. Gregory quoted from Lewis' account of the debate with McKay. The *Daily News* used a *World Book* Science Service release May 25, 1968 illustrated with a picture of Mackal demonstrating the biopsy dart he hoped to use on Nessie. Back for another summer season Richard Lewis got one bit of new information—that Mackal no longer believed Nessie to be a sea serpent or a supposedly extinct plesiosaurus, a giant marine reptile that roamed these areas about 70 million years ago.

From Drumnadrochit Lewis reported July 17, 1967 that he did not believe the recent discovery of the 150-million-year-old skeleton of a 30-foot reptile in a clay pit near Stamford, England fortressed the belief that Nessie is a descendant or survivor of prehistoric times. July 25 Lewis reported from Clifden, Ireland that Mackal went there to investigate reports of Glan Lake's Duffy, called the cousin of Nessie, and some other presumed Irish monsters. Lewis described Glan Lake as about the size of Chicago's Soldier Field and 20 feet deep. Two days' effort to stir up any denizens ended in failure.

July 29, 1968 Lewis reported that Nessie "keeps turning up for the wrong people." Mackal in his rowboat had no chance to shoot his harpoon gun, but several laymen told the reporter about their experiences. Lewis also revealed Field Enterprises had invested another $10,000 in the venture.

The Associated Press sent a story from Dublin that the *New York Times* used June 9, 1968 about the supposed sighting of a sea monster in Glendarry Lake, the description of which resembled that of Glan Lake in Lewis' accounts. The AP's account of the discovery of the prehistoric skeleton in a clay pit at Stamford was published at least in the *Harrisburg* (Pa.) *Patriot Ledger* for June 7, 1968 and the *Christian Science Monitor* for June 29.

Back in Scotland Lewis reported Aug. 4, 1968 that "Whether or not there are monsters in Loch Ness, some kind of critter broke a 10-pound nylon test line and made off with a canister of bait the size of a cooky jar."

Surface surveillance and underwater photography having proved fruitless, Nessie chasers put their faith in sonar near the end of 1968. The
Milwaukee Journal Dec. 15 and the *Chicago Sun-Times* Dec. 16 used a
London Observer special from London telling of the success of Birmingham
University scientists. Using new equipment developed in their laboratory,
they established the existence of live objects, uncharacteristic of fish,
living in the loch. Dec. 18 the *Daily News* reported that, although encouraged by the report, Mackal cautioned, "We still have no idea what such
creatures, if they truly exist, might be."

The *Chicago Tribune Magazine* for Jan. 12, 1969 featured a detailed
first-person account by F. W. Holiday, a Welshman, whose trip to Inverness in 1962 was rewarded by a glimpse of Nessie one dawn. Later he wrote
a book, *The Great Orm of Loch Ness*.

Evidently just to keep the story alive, the *New York Times* used a
lengthy rehash of Mackal's ideas and ambitions Jan. 27, 1969, illustrated
with photographs provided by the *World Book*. Only new point was
Mackal's statement that he now believes that Nessie is "an overgrown
fresh water adapted sea cow—a very shy seacow—Ferdinand the Bull of
the Sea."

The *Chicago Daily News* picked up the story again April 12, 1969 when
it ran a *World Book* Science Service article by Leonard Reiffle and a
sidebar to announce that Field Enterprises would be at it again come
summer. The Reiffle piece eulogized the Birmingham sonar experiment
May 9, 1969. The paper announced the arrival in Drumnadrochit of Taylor
and his yellow submarine and quoted the project leaders' assurance that
Nessie would not be injured by the attempt to get a biopsy. May 16 the
paper ran a picture of the sub. Taylor and Mackal repeated the assurance of
safety after the head of a Scottish clan, Lord Lovat, a World War II
commando leader, declared, "I think it's just damnable to bully this creature. I don't know who has given authority for bullying this animal." The
Sun-Times had a similar story and picture the day before, May 14. It also
had an AP story from London May 15 elaborating on Lord Lovat's complaint. May 26 the suburban *Arlington Heights Herald* editorialized on
"The Monster Never Hurt Anyone!" strongly supporting Lord Lovat. The
paper said Nessie is as real as fairies and Santa Claus "and just because
you haven't seen him is no proof that he doesn't exist. And that's the way it
should remain. It is no more right to plumb and probe the depths for him
than it is to spy for Santa or set a trap for a fairy."

The first of *Viperfish's* new troubles to be reported in a paper outside
the Chicago circulation area was in the *Salt Lake Tribune,* which carried a
Reuters dispatch from London July 8, 1969. Engine trouble developed
before the first submergence and then there was a further hitch with the
breakdown of the crane being used to lower the sub. That repaired, a leak
was discovered in a seal in the hatch. Earlier, the *Chicago Daily News* of
May 31 had reported that much of the electrical equipment had to be

reinstalled after the journey from the United States but that delay was downplayed as merely routine. July 9, 1969 the *New York Times* ran a similar AP story. The same day the *News* ran a lengthy article by David M. Nichols from London under the headline, "Gremlins help Nessie." Its recitation of grievances that began after an hour in the water, spent mostly in adjusting ballast and some tentative starts of the main motor, Taylor discovered that the hatch of his 20-foot do-it-yourself sub had developed a leak. After two days spent trying to repair it, new hatch seals were installed.

Next it was discovered that the brushes of the main motor had failed. Then, when it was believed a descent could be made, the brake drums of the mobile crane that was to hoist the sub from its carrier failed and had to be replaced. Frogmen from the Vickers submarine *Pisces,* nearby for use in connection with a motion picture, *The Private Life of Sherlock Holmes,* helped guide *Viperfish* through the brush to the lake shore.

The *New York Times* picked up the story July 13 with a report from Glasgow under the headline, "Loch Ness Gremlins Plague Yellow Submarine." It reported that *Viperfish* sank at its moorings after a leaking stern plate caused flooding of the ballast tanks. The story also included the information that the movie sub, which it called *Discus* not *Pisces,* had charted a depth of 820 feet whereas formerly it was believed Loch Ness was no deeper than 754 feet.

In faraway Provo, Utah readers of the *Daily Herald* read an editorial, "Three Cheers for Nessie," which exulted in Taylor's difficulties. In part the editorial read: ". . . while we are not about to admit being superstitious or to standing in the way of man's advances of the frontiers of knowledge, secretly we're on Nessie's side. In an age when man is taking his first steps toward unraveling the secrets of the stars, it's somehow comforting that an age-old mystery right here at home still defies solution. If Nessie has her (or his or its) way, man will never be a know-it-all."

July 17 the *Provo Herald* ran a UPI story from London that the House of Lords had been assured Nessie would not be hurt by a biopsy. The parliamentary secretary, Lord Huges, however, said the 1876 Cruelty to Animals act does not apply to invertebrates so its application in this instance must wait until Nessie's identity is established.

Just as the repeated failures of all attempts to identify Nessie seemed to be hurting the tourist trade, interest was rekindled by the announcement that two fishermen had been attacked by an aquatic creature in Loch Morar 50 miles from Loch Ness. According to the *Chicago Tribune* for Aug. 19 and the *Provo Herald* which used a UPI story Aug. 20, the what-is-it bit off the end of an oar before one of the boatmen shot it whereupon it sank. The only discrepancy between the two accounts was the depth of Lake Morar. The UPI said 1,017 feet whereas the *Tribune* said 4,200. Aug. 25 Reuters reported, "The Loch Ness Monster is in danger of becoming a has-been." Whereas the road to Loch Ness was quiet for the first time in the season, that to Loch Morar was crowded, with those trying to get a glimpse of the new what-is-it, promptly dubbed Morag. Sure enough, in the crowd were David James and Roy Mackal while Taylor was reported waiting for sonar equipment. The next day, Aug. 26, the *Christian Science Monitor* ran an encouraging story by its correspondent Alan T. Band that "despite the diminishing arguments of 'unbelievers' there seems to be little doubt that there is something strange" in Loch Ness.

The *New York Times* caught up Sept. 7, 1969 when it used a UPI story from Loch Morar headlined, "Loch Ness Monster Has a Neighbor Now." The *Chicago Sun-Times* used a brief item Sept. 15 that the search for Nessie finally got under way and would be the most thorough since the first claimed sightings in the '30s. The next day the paper had an AP story from Inverness that Ladbroke's, one of Britain's top bookmaking firms, shortened the odds on the discovery of Nessie from 10-1 to 6-1. James said $48,000 would be spent on the project this season. In parentheses the *Sun-Times* refreshed memories that Field Enterprises helped raise the money. The *Wall Street Journal* had a brief item on the matter Sept. 18.

A new feature was reported in the *Chicago Daily News* Sept. 15. An AP story from Inverness that two British businessmen had found a monster-sized bone 4 feet 2 inches long, on the edge of the loch. Sept. 18 the *New York Times* ran an AP followup that the curator of the natural history department of York Museum had identified the bone as the lower jawbone of a whale which had been stolen a fortnight earlier from his rock garden. He had put it there after the museum discarded it as worthless. The "businessmen" remained anonymous.

A scene from the movie that was made in part on location at Loch Ness was used by the *Chicago Sun-Times* Oct. 18, 1969 and the *Boston Herald Traveler* Oct. 19. It showed the theatrical monster upsetting a boat with three occupants. According to the cutlines the mechanical monster disappeared in the water and a San Francisco insurance company was being billed for $25,000.

Defeated but determined to try again, Dan Scott Taylor, Jr. returned to Atlanta according to a *Chicago Daily News* story Oct. 27, 1969. Taylor said he got within 20 feet of Nessie but lost the race to get pictures or biopsies because his submarine made only 2 or 3 knots whereas Nessie makes 12 knots.

An audience of 250 in the lecture hall of the Philadelphia College of Pharmacy heard J. Houston House, president of the Amalgamated Loch Ness Society, say that Nessie must be twice the size of a hippopotamus, swims like a dog and has one or more humps on its back. Nessie must be a meat eater because the loch has little plant life. All this was reported in the *Philadelphia Daily News* for Dec. 6, 1969.

The year's accomplishments were summarized in a report by the *World Book* Science Service, which the *Chicago Daily News* published Jan. 3–4, 1970. Based mostly on an interview with Robert Love of Joliet, Ill., now the bureau's engineer, it was stated that sonar had picked up an aquatic object 500 feet below the lake's surface and tracked it for 2 min. 10 sec. Mackal, also present at *World Book* headquarters, explained that dead animals do not bloat and float because of the coldness of Loch Ness. And he added with a shrug, "There is always the possibility that we have here animals of a type hitherto simply unknown to us."

June 14, 1970 the *Chicago Sun-Times* devoted a half-page to an account of Love's testing his hydrophone about 20 miles offshore in Lake Michigan, a "warm up" for the fall season in Scotland. Love was identified as 42, who has lived and worked as an engineer, oceanographer and scuba diver in 79 countries and at least a dozen seas.

In the interim there had not been much Nessie news. In their *Daily News* column Jan. 8 Jon and Abra called the new interest in hunting for Morag in Loch Morar "bad news" for Nessie. June 9 David Nichols did a story for the *Daily News* from London about a Chicago bartender, Bert Heron, who hired two scuba divers who made a futile search for a case of Canadian whiskey that the company advertisements in *Life* and *Look* said had been dropped into Dores Bay on the south side of the 26-mile-long, one-to-two-mile wide loch. July 13 the *New York Times* announced that a group of 25 aquatic biologists intended to make a six-week search. July 27 both the UPI and AP reported that Douglas Drysdale, lecturer in visceral physiology at the British College of Naturopathy and Osteopathy, believed that pollution had killed Nessie. Bob Cromie commented on this sad news in his *Chicago Tribune* column for Aug. 5. Among the angry retorts from Nessie fans was that of Alexander Campbell, the original sighter who denied the water was bad, saying "I've drunk it myself for 40 years." Peter Davis said there probably are more than 20 monsters and the bureau reported 9 new sightings.

The fall season began with an altered plot and an enlarged cast. The Associated Press reported Sept. 23, 1970 from Drumnadrochit that the Loch Ness Phenomena Investigation Bureau was using the fishy equivalent of a love potion—the ground-up reproductive organs of eels, sea cows and other piscatorial goodies. One unnamed cynical native was quoted as saying, "I don't know what these scientist chappies think our wee Nessie is, but no self-respecting monster would be attracted by minced eel, no matter what part of the eel it comes from." His words were prophetic as all knew by season's end.

Supplementing—or duplicating—the work of the nine-year-old bureau were several newly formed groups. One sponsored by the distillery that makes Black and White whiskey employed Jack Ullrich, noted authority on paleontology, glaciology, archeology and geology who used an infrared camera able to take pictures in the dark, important because a few feet down Loch Ness becomes thoroughly dark, mostly because of the peat deposited from 40 rivers and streams. So confident was Ullrich that he placed a $50 bet with Ladbroke at 10 to 1. Two months later, according to an Enterprise science story by Joyce Gabriel that the *York* (Pa.) *Daily Record* used Dec. 4, 1970, Ullrich declared he believes there are 20 or 30 animals of one species in the loch. However, he lost his bet that his cameras would "prove the existence of a creature not less than 30 feet long, hitherto unknown in Britain and positively identified as such a monster before Nov. 1." The loch's physical characteristics is one of the factors handicapping all explorers. It is part of a geological rift or major fault in the earth which runs 100 miles northeast to southwest. Inverness is 4 miles north of the 23 miles that comprise the lake proper. There are 80 locks between St. Augustus at the northern tip to the North Sea and 17 locks at the southern end. When the last Ice Age retreated 10,000 or 15,000 years ago, the melting water raised the sea level 200 feet, flooding glens and valleys that turned into fjords. Loch Ness is believed to have been a fjord but was cut off from the North Sea by earthquakes, including that which destroyed Lisbon in 1776. Loch Ness is 52 feet above sea level and is a fresh water loch.

The most important newcomer was the Academy of Applied Science of Belmont, N.H., organized by Dr. Robert H. Rines, a Boston patent lawyer and dean of the Franklin Pierce Law Center at Concord, N.H. His honorary title was bestowed upon him by National Chaio Tung University in Taiwan. Rines hoped to entice Nessie to show him or herself by means of the sex bait or loud noised tape-recording of sea lions and other aquatic creatures. Sept. 30, 1970 David M. Nichols reported to the *Chicago Daily News* that Rines believed "a great scientific discovery is just waiting to be made." The scientists, Nichols reported, have stopped using the term "monster." Instead, they speak of "large animal objects." Sophisticated sonar equipment made four contacts with mysterious somethings, Rines said.

The next day Reuters reported that the new sonar contacts were better than those made by the Birmingham University expedition of 1968 and those of Robert Love in 1969. The *Boston Globe* used the story Oct. 1, 1970.

The biggest journalisttic smash of the year was David M. Nichols' piece in the *Chicago Daily News* for Oct. 3–4, 1970. It reviewed the entire history of the monster hunt and surmised that professionals now had replaced amateurs in the effort. A stroboscope was to be used by Prof. Harold Edgerton of the Massachusetts Institute of Technology, who invented it. Robert E. Love, the engineer, established his own Atlantis Scientific Foundation for Underwater Archeology and Exploration and was acting as director of underwater research for the bureau. There also was Kenneth Wallis, a retired RAF wing commander, who flew his own tiny autogyro to skim the water or hover at about 15 miles per hour to penetrate the murky waters for about 15 feet.

At year's end there was not much progress to report. Nov. 29, 1970 the *New York Times* had two stories, one by its own correspondent and the other a Reuters dispatch. The news was that a group of London University scientists reported that 27 persons sighted the Loch Morar monster, described as black, smooth and hump-backed. Nov. 30 the *Memphis States-man* had a similar story.

Dec. 2 Nichols reported that Love had recorded sounds not characteristic of those made by any known aquatic animal. Dec. 4 the *York* (Pa.) *Daily Record* ran an AP story from London that a group of scientists had told the Zoological Society of London they saw moving objects in Lake Morar. Dec. 6 the *Minneapolis Tribune* had a travel piece describing the Loch Ness area and reciting some of the monster lore.

Despite their persistent failures Nessie searchers continued to grow in number and support increased. April 21, 1971 Bob Herguth revealed in his *Chicago Daily News* column that the Scottish firm that makes Cutty Sark whiskey had offered $2.6 million to anyone who would bring Nessie to shore alive and unharmed by May 1, 1972, with a statement from the curator of the London History Museum that Nessie is a real monster, not just a big fish.

And April 25, 1971 the *New York Times* ran a full-column interview with Tim Dinsdale of Reading, England, Robert Rines and Isaac Blonder, chairman of the board of Blonder Tongue Laboratories of Old Bridge, N.J. who would provide the electronic equipment and expertise for the 1971 quest that Dinsdale estimated would cost $100,000.

Dedicated to the responsibility to keep readers informed about Nessie, the *New York Times* devoted almost a full page Jan. 15, 1972 to an article by Martin Kasindorf, deputy chief of the *Newsweek* bureau in Los Angeles. He summarized: "It has been a terrible year for monster seeking" because the weather was cloudy and windy. There had been 15 sightings but none by bureau personnel.

By contrast Jan. 14, 1972 the *Atlanta Journal* used a UPI story from Drumnadrochit that the bureau in its annual report said "the mild weather last year made it exceptionally good for monster sighting."

April 1 the *Chicago Sun-Times,* a morning newspaper, had a sizable AP story from Inverness about the discovery of a "green and scaly" creature found dead on the shore of Loch Ness. Don Robinson, curator of the Flamingo Park Zoo in Scarborough, was quoted as saying, "This is definitely a monster, no doubt about it." The same afternoon, however, the *Chicago Daily News* had a UPI story that the curator of the Edinburgh Zoo said it was a young deep-frozen elephant seal, an April Fool's Day prank.

The next day, April 2, Robert Merry began his *Chicago Tribune* story from Edinburgh: "Scotland's tourist industry breathed a sigh of relief today when it was officially proclaimed that an Englishman had hoaxed the nation into thinking Nessie, the Loch Ness monster, had at last been caught." The Associated Press story that the *Sun-Times* used that day explained that the zoo director confessed that the zoo's education officer, John Shields, admitted he was just trying to fool a few friends.

And the light touch was added to the running story April 26 when Reuters reported from Glasgow that Cutty Sark had received only one claim for the $2.6 million reward. It came from a Jackson, Miss. woman who wrote, "I have been living with the monster for the past 20 years." In October 1972 the *Tulsa Tribune* editorialized on "Monstrous Ideas," the first sentence being as follows: "The Scottish Society for the Propagation of Wild Tales About Sea Monsters is at it again." And in an editorial that the *Philadelphia Inquirer* reprinted Nov. 24, 1972, the *Washington Star-News* concluded: "If there's really a whopping great monster down there, we hope it remains secure in its privacy a while longer. There are all too few mysteries left to titillate us and we presume that monsters have rights too."

June 3, 1973 the *Chicago Sun-Times* devoted a full page in its *Midwest Magazine* to a question and answer interview Philip Nobile had with Robert Rines. As a result of sonar soundings and underwater photographs Dr. Rines was positive in his belief in Nessie's existence and eager to obtain additional evidence during the 1973 season. As it turned out, however, the space otherwise reserved for Rines and his Academy of Applied Science was usurped by the ventures of a group of Japanese.

The best accounts of the Japanese fiasco appeared in *Midwest Magazine* for Nov. 18, 1973 and the *New York Times* for Feb. 3, 1974. Organizer of the project was Yoshio Kou, 36, a fabulous impressario who made a reputation by bringing to Japan at different times Muhammad Ali, Tom Jones, Elvis Presley, the Bolshoi Ballet and the entire Indianapolis 500 in a repeat in Tokyo of the American event with all 33 original drivers and cars. With $510,000 underwritten by some Japanese businessmen Kou announced his intention to charter a French submarine and to capture Nessie, using tranquilizers and nets. A Tokyo dispatch by Robert Whymint of the *Manchester Guardian* June 11, 1973 revealed that the Japanese foreign ministry had informed Kou that he and his team would not be welcome in Scotland. An official of the British Embassy pointed out that Kou would need a license from the Home and Health Office in Scotland for his tranquilizer gun and "In any case it seems most unlikely that Mr. Kou would be allowed to take the monster out of the country."

Three months later than originally planned, Agence France-Presse reported Sept. 6, 1973 that the Japanese reached London led by Shinsaku Yoshida to begin "the biggest Loch Ness monster hunt of all times." "We only want to shoot her with cameras," he said. Tom Lambert of the *Los Angeles Times* wrote a detailed account of the expedition's plans to use submarines to descend to the lake's bottom and photograph denizens of the deep. Holly Arnold, secretary of the James-Mackal group, was pessimistic about the chances of Nessie not being frightened by the submarines according to the account that the *Austin* (Tex.) *Statesman* used Sept. 21, 1973.

Dan Greenburg's account of his adventures accompanying the Japanese expedition in *Oui* for May, 1974 is a hilarious account of delays, procrastination, blundering and mishap "to solve the biggest unsolved mystery of the 20th century." Kou held innumerable press conferences in

London and elsewhere while his equipment remained unclaimed in customs or unpacked in Scotland. As one piece of needed equipment was obtained another was discovered to be missing: weight belts, trawler, sonar truck, air compressor, decompression chamber and more. There was trouble getting a submarine that would serve their purposes and Nov. 11, 1973 the AP reported from London that the Japanese ended their two months' foray with "a pile of bones and some weird noises," and were heading homeward, presumably to return another year.

In his resumé of the episode in the *New York Times* for Feb. 3, 1974, Roy Bongartz quoted Kou's answer when asked what he would do with the monster if he caught it: "It all depends on Her Majesty the Queen. If she asks me to catch it, I will catch it. But there are many monsters and with such permission I will present one to the queen, then another to Emperor Hirohito, another to Mao Tse-tung and one to Chiang Kai-shek." Kou has ties with China through a Chinese father and hopes to unite the Chinese through gifts of lake monsters.

In a letter to members of the Loch Ness Phenomena Investigation Bureau in November 1974, David James remarked: "In August last year a Japanese group came over and we agreed to advise and help them for a fee. We were, therefore, able to re-engage Holly Arnold and Dick Raynor to assist them and brought Prof. Roy Mackal over from Chicago to advise. Unhappily, they did not see fit to benefit from our experience and left abruptly without paying the agreed fee in full. They are now paying the balance of it in installments and so at long last we have a credit balance with which to meet the cost of this mailing."

In a letter to the *New York Times* Travel Section for Feb. 17, 1974 Donald Muro objected to Bongartz's declaration in his Feb. 3 article that few photographs existed of Nessie. Muro said Frank Searle, a professional, had taken many photographs "which clearly show the existence of some large living object." The author replied: "Any really clear photograph wouldn't just show 'some large living object.' They'd show a lake monster, wouldn't they?"

As the 1975 tourist season approached, the *St. Paul Pioneer Press* ran a UPI story by Robert Musel March 30, 1975. The journalist told of his personal sighting of Nessie several years earlier. Most interesting new fact was that six swimmers participating in a race the preceding summer insured themselves against injury by a monster, the first time anyone ever took out anti-monster insurance.

In an interview with Joe Ward for the *Louisville Courier-Journal* of April 2, 1975, Tim Dinsdale related the anecdote of some archeological divers who inspected a sunken ship in the loch. Some sonar and sex bouy experiments were being conducted at the time and two divers felt fish brush against them. Thereupon the insurance company forbade diving while sex tests were being conducted.

Sex was the essence of the next rash of Nessie publicity stories. Aug. 5,

1975 the *Chicago Daily News* printed an AP story from Hemel Hempstead, England. Hertfordshire firemen had devoted six months to the construction of a papier-mâché female effigy of the Loch Ness monster, complete with flashing green eyes and long curly eyelashes, able to float and snort water vapor and, most important, equipped with an electronic mating call. The *Washington Star* had Ear notices of the money raising stunt Aug. 3 and 10. Nothing happened, at least journalistically, thereafter.

A month later, however, began a chain of events involving scholarly controversies and further expressions of outrage by Scots. Saturday, Nov. 22, 1975 the *Boston Globe* ran a copyrighted story quoting Robert Rines that his Academy of Applied Science had developed photographs that proved the existence of the Loch Ness Monster. "There is no chance of a hoax at all. All of us are making our livings on the basis of our integrity and we wouldn't risk it for something like this," Rines said. The others to whom Rines referred were his associates in the academy. In its account that the *Milwaukee Journal* ran Nov. 22, the AP quoted George Zug, a Smithsonian Institution geologist who had examined Rines' pictures and considered them exciting and "additional proof there is a population of living animals in Loch Ness."

Support also came from John Prescott, executive director of the New England Aquarium. The photographs were taken in 1975 with a high-speed camera system developed by Dr. Harold Edgerton, the MIT electrical engineering professor.

The next day, Nov. 2, the *Washington Post* declared that another supporter was a famed British naturalist, Sir Peter Scott, son of Antarctic explorer Robert Falcon Scott, head of the World Wildlife Fund and chancellor of Birmingham University. During a news conference at Slebridge, England, Scott said the photographs showed parts of what appeared to be a flipper and head, suggesting Nessie might be a pleisiosaurus, thought to have become extinct 70 million years ago.

Prescott said four of the photographs showed "sort of a dumpy round body" in silhouette, with "an appendage that looked like a fish fin or a whale flipper, and a long tail."

An Associated Press story from London that the *Austin Statesman* used Nov. 3 quoted Scott as "violently against" any attempt to capture any of the creatures of which he believes there are 20 to 50.

David James, M.P., co-founder of the Loch Ness Phenomena Investigation Bureau, shared Scott's viewpoint. Raymond R. Coffey reported for the *Chicago Daily News* of Nov. 24 that James asked the government immediately to add the monster to Britain's list of protected species along with such endangered species as the Natterjack toad and the large blue butterfly. At the same time Maurice Burton, 77, for 30 years an expert on prehistoric animals at the Museum of Natural History, repeated his conviction that "there is nothing more monstrous in Loch Ness than a family of otters."

"None of the photographs is sufficiently informative to establish the existence, far less the identity, of a large living animal in the Loch," the zoologists of the museum declared in a statement, according to the *Chicago Sun-Times* for Nov. 25, 1975. The scientists refrained from making a detailed report as they had promised to refrain until after Rines made the photographs public at the two-day conference called for Dec. 9–10 in Edinburgh.

The museum scientists did admit that computer enhancement of one frame produced a flipperlike image which, however, they believed did not enable them to attempt "even the broadest identification."

The computer-assisted study to which the museum scientists referred was conducted by Alan Gillespie at the Jet Propulsion Laboratory in Pasadena, Calif. Gillespie used techniques with remarkable success on pictures of the planet Mars taken by Mariners 6, 7 and 9. Gillespie told the *Los Angeles Times* that "there seems to be something in the loch" and that he could detect no fraud. The *Louisville Courier-Journal* and *Times* used the *Times* story Nov. 27, 1975. It contained considerable description of the pictures but not the pictures themselves. Gillespie called Rines "sincere, serious and honest." "As a paleontologist I need bones," wrote Adrian J. Desmond of Harvard in the *Times of London*, the *Washington Post* reported from London Jan. 1, 1976.

The controversy was waged by scientists in the press, without waiting for the release of the cause of it. Some newspapers took sides. Nov. 8 the *Washington Star* commented editorially, "We are inclined to think that the Loch Ness monster is a delightful imaginative product of Scottish drollery . . . We heartily call for cancellation of the international monster conference next month."

The next day in the *Washington Post* Ann Cottrell Fine, on the board of the Rachel CarsonTrust for the Living Environment, wrote, "Verification will be a body blow to the ever-elusive world of elves, trolls and giants. For it means goodbye to the days when you could look across the great loch and as the wind and light change, see humps, a head, horns, a tail—a monster of your own making." The *Manchester Guardian* commented, "Nothing would be sadder than for Nessie's existence to be established beyond doubt." The paper added that discovery would put a crimp in the loch's flourishing tourist business and besides "a world where dodoes are dead and phoenixes fabled needs the odd mythical beast."

Such ridicule added to the opposition of many scientists killed the proposed two-day symposium. Dec. 1 the Associated Press reported that the Royal Society of Edinburgh, the University of Edinburgh and Heriot Watt University, organizers of the two-day symposium, canceled the plan because "no useful or impartial discussion" could be held—"against a background of leaks and rumors it could not have been possible to hope to take a cool clinical look in the normal manner as to this discovery."

Robert A. Semple, Jr. enumerated what Nessie had done in the *New York Times* for Dec. 5, 1975:

Caused any number of harsh words to be passed among eminent members of the British scientific community.

Embarrassed a few newspapers that concluded without seeing them that photographs taken by an American from Boston incontrovertibly proved the monster's existence.

Sent the odds on Nessie's existence at Ladbroke's, the big London betting organization, bouncing up and down like a yo yo.

The letters column of the *Washington Star* Dec. 6 had two letters commenting upon the Nov. 26 editorial, "Nailing Nessie." In one Curtis D. MacDougall called Nessie "the most successful public relations stunt of the 20th century." In the other Dr. Sandy Grimwade, assistant editor of *Nature,* said his magazine would publish Rines' pictures, which "should convince skeptics that Nessie is not an invention of the Scottish Tourist Board." Dec. 12 Paul J. Willis, president of the International Fortean Organization, accused MacDougall of the "naive smugness of a knee-jerk dismissal."

Taking a somewhat different position than his assistant, David Davies, editor of *Nature,* told the UPI Dec. 10, 1975 that publication of three of Rines' photographs in the magazine's Comment and Opinion section did not confer the authority of the magazine on the subject.

With the two-day symposium called off, Rines and Scott called a press conference in a House of Parliament committee room to reassert their claim to having proved Nessie's existence. They said that the creature should be named Nessiteras rhombopteryx as a first step in protecting it as a threatened species.

Another believer who refused to withdraw from the foray was taxonomist George R. Zug, curator of reptiles and amphibians of the Department of Vertebrate Zoology, National Museum of Natural History of the Smithsonian Institution. Back from the House of Commons news conference he was interviewed by John Sherwood for the Dec. 20 *Washington Star.* He strongly reasserted his belief in Nessie's existence and favored more underwater pictures and opposed trying to remove Nessie from the loch.

The time obviously had arrived to let the public in on the debate by making public the controversial photographs. The New York *Village Voice* revealed Dec. 29, in an article by Anthony Haden-Guest, that publication was being delayed because Rines wanted to sell them for a sum of almost six figures which the *National Geographic, National Enquirer* and *Time* all had refused to pay. The article related some of Rines' background. Previous enterprises included an attempt to find the fleet of King Jehoshaphat in the Red Sea and searching for Bigfoot. Haden-Guest also summarized the activities and opinions of some half-dozen zealots dotted around the shore. "And it would be pleasant to report that they are working in unison, but such regrettably is not the case," he wrote. "Discussing monster theory with monster watchers is, as a matter of fact, a bit like discussing fine points of church doctrine with opposing sects in the Middle Ages." He cited Frank Searle, former paratrooper; Clem Shelton, an ex-Pauline monk; Ted Holiday; the Reverend Osmond, an exorcist, and Basil Cary, a former RAF wing commander, and his wife, Winifred, a psychic.

Village Voice used one of Rines' 1972 photographs, supposedly of "a flipper-like appendage to a large-textured body of indeterminate extent and identity."

And so the photographs were reproduced in newspapers and magazines from coast to coast. The *Chicago Tribune* Jan. 5, 1976 devoted an entire page to them and to artist drawings and maps in color. In the accompanying article Ronald Kotulak, science editor, gave some of the lineup of scientific supporters and critics. Prof. Roy Mackal was quoted as now thinking Nessie belongs to a family of amphibians called eogyrinus, believed extinct for 250 million years. Most readers probably took the word of the author that the blurred images showed "a hazy rust-colored object and two appendages gliding through the murky depths of the loch" and a monster, with mouth open looking directly into the camera.

Much more believable was the drawing based on a June 20, 1975 underwater photograph. Its features were two horns, eyes and nostrils, still not easy to recognize without the cutlines. In his accompanying article Walter Sullivan mentioned scientists formerly skeptical but now advocates of further research.

Explaining why he intended to return to Scotland in the summer of 1976, Dr. Harold E. Edgerton of MIT said, "It took five years to get these lousy pictures we have now," according to Thomas O'Toole in the *Washington Post* for April 9, 1976. An article by Edgerton in the March–April issue of *Technology Review,* edited at MIT, explained how the strobe lights and other equipment have been improved since 1970, according to the *Village Voice* for April 11, 1976.

In a letter to the *New York Times* April 15, 1976 Eliot Stanley of Dobbs Ferry, N.Y. pleaded for a cessation of attempts to identify Nessie who never hurt anyone. Judith Martin said virtually the same in the *Chicago Sun-Times* for April 24, 1976. She mentioned the MIT magazine article and a similar one in the Museum of Comparative Zoology *Newsletter* from Harvard but disagreed that there should be more expeditions. Wrote Martin: "If any creature on Earth has sincerely and consistently tried to lead a quiet life, free of the rewards as well as the drawbacks of celebrity-dom, it is the Loch Ness monster."

In her review of Roy Mackal's book, *The Monster of Loch Ness,* in the *Chicago Tribune* for May 2, 1976, Penelope Mesic summarized the difficulties Nessie hunters encounter: "It is close to impossible to gather information about the Loch Ness animal. Not only is the beast shy but the loch is large, deep and inky black, clouded with particles of peatmoss. The best new evidence is that of underwater sonar photographs but even these show vague outlines and no details. Therefore Mackal quite rightly stresses that his conclusions are to be taken not as fact but as hypotheses."

In his book Mackal wrote that Loch Ness animals are related most closely to eels, or more probably to Urodele Embolomeri, a large form of extinct (250 million years) amphibian. In his review of the Mackal book in the *Chicago Daily News* for May 15–16 David M. Walsten, editor of the Field Museum of Natural History *Bulletin,* wrote: "There is no shred of hard evidence—no fragment of bone or drop of blood—to tell us what manner of creature for centuries has been the cause of nightmares . . ."

The *New York Times School Weekly,* a supplement to the *Chicago Daily News* for the week of May 10, 1976, summarized an article in the March–April *Technology Review* that said of the activities of the Boston Academy of Applied Science: "On the first expedition in 1970, moving targets 10 to 40 times larger than fish were detected by sonar." In 1972 and 1976 underwater photographic equipment developed by Harold E. Edgerton was added to the sonar and photographs showed what seemed to be a 4- to 6-foot "flipper" and a long neck with a 2-foot head on it, as well as several more ambiguous pictures. On the last expedition the camera and the lake bottom were also disturbed, presumably by a large moving object.

Instead of a book review the *Washington Star* devoted more than a half-page May 20 to a Question and Answer interview with Mackal by staffer Vernon A. Guidry, Jr. All the familiar angles were explored and, in addition, Guidry asked, "More and more scientists are taking your evidence and the Loch Ness animals seriously. Yet you say the stigma of the crackpot still attaches. Why?" Mackal answered: "Once ridicule has been attached to a subject, it's pretty hard to change directions."

Then came the startling news that Nessie would have no peace in 1976. Judith Martin revealed in the *New York Times* May 15 that that newspaper had purchased the exclusive rights to whatever is discovered about Nessie by Rines' Academy of Applied Science in Boston. Surmised Martin: "Perhaps the most excited about this is the *Times* subsidiary sales office which markets such products as shower curtains with the front page of the *Times* on it, T-shirts, scarves, mirrors which declare you Man (or Woman) in the *News* and canvas bags. All they need is a photograph of the monster, a spokeswoman said yesterday, and there's no limit to what they can do for it. A *New York Times'* Loch Ness Monster Doll is already planned."

Assigned to accompany the expedition and copyright everything the scientists said or photographed was John Noble Wilford, the first of whose articles consumed almost a full-page of the *New York Times* for May 28, 1976. "Now," he wrote, "after centuries of amateurish observation and scientific debate, a team of engineers and scientists is to undertake what is planned as the most thorough and technologically sophisticated investigation to date into the phenomenon, whatever it is."

Wilford enumerated the cast of characters. In addition to Rines and Edgerton it included Charles W. Wyckoff, of Applied Photo Services in Needham Heights, Mass.; George Newton, M.I.T. engineering professor; Martin Klein, president of Klein Associates Inc. of Salem, N.H.; an undersea search and survey company; and Dr. Christopher McGowan, curator of vertebrate paleontology at the Royal Ontario Museum in Toronto. Most of the article described the nature and use of equipment and a history of sightings of Nessie beginning with the St. Columba legend.

May 30, 1976 the *New York Times* declared that it was reviving a lately quiescent tradition, that of newspaper sponsorship of expeditions. It cited the *New York Herald's* sponsorship of Henry Stanley's successful search for the missionary Dr. David Livingstone in 1871 and the *Times'* own backing of Admiral Richard Byrd's South Pole expedition in 1929. *Life* bought the exclusive rights to the earlier Apollo flights but the *Times* obtained them for Apollo 15.

May 30 the *Chicago Tribune* announced it had bought the *New York Times* series and published Wilford's first article slightly altered. So did the *Madison* (Wis.) *State Journal* and doubtless many other papers.

Beginning June 4, 1976 Wilford's articles were datelined Drumnadrochit, Scotland. In the first he rhapsodized regarding the beauty of the Highlands: "In the afternoon the stillness fell over the Great Glen. The morning drizzle drifted beyond the green hills, the wind died down and Loch Ness could settle itself. The dark waters became like a smooth sheet of shining obsidian, a mirror reflecting the steep hills, gray clouds—and some may say—the imaginations of those who had come here in search of the Loch Ness monster."

Wilford gave a detailed account of the unloading and setting up of equipment and of the routine performances of duties by Rines, Edgerton, Wyckoff and others. He reported that Edgerton gave some color postcards to some children who were onlooking. The photographs were of a bullet ripping through an apple. He had taken the picture to demonstrate the virtues of his high-speed photographic technology. He told the children, "This is how we make applesauce in America."

In his June 5 piece Wilford recalled the lore of the Highlands replete with monsters, "fabulous goblins" and water spirits known as kelpies or water horses. He gave the highlights of the St. Columba tale and several others, including a 1570 record of "a monstrous fish seen in Lochfyne." A 1653 map noted that Loch Lomond, near Glasgow, has "waves without wind, fish without fins and a floating island." In his account of a tour of the Hebrides with Dr. Samuel Johnson in 1773 James Boswell related a story, told by his guide, that a sea horse had devoured a girl. Sir Walter Scott wrote in a letter in 1815 that "a monster long reported to inhabit Cauldsshield Loch has of late been visible to sundry persons." On the isle of Skye in 1870 a laird had an idea about capturing a monster by dragging the loch with a long net. When the net caught on a snag the crowd of watchers became frightened and scattered. In 1880 a diver said he came across the beast with eyes "small, gray and baleful."

June 6 the *Times* announced that the hunt had begun the preceding day, when Rines got 8,000 color-pictures, not yet developed. With most of the equipment donated by American companies that specialize in photography and underwater exploration, the cost of the Academy of Applied Science was estimated at $75,000. A film crew from the National Broadcasting Company, which had exclusive television rights, was on hand. Wilford reported the activities of the ten explorers in minute detail. In a lengthy second article Wilford described the geological history of the area and the likelihood that seafaring animals could adjust to fresh water if cut off from the sea.

Wilford's June 7 story pertained to the full array of cameras and lights now in operation. June 10 he revealed that the expedition was finding more evidence of Murphy's law (that whatever can go wrong will go wrong) than of Nessie. The weight of the underwater television made it impossible to shift equipment about. Water was discovered in the strobe light. Moisture seeped into the cylinder containing the Polaroid camera, the mechanism triggering the camera's flash unit failed to work, and so on. June 12 Robert B. Semple, Jr. joined Wilford and did a long piece based on interviews with residents, some of whom believed they had seen the monster. Jimmy McLennan, 62-year-old crofter who never saw the monster nevertheless expressed the attitude of many that any creature should not be removed as they feared the Japanese wanted to do. Said McLennan: "Those little fellows couldn't speak a word of English. They just sailed around in a little boat, mostly in circles." June 14 Wilford told of how the sonar equipment was being moved about. June 21 he wrote: "Certainly no business in research at Loch Ness . . . for nearly a month now and . . . yet to find any evidence to explain the legendary phenomenon." July 17 Semple used up a lot of space to repeat that the search proved fruitless. Aug. 3 he reported that, despite many letters of encouragement, Rines had decided to streamline the operation, leaving three Scots in charge while he returned to Boston. His faith in the existence of Nessie remained undiminished.

"Though frustrated in the search this summer for the Loch Ness monster," Wilford, back in New York, wrote in the Aug. 28 *Times,* "an American team of engineers and scientists has reported a discovery that could be of considerable archeological interest—some apparently ancient stone formations in the shallow end of the Scottish lake." It was speculated that the distinctive rings seen on the sonar charts could be the ceremonial stone circles of burial chairs associated with the early Celts, the most striking of many throughout the British Isles and western Europe being the Stonehenge ruins in England.

In a much delayed review of Mackal's book Sept. 10, Gerald Jonas recalled that formerly people asked, "Is there really a Loch Ness monster?" The *New York Times* and Academy of Applied Science mounted an all-out expedition to find the answer. "Unfortunately," Jonas commented, "the news from Scotland has been so sparse since then that people now have begun to ask 'Is there really a Loch Ness Monster expedition?' " Oct. 10 Wilford wrote that Rines, Wyckoff and some others planned to return to Loch Ness in November, hoping that salmon would be running and would attract the creature. Archeologists from Edinburgh University, Rines said, would assist, hoping to learn more about the stone formations revealed by the sonar. Dec. 6 Wilford finally wrote: "The 1976 search for the so-called Loch Ness monster has come to an end with results that were —well, in a word—disappointing but the searchers hasten to add, not discouraging." The rest of the article reviewed the summer's activities and quoted Rines, Wyckoff, Edgerton, Klein and others as still convinced that there is a Nessie. The *Chicago Tribune* used the story Dec. 12, 1976. Dec. 20 the *Times* revealed that of 108,000 pictures taken by Rines' academy, none showed signs of the monster or very much else.

Despite the *New York Times'* news monopoly, throughout the summer other news media remained on the alert for occurrences that would be newsworthy and common property. June 8 Charles and Robert G. Hahl voiced the opinion in the *Washington Post* that what onlookers have seen for centuries was caused by methane gas accumulating between layers of compressed organic material, bouncing up and breaking loose large, irregular sections of those mats, having several ragged appendages.

June 7, just a week after it began publication of the *New York Times* stories from Scotland, the *Chicago Tribune* gave two columns to Ronald Yates who wrote from Kawayu, Japan that Kussie, named for Lake Kussharo, though seen since 1973 by only 53 persons, nevertheless was exciting Japanese scientists, journalists and government officials.

The *Tribune* also printed a cartoon June 9 showing a UFO landing while a Loch Ness Monster hunt leader asked a worker, "You mean you put all the cameras underwater?" Arthur Hoppe wrote a satirical story about the capture of Nessie by Mr. and Mrs. Milton Haberdash of Waco, Texas for the *Philadelphia Inquirer* June 27. It was in the same vein as Russell Baker's *New York Times* column for June 19 in which the paper's publisher, Arthur G. Sulzberger, and other *Times* personnel, including James Reston, Red Smith and A. M. Rosenthal, discussed the implications of a captured Nessie.

July 10 the *National Observer* gave a full page to a descriptive piece by Gerald S. Snyder. The *Washington Post* did the same Aug. 17, Paul Richard's article being illustrated by photographs, including one by Frank

Searle who says he saw the monster more than two dozen times in seven years.

Dec. 31, 1976 the *Chicago Tribune* used the 1934 picture with the caption "Where's Nessie?" and brief cutlines telling of the failure of the Rines–*New York Times* venture but quoting Wyckoff as saying, "I'm not discouraged. I'm still convinced in my own mind that there's something there."

Jan. 8–9, 1977 the *Chicago Daily News* used a three-column blowup of the same picture with an Associated Press story citing Wyckoff's report in the *Technology Review* that the severe drought that gripped the United Kingdom might have lowered the level of the loch so much that there were no salmon swimming in the shallow areas "to bring the animal up from its usual depth to feed."

Jan. 31, 1977 the *New York Times* used an article by Christopher A. Wren from Moscow that a member of the Soviet Geographical Society had seen a leviathan 50 feet long in the Lake Kol-Kol in southern Kazakhstan. And, as though nothing had happened, the *Chicago Sun-Times* headlined a story by Thomas J. Dygard Feb. 8, 1977, "Loch Ness Monster Lives—There's No Doubt About It." The article contained absolutely nothing that hadn't been published many times before, but it crowded out real news.

Never-give-up Robert Rines returned to Scotland for another try, John Noble Wilford reported in the *New York Times* for June 12, 1977. This time he expected to be joined by archeologists from the University of Strathclyde and divers from Underwater Instrumentation investigating what appear to be ancient stone rings in the shallow north end of the lake. Oct. 9 in its "Follow-up on the News" the *Times* again quoted Wyckoff as absolutely certain. It did not, however, recall what Jane E. Brody wrote in its issue of July 4, 1976, inspired by Angus Hall's book *Monsters and Mythic Beasts*. Wrote Brody: "Whether Nessie is discovered or not, people will continue to believe in such creatures as they have throughout recorded history."

"A belief in monsters, psychologists say, seems to fulfill a universal human need to explain the unknown, to reach beyond the dullness of ordinary life, to give form to undefined fears and hopes for a brighter future."

Another journalist who was overwhelmed by the beauty of Loch Ness and its environs was Philip R. Smith, Jr., who began his feature for the July 10, 1977 *Washington Star* from Inverness: "It is little wonder that so many of the sightings of the Loch Ness monster have been from the setting of Urquhart Castle on the shore of the loch." Smith got both his historical and geological background a bit twisted but he was on sound ground when he wrote: "On the hillside above the castle the spectacular beauty of the area struck us with full impact." The *Chicago Tribune* ran virtually the same story by Smith May 28, 1978. "The most picturesque castle ruins in the British Isles" was the headquarters of almost all of the expeditions and was regarded as the best spot for tourists to wait for a glimpse of Nessie. In a book note in the *Chicago Daily News* for July 22, Dennis Meredith, author of a book dealing chiefly with the Robert Rines ventures, *Search for Loch Ness,* is quoted as believing the shy creature is an elasmosaur. Also mentioned is the capture by a Japanese trawler off New Zealand of a similar monster. More details of that incident were included in a UPI article from Chicago quoting Leigh Van Valen as saying that if the Japanese scholar, Tokyo Skikama, ancient animal expert at Yokohama National University, is correct, it would lend credence to the belief that Nessie is a plesiosaurus. The *Wall Street Journal* used the story July 26, 1977.

Another believer in the plesiosaurus identity is Frank Searle, a retired British soldier who has spent 25,000 hours of monster watching, 15,000 in boats. He claims to have seen Nessie 25 times, according to a long feature in the New York *Village Voice* for Feb. 12, 1978 but says few of his pictures have turned out well because of the lack of proper background.

Agence France-Press announced the first public appearance of Nessie of the year as having been seen by fisherman Bill Wright. The *Milwaukee Journal* used the story June 25 and the *Chicago Sun-Times* did so June 26. Otherwise nothing seems to have happened the rest of the year or, in fact, until late spring of 1979. Then, April 4, the *London Daily Telegraph* had a story by Christopher Leake in Edinburgh that the British Broadcasting Company admitted its supposed exclusive picture of Nessie was really a duck, difficult to distinguish from a distance.

And May 23, 1979 the Associated Press reported from New York that two dolphins were being trained in Florida to assist Dr. Robert Rines by carrying cameras and strobe lights to survey the deep waters. Reuters had the same from Boston March 22. It mentioned the anxiety regarding whether dolphins who live in salt water could adjust to fresh water. Howard Curtis, executive vice president of the academy, said it could be done but Louis Garibaldi, curator of the New England Aquarium in Boston, was skeptical.

Reuters also reported that a British Broadcasting Company film showed only a black spot on the surface of the loch. Peter Leddy, a television cameraman, thought he had gotten 15 minutes of pictures showing Nessie in motion. He described her as having a round head like a seal.

March 24, 1979 the AP had a story from Miami about the progress Harold "Rusty" Nielsen was making in training the two dolphins. He would not show the equipment being used and made the reporter, Martin Merzer, promise not to reveal the location of the training ground. He did declare dolphins are being used "because of their built-in sonar system, their intelligence, their mobility. They can 'see' sound and find the animals."

Even more startling was the extra-long AP dispatch from London Aug. 5 that two American scientists claimed that the seldom-seen denizen of the murky Scottish lake might be an elephant. The two were Dr. Donald Johnson, a research associate in geography at the University of Illinois, and Dr. Dennis Power, director of the Santa Barbara Museum of Natural History, who wrote an article for the British magazine *New Scientist.* They studied reports of many who reported seeing Nessie and compared the descriptions with those of an elephant swimming.

By the time William Tuohy interviewed him for a story in the *Los Angeles Times* Sept. 20, 1979, Frank Searle claimed to have seen Nessie 31 times from his trailer home of ten years. He scoffed at Rines' plan to use dolphins as a "gimmick." "It's all a stunt supported by the media," he said. "It's another one of Rines' publicity stunts. Look, the water down there is so dark you'd have to get a camera within five yards of any creature to get a proper image . . . there's no way a dolphin's going to swim that close to a predator."

The dolphin plan never materialized because one of the two trained in Florida died in Massachusetts before it could be shipped abroad.

Tuohy's article was a fine summary of the efforts to prove Nessie's existence. He concluded by quoting Lt. Col. McLean, a former tourist official: "The worst thing for tourism would be to find scientifically that Nessie doesn't exist. But the second worst thing would be to prove that she does. It's the mystery that counts. When you come down to it the story is more important than the reality."

Thwarted in his effort to convince the world of Nessie's reality, Dr. Roy Mackal turned his attention to the African Congo in search of the so-called Mokele-mbembe, a legendary animal first written about in 1776 by a French missionary, according to an interview that Rick MacArthur reported in the *Chicago Sun-Times* for March 31, 1980. During a 30-day journey through the Likouala region jungle, Mackal, two associates and four pygmy porters found natives who gave eyewitness accounts of an animal up to 15 meters long with a snakelike head and a neck two or three meters in length, a long tail and reddish brown to gray in color. Mackal hopes the Congolese government will appropriate money for further research. April 10 the *Chicago Tribune* also ran an account of an interview with Mackal by Jon Van. Mackal repeated a story told among the pygmies about a Mokele-mbembe whose movement within a river disturbed the fishing, causing a group of pygmies to kill the beast, dress it and eat it. All who ate the meat died. Mackal wants to visit the site to hunt for monster bones.

Sept. 24, 1980 the *Sun-Times* used a full-length feature about Mackal's African venture by Jane Gregory. She revealed that an American missionary and his wife, Eugene and Sandy Thomas, of whom Mackal learned from a Fulbright scholar just back from the area, were a great help. Mackal also won the confidence of Congolese government officials by repairing television sets and other machines.

A third journalistic boost for Mackal appeared in the *Sun-Times* for

Oct. 15. The professor hoped to raise $20,000 so he and a scientific colleague, James Powell of Plainview, Tex., could make the trip during the summer of 1981.

About the same time, according to the *New York Times* for Dec. 26, 1979, one of Mackal's early associates in hunting for Nessie, Jack Grimm, a millionaire Texas oilman, announced he would try to find the *Titanic* which sank April 14–15, 1912 after striking an iceberg in the north Atlantic.

That wild-goose chases are an obsession with Grimm was revealed in an Associated Press story from New York that the *Chicago Sun-Times* ran Aug. 31, 1980. Not only had he participated in the Loch Ness enterprise but he also hunted Bigfoot in the Northwest and financed expeditions to find Noah's Ark in Turkey. He offered $500,000 for the first conclusive photos of Bigfoot and went to Israel to investigate reports of miracle healings. He disclaimed any intention of attempting to raise the *Titanic*. "What would you do with it if you got it up?" he asked. "You'd have to tow it 1,000 miles to New York. Besides it's the tomb for 1,500 souls. It shouldn't be disturbed."

Grimm conceded he gets a special kick out of using his money to chase the few great remaining mysteries of modern life. He said: "It gives me a great deal of pleasure to do these projects and share them with the world. A lot of people live vicariously through my adventures. I enjoy that. To me life is a series of adventures."

June 21, 1981 the AP reported from Abilene, Tex. that Grimm would sponsor another expedition to pinpoint where the *Titanic* could be found. July 14 the *Los Angeles Times* had a lengthy profile of Grimm by Kathy Maxa. Hoping to convert Russians by proof of biblical stories he joined a futile attempt to find the remains of Noah's Ark in Turkey, recouping his losses with a successful motion picture, *Ark of Noah,* in 1974. Grimm said all of his searches, including those for Bigfoot and Nessie, are motivated by business reasons and he takes tax exemptions for them. By the end of 1981, it was estimated, he had sunk about $2 million on the *Titanic* project.

July 29, 1981 the *New York Daily World* published pictures of the *Gyre,* the explorers' vessel, and an account of the return to Boston of the expedition leader, Mike Harris, and his companions who said they had taken underwater photographs of the sunken ship.

A plan to dredge Loch Ness with a motorized raft and to catch Nessie in a net was reported in the *Boston Globe* for Aug. 5, 1980. Leader of the expedition was Adrian Shine, a British plastics manufacturer. The next day, Aug. 6, the *Chicago Sun-Times* ran an Associated Press story from London quoting Shine as expecting the expedition to cost about $140,000 and to take three years.

In what the *Bakersfield Californian* for May 28, 1982 called an "ambitious . . . renewed effort to find the elusive Loch Ness monster," Tim

Dinsdale and representatives of the Great Britain Exploration Society planned a four-day mission in the Goodyear blimp *Europa.*

"Theories on the Loch Ness monster get stranger every year," Michael West reported Aug. 6, 1982 from London for the Associated Press. The *London Daily Telegraph,* Field News Service and other news media reported similarly that a retired electronics engineer, Robert P. Craig, had written an article for the British magazine *New Scientist* saying Nessie probably is a pine log propelled from the bottom of the lake to the surface now and again by a buildup of natural gas.

In the *San Francisco Chronicle* for Sept. 14, 1982 Charles McCabe devoted his entire columnlong article to mock grief. Dec. 5, 1982 the *Chicago Sun-Times* ran a half-page *Discover* article elaborating on the Craig theory. May 15, 1983, however, the same paper gave an equivalent amount of space to George Will's syndicated column exaggerating the evidence for Nessie's existence.

15

Healing, Medical and Psychic

There are some newspapers, though not so many as formerly, that occasionally displease medical authorities by premature or overly optimistic accounts of the discovery of a new cause for disease or new cures or surgical innovations. Such stories cruelly raise the hopes of some sufferers from diseases of which the causes are still unknown or for which no remedy has been developed. Ignorant health reporters can describe some practice as new when the medical profession has been familiar with it for some time.

The journalists' defense against these and similar charges is that they rely on supposedly reputable members of the medical profession whose colleagues should exercise more discipline over them. As the number of journalistic specialists in this field grows, the bad reporting diminishes. Furthermore, in this as in no other area the press has been aggressive in attacking superstitions. The debunking has been mostly in health columns conducted by distinguished medical authorities. One of the first to lead the crusade was George W. Crane, holder of both an M.D. and a Ph.D. in psychology from Northwestern University. For instance, in his "Case Records of a Psychologist" for Jan. 11, 1936 he dealt extensively with myths about birthmarks which, he wrote, "are not due to an unsatisfied maternal wish for strawberries or cherries or any such peculiar appetites."

Another pioneer was Dr. Logan Clendening. His June 6, 1936 syndicated column debunked the myth that aluminum cooking utensils are harmful. June 16, 1936 the International News Service reviewed an article by L. W. Bryce of Ronceverte, W.Va. in *Hygeia* concerning superstitions prevalent in remote parts of the United States, such as "a sty in the eye will quickly disappear if rubbed with a gold ring" and "a red string worn about the little finger will check a tendency to nose bleed." A similar story was reported Aug. 3, 1936 from Martins Ferry, Ohio by the United Press. A sufferer from a siege of hiccups received 16 suggestions from all parts of the state, including "hold one hand in hot water and the other in cold for five minutes" and "eat two crusts of dry bread." An Associated Press story Feb. 24, 1982 from East Islip, N.Y. helped to dispel faith in old remedies. It reported that a 10-year-old girl had eaten crackers, drunk water, held her breath, put a paper bag over her head and tried other remedies for eight months. Then surgery realigned her vertebrae and the hiccuping stopped.

The syndicated Hearst *American Weekly* for June 20, 1937 included a feature, "Queer Medical Superstitions." It quoted Dr. Charles F. Bolduan, of the New York City Department of Health, that it is not only backwoods and ignorant people who believe in fantastic and useless cures such as treating asthma patients with a broth of lizards boiled in milk, using spider webs to attempt to stop a cut's bleeding and using a poultice of red clay and vinegar for a sprained ankle or wrist.

Another New York doctor, August A. Thomen, was the main authority on which the *Kansas City Star* based an opposite-editorial-page article, "False Health and Food Ideas Still Fill a Large Volume," Aug. 20, 1941. The big book was Dr. Thomen's *Doctors Don't Believe It, Why Should You?* Among the foolish beliefs it warned against was that one should not mix lobster and ice cream during the same meal and that it is harmful to have flowers in a bedroom at night. "Probably the most widely held fallacy in the world is the one about the dangers of wounds caused by rusty nails," the article by Berton Roueche read.

For several decades a generation ago Dr. Arthur Evans issued warnings against quacks and debunked frauds in the health field in his *Chicago Tribune* column. Dr. Evans' successor was Dr. Irving Cutter, dean of the Northwestern University School of Medicine. An example of what the two crusaders did was the latter's column for Aug. 6, 1942, entitled "Health Superstitions." In it he blasted many old wives' tales such as that possession of a particular coin, luck piece or button insulates against disease, that necklaces ensure easy teething, a horse chestnut or buckeye can ward off rheumatism and beads of amber forestall goiter. He wrote:

Volumes have been written setting forth the horrible consequences which will ensue should certain foods be eaten in combination. For example "You cannot eat fish and drink milk at the same meal." "Don't employ proteins and carbohydrates in the same menu." Such sayings ignore the fact that milk— the universal food of nature—is an ideal mixture of proteins, carbohydrates, fats and minerals.

Dr. Cutter also debunked the notion that birthmarks result from a pregnant mother's having been frightened. In his *Sun* column for March 8, 1947 Dr. Edwin P. Jordan considered birthmarks at greater length, saying that everyone has some blemishes but worries only about those that appear in conspicuous places. He explained the different kinds of birthmarks and advised as to their treatment.

In another column, Aug. 3, 1947, Dr. Jordan debunked many other superstitions regarding pregnancy and infant care, such as that the activities of an expectant mother can determine the taste and disposition of her offspring, a baby's clothes should not be put on over its head, an infant should not be allowed to see itself in a mirror during the first year of life, and many more he encountered in his practice.

By far the most vigorous campaigner against health superstitions was Dr. Morris Fishbein, editor of American Medical Association publications and columnist for the *Chicago Times*. Warts, the doctor wrote Sept. 28, 1942, do not result from touching toads and do not disappear if they are rubbed by a carrot that is buried in a cemetery after the sufferer has walked around the graveyard three times. Feb. 21, 1943 he went after the notion that the way to rid oneself of venereal disease during wartime is to have intercourse with someone not infected. Jan. 28, 1948 he scoffed at the idea that a woman, on a first visit to a newborn baby, should not hold it in her arms unless she wants to become a mother shortly; also if a married woman is the first person to see a recently born infant she will have the next baby, and so on. Aug. 11, 1948 Dr. Fishbein denied that wrapping the skin of a rattlesnake around the affected part or use of bent horseshoe nails help cure rheumatism.

These accounts would be humorous if they were not harmful in that they cause people to avoid effective treatments while relying upon the useless ordeals. Dr. Floris van Minden, dentist, warned in a *Chicago Sun* column for Aug. 7, 1947 that it is not so that a mother must lose a tooth so that the newborn baby can have enough lime salta (calcium) for its own teeth.

Despite these columns by medical experts, the *Chicago Daily News* reported Aug. 26, 1949 that one-fourth of all questions that young expectant mothers ask doctors are based on superstitious notions, such as that it's bad luck to cut a child's hair before it is old enough to patronize a barber, that a baby will have cross-eyes if it looks at the sky and that crawling between someone's legs will stunt a child's growth. And June 3, 1953 the same paper ran an Associated Press story from New York under the heading "Claims Unborn Tot Can Be Neurotic." It was the report of a speech by a Chicago gynecologist. And there continue to be persons who won't eat oysters in months without an "r" in them, some still wear red flannel to cure colds and don't allow canned food to remain in a can once it has been opened.

According to Dr. Ralph W. Sockman in his syndicated column for May 18, 1952, "A superstition is a belief resting on emotion or fear rather than reason. It is a kind of cobweb in the corner of the mind and we like to think that our mental attics have been swept clear of such falsehood." Dr. Sockman said the church should abandon "many irrational ideas that should have been discarded with the Dark Age."

Another medical journalist was Dr. Walter C. Alvarez whose column the *Sun-Times* used. His Feb. 25, 1955 piece, "More Curious Beliefs That Have No Bases," was especially good. In it he debunked the prenatal cause of birthmarks, the notion that food should not be cooked in aluminum pans, that it's bad to swim after eating, that one should "feed a cold and starve a fever" and many more. May 27, 1956 he wrote "The Folly of Seeing Quacks," because many ailments clear up without treatment and others, such as arthritis, flare up no matter what is done. Sept. 15, 1948 the *Tribune's* health editor, Dr. Theodore van Dellen, explained how quacks work.

In *Parade* for Oct. 29, 1961 Robert P. Goldman wrote "10 Myths About Your Teeth." They included: "An unborn baby draws off calcium from its mother's teeth," "Dental troubles end when you have a full set of false teeth" and "Most teeth are lost because of tooth decay—plain old cavities."

An early critic of the press' handling of health news was Dr. Watson Davis, editor of Science Service. He was reported in *Publishers' Auxiliary* for Dec. 23, 1961 to have told a University of Michigan audience, "The mass media have failed to apply the rigorous criteria of scientific truth in fields of utmost concern to public health and well being." He chastised newspapers that carried horoscopes or failed to campaign for the fluoridation of water. He supported voluntary birth control, warned against medical nostrums, favored immunizations for controllable diseases and cited many other areas in which journalists could be more helpful.

In their book, *Take Warning: A Book of Superstitions,* Jane Sarnoff and Reynold Ruffins debunked unscientific ideas about warts; the *Chicago Sun-Times* reprinted several paragraphs Sept. 24, 1979. Among the false ideas the authors exposed was "Cut an apple in half and rub each wart with each part of the apple; then fasten the apple together and bury it. As the apple rots it will take the warts with it."

More recently in his column in the *Chicago Tribune* for Dec. 20, 1980, Edward Barry said: "A word to the wise: What you 'know' can hurt you too." For instance, "if a child swallows poison vomiting should be induced immediately," "feed a cold and starve a fever" and "a person who drowns surfaces twice before going under the third time," are all untrue.

In addition to debunking health myths the press has waged numerous campaigns against medical quackery, usually with the cooperation of the American Medical Association or some other medical organization. Impressive-appearing machines, useless in either diagnosing or treating disease, illustrated a full-page article, "Medical Quacks," by William Kiedaisch in the rotogravure section of the *Chicago Daily News* for Feb. 18, 1956. The *Chicago Sunday Tribune* for Sept. 14, 1958 advertised a forthcoming article by Dr. van Dellen, "Quack psychology—how crooks get away with fooling the sick." Sept. 28, the *Chicago Sun-Times* ran Robert S. Kleckner's article, "AMA Official Bares Sales Approaches Made by Quacks," based on an interview with Oliver Field, director of the AMA's Bureau of Investigation.

"Ten million overweight Americans will waste 500 million dollars this year on quack diets, fake reducing pills and other non-scientific junk," the UPI reported Sept. 27, 1959 from Washington on the authority of Helen S.

Mitchell, dean of the University of Massachusetts school of home economics. Her warning was included in the annual year book of the Department of Agriculture titled *Food.*

Similarly Sarah Boyden warned in the *Chicago Sun-Times* for April 24, 1960 that "Today in the U.S. some 5,000,000 people suffering from arthritis pay over $250,000,000 annually in hope of getting relief. The tragedy is that the remedies they buy are utterly worthless. In some cases they are harmful to the hopeful user."

The economics expert Sylvia Porter began her column March 30, 1962, "Close to three-quarters of a billion dollars is plucked each year from the hands of millions of Americans—ranging from the gullible to the desperately ill—by health quacks." Marilyn Preston said it more forcefully in *Chicago Today* for Sept. 27, 1970: "We are a nation of suckers." The full-page article was headlined: "Quackery—the deadliest hoax of all."

The history of attempts to protect the public against quackery by acts of Congress was summarized by William Hines in the *Chicago Sun-Times* for Aug. 14, 1977. The review was timely in view of pending legislation to weaken the 1962 Kefauver amendment to the Food, Drug and Cosmetic Act by relieving a drug manufacturer of the obligation to label his products as effective. The crippling legislation, sponsored by Sen. Jesse Helms (R., N.C.) and Rep. Steven Stymmo (R., Id.) was intended to permit use of the controversial cancer cure, laetrile. Hines quoted an FDA historian as saying, "A new quack remedy for cancer appears every ten years." He elaborated, "Before Laetrile in the '70s there was Krebiozen in the '60s, the Hoxsey naturapothic treatment in the '50s, Dr. William Koch's glyxolide in the '40s and the celebrated orgone mumbo-jumbo of Sigmund Freud's protege Wilhelm Reich in the '30s."

Writing from London, England for the *Chicago Tribune* April 12, 1978, Robert Merry wrote: "In an age of wonder drugs, chemotherapy, and laser-beam surgery, it is easy to forget some of the disreputable ancestors of modern medicine." He then reviewed Eric Maple's new book, *Magic, Medicine and Quackery,* in which the author declares, "Quacks were dedicated amateurs with a mission or villains with a heart." He traced the development of British medicine over several centuries and speculated on the origin of the word *quack.*

About the best source of information about medical quackery is the National Museum of Quackery in St. Louis. Howard Wolinsky described some of the exhibits in the *Chicago Sun-Times* for May 16, 1982. The oldest are Perkins Tractors, which in the 1790s Elisha Perkins said would "draw out noxious electric fluids" and cure disease. There also is the Somus-Filmo-Sonic, a sort of tape recorder to cure ailments by different tunes, "Holiday for Strings" for cancer, "Smoke Gets in Your Eyes" for high blood pressure and many more.

From nearby Purcell, Okla. the United Press had reported Aug. 25,

1938 that a century-old "mad stone" was on exhibit. Wrapped in a piece of red flannel cloth from the baby gown of Gen. Sam Houston, it reputedly had saved the lives of dozens of persons bitten by rabid dogs and poisonous snakes.

To its credit the press had not confined itself to generalizations about the quackery evil. Rather, journalistic investigations have been instrumental in exposing quackery and thereby goading public officials to perform their duty to protect the public from injury and monetary loss. Norma Lee Browning fulfilled several such assignments for the *Chicago Tribune*. One of the first, Oct. 18, 1953, headlined "She Battles the Medical Fakers," was about the career of Charlotte Hermes, investigator for the Illinois Department of Registration and Education. Newspaper exposés helped check the spread of a post-war racket, uranium tunnels, in which sufferers from almost any imaginable illness supposedly could obtain relief by absorbing radioactive rays from uranium-lined tunnels. Robert S. Kleckner quoted Illinois state officials doubtful of their value. One operator of a Chicago room he called a tunnel admitted he had no idea what the amount of radioactivity was. "I haven't got a geiger counter. Those things cost $60 or $70," he told Kleckner for publication in the *Sun-Times* Dec. 5, 1954.

By July 18, 1955 Arthur J. Snider was able to report in the *Chicago Daily News* that "Wisconsin has sealed off the last of its uranium tunnels, the 1955 counterpart of the oldtime medicine show." He quoted Oliver Field, of the AMA's Bureau of Investigation: "The mines are a monument to the gullibility of the public." The tunnels were really rooms whose walls were lined with uranium rocks from worn-out western mines. They contained no more radioactivity than does the luminous dial of a watch.

In its issue of March 15, 1959 the *Chicago Tribune* helped find innocent victims of radium poisoning. Roy Gibbons' article was headed, "Vast Search Is On for Radium Fad Victims of 30 Years Ago." In a series of four articles Jan. 5–8, 1959, Miller Davis of the *Daily News* exposed quacks who mulcted the public with fake cancer cures, herbs that were supposedly good for almost anything and diets to prolong life. In the same paper Jan. 9, 1959 Arthur J. Snider debunked reducing pills on which the *Tribune* revealed, in a UPI Washington dispatch Sept. 27, 1959, 10 million Americans waste $500 million annually. Dec. 19, 1959 the *Sun-Times* publicized a new book in which Dr. Morris Fishbein revealed how he exposed an Escanaba woman who claimed to be running a high fever, up to 120 degrees; she succeeded in baffling many by means of a hot water bottle hidden under the sheets.

Injurious face-lifting treatments were exposed by Gabriel Favoino in the *Sun-Times* for Feb. 19, 1960 and in a series that began March 3, 1960. However, despite the insistence of scientists that copper bracelets have no curative value, the *Sun-Times* gave a half-page illustrated feature to the fad Sept. 6, 1970. Bert Yancey and Van Johnson endorsed treatment and it was noted that the Duke and Duchess of Windsor both wore copper bracelets. A few derisive prominent medical authorities were quoted.

Although unidentified medical authorities were quoted as charging "quackery and gimmickry," an alleged epidemic of interest in brain waves received almost a full page in the *Chicago Daily News* for April 6, 1972. Presumably brain waves, especially alpha waves, improve lives, control minds, stop headaches and wipe out other assorted human frailties, Patricia Moore reported.

Obviously in exposing quacks the press sometimes advertizes them despite the intentions of the reporter. Such seems to have been the case when Don Bishoff interviewed Ms. Doris Powell for the April 15, 1977 *Eugene* (Ore.)*Register-Guard* about her trip to Urissaden, Germany where she spent $1,500 for three injections of immunobiological transformation, a serum banned from the United States. Insisting that she had been cured of many aches and pains, Powell said that Dr. Theodore Bruck operated a Fountain of Youth.

This was one of the first such claims since the Associated Press reported March 14, 1949 from Moscow that the Soviet magazine *Ogonek* reported a Lake of Life had been discovered in the Ural mountains. It was not the first time, however, that Americans traveled abroad for seemingly magical cures not available to them at home. For years after Dr. John R. Brinkley was forbidden to perform goat gland operations in Kansas, patients went to him in Mexico from where he broadcast on a radio powerful enough to reach his old neighborhood. At another time hordes of Americans went to Williamsburg, Ontario to have their feet twisted by Dr. Mahlon Locke.

As for Doris Powell, shortly after her 59th birthday she told Ron Bellamy of the *Register-Guard* that she hadn't aged in four years. Occasion for the interview which the paper published April 28, 1981, was a lecture by Dr. Bruck in Eugene. In it the good doctor said his serum does not prolong life but makes it more endurable.

By far the most famous (or infamous) of the unorthodox medical miracle men was Edgar Cayce of Virginia Beach, Va. During 40 years of practice before he died in 1945 he is believed to have given more than 30,000 "readings," as he called them. Twice daily he went into a trance to respond to letters in which sufferers described their symptoms. It mattered not whether the petitioner was in the same room or hundreds of miles away. Cayce diagnosed and prescribed to the satisfaction of thousands who sang his praises. There still is a Cayce claque. On the 100th anniversary of his birth the *New York Daily News* reported March 18, 1977, "200 plus assorted psychic healers, hypnotists, parapsychologists, dream interpreters and Kirlian photographers" met at the National Council for Geocosmic Research convention at Christ Church, Manhattan. Tom Hodge wrote a column about Cayce for the *Johnson City* (Ill.) *Press-Chronicle* June 5, 1980. There was no occasion, such as an anniversary, just the journalist's memory. In his book *Myths of the Space Age* Daniel Cohen wrote of Cayce that "generally his treatments were harmless enough; he was big on such things as castor oil packs and spinal manipulation . . . No doubt Cayce and the other healers do have a certain number of spectacular 'cures.' Faith is a powerful force, especially when dealing with psychosomatically induced ailments . . . Eventually many diseases will simply run their course and go away whether they are treated or not."

Helping to keep the Cayce memory alive, in vol. 4, no. 1 of the magazine *New Realities,* the psychic's son, Hugh Lynn Cayce, contended that "various body tissues seem to acquire memories that can automatically be stimulated to respond in a fixed pattern." In that way, the son wrote, his father's cures could be explained.

When the Rev. Harmon Bro of the Park Ridge (Ill.) Community Church visited Madison, Wis. the *Wisconsin State Journal* interviewed him, mostly about Cayce whose biographer he is. In the paper's issue of April 11, 1981 Bro was quoted as not doubting Cayce's psychic ability. He said he is uneasy because too many people want to deal with psychic experience without grounding it in traditional Christianity. He said that Cayce taught that "ultimately the only power that works in the psychic area is power that is rooted in love."

The most expensive drama in the history of Off Broadway was *The Freak,* a play based on the life of Edgar Cayce. It really was a revival, Diana Maychick pointed out in the *New York Post* for June 8, 1982 because it was produced by the Theater Project of the WPA in the '30s. Maychick's article was mostly a summary of Cayce's career with no analysis of Granvile Wyche Burgess' play. The same day the *New York Daily News* reported that *The Freak* was closing after 9 previews and 22 performances.

Whereas Cayce didn't touch patients, psychic surgeons rub and knead supposed diseased parts of the body and, without leaving a scar, extract bloody tissue that they say was an ulcer, cancer or some other foreign matter for relief from which most patients seek psychic help after becoming discouraged because of the failure of treatment by physicians.

The quest for magical cures naturally results in tragedies. Two Canadians and 108 Americans from Wyandotte, Mich. and other places in the Detroit area went to the Philippines to be treated, their expenses paid by parishioners of three Wyandotte churches. Their arrival in Manila was reported Oct. 6, 1967 by Albert Ravenholt in the *Chicago Daily News*. Most of them came in wheelchairs or on crutches. After they had been treated by Dr. Antonio Agpaoa at Baguio City, they returned home on crutches and in wheelchairs, Gary Blonston reported to the *News* Oct. 10, 1957 from Bauang, Philippines. Two days later the UPI reported from Manila that the party left "without visible signs of success." There were some who said they were cured and praised the psychic surgeons. One such was Dr. L. P. L. Katigbakwho, who Blonston reported had an infected tooth extracted painlessly. As a result of the failure of the pilgrimage Filipino authorities moved to charge Agpaoa with practicing medicine illegally, of which he had been convicted in 1959.

After thousands of Americans had been lured to the Philippines to undergo psychic (or spiritual) surgery, Federal Trade Commission Judge Daniel Hanscom said the psychic surgery they sought is "pure and unmitigated fakery," the press associations reported from Washington March 15, 1975. This was similar to the charges made by the American Medical Association. In the *Chicago Tribune* for Jan. 19, 1975 Ronald Kotulak began his story by quoting V. B. Powell, a blind assistant of the psychic surgeons who denied they were fakes. Numerous investigators who possess eyesight, however, have described the sleight-of-hand magic they said was performed. Kotulak quoted the AMA that health quackery costs $2 billion annually and takes more lives than all crimes in the United States.

Beginning June 9, 1975 the *Chicago Daily News* ran a series of eight articles by Dr. William A. Nolen extracted from his book *Healing: A Doctor in Search of a Miracle.* In one installment he told of viewing motion pictures of psychic operations in the Philippines. The patients thought the films confirmed the psychics' claims, but Dr. Nolen said he detected the trickery and the tumors and other offending parts removed by the surgeons, usually to be hastily burned, in no way resembled what his lifetime of practice made him know was the truth. He and others say that the objects are from chickens and small animals. Karen Hasman visited Chicago offices of psychic surgeons, finding them ill equipped and unsanitary. In part she described the performance: "The healer kneads the skin, then pulls out what appears to be bloody tissue. In reality, according to the testimony of former helpers, the healer palms a capsule containing animal blood and tissue."

The *National Observer* for March 30, 1974 contained a half-page article by John Peterson on the history of the FTC's action and the pros and cons of psychic surgery, quoting numerous authorities. A pertinent paragraph from the article follows:

> Faith healing or psychic healing is hardly new. Sickness, pain and approaching death can turn normally cautious conservative people into desperate seekers of any chance to prolong life. It is a field rife with frauds and charlatans, but from Jesus Christ down through the ages to Oral Roberts and Kathryn Kuhlman of today, faith healers have attracted huge followers.

United Press International allowed Kenneth R. Clark approximately 2,000 words to describe the performance by James Randi, prominent magician, demonstrating the trickery of the Filipino psychic surgery. When he drove his right hand deeply into a patient's abdomen, blood spurted in a crimson arc. "A malignant tumor," said Randi as he dug deeply and came up with a bloody handful of flesh while more blood spurted onto the floor. Then the Amazing Randi, as he is known professionally, told the audience,

"I'm a magician. I'm a fake, a liar, a cheat and a fraud, but at least I do it with panache."

Randi said he wished he had a regular television program to offset much fakery that misleads the American public. He also said he would pay $10,000 to anyone who could do anything he was unable to duplicate.

Sometimes invalids recover without medical aid or after physicians and/or surgeons have abandoned hope. Such cases are called proof of faith healing provided the patient or someone else on his/her behalf has pleaded for supernatural aid. And the press likes to publicize such cases, as the *Chicago Times* did Oct. 5, 1945 when it reported that a woman crippled for 16 years had three visions of God whereupon she was cured of spinal meningitis. Aug. 26, 1946 the *Times* reported a 12-year-old boy came out of a three-month coma following an accidental fall of four stories. Doctors (unnamed) were quoted as believing the headline over the story and three-column picture, "Mother's faith works a miracle."

A month later the *Chicago Sun* headlined, "Boy, 8, Smiles in Coma As Cardinal Prays for Him," with the overline, "Drama in Attic Apartment." The boy was a two-year victim of sleeping sickness. Dec. 22, 1946 the same newspaper used a large two-column Associated Press wirephoto showing a 4-year-old boy before a crucifix in his Bayonne, N.J. home after overcoming infantile paralysis, the cure being attributed to St. Francis Xavier Cabrini, Chicago saint. Jan. 20, 1947 the paper reported that a Purple Heart veteran had recovered his sight following an explosion in a furnace. Doctors were quoted as saying the blindness was caused by shock, not physical wounds. There was no mention of supernatural influences.

March 8, 1948 the *Chicago Herald-American* carried a story from New York about the prayers that members of the Wesleyan Methodist Church said saved the life of Hattie Curl, overcome by gas fumes that killed her husband. Less common today than they were a generation ago such stories are still much more common than the AP story Sept. 16, 1980 from New Castle, Pa., where two elderly women starved to death while believing God would save them from their fast.

A melodramatic account from one installment of a series on "The Living Religion" by the Rev. Ivan H. Hagedorn, of the Philadelphia Bethel Evangelical Lutheran Church, was published March 23, 1955 by the *Chicago Daily News*. The anecdote was of the Easter morning recovery of her sight by a girl who had undergone extensive medical attention and went to the faith healer as a last resort. Similarly Reuters reported Aug. 17, 1967 from Rome that a Brazilian woman regained her sight during an audience with Pope Paul VI. And Nov. 25, 1961 the AP distributed a picture of a 4-year-old girl who recovered her sight after three months of blindness. Pictured with her was the Episcopal missionary in Sherwood, a Cumberland Valley village, who said there had been a miracle.

For its State Weekender for Sept. 7, 1974 the *Cleveland Plain Dealer* used an AP story from Newark, Ohio under the headline, "Ill. Woman

Better with Bench's Help." It told of the famous Cincinnati Reds' catcher visiting the 22-year-old tumor victim for whom he was a hero.

Not infrequently the press publicizes instances of medical attention being rejected by patients or parents for religious reasons. Sept. 27, 1968, for instance, the *Chicago Sun-Times* told of a 9-year-old boy who died of injuries received when he was struck by an automobile, because his Christian Science parents would not permit medical assistance. The same paper Aug. 27, 1973 headlined, "Diabetic boy dies after parents turn to faith healer." The story was sent by the UPI from Barstow, Calif. Members of the Assembly of God church crowded the funeral parlor where, despite their prayers and lamentations, the boy stayed dead.

July 22, 1982 the UPI reported from Lexington, Ky. that 14-year-old Tim Clark said that God had given him a sign "to come home." So he ordered an end to 3½ years of dialysis and died. In Fort Wayne, Ind. officials ordered surgery to remove a basketball-sized tumor from a 5-year-old girl despite the objections of her parents, members of the Faith Assembly Church. The AP reported the story Nov. 22, 1982. May 3, 1983 the UPI reported from nearby Warsaw, Ind. that 52 persons linked to the church had died because of lack of care.

It is news whenever a faith healer becomes involved in any way with a celebrity. June 14, 1956, for instance, the UPI reported from Amsterdam that Prince Bernhard did not share the confidence his wife, Queen Juliana, had in a 61-year-old faith healer, Greet Hofmans. More ominously the *New York Times* reported from The Hague July 5, 1956 that some close to the Dutch throne feared either a divorce or abdication might result because of the controversy over the faith healer. The queen and prince appointed a three-man commission to investigate why the foreign press was making so much of the issue.

When Gov. George C. Wallace of Alabama consulted a faith healer it was news and the UPI reported it June 26, 1973 from Montgomery. Wallace still remains paralyzed from the waist down as a result of a would-be assassin's bullet during his campaign for president in 1972.

Conversion of a celebrity to belief in faith healing is newsworthy whereas ordinarily the religious beliefs of a person in public life are respected as his/her private business. Nevertheless, May 31, 1973 the *New York Post* gave a column to the views of astronaut Capt. Edgar D. Mitchell, who said, "Psychic healing is an observable fact." Although he does not know its source, Mitchell believes "The healing energy is apparently channeled by the focusing of thought processes."

When her brother was a candidate for the presidency and thereafter, Ruth Carter Stapleton was the subject of many feature articles. One of the first was by Myra MacPherson in the *Washington Post* for March 26, 1976, and her techniques were described in part as follows: "Mrs. Stapleton calls upon Jesus to heal the emotional wounds of the 'inner child' of each one's long ago past. As she asks them to close their eyes and relax, Mrs. Stapleton invites Jesus to enter their imaginary world, punctuating her sentences with the fervent, almost hypnotically repetitious, 'And we thank you Jesus.' " In May 1983 it was reported that Mrs. Stapleton had cancer.

On the whole the press' handling of news involving faith healing has been objective and sympathetic, with few exceptions. One was the Family Doctor column syndicated by Dr. Morris Fishbein Feb. 1, 1950. After tracing briefly the development of belief in "laying on of hands" the medical authority wrote, "These cures—which depend for their success on making people think they are better—are on a par with carrying a buckeye in the pocket to relieve rheumatism or burying a cucumber in a graveyard at night to relieve warts."

Although she gave favorable writeups to many psychics of one kind or another, Norma Lee Browning of the *Chicago Tribune* wrote that "Doctor" William Estep became "an ace medical quack by capitalizing on public interest in vitamins, glands, religion and science." In about a half-page article in the Aug. 2, 1949 issue of her paper, she wrote, "Even more incredible than Estep's atom were the suckers who fell for it—with 1, 5 and 10 dollar bills for the collection plate—little knowing that Mahatma Estep, as he calls himself, is one of America's most notorious phonies and a chronic fugitive from justice."

Unquestionably one of the most subtle exposés of faith healing was that of Bob Greene in his *Chicago Sun-Times* column for Sept. 22, 1976. It pertained to a visit to his office by Little Michael, 9-year-old faith healer and evangelist, who had received much exposure on television news and talk shows. Bob was unsuccessful in attempting to get the child to lay hands on a copy reader who made corrections in Greene's column.

One way to expose charlatans and, hopefully, make the public and newspaper editors less gullible is by the carefully planned hoax. One successful practitioner of the art of deception is Joseph Skaggs who teaches journalism at New York's School of Visual Arts. In 1976 he took out newspaper ads for a "bordello for dogs" that won him mention on local television. In 1977, as Giuseppe Scaggoli, he made *Ms.* magazine for founding a "celebrity sperm bank." His biggest success was the announcement that a New York research group called Metamorphosis, headed by Josef Gregor, had successfully tested cockroach pills as a cure for acne, anemia and nuclear fallout.

The UPI put the story on its wires and it was used by the *Washington Star, Philadelphia Inquirer, Chicago Tribune, Pittsburgh Press, Dallas Times-Herald, Louisville Courier-Journal, Bend* (Ore.) *Bulletin* and about 175 other newspapers according to the story David J. Blum wrote for the *Wall Street Journal* of Sept. 28, 1981. In on the hoax were Skaggs' 50 students of whom he said, "I'd been telling them how easy the media can be duped, but I wanted to show them."

"Voodoo healers, spirit workers, rootworkers, charismatic faith healers—they have no licenses and many don't even have a grade school education. But now psychologists are beginning to accept them openly as colleagues," Philip J. Holts began his article in the *Washington Post* for Aug. 21, 1981. He quoted scientists that the effort to make immigrants abandon their folk practices had not succeeded very well and a grim fact was that often the unorthodox treatments worked.

An excellent explanation of native American Indian health practices was published by the *National Observer* June 26, 1976. It was excerpted from *Innovations,* an experimental magazine published by the American Institute for Research in collaboration with the National Institute of Mental Health. An idea of its slant can be surmised from the statement it quotes from psychiatrist E. C. Townley, chief of mental health programs for the Indian Health Service and the first Indian to hold that position, who said: "Medicine men excel in the prevention and treatment of mental and psychosomatic illness. The mental health staff of the Indian Health Service has learned to join forces with them whenever possible. Consultation with traditional healers helps Indian Health Service doctors better understand the needs of their patients." Carl Gorman, a Navaho who is director of the Office·of Native Healing Services, Navaho Health Authority, said, "The medicine man is actually a doctor, counselor, priest and historian. He is the repository of ancient myths that are religious—even today they cannot be written down—and he uses the wisdom of these myths for insight into human behavior and to explain psychological and behavioral problems."

How orthodox medicine is being influenced by ancient American Indian concepts was reported in a full-page article by Sandy Rovner in the *Washington Post* for Sept. 26, 1982. Acting on instructions received in a vision, a Chippewa medicine man, Sun Bear, conducts Medicine Wheel Gatherings attended by hundreds. Believing that the time has come for them, as caretakers of life, to "speak out clearly," he and several others travel and lecture, mixing ancient Indian ceremonies with latter-day humanism and dancing, chanting and pipe-smoking in the weekend seminars.

A psychiatrist-nurse who says, "I believe very much in the intuitive powers of each individual," was written up by Jacqueline Novak for the *Baltimore Evening Sun* of July 30, 1930. The woman, a Johns Hopkins graduate, had worked with eagle feathers and crystals in Indian healing and credits her Indian background for at least part of her own powers.

The number of folk healers of all sorts has been estimated in the tens of thousands and about 80 percent of all mental or physical illnesses in the United States are treated not by M.D.s but with home remedies or folk cures regardless of whether they contradict medical knowledge, the *Washington Post* for Aug. 26, 1981 quoted Vivian Garrison, a psychologist of the New Jersey Medical School, as saying.

The long article contains evidence that spirits, magic seers and other mystical folk healers are being brought into hospitals and mental-health clinics to assist in treating patients with widely different ethnic backgrounds. American psychologists are coming to accept them as colleagues, the article states. A typical quotation of Americans who are accepting the native faith-healers is that of Dr. Jerome Frank, a Johns Hopkins psychologist, "There is no question that psychotherapy and folkhealing have features they share. They provide a patient with acceptance. They create hope."

Uncanny as psychic Henry Rucker's claim that he can look into a patient's body without X-rays may be, some doctors regularly take him with them on their rounds in clinics in Wisconsin, Ohio and Texas. Howard Wolinsky reported from La Crosse, Wis. in the *Chicago Sun-Times* for May 31, 1981 that Dr. William Barclay, editor of the *Journal of the American Medical Association,* said, "If one is trained scientifically you have to reject the claims that a man can see inside a body." Answered Dr. C. Norman Shealy, who has used Rucker, "Psychic powers are not explained by any science. We also can't explain how anesthetics work but I wouldn't do surgery without them." On all of this Rucker commented, "I see what I see because God wants me to."

Such attitudes of some reputable scientists naturally have caused considerable debate on the subject. An early indication was the report of a committee of the United Presbyterian Church of the U.S.A. according to a story from Pittsburgh by David Meade for the *Chicago Daily News* of June 2, 1958. In part summary the report said: "We believe that however many or grave the dangers in the practice of a ministry of healing, there is the greater danger of our limiting the power of God by our fear and timidity and of our failing to fulfill our Lord's own concern for the well-being and harmony of the whole personality when brought into obedience in the will and purpose of God."

Colin Dangaard began a series on "Psychic Healers at Work" Aug. 25–26, 1973 in the *Chicago Daily News* with a half-dozen testimonials by practicing doctors of the curative powers of a number of faith healers. He wrote: "All over the United States psychic healing, faith healing, the laying-on-of-hands—call it what you will—is being taken seriously in quarters where its mere mention a decade ago would have brought laughter. The age of the mind has arrived . . ."

The attraction healers have over medical doctors was explained by Dr. William A. Nolen, Minneapolis surgeon, about whose views the Newhouse News Service distributed an article by Victor Wilson Feb. 8, 1975. A doctor does not extend much sympathy to patients with trivial ailments whereas faith healers provide greater comfort as they also do to the incurably ill who refuse to accept a doctor's gloomy prognosis.

Both this article and most reviews of Dr. Nolen's then-new book, *Healing: A Doctor in Search of a Miracle,* left it up to readers to decide for themselves. In the *Chicago Sun-Times* for Jan. 25, 1975 Clifford Buzard expressed surprise to learn that people consult faith healers because doctors have let them down. In the *National Observer* for Feb. 15, 1975, L. L. Davis pointed out that Dr. Nolen concedes that faith healers may actually "cure" as many as 70 percent of their patients—the 50 percent who are going to get well anyway, due to the body's natural healing powers, and the 20 percent who are suffering from psychosomatic disorders that are equally susceptible to treatment by a skilled physician or psychiatrist. "The remaining 30 percent are those afflicted with organic disorders—cancer, arthritis, withered limbs, ulcers and the like—and to these people, a faith healer can do no good and much harm," according to Davis.

On the other hand the press has noted the increase of interest in faith or spiritual or psychic healing and has given ample publicity to individuals and organizations promoting the cause. From Palo Alto, the *New York Times* Service distributed a story that the *Chicago Tribune* used Oct. 9, 1972. It was about a four-day symposium sponsored by the Stanford University Department of Industrial Engineering and Materials Science and the Academy of Parapsychology and Medicine of Los Altos. Under discussion was the transfer of psychic energy from one person to another or to other objects. Dr. Thelma S. Moss of the University of California at Los Angeles said she could restore the vitality of a sickly leaf by simply laying a hand over it for a few minutes. She also said after a healing session of laying- on- hands the inertia auras of the healer are usually smaller while the auras of the persons being healed are larger.

Dec. 8, 1972 the *Tribune* used a *Washington Star-News* story concerning the experiments with mice that caused Dr. Barnard Grad, McGill University psychiatrist, to believe laying on of hands is an actual force. Mice recovered from different diseases faster if their boxes had been handled.

During the 16th annual conference of the Spiritual Frontiers Fellowship in Chicago May 18, 1973 James H. Bowman, *Chicago Daily News* religion editor, interviewed Gordon Turner, one of 8,000 members of the National Federation of Spiritual Healers in England. Healing, Turner said, is love. His hands often tingle "like electricity" and get warm when he heals either persons or animals.

So respectable had psychic healing become that New York University School of Continuing Education offered a course in the subject beginning with the Fall 1974 term, the *Village Voice* reported Aug. 22, 1974. Instructors were Judith Skutch, president of the Foundation for Parasensory Investigation, and Hilda Brown, psychic healer.

Feeling the competition of the ever-increasing army of psychics many established churches have resumed practicing faith or psychic healing, sometimes after centuries. Today they sponsor classes and/or centers. One such church-healing center is sponsored by the St. Patrick's Catholic Church of the Antioch-Malabar Rite in St. Paul. Nancy Livingston wrote about it and its director, the Rev. Robert Parker, in the *St. Paul Dispatch* for March 11, 1975.

"The Occult Goes Kosher" was the heading the *Village Voice* put over an article about the Dynamic Judaism being preached by Rabbi Alvin J. Bovroff who challenged the Talmudic taboo against mysticism. In its issue of Aug. 7, 1977 the paper told of the visit of an Israeli, an orthodox Jew named Yehuda Isk, shown in an accompanying picture "recharging Rabbi Bovroff's battery." Isk said he could "zap" a roomful of 2,000 people with his "electric hands."

The extent to which the charismatic movement has spread was provided when the Rev. Ralph Di Orio of St. John's Church in Worcester, Mass. appeared before more than 1,000 people in Chicago. It took the *Sun-Times* Dec. 17, 1977 one and a half pages to allow Maurice Possley to describe the occasion, beginning with a quotation from a Roman Catholic woman, "It's about time we had one," meaning that hitherto most faith healers were Protestants. Di Orio's performance was reminiscent of a Kathryn Kuhlman meeting. He announced that he felt a healing was occurring somewhere in the audience. Before long there was a parade of believers who said they had been freed of their illnesses, from ulcers to cancers. Many fainted upon being touched by Father Di Orio while a guitar ensemble made soft music in the background.

Ignoring the matter of their prowess, faith healers are considered extremely newsworthy by most editors. Let one pitch his tent in the neighborhood and the small newspaper gives him or her top billing. This happened in Vandalia, Ill. during the last week of June, 1947. At least half of the 9,000 inhabitants attended some of the meetings held by a former Indiana game warden, the Rev. William Branham who claimed to have cured 35,000 persons during the preceding 11 months. Ambulances and station wagons brought sick persons from several nearby states, two of whom died before they had a chance to visit the healer.

Saying that Jesus was working through him Branham attended personally to hundreds in wheelchairs and on crutches, telling them they had to have faith. The local newspapers, the *Leader* and the *Union,* reported the behavior of quite a few invalids who rose from their beds and claimed to be cured. Much was made of the report that Walker Beck, 20, born deaf and dumb, had spoken two words, "daddy" and "amen." The next day, however, he was as afflicted as ever. When that fact was reported to Branham, the *Leader* reported, he declared, "I hear that Walker has smoked a cigarette after I told him he would have to give them up. Because of this he will not be able to hear or talk and in all probability he will be afflicted with some greater trouble—perhaps cancer."

Because of the publicity that the Chicago papers, especially the *Chicago Times,* gave the Vandalia story and because I happened to be spending the Fourth of July weekend in nearby Springfield, accompanied by my father-in-law I visited Vandalia shortly after Branham departed.

Townspeople were willing to discuss the affair. The comment of one was typical: "There are lots of different kinds of people so you have to have different kinds of religion to satisfy them."

One of the most charismatic faith healers is Prophet Johnson (real name J. J. Rogers), who declares that God gave his left hand the power to heal. B. J. Mason told his Chicago ghetto story in the *Chicago Sun-Times* for March 10, 1974. It included weird details of Johnson's youthful fight with the devil and his hesitation in accepting the call of God. "If I can't heal them," he told Mason, "there's something wrong with their souls."

Capitalizing on the current interest in mystical and occult rites, the Spiritual Frontier Fellowship experienced great growth during the '70s. Roy Larson, *Chicago Sun-Times* religion writer, attended one service in the Garrett Theological Seminary in Evanston, climaxed by laying on of hands by the Rev. J. Gordon Melton and his wife, Dorothea. Said he of her: "When my wife is healing she relaxes and lets her hands go limp. Then her hands go into a trance and she permits her hands to go wherever, in a sense, they want to go."

Dean Kraft, today called New York's leading healer, got his first journalistic break when the *Village Voice* gave more than two pages Dec. 23, 1974 to an article by Brian Van Der Horst. Kraft explained that he blanks his mind, then pinpoints what ails the patient, after which he projects a good feeling, love. He doesn't know how passing his hand over the sick part or even touching the person effects a cure. He only knows it works.

March 10, 1977 the *New York Post* reported that Dean Kraft had luxurious offices on New York's east side. The item said that Kraft was discovered by John Lennon and Yoko Ono, a fact overlooked by Van Der Horst in his *Voice* article but apparently to be included in a biography of Kraft.

In the *New York Daily News* for Aug. 12, 1979 Charles W. Bell told a weird story of how Kraft discovered his psychic powers. When the electric door of his boss' car clicked, he jokingly asked if there were spirits present. Soon a code involving number of clicks for letters in the alphabet was worked out and the unseen power revealed his name was G-O-D.

Aug. 30, 1981 the *Chicago Sun-Times* gave another page and a half to a Catholic priest healer, the Rev. Dennis Kelleher. Howard Wolinsky told of a healing service attended by a capacity crowd of more than 1,000. Catchers were needed to shorten the falls of those who swooned upon being touched, "slain in the spirit by God," as the faithful say. In a second story in the same issue Wolinsky summarized the history of faith healing of which there was evidence in cave paintings 15,000 years old. Many medical authorities today agree that the laying on of hands causes physical reactions but, as Dr. William Nolen is quoted as warning, what seem to be cures during the excitement of a meeting might not prove permanent in the calm of the next day.

Maybe before another 15,000 years have passed faith healing will no longer be a mystery. Now that the medical profession and the church have joined the psychologists in attempting to explain it, there may be an answer. In the meantime psychic or faith healing has become a very lucrative profession. In a page-and-a-half article, "The Hands of a Healer," in the *New York Daily News* for Sept. 18, 1981, Ryan Vollmer reported that it costs $50 for a first visit to a professional psychic. His article is mostly about Elizabeth Stratton whose patients form a waiting list three months long. Healers like Stratton, Patricia Sun in California and Olga Worrall in Maryland "are part of a national network of contemporary city-based healers who combine faith, modern medicine, humanistic psychology and Eastern religion in their work. They believe that a person's susceptibility to illness is rooted in psychological malaise. Anything from severe grief over the loss of a loved one to long-forgotten anger of a parent can be the root cause of illness. Disease is merely a symptom of a deep psychological problem that the person probably isn't even aware of. Once the cause is brought to light and resolved, susceptibility decreases. This way of thinking is not new. Eastern religion has long held this belief . . . What I look for, Stratton says, is why they created the illness and why they're holding onto it."

Sounds very much like what most psychiatrists have made out of Sigmund Freud. And yet today they dope their patients with lithium, vallium and other drugs to keep them quiet.

Olga Worrall was the subject of a feature by Sandy Rovner in the *Washington Post* for Nov. 7, 1981. Her husband, also a healer, believes that her healing power is what he calls paraelectric. Among her claims are these: changed the surface tension of water, sensed an earthquake seconds before it registered on a Mt. Hood seismograph, dowsed for water by marking a map and accelerated a reversion to order of chemical mixtures in a physics laboratory. She was in Washington for a Healing in Our Times conference sponsored in part by the American Holistic Health Association.

Three days later Rovner interviewed several others among the 2,000 who attended the conference. Among them was the Russian Yefim Gregorievich Shubentsov, who said American research is "kindergarten" in comparison with that of the Soviet Union. Reported Rovner:

> That there does exist a healing energy that can be measured electrically, photographed, demonstrated in scientific laboratory studies—whether it emanates from the hands of an energetically endowed healer or from the stimulation of an electric prod. Moreover it is available to almost anyone and almost anyone can be taught to use it in a greater or lesser degree.

That was the reporter speaking, not quoting any delegate.

Journalistic interest in holistic health is growing with the movement. The third annual congress of the Himalayan International Institute was held in Chicago where Ellen Holstein interviewed its medical director, Dr. Rudolph Ballentine, whose patient she was. In the *Chicago Tribune* for June 21, 1978 she wrote, "The holistic physician views the patient as a unity of mind, body and spirit. All must be of concern, if the goal of total health and prevention of degenerative disease is to be achieved."

Another leader in the holistic health movement is Dr. Alan Hymes of the University of Minnesota who Donna Joy Newman interviewed for the *Chicago Tribune* of July 5, 1978. He is a pioneer in combining breathing methods practiced for centuries by meditating yoga with the modern Western practice of medicine. He said: "Any disturbance in the mind will be reflected in the body."

Granger E. Westburg, founder of Holistic Health Centers, was the subject of an article by Bruce Buursma, religion editor, in the *Chicago Tribune* for Nov. 12, 1981. A former Lutheran pastor, Westburg said that church should be "a place for the spirit, the mind and the body," and explained, "I'm just trying to get the church back in the business of living out the gospel message of health and salvation."

Among the most successful of the contemporary miracle workers was Kathryn Kuhlman who caused supplicants to faint by merely touching them. Most described the sensation they received as resembling an electric shock, James H. Bowman reported in the *Chicago Daily News* after attending a Kuhlman overflow meeting in Chicago's Conrad Hilton Hotel. In an extract from his book *Healing: A Doctor in Search of a Miracle,* published in the *News* for June 10, 1975, Dr. William A. Nolen noted the same masterful Kuhlman showmanship that Bowman had mentioned: her announcing that some sufferer in the audience was being cured at the moment. In response to her request that such a person identify him or herself, victims of bursitis, lung cancer, infantile paralysis and other ailments arose and limped to the stage insisting they had been cured. Following open heart surgery Kuhlman died Feb. 20, 1976 of pulmonary hypertension in Tulsa, Okla. In its obituary notice the Associated Press revealed Kuhlman was an ordained Baptist minister and contributed $2 million annually to the Kathryn Kuhlman Foundation in Pittsburgh, an organization that promoted foreign missions, drug rehabilitation and education of the handicapped. In the March 13–14, 1976 *News,* Bowman speculated on who would succeed Kuhlman. In a half-page article he cited a dozen or so aspirants but concluded, "Maybe no one will take the place of the late Kathryn Kuhlman, but it won't be for lack of aspirants."

Bowman followed his roundup piece with a series of four articles June 19–20 through June 23, 1976 about the Rev. Lowell I. Torgerson, Jr., pastor of the Community Lutheran Church of Oak Park, Ill. He explained his purpose thusly: "Because of the growing interest in faith healing the *News* traced the medical histories of one man's 'miracles,' people who say they were cured by the healing hands of Mr. Torgerson." The doctor who performed breast surgery on one of the women said there was nothing unusual about her story of the disappearance of tumors after the minister prayed, spoke in tongues and touched her. The surgeon said the woman's tumors were not cancerous and it is not unusual for benign cysts to disappear spontaneously no matter how large.

The physician of another woman presumably cured by Torgerson said she never had a blood-sugar problem from which she believed the minister cured her. It is doubtful whether any of the Torgerson parishioners lost their faith in him as the result of a mildly iconoclastic newspaper feature.

Torgerson discovered what he believes to be his gift of healing after being "baptized in the Holy Spirit." He says faith healing is in the Christian tradition.

Another Oak Park healer whose "magnetic personality and seductive stage presence" William J. Cromie described in the *Chicago Daily News* for Feb. 7-8, 1976, is Burton Seabey, founder of World Outreach Evangelism. Friday nights he holds healing services in Bethel Temple Assembly of God in Oak Park. Cromie summed up what he observed at one of the sessions:

> They complained of back pains, stiff legs, poor eyesight, blank spots in the memory, family trouble and sore throats. When the big man with the soothing voice laid hands on them, many swooned and fell over backwards.
>
> Some shook violently and spoke in tongues. They said they felt heat or electricity when the healer prayed over them. Then came a relaxed floating feeling as they toppled back into the arms of waiting ushers. They lay on the floor, some quietly, and some shaking and writhing, some babbling in tongues.
>
> When they arose many said they were cured of their illness.

Cromie concluded that "certainly a kind of spiritual healing takes place at these meetings. People are visibly uplifted and appear relaxed and joyful in many cases."

Another Chicago-area healer, who calls himself "just a television set for God," is Joseph Pawlak who holds Miracle Healing sessions every Friday night in the Dolton Bridge Club. Mark Fineman wrote about him in the *Suburban Sun-Times* for Aug. 11-12, 1976. Pawlak says he saw a vision of Jesus as tall as a telephone pole walking on water in 1969. He does not touch people, merely tells them of messages he receives during visions.

Although Dr. Daniel Friedman, University of Chicago psychiatrist, was quoted as saying that "medicine has traditionally rejected anything that cannot be explained scientifically, or rationally," Ronald Sullivan reported in the *New York Times* of Nov. 6, 1977: "An unorthodox therapy in which nurses attempt to make sick patients feel better by 'laying hands' on them is being introduced in hospitals and nursing schools throughout the country."

Subject of the article was Dr. Dolores Krieger, Ph.D. and a registered nurse who insists that her "therapeutic touch healing affects the healer's brain waves, elicits a relaxation response, relieves pain and seems to invoke a sense of self responsibility for his/her health," to quote from Barbara Somerville's article in the *West Palm Beach Post* for Feb. 17, 1982. "But," Krieger is quoted as saying, "it is the patient who heals himself. The transfer of energy from the person playing the role of healer is usually little more than a booster until the patient's own recuperative system takes over. The healer is just accelerating the healing process." Krieger learned her technique from Col. Oskar Estebany who learned he could heal horses when he was in the Hungarian cavalry, after which he learned he could heal plants and people too. She now cooperates with Oh-Shinnah, an American Indian psychologist whose great-grandmother, a Mohawk, taught her how to heal using crystals.

Dolores Krieger is among those sidebarred in the three-article series "Faith Healing: It's Booming," which Charles W. Bell wrote for the *New York Daily News* Aug. 12, 13 and 14, 1979. Other practitioners, Bell wrote, "include highly-respected Main Line Protestant Churchmen in the suburbs, voodoo priests in Harlem, speaking-in-tongue Pentacostals in the Bronx, licensed nurses, vegetarian gurus and the Rev. Ike and other psychic 'new church' theologians," so that the booming healing business "has become as real as confession to Catholics, as important as prayers to Protestants and as natural as meditation to thousands of troubled men and women."

Mental healing, Bell explained, falls into six main classifications:

Faith, prayer or spiritual. Usually this involves a religious belief by the sufferer, especially a belief in the healing powers of God and/or Jesus Christ.

Mind cure. This rests on the ideas that all diseases and ailments are caused by abnormal conditions in the mind, and that healers have mental powers to cure or relieve pain.

Christian Science. This rests on the belief that all matter (and thus the body and illness) exists only in the mind.

Spiritualism. This is based on the idea that the spirits of the dead, operating directly or through living mediators, exercise healing powers.

Mesmerism. This rests on the theory first proposed in the 19th century by a German philosopher that there is a "healing" or magnetic force or fluid in every person that somehow flows into other persons to restore them to health.

Suggestive hypnosis. This rests on a belief that people with the ability to hypnotize others also can—through the power of suggestion—modify bodily functions, suppress pain, etc.

As much that has preceded has indicated, "Psychic healing is trying to become respectable," to use the words with which William M. Kutik began his article in the First Person section of the *New York Daily News* for Dec. 15, 1980. "Buoyed by the sensitive portrayal of healing in the Ellen Burstyn film, 'Resurrection,' conservative psychic healers are gently tapping on the door of the medical establishment and asking to be let in. The front door hasn't opened yet and probably won't for many years. But there are cracks."

The article paid attention to the pioneer work of Dr. Dolores Krieger and also Sister Justin Smith of Buffalo, Olga Worrall of San Francisco, Abraham Weisman, Dr. Lawrence LeShan, Bryce Bond, Dean Kraft and Rosalyn Cruyere, all of New York.

Augmented interest in faith or psychic healing has become epidemic throughout a troublesome world in which people seek security and comfort. For example Virginia Prewitt reported from Rio de Janeiro in the *Chicago Sun* for Oct. 3, 1947 that because "reports of undeniable cures have been numerous. . . science and religion both recognized the authenticity of miracles performed by Antonio Pinto, a village priest."

As Charles Fernandez began his article from Bogota, Colombia for the April 25, 1949 *Chicago Daily News:* "Ailing mankind never ceases to pray for the miraculous." The lengthy profile was of Tomas Rodriguez, known as the Miracle Monk of Columbia who also ministered to the poor in Ecuador, Venezuela, Panama and Peru. Asking for no symptoms, checking no pulses and listening to no heartbeats, he simply looked into a patient's eyes with a small magnifying glass. He then diagnosed and prescribed herbs. Because of public clamor in his behalf, El Lego (the lay brother) has defeated attempts to prevent his medical practice.

May 11, 1956 the AP reported from London that the British Medical Association issued a report on spiritual healing that declared, "Many aspects of healing are still outside our present knowledge and this we should honestly and humbly admit." In the last of three articles on "Psychic Healers at Work," in the *Chicago Daily News* for Aug. 28, 1973, Colin Dangaard wrote, "Not only are medical doctors starting to consider the powers of the psychic, some actually are utilizing them," followed by examples of doctors doing so in different parts of the country.

Another who insists he's merely "an agent of God" is E. G. Fricker who visited the United States to plug his book, *God Is My Witness,* and was interviewed for the *Chicago Sun-Times* of May 26, 1977 by Barbara Varro and by Daniel St. Albin Greene for the *National Observer* of May 30, 1977. Fricker operates the Healing Center in London where he said he has healed one million persons in 25 years and has 20,000 on his waiting list. Fricker says he began hearing voices at the age of five years and believes he lived before and observed Jesus minister. Many of his cures are not immediate and he instructs patients how to have a relative or friend rub or stroke the afflicted part of the body. Greene wrote that Fricker's accounts are "long on stranger-than-life anecdotes but short on details and documentation."

One of several self-styled Oriental wonder-workers is Chun Kan, a shopkeeper in Hong Kong from where the UPI Dec. 15, 1981 sent a long article about him by Julie Brossy. He is reputed to be guided by the

Monkey God with power to protect people from evil. The legend of the Monkey God portrays him as one who learned the secret of immortality. Chun does not like the trances he experiences, usually without warning, but he says they enable him to travel 100,000 miles in a single somersault. Once he fell 16 stories without injury. He walks on hot beds of coal and in other ways endears himself to the squatters of Hong Kong.

The editorial "Heal, Yes" in the *Village Voice* for Nov. 8, 1976 was encouragement for the idea of a World Federation of Healers being promoted by Douglas Dean.

Strong evidence that the faith healing fad was spreading worldwide is contained in some articles from Moscow. The *New York Times* for instance, ran a story Aug. 18, 1980 about the popularity of Dzhuna Davitashvili who presumably cured thousands with the "biological force" of her hands. Among her performing wonders is reviving dead roses by passing her hands over them. More important, she is accredited with having improved the physical appearance of President Leonid I. Brezhnev. Jan. 28, 1981 the UPI reported from Moscow that the respected Soviet magazine *Ogonyok* advocated more research into the phenomenon of faith healing.

What has become the greatest influence of Russian science on American since Pavlov has received little attention from the press to date. One of the few, if not the only, full length treatment of it appeared in the *Wall Street Journal* for July 24, 1973. Of the new photography invented by Dr. Semyon D. Kirlian, Richard R. Leger wrote: "The resulting pictures are remarkable in that they capture on film previously invisible emanations from the human body (and from plants) that change in color and size."

Some psychics have insisted for years that people and things are surrounded by auras like halos, which they can see and others cannot. They say that the intensity changes as energy flows to or from the person or thing. Dr. Kirlian's principal disciple in the United States, Thelma Moss, assistant professor of medical psychology at UCLA, hails the procedure as "a laboratory tool, perhaps the equivalent of the EEG (electroencephalograph), a device used to detect and record normal and abnormal brain waves." She believes it may be possible to measure states of anxiety which would be a major diagnostic advance in the treatment of emotional disorders.

Kirlian photography is one of the major interests of Mankind Research Unlimited. According to Kenneth Turan and Nancy Meadors Klein who wrote "Scientist in a Strange Land" for the *Washington Post* of July 22, 1973, Carl Schleicher, MRU's director, "sees in Kirlian photography what he sees in everything else he deals with—something that can be applied to a problem, to possibly diagnose sickness, to identify abnormal mental states, even to spot potential hijackers."

Some suggest it may be the aura or life force that is recorded. If psychic healers lose glow during a treatment it indicates to them that there is a transference of energy from healer to patient. Stanford's Prof. William A. Tiller says the radiations are a "corona discharge."

Another convert is Dr. Bernard Murstein of Connecticut College whose views the AP reported July 10, 1975 from New London. He said his experiments showed that people who like one another emit strong auras and those disliking one another have no emissions.

For any critical analysis of Kirlian photography it will be necessary to wait until the learned journals discover the subject. In the *New York Times* for June 4, 1972 A. D. Coleman mentioned it in an article entitled "Spirit Photographs: Are They All Hoaxes?" At the time there was an exhibit at the Floating Foundation of Photography of "Phantoms of the Camera," including the pictures that Ted Serios takes of his own thoughts. In the *Wall Street Journal* for Oct. 12, 1976, Jerry E. Bishop reviewed an article in *Science* magazine reporting that tests by scientists sponsored by the Department of Defense explained the photographs easily by a well-known electrical phenomenon related to the amount of moisture in the skin.

April 15, 1982 the Associated Press distributed a picture of a man in a sea grape tree with a crowd of people holding out their hands for a piece of bark or wood. The cutlines explained the situation: "Residents of the Little Havana section of Miami gather around a sea grape tree they say has healing properties. A few days ago 92-year-old Alfred Varona, who suffers from cataracts, rubbed his eyes with sap from the tree. He now says he has clear vision. Experts say the sap contains tannin, an astringent found in plants, and that may be responsible for the so-called miracle effects."

Four days later, April 19, the UPI reported from Miami: "The 'miracle tree' of Little Havana has been reduced to a stump by three men who hoped to sell it for $1 a chunk." Most people, however, used knives and hatchets to get their own souvenirs from the stump. Many rubbed sap from the tree over afflicted parts of their bodies. Reported the UPI: "They showed up with children in wheelchairs, people on crutches, leading the blind, all with hope that God was somehow working through the tree in a miraculous way."

The same day the *Chicago Tribune* had its own story in which John O'Brien quoted an unnamed spokesman for the University of Miami that people, particularly Cubans, "have used the sea grape bark fluid as a folk remedy for hundreds of years. It helped stop diarrhea, dysentery and hemorrhages because it is an astringent. But it does not make the blind see."

The Associated Press quoted Dr. Julia Morton, author of *The Atlas of Medicinal Plants of Middle America,* that Varona's sight might have been improved because tannin can clear the mucous caused by cataracts.

The Creative Ones are turning to the New Wise Ones, according to Georgia Dullea in the *New York Times* for July 24, 1979. Creative people, she explained, often lack the time—and sometimes the faith—required for traditional therapies. So, "Enter the chiropractor, who manipulates the best of spines; the acupuncturist who twirls the needles that banish wrinkles and pinched nerves; the astrologist who tells when the signs are auspicious for signing a contract, making a movie or taking on a new mate."

The unreconstructed conservative attitude toward all of this was expressed by Dr. Arthur Kornberg, a Stanford University physician who won the 1959 Nobel Prize for medicine. March 18, 1981 the *Washington Star* quoted him as believing that science is falling prey to "the cultists, the misfits and the fools" because scientists have failed to explain and defend their profession. He told a medical audience in Anaheim, Calif. that "society, by ignorance, is as captive to creationists, astrologers, evangelists, food faddists and all kinds of gurus as were our ancestors [held captive] by fears of thunder and lightning."

16

Witchcraft

For several months in 1692 the peace of Salem, Mass. was disturbed by charges of witchcraft against scores of citizens. Under a 1641 law making witchcraft a capital offense, 30 persons were convicted; of them 19 were hanged and one crushed to death.

Their accusers were ten teenaged girls who belonged to a group that studied fortune telling and magic at the home of the Rev. Samuel Parris. When the children's behavior became irrational (barking like dogs, screaming, having hallucinations, etc.) a physician announced that the girls were practicing witchcraft. They then accused a slave girl from the West Indies of having bewitched them. The girl, Tinuta, was tortured until she confessed after which she was the first to be hanged. The girls therewith hysterically blamed others for their condition and it wasn't until they named several prominent citizens, including a minister's wife, that the governor ordered the release of all others who had been jailed.

In 1703 three successfully petitioned the court to reverse the attainders against them. In 1711, following an investigation by a committee of the General Court, the attainders were lifted from 22 others whose reputations or those of relatives had been injured. Money compensations were granted.

In the 20th century several attempts have been made to persuade the Massachusetts legislature to reverse the convictions of the seven women not yet exonerated. However, since the attainders were set by the English government, only the English could reverse them. According to the Essex Institute, a Salem historical society, "an attempt was made to have Queen Elizabeth grant a pardon but she apparently saw no point to it."

A UP story from Boston Jan. 14, 1945 reported the essence of one unsuccessful petition but incorrectly said the 1692 hysteria ended when the governor's wife was accused. In 1955 the state senate defeated a bill to exonerate the victims on the grounds that to declare the witches innocent would injure the tourist trade. "Reminders of witch hunt days echo in Salem" was explained in a lengthy illustrated feature by Bill Thomas in the *Chicago Tribune* for Oct. 17, 1974. Over the years similar stories have appeared on the travel pages of most papers.

One of the best was "Salem Is Bewitching Still," by Jason Marks in the *New York Times* for Aug. 25, 1974. The *Minneapolis Tribune* used the same story Dec. 8, 1974. Doubtless other papers that subscribe to the *Times'* syndicate service also used it.

A strong editorial favoring a pardon appeared in the *Chicago Sun-Times* for Oct. 23, 1949. It summarized briefly what happened in Salem and supported the efforts of Repr. Daniel Rudsten, quoting several approving letters he received. The editorial endorsed Marion L. Starkey's book, *The Devil in Massachusetts,* and quoted from an article by Bernard DeVoto in *Harper's,* "There is loose in the United States today the same evil that once split Salem Village between the bewitched and the accused and stole men's reason quite away." He became specific, citing the FBI's spying on citizens.

A succinct article, "No Witches Burned in Salem," in *Parade* for Oct. 11, 1981 set the record straight: 19 persons were hanged and one was crushed to death by heavy stones. In all 170 were tried, the youngest a 5-year-old girl; the oldest was 100 and the first acquitted. None of the 55 who confessed to being witches were convicted.

A mother strongly objected to the illustrations in a coloring book sold at the Salem Witch Museum. They show a man hanging, another being crushed and women in cages. Jan. 14, 1982 the *Chicago Sun-Times* Action Time gave the answer of the Salem museum director: "The scenes are historic renditions of the events that took place in Salem Village during the witchcraft hysteria of 1692." The souvenir remains on sale.

In 1957 the Massachusetts General Court passed a resolution that, since the whole witchcraft episode was shocking and the laws under which the proceedings were conducted have long since been outmoded, no disgrace or cause for distress attaches to any descendant. Supporting the resolution John Beresford Hatch stated: "Some 700 honest, respectable and law-abiding citizens . . . were wantonly accused, publicly humiliated and insultingly examined for allegedly committing hypothetical crimes of witchcraft and wizardry . . . Wild accusations and hysterical prosecutions for these imaginary crimes . . . were so foul and illegal as to nag the conscience of civilized people ever since . . . Contrary to all civilized law, before or since, guilt was established by spectral, or make believe, evidence and on the hysterical testimony of confessed liars, some witty, some witless . . . the 'witches' and their kith and kin . . . were placed at the untender mercies of avaricious adventurers . . ." who took their goods, money and good name, according to Frank Collier in a newspaper feature for Feb. 18, 1957.

Hatch's enlightened and rational viewpoint has not been majority opinion throughout most of history, or today. In fact archeologists believe that figures carved on rocks and painted on the walls of caves indicate that witches were believed to exist in Spain about 30,000 B.C. Cotton Mather and other fundamentalists who preached hell and damnation and approved the Salem trials, cited Exodus 22:18: "Thou shalt not suffer a witch to live." Homer, Horace and Greek authors mentioned witchcraft and during the Renaissance and Inquisition the Roman Catholic church punished witches as disciples of the devil. Torture was used to obtain confessions.

The encyclopedia definition of witchcraft is "the human exercise of supernatural powers for antisocial evil purposes, so-called black magic."

Most witches have been thought to be female and called witches or sorcerers; their masculine counterparts are warlocks. Many are their attributes according to folklore, primitive and contemporary. Most feared is their alleged ability to cast spells on other persons, possibly by sympathetic magic through the use of effigies.

Witches supposedly are organized into groups of 12 called covens led by a 13th priest or priestess and meet at least four times annually for sabbaths, one of which, Halloween, is still observed but not seriously by everyone in the Western world. Witches presumably can change themselves into animals or reptiles and can fly through the air on broomsticks. They provide herbs and potions to aid a petitioner to be loved or to injure another.

The closest equivalent of Salem, Mass. anywhere else in the world is Loudun, France where the 17th-century curate of the parish church was charged with bewitching a convent of Ursuline nuns and burned alive at the stake Aug. 18, 1634. Nan Robertson reported in the *New York Times* for March 16, 1974 that even the children know the story of his life and death. Robertson described the city as it is today contrasted with its past.

In England a significant landmark is the Witches House that Cecil Williamson, a practicing sorcerer, runs in Bocastle. Over a quarter-century Williamson has collected perhaps the world's largest museum of mementos of black magic and witchcraft. Among the treasures is the skeleton of Ursula Kemp, an Englishwoman executed for witchcraft July 5, 1689. There also are paintings by Aleister Crowley, a notorious diabolist once called "the wickedest man in the world." Peter Bloxham described all the rest of the exhibits in the *New York Times* for April 19, 1970.

A compact history of Halloween appeared in the *Fairbury* (Ill.) *Blade* for Oct. 25, 1977. Nov. 1 marked the New Year's Day for the Celtic tribes of Wales, Ireland and Scotland who practiced the Druid religion. In the 8th century Pope Gregory III moved the church festival of All Hallows or All Saints Day to Nov. 1 and in the following century Pope Gregory IV decreed that the day was to be observed universally. Honored were all saints who died without official church recognition and All Hallow E'en became known in the Middle Ages as the time most favored by witches and sorcerers. The customs—masks, costumes, etc.—came from several different countries.

A few additional facts of interest were told to Steven Pratt by a pseudonymous Margaret for an article in the *Chicago Tribune* for Oct. 30, 1975. Witchcraft, she said, is a pantheistic religion with many gods and goddesses dating back before Christianity. She condemned some contemporary witches who show off and perform bad tricks. She explained that they are not hereditary witches as most witches were killed during the Inquisition. So today's witches are converts and converts of any kind are often fanatics. Yes, she said, she can cast spells; in fact she did so to get her husband.

In the same newspaper for April 30, 1982 Timothy J. and Magdalene Wise Tuomey wrote that, in Satan's kingdom, Walpurgis Night is even bigger than Halloween. According to a German legend Walpurgis Night, April 30, was the occasion for devils to gather and howl and curse the moon atop Brocken, the highest peak in the Harz Mountains. In the 8th century an English woman who became St. Walpurgis championed the people's case against these pagan rites and taught them to fight evil spirits with fire and light; she became the protectoress against evil spirits. Today she is honored by festivals in many parts of the world. Some of the groups are gags, as is Chicago's Bushmanic Society in honor of a deceased Brookfield Zoo gorilla.

The last witchcraft trial in England was held in 1712 but in 1736 Parliament deprived witches of legal standing by repealing the witchcraft statute. Nevertheless, legends persist, as Elizabeth Dickens recounted in an article, "A Witch-Hunting Jaunt in Jolly Old England," in the *New York Times* for Nov. 17, 1973. She wrote mostly of the Witch of Wookey, a hag who put the evil eye on most of her neighbors until destroyed with holy water by a monk. In 1916 the English Spiritualists Union tried to persuade Parliament to repeal the 1736 act because it had "an oppressive effect" on genuine mediums.

Despite the enlightened attitude on the part of both governmental and religious institutions, belief in and practice of witchcraft persists and the press' role has been mostly one of neutrality. No matter what publishers and editors may believe personally they consider only potential reader interest when exercising news judgment regarding the subject of witchcraft. Many Americans smugly believe that witchcraft persists only in backward areas, mostly in Africa, the South Pacific and the islands of the Caribbean. A fair sampling of the objective reporting to appear in American newspapers during the past few decades follows.

Aaron Brown wrote an eyewitness account of a voodoo dance and sacrifice of a chicken at Port-au-Prince, Haiti for the *Chicago Tribune* of April 28, 1939. He explained, "Voodooism or black magic worship of the Haitians is a reverberation of the religious worship once practiced in deepest Africa. When the original slaves were brought over to the Antilles in the 16th century they brought with them their incantations, their adoration of the dead spirits and their feverish dances."

Differing from voodoo because it has no formalized creed or organized service of worship obeah (or obeeyahism) "Is a Fact of Life and Afterlife in the Caribbean," as described by Lindsay Haines in the Sept. 10, 1972 *National Observer*. Brought from Africa by slaves it persisted underground after the plantation owners forbade open practice of old religions and customs. So it represented a way of revenge. Explained Haines in his two-page article, "A person might turn to obeah if he yearns to see his competitor's business fold, or if he wants to clinch a promotion or if he needs a spell that will make him irresistible to the opposite sex . . . The powers of obeah protect fishermen, aid farmers' crops, get a man's boss to offer him a raise, make a man's shop profitable, help a lawyer win the case by tongue tying his opponent in court, or drive off that evil spirit which has brought one down on one's luck." Specific instructions include the following: "Git your enemy's footprint and gather up dirt where he walked into a bag. Add salt and tie de bag on the wall. Then stick pins in the bag. Right away, wherever he may be, da foot or arm goan swell up and take sores."

A United Press story March 31, 1947 from Bombay, India by John Hlavacek told of Yogi Ramanand Swami who survived 24 hours in a supposedly air-tight, cement-lined grave. There was no mention of the fact that the trick was known to Harry Houdini and some other American magicians.

Another United Press story July 9, 1948 from Sago, Japan told of the merciless killing of one of twin babies and the divorcing of the "animal-like" wife who brought such a disgrace on the husband's family. Buddhist Japanese believe that twins are the reincarnated forms of persons who died in double suicide pacts.

June 1, 1949 Ernie Hill, *Chicago Daily News* foreign correspondent, reported from Accra, Gold Coast that the illnesses of several British governors were caused by terrible hexes in the opinion of tribal chieftains, as part of a nationwide campaign against colonialism. The principal tourist attraction in Port-au-Prince, Keith Wheeler reported in a two-page illustrated article in the Dec. 10, 1950 *Chicago Daily News,* is voodoo dancing, "genuine voodoo too and not a tourist attraction."

The AP reported March 20, 1955 from Guatemala that authorities charged a woman with practicing witchcraft against President Carlos Castillo Armas. Presumably she placed a small rag doll in a jar containing a thick liquid, pieces of garlic, onion and tomato and some buckshot, after which she stuck pins in the doll's head, then sent her maid to the cemetery to bury the jar. The woman was the sister of an exiled political rival of the president.

April 29, 1957 the *Chicago Sun-Times* reported that an epidemic of a virus disease affecting children was believed by many Tlingit, Alaska villagers to be caused by witchcraft. A teenaged girl confessed she had turned into a cat when touched by a bone held by a witch and the chief of police said he saw a man turn into a bird.

July 1, 1961 the *Chicago Daily News'* Smith Hempstone reported from

Nairobi, Kenya the sentencing to death in Tanganyika of two women charged with the witchcraft murder of a 4-year-old boy. Hempstone explained the purpose of magic to win the support of the spirits to one's side. Even whites solicit the services of practitioners of white magic.

The Associated Press reported Jan. 24, 1968 from Mexico City that a couple accused of witchcraft in the death of a girl were lynched by villagers.

Cutlines for an AP picture Oct. 25, 1968, "Woman Doctor," explained that the African witch doctor finds lost possessions, communicates with the dead and makes straying husbands return to their wives.

The AP also reported Jan. 1, 1969 from Dar-Es-Salaam, Tanzania that a member of Parliament wanted witches and wizards rounded up to prevent their incantations which drive people from the villages.

An AP dispatch from Rome Feb. 8, 1969 told of a demonstration before the Chamber of Deputies by a dozen wizards who promised they would end traffic jams in Rome if given legislative recognition.

An AP story June 3, 1970 from Lusaka, Zambia related that losing football teams charged that they were bewitched by their opponents. They intended to import their own witches from Malawi to protect themselves.

Black magic practitioners have pillaged graves, induced suicides by curses and dismembered corpses for ceremonies, Anglican church leaders charged according to an AP story July 30, 1970 from London.

One of the first attempts in recent times to defend witches was Martin Knelman's review of a motion picture and book in the *Toronto Star* for Nov. 17, 1970. The film was *Witchcraft 70* "which raises a matter of conscience for all of us: are witches really just the most persecuted, misunderstood minority group in our society?" The book, *Witchcraft Today* by Gerald B. Gardner, advanced "the concept of witches as gay, fun-loving hedonists." Witches, Gardner wrote, confessed to signing pacts with the devil only because they were tortured.

A furor caused by a television performance by a woman claiming to be a reincarnation of a voodoo spirit led the two Brazilian networks to ban such programs, the AP reported Sept. 10, 1971 from Rio de Janeiro.

A 70-year-old widow was shot to death by villagers of Santa Ignacia because they suspected her of being a witch according to a UPI story from Manila April 10, 1972.

In announcing the opening of Canada's first occult supermarket Barbara Klich quoted John Rode, the owner, in the *Toronto Globe and Mail* for July 20, 1972: "It was necessary in the 13th century to degrade witches because of orthodox religion . . . We look to the orthodoxy in witchcraft craft and find a great deal in it."

"Now Why Would a Grown Man Be Riding a Broomstick?" Barry Conn Hughes asked in *Canadian Magazine* for Oct. 21, 1972 and answered, in the subhead, "If he's Roy Dymond it's to make the crops grow." In the article, Dymond, a white witch, explained, "Witches do have a fertility ritual that involves hopping along on a long staff like a hobbyhorse and some observer centuries ago must have got the wrong idea. While the ceremony may have sexual overtones, the 'fertility' refers to the earth. Witches leap high to encourage crops to grow."

Ostensibly to dispel myths about them, a coven allowed a *Toronto Star* reporter, Bruce Kirkland, to observe its Halloween ceremony. In the Nov. 1, 1972 edition of his paper he quoted the coven's high priest as saying, "We believe we are the oldest religion in the world . . . The ceremony you see is the same one you would see in pagan times." The priest's wife said the present is her seventh or eighth reincarnation. Everybody has the power to be a witch, they both said.

Interest in witchcraft is alive even in strongly Catholic Spain, the AP reported Nov. 5, 1972 from San Sebastian, Spain. More than 400 attended the First National Congress of Studies in Witchcraft, whereas only a handful had been expected.

The New Diabolist, "an example of a resurgence of devilry the likes of which earned countless early practitioners a stake inside a bonfire" was described at length by Daniel St. Albin Greene in the *National Observer* for Sept. 1, 1973.

The *Washington Post* reported Sept. 23, 1978 that a psychologist in Pretoria told a convention of the Psychological Institute of South Africa that witch doctors are far from obsolete and should be integrated into present society.

The diabolists are denounced even by the rest of American occultism for following the "left-hand bath" and trying to harness the "dark powers," according to Greene. The secret of the appeal, he wrote, "is the extent to which diabolism offers what proselytes failed to find in hallucinogenic drugs, mysticism, Jesus freaking or any other 'trip' they'd tried. After two years as an observer-participant in the Church of Satan in San Francisco Edward J. Moody, anthropologist now at the Queen's University of Belfast, concluded that the church's "beliefs and practices provide the witch and warlock with a sense of power, a feeling of control and an explanation for personal failure, inadequacy and other difficulties."

In an article from Rio de Janeiro for the *Washington Post* of Jan. 1, 1974, Bruce Handler told of tens of thousands of white-robed voodoo believers, mostly also good Roman Catholics, who jammed the beaches for the annual New Year's Eve homage to Iemanja, mystical goddess of the sea whom the cultists consider as important as the Virgin Mary.

Aug. 9, 1974 the UPI reported from Buenos Aires that police saved a mystic from lynching by a posse of women who accused him of bewitching some prostitutes.

The failure of the Roman Catholic church to lure Brazilians from their cults was reported by Marvin Howe in the *New York Times* for Dec. 31, 1974. Thousands chanted and clapped and made presents while observing the rite of Iemanja. It is believed that New Year's Eve spirits of African ancestors enter the minds and bodies of believers who stagger in a trance, fall and writhe in the sand. The African deities came to Brazil on slave ships between 1530 and 1850 when 10 to 15 million blacks were brought there.

The First World Congress of Sorcery ended in Bogota with the 2,500 delegates divided. Some cried "fraud" but the sponsor, a travel agency, said it lost $100,000, the *Washington Post* reported Aug. 31, 1975.

Maxine Sanders, England's "witch queen," pointed out the difference between two types of contemporary witches in an interview with Robert Merry for the *Chicago Tribune* of Oct. 31, 1975. One type is garbed in long black robes or cloaks; the other is sky-clad or naked. Most modern behavior is derived from ancient practices. Herbs, for instance, always have been an integral part of the occult since antiquity so some modern witches study herbs. Ohers mix batches of noxious brews to make salves called "flying ointments," said to be smelly, oily, greenish and hallucinogenic. Witches would grease themselves and their broomsticks with the salve to get a sensation of flying and of meeting weird supernatural creatures and demons. Said Sanders: "We work to free the mind. We believe in complete personal freedom. We try to remove the mental blocks put upon a person by the conformist society. Essentially it is a case of helping a person find his real self."

In the *New York Times* April 14, 1975 Ruth Berenson told of the ministrations of a voodoo practitioner in Haiti after she sprained her ankle. What ordinarily would have taken weeks to heal was better in less than a day.

Just back from Africa Dr. Paul Gekas told the *Chicago Sun-Times* June 7, 1976 that a big obstacle to better health on the continent is the continuing influence of witch doctors. Typical case: a witch doctor made razor cuts to allow evil spirits to escape from a woman's infected knee. On the other hand a Western-trained doctor was quoted Aug. 30, 1969 in an Associated Press story in *Newsday:* "Witch doctors who apply their Stone Age wisdom to bags of bones and seashells stand as good a chance of curing psychological disorders among African urban blacks as does modern medicine." What Western medicine has to learn from witch doctors was the subject matter of an article in the *Chicago Tribune* for April 18, 1981 by Norman Myers. Mostly there has been increased knowledge of plants and herbs with proven medicinal value. In reply to Myers' question of how he knew his prescriptions would work, one witch doctor replied, "How does anyone know and what difference does it make? If it works why waste time figuring out how?"

John Parcell wrote "Rural Mexican Cure-All: With a Raw Egg" for the Aug. 17, 1976 *Washington Post* from Mexico City. The treatment, almost universal among Mexican witches, is to wave an unbroken raw egg over the clothed body of a patient to remove both physical and psychological conditions. Practitioners are either brujas, who cure physical disorders by magic and put the evil eye on offensive neighbors, or curranderas, who deal mainly with physical manipulation of bones or internal organs and use remedies made from recipes using herbs and grasses.

Stan Delaplane began an article in the Around the World column in the *Chicago Sunday Tribune* for Oct. 4, 1981: "Each culture has its own superstitions and taboos." He then related samples from Tahiti to Jamaica. In the former place an entire hotel staff walked out when a stone tiki was brought into the building. They believed it was a living fearsome god able to destroy people. Their fear disappeared when the stone was chained to a coconut tree until it cooled.

In the *Chicago Sun-Times* for July 4, 1982 Victor Zorza gave an eyewitness account of a shaman's body being used by the goddess Kali to express displeasure at the lack of homage paid to her in a Himalayan village. Sacrifices of food and money evidently pacified her.

Much earlier in a full-page feature, "When Civilized Folk Make Magic and Savages Don't," copyrighted in 1935 by *Everyweek Magazine,* Emily G. Davis wrote, "There's just one community on earth where no vestiges of superstition are found—and it is neither New York, London nor any other great city, but a tribe of pigmy savages far back in a deep jungle of the Philippine Islands."

The witch doctors gained respectability when Dr. E. S. W. Bidwell of Gambia told the World Health Organization in Geneva, Switzerland that "Health development in Africa is a complete nonstarter without these people. They will continue to be the primary deliverers of health care until 2000," the *Chicago Tribune* Press Service reported Sept. 30, 1981.

To match such accounts of the prevalence of witches in many other parts of the world there are reports of the persistence of such practices in the enlightened United States. To tell the "Weird Story of the Louisiana 'Devil Man' " Maurice Ries needed a full page in the Dec. 18, 1938 *Chicago Times.* Especially in New Orleans people have panicked and suffered injury and death while fleeing "the Devil Man" of which all sorts of rumors circulate. Among them: that a man in a saloon made glasses walk up and down the bar, and disappeared when the clerk came, and another man turned bright scarlet for a few minutes at a dance.

Sept. 25, 1949 the lead of an AP story from New Orleans was "Voodoo still slinks in the dark corner of ancient New Orleans but it's a dying business. There are some who claim voodoo's curse rid the world of Hitler and Mussolini." This was accomplished by burying pictures of the two dictators in a graveyard and laying ancient curses on them, indicating the manner of their deaths to come, Hitler by shooting and Mussolini by hanging.

An example of the extent to which the practice persists in the United States was a half-page article "Conjure Woman—She 'Talks With the Devil.' Keeps the Negro in Terror With Her Spells," by Jack Kytle in the *Milwaukee Journal* for March 26, 1939. The article begins by extoling the prowess of Earthy Ann of Livingston, Ala. and continues, "If Earthy Ann worked along in voodooism and conjuration, her existence would not be worth mention. A hundred conjure men and women might not be enough to cause concern. But there are several thousand of them spread like a giant octopus over the South. Year after year they prey upon the helpless, exacting an annual harvest of tribute, creating untold mental torture, provoking homicides and even casting their shadow across the courts."

The South, however, has had no monopoly on witchcraft cults. An exiled Japanese operating from Canada controlled Worshippers of Allah in northern states. The UPI reported from Detroit Jan. 21, 1933 that a woman and child were in hiding for fear of being boiled alive as a sacrifice to Allah.

Because Delaware's colonial law against witchcraft never was repealed, several clients of a handwriting analyst caused a Wilmington woman to be arrested, the AP reported March 14, 1950. March 23, 1950 the AP reported that Mrs. Helen Evans would be tried under a 1603 British law. Mrs. Evans admitted she believes in the efficacy of bread and sugar wrapped in a handkerchief and in little charms and religious medals. Judge Herlihy said, "It is unbelievable that a charge of practicing the art of witchcraft could be brought in the enlightened state of Delaware."

The persistence of conjuring in the United States was described in the *National Observer* for Feb. 7, 1965. Several incidents that occurred on the McLemore plantation near Montgomery, Ala. were related. In one instance William McLemore threatened to fire a woman supposed to have hexed another unless she lifted the curse. In another case a woman died although doctors could determine no cause. The article's anonymous author wrote: "Those who believe in the power of conjure will never identify the conjurer's name for fear that they too will be cursed. But the conjure women are sometimes identifiable because amid poverty they are relatively better off and usually smarter and shrewder. They make their money selling crude charms—broken glass, a bag of animal bones and the like. They prosper because some of the Negroes believe in their power and believing makes it so."

That psychologists are beginning to accept voodoo and faith healers openly as colleagues was the gist of an article by Philip J. Hilts in the *Washington Post* for Aug. 21, 1981. Vivian Garrison, a New Jersey Medical School psychologist, was quoted as believing 80 percent of all episodes of mental or physical illness in the United States are handled not by M.D.s but with home remedies or folk cures.

Physical evidence that some living persons attempt to practice ancient forms of witchcraft was discovered near Bentonville, Ark. in the form of stone altars with skulls, knives, candles, other material and especially stones with strange characters on them. A sheriff's deputy found the clue in some books on demonology. One stone was inscribed with a warning, "Zyto's wrath is upon you."

An ancient sorcerer named Zytho was mentioned in one of the books. A University of Arkansas anthropologist said animal mutilations that had become common in the area probably were related to the altars. He consulted old astrological charts and correctly predicted when the next ones would occur. The full details were included in an article by John M. Crewdson in the *New York Times* for June 30, 1978.

By far the most important witches' conclave in the United States is the 10-acres settlement near Beaufort, S.C., the nature of which is stated in a road sign that greets visitors: "Notice: You are leaving the U.S. You are entering Yoruba Kingdom. In the name of his Highness King Efuntola, Peace. Welcome to the Sacred Yoruba village of Oyu-Tunjim, the only village in N. America built by priests of the Orisha-Voodoo cult. As a tribute to our ancestors, the priests preserve the customs, laws, and religion of the African race. Welcome to our land."

J. E. McTeer, a 70-year-old white man who served 37 years as "the high sheriff of the low country," believes the "best and truest witchcraft in America is practiced in the Beaufort area, B. Drummond Ayers, Jr. reported in the *New York Times* for Dec. 31, 1973. The colony was established in 1969 by a former Harlem follower of Marcus Garvey, leader of an unsuccessful movment in the '30s to persuade American Negroes to move to Africa.

In 1959 the leader, Walter Serge King, once a member of Katherine Dunham's dance troupe, was initiated into a voodoo cult in Cuba. He returned to New York convinced "that you'll never be able to do anything with the blacks in the cities because their lives are politically, culturally and economically controlled by the cities. And the only way you'll be able to change the blacks, even for their own benefit, is to control their lives completely. So I concluded about 1961 or '62 that we'd have to build our own towns and villages. I never lost sight of that dream."

In a long article on the colony in the *National Observer* for Nov. 29, 1975, Daniel St. Albin Greene wrote: "The voodoo revival is also a manifestation of the emerging cultural consciousness of some disaffected black Americans. Many of them are convinced that blacks are oppressed by white-dominated society and will remain so unless they free themselves from the 'cultural amnesia.' "

In 1973, Ayers reported, the Yoruba Kingdom had a population of 35. In the *Chicago Sun-Times* for May 26, 1979 Kevin Horan said it had increased to 130.

Familiar to sightseers in eastern Pennsylvania are hex signs on barns and other buildings although even modern Pennsylvania Dutch (Germans) have less faith in them to ward off evil spirits and bring good luck. An inquirer regarding them was informed by the *Chicago Daily News* Beeline March 24, 1972 that the Philadelphia Phillies had three hex signs over their dugout, but maybe "ought to switch the signs to the visiting team's dugout." A full page of hex signs in color, with accompanying explanations, appeared in the *Chicago Tribune* for Aug. 19, 1978.

Reflecting the general public's more tolerant and less fearful attitude toward witchcraft, the press has been objective, even sympathetic in its treatment of the subject during the past decade. Michael Miner wrote in the *Chicago Sun-Times* for Feb. 8, 1971 of meeting a self-proclaimed witch on a bus. The charming young lady was secretive regarding her coven's activities but by no means threatening.

Instead of discarding the letters seeking information concerning aspects of witchcraft the *Chicago Daily News'* Beeline provided sympathetic answers. July 9, 1971 one correspondent was advised on how to obtain a do-it-yourself witches' kit; Aug. 23, 1971 another writer was told how to contact Witch Hecate by use of incense and incantations in a graveyard in the light of a full moon.

Growth of widespread public interest in, if not acceptance of, modern-day witchcraft is indicated by such stories as the one Patricia Shelton, *Chicago Daily News* fashion editor, wrote March 30, 1972 about Marvin Berkman, a custom jeweler who was fast becoming a custom jeweler to witches.

Because theological colleagues neglected black magic, the Bishop of Petersborough invited Dennis Wheatley, expert on the subject, to speak to 150 clergymen, the *London Express* reported in an article that the *New York Post* reprinted June 13, 1972. The bishop expressed concern over the increase of occult activities and wanted his priests to be informed.

About the same time the *New York Times* publicized efforts to combat the growth of witchcraft. Aug. 6, 1972 it had a special dispatch from San Diego about an anti-occult mobile unit sponsored by Morris Cerulla, founder and president of World Evangelism. To appeal mostly to youth in 45 cities he had a display of potions, voodoo oil, a Satanic altar, a goat's hoof, the Satanic "bible," a human skull and other paraphernalia whose use leads to "mental derangement, criminal tendencies and self destruction."

Another special to the *Times* from Brentwood, L.I. Oct. 30, 1972 was about Raymond and Rosemary Buckland who operate a Bay Shore Witchcraft Museum and every six months have ceremonies whereby he, a Ph.D. in anthropology, becomes the high priest for six months, after which she rules as high priestess. "The position of women in witchcraft has been slightly more important than that of men since the earliest times," he says.

The intention of Paul Kovi, manager of the Four Seasons, to write a cookbook on witches' recipes, to be called *The Warlock Cookbook,* was reported by Leonard Lyons in his *New York Post* column for Dec. 26, 1972.

In the *Chicago Tribune* for Dec. 9, 1973, Pat Colander gave detailed instructions on how to be successful in a romance as Ann Grammary tells it in a book, *The Witches' Workbook;* slightly different procedures were explained in the *Chicago Sunday Tribune*, Oct. 9, 1973.

Because "three-fourths of all witches are former Catholics," a Dominican priest, Richard Woods, became a student of the occult. He is the author of *The Occult Revolution: A Christian Meditation.* He talked to Margo,

Chicago Daily News columnist who quoted him Feb. 19, 1972 as saying, "The kids are turned off by modern society. They're looking for relationships in nature, animals and the cosmos. They want an alternative to Establishment religion and Establishment science. When the structure of society breaks down, there's a need for ritualistic behavior and traditional religions don't meet that need today."

In the *Wall Street Journal* for Oct. 21, 1969, Stephen J. Sansweet told of a lecture series about witchcraft at the University of South Carolina, an adult education course in the subject at New York University and a course in a Langley, Va. high school. In the article headlined "Americans Show Burst of Interest in Witches, Other Occult Matters," Sansweet wrote: "Periodically throughout history there have been surges of interest in the occult but psychologists and others suggest that there are newer explanations for the current fascination with mysticism. The closer we get to a controlled, totally predictable society, the more man becomes fearful of the consequences." He quoted Mortimer R. Feinberg, a psychology professor at City University of New York, "Interest in mysticism is a regression to a childlike state of mind" that relieves man of many of his worries. Others say the trend is due to increasing dissatisfaction with science and frustration over what scientists can't accomplish. The occult, some say, provides meaning to life and a feeling that man can control his life. Still others see the increased interest in the occult as a hoax perpetrated by those who stand to profit financially by it.

Three practicing witches attending Southern Illinois University at Carbondale, Ill. were interviewed by the student newspaper, the *Daily Egyptian,* March 10, 1972. They defined witchcraft differently. Jane said it is "mental telepathic persuasion," an attempt to control people's actions through thought waves. Mary said witchcraft is the projection of thoughts to other people and the reading of other people's minds. For Joe witchcraft is "more fulfilling than any other comparable religion."

According to an AP story from Madison, N.J. Jan. 14, 1974, a course in voodoo was added to the curriculum of Fairleigh Dickinson University. The same day the *Austin American-Statesman* told of the announcement of a new University of Texas course on "The Vampire in Eastern Europe." The same paper carried an AP account from New York of a new course in demons, witches, demonic possession and devil worship at Fordham University. The cutlines to an AP photograph May 8, 1974 said Laurie Cabot who runs The Witch Shop in Salem, Mass. teaches informal classes of teenagers and others on mind control, natural law and mysticism. According to an AP story from Salem that the *Miami Herald* used Nov. 14, 1974, Ms. Cabot was teaching a course in her craft at Salem State University; Baptist church parishioners were objecting to her speaking in public at Georgetown.

About 12,000 students took the correspondence course in witchcraft of the School of Wicca, operated by Gavin and Yvonne Frost from Salem, Mo., where they moved after an injunction prevented their filling a speaking engagement at St. Charles, Mo. High School. The Frosts use spiritual and telepathic healing, along with penicillin, to care for any ailing hog on their farm, explaining "Our form of witchcraft is very pragmatic."

In the *New York Times Magazine* for Dec. 31, 1972 there appeared a controversial full-page advertisement inserted by the New York University School of Continuing Education. In large type that consumed almost half of the total space, it read: "On Feb. 5th, he'll challenge a witch to turn him into a toad at NYU." There were small pictures of a man and a toad. What it was all about was a course in Witchcraft, Sorcery and Astrology taught by Owen Rachleff. Among the promises to students was ability to predict the future "with the same accuracy and frequency as Jeane Dixon."

There is no way of telling what the reader response as a whole was. In the *Times* for Feb. 8, 1973 Philip H. Dougherty commented on both the NYU ad and several others prepared by the same advertising agency that said tests in split-run newspapers indicated they outpulled others by as much as two to one.

In the *New York Daily News* for Aug. 21, 1973 Rachleff was quoted as saying his witchcraft course draws over 80 students a semester whereas his Bible as Literature course draws only 15. He brightens his course with what he calls "debunking the cultniks and occultniks."

Rita Reif wrote in the *New York Times* for Jan. 17, 1973 of a show that "accomplishes best by its wide-ranging selection of more than 115 objects, to indicate the surprising breadth and depth of spiritualist traditions in this country." It was opened in the Museum of American Folk Art by members of the Coven of Welsh Traditionalist Witches who wore ceremonial robes and chanted. Experts in fortune telling by palm reading, tarot cards, numerology, psychic reading and other ways were ready for customers in separate booths.

In an article written from Los Angeles for the *London Observer* and reprinted in the *Houston Chronicle* for July 31, 1973, Charles Foley estimated that between 5 and 6 million Americans are devotees of some cult, sect or society, with at least another 25 million sympathetic and interested onlookers. He wrote: "Theories as to why the world has suddenly swung back toward a belief in the supernatural are legion. The consensus is that it is a substitute faith, the outcome of modern man's disillusion with a civilization that lacks ideals and his craving for another world of deeper meaning."

Foley quoted from Paul Godwin's *Occult America:* "A civilization that reaches a stage of uncertainty in its own quest seeks aid from supernatural forces. The occult renaissance is a sign that the people are troubled." Also, Prof. Iden Goodman, who teaches a course about dreams at San Francisco State University, believes, "The huge desire for occult studies is a reaction to the grossly materialistic culture."

At Oakland University, Michigan, Prof. Philip Singer lectures on

"Ethnopsychiatry" which he says is the study of curing mental disorders through psychic means—witchcraft. Pepperdine College in Los Angeles had a course in "The World of the Supernatural" and the Seattle campus of the University of Washington had extrasensory perception and Yoga courses.

His study of the ancient secrets of primitive witch doctors led Dr. Bruce Halstead to believe poisons in fish, reptiles and plants cause hallucinations, depressions and other abnormal mental states, the Associated Press reported Sept. 30, 1959 from Colton, Calif. Dr. Halstead was quoted as follows: "Many of the so-called miraculous cures attributed to witch doctors have no basis in fact. They make their patients sick with certain poisons of short duration, then claim a cure when the effect wears off."

Years later, in an article in the *Washington Post* for March 31, 1976, Linda R. Caporael, a graduate student in psychology at the University of California at Santa Barbara, was quoted as believing the Salem villagers who swore to seeing "diabolical deeds and distempers" might have been under the influence of ergot, a component of which is the hallucinogen commonly known as LSD. Two Carleton University professors commented that the Salem children did not show any of the symptoms usually associated with ergot poisoning, such as nausea, vomiting and then enormous appetite. Support for the Caporael theory did not come until late 1979 when a University of Maryland history professor, Mary K. Matossin, said, in *Psychology Today,* that her study of the social consequences of taking LSD led her to believe Caporeal was right. Walter Sullivan reported her findings in the *New York Times* for Aug. 29, 1982. In the paper's Oct. 5 issue Mary Cantwell reviewed letters to the editor on the subject. The *Chicago Tribune* had a story Sept. 13, 1982.

For the do-it-yourself witch a book, *How to Make Amulets, Charms and Talismans: What They Mean and How to Use Them* by Deborah Lippman and Paul Colin, was a big help. Tom Donnelly gave it a half-page review in the *Washington Post* for Aug. 8, 1974. Amulets can be either personal or general; they cannot do harm. On the other hand, talismans relate to specific purposes and can be good or evil. The recipes are easy to follow but not all the ingredients are likely to be handy in the ordinary home: copper tubing, Elmer's glue, eggs, candles, carraway seeds, toothpicks, corn husks, embroidery hoops, scissors, hammer, butane torch, soldering gun, longnosed pliers. What you make yourself, however, is better than store-bought amulets.

"A growing interest in the occult and the devil in Chicago" was explained by Diana Milesko-Pytel in the *Chicago Daily News* for July 20, 1974. The reporter visited the Occult Bookstore, the Temple of the Pagan Way and several other places with a similar interest. She concluded that "all of them are centered around the importance of man in nature and in the universe. The most striking difference between occult religions and the

Judeo-Christian faiths is that occult beliefs recognize the possibility of many gods; the Judeo-Christian only one. The devil who represented Evil Personified seems to be distasteful even to occult people."

To act as a clearing house and reference source there is the New York Center for the Strange. A survey of 280 witches was reported Oct. 31, 1973 by the UPI. Among the forecasts: Vice-President Ford would resign, a woman would become president of a leading labor union and the Dow Jones average would hit an all-time 1,100 high. Nov. 1, 1974 the UPI quoted Robert Carson, the center's public relations director, as saying, "Some of the straightest people are witches," including two members of Congress. The center polled 275 witches for their predictions. The 75 who answered were wrong in forecasting the resignation of Henry A. Kissinger as secretary of state in May 1975. Oct. 30, 1975 UPI reported from New York that a survey of 280 witches revealed that Hubert Humphrey would be elected president and that medical researchers would conclude that kissing is a serious threat to the nation's health. According to a UPI story May 31, 1976, however, they correctly predicted the election of Jimmy Carter by a small margin in 1976. As reported by the UPI Oct. 31, 1980 the majority of the 290 who responded said Carter would beat Reagan; Billy Carter would become a citizen of Libya; scientists would turn sea water into gold; people from outer space would send a message to Earth containing profanity and the United Nations would move its headquarters from New York to Casablanca, Morocco.

"Today witches are treated like refugees from a psychotic ward," Leo Martello told Philip Nobile who devoted a page in the *Chicago Sun-Times Midwest Magazine* for March 24, 1974 to the leading witch's complaints against the persecution and discrimination of the past and today. He lamented that a sacred holiday, Halloween, has been turned into a ceremonial enterprise, but he was optimistic about the future. "The Mormons and Christian Scientists began right here in the United States," he said. "They own millions of dollars of property and have full rights. I don't like to go into the numbers game but there are at least 4,300 covens with 13 witches each in the United States."

An outstanding example of how hysteria is created and spread was provided by the *Pioneer Press* July 24, 1973 with an article by Bill Choyke entitled "Helen Miller: a witch or just misunderstood?" The article consisted of four pages of quotations of neighbors that an admitted witch is corrupting youth, selling narcotics and engaging in other unspecified anti-social activities, together with statements by police authorities that their investigations have yielded nothing. The woman admits having a pet snake in her Round Lake Beach home. "I've liked snakes since I was a child Does that make me evil?" is Mrs. Miller's retort. Complaining witnesses have a habit of not appearing in court, causing charges to be dropped, and others complain because nobody else does anything.

To avoid being transformed into "some kind of a rent-a-witch clearinghouse," the *Chicago Sun-Times'* Action Time answered a reader who wanted to know if there were "any real witches in Chicago" by giving her the name of a shop whose owner agreed to put her in touch with one of his mystical clients. Less timid, the *Chicago Daily News'* Beeline Oct. 29, 1975 quoted an Occult Bookstore owner that there are about 2,000 witches and wizards in Chicago, about which a reader was curious.

In connection with a jocose piece on Halloween, "Masked marauders on the prowl" by James Kloss, the *Chicago Daily News* for Oct. 31, 1975 used an Associated Press picture of Babette Lanzill, a self-proclaimed witch, who planned a "charger ceremony" in the temple behind her sorcerer's shop in Los Angeles. The caption was "Her night to Howl."

About the most popular self-proclaimed "white" witch in Chicago is Ruth Revzen who manufactures "Body Spirits" perfumes known as Love Potion, Enlightenment and Goodness with results that the titles indicate. Patricia Shelton gave her a lengthy writeup in the *Chicago Daily News* for Jan. 2, 1976 and Jason Thomas did the same in the *Chicago Sun-Times* for July 22, 1976. Thomas reported that Revzen had modified her products to conform to federal standards.

"Parents glad daughter became witch" was the headling the *Sun-Times* gave to a UPI story from Portsmouth, Va. Aug. 29, 1976. The parents are the priest and priestess of "a group of self-proclaimed witches in the Tidewater section of Virginia that includes a doctor, a housewife, a music composer, a radio announcer and an electrician." They insist they do not worship the devil.

Michael Aaron, a supervisor at the Revlin distribution center in Edison, N.J., bought a "Tour of Occult New York" for $150 at a Channel 13 auction. What he got for his money was reported Sept. 2, 1976 in the *New York Times*. He took part in a "full-moon ceremony" with six members of a Passaic, N.J. coven, received a "laying-on-of-hands" treatment by Dean Kraft that left his crushed left leg as bad as ever, had his fortune told with tarot cards, saw a slide show of levitating furniture shown by Ed and Lorraine Warren and had a Kirlian photograph taken of his fingertips.

In a two-column-long article in the *Wall Street Journal* for Oct. 25, 1976 Earl C. Gottschalk, Jr. told how and why the leading motion picture producers were planning films dealing with the devil. The success of such pictures as *The Omen, Rosemary's Baby* and *The Exorcist* showed that young people are intensely interested in mysticism, the supernatural and psychic. Thus, says Samuel Z. Arkoff, chairman of American International Pictures, the appeal is a kind of "pop religion" or "religioso."

Gottschalk quoted from reviews in several religious publications, all condemnatory of the current trend.

It is not only the motion picture industry that has benefited from the current revival of interest in witchcraft and demonology. As Marjorie Gottheimer pointed out in *Newsday* for Oct. 31, 1976, it also has "created a seemingly boundless market for literature, both sensational and serious, on the devil, satanic erotica, witch trials, torture, possessions and exorcism." After citing a score or so books, she concluded:

> The decline of magic and witchcraft by the 19th century was related in part to the optimism generated by scientific and technological advances that seemed to promise control over the environment. The current revival of interest in the supernatural may indicate that technology is not supplying us with enough to keep us confident.

Billie Jo Selph is the witch of Coshocton, Ohio to whom Bob Greene devoted his column March 10, 1977 in the *Sun-Times*. She insists she does not worship the devil and she made news when she complained to the Ohio Civil Rights Commission that she was discharged as a bartender because of her religion. Greene quoted her: "A lot of people think that witches are evil, but that's just a stereotype. If you're evil it has nothing to do with whether you're a witch, a Christian, an atheist or what. You're just evil."

Unfortunately for the witches not everyone is tolerant. Dec. 11, 1970 the *News* ran a picture of Mrs. Ann Stewart, a high school teacher in Tucson, Ariz. for 11 years, who was suspended while charges that she taught witchcraft in her classes were investigated. On the other hand, an AP story from Topeka, Kan. related that the Kansas Civil Service Board ruled that practicing witchcraft was not in itself sufficient reason to dismiss the chief psychologist of the state Industrial Reformatory.

What was "certainly the most violent and unfriendly reception we've ever had anywhere" was experienced by the Church of Wicca when it tried to hold its eighth annual Samain Seminar in Amarillo, Tex. Oct. 18, 1980. According to a *Chicago Tribune* article Oct. 10 and an AP followup Oct. 20, 300 fundamentalists, led by a reformed prostitute, picketed the motel where 75 witches were meeting. A bomb threat caused the evacuation of the motel. Across town a "pray in" led by a reformed heroin addict was held in a Baptist church to ward off demoniac spirits that might appear because of the convention. The leader said the witches "are all going straight to hell. They are going to bust hell wide open." The witches answered that they do not believe in hell.

The Baptist reaction was not entirely a surprise. In a dispatch to the *New York Times* for publication Sept. 28, 1980, nearly a month earlier, William K. Stevens told of the unsuccessful attempt to persuade the Holiday Inn to cancel the Wicca meeting because the Baptists planned a marriage encounter seminar at the same time and place. Analyzing the attitude of townsmen, Stevens wrote: "Amarillo has found itself with perplexing new problems: it is in the midst of an alarming upsurge in crime, particularly rape, that has preoccupied its citizens for months. So it was the difficulties of modernity and the presence of self-professed witches came to be linked in the minds of some of the many Amarillo residents who adhere to the fundamentalist Christianity of their forebears." Three years earlier a teenager had been shot to death when a youthful mob besieged the home of two avowed members of the Church of Wicca.

In his followup story for the *New York Times* of Oct. 20, 1980 William K. Stevens quoted a Wicca leader, Sabrina, as saying, "Wicca has got to change. It's got to come out of the broom closet. It's no wonder there are 500 Baptists out there screaming. They don't know what we do." The rest of Stevens' long article was a recitation of Wicca beliefs and practices.

Despite such harassment witches are becoming increasingly bolder in confessing their identity. They insist that they are "good" witches and do not engage in any evil practices injurious to others. Nevertheless, they are secretive as regards their rites and even their beliefs. Some talk freely to journalists but insist that their real names be concealed.

Bill Hazlett used a fictitious name, Cassandra Salem, for the subject of his article "Who is *your* friendly, neighborhood witch?" which appeared in the *Midwest Magazine* of the *Chicago Sun-Times* for Aug. 30, 1970. The woman who runs a consultative service in addition to performing wifely household duties said, "Witchcraft is actually a return to nature, a worship of the natural gods as opposed to the chrome and glass gods you find in society. We're more interested in finding powers within ourselves, in broadening our own minds."

The hundreds of chants and spells listed in witch books range from a way to stop bleeding to how to prevent thieves from entering your home. Cassandra became explicit, "Suppose a burglar has entered your home and you want to stop him from returning, well it can be done by witchcraft. In this case I need three pieces of hog fat, three pieces of bread and three pieces of salt. These are cast on an open fire and burned while reciting particular spells. This will stop the thief from coming back."

The pagan ceremonies observed at a weekend celebration of the summer solstice at Bangor, Wis. did not seem diabolical to a reporter from the *LaCrosse Tribune,* on the basis of whose report the Associated Press prepared a dispatch for June 23, 1981. The 200 participants created a "totally pagan environment" by pitching tents, having campfires, dancing and chanting. Not so harmless seemed the rituals of voodoo or black magic followers who were written up by Lee May of the *Los Angeles Times* Aug. 18, 1981 from Washington. Earnest Bratton of Alexandria, Va., who calls himself Dr. Buzzard, explained how his hex paraphernalia works: red peppers sprinkled in someone's tracks will send him away; nutmeg and lodestone dust bring luck in gambling and so on.

James H. Bowman called a married couple of witches Jane and John Doe in his article "Love Those Witches" in the *Chicago Daily News* for Feb. 18, 1971. They lighted candles and sang and danced around an altar with a "love feast" to follow to celebrate Candlemas. There was no nudity, sex or degenerate behavior, the Does said. They added: "We are not satanists (disciples of Satan). We are pre-Christian."

Lightning in the middle of a snowstorm was a salute from the occult to herald her arrival in Chicago, Starr Maddox, a *Playboy* bunny from Miami, told Sandra Pesman according to the *Chicago Daily News* for March 30, 1972. She was in town to help promote the Playboy Theater's production of *Macbeth*. She praised the motion pictures *Rosemary's Baby* and *Bewitched* and told how she sends her soul out of her body to fly around the room and watch her body bent over in prayer. As is true of most confessed witches, she believes in reincarnation, saying she once was burned at the stake for witchcraft and also was a cat. "That's why I move so gracefully," she explained.

The explanations of modern Wicca leaders and their pleas to be treated normally haven't quieted the fears of many. Fear-struck nuns from a convent near Westchester, N.Y., for instance, cooperated with police in trying to discover the source of chants, gunshots and rock music. They feared some Satanic rites were being performed and rumors told of sacrifices of dogs and cats, the *New York Post* reported Aug. 17, 1979.

On nearby Long Island *Newsday* reported Oct. 29, 1979 there are 4,000 witches who worship Mother Earth and not the devil. David W. Hart described the church as a "back to nature" movement.

A resumé of the persecution witches have suffered was given in a lengthy article by Alicia Murray in the *New York Daily News* for June 22, 1980. Between the years 1350 and 1750 estimates of the number of witches put to death range from 500,000 to 9 million. Interest in witchcraft waned as a result, but in the 1920s an English anthropologist, Margaret Murray, revived it. In 1951 England repealed its last anti-witchcraft law. Thereafter the religion grew in strength in England and the United States, Catherine Poe, local leader, told Murray.

Real witches resent the commercialization of Halloween and the picturing of them as evil-doers. Alina Tugend wrote from Los Angeles Oct. 30, 1981 for the UPI. "Members of the witchcraft community are beginning to sound like any other beleaguered minority—they don't like the press they are getting," she wrote. Babetta, a high priestess, complains because their wearing black is considered ominous. She points out that priests and judges also wear black. In the witchcraft religion, Mother Nature or woman is supreme; they are matriarchal, not patriarchal.

The Nov. 14, 1981 *Los Angeles Times* carried an interview by Elizabeth Mehren with novelist Erica Jong with her "finest creation," 3-year-old daughter, Molly. She stressed that witchcraft "should be viewed in terms of a matriarchy." She defined a witch as "one who uses magic to bend things according to her desires. Or his desires."

"For 6,000 years," Jong said, "the Judeo-Christian culture has resulted in the most pernicious misogyny the world has ever known. The whole Judeo-Christian mind set has led to a situation where women have been consistently kept down." Jong also got a journalistic boost from Beverly Stephens in the *New York Daily News* for Oct. 30, 1981. Stephens called Jong's book *With Witches* "a lively mix of history, poetry and myth . . .

complete with magic spells and recipes for potions." She dispelled the myth that witches are ugly old hags and quoted Jong as believing "Today's image of the witch is a sadly reduced remnant of the Great Mother Goddess."

During the '70s the only important bad publicity witches got resulted from several instances of grave robbing. Nov. 18, 1977 the *New York Times* reported that four suspects were arrested in the vandalizing of two cemeteries in Queens to obtain skulls and jewelry to be used in the rituals of a black magic cult. The *New York Post* ran a much longer article naming names. Police said they had broken up a grave-robbing ring made up mostly of teenagers. In an unrelated case police also found an unoccupied apartment to contain an altar, human skull, goat skull, dried blood and feathers.

The *New York Daily News* went a bit further than either the *Times* or *Post* with the information that the robbers expected to receive $500 from a witches' cult.

One of the few open defenders of witches is Steve Kaplan of Queens, about whom Frank Lombardi wrote a column in the *New York Post* for Oct. 31, 1978. Not a witch himself, Kaplan founded Witches of America because he resents the treatment witches have been and continue to be accorded. He writes articles and talks on radio to plead for justice.

Then, the *New York Post* reported Dec. 20, 1981 from Freehold, N.J., a Wicca high priestess and two warlocks went to trial charged with extorting $4,000 from a young woman on a promise of casting a spell to cure her of diabetes. March 4, 1982 Frank McKeown and Marcia Kramer reported for the *New York Daily News* that one witch and one warlock had been convicted. No mention was made of a second warlock. The defense that failed was that "black witches" had interfered with the cure so more money was needed to hire another black witch to ward off the evil spell cast by the first.

When he received a brown bag containing four pennies and an apple pierced with a small wooden cross, Judge James Rainwater didn't know if it was a gift or a warning and, if the latter, of what. Prof. Jack Kapchan, University of Miami, said it seemed to be from the Cuban Santeria cult, the purpose probably being merely to confuse His Honor, the Associated Press reported April 29, 1982 from Miami.

By far the most celebrated witch in this generation was the English-born Sybil Leek, who died Sept. 26, 1982 in Melbourne, Fla. of cancer at the age of 65. She came to America in the early '60s after she was evicted by her London landlord, according to the *Chicago Sun-Times* Action Time for Dec. 30, 1976. Shortly after her arrival she told Milt Freudenheim of the *Chicago Daily News* in New York that she received 1,000 letters a week from all over America. There are about 6,000 witches in England, she said, but British newspaper accounts of naked orgies and fertility rites are "good journalese." In Boston to promote a book Leek complained to an Associated

Press reporter that she had decided not to discuss witchcraft any more because she was misquoted and misunderstood too often. The *Chicago Sun-Times* used the story on Halloween, Oct. 31, 1969. The same day the *Chicago Daily News* used an interview by one of its own reporters, Diane Monk, for whom Leek estimated there are about 8 million witches worldwide. She expressed dislike of both the *Rosemary's Baby* novel and film. Also on the same day the *New York Times* ran a feature story by Judy Klemesrud, "Some People Take This Witch Business Seriously." The views of three witches were elucidated: Mrs. Raymond Buckland, Mrs. Florence S. and Sybil Leek, all "a part of the big boom in mysticism in this country in which Americans are turning not only to witchcraft, but to astrology, fortune telling, Satanism, the psychic phenomena and other occult practices in what appears to be either a special spiritual experience—or a few laughs."

Leek told the interviewer, "We are entering the Age of Aquarius, and people are searching for a religion where they don't have to live a Godlike life, a religion that acknowledges them as human beings. Witchcraft is a return to a nature religion."

The *Times* article described the ceremonies in the Buckland home with all members naked while soft music played and incense burned. Inside a circle the members sing, chant, dance with broomsticks in commemoration of an ancient fertility rite, drink tea and wine and listen to their high priestess read from *The Book of Shadows*.

As for Mrs. Florence S., she proved very secretive about not only her name but also her activities. She did declare a boy skater whom she blessed won every race he entered. She hands out good luck charms and her husband corroborates her statement that she once caused the wind to blow.

Leek told Sally Quinn of the *Washington Post:* "Witches are the working class. Druids are the priests." Leek was a Druid, probably No. 1 in the world in her day. In the *Post* for May 1, 1970 Quinn related some anecdotes of how Leek used her power perhaps incorrectly. Once she stared so steadily at a singer on the stage that he burst out laughing; another time she put a dramatic producer to sleep daily at 4 P.M. A witch's spells are not written but are handed down orally, in Leek's case since the 10th century.

She said she dealt in prophecies regarding important world events rather than in individual horoscopes. For example, as Frank Beacham reported in *Chicago Today* for Aug. 18, 1972, she considered the reelection of President Nixon doubtful. However, although Senator McGovern might win, his stars were unfavorable and the victory would be close.

Leek told reporters in Los Angeles that she was "not the Billy Graham of witchcraft," according to the *Toronto Star* for Sept. 7, 1972. She said her religion was personal and derived from the Druids.

A revealing question and answer interview with Sybil Leek appeared in the *Grey City Journal* and was reprinted by the University of Chicago *Daily Maroon* for Nov. 21, 1969. Aug. 24, 1974 the *Daily Illini* reported that of Leek's nine businesses the most important was a design and movie business. The author of about 50 books, she enjoyed writing. As she did in most interviews she stressed the fact that witches believe in reincarnation, not in heaven and/or hell.

In her half-page article on "A Gentle Woman Who Is Also a Witch" in the *Chicago Tribune* for Dec. 2, 1972, Mary Daniels emphasized Leek's great financial success and the important clients she had: Aga Khan, Queen Marie of Rumania, Somerset Maugham, Charles deGaulle among them.

The substance of Ed Prickett's article about Sybil Leek in *Chicago Today* for March 14, 1974 was contained in the headline, "High Priestess Boils Over Anti-Witch Bias." The incident that annoyed her most at the time was the inquiry by a Fort Lauderdale realtor through whom she wanted to buy a house for her son. He wanted to know her religious beliefs and whether there would be seances held in the house.

Over the years witches have been newsworthy, especially when they land in court or cause others to do so.

Many of the most sensational stories that attract nationwide interest originate in the hex country of southeastern Pennsylvania and nearby New Jersey. For example, the generally sober and dignified *St. Louis Post-Dispatch* devoted more than a page in its magazine section for May 13, 1934 to the "dark superstitions and medieval practices behind the crime of young Albert Skinsky" who, as the story's title stated, "Committed Murder Because He Thought He Was Hexed." Although confined to an insane asylum in Pottsville, Pa. "his mind is at peace at last" since he shot and killed elderly Mrs. Susan Mummey who he was convinced cast a witch's spell on him seven years earlier.

The article made mention of several earlier hex murders and stated: "The cult of hexerel remains a potent force in the lives of many of the men and women who live in the mining and farming regions of the Pennsylvania Dutch country. Belief in demons, witches, spells, omens, incantations and the like, brought from Europe by the early German settlers, persists in many of their descendants today, coloring the daily routine of their existence."

I lived for a year with an Italian family in Bethlehem, Pa. They had lost three sons in infancy or early childhood and were so concerned about their surviving 4-year-old that they took him to both a medical doctor and a hex pow-wow. The latter told them to make a mark on the wall six inches above the child's head; when he grew beyond the mark he would have no more temper tantrums. By then, he would be at least five years older. One evening, after a dinner of plums, ice cream and beer, the boy had convulsions and died with the medical doctor at his side filling the room with heavy smoke from his cigar.

At another time a jury refused to acquit one neighbor who broke into the house of another and murdered him, declaring that the Angel Gabriel had ordered the act. Priests made periodic visits to all homes to sprinkle holy water in every room.

The *American Weekly,* a syndicated feature service of the Hearst organization, produced a two-page center-spread feature, "The Witch Hunters' Bible." It consisted of extracts from an early 19th-century book, *The Long Hidden Friend,* by a German, John George Hohman, from which Pennsylvania hex (pow-wow) doctors learned the spells, magic rites, incantations, enchantments and talismans to cure ills and protect man and beast from harm. One short example: "Whoever wears a dog's heart on his left side no dog will bark at him; they are all dumb before him."

Courts often, perhaps most often, do not sympathize with litigants who accuse others of witchcraft. The Associated Press reported from Philadelphia April 12, 1936 that a magistrate called for $3,000 bail for a woman charged with collecting money under false pretenses. She allegedly extorted $2,000 from another woman to bring good luck to her boarding house.

Three Woodbridge, N.J. women were admonished by Recorder Arthur Brown, "I cannot understand how people in this modern age can profess the belief in things that were forgotten 200 years ago. You defendants are dominated by sheer ignorance." The women, supported by two witnesses, were there because a neighbor took them to court, according to the Associated Press Oct. 3, 1936. Despite the court's admonition they insisted they had seen their neighbor change herself into a horse and walk on her hind legs, change into a dog's head, cause her head to shrink to the size of a fist and perform other feats of necromancy.

For five ensuing days the *Philadelphia Record* followed the story with accounts by its own reporters and the AP. Mrs. Theresa Czinkota spoke in Hungarian which was translated by an interpreter for the benefit of George R. Burns, *Record* reporter. She said her neighbors misinterpreted shadows and religious pictures on her walls and the purpose of a potion she made with herbs for her husband who had rheumatism. In his Oct. 4, 1936 article Burns recalled the 1928 murder of a York County man accused of witchcraft and a physical attack on a supposed witch in Philadelphia a few months earlier.

Calm began to be restored when the parish priest, the Rev. Vincent Lenyi, told 1,600 parishioners, mostly of Hungarian ancestry, that "devil worship is opposed to the principles of the church," the AP's Oct. 5, 1936 story told. The next day police began a search for three itinerant "miracle workers" who had extracted considerable money from Hungarian-speaking women for fantastic rites and foul potions. The fakers presumably inspired the accusations against Mrs. Czinkota.

Oct. 10, 1936 the *Philadelphia Record* used an AP story from Carlisle about a farm woman seeking court protection against three neighbors who accused her of putting a hex on their barnyard. They said a witch doctor had consulted a crystal ball to inform them of the hex's origin.

The same day the AP reported from Rockaway Beach, N.Y. that a magistrate had admonished two tenants and a landlord who had made countercharges of witchcraft against each other: "All the witches died 250 years ago. Go home and behave yourselves."

An amateur hypnotist was believed to have shaken Stephen Richardson's belief he was slowly dying from a witch doctor's hex, the UPI reported March 15, 1947 from Louisburg, N.C. A few weeks earlier the conjurer was murdered by one of Richardson's friends who feared he might also be hexed. From Jarrow, England the UPI reported March 22, 1947 that a father and son testified they had beheaded their wife-mother because of "visions" and "evil spirits." The *Chicago Sun* used the story. The *St. Louis Globe-Democrat* had an illustrated AP story from Weehawken, N.J. that a man told the court his estranged wife had dug a grave in her backyard and placed his picture and old hat in it as a hopeful hex. She explained that she did it "because I had a dream he is going to die there." Police Magistrate Abraham Liebermann made the wife promise to permit her husband to visit their children and told her that her pains resulted from illness, not a husbandly hex. He told her to close the grave and consult a doctor.

In what the *National Observer* said Oct. 28, 1960 was "one of the stickiest issues in its history," the National Labor Relations Board considered the charge of the General Cigar Co. plant in Puerto Rico that workers were induced to vote for representation by the International Association of Machinists because union representatives cast spells over them. The union won the election, 255 votes to 222. An IAM official commented: "The charges were greeted with hilarity and are an indication of the contempt the company holds for its employees. It's pretty ridiculous for these charges to be taken seriously. Our organizer there drove to work in his Ford; he denies he ever rode a broom."

In Dixmoor, Ill. a woman who seemed to be in a trance reported to police that she fatally shot her husband and two women at a wedding reception. According to the police she said a voodoo doctor told her she had a snake moving around in her stomach. A second witch doctor said the husband was "administering powers to her."

In Fayetteville, Ark. the UPI reported Feb. 26, 1970, a husband and his mother tortured his wife and her sister whom they accused of casting a spell on his 5-year-old epileptic daughter. The explanation: the Voice of God was instructing them to drive the evil spirits from the sisters, who, they said, were witches.

Illinois State Sen. Edward McBroom, Kankakee Republican, went to San Jose, Calif. to obtain custody of his son, Victor, 21, who, he charged, had been bewitched by Mrs. Patricia Schneider of Kankakee, who took him to a former Kankakee resident, Mrs. Sara Chaney in San Jose. The father charged that Mrs. Schneider "introduced Victor to her witchcraft and spiritual meetings, including seances, and induced him to take and use drugs, narcotics and other substances detrimental to the health and welfare of Victor." The story was told in the *Chicago Sun-Times* editions of Dec. 30 and 31, 1970.

Narcotics agents said it was not drugs that caused 15 girl students in the Sand Flat High School of Mount Pleasant, Miss. to fall to the ground writhing and kicking, crying "Don't let it get me." The principal called the phenomenon hysteria and refused to give credence to charges that another girl student had cast a witch's spell on her classmates. Nevertheless, parents kept their children at home for a while.

An autopsy revealed that Mrs. Dorothy Ramsey of Morganton died from excessive use of alcohol and drugs and police found a suicide note. Nevertheless, the dead woman's family brought charges that Mrs. Joan Denton had violated the state's 330-year-old law forbidding the practice of witchcraft. The *Chicago Sun-Times* gave the story almost a full page April 17, 1976 and used a picture of Mrs. Denton holding a plastic skull. April 27, 1976 the *Chicago Daily News* carried a brief undatelined item that Joan Denton would not be prosecuted because Mrs. Denton, whom they called a self-proclaimed witch, did not actually predict Dorothy Ramsey would die on a certain day.

Acting, she said, on the advice of Elvis Presley in a dream, Joan Denton ran for mayor of Morganton, getting 200 of the 2,000 votes cast. Later she attracted attention by staging her own funeral services, stopping just short of interment. Thereafter she kept her coffin in her home. The *Chicago Tribune* gave a half-page to a Knight-Ridder feature by W. J. Speers Nov. 15, 1981.

A directive forbidding use of "voodooism, witchcraft, spiritualism or any kind of mind control over any of the clients" was issued by Dozier T. Allen to Calumet Township (Gary, Ind.) caseworkers according to the *Chicago Sun-Times* for Sept. 22, 1979. The order followed discovery that a caseworker had convinced a client that she had supernatural powers. Under her direction the client returned half of a huge food order to the caseworker for her own use.

Two members of the Church of Arianha, a branch of the Church of Wicca, were to be tried on charges that they shot and killed a 15-year-old Mexican-American girl on a Halloween night when teenagers cruised around the home of Louise and Loy Bean Stone, both 49. The AP covered the story from Plainview, Tex. but the *Chicago Sun-Times* ran no followup.

Yvonne Kleinfelder, a devil worshiper and the head of two covens of witches, was found guilty of murdering her roommate, John Comer, because he mistreated her cats. She beat and poured boiling water over him. She refused to obtain medical aid but attended Pentacostal prayer meetings where she prayed for his recovery.

On the whole books on witchcraft, both those supporting and those condemning it, receive reviews in most papers with book review departments. Especially good were Ralph Thompson's review of *Witchcraft: Its*

Power in the World Today by William Seabrook in the *New York Times* for Sept. 5, 1940 and Alden Whitman's review of *Europe's Inner Demons: An Inquiry Inspired by the Great Witch Hunt,* by Norman Cohn in the *New York Times* for May 3, 1975. Neither this paper nor many others, however, take an adversely critical view of novels, motion pictures and television shows that present some phase of the supernatural as credible. Syndicated advice columnist Abigail Van Buren (Dear Abby) March 28, 1981 advised a correspondent who was convinced he was under a witch's spell to consult a psychiatrist. She said the physician who laughed at his patients' worries should have done so.

A Georgia Supreme Court ruling granting tax exemption status to the Ravenwood Church of Wicca in Atlanta was hailed as a victory for religious freedom for minority religious groups, the AP reported April 12, 1982 from Atlanta. In her syndicated column March 27, 1982 Carol Mathews told a reader she could deduct $5,000 that she gave the church of a psychic who put her in touch with her long-lost family.

That witches can overcome prejudice and live at peace with neighbors was suggested by John Belanger, writing July 21, 1982 for the Cox News Service from Toronto. The Wiccan Church of Canada, the first of its kind to be recognized in Toronto, has so established itself since 1979 that it is applying for tax-exempt status federally and for the right to perform legal marriages. It already had received ministerial privileges in the jails.

Also thriving is the New Bern, N.C. correspondence school in witchcraft conducted by Gavin and Yvonne Frost, who receive from 300 to 1,000 answers to their advertisements weekly. Fellow townsmen, including the mayor, speak kindly of them, according to Jim Spencer's story in the *New York Times* for Aug. 18, 1982.

One form of witchcraft that has baffled researchers for centuries is water witching, which the 2,200 members of the American Society of Dowsers, with headquarters at Danville, Vt., say is not the result of supernatural influence. Ancient Egyptian drawings show figures in strange headgear carrying forked sticks at arm's length in front of them and Emperor Kwang Su of China is depicted in a statue dated 2200 B.C. carrying an identical object, Dr. Lyall Watson, a biologist, reveals in his book *Supernature.*

Dr. Watson's book is only one of many that have been written either to fortify belief in the ancient art or to disprove its possibility. Foremost among American writers who believed in water witching was Kenneth Roberts who wrote *Henry Gross and His Divining Rod* about a leading New England dowser, to use the English term. Outstanding among the books debunking water witching is *Water Witching, U.S.A.* by Evon Z. Vogt, University of Chicago anthropologist, and Ray Hyman, formerly Johns Hopkins and now University of Oregon psychologist. In the *Skeptical Inquirer* for Fall 1979 James Randi reported on controlled experiments with professional dowsers that ended disastrously for them.

About the only attempt at a scientific explanation of the phenomenon was that of Dr. Z. V. Harvalik, a physicist working at an Army research center in Alexandria, Va. at the time he was commended by John Fischer in his Easy Chair column in *Harper's* for January 1970. It was that the human body is quite sensitive to changes in a magnetic field. One way in which the body reacts is with a slight, involuntary twitching of the forearms. Thus it is not the forked stick that is affected by underground water but the holder of the piece of wood or metal rod.

Newspapers mostly have stayed out of the controversy and have not considered dowsing especially newsworthy. There have, of course, been exceptions. Jack McPhaul ridiculed the instructions for making your own divining rod as advertised in a pulp magazine. His article in the *Chicago Times* for July 6, 1945 was the last of a series based on responses he received from mail order houses. Sept. 15, 1947 the *Chicago Sun-Times* used a short story about Edward Riebel of Udine, Ill., who estimates he has found water for approximately 400 wells during the 27 years he has practiced the art. The 1955 *Agriculture Yearbook,* published by the Department of Agriculture, was devoted entirely to the subject of water. In it Arthur M. Sowder, an extension forester, described how he dowsed but admitted most scientists were skeptical. The *Chicago Daily News* quoted from the book Dec. 13, 1955 in a sidebar to a story from Addis Ababa, Ethiopia by its correspondent George Weller that Emperor Haile Selassie had ordered an American well-drilling team to transfer its efforts from an airfield to the capital to find water for the emperor's new swimming pool.

Divining rods were used to discover tunnels that the North Vietnamese might use to attack American Marines defending Khe Sanh in northwest South Vietnam. John Randolph wrote a lengthy description of the operation for the *Los Angeles Times* March 24, 1968. The next day, in its Answer column, the *Los Angeles Herald Examiner* said the evidence against the magical power of willow sticks outweighs the claims of psychics and others.

How Hubert Wyant, 67, made use of what he said was "a gift from the good Lord" was related in an AP story April 8, 1974 from Hurricane, W. Va. Since he learned the practice at the age of nine from his father, Wyant said he found 25 or 30 wells annually, mostly without a fee.

After searching for years without success for a fortune his grandfather supposedly buried somewhere in the Ozarks, a reader asked the *Chicago Tribune* Action Express for help. Although expressing disbelief the column's conductor June 28, 1974 directed the fortune hunter to a few dowsers.

In her syndicated column for Oct. 5, 1975 Dorsey Connors gave detailed instructions in how to make a divining rod out of wire coat-hangers.

Although most dowsing has been for water there are some water witchers who use it to detect metals, including gold. John Noble Wilford covered the 16th annual convention of the American Society of Dowsers in Danville, Vt., reporting on it Sept. 21, 1977 in the *New York Times*. Several failed in their effort to find gold believed to have been left in a burned-down house. Raymond C. Wiley, the society's secretary, defended dowsing as "an exercise of a human faculty which allows one to obtain information in some manner beyond the power and scope of the standard human senses."

In 1979 Harold Johnson retired as mayor of Hatton, Wash. (population, 74) to be cited in the *Guinness Book of World Records* for having been a mayor the longest, 48 years. The UPI story Aug. 22, 1979 of Johnson's retirement, however, stressed the fact that he was a water witcher, getting his start when the town's well ran dry early in his administration. He used a hell-horn can.

Under the caption "A Big Dipper," the *New York Sunday News* devoted three pages Dec. 7, 1980 to the proper directions George Kaufman, 67, gave Consolidated Edison workers to enable them to uncover a k2-strand copper cable whose location was improperly marked on their street map. The old man insisted that the Rockefellers kept an Indian dowser on their payroll and that Nelson Rockefeller had 12 divining rods. Also Albert Einstein practiced dowsing, the article said, and Herbert Hoover used German dowsers to rediscover lost tin mines in England.

Oil companies maintain dowsers as backup advisors to geologists and plumbers and electricians can underbid competitors by dowsing to find leaks and other complications, according to Sandy Stalnaker in a story in the *Glendale* (Calif.) *News-Press* for March 12, 1981, inspired by a seminar on dowsing at Glendale College. And at Green Forest, Ark. the Associated Press reported Oct. 3, 1981 that during the preceding decade Steve Work found water 40 times in 40 tries, but Orville Wisc, a geologist, said there's no evidence that dowsing is anything but tomfoolery.

In the late '40s a 17-year-old South African named Pieter Van Jaasvelt attracted the attention of several American magazines because of his X-ray eyes, so-called. Merely by staring at the ground, without the aid of a forked stick or other implement, Pieter was said to have discovered thousands of dollars worth of coal, gold and diamonds as well as water. *Life* wrote this up April 25, 1949.

Sept. 22, 1975 the AP sent a story from Caledonia, Ohio about a retired welder who says he's never missed when he used a forked stick to find water. After years of donating his services he now charges. He doesn't know how he does it and only the *Chicago Sun-Times* editor who played the story on page 4 knows why it was supposed to be news. Perhaps it was meant to coincide with the American Society of Dowsers' convention being held in Danville, Vt. about which the *New York Times* had a brief item Sept. 26, 1982.

17

Fundamentalism

Evangelists and revivalists always have enjoyed a good press in the United States. With few exceptions their words and deeds have been reported objectively, almost reverently. Even Elmer Gantry-type frauds have been treated with respect. Most of the churches or movements started by evangelists, however, have not outlived their founders by many years. Exceptions are the Christian Science church, founded by Mary Baker Eddy (1821–1910), Church of Jesus Christ of Latter-day Saints, commonly called Mormons, established in 1830 by Joseph Smith (1805–1844), whose long-time successor was Brigham Young (1801–1877), and Jehovah's Witnesses, an outgrowth of the International Bible Students Association in Pittsburgh led by Charles Taze Russell (1852–1916), whose successor, Joseph Franklin Rutherford (1869–1942), named it in 1931.

During the past century the principal headline grabbers among the evangelists and revivalists have been:

—Dwight L. Moody (1837–1899), who believed in a literal translation of the Bible and the imminence of a second coming of Jesus. In 1889 he founded the Moody Bible Institute in Chicago, where the instruction is still fundamentalist.

—William Ashley (Billy) Sunday (1862–1935), a major league baseball player who "struck out the devil" and preached a gynmastic fundamentalism as an ordained Presbyterian minister, converting perhaps 75,000.

—John Alexander Dowie (1847–1907), an Australian Congregational minister who came to Zion, Ill. in 1888 to become the First Apostle of the Lord Jesus Christ and General Overseer of the Christian Catholic Apostolic Church. In 1906 the church ousted him for misuse of investments, tyranny and polygamy.

—Wilbur Glenn Voliva (1870–1942), Dowie's successor and for 35 years despotic ruler of Zion. Ownerships of all industries were in his name; there were no paved streets and laws were strictly enforced against smoking, profanity, cosmetics, oysters, pork and cigarets. In 1914 he won worldwide attention by declaring the world is flat. He also obtained worldwide publicity for his prediction that the world would end Sept. 10, 1934, later changed to 1943, by which time he was dead. The *Chicago Daily News* had two long Beeline answers on Voliva in its issues of July 26, 1971 and Feb. 10, 1978. Sept. 5, 1973 it also gave the address, Box 2533, Lancaster, Calif. 93534, of the International Flat Earth Research Society of the Covenant People's Church together with a map of the world as Voliva saw it and an explanation of the basis for the belief.

—Benjamin (King Ben) Purnell, who from 1903 until his death in 1927 presided over the House of David in Benton Harbor, Mich., where presumably the "chosen descendants of the 12 lost tribes of Israel" still await the millennium in 2000. In 1892 Ben declared himself the Seventh Messenger of the Kingdom of Heaven assigned to gather 12,000 members from each of the 12 tribes to obtain immortality at the millennium. A year before his death Purnell was convicted of morals charges brought by some young women colonists. In a much publicized trial it was revealed that King Ben, who required celibacy among the membership, appointed himself "cleaner of the blood" in charge of deflowering the daughters of parishioners. Answers to inquiries appeared in the *Chicago Daily News* Beeline for June 13, 1970 and the *Chicago Tribune's* Action Line for Dec. 12, 1974.

—Aimee Semple McPherson (1890–1944), who established the International Church of the Four Square Gospel in 1926 with headquarters in her Angelus Temple in Los Angeles. Her platform antics were reminiscent of those of Billy Sunday. She lost credibility when she disappeared while swimming in the ocean and reappeared wandering alone in the desert to tell a story of having been kidnapped. It was noted that her radio operator was absent during almost the same time.

—Father M. J. Divine (1881–1965), born George Baker in Savannah, Ga., who established the Kingdom of Peace with numerous "heads" in and near New York City. His resident disciples, called angels, transferred all their worldly belongings to him. He claimed 15 million followers worldwide and he survived numerous exposés of misconduct.

—William Franklin "Billy" Graham (b. 1918) has conducted crusades for fundamental Christianity since shortly after his graduation from Wheaton College, Wheaton, Ill. Without question he has outstripped all rivals with the crowds his revival meetings all over the world have obtained and the publicity his crusades have received. He has been the confidante and golf companion of every president since Truman and his pronouncements on political matters get headlines, as when he told Ernie Hill of the *Chicago Daily News* Dec. 15, 1952 that he had a way to end the Korean war that he would present to President Eisenhower. March 22, 1973 the UPI reported from Johannesberg, South Africa that Graham advocated castration for rapists and the death penalty for many crimes. Near the end of the Vietnam war he received headlines for saying the war had been a tragedy. His theology was expressed in a quotation that the *Chicago Sun-Times* published June 5, 1971: "The devil and his legionnaires are gathering steam for a great last campaign of conquest on this Earth."

Headquartered in Minneapolis, the Billy Graham Evangelistic Enterprises include a television production company and a movie company, the total budget exceeding $30 million annually. Graham is in the Religious Broadcasters Hall of Fame and is considered by many to be the father of modern "electronic evangelism," which now consists of 1,400 Christian-owned radio stations and three television networks. In a lengthy profile in the *Washington Post* for Jan. 19, 1981, Megan Rosenfeld related the change in Graham's attitude toward nuclear warfare from indifference to outright opposition. In May 1982 he went to Moscow for the World Congress of Religious Leaders Against Nuclear Wars and preached in Moscow's only Baptist church. He came in for considerable adverse criticism when he said there is much more religious freedom in the Soviet Union than most Americans believe. Anthony Barbieri, Jr. of the *Baltimore Sun* reported Graham's words May 13, 1982, "I went to three Orthodox churches Saturday night and they were jammed to capacity. You'd never see that in Charlotte, N.C."—his home town. A few days later he explained that North Carolinians don't go to church on Saturdays. Typical of the editorial comment was what Irv Kupcinet wrote in his *Chicago Sun-Times* column for May 13, 1982: "The Rev. Billy Graham is walking the tightest rope of his life while attending that convention . . . He's avoiding any mention of human rights lest he offend the host nation and is confining himself to the glory of religion. His silence on human rights is deafening. It is unlike Graham and is impairing his image."

The AP reported May 17 the explanation Graham gave for his trip on ABC's "This Week With David Brinkley" was that Jesus said "Go ye into all the world and preach the gospel." He didn't say, "Go into capitalist countries only." May 20 the UPI quoted Graham from New York as saying, "I am not a Communist" and denying that he was used.

A generation ago the Rev. Charles Coughlin of Royal Oak, Mich. and Bishop Fulton Sheen, both Roman Catholics, were pioneers in the use of radio for religious and political advocacy. Today preachers of many faiths make more use of the airways than they do of the pulpit or platform. Brian J. Kelly did a roundup, "Evangelicalism: From Tents to the Big Time" for the *Chicago Sun-Times* of Nov. 13, 1977. His evaluation of the five he considered the most potent follows:

> Oral Roberts, with annual income for operations of $50 million a year, who built Oral Roberts University from 500 acres of farmland into a major university with $150 million worth of buildings in less than 10 years. He's now raising $100 million for "the greatest project of my life"—a 60-story hospital and medical research complex.
>
> Bill Bight, whose Campus Crusade for Christ is now a $34 million corporation with 6,000 employees worldwide and a broad range of publishing and media services, and who may have substantial Washington clout.

Rex Humbard, the godfather of evangelical television, who reaches 250 stations from his Akron (Ohio) Cathedral of Tomorrow and takes in $12 million a year in contributions.

Garner Ted Armstrong, who runs the Worldwide Church of God and a religion empire that includes schools, publications, television and radio broadcasts as well as a lavish life-style for himself and many of his executives. Estimated annual income for his operations, $60 million.

M. G. (Pat) Robertson, founder of the Christian Broadcasting Network, which is on the verge of forming a fourth television network to offer "alternative wholesome programming." His sophisticated facilities include a number of satellite stations, enabling him to broadcast around the world.

Since Kelly's article the City of Faith, to which the *Daily Oklahoman* of Oklahoma City referred Feb. 12, 1981 as "this gleaming $120 million showcase of superlatives," was opened Dec. 2, 1981. Reporters who covered the opening reported, as did Bruce Buursma in the *Chicago Tribune,* that Roberts told a crowd of 10,000, "I saw Jesus and he looked about 900 feet tall. Now some of my fellow ministers thought I was crazy—one of them said that Jesus was 5 foot 7—but the eyes of my soul can see real good."

On the Phil Donahue show May 6, 1982 Roberts reiterated that he saw the gigantic Jesus "with my inner eyes, not my physical eyes," the AP reported May 7 from Tulsa.

Roberts says that God healed him of tuberculosis and stuttering when he was 17 and called him to the ministry four years later. In the *New York Times* for April 22, 1973 Edward B. Fiske reported that by then Roberts had laid his hands on one million persons, there being no way to determine how many were cured. Roberts' organization, with a $17 million annual budget, received lengthy sympathetic feature treatment by Jerry le Blanc in the *Chicago Tribune* for April 4, 1972, by Paul Galloway in the *Chicago Sun-Times* for Nov. 5, 1972 and by Bruce Buursma in the *Chicago Tribune* for Jan. 3, 1982.

After considerable controversy because of the Christian oath demanded of students, the School of Law of Oral Roberts University at Tulsa was accredited by the American Bar Association. Lee Shobel wrote a comprehensive piece on the issue for the *Chicago Tribune* of Aug. 10, 1981.

Another *Tribune* columnist, Jack Mabley, went further than any of his contemporaries in sideswiping Roberts. July 2, 1981 his piece began as follows:

Oral Roberts keeps asking me for money. "Dear Brother Mabley," says the Oklahoma evangelist, "WE HAVE AN EMERGENCY. And because I feel you are a part of this family, I must tell you about it. . . .

"Brother Mabley, we don't discuss our business with just anyone, but this is big. This emergency is bigger than Evelyn and I both. And if I can't talk to you, then who can I talk to?"

Brother Roberts, somebody in your mail room goofed, because the last I heard I was on the side of the devil. I'm one of the forces of evil who said you shouldn't get a permit for your grandiose hospital because Tulsa already has enough hospitals. I also expressed doubt that Jesus picked up the building in his arms, though you say you saw him do it.

Brother Roberts needs an EMERGENCY MIRACLE because his City of Faith Hospital is to open Nov. 1 and he needs millions of dollars to pay subcontractors and their laborers and for equipment and the payroll for doctors and nurses and technicians.

When his son, 38, a dope addict, committed suicide Roberts said, "The devil has played his last card. I sometimes feel at peace."

In reporting activities of a minor or little-known religious sect the press generally attempts to explain the group's main characteristics. The UP did this Feb. 21, 1936 when it reported the death of a magazine writer in Albuquerque supposedly killed by members of the Penitente. The cultists were not guilty but got more than a column of publicity in papers throughout the country. Furthermore, April 11, 1936 the Associated Press covered the Penitente convention in New Mexico. Throwbacks to the Penitentes of the Middle Ages, the members carried heavy crosses up mountainsides on feet stuck in shoes filled with sharp pebbles and with circulation cut off by wire bindings. At other conventions Penitentes beat themselves and each other with cat-o'-nine-tails. The same day, the last day of Lent, the United Press reported from Albuquerque that the tortured body of a man was to be cut down from a cross. If alive he would be taken to Les Hermanos se Penitente for medical attention; if dead he would be buried on a hilltop. In either case he would be honored for his part in the 40 days of self-torture, which included rolling on cactus beds, beating themselves, cutting their flesh and inflicting other injuries to their bodies.

April 17, 1983 the *Chicago Tribune* devoted almost a full page to an illustrated article by Robert Cross about Los Hermanos Penitentes with headquarters at San Antonio, Colo. The members are mostly Hispanic Americans who carried on the traditional activities for decades during which Catholic clergymen did not dare enter the territory. The church finally recognized them in 1947.

While 4,000 watched, for the sixth consecutive year Juanito Piring, a laborer, was nailed to a 16-foot wooden cross on Good Friday, April 12, 1974, the AP reported the next day from San Fernando, Philippines. Piring wore a white loin cloth, a curly wig and a crown of thorns and the man who drove the nails through the palms of his hands was dressed like a Roman soldier. Piring remained aloft only about ten seconds.

July 14, 1938 the *New York Times* devoted almost a column to AP and UP accounts from Chichester, England that a son had been virtually excommunicated from the Church of England for failure to obey the commandment "to honor thy father and thy mother." According to a suicide note left by his parents, he had not aided them when they were in dire financial need.

"For the 26th time in as many years sinners by the score rushed to the prayer rail of the tabernacle of the Pillar of Fire sect" on the campus of Alma White College at Zarephath, N.J., the *New York Herald Tribune* reported Aug. 25, 1936. Leading the militant assault on that "satanic devil Lucifer with his heart as black as Hell" was Bishop Alma White, 74, founder and leader of the sect which assigns to everlasting damnation bridge players, cinema lovers and the devil's wife, Dame Fashion.

Equally adamant in her condemnation of modernism was 8-year-old Renee Martz, the AP reported Feb. 5, 1948 from Los Angeles. The child, already an evangelist like her two parents, was credited with having "led 6,000 souls up to the altar to confess their sins and accept Jesus Christ." She told a reporter: "You are not interested in movies, you don't even go to see them if you are saved."

Members of the Holiness Church of God in Jesus Christ believe that snakes represent the devil and if one can handle them s/he is a channel for God's power over Satan. Sept. 13, 1947 the Associated Press distributed pictures and story of a service at Hall Station, Ga. at which "fanatic hill folk groveled in the dust of a backwoods clearing in clamorous and convulsive rites which bid the faithful to handle serpents and sometimes to drink poison." A fortnight earlier a man died after taking poison but the minister was acquitted because there was no law against carrying poison.

Oct. 13, 1947 the United Press covered a similar service at Stone Creek, Va. The accompanying picture showed a 13-year-old girl fondling a snake that had bitten her but from whose bite she recovered despite a paralyzed hand and gangrene. When Virginia highway patrolmen arrived to enforce the state's anti-snake handling law the cultists stepped a few feet away to be in Kentucky. Although 29 persons were reported to have died from snake bites incurred during religious rites before Lisa Alther attended a service in Carson Springs, Tenn., members fondled copperheads, cottonmouths and rattlesnakes for photographers. The illustrated story appeared in the *New York Times Magazine* for June 6, 1966.

"Serpent handlers' worship God . . . to their own conscience" was the two-page streamer headline on a doubletruck feature on the Holiness Church of God in Jesus Christ in the University of Tennessee *Daily Beacon* for April 30, 1973. The author, G. Frank Munger, attended services in Carson Springs Community Church of Cocke County, interviewed the pastor, Liston Pack, and observed him and some others in the congregation of 48 handle poisonous snakes. Pack's brother Buford Pack, and the assistant pastor, Jimmy Ray Williams, had died in convulsions after drinking a mixture containing poisonous strychnine. The tragedy was only one of several incidents to make headlines since the church's founding in 1969. Pack explained that one is immune to poisonous snake bites or liquid doses when he feels anointed.

To find out how snake cultists perform rites with poisonous reptiles and stay alive, the *Chicago Daily News* interviewed Bert Tschambers, head of the Lincoln Park zoo reptile house. Oct. 25, 1947 the paper quoted him as believing the snake worshipers probably use "pre-handled" snakes and species less potent than many others. Almost any snake, he said, will strike the first time it's picked up; thereafter the snake enjoys having its head stroked. But he said, "Anyone who handles poisonous snakes when he doesn't have to is crazy."

In 1963 Robert Grimston and a handful of likeminded people in London, England formed the nucleus of the Process Church of the Final Judgement. March 20, 1971 Roy Larson reported in a full-page article in the *Chicago Sun-Times* that there were chapters in most large American cities. Church members, believers in the imminence of Doomsday, worshiped "the three great gods of the universe—Jehovah, Lucifer and Satan, in the belief that "all three of the gods exist to some extent in every one of us and the individual achieves salvation "through the reconcilation of opposites." Aug. 21, 1971 the *New York Times* devoted two of its long columns to an article by Eleanor Blau based on interviews with church leaders in Cambridge, Mass., one of the four centers, the other three being Chicago, New Orleans and Toronto. Father Christian, a Britisher whose secular name is Jonathan DePeyer, said: "Theology is based on the unity of Christ and Satan. They are two sides of one coin with Jesus representing love, the ultimate good and evil the absence of love."

A short three years later Eleanor Blau reported in the *Times* for Dec. 1, 1974 that a majority of the estimated 6,000 members had broken with Grimston to form the Foundation Church of the Millennium. Father Micah, a minister of the new church, explained, "The idea of loving Satan seemed very logical but when you tried to live it day to day it just didn't work." The Rev. Richard Wood, a Roman Catholic priest and professor at Loyola University in Chicago, commented on what he called "an almost classic example of the development of a sect into a denomination."

In Chicago Father Lucius, chief spokesman for the new church, told Clarence Page of the *Chicago Tribune* that the old church fell prey to "pathetic fatalism."

One of the most fulsome accounts of a religious movement appeared in the *National Observer* for Oct. 10, 1964. Based on first-hand observations, interviews and scholarly research, it explained the nature of the Pentecostal movement, the main feature of which is talking in tongues. During the second half of the present century the movement has spread to virtually every Christian denomination.

" 'Praise-the-Lord-and-pass-the-snake' service is a trip, if you can handle it," was the steamer headline the *Chicago Tribune* gave April 3, 1983 to a half-page article by Garrett Mathews. The illustrated feature described snake worshiping by several small sects in the Appalachian mountains.

"Down through history speaking in tongues has been quite common at the beginning of great religious revivals," the paper reported. "The new tongue speakers differ in many ways from the old-time Pentecostals. They have no intention of splitting off to form new churches, but try instead to make tongue speaking an added dimension of the Christian experience in mainstream churches . . . The Pentecostals tend to regard speaking in tongues as the only conclusive evidence that a person has been filled with the Holy Spirit and thus as the only road to salvation."

After tracing its development from the historic camp meeting in 1801, James H. Bowman March 24, 1973 in the *Chicago Daily News* revealed the existence of 400 to 600 Catholic adherents to Pentacostalism, the charismatic movement that includes speaking in tongues, healing by laying on hands and New Testament neo-fundamentalism. Regular prayer groups meet on the Loyola University campus and other places. Two days later, March 26, 1973, Bowman wrote that Pentacostalism in "probably the fastest growing Christian movement in the United States." In articles March 27 and 28, 1973 he described the movement among Roman Catholics and others.

Charismatic religious leaders make news. May 22, 1972 the UPI reported from Jackson, Miss. that the Rev. W. L. Jenkins, who claims to be the third prophet of God, canceled plans to walk on water at Ross Burnet Reservoir because of a wounded foot.

Prophet Jones, a flamboyant preacher who said that God spoke to him through a gentle breeze fanning his right ear and who once claimed to be the spiritual leader of 6 million, died at 65 in Detroit, Larry Green reported for the Aug. 13, 1971 *Chicago Daily News*. He called his cult the Church of Universal Triumph, the Dominion of God.

The Rev. Jack Lundin of Community of Christ the Savior sees Jesus Christ as a clown figure; one who falls down and gets up again, and so he took his 30 youngsters to meet the clown, an aerial ballet performer and ringmaster of the Ringling Brothers and Barnum & Bailey circus. James H. Bowman reported the affair in the Oct. 14, 1971 *Chicago Daily News*.

A story that Dick Griffin, financial editor, had written in December 1972 was reviewed for an inquiring reader by the *Chicago Daily News'* Beeline July 2, 1973. It was about John Richard McDermott, whose 15-year-old daughter Ellen suddenly began relating parts of the Bible, including the entire 68 chapters of Isaiah although she had never read the Bible. A witness was the Rev. William McMahon, pastor of St. Peter's Catholic church, the only formally established Catholic Pentecostal parish in the United States sanctioned by a Catholic bishop.

The *News* also used a UPI story from Jacksonville, Fla. April 25, 1974 about the arrest of 95 traveling evangelists of the Christ is the Answer church of Weldon, Ill. Customers in a shopping center complained that the missionaries made a nuisance of themselves.

In a column in the *Grand Forks* (N.D.) *Herald* for Oct. 8, 1971 the Rev. Lester Kinsolving lambasted the "paper priests" of California, especially Michael Itkin who dubbed himself President and Metropolitan Bishop-

Abbot of the Holy Orthodox Catholic Synod of the Syro-Chaldean Rite Evangelical Catholic Communion Brotherhood of the Love of Christ, Incorporated.

The largest and most influential college dedicated to the promotion of fundamentalist doctrines is Bob Jones University at Greenville, S.C., "a nondenominational, coeducational, Christian, liberal arts university standing without apology for the old-time religion and the absolute authority of the Bible." It has been the object of quite a few hypercritical magazine articles, such as "New Curricula for Bigotry" by Robert G. Sherrill in the March 8, 1965 *Nation* and "The Buckle on the Bible Belt," by Larry L. King in the June, 1966 *Harper's*. Typical of the respectful treatment the nonaccredited school gets from the press was "Bob Jones U—No Compromise With Satan" by Dana L. Spitzer in the *St. Louis Post-Dispatch* for July 25, 1971. The facts are there, so readers can draw their own conclusions: no blacks or Jews admitted; dating allowed only with a chaperon present; a completely debt-free $37,000,000 campus and a $7 million annual budget raised through tuition fees and gifts that "come from God." Bob Jones III, whose grandfather founded it in 1928, told the St. Louis reporter the school is nonpolitical except when an outstanding candidate is on the ballot. In such cases the school endorses him, as it did Barry Goldwater, George Wallace and Strom Thurmond.

When the Department of State refused to grant a visa for the Rev. Ian Paisley of Northern Ireland to speak at the University, President Bob Jones called Secretary of State Alexander Haig, a Catholic, "a tyrant of the worst sort, a monster in human flesh and a demon-possessed instrument to destroy America." According to the *Buffalo Evening News* for April 4, 1982 Jones called on God to smite Haig "hip and thigh, bone and marrow, heart and lungs."

In October 1982 the United States Supreme Court listened to a prominent Negro lawyer, William T. Coleman, Jr., defend the Internal Revenue Service's ruling that Bob Jones University could not be tax exempt because of its racial policies. In his Oct. 2, 1982 syndicated column, James J. Kilpatrick took an opposite view. The *Chicago Sun-Times* had a comprehensive article on the situation Oct. 13, 1982. By an 8 to 1 vote May 24, 1983 the United States Supreme Court affirmed the authority of the IRS to deny tax exemption to private schools and colleges that discriminate on the basis of race.

James H. Bowman explained seven little-known and small religious movements. For instance, in the *Chicago Daily News* for March 17–18, 1973 he told of the Chicago branch of the Ramakrishna order founded in Calcutta in 1886 to practice a form of Hinduism known as the Vedic religion. It takes ten years of training to be eligible to take vows as a swami or monk. Chicago candidates included former Jews, Lutherans and Presbyterians.

Jan. 31 and Feb. 1, 1974 Bowman's space was filled by a reprint of an article on Brother Lester Roloff that Molly Ivins wrote for *New Times* magazine. The personification of Sinclair Lewis' character, Elmer Gantry, the ex-Baptist minister operated several enterprises, including homes for unwed mothers and elderly, alcoholics, drug addicts and delinquent teenagers. In part Ivins described Brother Roloff's prowess as a preacher: "Pathos, bathos, ridicule, threats, pleadings, promises all whirl in and out of a Roloff sermon. Tears veritably spurt from his eyes . . . and he shuts them off just as suddenly as he starts them." Finally the House Human Relations Committee investigated charges of mistreatment of girl students and Brother Roloff had to curtail his activities. The faithful, however, continued to respond to his radio appeals with thousands of dollars daily. Brother Roloff was killed in an aviation accident Nov. 2, 1982.

The Holy Order of Mans is "a new nondenominational sect with many of the trappings of old-time religion," according to Roy Larson, *Chicago Sun-Times* religion editor, who wrote of his attendance at a service in the Oct. 27, 1978 issue of his paper. In the first five years after the Rev. Earl W. Brighton, a 70-year-old former engineer, founded it in California in 1961, 1,000 men and women took "life vows" pledging themselves to lifetimes of poverty, obedience, humanitarian service, humility and purity. Communicants wear Franciscan garb.

Details of the way members live and operate were given in a long *New York Times* article from San Francisco Aug. 12, 1973. Brighton was quoted, "We are doing things the same way they were done in Paul's time. We help people, we heal the sick, we pray for them."

In the March 25, 1974 edition of his paper, Larson gave a sympathetic description of the Center Group in Evanston, which studied the philosophical ideas of the ancient Chinese sage Lao-tzu under the leadership of a social worker, Eugene Burger. In the Suburban Week section of the same newspaper June 19 & 20, 1974, Neil Goldstein was given two full pages for a writeup of the Evanston Reba Place Fellowship, "a church, a commune and a not-for-profit corporation of about 180 people." It was originated in 1957 by a group of three, sponsored by the Mennonite Church Central Committee.

Still another Larson story was published Jan. 18, 1975 after 53 clergymen and clergywomen, several psychiatrists and psychologists and other mental health specialists spent a day in a Des Plaines hospital with Sri Sunyata, an 84-year-old Dane who turned Buddhist and spent 40 years as a semi-hermit in the Indian Himalayas. The charismatic mystic was introduced not as a guru or a lecturer but as "a presence" who believes Western churches are in decline as youths turn to ancient Eastern religions.

Equally fascinating, Charles Hillinger made it seem in the *Los Angeles Times* for June 16, 1974, is the Temple of the People in Halcyon, Calif., a small community established in 1903 by a group of Theosophists from New York. At the University of Halcyon students are taught to revere Hiawatha, Indian chief who engineered the formation of the Iroquois nations, inspired Benjamin Franklin in planning the Federation of American States and was immortalized in an epic poem by Henry Wadsworth Longfellow. The Halcyon believers rank Hiawatha as a master like Jesus, Buddha and Confucius, all three of whom they believe are alive somewhere today in some form.

One of the most attractive child ministers has been Roy Pheden, Jr., who at 11 was licensed as an associate minister by the King Solomon Baptist Church of Louisville from which place the AP told his story Aug. 3, 1974. The boy declared his "calling" came while he was watching TV and "a strange hail began to fall and I was in heaven with Peter and Paul and Jesus. They called for Gabriel and his horn."

Another tiny religious band threatened with extinction is the United Society of Believers in Christ's Second Appearance, commonly called the Shakers. According to a feature originated by the *Christian Science Monitor* Bureau, published by the *Minneapolis Tribune* March 2, 1975, the membership had shrunk to a mere dozen from the 300 who fled to America from England in 1774. Their basic tenet is celibacy. They have counted on conversions and adoptions to swell their ranks but the dozen now residing in Sabbathday Lake, Me. and Canterbury, N.H. are the survivors of defections from a peak membership of 6,000 a century ago.

Steve Sonsky provided more details in his account in the *Chicago Tribune* for Dec. 27, 1981, after he interviewed a half-dozen members. They told him the nickname Shaker resulted from the enthusiastic ritual dancing in which they formerly engaged. They are respected for the high quality of the functional furniture they manufacture. The Metropolitan Museum of Art in New York has a permanent exhibit and antique collectors constantly search for genuine articles. The Shakers themselves would rather be remembered because of their lifestyle which Sonsky described as "simple, communal, agrarian, founded on these precepts: united inheritance and community of goods, celibacy, nonviolence and openness of mind."

Pleasant Hill, Ky. or Shakertown as it is popularly known, has been designated a national landmark by the U.S. Department of the Interior and in 1981 was visited by 122,000 paying tourists, according to a half-page feature article by Gay Pauley in the *Chicago Sun-Times* for June 6, 1982.

"On any given day in these United States a wife will sweep her kitchen floor with a flat broom; a husband will perform carpentry with a circular saw; someone will wash clothes and employ wooden clothespins to hang garments out to dry; and still another will use a metal point pen to write a letter." That was the first paragraph of a half-page article June 17, 1982 in the *Chicago Tribune* by Hal Butler. He was describing how the sect's members lived in Shakertown, Ky., whence he wrote.

As hard working as the self-sufficient Shakers are the members of the Brotherhood of the Sun in Santa Barbara, Calif., about whom Joan Zyda wrote in the *Chicago Tribune* for July 28, 1976. Under the leadership of Norman Paulsen, a former Los Angeles bricklayer, in seven years the 260 volunteers have built a flourishing, respectable business with their own farm, orchard, a truck fleet, a restaurant and a fishing schooner. The commune has a strict morals code and stresses hard work in addition to meditation and religious sessions. It attracts reformed alcoholics and drug addicts but anyone adverse to hard labor is not happy there.

Although there are probably only 5,000 Tibetan Buddhists in the United States, 25 of them in Chicago, when the Karmapas, the spiritual leader of one branch of the faith, came to the nation's second city, Paul Galloway was assigned to write a half-page article for the *Sun-Times* of Jan. 30, 1977. Galloway opined that there are not more American converts because of the rigorous demands of time, money and intellectual development and also because Tibetan Buddhism doesn't guarantee bliss, relaxation or happiness. One member explained: "It's more of a spiritual practice than a religion. It's not theistic in that we don't believe in God." Nov. 23, 1982 Don Hayner reported in the *Chicago Sun-Times* that there now are about 40,000 Nichiren Buddhists in the United States, about 6,700 of them associated with a temple in DuPage County, Ill., which he visited. Shudo Sugano, the chief priest, explained its operation to him.

The current fascination with Eastern philosophies and spiritual beliefs motivates editors to assign reporters to cover all foreign visitors and natives alike who are converts to any of them. Steve Brown visited the Temple of Ra-Heru-Khuti in the Bolingbrook home of Mrs. Rosemary Clark who founded it in 1975. Brown attended a ceremony reenacting the Egyptian rites of the new moon. Candles and incense and prayers invoking the powers of Ra, ancient Egyptian sun god, contributed to the members' efforts to develop personal qualities often not stressed or actually neglected in modern Western society. Brown's account appeared in the June 25, 1977 *Chicago Daily News*.

The same paper Sept. 21, 1977 used Bonnie Gross' half-page feature about Rochunga Pudaite, a native Indian who established Bibles for the World to mail free Bibles to foreign countries from his Wheaton, Ill. headquarters. The evangelist describes himself as from a primitive backward tribe in northeast India. In 1910 his father was the only convert to Christianity in the area.

"Preacher Will" Campbell came alive in a half-page feature by Roy Larson in the Dec. 12, 1977 *Chicago Sun-Times*. Campbell, director of the Committee of Southern Churchmen, has enraged both conservatives and liberals by his neutrality on social issues and his attempts to minister to aggressors as well as the oppressed.

In his paper March 6, 1978 Larson did a half-page piece on "one of the major success stories in contemporary American religion." The subject was Dr. Robert H. Schuller of Garden Grove Community Church in Garden Grove, Cal. Wrote Larson: "The fast-paced service geared to rhythms of the

Age of Television and the Age of the Expressway began with a bang and ended with a bang. In between there was no dead time."

Bob Greene used a Q and A technique to let Ben Adkins explain Astro Soul in his *Chicago Tribune* column for May 1, 1978. Although he confessed that he considered self-improvement programs to be "by tootie-footies for tootie-footies," Greene made no editorial comments when Adkins, who made a living as a meat salesman, told him there is no death because energy is indestructible. He insisted that a haze Greene thought he saw was the aura of his female companion who backed up against the wall for the experiment.

Gene Muztain used a similar tactic to introduce *Chicago Sun-Times* readers to the Rev. Frederick J. Eckerenkoetter II, ordinarily known as Rev. Ike, the flamboyant black founder of the United Church Science of Living Institute in New York City, a multimillion-dollar operation promoting Ike-isms on more than 1,000 radio and television stations and to 2-million-plus circulation magazines. Asked to "say cheese" by a photographer, Rev. Ike replied, "Say money. With money you can buy all the cheese you want." Despite the man's wisecracking the reporter was able to learn that "the message" was a black man's version of the positive mental attitudes Norman Vincent Peale and W. Clement Stone have been talking about to whites.

If one can believe Fern Schumer's story in the *Chicago Tribune* for Dec. 2, 1981 Rev. Ike has a rival for the title of "most charismatic" in the Rev. Wilbur N. Daniel whose histrionic tactics resulted in an increase in membership in the Antioch Missionary Baptist Church of Englewood from 600 to 4,500 between 1959 and 1981. A Bible thumper, he meets the needs of the black community. Parishioners dance, writhe, moan and have convulsions during his raucous services. According to the headline writer the Rev. Mr. Daniel is "politicking for the Lord—a power broker for the Lord's children."

Another religious leader who boasts about money making while he battles the Internal Revenue Service is Kirby J. Hensley, founder of the Universal Life Church centered in Modesto, Cal. Scott Forter wrote a full-page article about him and his colleagues for the Aug. 29–Sept. 4, 1979 issue of *In These Times*. Hensley got his start by the mass ordination of thousands of youths who wanted to avoid military service in Vietnam and who donated one dollar each to Hensley's organization which the IRS finally gave church status and tax exemption. Keith L'Hommedier, head of the ULC Sacerdotal Order, retired from the real estate business and began selling ministerial credentials, from 50 to 500 a week, according to different estimates. Hensley says ULC is the only organized church in the world with no traditional religious doctrine. He also admits religion is the freest when it is profitable.

In an interview with Don Bishoff that appeared in the *Eugene Register-Guard* for May 11, 1977, Hensley raised the number he had ordained to 6 million, making his "the fastest growing church" in America. He told Bishoff:

> I was first in mail-order ministry. I was first in baptism through the mail. I was first in trial marriage—I done a one-year trial marriage over television.
>
> I've married through the mail and over the phone. Dozens and dozens of things I'm doing no other churches have done.
>
> I will make a saint out of you which only the Catholic church does now, through the mail. Give us five dollars to help support the church and we'll give you a beautiful certificate with a gold seal on it, to prove it. Then you can put "Saint" in front of your name and can't nobody make you take it off.

Bishoff concluded that Hensley is "a con man, a philosopher, a religious nut, an anti-religious nut, a put-on of a crusader," all of the above.

The Internal Revenue Service was reported by the *New York Times* Aug. 24, 1980 to be alarmed over the growth of "mail order ministries," which for a "donation" provide church charters and ministers' credentials to persons who use them to avoid paying large taxes. The Universal Life Church of Modesto, Calif. was cited as having ordained some 10 million ministers by mail and with issuing 50,000 charters, according to its founder Kirby J. Hensley, a self-appointed bishop.

Another headache for the IRS is the Ethiopian Coptic Church, a 2,700 member Jamaica-based sect with Miami headquarters. Lynn Emmemerman reported in the *Chicago Tribune* Sept. 29, 1980 that up to that time the church had not paid $2.3 million in back taxes nor a $15 million fine imposed by the U.S. Customs Service for illegal imports. Brother Louv, onetime Thomas Frances Reilly, Jr., the church's spokesman, said: "We smoke marihuana to get closer to God. It's the sacrament, the body and blood of Jesus Christ."

Just about every Christian sect today faces the demands of feminists for full equality, including ordination and ministration of the sacraments. In Waco, Texas the feminist revolt took a new direction with the demand of a group led by Mrs. Lois Roden to recognize the fact that the Holy Spirit is a woman. As the *Waco Times Herald* reported Dec. 28, 1980, most of the men withdrew from Mrs. Roden's branch of the Seventh Day Adventist Church but are slowly returning.

All of the examples cited so far in this chapter illustrate the extent to which the press attempts to describe and explain the beliefs and activities of lesser known religious groups. Religion pages in large newspapers contain accounts of discussions and enactments of procedures, creeds, dogmas and the like. Theological differences are neither played down nor sensationalized. Matters of concern to members of a church are reported objectively.

In addition to such news there is much that is of interest to the general public for a variety of reasons, as illustrated by the following events that received headlines within the past generation.

A love cult led by a Monsieur Boe, self-proclaimed spiritual son of Jesus, was broken up by police upon evidence that he whipped disciples to cure them of bodily ills. The AP sent a story from Bordeaux Sept. 6, 1936. The AP also reported July 7, 1936 from Cape Mount, Liberia that the Human Leopards, a dreaded secret cult, successfully abducted two children before being driven away.

The modern nation of Israel was not a year old before a Dutch man signing himself H187 asked the Israeli supreme court to review the trial of Jesus Christ. The plaintiff assumed that the court is the direct and legal successor to the Jewish high court under the Romans that condemned Jesus to die on the cross for blasphemy. The petition was filed Dec. 15, 1948. The AP distributed an account Jan. 31, 1949 from Jerusalem.

From Nelson, British Columbia the UP reported Dec. 1, 1949 that the Doukhobors were accused of trying to blow up a Canadian Pacific Railway bridge, the third such incident within a fortnight.

After ten women members of the Sons of Freedom division of the Doukhobors were sent to prison for 2½-year terms for stripping, police were on guard for more outbreaks of arson, according to a UP story from Krestove, N.C. April 28, 1960. Within a ten-day period 18 homes had been destroyed by fire with naked Freedomites in 41-degree weather chanting Russian hymns.

Conversion of a celebrity, especially a glamorous movie star, to a religious life always is news. Colleen Townsend, a promising starlet, told a Youth for Christ rally in Chicago that she would quit Hollywood for a theological seminary, the *Chicago Daily News* reported Feb. 3, 1950. Three days later, Feb. 6, the AP reported from Punxsutawney, Pa. that the actress attracted 1,200 to hear her preach in the Norman Gothic Presbyterian Church where usually only 300 attend services.

From Hollywood the UP reported Feb. 8, 1950 that 25 movie celebrities, including Jane Russell, announced they had banded together "to bring God and religion to show business." That this was not unusual was the gist of a roundup article from Hollywood by Sheilah Graham that the *Chicago Daily News* used Feb. 18, 1950. Graham mentioned 25 or more actors and actresses who teach Sunday School classes, sing in choirs, donate earnings to religious groups and are devout worshipers. Her article mentioned Gale Storm, Roy Rogers and Dale Evans, Loretta Young, Ann Blythe, Ginger Rogers, Ann Moorehead and others, altogether a prestigious bunch.

When, three years later, June Haver quit show business to become a nun the UP broadcast another comprehensive piece Feb. 6, 1953. In addition to those cited by Graham, the story mentioned Virginia Mayo, Tim Spence, Connie Haines, Marilyn Monroe and several others.

Also newsworthy are religious athletes to whom James H. Bowman gave almost a full page in the March 27–28, 1976 *Chicago Daily News*. About 1,000 groups of high school students, 250 college groups and 300 adult groups are affiliated with the Fellowship of Christian Athletes, organized in 1955 by Don McClanen, an Oklahoma coach who had the assistance of major league baseball stars George Kell, Carl Erskine and Alvin Dark and the owner-manager Branch Rickey. John Erickson, former basketball coach at the University of Wisconsin, its president, explained the PCA's purpose: "to confront athletes and coaches, and through them the youth of the nation and get them to witness the life of Christ in their sports."

When Brock Davis was sent to the minors by the Chicago Cubs in 1971 he consulted a fellow Christian, Don Kessinger, who advised Davis to pray harder. He did and a month later was brought back to Chicago, according to Bill Gleason's article in the *Chicago Sun-Times* for June 10, 1971.

A newer organization with a similar purpose is Athletes in Action sponsored by Campus Crusade for Christ. Its members among professional teams keep many speaking engagements at high schools and youth rallies.

Whenever college students swallow goldfish, streak or perform other unusual acts the press accommodates by giving them the publicity they desire. The rule holds true when a campus becomes imbued with a revival fever as happened in February 1950 at Wheaton College, Wheaton, Ill., Billy Graham's alma mater. "1,500 Students Pray 21 Hours" was the 4-col. 2 line headline in the *Chicago Daily News* for Feb. 9, 1950. The subheads summarized the story: "Fervor Grips Wheaton Hall" and "Each Rises to Publicly Repent in Spontaneous Revival." The page 1 story was accompanied by a 4-col. picture, "Students Listen Intensely to Revival Talks." An inside page was devoted completely to pictures of the event. The next day's streamer headline was "College Halts Revival," and "Press Steps in, Classes Renewed," together with more pictures of prayerful youths. March 4, 1950 the *News* had a followup, "How Wheaton Revival Affected Student Lives." The consensus of a half-dozen students was that there was much less griping about the meals and other matters. A decade later, Dave Meade, religion editor, did a "Stranger Goes to Church" piece for the Jan. 11, 1960 *News,* "Wheaton College's Beliefs Unshaken by Darwin Theory." The school was founded in 1860 shortly after publication of *The Origin of Species*.

Another marathon revival lasted for five days beginning Feb. 24, 1950 at Asbury College in Wilmore, Ky. It began when one student stood up in chapel and asked to speak. From then on students, faculty members and townspeople joined in praying, singing and relating religious experiences. After the revival passed the 48-hour mark a professor told the AP, "This is not some kind of emotional experience, like that at Wheaton." At the end of the 100th hour there were still 150 in the auditorium and students from nearby colleges came to participate for short periods. After that press association coverage petered out.

"They've given the old time religion a boogie beat and it's packing them in by the thousands down in Dixie," was the lead paragraph of an AP story March 2, 1952 from Thomasville, Ga. It told of the popularity of all-night concerts of religious music by quartets and trios of entertainers. "It's the kind of music you never hear in church. Swaying, whirling and often leaping in the air in exuberation; they've put everything they've got into such ditties as 'I Got Happy When I Got Saved,' 'Better Get Down on Your Knees and Pray'," and so forth.

When someone comes foul of the law because of his/her religious beliefs, it's often news. The *Chicago Tribune* used a story Aug. 29, 1951 from a special correspondent in Toledo about two brothers who faced loss of their jobs because they refused to join the Brotherhood of Locomotive Firemen and Engineers which had a union shop agreement. They belonged to a religious group known as the Plymouth Brethren and invoked II Corinthians, sixth chapter and 14th verse, "Be ye not unequally yoked together with unbelievers, etc."

The question "What is a Christian?" became the main issue in a suit to break the will of a Waterloo, Iowa man who directed that his trustees distribute "to such persons and for such purposes as they may feel are directed by God the Father, Jesus Christ the Son and the Holy Spirit." Headlines over the AP story went to the testimony of a Unitarian minister that it is not necessary to believe in the divinity of Jesus to be a Christian and exactly contradictory testimony by a Roman Catholic chaplain.

A St. Paul man was charged with the deaths because of floggings of his grandmother and wife as part of a religious cult ceremony, the UP reported Oct. 18, 1951. The man, who also had welts as the result of beatings, said his group believed in "beating the Devil" out of its own members who otherwise read the Bible and sing hymns.

From Montgomery, Ala. the AP reported May 8, 1952 that a Baptist minister said his congregation dismissed him because "I am too strict in preaching God's word. I am too strict in my beliefs in God's book." What he did to antagonize his congregation was to say in a sermon: "We have among the membership of this church, theft, robbery, dishonesty, falsehood and open adultery—not to mention the so-called little sins."

It took 25 policemen to quell a riot in which two priests of the St. Nicholas Ukrainian Catholic Cathedral in Chicago were injured by angry parishioners demanding that the Feast of the Epiphany be observed according to the old Julian calendar, Jan. 19. In vain the priests tried to quiet the worshipers, mostly immigrants from eastern Europe, telling them the church had adopted the Gregorian calendar which meant Epiphany on Jan. 6. Hugh Hough covered the incident for the Jan. 20, 1968 *Chicago Sun-Times*.

Another church had legal troubles when Mrs. Emma Bolton sued the Church of the Covenant of Lake Forest, Ill. to recover $10,000 she had given it on the persuasion of her second husband and the pastor. They told her the money was needed to appease the spirits that were guarding her first husband who had been a sinner, the *Sun-Times* reported Dec. 3, 1971.

Court orders are needed sometimes to overcome parental objections to medical treatment for a member of Christian Science, Jehovah's Witnesses or other denomination. Such happened when a 15-year-old boy was badly hurt in a motorcycle accident and police could not persuade the boy's father to permit even the use of splints, Larry Ingrassia reported for the *Sun-Times* Aug. 30, 1974.

Religious fasting that leads to a fatality often obtains journalistic headlines. One such story was reported Nov. 11, 1974 from Mayhill, N.M. by the UPI. A Pittston, Pa. psychologist and his 13-year-old daughter died of starvation in a van parked on a desert roadside with window signs including "We serve God and man" and "You like your beliefs to be respected so please respect ours." The wife-and-mother also was near death as were three young sons.

In Finland, Reuters reported May 21, 1975 from Rovaniemi, an extreme brand of Lutheranism started a campaign to save people from going to hell by smashing their television sets as they did radios in the 1920s. The sect, Laestadians, was established in the 19th century by a Swede, Lars Levi Laestadius.

It is possible for one to have the law on his/her side and still be punished by a religious group. That is what was predicted for Robert Bear who was excommunicated by the Reformed Mennonite church for "railing," which means criticizing a church doctrine. Bear's wife obeyed the church's order that she shun her husband; she refused even to talk to him and alienated his children from him. Bear brought suit in Cumberland County Court according to a UPI story from Carlisle, Pa. Nov. 24, 1975.

Although he lost his alienation-of-affections suit against the church, the UPI reported Sept. 27, 1978, Bear continued to try to woo his family back. He said it was like living with a girlie show as his wife would allow all intimacies except intercourse for fear she would be damned. He refused the church's offer to reinstate him if he apologized. He charged the church with "playing God." Dec. 5, 1979 the *Chicago Sun-Times* reported that Bear was acquitted by a jury of having abducted his wife whom he restrained for 30 minutes in his truck.

Nov. 30, 1981 the UPI reported from Plainfield, Pa. that Bear tried to see some of his ten children who had shunned him for a decade. He asked two girls how to find his son whom he knew was working nearby. Belatedly he realized that one of the girls was his daughter.

The *Honolulu Star-Bulletin* reported Aug. 30, 1976 that eight members of a religious sect called the Source fought a court order to surrender the body of a co-worker who was an accident victim. The sect believes it takes 3½ days for the soul to leave a body.

Douglas Ray Sumner of Tampa, Fla., who belonged to what a Baptist minister called "a way-out religious group," apparently spent two weeks chained to a tree before he died in a thicket near the Gulf of Mexico, the *Chicago Daily News* reported Sept. 22, 1978.

Several cities have experienced attempts to prevent the use of public property for nativity scenes during the Christmas season. The UPI reported Dec. 19, 1979 from Denver that the United States Appellate Court had upset a District Court order to the city to remove the $25,000 display at the City and County building. The suit was brought by the American Civil Liberties Union and Americans United for Separation of Church and State. Only one of 12 councilmen voted against a resolution backing the mayor's action favoring the display.

In an attempt to evaluate the effect of the evangelist movement, the *Chicago Sun-Times* devoted most of its Views section Aug. 8, 1976 to the subject. Michael Novak, a Roman Catholic theologian, wrote a full-page article, "U.S. evangelism revealing its long-overlooked power," the gist of which is suggested by its subtitle, "Jimmy Carter taps a hidden well-spring." Another two pages were devoted to Roy Larson's piece, "Old-time religion lives in suburbia," based on visits to numerous churches in the vicinity of Chicago. A quotation from Gary Wills, syndicated columnist, summarized the findings of the two authorities: "Hard as it is to arrive at the exact size of the evangelical movement, since it is not confined to any one denomination, it has become a general tendency in American Protestantism—one that seemed to be losing out to liberal theology in recent decades but that now has made a stunning comeback. It has, in fact, become the major religious force in America, both in numbers and in political impact."

In part confirmation John Dart wrote a critical analysis of Gallup polls on the subject for the *Los Angeles Times* July 29, 1977. The headline the *Sun-Times* gave the reprint two days later was, "Americans 'believe' but religion's influence is slipping." The story began: "Americans, as Gallup polls have shown, are big on beliefs. Some 94 per cent say they believe in God or a universal spirit; some 68 per cent say they believe in a personal, observing God and in life after death; 58 per cent say their religious beliefs are 'very important' to them." Dart interviewed quite a few religious leaders to conclude that such beliefs do not play so big a part in everyday life as in years gone by.

Maybe not, but June 2, 1979 the *Washington Post* carried a story from New York by Lee Lescare, "Rally for Jesus Attracts Cheering Throng of 35,000 in Shea." Christians of all denominations took part in an all-day revival meeting. Such affairs, Lescare declared, "until recently were shunned by more establishment-minded Christian churches." Pope John Paul II even sent his blessing to the rally.

That "In America as in Europe, an amazing turn to the ancient religions of the white race is in progress" was the theme of a full-page article, "Old Time Religion Gaining" by Sean O'Tighearnaigh in the Jan. 4 & 11, 1982 issue of *Spotlight*. The new-old movement claims some two million in France where Alain de Benoist, editor of *Nouvelle Ecole* is its principal proponent. Most of the article, however, deals with the Odinists, who along with the Druids are part of a slowly developing back-to-"pre-Christianity" movement. Odinists do not believe in original sin or in having a guilt-complex outlook on life. American leader is Californian Terry Oaks.

Most important organizations are the Asatru Free Assembly in California and the Odinist Federation in Florida.

Other organizations with a fundamental religious orientation are the Right to Life, dedicated to abolition of abortion, and the Moral Majority, led by the Rev. Jerry Falwell which wants prayers and Bible readings restored in public schools and strict censorship of literature and art it considers pornographic or blasphemous. Its scapegoat is secular humanism whose proponents the Rev. Tim LaHaye, chairman of Californians for Biblical Morality, charges want to "turn traditionally moral-minded America into an amoral, homosexual humanist country." Other leaders have been quoted as saying, "We do not want a democracy in this land because if we have a democracy a majority rules," according to the Rev. Charles Stanley and "If necessary God would raise up a tyrant, a man who might not have the best ethics, to protect the freedom interests of the ethical and the godly," according to the Rev. James Robison.

A thoroughly objective resumé of both the historical development of humanism and of the present-day attempts to blame it for virtually all social problems was contained in an article by Russell Chandler in the *Los Angeles Times* for July 16, 1981. Humanists trace their intellectual origin to Pythagoras, the 5th-century B.C. Greek philosopher, who said, "Man is the measure of all things." It thrived during the Renaissance and the Englightenment. The dictionary definition is "the character or quality of being human, devotion to human interests." According to H. Edward Rowe, an evangelical economist, "The moving force behind humanism is Satan. Humanism is basically Satan's philosophy and program."

An objective analysis of the rise of right-wing religious politicians was written by John Herbers for the *New York Times* of Aug. 17, 1980. He explained:

> Abandoning a long-held belief that political activism is incompatible with their faith, ultraconservative evangelical Christians are forming a growing new force that is affecting elections and government at federal, state and local levels.
>
> Organized in great part by television preachers and driven by a belief that a moral and spiritual decline is endangering the nation, hundreds of thousands of evangelicals have registered to vote in a drive to support conservative candidates, most under the Republican label.

That all religious fanatics are not Christians was evident in the news from many parts of the world, including Iran where Ayatollah Ruhollah Khomeini executed thousands of opponents of his attempt to restore rigorous customs. Editorializing about the proposal for an alliance between

Egypt and Libya the *Chicago Sun-Times* Sept. 1, 1973 cited the leadership of Libya's President Muammer Kadafi of a cultural revolution to involve "the burning of books that contain imperialist, capitalist, reactionary, Jewish or Communist thoughts," the only permissible ideas being "those emanating from the Koran."

18

Cults

The appeal of evangelists and revivalists is greatest to middle-aged and elderly churchgoers whose faith is buttressed by Bible thumping, hell and damnation preaching and soul stirring martial music. Loyalty to one's church is strengthened; there are few conversions from one sect to another and movements that depend almost entirely on the charisma of one leader seldom survive his or her passing.

For younger people, however, the old-time religion is not enough. In fact, youths renounce or at least largely ignore the faiths of their fathers, as they reject many other aspects of contemporary life. Although parents have worried about their wayward sons and daughters since ancient times, Egyptian hieroglyphics indicate, the post-World War II American youths, now possessed with the right to vote, have challenged traditional lifestyles more than any of their predecessors did.

Widespread dissillusionment developed when a brave new one-world was not achieved by World War II which had been supported, especially by idealistic youths, as a crusade for utopia. With Franklin Delano Roosevelt dead, the altruistic Atlantic Charter and the Four Freedoms were forgotten and the blueprint for American foreign policy was the American Century postulated by Henry Luce and sold to Harry S Truman by James Byrnes, James Forrestal and John Foster Dulles. High school and college graduates could not, as a last resort, join their fathers' businesses because their fathers no longer were small independent businessmen but employees of gigantic impersonal corporations. Military expenditures, instead of diminishing with the close of hostilities, skyrocketed, resulting in inflation, high taxes and high unemployment.

The first effort of young people to throw the rascals out of public office was an increased active interest in politics. They licked stamps, addressed envelopes and rang doorbells for worthy candidates and parties, only to feel let down as few if any of the liberal planks in their heroes' platforms became enacted into law.

So the young joined groups that supported progressive causes. They became important segments of the civil rights and peace movements. Thus they marched with Martin Luther King in Alabama, risked their lives as Freedom Fighters in Mississippi to assist Negro voters and rallied before the Lincoln Memorial in Washington. When their efforts led to violence and death, as at Jackson State and Kent State, they struck to close most of the nation's institutions of higher learning.

Still no encouraging results. Rather, whitewashes, violence and a series of phony conspiracy trials involving the Chicago 7, Dr. Benjamin Spock, the Berrigan brothers, Angela Davis and others. Although the jury system worked to thwart the government's program to stifle dissent, youth remained hopelessly impatient for long-overdue reforms. And increasingly youngsters revolted against conventional forms of behavior. They wanted none of contemporary society's life-style. If they couldn't change the environment they'd ignore it. Result: outlandish clothing and symbols (beads, moccasins, etc.), defiance of moral codes, marriage and divorce laws, hair fashions, vocabulary and the substitution of loud noise for music. The first youthful rebels were called beatniks and their activity center was the Haight-Ashbury region in San Francisco. There they withdrew from square society for one of their own. Later, they came out of retirement for political activity again; it was disruptive and terroristic by malcontents who called themselves hippies.

The most serious and lamentable effort to escape the lousy world was by means of narcotics. In the '60s a Harvard University psychologist, Timothy Leary, conducted a nationwide campaign to encourage the use of psychedelic drugs while preaching "Tune in, turn on and drop out." Most popular and effective was lysergic acid, diethylamide (LSD), of which Henke Gratteau wrote in the *Chicago Sun-Times* for July 26, 1981, "A synthetic hallucinogen, LSD alters perception, sensation, thinking, emotions and self-awareness. It can cause changes in time and space perceptions, delusion—thinking you can fly—and hallucinations . . . Longtime effects include anxiety, depression and breaks with reality."

When the bad side-effects of LSD became recognized, even by the beatniks of San Francisco's Haight-Ashbury section, there was a shift to phencyclidine or PCP or angel dust. Cocaine, heroin, marijuana and other drugs also helped people to forget their troubles momentarily. When, however, they returned from their dope-induced "trips," the evil society was still there. So then they emulated distraught, insecure and fearful people throughout the ages; they turned to the unworldly, the supernatural. This last phase of the revolt of youth has taken many different forms and has affected adults as well as youth. Some of them have been examined in previous chapters: astrology, spiritualism, witchcraft and others. Such forms of escapism are not institutionalized. The religious cult, with its guru, *is* institutionalized and has become a prominent phenomenon of our times.

Among the first journalists to note the spread of the resurgence of interest in the occult on college campuses was Andrew M. Greeley, a Roman Catholic priest who also was program director of the National Opinion Research Center of the University of Chicago. In the article "There's a New-time Religion on Campus" in the *New York Times* magazine for June 1, 1969, he described the forms the phenomenon took on many campuses in all parts of the country, a typical one being WITCH (Women's International Terrorist Corps from Hell), on the Chicago campus. He quoted Prof. Huston Smith of the Massachusetts Institute of Technology concerning a seminar of some of the school's best students:

> I cannot recall the exact progression of topics, but it went something like this: Beginning with Asian philosophy, it moved on to meditation, then yoga, then Zen, then Tibet, then successively to the "Bardo Thodol," tantra, the kundalini, the chakras, the I Ching (ee-ching, a book presenting an ancient Chinese divination device which enables one to make decisions—a sort of pre-I.B.M. computer), karate and aikido, the yang-yin macrobiotic (brown rice) diet, Gurdjieff, Maher Baba, astrology, astral bodies, auras, U.F.O.'s, tarot cards, parapsychology, witchcraft and magic. And, underlying everything, of course, the psychedelic drugs. Nor were the students dallying with these subjects. They were on the drugs; they were eating brown rice; they were meditating hours on end; they were making their decisions by I Ching divination, which one student designated the most important discovery of his life; they were constructing complicated electronic experiments to prove their thoughts, via psychokinesis, could affect matter directly.

About the first to note the extent of the evangelical movement among youth was Edward B. Fiske, *New York Times* religion editor. July 4, 1971 he wrote of the Jesus People as "part of a nationwide movement that is giving a new (and often bearded) face to fundamentalist Christianity and taking on all the marks of a minor religious revival." They have, Fiske wrote, "attracted a deal of publicity." Fiske mentioned their "hippie style and unusual language" and described them as "young rebels against middle class culture who find that acceptance of Jesus Christ as Savior has given them a whole new purpose in life. They preach traditional fundamentalism, with belief in heaven and hell and literal interpretation of the Bible, but their suspicion of middle class institutions extends to fundamentalist churches which they usually see as lacking in passion for the radical demands of a Gospel life style. A high proportion are former drug addicts who now prefer to 'turn on to Jesus.' "

In a half-page article, "The Jesus Movement Spreading on Campus," in the *New York Times* for Dec. 26, 1971, Douglas D. Kneeland, from Palo Alto, Calif. presented the results of a nationwide roundup that showed, "Just as the radicals gained adherents because of the wide disenchantment among the young with existing political and economic institutions, the

Christian movement is attracting many who are disillusioned with the established churches and the quality of American life, including some facets of the so-called counterculture."

According to B. Davies Napier, dean of the chapel and a professor of religion at Stanford, "The Jesus Movement is not going to lift a finger to change the status quo. They're waiting for the Second Coming and Christ is going to take care of all that."

It wasn't long before Jesus People became Jesus Freaks, a term which, Kneeland reported, the members resented because it usually is one applied to street people who have frequently dropped out of the drug scene and occasionally out of radical politics, whereas the students in the new fundamentalist drive come mostly from middle-class and upper-middle-class homes.

Nevertheless, George Will used the terms Jesus People and Jesus Freaks interchangeably in his syndicated column for July 31, 1971. "They were bearded, scruffy," he wrote. He recalled the God Is Dead movement of a few years earlier, when most theologians said the name meant little any more. "And now," he wrote, "here come the freaks—against all the best analysis—saying that God-talk does mean something to them."

The Associated Press reported from London July 6, 1971, in a piece to which the *Chicago Daily News* devoted more than a column, that Britain's top pop-singer was Cliff Richard, a former rock and roller who became an evangelist after meeting Billy Graham and won the Songwriters' Guild annual award. "Richard packs them in," the AP reported.

What surprised Robert C. Marsh when he covered the Aug. 6, 1971 performance of *Jesus Christ, Superstar* at Ravinia for the *Sun-Times* was that the largest audience in the outdoor theater's history was "very cool, well mannered that put up with the inconvenience of standing in line for everything, listened to the music and liked what it heard . . . those who prophesied an invasion of dreadful hippies and drug pushers and trouble makers saw instead thousands on thousands of predominantly North Shore youth."

In the *National Observer* for Dec. 25, 1971 Arthur C. Tennies answered the question that was the article's title, "Why Is Jesus Christ Now a Superstar?" He contended: "Many people, because they cannot believe in God and have lost their faith in mankind are reduced to despair . . . The renewed emphasis on Jesus is an attempt to build a faith in a God who is in this world . . ." As a consequence of the rock opera *Jesus Christ, Superstar,* "Jesus Christ has suddenly become a popular hero. Here at last is one person in whom one can believe. He is an authentic person of integrity in contrast to other heroes who are false."

After attending quite a few Jesus movement meetings, the columnist Garry Wills wrote Nov. 27, 1971, "I noticed a mood of undifferentiated assent. Everything is accepted—tongues, healings, miracles—unhesitatingly, without question. Mutter whatever you like—tepid Latin obcen-

ities or gibberish—and your neighbor will mutter back. 'Praise the Lord.' "
He wrote further: "You must join or leave; you cannot simply observe or
question. These people are too happy. Reality has not got to them, or they
are blocking it out."

"God comes to Fraternity Row" was a full page written for the Dec. 16,
1971 *Chicago Today.* The article was a summary of the extent to which
Jesus Freak groups and others had taken over abandoned fraternity
houses on the campus of the University of California in Berkeley. Among
the takeovers were: Zeta Beta Tau by the Franciscan School of Theology;
Acacia by One World Family Commune, a part of Messiah Allen's World
Crusade, part of the long awaited new order of the Kingdom of God; Sigma
Phi Epsilon by Joaquin Murrieta; Chicano Student Cooperative and Phi
Delta by the International Society of Krishna Consciousness.

A former Jew and assistant professor of religion at Temple University,
Lowell D. Streiker, told Roy Larson, *Chicago Sun-Times* religion editor,
"The whole generation is one death trip. They can't seem to take the input
of society and they're running away from responsibility and reality,
searching for a simple life and easy answers. At least the Jesus trip is a
safer trip than the drug trip." Larson used the quotation in a review of
Streiker's book, *The Jesus Trip,* in the Jan. 8, 1972 edition of his paper.

Columnist Harriet Van Horne wrote in *Chicago Today* for Feb. 7, 1972
that she doubted the so-called Jesus Movement was "headed up the right
road." Many, she wrote, regard it as a travesty, the disciples as a scruffy lot,
many of them former dope addicts, their frenzied worship a kind of blasphemy." However, she added, it is heartening that some young people
searching to solve the crises of authority and identity should find evangelical religion "more socially acceptable" than tranquilizers and other drugs.

In the *New York Times* for Feb. 13, 1972 Andrew Greeley mentioned at
least a score of new books on some aspects of the new religion movements in
the United States. In the same paper March 1, 1972, Edward B. Fiske
predicted that the '70s would be known as the decade of religious revivals.
"But," he wrote, "the revival does not mean that there is a decrease in
over-all church membership and attendance: it means merely that there is
a trend toward conservatism in religious thinking."

By late spring of that year the movement was still going strong as
evidenced by the 200,000 who attended the Jesus Music Festival, otherwise known as Godstock, in Dallas June 17, 1972; of them 85,000 had
attended Explo, a weeklong training session. Michael Kernan reported for
the *Washington Post* that the purpose was "to bring the public into contact
with the proselytizing young Jesus Movement people who make a point of
checking every stranger's religion."

"What sets Jesus People apart from other Christians is that generally
they came out of the counterculture of the 1960s," according to Donna Joy
Newman in her article "The Young Turn on to Christ" in *Chicago Today*
for Feb. 12, 1974. "Though a communal lifestyle has been closely as-

sociated with the Jesus Freak movement since it blossomed in California in the late '60s, many young people who have shared in the religious beliefs continue to live normal, independent lives."

During the presidential campaign of 1976 the general public became aware of the "born again" movement when Jimmy Carter answered a question, stating that he had been born again, adding that any southerner would understand what that meant. Maybe so, but many northerners and others were as confused as a reader who asked the *Chicago Daily News'* Beeline, "Pardon my ignorance, but I am not a Christian. Just what does it mean to be born again?" July 16, 1976 the paper explained the phrase comes from John 3:3, where Jesus tells Nicodemus, "Except a man be born again he cannot see the kingdom of God," and further explained, "That which is born of the flesh is flesh and that which is born of the spirit is spirit." Jimmy Carter, at the spiritual age of 9, said he "established a more intimate relationship with Christ."

Calling the "born again" movement the top religion story of 1976, in the 1, 1977 edition of the *Chicago Tribune,* James Robison cited Carter's declaration, the book by Charles Colson, former aide to President Nixon, and the profession by Eldridge Cleaver, onetime Black Panther leader. Also a Gallup poll showed one-third of all Americans said they were born again too. Robison defined the phenomenon as follows: "It's a (spiritual) experience among those Christians who call themselves 'evangelicals,' whose faith is conservative with heavy emphasis on personal morality versus social action. They usually base their belief in Jesus Christ."

Jan. 6, 1977 James Bowman reported in the *Chicago Daily News* on a speech by Cleaver at Wheaton College. In it the onetime rebel told of seeing a vision of Jesus Christ in the moon from his home in southern France that caused him to tremble, weep and read the Bible before turning himself in to face criminal charges.

Typical of the serious, almost reverent treatment that the press gives the "born again," was the feature "How John Costello Found Jesus and Happiness" in the *Chicago Tribune* for Dec. 21, 1980. The anonymous piece related in part: "John cannot exactly explain how his 'born again' thing happened . . . But God just sort of seeped into his inner being and filled him up until one day he knew it had happened for real . . . He knew because the changes in his life weren't abstract, the kind of changes as he sees it that could only have come by the Creator's taking those things in his life that he had bottled up and giving them back to him, a second chance."

During the 1980 presidential campaign an all-day Washington for Jesus festival attracted speakers linked to the Religious New Right and an estimated 200,000 to 500,000 churchgoers. Recalling the affair, Bruce Buursma, the *Chicago Tribune's* religion editor, predicted Aug. 8, 1981 150,000 midwesterners would attend an America for Jesus rally Aug. 15, 1981 in Chicago's Grant Park. After it occurred Buursma reported in the Aug. 16, 1981 *Tribune,* an attendance of tens of thousands and quoted the organizers that it was "the most historic rally that's ever occurred in Chicago." The Rev. John Gimenez of Virginia Beach, Va. told the worshipers, "My vision is America for Jesus and Jesus for America . . . No enemy has touched the shores of our land, not because we're big and strong but because the angels of God have protected us."

Without estimating the size of the crowd, in the Aug. 16, 1981 *Chicago Sun-Times,* Cindy Skaugen related some of the history of the America for Jesus movement, tracing its start to the experience of a California dairy farmer during World War II. About one-third of his herd was stricken with tuberculosis but six weeks after a Brother Glover prayed in the center of the corral no animal was diseased.

Maybe the Chicago rally fell short of expectations because of the influence of the devil, belief in whose existence is deeply rooted in the Christian religion and many others as well. As *Time* explained March 10, 1952, "The idea of an Evil Being is as basic as is belief in a supreme God. Devils were a keystone of belief among the Aztecs, the Assyrians and the ancient Chinese. In the Buddhist scriptures the Devil Man appears at the head of an army of demons with 'bodies of flame . . . with the skin of oxen, asses, boars . . . spitting snake venom—and swallowing balls of fire.' "

Throughout history in Christian mythology the devil has lost much of his ferociousness. No longer is he the three-headed giant of Dante's *Divine Comedy*. He has mellowed considerably since Goethe and Milton and often has been described as more a comic than a tragic spirit. During the '70s as the Jesus People mushroomed so did Satan cults. June 4–6, 1970 the *Chicago Daily News* ran a three-part series on the "sometimes funny, sometimes frightening world of the occult." The series by Jacquin Sanders originated with the *Newsweek* Feature Service and was lavishly illustrated by pictures of bald-headed, droopy-mustached leaders with piercing eyes, black robes and typical figures prominent in the "Big Boom in Black Magic" and practitioners of the black mass. Sanders accredited the rise of "some of the most outlandish beliefs and rites in the history of civilization" to "the shortcomings of science." "What is new," she wrote, "and it has developed during the last five years—is a rebirth of interest in the causes and a willingness to accept the irrational as an answer. It may be that reality in an increasingly controlled and overpopulated society has become too unpleasant for many people to accept."

"Satanism," she wrote in the installment entitled "Sex and the Black Mass," "is the dark side of the occult. It involves a reversal of all moral values. It is evil incarnate and unending."

The mass Sanders attended consisted mostly of the showing of a "medium heat pornography" motion picture in which a naked man is beaten, other nudes bounce in and out and a girl writhes about with a 6-foot boa constrictor. The ritual centers on three emotions: lust, vengeance and something called "compassion for one's self."

Leader of the First Church of Satan is Anton Szandor LaVey—the

"Black Pope." "Exarach of Hell" or "Satan's Emissary on Earth," a one-time circus lion tamer and calliope player, and a former police photographer.

A full-length personality study of LaVey appeared in the *Chicago Sun-Times* for Aug. 30, 1970. It was written by Dave Smith of the *Los Angeles Times,* who visited the First Church of Satan, which LaVey founded April 26, 1966 in San Francisco. LaVey admitted that the nude Satanic wedding and a funeral to consign the soul of a sailor to the devil were mostly for publicity purposes. His church, he explained, is a mirror image of Christianity, which he says is "going down the drain" because it had "almost 2,000 years to fill the bill and failed miserably to redeem mankind." LaVey's denials, however, have not ended rumors of orgies, sex, drugs and even the sacrifice of human babies.

"With California taking the lead, the interest (in the Satanic majesty) or obsession has spread to colleges, hippie gathering places and even to suburban housewives," according to Edward C. Burks, to whose article " 'Satan Cult' Death, Drugs Jolt Peaceful Vineland, N.J." the *New York Times* gave almost a full page July 6, 1971. High school students who were among an estimated 80 or 90 former drug addicts told authorities the drowning of a youth found with hands and feet tied was a ritualistic murder with assistance; friends bound the youth who insisted he had to die violently in order to be put in charge of "40 leagues of demons." A number of teenaged boys and girls declared they had been saved by Jesus. A skeptical official commented, "Yeah and what happens when the kids get bored with being Jesus People?"

Despite a series of articles by Roger Simon in the *Waukegan* (Ill.) *News-Sun* beginning May 1, 1972, after two months' investigation Lake County Sheriff Orville Clavey said there was no evidence that there were Satanic cults in the area. He did admit there were parties at which high school students consumed alcohol, used narcotics and engaged in sex but denied there were killings of animals and babies and Satanic rituals in a cemetery.

The newspaper's exposé was based on the testimony of at least a half-dozen boys and girls who had been participants in the orgies. The operator of a drug counseling service said that in 11 months she received calls from 42 persons who belonged to witchcraft or Satanic groups. She said, "They meet in motels, apartments, homes when the parents go out. These kids are caught in a web, a web of booze and drugs and fear. When they want to get out they find they can't."

May 4 the newspaper reported that despite Clavey's disbelief he was assigning two deputies to investigate. Also libraries and bookstores reported a greatly increased interest in books on Satanism. Also, it was reported in a second story that one of the newspaper's sources, all of whom were promised confidentiality, had talked to Chief Circuit Judge La Verne Dixon. May 6 it was reported that 19 adults and 3 juveniles were arrested in two raids on dope parties but no Satanic tieup was found. In another story, however, Mayor Robert Sabonjian pledged a full-scale police investigation of Satanism.

The situation as regards Satanic cults in California was described by Simon May 12, the story being headlined "Manson's Cult Gave Satanism New Impetus." The next day Simon wrote about exorcism, citing several examples of supposed casting out of devils here and abroad. The story was illustrated by a picture of the Rev. Rudy Evans, ordained by both the Baptist and Pentacostal churches but who operates his own Gospel Ranch near Lake Villa, Ill.

That drugs are easily obtainable was the subject of Simon's May 16 article following interviews with several teenagers.

Sheriff Clavey's announcement that his investigation resulted in no evidence of the existence of Satanic cults was reported June 29, 1972. June 30 the *News-Sun* editorialized on "Satanism officially ruled invisible." The paper said the sheriff's announcement recalled an old joke about the Brooklyn visitor to the Midwest. He told a friend, "Look at the boid." To which the friend replied, "That's no boid; it's a bird." Muttered the visitor: "That's funny. It looks just like a boid and it sounds just like a boid." In other words, the sheriff didn't know what he saw.

In his *Waukegan News-Sun* column for June 13, 1972 Craig Anderson reasoned that the increase in sales of occult books and items made it "hard to deny that there is a definite interest in devil worship in the local area."

Mike Warnke, onetime Southern California Satanist High Priest with 1,500 parishioners, spoke Jan. 8, 1973 in the Cary Grove High School. His coming was announced in the *Waukegan News-Sun* for Jan. 2 and Doug Weatherwax covered his appearance for the Jan. 9, 1973 paper. The meeting began in orthodox evangelical style with children singing hymns and the capacity audience of 700 answering loudly the missionary's demands that they tell whether they love Jesus.

Warnke described himself as "a filthy, no-good, rotten sinner." He escaped from the Christians by joining the Navy and was born again mostly because of the influence of two shipmates.

March 24, 1973 Warnke was announced as the speaker at a Jesus rally at Chicago's McCormick Place to expose "the fastest growing and most deadly occult religion in the world," drawing on his book *Satan-Seller*. Jan. 23, 1974 he was announced as the speaker at the College of Lake County. He now devotes full time to his anti-occult counseling, known as Alpha Omega Outreach.

Dr. David Breese, president of Christian Destiny, was announced as the speaker Jan. 12, 1974 at Immanuel Baptist Church, Waukegan. His topic: "Satanism."

The rapid growth of Satanic cults in many countries caused Pope Paul II to devote an entire sermon to "that evil which we call the devil," according to an Associated Press story from Vatican City Nov. 16, 1972.

"We all are under an obscure domination," the pontiff said. "The devil is the occult enemy who spreads errors and disasters in human history. He is the evil and crafty deceiver who knows how to creep into us."

In comment, a liberal Protestant clergyman, Dr. Marion Marty, charged that the pope "sees strange new possessions by the devil all around him. He drops devil talk casually onto a scene where theologians have had enough trouble with God-Talk." In the *Chicago Daily News* for Jan. 13–14, 1973, James H. Bowman reviewed a book by the Rev. Mike Warnke, "a former hophead, sexual libertine, speed freak and field organizer for a California-based Satanic group and now a minister of the gospel." Warnke wrote: "Satanism is a gigantic ego trip. You climb to achieve power and you hate anything that gets in your way."

March 3, 1973 Bowman edited four full pages of a symposium, "The Supernatural Joyride: Should We Blame It on the Devil?" to which a half-dozen reporters and others contributed. Hassan Haddad, professor of history at St. Xavier's College, was quoted as believing the devil "is part of the background of Christianity." John Miles, Loyola University Bible scholar, said, "When things went bad for the Jews, as in the Babylonian exile, the Bible writers needed something to blame." Vanessa Whitlock, a high priestess of the Satanic Church, said, "We are not devil worshippers per se. We don't drink blood. We don't sacrifice babies. We don't stomp on the crucifix and we don't say a black mass. We believe in God as the creator of the universe and he created Satan, the holder of all knowledge." Other writers described the activities of Satanic groups in the area.

More comprehensive because it was based on a nationwide survey was the two-page feature "Satan Lives!" subheaded "So Say Believers Who Call Him God," by Daniel St. Albin Greene in the *National Observer* for Sept. 1, 1973. The article spelled out the thesis: "What Hugh Hefner did for sex, LaVey did for Satanism—packaging and selling it as a voluptuous philosophy and life style and the social trend of the future." The article cited numerous ventures in different parts of the country and summarized: "The one thing that unites all diabolists is the quest for power over personal destiny. Consequently most satanic ceremonies are for specific purposes: to cure enemies, to ask for favors (money, success, sexual gratification), to vent basic urges (hatred, lust). It's a practical, hedonistic, self-deluding faith."

Charging that his constitutional right of freedom of worship was violated, an inmate in the Texas state prison at Huntsville filed a class action suit against prison officials in federal court, the *Houston Chronicle* reported July 20, 1973. Another legal action regarding Satanism was reported in the *Chicago Daily News* March 27, 1974. Mrs. Margaret Taylor asked the court to prevent her former husband from influencing their daughter, Susan, 10. The father, high priest of the Satanic Church of Chicago, allegedly took his daughter for rides in a hearse and showed her a coffin in which he slept. April 11, 1974 the *Chicago Sun-Times* reported that a Circuit Court judge ordered the father to stop bedeviling the girl.

The prodigious popularity of the novel *The Exorcist* and the motion picture based upon it caused Dan Miller to begin a half-page article in the *Chicago Daily News* for Jan. 21, 1974: "The devil is getting his due." Illustrated with eerie photographs, the article had a streamer headline, "Satan business: a New Industry is Born" with the two-column subhead "Devil dollars fill publishers' tills."

According to an Associated Press story from New York that the *Austin* (Tex.) *American Statesman* used April 4, 1974, a Center of Policy Research study showed that the proportion of the United States population completely convinced the devil exists rose in nine years from 37 to 48 percent, with another 20 percent considering his existence probable. The study was made before *The Exorcist*.

In the third of their series on Satanic cults, in the *New York Daily News* for Oct. 8, 1980, Michelle Smith and Dr. Lawrence Pazder described the black mass, which they called "a eucharist of dead babies." Illustrating the two-page article was a chart of the arrangement for the black mass, including the pulpit from which Satan delivers his sermon, his vision; the altar, where the living victim is sacrificed and where Satan penetrates and inseminates his bride and the points of Vision of Despair and Vision of Hell. If it sounds hard to understand, it is. The entire series is based on what Michelle remembered of when she was five years old.

As David Selfman reported it for the *New York Post* Feb. 21, 1980 homicide detectives were studying Satanism and the occult in an attempt to solve the brutal ritualistic murders of a Brooklyn painter and his dress-designer girlfriend. Both were bludgeoned on the left side, each had a right eye wound and similar cuts and bruises about the knees and groin. Friends said the two were students of the occult.

Because he believed his six-month-old son was possessed by the devil, a 16-year-old father threw the baby out of a fifth-floor window. Luckily the infant landed on a pile of garbage and lived. The father was charged with attempting homicide, according to Larry Sutton in the *New York Daily News* for Aug. 2, 1980.

Nine books, all concerned with the occult and intended for young readers, were reviewed by Christopher Davis in the *New York Times* for May 5, 1974. Davis wrote: "The reasons behind the occult rage have been well explored. We know the times are particularly insecure; that institutional religions are casting down old hollow figures, hoping to strengthen their base; that parents, unruled, become mere tall children appealing for assurance of immortality to their own offspring who, in turn, lost, light up and go to the devil. A species under the sort of pressure ours endures is bound to invent gods and their opposites and worship them fervently or put them on the shelf, depending upon the times, the weather, the wars, the kings. Fallen on evil days and when religion and government are about the same, we get cathedrals and witches. In our own difficult times, the state secular, we are getting, one hopes briefly, pop black magic."

Another motion picture that aroused controversy was *The Omen,* in which the anti-Christ mentioned in the Book of Revelations appears on Earth. Mark Fineman solicited the opinions of many for the Suburban Week of the *Chicago Daily News-Sun-Times* of July 28 & 29, 1976. Psychic Irene Hughes said she has long predicted the appearance of a figure that would be known as the anti-Christ. A Catholic theologian said he interpreted the Bible's statement as symbolic, not realistic. A second Catholic theologian said the biblical story is allegorical and no anti-Christ ever will appear.

Of special value to the Satanists must have been the long confessional "Was It Satan At Work?" that Arch Oboler wrote for the *National Observer* for Aug. 28, 1976. Oboler, author of a "tongue-in-cheek tale about an ordinary family cursed by a grandmother in league with the devil," experienced a series of frightening occurrences that caused him to doubt the validity of his doubts. Doors opened mysteriously, loud sounds disturbed him, dogs howled and similar incidents remained unexplained.

One ramification of the growth of Satanic believers was reported by Jack Anderson in his syndicated column for May 24, 1978. Army chaplains were unable to assist the cultists. For $30,000 a private firm offered to instruct chaplains in how to minister to the needs of members of the Church of Satan, Council of Witches and Native American Church.

Another example of the extent to which the movement has developed is the campaign by an evangelical minister from Hutchinson, Kan. to purchase all copies of the game Dungeons and Dragons. Larry Weintraub reported in the *Chicago Sun-Times* Public Eye column for June 25, 1981 that the minister insists, "When you deal in any way with demonic spirits, they're alive and they've got power."

In Texas City, the *New York Daily News* reported May 8, 1982, members of the First Assembly of God Church ripped to pieces thousands of books, records and figurines in a fight against the devil. Among the objects confined to the fire were the music album *Urban Cowboy,* Star War figurines, Walt Disney stories that speak of witches, rock and roll records from *The Omen, Little Red Riding Hood* and many others.

About the same time California Assemblyman Phil Wyman sought a law to require any records containing messages discernible when played backwards to be labeled accordingly. Focus of attention, according to an AP story from Los Angeles, is Led Zeppelin's *Stairway to Heaven,* which supposedly pays homage to the devil in a song that criticizes drug use.

In her story May 3, 1982 UPI's Sandra Michioku cited the song *Snowbound,* under attack because it allegedly contains a Satanic message, "Oh Satan move in our voices" that can be heard if the record is played backwards on a turntable or tape recording. One record maker said any such message would have to be done by the devil as the only one capable of performing the trick. Another producer said, "It's a hoax."

To test the validity of Wyman's charge the *Chicago Tribune* hired the Universal Recording studios to play backwards a number of records, those under suspicion and some others. Only such a technological organization had the equipment with which to do what Wyman seems to think any rock and roll fan can do. Most of the transcriptions were unintelligible. Wyman charged that Led Zeppelin's song included the words, "Here's to my sweet Satan." Not even the engineers were able to detect that or any of the other alleged messages until told what exactly to look for. Then they heard, "Here'sh to my shwweet shatin," or something of the sort. Howard Reich wrote a complete report on the experiment for the June 6, 1982 *Chicago Tribune*.

Aug. 8, 1982 the *Tribune* ran a column-long satirical article by Douglas Hand, a New York free-lance writer. Hand experimented with his record player and succeeded only in ruining it and getting very garbled sound. At the end, he said, when he played "The Ballad of Davy Crockett" backward he heard "The Giants win the pennant," which is what Russ Hodges shouted after Bobby Thompson's homerun. "So now we know," Hand wrote. "The devil did it. And all these years I'd thought it was the hand of God."

In her *Boston Globe* column March 14, 1983 Diane White told of her interview with the Rev. Don Hutchings of Hot Springs, Ark., who blamed the press for the defeat of a bill similar to the one Phil Wyman promoted in California.

The Arkansas House passed the labeling bill 86-0 but the Senate defeated it after newspapers ridiculed it.

Some people who are always on the alert to ferret out heretical or subversive messages circulated the rumor that more than 15 percent of the employees of Procter & Gamble are Satan-lovers. Someone on either the Phil Donahue or Merv Griffin show allegedly made the claim, although no P & G official ever appeared on either show. Since the rumor originated in fundamentalist churches on the West Coast, it was natural that the *Los Angeles Times* be the first to take cognizance of it. Pamela Moreland wrote the first article for the Jan. 22, 1982 issue explaining that the company's symbol of a moon and 13 stars originated in 1840 to identify crates of Star Candles and had nothing to do with the Unification Church of Dr. Moon.

The campaign of Procter & Gamble to squelch the rumor got a page 1 streamer-headline story in the *Chicago-Tribune* for July 18, 1982. The *New York Times* got into the act July 27 with a couple of columns by Sandra Salmans.

The *Chicago Sun-Times* Action Time for May 11 quoted a P & G official denying the rumor. Dear Abby did the same Aug. 3 and Ann Landers followed suit Sept. 6.

June 25, 1982 the *Wall Street Journal* ran an article by Margaret Yao telling of the appeal Procter & Gamble made to the Rev. Jerry Falwell, president of the Moral Majority, and the Rev. Donald W. Wildman, chairman of the Coalition for Better Television, to disabuse their parishioners of the belief the company is run by Satanists.

July 2, 1982 Dean Rothart reported in the *Wall Street* Journal that Procter & Gamble brought separate libel actions against Mike Campbell of Doraville, Ga. and Mr. and Mrs. William J. Moore, Jr. of Pensacola, Fla. Lawyer for the company was Griffin Bell, United States attorney general in the Carter Administration. The UPI reported from Cincinnati that Procter & Gamble was receiving 12,000 calls a month asking if the rumor was true. Sandra Salmans reported in the *New York Times* that there never was any discussion of the matter of the Phil Donahue show. Aug. 13 the *Wall Street Journal* reported that Procter & Gamble had dropped its libel suits after receiving formal apologies from a television weatherman in Atlanta and a Tallahoma, Tenn. couple.

Aug. 29, 1982 Terry Kinney reported for the Associated Press from Cincinnati that Procter & Gamble had dropped libel suits after the defendants apologized. During June the company received 12,000 phone calls and 2,000 letters to inquire about the rumors. Kinney gave more details of the origin of the trademark. Originally the stars were merely crosses to distinguish candle from soap crates. William Procter decided to increase the number from 3 to 13 to match those of the American flag. In 1882 the design was registered with the U.S. Patent Office.

Possibly because they share that feeling an overwhelming majority of those in search of spiritual peace prefer any of a quantity of other available sects. Most popular are those with a strong leader or guru, preferably with a mystical Indian or Oriental background.

One of the most venerable native-born sects is the Mighty I Am Presence, founded in 1934 by Guy Ballard, who said that in 1930 St. Germain appeared to him on Mt. Shasta, where he was working as a mining engineer. Members of the cult revere St. Germain more than they do Jesus; both are Ascended Masters, as was Ballard. Because of its troubles with the post office and Internal Revenue Service as well as because of the apparent weirdness of its doctrines, I Am never has had a favorable press. *Time* gave it a mild sneer Feb. 28, 1938 and in his syndicated column Oct. 25, 1939 Westbrook Pegler wrote, ". . . Members of this cult, not being legally insane, have deliberately become accessories to the most revolting travesty in the entire record of religious eccentricity in the United States."

When Ballard died in 1940 he claimed 700,000 followers. In the *Chicago American* for April 4, 1959 Mervin Block said the national membership total probably was about 10,000, of whom 1,000 were in the Chicago area. Headquarters of the cult still are in Chicago's loop, where there also are reading rooms, a print shop, a discount store and a mission. Mrs. Edna W. Ballard, who succeeded her husband as the cult's leader, received a brief obituary in the June 4, 1971 *Sun-Times*. Because the

Santa Fe New Mexican ran accounts of Mrs. Ballard's conviction for
fraud in 1942, a posse of women members of I Am raided the newspaper
office, the Associated Press reported Jan. 7, 1951. Most of the time before
and since the press has generally ignored the movement.

Another native American cult is Children of God, called "God's Hippie
Children" by the *National Observer* which ran Daniel St. Albin Greene's
long account of it April 15, 1972. It is an offshoot of the Jesus Movement.
Greene quoted a leader of the orthodox group regarding what he called
"fringe cults," and declared: "We called them Jeremiah prophets because of
their creed of doom. They never ministered in love like the normal Jesus
people. They had a double gospel: a gospel of Jesus Christ but also a gospel
of the destruction of America." Founder and determiner of the cult's doctrine was David Berg, an itinerant fundamentalist preacher, who changed
his name to Moses David and fled to England in 1972 to escape the Internal
Revenue Service. From there Mo, as his devout followers call him, writes
letters to the faithful to interpret the Bible to forecast a period of Great
Confusion before God's anointed will be rewarded. Extracts from the letters appeared in the two-part series on the Children of God in the *Chicago
Daily News* for April 5–6 and 7, 1975. Writing in the Sept. 4, 1973 *ids,*
publication of Illinois Wesleyan University, Nancy Scudder quoted Mo,
"God will shake up this nation because he loves them, in the form of
plagues, international revolutions and sabotage."

From New York the UPI reported Oct. 15, 1974 that New York State's
attorney general had issued a report charging the Children of God practice
brainwashing, physical coercion and sexual abuse on members. Nevertheless, the sect continued to claim 3,000 members in 120 communes in 165
countries.

Still another splinter sect, with a membership in all 50 states and 50
foreign nations, estimated variously from 40,000 to 100,000, is The Way
International. It was organized in 1957 by a former fundamentalist minister, Victor Paul Wierville, in New Knoxville, Ohio. Its organizing activities were conducted quietly for two decades by missionaries sent in
pairs to all parts of the world. Then, in the mid-'70s it began to attract
attention along with other cults that aroused parents by enticing away
their sons and daughters. The *Chicago Sun-Times* introduced its readers to
The Way with two articles by Zay N. Smith Aug. 17 and Sept. 14, 1980.
"The doctrine," Smith wrote, "is the Bible according to Victor Paul Wierville as revealed to him many years ago by God who made him an apostle.
The Holy Trinity denied speaking in tongues is a repeated ritual. Healing
happens all the time. And you can correct your calendar: Christ was
crucified on a Wednesday and raised on a Saturday."

The value of property owned by the sect, including 147 acres in Ohio, is
$10 million. The wealth is visible in the form of private planes, buses and
flashy wardrobes. The Way is appealing an Ohio tax commissioner's order
that all but six acres of the estate be returned to the tax rolls. Under attack

from critics is the regular weapon training that the cult says is only for public safety and hunting. Nevertheless, in a third piece April 17, 1981, Smith revealed that the FBI was investigating charges that The Way had infiltrated Chrysler and other plants.

The *Chicago Tribune* started to catch up in its handling of The Way with an article March 15, 1981 by Bruce Buursma, religion editor. Headlined "Way International Sect Stirs a Storm," it told that pressure by critics caused the cancellation of most engagements by Takit, the group's rock band. Also, it was revealed that two of Wierville's books were anti-Semitic. They are *The Hoax of the Twentieth Century* and *The Myth of the Six Million,* both denying that the German Nazis conducted a Holocaust of Jews.

Almost in a class by itself is Kinonia Farms in southwest Georgia. The name is derived from the Greek meaning "fellowship" or "commune" and most of its 200 inhabitants are not hippies or fanatical religionists; rather, they are formerly successful business and professional persons who agree with Clarence Jordan, who founded the commune in 1942, that Christians can like what they believe and the core of Jesus' teaching was: peace, brotherhood and sharing. Members use the profits from self-supporting industries and farms to build homes for poverty-stricken blacks at a cost of $25 to $35 a month and provide economic assistance in other ways. During World War II the commune underwent considerable harassment because of its pacifism. How they have gone their quiet way was related by Michael I. Malloy in the *National Observer* for March 11, 1972.

Mostly, as has been pointed out many times, especially in this and the preceding chapter, the press treats news regarding groups claiming to be religious, objectively, respectfully, even sympathetically. There have been several incidents of changes of heart and of desperate conflicts between reporters and reported. One such involved Synanon. Founded in 1958 by a former alcoholic, Charles Dederich, it enjoyed a favorable, indeed a highly laudatory press as a rehabilitation center for alcoholics and drug addicts in Santa Monica, Calif. Just about every important newspaper and magazine praised it as it grew into a $20-million enterprise with facilities in Santa Monica, San Francisco, Oakland, Westport, Conn., New York, Chicago, Detroit, Malaysia, Philadelphia, the Philippines, West Germany and Tomales Bay, Calif. Scholars came from all over the world to study Dederich's hardboiled therapeutic methods. Robert Sam Anson wrote in *New Times* for Nov. 27, 1978: "He was a journalist's delight. He was quotable. He made sense. 'Crime is stupid, delinquency is stupid, and the use of narcotics is stupid,' he told a *New York Times* reporter in 1965. 'What Synanon is dealing with is addiction to stupidity.' The force of his personality was overwhelming, almost hypnotic, and, to some, terrifying."

Such journalistic accolades, encomiums and eulogies continued until after 1968, the year Dederich ordained that Synanon was to become a life-style, not just a temporary place for a cure; also that "squares," outsiders not in need of rehabilitation, would be admitted. And then, as Anson put it, "a new Synanon story seemed to be emerging every week: shaved heads, mass vasectomies, group remarriages, threats of violence . . . talk about 'Imperial Marines,' 'hit lists' and 'dealing with the enemy.'"

As might be expected there were defectors who helped influence the press in its treatment of Synanon news. The most advertised incident of violence was the nearly fatal bites that an attorney, Paul Morantz, received from a poisonous rattlesnake that had been placed in his mailbox. Two Synanon inmates were indicted for the crime but the institution itself disclaimed any knowledge of the affair.

Synanon's effort to discourage and/or punish unfavorable publicity did not prevent the nearby weekly *Point Keyes Light* from winning the 1979 Pulitzer prize for meritorious service for a series of articles on Synanon. Synanon began a libel suit for $1,250,000 against the paper and Prof. Richard Oshe of the University of California at Berkeley, who assisted *Light's* editors, David and Cathy Mitchell. Although a prestigious Los Angeles law firm offered its services gratis and contributions were received from journalists all over the country, nobody was overconfident. In 1973 the *San Francisco Examiner* paid Synanon $2,600,000 in two out-of-court settlements, called the largest ever of their kind. The story considered most offensive by Synanon was printed in January 1972, based on information supplied by a former member who charged that Synanon no longer tries to care for addicts but "specializes in providing a zombie-like existence for fugitives from reality" and that Synanon is "the racket of the century." *Publishers' Auxiliary* summarized this and numerous other legal matters involving Synanon in its issue of Feb. 26, 1979.

There is no doubt that other journalistic enterprises have been intimidated by Synanon's rowdy tactics. An outstanding example was the retraction and apology by Capitol News Service for a column questioning the state of California's policy in selecting rehabilitation programs and the competence of Synanon to serve as such an agency. The syndicate backed down because too few of its 400 subscribers would back it in a legal battle.

An excellent source for information concerning Synanon is *Feedback,* quarterly publication under the auspices of the Department of Journalism of San Francisco State University, virtually every issue from that of Fall 1975 to the present.

Charging that San Francisco's KGO-TV's coverage of Synanon's purchase of 138 guns made it seem like a terrorist group, Synanon sued for $42 million, later reduced it to $21 million and finally settled for $1.25 million, the *Chicago Sun-Times* reported June 15, 1982.

The Winter 1979 edition of *Feedback* also is the best source for a play-by-play account of how the two San Francisco papers, the *Chronicle* and the *Examiner,* covered the 914 deaths in Jonestown, Guyana. Among the dead was Greg Robinson, a *Chronicle* photographer who accompanied Congressman Leo Ryan, who was investigating reports of conditions at the commune established and ruled by the Rev. Jim Jones of Peoples Temple, headquartered in San Francisco.

The mass murders-suicides commanded international interest and many asked why the press waited until after the tragedy to expose Jones as a dangerous charlatan who, it was revealed in the analytical and interpretative pieces, had at least once declared himself to be the reincarnation of Jesus Christ; at other times he said he was the reincarnation of V. I. Lenin, leader of the Russian revolution. Jones also told his congregation of 20,000 that he had cured many persons of cancer and other diseases and had raised 40 from the dead.

All of these and many other damaging facts were included in an early three-page resumé in the *Chicago Sunday Tribune* for Nov. 26, 1978, eight days after Congressman Ryan and four others were fatally shot at the Jonesville airport as they were about to return to the United States. At about the same time, seven miles away, Jones addressed a mass meeting of his 1,200 followers and 911 of them, evidently on his orders, committed suicide by swallowing cyanide. Jones died from a gun wound in the head.

In its "Deadline Guyana" piece in its Winter 1979 issue *Feedback* revealed that two years earlier Steve Gavin, the *Chronicle's* city editor, was so impressed by Jones that he refused to permit reporter Marshall Kilduff to examine the cult's affairs. The high esteem in which Gavin held Jones was shared by many others. Although unordained, Jones in 1950 became a pastor and directed an integrated community center in Indianapolis. Ten years later he was appointed director of the Indianapolis Human Relations Commission. In 1964 he was ordained by the Disciples of Christ and in 1974 was named one of the 100 outstanding clergymen in the United States by *Religion in America's Life*. In 1965 an article in *Esquire* concerning nuclear destruction caused Jones to predict the world would end in a nuclear holocaust July 15, 1967. Seeking sanctuary he visited several places in South America and then settled 150 of his followers in Ukiah, Calif. By 1972 his churches were well established in San Francisco and Los Angeles and other places. In 1977 he was appointed chairman of the San Francisco Housing Authority by Mayor George Moscone, for whom he had provided 200 precinct workers on election day. Shortly thereafter Jones defected with 1,200 followers to Guyana.

When he was thwarted in his attempt to expose Jones in his newspaper, the *Chronicle*, Marshall Kilduff did an article with Phil Tracy for the July 18, 1977 *New West* magazine. The failure of public officials to act on complaints of former followers against Jones was explained by Larry Remer in *In These Times* for Nov. 29–Dec. 5, 1978, partly as follows: "The key to Jones' political influence came from his willingness to mobilize Peoples Temple on behalf of various political candidates. In nearly every election in this decade, Peoples Temple has provided foot soldiers for liberal and Democratic candidates. Jones and his followers have been wooed by every left-of-center politician to campaign in San Francisco,

including San Francisco Mayor George Moscone, California Governor
Jerry Brown, U.S. Senate candidate Tom Hayden, State Assemblyman
Willie Brown and—during the 1976 presidential campaign—Rosalyn Car-
ter on behalf of her husband, Jimmy."

After the *New West* exposé Jones obtained endorsements from many of
his political friends to use in an advertisement in the *Sun-Reporter,* an
influential Negro publication. His lawyers were two outstanding liberals,
Charles Garry, defense counsel, and Mark Lane, iconoclastic assassination
theorist. Both were in Guyana at the time of the tragedy and each said the
other knew Jones' plans in advance.

Two years after the tragedy Prof. Jonathan Z. Smith of the University
of Chicago, wrote an article, "Jones: Messiah or Madman?" for the *Chicago Tribune* of Nov. 18, 1980. "Since the event in Jonestown," he wrote, "I
have been selecting clippings from newspapers, magazines and the religious press and the subsequent slapdash literature. I have also searched
through the academic journals for some serious study, but in vain. Neither
in them nor in the hundreds of papers on the program of the American
Academy of Religion has there been any mention."

"The press," Smith charged, "by and large featured the pornography of
Jonestown. Space was taken over by lurid details of beatings, sexual
humiliations and public acts of perversion. The bulk of them focused on
Jones as a 'wrathful, lustful giant.' " Concealed by religion scholars especially was the fact that "Religion has rarely been a positive liberal force.
Religion is not nice; it has been responsible for more death and suffering
than perhaps any other activity . . . The fundamental fact about Jones is
that he sought to overcome distinctions."

The type of article that Smith thought shallow was "One Year After
Jonestown, Cults Still Unchecked," by Kenneth Wooden in the *Chicago
Sun-Times* for Nov. 18, 1979, in which Jones was called "a madman who
skillfully used psychological techniques and financial chicanery to lure
hopeless and innocent people into joining his cult, the Peoples Temple, and
to hold them as hostages to his will." Wooden warned that a number of
other religious groups, called cults by the majority churches, had used
methods similar to those Jones used to manipulate and dominate his
disciples.

Another critical analysis of the press' handling of the Guyana story was
made by Frank Harris for a master's thesis in journalism at the University
of Texas in Austin under the direction of Dr. Gene Burd. He analyzed 203
editorials in 328 newspapers selected at random from the 1,744 American
dailies. He found that 42 percent never editorialized on the incident at all.
Only 12 percent of the editorials dealt with the issue of race, press and
society that Harris who, like Professor Smith, thought crucial for an
understanding of the deaths and prevention of such in the future. The
suicides, he wrote, "are a symptom, a warning sign of something grossly
wrong in America."

Harris said 88 percent commented on the "safer" and more superficial aspects of the tragedy cults.

Facts concerning the tragedy have continued to be revealed since their occurrence. Almost immediately three male survivors told the press that Jones' mistress had entrusted them with approximately $500,000 to be delivered to the Soviet Embassy in Georgetown. Also specific details were given of the harsh disciplinary methods and the organized military drills; most important, the suicide drills. Dec. 3, 1978 the *Cleveland Plain-Dealer* published an interview with David Hill who headed another religious cult of 8,000 in Guyana. Hill, who had fled Cleveland seven years earlier after a conviction for blackmail, said his followers would do anything for him, including committing suicide. When he established the House of Israel Hill he changed his name to Rabbi Edward Emmanuel Washington.

The fanaticism of the Jones' followers was demonstrated in 900 hours of tapes that James Reston of the *New York Times* obtained through a Freedom of Information Act request. April 16, 1978 Reston declared the tapes demonstrate "the slavery of the followers and the power and sacrilege of Jim Jones."

Inevitably court actions followed the tragedy. Sept. 18, 1981 the AP reported the defense testimony in the trial of Larry Layton, accused of participating in a conspiracy to kill Congressman Ryan. A *New York Daily World* story Oct. 16, 1981 reported that the Layton case ended in a mistrial. More recently, three who were wounded in the attack on Ryan and relatives of several dead cult members brought suit against former Secretary of State Cyrus Vance and former CIA director Stansfield Turner charging that the CIA took part in sinister mind-control experiments on Peoples Temple members.

The Associated Press reported Aug. 8, 1982 from San Francisco that the last 120 of 600 claimants will receive $9 million from the assets of the Peoples Temple as a result of a federal judge's ruling.

In the meantime the jungle was recapturing Jonestown according to a UPI story Nov. 28, 1981 from Georgetown, Guyana. One former cult member was serving a five-year prison-term for a knife attack on a girl. The government was trying to prevent looting pending the outcome of all the legal battles.

Nothing perhaps demonstrated more clearly the power that modern religious gurus can exert than the revelation in the *Los Angeles Times* for Jan. 10, 1981 that Shannon Jo Ryan, 28-year-old daughter of the congressman who was murdered at Jonestown, had joined a cult that resembles Jim Jones' Peoples Temple. The guru is Bhagwan Shree Rajneesh of Poona, India, who, Ryan told the *Times,* she considers "a present-day incarnation of Jesus or Buddha or Mohammed." She does not believe there are parallels between the two movements, saying, "What Jones created was a prison and what Bhagwan has created is a way out of the prison of ordinary life. Just total freedom is what he is all about. Jones was trying to control people, while Bhagwan is trying to give people control of themselves."

Perhaps the most thorough and sober evaluation of the Jonestown tragedy is the book *Raven* by Tim Reiterman, a *San Francisco Examiner* reporter who was wounded at the Guyana airport but survived. He and his coauthor John Jacobs spent three years of delving into Jones' background which resulted in a story of a very maladjusted child and dishonest adult. Published in 1983 by Dutton the book was reviewed Jan. 12, 1983 in the *Chicago Tribune.*

19

Gurus

After the Charles Manson Family murdered actress Sharon Tate and four others Aug. 9, 1969 some critics demanded to know why the press had not exposed the cult as a group of drug-driven potential killers. Similar questions were asked after the suicides-murders in Jonestown, Guyana, and on other occasions when supposedly peaceful persons have gone berserk.

Probably many of the accusers were persons who also are loud in their condemnation of journalists at other times for allegedly invading the privacy of citizens, exaggerating scandalous situations to boost circulation.

In its handling of news of religion the press is probably more careful than in its treatment of any other kind of news. Unless a church is involved in some scandal, such as embezzlement by a church official or investigation by some governmental agency, newspapers try their best to be neutral, objective, sympathetic. On holidays and other occasions it is customary to explain the meaning of the occasion and the way it is observed. To some doubtless a factual description of the beliefs and rites of a strange group will be greeted with laughter or scorn, whereas others experience exactly the opposite reaction.

As related in the preceding chapters, in their early years Peoples Church, Synanon and other cults that later lost the public's respect received dignified treatment in the journalistic media. One outstanding exception has been the Church of Scientology, for full details about which the reader should consult *Cults of Unreason* by Christopher Evans (Farrar, Straus and Giroux, 1974), *The Scandal of Scientology* by Paulette Cooper and *Scientology: The New Religion* by George Malko (Delacorte Press, 1970).

It all began May 1, 1950 with the publication of a book, *Dianetics: The Modern Science of Mental Health,* by a widely known science-fiction writer, Lafayette Ronald Hubbard, 39. Almost without exception psychiatrists, psychoanalysts and other medical and scientific reviewers condemned the book as a rehash of discarded early Freudian doctrines. Typical blast was that of Dr. Martin Gumpert, a staff physician of Goldwater Memorial Hospital: ". . . a bold and immodest mixture of complete nonsense and perfectly reasonable common sense taken from long-acknowledged findings and disguised and distorted by a crazy newly invented terminology."

Only important defender of dianetics was Dr. Frederick L. Schuman, a Williams College political scientist, who insisted, "There are no authorities on dianetics except those who have tested it." To test it one lies on a couch with an auditor to direct the attention of the patient to disagreeable experiences in his/her past. The auditor then tries to place the patient in various periods of his/her life by merely telling him/her to go there rather than just remembering. All therapy is done, not by remembering but by "travel on the time track" that begins with life and ends with death. Incorrect data that caused emotional disturbance or physical pain or disorder comes from engrams, cellular recordings made and stored in the active mind when the analytical mind is inoperative because of unconsciousness. More simply put, engrams are buried memories of displeasure. An E meter is a mechanical aid, something like a lie detector, that indicates the patient's emotional state.

Although experts found it difficult to discover any new principles or techniques to combat psychosomatic illnesses, 60,000 laymen bought the book during the first four months. The press naturally could not ignore the movement. One of the first serious analyses was by Sid Kline in the *New York Compass* Sept. 24–26, 1950. At the end of a two-hour session during which he relived two operations, one a tonsillectomy and the other to strengthen an eye muscle, Kline was told he was a good pre-Clear, which was jargon for possible Clear, someone who had had enough therapy to be entirely rid of engrams.

Kline's article was descriptive, not argumentative. Oct. 26, 1950 he had an exclusive story on the resignation of three members of the Hubbard Dianetic Research Foundation, one of them the president of Hermitage House, which had published Hubbard's book.

Sunday, Oct. 22, 1950 the *Chicago Sun-Times* devoted a page to an article by Robert S. Kleckner, "Science or Quackery? Dianetic Disciplines Claim Cures." Kleckner was impressed by Hubbard's claim that "The creation of dianetics is a milestone for Man comparable to his discovery of fire and superior to his invention of the arch and the wheel." He explained the dianetic conception that there is a kind of memory impressed on human cells that consist of protoplasm. Kleckner quoted Dr. Morris Fishbein, eminent editor of American Medical Association publications: "The United States is overwhelmed with mind reading cults. A new one like dianetics simply adds to the fun and the fury. It's good stuff for resort conversation."

That was about as close as any newspaper came to balanced reporting in those days, but dianetics lent itself to good copy, especially when there were photographs of patients in a trance. Such was the illustration for a

414 SUPERSTITION AND THE PRESS

piece by W. A. Sprague and Richard Wild in the syndicated supplement *Parade* for Oct. 29, 1950. It was entitled, "Can We Doctor Our *Minds* at Home?" The authors concluded: "Like Coue's 'better and better every day' and the 'science' of phrenology (skull bumps) dianetics seems here to stay. Why?" Much of the rest of the article consisted of testimonials by patients who said they had been helped by dianetics, which came to be seen as a do-it-yourself or poor man's psychiatry.

The next year, 1951, Hubbard received considerable unfavorable publicity when his second wife, Sarah Northrup, sued him for divorce, claiming that he had attempted to abduct their 13-month-old baby. The newspapers reported the story under headlines such as "Cult Founder Accused of Tot Kidnap" and "Hiding of Baby Charged to Dianetics Author." More important than personal scandal in dampening the enthusiasm of followers in centers all over the country was the failure of the treatment to attain lasting results. A catastrophic experience for Hubbard occurred before an audience that packed the Los Angeles Shrine Auditorium. Hubbard introduced the world's first Clear, a pretty college student named Sonia Bianca. Although she was a physics major at Williams, she was unable to state Boyle's law or answer other elementary questions asked by Cy Endfield, motion picture director.

Dianetics began to change character when Hubbard discovered the existence of the thetan, the part of a human that "is aware of being aware." Thetans are not physical but are immortal and belief in them led easily to belief in reincarnation as pre-Clears began recalling traumatic experiences in previous lives. So in 1952 dianetics became Dianetics-Scientology. In 1955 Hubbard moved to England where he established clinics and training centers for Scientology. In 1959 he bought the elaborate estate of the Maharajah of Jaipur near East Grinstead, Sussex. A writer for *Lilliput* described Hubbard as "possibly the best informed man alive today beside whom Albert Schweitzer is a well-meaning medicalist and Aldous Huxley naive."

With Scientology slowly but steadily attaining popularity comparable to that Dianetics had enjoyed a decade earlier, July 21, 1955 the Founding Church of Scientology was incorporated in Washington, D.C. Jan. 4, 1963 officers of the United States Food and Drug Administration raided the headquarters, removing books, pamphlets and E-meters. The raid was a tactical error on the government's part as it made persecuted martyrs of the cultists.

In November 1963, suspecting that Scientology was being used for blackmail and distortion, the Australian Parliament appointed a Board of Inquiry into Scientology. This gave the movement international publicity which was a boon to the growing membership. That was so even after publication of the Australian report, which declared: "Scientology is evil; its techniques are evil; its practices a serious threat to the community, medically, morally and socially . . ." Scientology continued to grow. Near the end of 1965 Hubbard returned triumphant from an African trip to be greeted by hundreds of devotees, after which the movement experienced its biggest boom.

Soon, however, there was alarm over the extent to which Hubbard followers were infiltrating local schools and in March, 1967 the British minister of health blasted Scientology in the House of Commons as "a hollow cult which thrives on a climate of ignorance and indifference." Ignoring Sonia Bianca and some other alleged "first Clears," in 1966 Hubbard said that actually the title belonged to a South African named John McMaster; by March 1968 there presumably were 1,000 Clears. Parliamentary blasts continued. Foreigners working at Scientology centers were not able to obtain extensions of their work permits and students were not given extensions to stay in England. When Hubbard was sailing in the Mediterranean an order was issued to refuse him re-entry into England. Hubbard traded his yacht for a larger trawler and in 1967 bought a 3,400-ton former Channel ferry, the *Royal Scotsman*. From then on Hubbard operated mostly from a floating office, issuing bulletins and producing pamphlets and books in abundance.

The interest of American journalists in Scientology was rekindled in the late '60s. Aug. 25, 1969 the *San Francisco Chronicle* began a five-part series by Donovan Bess who noted that membership in the cult in California had more than doubled during the preceding year. The articles clarified and updated Scientology. Hubbard's edicts, constantly enlarged the therapeutic techniques so that there came to be six grades of Operating Thetan levels above Clear. McMaster was quoted as saying that the income of the worldwide church had increased from $10,000 a week in January 1968 to $140,000 in the succeeding six months. The American church claimed 250,000 members. The cost of getting Clear ranged from $4,000 to $6,000.

The seers suggested the developing program for answering critics. Defectors became known as suppressive persons, and one of the 185 imperatives in the Scientology Code of Honor is: "Never fear to hurt another in a just cause." From his flagship, the 5,000-ton *Apollo* in the Mediterranean, Hubbard supervised five ships of his Sea Organization; members are an elite. One of his best-publicized letters went wholesale to psychiatrists and clinical psychologists stating, "Scientology has no wish whatever to drive the individual psychiatrist from personal practice or injure him economically." Hubbard claimed "a near but unwanted monopoly on results in mental healing." He offered to teach a therapist at a 50 percent discount on Scientology services if he would (1) swear not to use shock treatment or brain surgery on patients; (2) promise to follow the code for Scientology auditors; (3) swear not to mix Scientology with older practices.

Bess digested his *Chronicle* articles for an article in *The Nation* of Sept. 29, 1969. It is a compendious summary of the history and practices of dianetics and Scientology. So also was John Leonard's review of George Malko's book *Scientology: the New Religion* in the *New York Times* for July 16, 1970. In an article entitled "Scientology Help or Hoax?" in *Chicago Today* for Sept. 30, 1970, Marilynn Preston concluded: "There is no simple explanation of Scientology. It is a history of the planets, a religious philosophy, a science and a plan for immortality all rolled into one mind-boggling whole, with heavy doses of psychoanalysis, reincarnation and group therapy games thrown in for good measure."

In a followup of the Bess article, *The Nation* ran an article May 22, 1972 by Clay Steinman entitled "Scientology Fights Back." It detailed the harassment of Paulette Cooper, author of *The Scandal of Scientology* who filed a $15.3 million suit against Scientology. She charged that the publishers of her book were threatened with libel suits, of which Scientology has filed more than 100 against a long list of magazines, book publishers and others, without, she points out, winning any of them. Steinman wrote: "Cooper also claims that, among other things, Scientologists tapped her phone, followed her 'closely and obstructively' on the street, made obscene phone calls to her late at night and tried to serve a process on her at 2:30 in the morning, after waking a 72-year-old neighbor to ask him questions about her. She says they tried to date her as a means of acquiring information. And they harassed her when she went to Scotland, serving a patently invalid process on her—which was never followed up with a valid one—as she got off the plane. She says Scientologists posing as FBI men, and with letters supposedly signed J. Edgar Hoover, questioned acquaintances about her."

Routine news about Scientology activities included an Associated Press report from Washington Oct. 24, 1973 that about ten tons of religious books and controversial E-meters were returned after ten years by the Food and Drug Administration. In 1971 a United States District judge said their seizure was illegal but ordered that in the future literature carry a warning that the E-meter "has no proven usefulness in the diagnosis, treatment or prevention of any disease nor is it medically or scientifically capable of improving any bodily function."

Jan. 5, 1975 the UPI reported that a federal judge in Hawaii issued a temporary restraining order to prevent the Central Intelligence Agency from destroying any files it had on the church. The Scientologists acted after they learned it was one of 99 organizations listed as "enemies" by the Nixon Administration. A church spokesman cited numerous instances of spying by the CIA.

May 25, 1975 the *New York Times* noted the 25th anniversary of the founding of the Church of Scientology. A church spokesman said Hubbard was at sea in either the Mediterranean or Caribbean and planned a trip to India as part of a study of ancient cultural conditions.

When the Evanston, Ill. church moved to larger quarters the *Chicago Sun-Times* Suburban Week edition for Jan. 28 and 29, 1976 ran an article,

"Scientology cult thrives despite charges" by Neil Goldstein. The Rev. Daniel Tinnes reported that in two years membership had grown from a dozen to 1,500 "who have some contact" and 60 students taking courses.

July 9, 1977 the same paper ran a story from its wire services, "Sect is accused of plot on IRS." The FBI, acting on a search warrant and an affidavit outlining allegations, raided church offices in Washington and Los Angeles to recover documents allegedly stolen from the offices of the CIA and IRS by church members who infiltrated the agencies.

A church spokesman said the raids were in retaliation because the church disclosed illegal trafficking in drugs by Interpol, an international police information agency with which the FBI is affiliated. Scientology doctrine "requires the church attack and destroy its enemies," he explained.

The UPI's story from Washington on the raids revealed that FBI agents used sledgehammers and crowbars to break down doors in two Hollywood locations. Aug. 16, 1978 the news services reported that nine persons identified as officials and two others described as "agents" of the church were indicted on 229 counts charging conspiracy, burglary and bugging of government offices and theft of IRS and Department of Justice documents. Principal defendant was Mary Sue Hubbard, wife of Ron. The efficiency of the church's spy system was indicated by the fact that a secret grand jury document had been obtained and published by the church two weeks earlier.

The biggest news about Scientology's legal battles was played down to a short two paragraph AP dispatch from Paris Feb. 15, 1978 that Hubbard was sentenced in absentia to four years in prison and fined $7,300 for fraudulent business practices. French authorities had no word on Hubbard's whereabouts. By contrast Mrs. Hubbard, through her attorney, said she would return to face the charges against her. The *Chicago Tribune* editorialized Aug. 18, 1978: "It is easy to believe that neither the FBI nor the Scientologists have always been wholly candid and above board . . . He who fights the United States government with dirty tricks not only may lose. He may in the process make life tougher for other people." In the *Tribune's* Voice of the People column Aug. 29, 1978, the Rev. Kenneth J. Whitman, president of the Church of Scientology, commented at length on the editorial, scoring this point: "The assault on the Amendment has interestingly paralleled the refusal of the Justice Department to indict the admitted criminals within its own ranks. Legislative bodies are being investigated and clergy and press incarcerated while FBI blackbaggers walk free. It is a trend that reeks of imminent danger to our American way of life."

It took the *Chicago Sun-Times* three pages Sept. 17, 1978 to do justice to its comprehensive article by Robert Rawitch and Robert Gillette, "The Gospel according to Hubbard. Vengeance is mine, saith Scientology." The authors recalled the fear jurors felt after they had awarded former Scientologist L. Gene Allard $300,000 for malicious prosecution by the church. The article also reviewed the cases of Paulette Cooper and several others. The "battle lines," as drawn by Hubbard, were listed: (1) combatting suppressive persons—"SP Order. Fair Game. May be deprived of property or injured by any means by any Scientologist without discipline of the Scientologists. May be tricked, sued or lied to or destroyed"; (2) counter-attacking—"If attacked on some vulnerable point, always find or manufacture enough threat against them to cause them to sue for peace"; (3) countering propaganda—"If there will be a long-term threat, you are to immediately evaluate and originate a black PR campaign to destroy the person's repute and to discredit them so thoroughly that they will be ostracized." The *Los Angeles Times* had a series of articles by Rawitch and Gillette Aug. 27, 28 and 29, 1978.

A legal case in Oregon that "brought a new wrinkle" led the *Chicago Sun-Times* to editorialize Aug. 21, 1979. A jury awarded a woman $2 million from the Church of Scientology because it didn't deliver the miracle cures it had promised—better classwork, heightened creativity and an improved IQ. In fact the woman charged Scientology damaged her psyche. The paper pointed out that freedom of the press is not absolute. Neither is freedom of religion, because it does not protect ritual murder and harassment. "Just as clearly," the paper said, "there is no constitutional right to defraud. On the other hand, there's also no law against being a gullible whinny."

It took the church two years to appeal the verdict to the Oregon Court of Appeals. Simultaneously, the *Willamette Week* reported Sept. 22, 1981, it distributed 5,000 copies of a pamphlet, *Freedom of Religion Denied,* to court officials, attorneys and others, presenting the church's side of the argument. The *Portland Oregonian* reported Sept. 29, 1981 that Court of Appeals Judge W. Michael Gillette strongly rebuked the church's attorney for the tactic.

Contents of the documents seized in the 1977 raid were made public Oct. 26, 1979 the AP reported from Washington. About 15,000 documents were taken from the IRS office alone, including reports on its investigation of the church's tax exempt status. One church memorandum listed 136 government agencies that were to be infiltrated by Scientology members. The next day, Oct. 27, 1979, eight high-ranking members of the church were found guilty of conspiracy. One was Mary Sue Hubbard.

Nov. 2, 1979 it was revealed that the American Medical Association and the National Institute of Mental Health had been infiltrated in an effort to discredit them. Nov. 24, 1979 it was revealed that the church planned to make bomb threats in the name of Paulette Cooper. The next day, the contents of more documents were revealed to show that the Scientologists stole IRS files on Frank Sinatra, California Gov. Edmund G. Brown, Jr., Los Angeles Mayor Tom Bradley and other prominent Americans in the effort to blackmail the IRS into doing a favorable audit of the church. A year later, the AP reported from Washington Nov. 27, 1980, two high-ranking Scientologists were convicted of burglary for ordering subordinates to infiltrate offices of the IRS and Justice Department to steal and copy documents.

Sept. 24, 1981 Bill Franks, founder Hubbard's successor as "executive director international," announced that the group's England-based top office had "gone adrift" and that some of the leaders would be replaced.

In December 1981 there was an organizational reshuffling and the Church of Scientology International was registered with the Florida Department of State as a California organization headquartered in Clearwater, Florida.

April 15, 1982 the *Clearwater Sun* reported that an advertisement announcing forthcoming public hearings into the sect's activities appeared in the *New York Times, Los Angeles Times* and *Washington Post*. Anyone knowing anything about law violations by Scientology were asked to communicate with a Boston lawyer, Michael Flynn. The next day reporter Will Prescott wrote that the attorney for the church demanded the firing of Flynn and contended the 1st and 14th Amendment rights were being violated. April 29 the news was that a federal judge denied a request by the church for an emergency hearing on its lawsuit against the city of Clearwater. He said he would consider a temporary restraining order to prevent the public hearing.

While all this was happening the United States Supreme Court upheld the conviction of Mrs. Hubbard. The Clearwater officials said the local organization is a "totally different organization" than the one with which Mrs. Hubbard was involved, the *Sun* reported April 20, 1982.

The public hearing before the Clearwater commission was held May 6–10. Lawyer Flynn presented 16 witnesses, including Paulette Cooper, founder Hubbard's eldest son, who had changed his name to Arnold De Wolf and several former members. Cooper told of her harassment by the sect. De Wolf said he considered his father to be insane, thinking only of power and intent on destroying anyone not submitting to his wishes. Ex-members told of disagreeable living and working conditions, one example of injustice being a week on only beans and rice for those failing to make the week's quota of fund raising.

The Scientologists refused to use the four days allowed to them. Instead, their attorney stalked out of the hearing, which he called "a Roman holiday." The church began an intensive public propaganda drive. The anti-Scientology witnesses spoke at a public forum for the Scientology Victims Defense Fund. The *Sun* reported May 23, 1982 that the turnout was a disappointment, about 350 instead of the 3,400 expected.

The American Civil Liberties Union agreed with the sect in a public statement expressing "disappointment and alarm" about the hearings, calling them, "neither fair nor public nor addressed to the stated purpose of investigating the need for a charitable solicitation ordinance," according to the May 21, 1982 *Clearwater Sun,* which gave elaborate coverage to the hearing day by day. May 22, 1982 it editorialized on "Scientology Ad," explaining why it accepted an advertisement from the sect. It was a repeat of a Nov. 15, 1980 editorial that included the following extracts:

> We would have preferred not to run this editorial. We continue to believe that the so-called church serves no meaningful public purpose and represents a grave threat to the health and well being of the Clearwater area.
>
> Nevertheless *Sun* readers have a right to know and we hope to understand why the *Sun* feels compelled to publish the advertisement. . . . The *Sun* shall never knowingly become a pawn of the Scientologists and we shall continue on our editorial page to raise a vigorous voice against the Scientology movement.

Nov. 1, 1982 the church sent a letter to Clearwater city commissioners summarizing its views concerning the pending lawsuits. Because the letter was released to the press in advance of delivery to the city officials the city manager branded it a mere publicity stunt. Nevertheless, the *Sun* summarized it Nov. 2, 1982.

In a copyrighted article Feb. 10, 1983 the *Rocky Mountain News* reported that Hubbard broke his 15-year silence by giving written answers to questions the Denver paper asked. Experts said Hubbard's handwritten letter was genuine because written with a pen with specially manufactured ink. In his statements to the paper and to a California court, Hubbard said he is alive and argued that the suit of his son to have him declared dead so as to inherit his fortune should be dismissed. The views of the son, Ronald DeWolf, were contained in an article in *Penthouse* magazine that Bruce Buursma summarized in the *Chicago Tribune* for June 4, 1983. June 13, 1983 a Riverside, Calif. judge ruled that Hubbard is alive and mentally competent and dismissed DeWolf's suit.

Whereas Scientology horrifies and frightens many, the International Society of Krishna Consciousness merely bores them, unless they happen to be the parents of young people who have become members. With bare shaved heads and dressed in flowing saffron-colored robes, the Krishnas are a nuisance when they attempt to peddle their literature in public places, so much so that cities and states sought legislation to thwart them. In 1981 the United States Supreme Court decided that it is legal to restrict the recruiting areas in which Krishnas or anyone else can stop persons to solicit support or sell their literature. Nevertheless, Norma Sosa reported in the *Chicago Sun-Times* for March 10, 1983, the Krishnas typically filed a $1.6 million damage suit against the city, the airport and some officials charging unconstitutional harassment.

Krishna means Supreme Being in Sanskrit. Founder of the Krishna movement, about 1950, was the Calcutta mystic A. C. Bhaktivedanta Swami Prabhupada, who introduced it to the Western world in 1965. Many of the British disciples were young self-exiled Americans. The support of

Beatles Paul McCartney and George Harrison was important. The Krishnas believed that there must be a rekindled interest in the teachings of Krishna, including an end to war, universal love, food and drink for all. Converts constantly chant a mantra, "Hare Krishna."

By mid-1974 the Krishnas had made inroads in many large American cites. Perhaps the first newspaper to pay attention to the movement was the *Los Angeles Times,* which used a descriptive article by Daryl Lembke about the three-year growth of Hare Krishna on the campus of the University of California in Berkeley. The *Chicago Sun-Times* reprinted the article Jan. 25, 1970. The *Sun-Times* for June 20, 1974 reported that they had invited 25,000 Chicagoans to a free vegetarian lunch in the Civic Center Plaza at which the 82-year-old Indian, His Divine Grace A. C. Bhaktivedanta Swami Prabhupada, would be present, fresh from a similar Rathayatra Festival in San Francisco.

There followed shortly full-length features. In the *Sun-Times Midwest Magazine* for Sunday, June 30, 1974, Rick Telander revealed that the cult had 30 temples and 3,000 devotees who lived austere lives as vegetarians, in scantily furnished homes, sleeping on floors and engaging in businesses to support themselves and followers in India. The Krishnas are the largest manufacturers of incense, commanding 20 percent of the American market. The master, Prabhupada, lives in a $250,000 temple in Los Angeles. Telander wrote: "Hare Krishna gives some middle-class, suburban youths a sense of values lacking in their 'other' life . . . Most of the Krishna members are in their late teens or early twenties and come from white suburbs."

July 8, 1974 Roger Ebert wrote a feature followup of the Civic Center rally, which 2,000 attended. He also had a short interview with the swami who put the nationwide followership at 6,000. He explained his coming to the United States: "I thought, everyone is following the Americans, is building the American skyscrapers. If Americans will follow then others will follow. In India they reject Krishna Consciousness. They reject, Americans accept. India is too much leaderless; now they are encouraging skyscrapers, drinking wine . . . but in the western countries people like the hippies have become dissatisfied with the materialistic life. They give up their possessions. In the western countries we are selling our books very nicely."

A mother whose five-year-old daughter was in the only school in North America for Krishnas, in Gurukula, Texas, wrote an article for the Nov. 16, 1974 *Montreal Star.* The mother, Bibhavati Dasi, was a close friend of John Lennon and George Harrison, both strong Krishna followers, in England. She related what a strict Krishna child-rearing program is like. For the first five years of a child's life it is very permissive, the rigid training beginning at five under the tutelage of the teachers at the school.

July 10, 1975 Peggy Constantine interviewed Swami Prabhupada for the *Chicago Sun-Times.* He told her a first-class man is hard to find and explained, "Woman is not equal in intelligence to man. Man's brain weighs 64 ounces. Woman's weighs 36 ounces. It is just a fact." In the *Chicago Daily News* the same day James H. Bowman, like Peggy, quoted the swami as saying there should be a caste system with four classes of men.

Peggy Constantine also covered a news conference during which Jerome Yanoff, a Chicago high school teacher, accused the Krishna of having assisted his divorced wife in kidnapping their 13-year-old son. As she reported in the paper for Dec. 11, 1975, although the sect denied responsibility, it urged the mother and son to come out of hiding.

Oct. 21, 1976 the Associated Press reported from New York that the American Civil Liberties Union was defending two Hare Krishna groups indicted on charges of brainwashing. The ACLU said that Hare Krishna is a recognized branch of Hinduism and is protected by the First Amendment. The defendants objected to the word "brainwashing," saying the movement used persuasion in the same manner as any convert-seeking religion.

An account of how a 16-year-old girl became dissillusioned with Hare Krishna after a year was told by Sherry Angel in the *Los Angeles Times* for April 7, 1976. She said she lost weight because of the lack of a balanced diet. Hare Krishna adherents pledge to obey rules of no meat eating, no illicit sex, no drinking, no gambling. The young convert also had to relinquish all material possessions other than the most basic necessities and to chant the name of the Lord Hare Krishna 1,728 times or for two hours daily. The article described the austere manner of living of the cult.

The *Chicago Tribune* devoted two full pages in its Suburban Trib supplement for May 5, 1978 to pictures and a description of Hare Krishna. It described a day in the life of a member of a unit, beginning at 4 A.M. Some really live two lives, since they often work in stores and offices wearing orthodox street clothes.

A Hare Krishna commune at Limestone, W. Va. has become a tourist attraction. The Associated Press reported March 7, 1981 that more than 100 visitors daily were attracted by the magnificent palace under construction as well as fountains and gardens. June 19, 1981 the *Charleston* (W. Va.) *Gazette* devoted the equivalent of a full page to describing the life 300 spend on the commune, their relationship with the community and future plans. Kathy Megan wrote the story with photos by Mitzi Kellogg.

Feb. 2, 1982 the *Chicago Tribune* devoted a full page to an account by Jane Engle of the daily life of Hare Krishna members at their Chicago north side headquarters, the illustrations showing how devotions are conducted.

Both Chicago papers had sizable illustrated stories May 22, 1983 to report the opening to the public of the $2.3 million Hare Krishna cultural center in East Detroit, Mich. The mansion was once owned by Louis Fisher, founder of the Fisher Body Co. and Cadillac Motors. Purchasers were Elisabeth Reuther, daughter of the late Walter Reuther, longtime leader of the United Automobile Workers of America, and Alfred Brish Ford, great grandson of the first Henry Ford, who founded the Ford automobile empire and fought Reuther's organizing efforts. Elisabeth and Alfred, both Hare Krishnas, were married in 1977.

The modern guru who has received more attention from the American press than almost all the others combined is Sun Myung Moon, the South Korean who founded the Holy Spirit Association for the Unification of World Christianity, ordinarily called the Unification Church, whose members have ceased objecting to being nicknamed Moonies. Within two years after Moon obeyed God's command and brought his message to the United States in 1972, the church claimed 25,000 American members among 2 million worldwide. The press began considering him seriously in 1974, when he imported 1,000 Koreans to help stage a rally in New York's Madison Square Garden.

One of the first and best comprehensive articles about the movement was written by Eleanor Blau for the Sept. 16, 1974 *New York Times*. It was not an exposé; rather, it was an objective summary of what Moon was telling audiences. Since he spoke only Korean, Moon's words were immediately translated into English by his close associate, Col. Bo Hi Pak. As he told it, in 1939, when he was 16, Jesus Christ appeared to him and informed him he had been selected for a great mission. There followed nine years of prayer and study and two years in a North Korean Communist prison, from which United Nations forces rescued him in 1950. From then until God in 1971 commanded him to take his message to decadent America, Moon built his church in Korea and Japan. Also, Blau revealed, he became a successful industrialist. He had heavy interests in a shotgun manufacturing plant, a paint and coating production company, a pharmaceutical company making ginseng tea, a handicraft company that makes vases and a titanium industrial company. There also are businesses in Japan, a printing company in San Francisco, home cleaning services in several states and a teahouse in Washington.

Moon does not claim publicly to be divine but in his book *Divine Principles,* the bible of the movement, he wrote that a new messiah would be a Korean. His heavenly purpose would be to achieve what both Adam and Jesus failed to accomplish, to establish the Kingdom of God on Earth. According to Moon, Adam and Eve were supposed to marry and have perfect children, but Eve was seduced literally by Satan and brought Adam into sin. Then God wanted Jesus to find a perfect mate and have perfect children, but again man failed him, crucifying Jesus and thus aborting his mission. Moon's followers believe he is the Third Adam.

According to Neil A. Salonen, president of the Unification Church in the United States, most of the American church's income comes from the street sales of candles, peanuts, candies and flowers. Sales must have been good as the church's 22-acre estate at Tarrytown, N.Y. reportedly cost

$85,000, a 255-acre estate at Barrytown, N.Y. purchased for an unknown price from the Christian Brothers, and a 26-acre property in Irvington, said to be worth $625,000.

Seoul sources are cited to explain Moon's arrests. The first, by the Communists, was for "disrupting the social order," specifically by promiscuous sex; the second was for remarrying without divorcing the second of his four wives; again in 1955 the arrest was for "disrupting the social order," specifically ritual sexual intercourse with women in the church.

In an article, "Ji-Whiz Religion," in the *National Observer* Oct. 19, 1974, Wesley Pruden, Jr. cited what Moon says are "signs that God is leaving America." Pruden quoted Moon: "Today there are many signs of decline in America. What about the American young people? What about your drug problems? What about the breakdown in your families? What about racial problems and the threat of communism? And what about the economic crisis? Why are all these problems occurring?"

Pruden noted the decline of older denominations. For example, Methodists contributed an average of $78 a year; Baptists, $83; Episcopalians, $112 and Presbyterians, $122. By contrast fundamentalists and evangelical sects did much better: Berean Fundamentalists, $429; Seventh Day Adventists, $389; Nazarenes, $235 and Pentecostal Holiness, $235.

"Moon's ministry, which began with a coast-to-coast tour last year, has suddenly been attacked by a pincers of the political left and the ideological right. Leftists don't like him because, they say, his teachings smack suspiciously of military regimentation. And they're still angry over his stout-hearted defense of the Nixon presidency. Evangelical conservatives attack Moon as the anti-Christ, accusing him of posing as a Christian evangelist but of rejecting the fundamental Christian doctrine of the Trinity.

A long article by John D. Marks, "Shadows on Rev. Moon's Beams," published originally in the *Washington Monthly,* was reprinted in the *Chicago Tribune* for Nov. 10, 1974. "Sun Myung Moon interweaves politics and religion in the best tradition of the medieval popes," Marks wrote. "His Unification Church operates a vast network of affiliate organizations in more than 40 countries under the distinctly temporal banner of the International Federation for Victory over Communism."

Potential converts, Marks wrote, "come to the sect largely from the ranks of disaffected young people and there is no shortage of those— chafing under an unhappy lifestyle and looking for a meaningful purpose in life . . . Absolutely taboo is premarital sex which Moon rails against as fornication."

Marks described briefly the activities of several Moon organizations: World Federation Institute to train students to fight Communism, *The Rising Tide* newspaper and lobbying. The annual budget of the tax-exempt church was $3 million, not counting the cost of supporting 2,000 "core" members who must be fed, clothed and housed for perhaps $5 million more.

In anticipation of Sun Moon's Chicago rally the next day, the *Sun-Times* carried a story Nov. 11, 1974 by Bob Olmstead to explain the major tenets of the Unification Church. Moon's visit was one stop on a nationwide tour that began with a Madison Square Garden rally that drew 20,000 on Sept. 18. Olmstead identified Pak as a former Korean army officer who was military attaché in Washington from 1961 to 1964.

Nov. 13, the day after the Chicago rally, S. K. Plous, Jr. reported in the *Sun-Times* that the 4,300 who attended wildly applauded the reading of a proclamation by Mayor Richard J. Daley naming the day "Rev. Sun Myung Moon Day" in Chicago. He quoted Moon: "Today Judaism is awaiting a messiah. The Christian church is awaiting the return of the messiah. The Unity church is proclaiming the Messiah." Before or after the meeting there was entertainment by the New Hope Band and the Korean Folk Ballet, affiliates of the church.

Moon's successful public relations efforts to gain prestige were described by Andrew F. Blake in the *Boston Globe* for Nov. 17, 1974. Of immediate interest was the Third International Conference on the Unity of Sciences that few of the 148 prestigious participants knew was sponsored by the International Cultural Foundation, a Moon enterprise. Blake opined that few of the Nobel Prize-winners would benefit much but Moon would gain plenty in prestige for such of his enterprises as the International Federation of a Victory Over Communism, which used the name Freedom Leadership Foundation in the United States. Two Cambridge University headliners, Lord Adrian and Lord Ashley, were quoted as not knowing of Moon's connection.

The close ties between the Unification Church and the very conservative South Korean government was documented by Andrew Ross and David McQueen in the July 2, 1975 *Guardian*. Radio of Free Asia, a Moon enterprise, was being investigated as possibly violating the Foreign Agents Registration Act. Colonel Pak, who has a $115,000 home in Fairfax County, was quoted: "Our movement is more important even than Martin Luther's 95 theses. The Rev. Moon's spiritual revolution will have a thousand times greater impact than the Christian Reformation."

Posing as a Unification Church recruit for six weeks, John Cotter, a reporter for the *New York Daily News,* underwent intensive indoctrination. He also observed the deprogramming of one Moon follower whose parents abducted him from the sect. The article appeared in the *News* and its sister paper, the *Chicago Tribune,* Dec. 18, 1975. A series of undistributed papers titled "The Master Speaks" showed, Cotter wrote, "that Moon is not above suggesting Watergate tricks of using beautiful young girls to try to influence senators. Furthermore," he confessed, "during my stay I battled the whirlwind of mind control and momentarily succumbed.

There were many glimpses of deceit and cunning; emotionally upset kids were told to reject their parents, a young girl was driven to tears when told she would have to give up her gift of art to truly serve the master," and more of the same.

Hustling money is the members' chief duty, Cotter wrote. Salonen said profits from street sales by 7,000 core members and some of the 23,000 supporters were $8 million annually.

Although the United States is Moon's chief target, he also said in a speech: "The present United Nations must be annihilated by our power. That is the stage for the Communist. We must have a new UN."

Cotter described the rigid regimentation to which recruits are subjected and the tremendous impact of the emotional appeals. There was no denying the church's political bias and activities. Before Nixon's resignation Moon was invited to the White House. He ran full-page newspaper ads to say: "At this time in history God has chosen Richard Nixon to be president of the United States. Therefore only God has the power and authority to dismiss him." In 1974 the Moonies worked for conservative Louis Wyman, Republican candidate for the U.S. Senate from New Hampshire, and helped defeat liberal Rep. Donald Fraser, Democrat from Minnesota.

The charge that the Moon campaign was intended to drum up anti-Communist sentiment and support for South Korean dictator Park Chung Hee was heard for one of the first times in the *Guardian* for June 2, 1976. As part of the buildup for a forthcoming Madison Square Garden rally the church spent more than $5 million to renovate and reopen the New Yorker Hotel.

In an article titled "The Rev. Moon: A Messiah—Or a Menace?" in the *National Observer* for June 12, 1976, Michael Putney updated the statistics on the church membership and wealth: 7 to 10,000 full-time workers, 30,000 part-time workers in America and 2 million active and associate members in 120 countries; property in New York city alone worth $16 to $17 million; another $10 million worth in Tarrytown and many other holdings throughout the country. He also told of the demonstrations and counter demonstrations at the June 1 Yankee Stadium rally when the 54,000 seat stadium was only two-thirds full. A sidebar to the article was a box containing Moon's comments on a dozen issues, including that congressmen are "just nothing," the Communists were responsible for Nixon's resignation, brothers and sisters in the movement are loved more than parents.

Susan M. Anderson began a series in the *Indianapolis Star* June 20, 1976 as follows: "A religious cult operating here 'brainwashes' its members into 'mental zombies' who engage in illegal fund raising activities which net more than $1 million annually, an investigation by the *Indianapolis Star* has revealed." The lengthy article described in detail the brainwashing techniques and quoted several former Moonies as to their effectiveness.

Moon's tie-in with the South Korean government was related during a Washington hearing by a House subcommittee. As reported by Marjorie Hyer for the *Washington Post* June 24, 1976, a former attaché testified that Colonel Pak was permitted to send messages on the Korean embassy's cable channel that presumably went only to the foreign minister, the director of KCIA, the prime minister or the president. Sept. 5 the *Post* ran an article by Janis Johnson telling of the plans for a Bicentennial God Bless America rally Sept. 18 at the Washington Monument. Plans of about 750 foreign followers to leave before being deported were coupled with the hint that Moon himself might shift his center of operations to Europe.

Sept. 16, 1976, two days before the rally, Robert Signer wrote from Washington for the *Chicago Daily News* that some congressmen and their staffs were offered chocolate-chip cookies, whereas others were offered all-expenses-paid trips to Korea. One of those who turned down the trip offer was Sen. Robert Dole of Kansas, who shortly thereafter became the Republican vice-presidential candidate on the ticket headed by President Gerald Ford. Moonie operations on Capitol Hill slowed down after the onset of investigations by a congressional committee and the Internal Revenue Service. Most congressmen were returning modest gifts of ginseng tea, tea bottles and plastic spoons.

The demonstrations in 1973 and 1974 opposing the impeachment of President Nixon were requested by the South Korean Central Intelligence Agency, it was announced by the Department of Justice, which was investigating South Korean attempts to influence American public opinion. The details were given by Scott Armstrong and Maxine Cheshire in the *Washington Post* for Nov. 7, 1976.

As a result of charges made before a congressional subcommittee that funds to establish the Diplomat National Bank came into the country illegally, the syndicated columnist Jack Anderson divested himself of holdings in the bank, the UPI reported from Washington Nov. 22, 1976. Anderson publicly stated he had no financial interest in the bank which he had helped organize to assist the Asian-American community to establish its first national bank. "I looked upon my affiliation as a service to the Asian-American minority," Anderson said.

Near the end of 1976 criticism of the Unification Church began to snowball. From New York, William Claiborne of the *Washington Post* reported Dec. 29, 1976 that leaders of three major religious organizations denounced Moon's church as a "breeding ground" for anti-Semitic, anti-Christian and anti-democratic beliefs. The leaders were spokesmen for the American Jewish Committee, the Catholic Archdiocese of New York and the National Council of Churches.

In an 11-page report, according to James H. Bowman in the *Chicago Daily News* for July 2–3, 1977, a commission of the National Council of Churches denied the Unification Church is Christian. It was denied membership in the Council of Churches in the City of New York. Citing "an informed source," the UPI reported from Washington Nov. 12, 1977 that the House investigating committee had "very reliable information" of the connection between Moon and the South Korean government. Documents presumably indicated that Moon's support of Nixon was "to bring new life to the archangel, Nixon—hence to make him aware of our significance."

A "positively bizarre" account of how Moon tried to make a small Alabama community, Bayou LaBatre, "an important hub in his booming business empire" was written by Ellen Warren for the *Chicago Sun-Times* of May 6, 1979. A group calling itself Concerned Citizens of the South vainly attempted to prevent the Moonies from buying much of the waterfront property, but the majority of the 2,500 citizens were indifferent or favorably impressed by the neat appearance and good manners of the newcomers.

Another journalistic view from within the Unification Church was provided by James Warren, whose full-page article, "My Four Days With the Moonies: Reporter finds they're anti-sin, anti-sex, and anti-semitic" appeared in the *Chicago Sun-Times* for July 8, 1979. The headline about summarizes the account. The Moonies, Warren said, tried to save him from "a decaying civilization." It didn't work, "But Lord, did the Moonies try." Church members, Warren found, are mainly American kids from small towns and foreigners with little prior religious experience. Among the "array of outrageous assertions" that the disciples accepted was that the DC-10 crash at O'Hare field was God-ordained because five of the passengers were members of the staff of *Playboy*.

In the fall of 1979 a special committee of the Illinois House of Representatives began an investigation of cults in the state. Patrick Hickey, director of the Unification Church in Illinois, immediately cried "witch hunt" and told Rep. Betty J. Hoxsey, committee chairwoman, "Prayer and God are now gone from our schools. Will the tax exempt status be next?"

Sept. 16, 1979 the *Tucson* (Ariz.) *Daily Star* ran a column-long Associated Press story from New York, telling of the direct-mail campaign to sell a $15 home study course in the Unification Church's beliefs. The goal was to solicit at least one million New Yorkers before invading other large cities similarly. The AP quoted liberally from Moon's six-page letter to prospects asking them "to put aside whatever you have heard about me and read this letter with an open mind."

Land purchases in Gloucester to expand the church's fishing business and give it a major new conference and training center in Massachusetts were reported in the *Boston Globe* for July 8, 1980 by James L. Franklin. He quoted the church's figures to show 10,000 active members in the United States and 40,000 associate members.

"I would not be standing here today if my skin were white and my religion were Presbyterian. I am here today because my skin is yellow and my religion is Unification Church," said Sun Myung Moon when he was arraigned on federal charges that he failed to report $162,000 of his income in his returns for 1973 to 1975. The UPI reported Oct. 23, 1981 from New York that 2,000 followers demonstrated in his support. The indictment was returned by a federal grand jury in New York Oct. 15 and was, of course, reported by the press associations and played prominently in most American metropolitan newspapers. Also indicted was a close associate, Takeru Kamiyama. Church officials denied the charges and said they are "a fundamental attack on all religions in America."

The CIA asked the United States Supreme Court to block what it called an unprecedented court order that it turn over "sensitive intelligence information" to the Unification Church. The CIA said the information should be withheld under exceptions to the FOI Act to forbid publication of matters injurious to "foreign policy or national security." The UPI reported on the case from Washington Oct. 23, 1981. Chief Justice Warren Burger granted the CIA a stay of the order.

By a 5 to 4 vote the Supreme Court struck down part of a Minnesota law that required religious organizations to disclose their funding sources if they collect more than half their money by public solicitation. The court said the law was discriminatory, not affecting all religious bodies equally. It was definitely intended to cripple the Moonies and Hare Krishnas.

The Unification Church won an even more important legal victory when the New York Court of Appeals unanimously decided it should be considered a religious organization for taxation purposes, the UPI reported May 7, 1982 from Albany.

The low esteem in which much of the public holds the Moonies was demonstrated when a Korean-born operator of two produce markets in New York City bought a third and much larger company. The rumor first appeared in the Gabby Tabby column of the weekly *Williston Times* that the church was the real owner. Although the paper retracted and apologized, Who Whang's business declined 25 percent. *Newsday* ran the story Feb. 14, 1982 under a Williston Park dateline.

May 18, 1982 the church published the first edition of a five-day-a-week newspaper, the *Washington Times*. It already published two New York dailies, the *News World* and the Spanish language *Noticles del Mundo*. Editor and publisher James R. Whelan said, "The *Washington Times* will represent the interest of no one religion, any more than it will close its mind or pages to any moral man or cause."

The next day a federal court jury found Moon guilty of conspiracy to evade taxes on about $162,000 in personal income for 1973, 1974 and 1975. The AP reported from New York May 19 that Moon expected to appeal. July 27, 1982 the press reported that Moon was sentenced to 18 months in jail and ordered to pay a $25,000 fine. Moon immediately appealed the sentence.

Aug. 20, 1982 a federal judge in Detroit ruled that Moon controls the Unification Church and can be held responsible for damages it may cause.

The case involved charges of a former member that she suffered emotionally as a result of five years as a member.

Paul Galloway was the author of a full-page report of an interview with
a disillusioned Moonie in the *Chicago Sun-Times* for Aug. 31, 1982. Oct. 4
Moon took out full-page advertisements in papers throughout the country
to denounce the movie critics for their review of *Inchon,* starring Laurence Olivier and financed by Moon's church.

Sun Moon's ability to receive free publicity from even an unfriendly
press was demonstrated when the *Chicago Tribune* devoted almost half of
its page 1 for July 2, 1982 to a picture of the mass wedding ceremony in
Madison Square Garden, New York, when 2,075 identically dressed
couples were married by Moon. All of the matches were dictated by Moon,
in whose judgment the newlyweds had complete faith, believing he transmitted the will of God. In an attempt to combat prejudice 546 of the couples
were interracially mixed, mostly Orientals with Caucasians. The *Tribune*
and, it believed, most other newspapers that covered the event declined the
church's offer to pay all expenses. In a July 4 followup the *Los Angeles
Times* revealed that all but a few of the couples would have to wait years to
consummate their vows, as the church insists on celibacy for 3½ years as a
prelude.

Tom Maier interviewed some of the couples from the Chicago area for
the *Sun-Times* of July 8, 1982. Ronald Koonce was to return to the church's
mission in Kentucky and his bride, Mei-yun Chen, was to return to her
export-import job in Taiwan. Asked when they expected to live together,
they said, "It all depends."

Ellen Goodman in her *Boston Globe* syndicated column for July 10,
1982 emphasized the difference between Moon's ceremony—"Everybody
now changes partners a-a-a-and MARRY"—and the traditional "ceremony
that celebrates something personal, a feeling that exists between one man
and one woman." She pointed out that "We demand love even in the most
stately sort of marriages. Prince Charles, great-nephew of a man hounded
out of the palace because he wanted to marry the woman he loved, was
hounded for evidence that he loved the woman he was marrying."

From Seoul the AP reported Oct. 15, 1982 that 5,887 couples from 83
countries were married there by Moon, who had determined the match-
ings.

20

More Cults

Shannon Jo Ryan's fascination with an Indian mystic was typically American. In a full-page article, "The Quest for a Guru," in the *National Observer* for Sept. 14, 1974 Michael T. Malloy quoted Baba Virsa Singh, a Sikh saint: "There is no place that God does not live. You don't have to come to India to get religion." Nevertheless, he estimated footloose young people make up a good share of the 400,000 visitors—more than 60,000 Americans—who come to India every year. Many (no estimates available) were converted to some offshoot of Hinduism before making their pilgrimage; others became converts after visits to holy men and places in the Himalayas. Malloy reported, however, that many best known in the West are almost unheard of and command little respect in India.

One such movement is Transcendental Meditation which a Buddhist monk told Malloy is virtually unknown in India. What caused the American press to advertise Maharishi (meaning Great Saint) Mahesh Yogi were the visits he received from famous entertainers. Perhaps the most important, the UPI reported Feb. 18, 1968 from Rishikesh, India, were Shirley MacLaine, Mia Farrow and the four Beatles. Sylvie Reice reported in the *Chicago Daily News* for Feb. 14, 1968 on a Yogi New York press conference during which the Beatles denied knowing how much money the rock quartet donated to TM. In a press conference of his own, according to the *Chicago Tribune* for May 20, 1968, John Lennon branded the Beatles' association with Yogi, "a mistake." Nevertheless, James Tuohy began his report of a press conference in the *Chicago Sun-Times* for Oct. 21, 1968: "The word of the Maharishi Mahesh Yogi, teacher of transcendental meditation to the Beatles and other show biz biggies, is being spread this week in Chicago." The word spreader was Charles Lutes, a salesman for the Blue Diamond Steel Company in Los Angeles. He induced 35 of his audience of 80 to invest $35 each to become mantras, or sponsors. Mrs. Nancy Jackson of Beverly Hills, Calif. dropped the names of numerous celebrities, including Efrem Zimbalist and Beatles Ringo and Paul. It seems that once a mantra, always a mantra.

When the Maharishi himself visited Illinois his picture with Gov. Daniel Walker appeared in papers of March 14, 1973. The Illinois General Assembly gave the Maharishi a standing ovation after he thanked it for passing a resolution that encouraged the spread of TM, the movement he began in 1959. He also was cheered by 400 delegates to a conference in Chicago of the American Association for Higher Education—his message, "a sublime plan for all mankind" so that there can be peace. The plan called for two 15-minute periods a day sitting in an upright position with eyes closed while the mind dwells on a meaningful humming sound known as a mantra.

May 2, 1974 the Top Line on page one of the *Chicago Sun-Times* was: "TM—the benefits behind the ballyhoo." According to Michael Kernan, author of the story, there were more than 300,000 American converts. Medical authorities as well as addicts were quoted as believing in the therapeutic value of TM—"expanding awareness, increasing intelligence, lowering body tensions and conquering addiction to liquor, tobacco and drugs." The story originated in the *Washington Post*.

Reader Bernard C. Colby admitted the value of TM, "a relaxing technique, more restful than sleep, that can be learned in a couple of hours." Because TM is a variety of Hinduism it should not be taught in public schools. Colby claimed there were 15,000 practitioners in the Chicago area alone.

While Yogi's followers pressured for public school instruction in TM, the Maharishi continued his own educational program. It was startling news for the *Chicago Tribune* and other papers Sept. 1, 1974 that the Maharishi International University had purchased bankrupt Parsons College in Fairfield, Iowa for $2.5 million and intended to move the school's campus from Santa Barbara to Iowa and to offer eight bachelor of arts and one master of arts degrees.

All of which made newsworthy a *Washington Post* article by Eugene L. Meyer that the *Philadelphia Inquirer* used Oct. 5, 1975 with the headline, "Meditation: Big Business Worth Millions." More than a million people worldwide—600,000 of them Americans—have made TM a $20-million business in the United States alone. The article gave details of the worldwide financial structure. Among other items of income $4.4 million was collected by the Maharishi International University in Fairfield, Iowa where the course centered on TM and the science of creative intelligence.

In an article written for the Associated Press and used by papers Dec. 24, 1975, Barbara L. Archer reported on an interview with Dr. Herbert Benson, cardiologist at the Harvard Medical School. The doctor corroborated findings that TM caused a "relaxation response," but enumerated several other ways by which the same result can be obtained without a four-day course costing $125 as the TM proponents recommend.

Another iconoclastic article appeared in the *Journal of Experimental Psychology* and was reviewed in the *Chicago Daily News* for July 12, 1976.

Author was Prof. William Plotkin of the University of Chicago who said the typical alpha brain wave rhythm of 8 to 9 cycles a second, which the TM advocates say results from their treatment, actually is the result of eye movement and nothing else.

Not content with success in teaching tense persons to relax, in late 1976 Yogi made public at TM headquarters in Seelisburg, Switzerland the possibility of some exciting by-products of TM. Called Siddihs, they are the abilities to fly and to become invisible. Nick Wolff, Chicago area media coordinator for TM, told Bill Gordon of the *Chicago Tribune:* "This is nothing new or spectacular. It's just an extension of what we've been saying all along." Gordon's article was published June 22, 1977.

A week later Abe Peck of the *Chicago Sun-Times* attended a lecture by Prof. Jonathan Shear, head of the philosophy department at MIU, which was advertised as being on "Highly-developed mind-body coordination, verified by direct experience of Levitation—command of the law of gravity, whereby the body lifts up, moves forward and comes down—inner experience of great freedom and bliss, release of deep stress . . ." The closest that the professor would come to demonstrating levitation was to inform his audience of 30 that anyone can master the art and learn to be invisible by taking a 10-week course costing $275 to $365 per week. Peck's story was published June 30, 1977.

About the same time the Associated Press sent Kay Bartlett to South Fallsburg, N.Y., site of TM's Capital of the Age of Enlightenment. It is there that the training in flying is given. Bartlett met quite a few TM practitioners who were skeptical of the flying program, fearful that it would be detrimental to the movement. Others said only time was needed to perfect techniques. There were no demonstrations and no picture taking. The AP feature appeared among other places in the *Chicago Daily News* for Nov. 12–13, 1977.

Early in 1979 a three-judge panel of the United States Court of Appeals for the Third Circuit in Philadelphia ruled that TM is a religion and should not be taught in public schools. Originally the suit was brought by a group of parents after five New Jersey schools began courses in Science of Creative Intelligence. To counter the defendants' denial of any religious aspect, the plaintiff quoted the chant that students were required to recite: "Guru in the glory of Brahma; guru in the glory of Vishnu; guru in the glory of the great Lord Shiva; guru in the glory of personified transcendental fullness of Brahma, to Him, to Shri Guru Dev adorned with glory. I bow down."

When a native Chicagoan and University of Chicago graduate returned to her home town to teach meditation, the *Sun-Times* had Paul Galloway write a full-page story for the Feb. 24, 1982 issue. The 42-year-old woman was born Joy Siegel and had been a leading New York choreographer, but after six years of study in Ganeshpuri, India, returned to the United States as Paramananda, which means supreme bliss, and as a swami, which means she is a leading teacher in an ancient order of monks, the Saraswati. She believes that the American "stressful, fast-moving, absolutely-positively-has-to-be-there-overnight lives are crying out for the venerable time-tested . . . dose of Eastern philosophy." She explains, "Siddha meditation is not a religion. It's a technique with a philosophy behind it. We can increase creativity, get relief from stress, realize our potential, enhance our spiritual lives with it."

The first and most important cultural importation into the United States from India during the present century is yoga, a system of Hindu philosophy that seeks through exercises to attain an exalted state of the faculties wherein they would be freed of all consciousness of the outer world. Yoga came to Broadway in February 1920 and, according to a long article in the *Kansas City Star* for July 3, 1936, was ridiculed by the New York press. In 1926 Hindu Yogi Wassan was received in Kansas City much more favorably. Then, in 1936, the *London Illustrated News* published pictures of Hindu Subbayah Pullavar suspended in midair. The pictures were taken by P. T. Plunkett, South India tea planter who "explained that Yogi's levitation was performed in a trance in which a virtual state of rigormortis was achieved, enabling the yogi to support himself merely by resting one hand on a cane. The picture was reproduced worldwide causing considerable controversy.

From then on interest in yoga grew steadily in the United States, where a flock of Indians came to lecture and establish groups. July 2, 1971 the *New York Times* had a big illustrated spread of about 60 Catholic nuns and priests attending the second annual Yoga Ecumenical Retreat at Annhurst College in South Woodstock, Conn. Leader was Swami Satchidananda, an Indian Hindu monk who founded the Integral Yoga Institute in New York and more than a dozen other cities. The Rev. George A. Maloney, professor of Eastern spiritualism at Fordham University, declared that the growing interest among Catholics was a direct outgrowth of the Second Vatican Council of 1962 to 1965. Several attendants said yoga can deepen their prayer lives and enhance their practice and understanding of Christianity.

How a young Chicago woman held funeral services for herself to become Ma Yogaleens instead of Linda Ardisana was told by Roy Larson in a half-page article in the *Chicago Sun-Times* for July 28, 1974. As Ma, she became overseer of the Himalayan International Institute of Yoga Science and Philsoophy at Prospect Heights, Ill. The institute was founded and directed by Shri Swami Rama who excited Ardisana's original interest by a speech at Chicago's Pick Congress Hotel.

A similar story of conversion appeared in the *Chicago Daily News* for Sept. 23, 1974. In it Kathryn Christensen told of two couples and a woman who were influenced by different leaders to adopt yoga as a way of life. One husband declared, "In a spiritual sense Kryananda represents God to me." One couple, influenced by Maharishi Mashesh Yogi, said TM is a technique, not a religion, to them. A former well-paid writer for *Esquire* and *Village Voice* had her life "turned around" by Swami Muktananda, world-touring Indian whom she said she adored, and for whom she does publicity.

The effectiveness of that publicity was seen when the holy man visited Chicago. Sept. 10, 1974 the *Tribune* gave an entire page to pictures and text. Under the heading, "Roses, Chants Greet Touring Guru," there were shots of shoes of followers piled up at the entrance to the guru's hotel room; a follower on his knees with his head touching the floor before Swami Muktananda who was holding court; the swami's sharing his throne with his pet dog; the license plate on his automobile, BABA, a term of affection for a saint, and a head shot of the sainted one. In the accompanying story James Robison quoted Muktananda as warning against fake gurus and saying too many people are seeking "cheap gurus."

"Meditation pro at Work," was the heading of the full page the *Chicago Sun-Times* gave the visiting celebrity Sept. 14, 1974. The wise man was shown giving a gesture of peace to a roomful of followers on their knees.

Roy Larson quoted the swami's answers to questions, including, "In a nutshell what is your teaching?" to which the interpreter gave the leader's reply: "Kneel to your own self. Honor and worship your own being. God dwells within you as you."

The same day the *Chicago Daily News* announced the swami's visit with a page-wide streamer headline. James H. Bowman quoted Agehananda Bharati, chairman of the anthropology department at Syracuse University, as saying that Muktananda is "one of the top five or six to come here from India." Most of the others he called "caricatures." Followers kneel and touch the master's feet because cosmic power presumably flows from the feet, he explained.

Sunday, Dec. 15, 1974, James Robison wrote: "Epilog. What Makes the Swami's Disciples Run?" His article was a lengthy recitation of the reasons three converts gave him, all adding up to an apparently satisfactory search for peace and inner security.

In June 1978 the third annual International Congress on Yoga, Meditation and Holistic Health was held in Chicago. Jeff Lyon seized the opportunity to interview the Swami Rama for the *Chicago Tribune* of June 12, 1978. He learned that the Oxford-trained founder and spiritual leader of the Himalayan Institute sleeps less than three hours daily and stopped his heart beat for 17 seconds several times at the Menninger Clinic and the University of Minnesota. He also said he can stop his blood flow and control the temperature of different parts of his body. And, he said, anyone can learn to do the same.

The extent to which yoga has influenced Americans of all kinds was shown by the large attendance at a panel on "Metapsychiatry: the Interface Between Psychiatry and Mysticism" at an American Psychiatric Association meeting, as reported by Ruth Winter in the *Chicago Sun-*

Times for Oct. 27, 1974. Dr. Stanley R. Dean, clinical professor of psychiatry at the University of Miami, crusades among his colleagues to bridge the gap between the medical and psychic sciences, He says that practitioners of yoga have learned to control the so-called "involuntary" functions. He also spoke sympathetically of Kirlian photography, which presumably shows auras around faith healers and patients.

In his *National Observer* article (see page 431) that appeared the same day as the Chicago eulogy to Muktananda, Michael T. Malloy wrote that educated Indians consider 75 percent of the gurus to be frauds. A newsman said of the America-based teen-aged Guru Maharaj Ji: "The Americans say, 'the guru has come.' The guru says, 'The money has come.' " And God is amused.

By the time Malloy made that observation the boy evangelist had made three visits to the United States while on round-the-world peace trips. The first, in 1971, when Maharaj Ji was 13, attracted little attention. Newsweek Feature Service did distribute an article by Peter Greenberg that appeared, among other places, in the *Pittsburgh Press* for Oct. 15, 1971. By quoting the answers to questions during a press conference in Hollywood's Divine Light Mission, Greenberg suggested the frustration journalists encounter when they attempt to get straightforward easy-to-understand answers to their questions. After Maharaj Ji said: "The aim and purpose of my life is to spread the true nature of the soul to humanity," he was asked, "Give me that knowledge." The guru replied, "I can't answer materialistic requests."

At that time Maharaj Ji claimed 3 million followers throughout the world, including 2,000 mahatmas in India. A mahatma is a "great soul," according to a comprehensive article, "The Guru Business," by Khushwant Singh, editor of the *Illustrated Weekly of India,* in the *New York Times Magazine* for April 29, 1973. The article also contained definitions of many other terms, including darshann (the blessing that flows from the sight of a saintly person); diksha (spiritual); gu (dark); run (light); bhagwans (gods); swamis (lords); rishis (sages); maharishis (great sages); acharyas (teachers); sants (saints); mantras (sacred words endowed with magical properties); ashram (hermitage) and Gurudev (guru god). The name given the youthful guru at birth was Pratap Singh Rawat. When at the age of 8 he succeeded his father as head of the Divine Light Mission, he became known as both Balyogeshwas (child god) and Shri Guru Maharaj Ji. By the time of Singh's article the Divine Light Mission claimed 4 million followers in 63 countries. Maharaj Ji, however, was no more definite in describing his mission. He told Singh that people come to him for knowledge and "I give them the maha (great) mantra. I tell them the true aim of human life. It is not to eat, drink and be merry; it is realization, the true realization of God. I am not God, I am only his servant."

In its issue of April 23, 1973 the *Times* devoted two full pages to letters commenting on the Singh article. "I was one who has experienced the 'knowledge' and found it to be the antithesis of what it purports to be," wrote Susan F. Lyman of Canton, N.Y. "True knowledge of God should not tell us to shave our heads or live adrift from society or even give up everything we own," wrote Thomas C. Swain of Greenlawn, N.Y. An anonymous correspondent wrote of "the evident destruction he has wrought upon our lives." Only one letter, from Dr. Edward S. Hanzelik, of the Divine Health Care Services, was sympathetic.

In an Associated Press story from New York Aug. 10, 1973, George Cornell called Divine Light Mission "an apparently snowballing movement—in assets, operations and fervent young crowds—building up around a teenage guru from India and his promise of 'the knowledge.' " Cornell reported that the movement has branches in 30 American cities, a monthly magazine, *And it is Divine,* with 90,000 circulation, a bi-weekly newspaper, *Divine Times,* with 60,000 circulation, and American head-quarters in Denver. The organization also had a public relations organization, a dance ensemble, a theatrical troupe, a food cooperative, a film-production agency, an aviation service and a wholesale firm dealing in electronics and office equipment.

Certainly such whirlwind success justified the streamer heading, "Teen guru finds fame, fortune" in the *Chicago Daily News* for Aug. 17, 1973. In the accompanying story Betty Flynn revealed that the movement now claimed 5 million adherents, 40,000 of them Americans who revered the boy as Divine Lord and Perfect Master. Flynn said the knowledge, achieved through meditation, faith and revelation, consists of four elements: the light, the word, the music and the nectar—"all revelations of God within one self." Two days later, in the *News'* Aug. 19–20, 1973 issue, Walter Morrison reported on the rally that 4,000 Chicagoans attended in the Auditorium theater. "For the most part," he wrote, "the audience sat in rapt attention. Some young women among the faithful had tears in their eyes. A few hecklers were in the audience and one irreverent listener let fly with eight letters of Anglo-Saxon barnyard disbelief." The guru apparently said nothing that had not been published before.

A few days later, however, Maharaj Ji made headlines not to his liking. From New Delhi Aug. 25, 1973 the Associated Press reported that before he was allowed to leave India he had to post a $13,300 bond because he was under investigation on a charge of smuggling. A year earlier, it was revealed, customs officers had seized $35,000 worth of jewelry, watches and foreign currency he and his disciples had with them when they returned from an American trip. The movement insisted the riches were used to support 3,000 Western devotees who came to India to meditate for a month. Chicago newspapers carried the story.

Better publicity was that which originated May 20, 1974 from Denver. The Associated Press reported two days later that Maharaj Ji had married his 24-year-old secretary, Marrolyn Lois Johnson, a former United Airline stewardess, after receiving special permission from a Juvenile Court judge, necessary because of his youthful age, 16. By then the Divine Light Mission claimed 40,000 American followers and 6 million worldwide.

In the first of two articles she wrote for the Knight newspapers (which the *Chicago Tribune* published July 14 and 15, 1974) Patsy Sims revealed that Indian authorities never filed charges against "the sausage shaped kid" for smuggling. After a visit to the Denver headquarters of the Divine Light Mission, she no longer was sure that it was just a passing fad. She found that the operation takes in and spends about $3 million a year; spares no expense on such extravaganzas as $1 million for a Millennium in Houston; had a plan for a $50-million City of Love and Light to be built near San Antonio; at least 56 cars plus another $80,000 worth of Maseratis and Rolls Royces reserved for God Junior and his family, with headquarters in at least 40 American cities and 36 foreign countries to serve 8 million followers worldwide, 50,000 of them in the United States. In addition to operating all of the other journalistic and business enterprises cited by earlier biographers, despite this opulence Patsy Sims quoted Kasturi Rauugan, correspondent for the *New York Times* in New Delhi, as insisting, "Indians know him only because of the United States publicity."

In the first of three articles on "The Mind Strokers," that began running in the *Chicago Daily News* Sept. 21–22, 1974, Kathryn Christensen said Maharaj Ji is the most famous of "the Indian gurus who've left their homeland and the Ganges river for the milk and honey of North America or Europe. Whether legitimate operations or outright frauds they usually enjoy a nonprofit status with the Internal Revenue Service."

"Little is known about Maharaj Ji's system because he refuses to reveal his techniques. He says he has the ability to teach 'perfect knowledge' which enables his devotees to develop a 'spiritual energy' that can be seen in the form of a divine light in their bodies," Christensen wrote.

As frequently happens when one member of a family strikes it rich, parents, siblings, offspring and others become involved in squabbles about how the proceeds should be split. The *Denver Post* for Dec. 1, 1974 carried a half-page account of the effort of Mata Ji, mother of the guru, to persuade him to return to India. A fortnight earlier it had been announced that she and another son, Bal Bhagwan, had taken over the London headquarters of the movement. Joe Anctil, the guru's press agent, about whom the *Post* ran a sidebar, belittled the matter, saying Mata Ji was acting as a mother would. "She feels her son is too young and she still wants some control. But the problem is not bitter or hateful." The mother also disapproved of her guru son's marriage to an American girl in a Christian ceremony.

The matter, however, wasn't so easily dismissed. From Lucknow, India April 14, 1975 the Associated Press reported that the guru said he is still a "perfect master" worthy of worship. This was his answer to his mother's declaration a fortnight earlier that he led "a despicable, nonspiritual way of life in the United States." Police withdrew permission for a Divine Light

Mission festival, fearing that a test of the rival strengths of mother and son would lead to rioting. Maharaj Ji said he intended to see his mother. He put his movement's strength at 500,000 in the United States and 8 million in India.

Feb. 26, 1979 Virginia Culver reported that Marahaj Ji spoke to 8,000 followers in the Denver Coliseum. There was much music and gift giving. The guru told the audience he could give all knowledge leading to "perfect-ness," but not unless they "open up to let in the knowledge and surrender confusion."

Another dissenter received almost a full page in Virginia Culver's article in the *Denver Post* for March 2, 1979. He is Ron Isaacks who said, "Instead of being the liberating experience I had joined to have, I ended up feeling quite limited, held seemingly helpless by the fear of leaving . . . I decided to leave the cult because I noticed dangerous similarities to the Jim Jones cult in Guyana."

March 7, 1979 Virginia Culver reported that the cult was moving its national headquarters from Denver to Miami because of the latter place's accessibility to overseas flights.

After the Peoples Temple disaster in Guyana, a former president and former vice president of the Divine Light Mission called a press conference to say that a similar catastrophe might occur as the result of the sadistic actions of Guru Maharaj Ji. Specifically they accused him of beating cult members with sticks and smearing their bodies with abrasive chemicals. They also accused Maharaj Ji of disobeying cult laws against drinking, drug smoking and eating meat. Jim Kirksey covered the story for the *Denver Post* of Nov. 25, 1979. The next day the same reporter quoted the two accusers as saying some devotees took pride in being abused by the guru.

Dec. 2, 1979 Marahaj Ji, who lived with his family in Malibu, Calif., was reported as intending to ignore the attacks on him. Dec. 15, 1979 in a half-page feature by Virginia Culver, the *Denver Post's* religion editor, the sect's public relations man, Joe Anctil, said the guru's mission was "peace and love" and he "has no intention of getting in fights with critics or wasting time in court battles with every crackpot that comes along." Anctil said the cult has 1.2 million members in 59 countries—15,000 in the United States.

To obtain the right to have their own religious services within the Denver county jail, two members of the Divine Light Mission brought suit in U.S. District court in Denver, Brad Martisius reported for the *Denver Post* of Feb. 25, 1981. Settlement of the case whereby the inmates won the right was reported Sept. 3, 1981 by agreement, whereupon the two dropped their suit.

Another of the many recently organized California sects is the Church Universal and Triumphant, originally called the Summit Lighthouse, organized in 1958 by Mark Prophet in Washington D.C. In 1961 Prophet, 42, married Elizabeth Clare Wulf, who says that when she was 3 or 4 years old she realized she had lived before on the Nile in Egypt. When Prophet died of a stroke in 1973, his widow waited eight months before marrying a Summit member, Randall King. They changed the name of the sect, purchased the old Claretville Seminary in Calabassa, Calif., and changed the name to Camelot, where they operate a tremendous financial organization with many ramifications.

Russell and Norman R. Chandler wrote a full-page article on "Guru Ma—Leader of Multimillion-Dollar Church" for the *Los Angeles Times* of Feb. 11, 1980. It was mostly biographical of Mrs. King, her early espousal of the I AM concept of "ascended master" and reincarnation through karma, and especially of the many business enterprises about which the church declines to make disclosures. In a full-page advertisement, "Church Challenges Times Portrayal," in the *Times* for April 8, 1980, Guru Ma's representatives protested that "Inconclusive rumors distort truth of economic individualism, healing and the awakening of self-worth in Jesus Christ." Unchallenged, however, was the Chandlers' statement: "As the name suggests, the aim of the organization is to guide disciples, or *chelas,* into the summit of their potential through the teachings of the ascended masters." Among the ascended masters are Jesus, Buddha, Zoroaster, Lao-tse, Confucius and St. Germain, who, they believe, was embodied as St. Joseph, husband of the Virgin Mary, a priest from the lost continent of Atlantis, Merlin the Magician, Christopher Columbus and Francis Bacon, among others.

In their reply the church leaders wrote, "The church's steady and stable growth is a testimony not to murky finances but to the ability of our ministry and the teachings of the ascended masters to satisfy the deep spiritual needs of our parishioners."

As happens to so many new sects, that of Guru Ma ran into trouble with different governmental agencies. Feb. 22, 1981 James Quinn reported in the *Los Angeles Times* that the architect publicly asserted that the church violated many building code restrictions in its remodeling of the Calabassas property into Camelot. That brought county inspectors and warnings from their superiors. In that and other stories the desire of the National Park Service to acquire the property for inclusion in the Santa Monica Mountains National Recreation Area is mentioned. Sept. 22, 1981 Russell Chandler reported in his paper that the Church Universal and Triumphant had purchased a 12,000 acre ranch adjoining the Yellowstone National Park from magazine publisher Malcolm F. Forbes. In a letter soliciting contributions to help raise the $7 million purchase price, Guru Ma had written it would ensure "protection from economic collapse, bank failure, civil disorder, war and cataclysm."

Another group that moved to obtain seclusion is that devoted to the "free-sex guru," as Bhagwan Shree Rajneesh is nicknamed. In June 1981 he quietly left his six-acre Ashram in Poona, India on a one year's tourist visa to settle on Muddy Ranch, an overgrazed and played out 64,000-acre ranch 17 miles from Antelope, Oregon.

Carol Oppenheim wrote a half-page detailed article on the nature and history of the sect for the *Chicago Tribune* of Oct. 25, 1981. In three months the disciples, their number approaching 200, planted and irrigated 150 acres of sunflowers and cleared another 2,200 acres for sowing winter wheat. They graded and graveled miles of dirt roads, and raised a half-dozen buildings for a school, a medical clinic, a communications center and a communal cafeteria. The nearby 40 residents of Antelope became worried when the newcomers made some property purchases but relaxed somewhat when the sect petitioned the county to be incorporated as a town, details of which Oppenheim related in another article Nov. 11, 1981.

Bhagwan means "The Blessed One, He Who Has Recognized Himself as God." His disciples became unpopular in Poona largely because of their caressing and kissing in public. Of their beliefs, Oppenheim wrote:

> The Bhagwan's philosophy has been described as giving up one's ego to create a "life-affirmative religiousness." In one of his lectures he urges people not to long for nirvana but to live life totally in order to be free. Critics say this is a form of mind control and could lead to losing touch with reality.
>
> At Poona he combined traditional Eastern mysticism and meditation techniques with a smorgasbord of modern Western encounter group theories, such as primal scream, rolfing, Sufi dancing, massage hypotherapy, rebirthing, awareness training, tai chi, and Gestalt, to name a few.

The most controversial was the tantra in which disciples were instructed to shout, fight, and act out their sexual and other fantasies.

According to the Associated Press reporting March 12, 1982 from Antelope, the city council voted unanimously to hold an election to consider abandoning the town's 1901 charter. In that way, it was felt, the guru and his followers would not be so interested in taking over the place. Attorney for the commune said the group, now 280 strong, wanted to have its own town. July 5, 1982 the *Chicago Tribune* used a 4-col. UPI picture of 7,000 attending the cult's festival of Meditation on the former Big Muddy Ranch in Oregon.

In his inimitable subtly sarcastic style, Mike Royko printed and commented pointedly on money-raising letters from the Rev. Don of Phoenix, one of the less affluent Bible thumpers who scramble for the dollars that go mostly to the leading evangelists. Typical extracts from the Rev. Bob's correspondence follow:

> My ministry is in your hands! I have to talk to you. If I can't talk to you then who will I talk to?

Just when God is giving us the nations of the world, Satan has popped his head up to destroy everything God is doing . . .

We are facing going off TV, canceling tent crusades. A miracle has got to take place and God let me know that you are going to be part of it . . .

The roof is caving in. I can't go on until I hear from you.

After quite a bit more of this, Royko concluded: "I'll say this for the Rev. Don. If he ever runs out of people who send him $20 and has to give up mail-order preaching, he would make one heck of a hotel clerk."

Over the years cults have been newsworthy in a number of different ways, for example:

In a copyrighted story Feb. 9, 1926 from Madras, India, the *Chicago Tribune* announced the forthcoming ceremony to proclaim J. Krishnamut as the new Messiah, recalling the sensational statement by Mrs. Annie Besant, leader of the Theosophists, that the King of the World had told her that a teacher was returning to Earth to reestablish decadent religion.

Dec. 3, 1937 the tabloid *Chicago Daily Times* gave almost a full page to a copyrighted interview with "Father" Giuseppe Maria Abbate, who said: "The divine power is in me. I am his Holy temple . . . I am the one God promised to send." In his syndicated columns for Dec. 4 and 5, 1939, Westbrook Pegler was not so generous with Dr. Frank B. Robinson of Moscow, Idaho who operated a correspondence course called Psychiana to teach his religious philosophy. Pegler expressed skepticism about Robinson's alleged conversation with God and his nonpecuniary interest in his enterprise. This was one of the very few criticisms of any religious leader or group in a generation.

What was believed to be the last organized center of polygamy was destroyed when a caravan of more than 50 carloads of state police arrested 76 men and 86 women and took 263 children into custody at Short Creek, Arizona. Gladwin Hill wrote a detailed account for the July 27, 1953 *New York Times*. Organized in the '30s under the name United Effort, the commune was disowned by the Church of Jesus Christ of Latter Day Saints, commonly called the Mormons, which forbade polygamy in 1890 after the United States Supreme Court upheld anti-polygamy laws. Gov. Howard Pyle of Arizona termed the community a lawless commercial enterprise using religion as a screen for white slavery.

Bishop Homer Tomlinson, overseer of one faction of the Church of God, was arrested when he tried to enact the role of Moses by destroying the 5-foot concrete lettering spelling out the Ten Commandments at the Field of the Wood, the AP reported Oct. 28, 1953 from Murphy, N.C. The commandments had been carved in the mountainside by the bishop's brother, a church overseer. The bishop said he could not permit idolatry any more than Moses could permit his brother Aaron to make a golden calf. It was on this site that the brothers' father, A. J. Tomlinson, said he saw a vision that led him to found the church.

When a lecturer in eugenics at London University College told a scientific gathering that rabbits, cats, mice and ferrets had given birth without contact with males and that the same thing might happen to humans, the London *Sunday Pictorial* asked all women who had had virgin births to make the fact known. The medical profession received a jolt when an eminent doctor wrote in the prestigious *Lancet* that it was impossible to disprove the claims of 19 mothers, according to a UP dispatch from London June 29, 1956. A decade later the UPI reported from Moscow Oct. 12, 1966 that Dr. Igor Goldman of the Soviet Genetics Institute believes that a virgin birth is scientifically possible but the child would be a girl and an exact double of her mother.

The founder and eight followers of the Fountain of the World movement died when a bomb exploded in their headquarters at Chatsworth, Calif., the AP reported Dec. 10, 1958. The next day the *Chicago Tribune* devoted two full columns to the account of the incendiary action against 53 cultists. The cult was founded in 1949 by a San Francisco longshoreman, Francis Heindwater Pencovic, who took the name of Krisha Vesta, proclaimed himself the reincarnation of Jesus Christ and stated his purpose to be economic security, scientific advancement and spiritual uplift. The movement's aims were wisdom, knowledge, faith and love.

Thirty believers in the cult of St. John the Baptist refused to reveal the secret of their faith that allowed them to walk barefooted over ten feet of coals heated to 1,472 degrees. The AP reported from Buenos Aires June 25, 1962 that 15,000 observed the cult's leader, Angel Ali, whisper secret words to his followers, who showed no signs of injury from the experience.

Oct. 4, 1982 the UPI distributed a picture from Hong Kong showing a man who claimed miraculous powers from the Monkey King, a Chinese god, walking or running through fire on the monkey's birthday.

The power of another self-styled bishop was broken when two of his nuns escaped from his Brooklyn church and charged their leader with kidnapping, assault, illegal possession of a revolver and narcotics. Raiding police found that ex-convict Devernon LeGrande had a harem of 11 women, seven of them pregnant, and 47 children. The nun-clothed women were chauffeured to areas where they begged to raise $100 a day. The UPI reported the story Sept. 3, 1965.

After traveling 8,000 miles in a vain search for a site for a Shrine of Beauty, Walter and Lao Russell obeyed the Lord and obtained an abandoned country club at Swannanoa, Va. There they established a University of Science and Philosophy to operate a correspondence school whose courses on the Science of Spiritual Man had been taken by 50,000 mail-order students when Hank Burchard wrote a long feature for the *Washington Post* on Sept. 10, 1967.

Walter Russell, once touted as the man from whom Einstein stole secrets, died in 1963 on his 92nd birthday. Lao continued to lecture, mostly to chiropractor and Unity Church gatherings. Tourists visit the 52-room Italian villa and grounds where much artwork and sculpturing is displayed. There are pamphlets on Cosmic Consciousness with answers to such questions as: What is God? What is my soul? What is my mind? and What relation is electricity to thinking and to matter?

Failure of the American astronauts to find "dwarfs with voices like thunder on the moon" would disappoint members of the New Church of Jerusalem, its minister, the Rev. Ian Johnson, was reported to have said according to an AP story July 17, 1969 from Birmingham, England. The cultists are followers of philosopher Emanuel Swedenborg. If the dwarfs were not there, Johnson said, the reason could be that they had moved to another planet.

Almost a year after the moon flight two *Chicago Daily News* reporters, James K. Batton and Clarence Jones, questioned 1,721 persons selected at random on the streets of Philadelphia, Miami, Akron, Detroit, Washington, Macon and several small Carolina communities to discover that from 2 to 54 percent did not believe men actually had walked on the moon, they reported in their paper for June 19, 1970. During a radio talk-show in Chicago in which I participated a woman insisted that the moon walks were a hoax perpetrated by the Mobil Corporation.

The "hottest psychic just now in that crowded field of mediums, psychic surgeons, astrologers, fortune tellers, witches and medicine men," according to Wesley Pruden, Jr. in the *National Observer* for Jan. 19, 1974, was Gilbert Holloway of the Christ Light Community in Albuquerque, N.M. Being careful not to break the laws against fortune telling and practicing medicine without a license, Holloway conducted what station officials called "the most successful talk show" over radio station KOB. He demonstrated his ESP by describing callers' ailments and their fears and plans.

Perhaps the zaniest group anyone ever wrote about was the Church of the Living Apathetics whose founder, Gene Townsend, answered questions as reported in the *Chicago Sun-Times* for Jan. 23, 1976. It has to be read to be appreciated. A sample extract follows:

> "Do you have any scriptures?"
> "Yeah, it's a book filled with blank pages."
> "What's your chief symbol?"
> "It's a gray rectangle. It symbolizes nothing."

Another small and not too easy to understand organization is Eckankar. The *Chicago Daily News* Beeline March 22, 1976 obtained the following explanation from the Menlo Park, Calif. headquarters: "Eckankar is a non-profit, religious-education organization with over 3 million followers worldwide. The teachings of Eckankar are concerned with the preservation of the individual throughout eternity, and stress personal spiritual development as a result of conscious contact with the ECK., the audible creative life stream." So now you know.

When Milwaukee was being flooded with letters from Gene Ewing of the Church by Mail in Atlanta, the *Milwaukee Journal* investigated. Jan. 13, 1980 it reported that the letters were sent to street addresses, not persons. Recipients were asked to put a "faith handkerchief" in a Bible overnight and then return it, preferably with a $5 bill. Ewing promised to pray for all who responded and asked them to designate their worries. Better Business Bureaus and postal authorities were investigating.

The *New York Times* reported May 24, 1980 on a police raid of a tenement that interrupted a primitive religious rite involving the slaughter of animals. It was the first time raiders had witnessed the rite by a cult known as Santeria, derived from a West African religion called Yoruba, taken to Cuba by slaves in the 18th century.

To shock young Bible students into listening to God's word, the Rev. Dwight Wymer of the Immanuel Baptist Church of Grand Rapids, Mich, wired the pupils' stools to a 12-volt battery and screens were placed on the seats. The AP reported the story July 10, 1981. The next day, the *Chicago Sun-Times* reported the minister had succumbed to criticism and questioning by authorities and agreed to discontinue the practice.

The AP reported Dec. 20, 1980 from Burlington, N.C. that 125 members of the Truth Tabernacle Church tried Santa Claus as an imposter, found him guilty and hanged him in effigy. The sect says Christmas is the work of the devil; it allows no Christmas trees or presents. The *Burlington Daily Times-News* had devoted a half-page Dec. 15, 1980 to pictures and stories about the hanging. The children cheered and jeered and Elder R. R. Robertson explained that the real reason for boycotting Christmas is because it comes on the birthday of Tammuz, a pagan god.

Because, as members of the Foundation for Ubiquity cult, they believed they would be resurrected in three days, Kate and Keith Hagler hijacked a Continental bus and, when police refused to kill them, Kate killed her husband and then herself, the UPI reported July 4, 1982 from Jasper, Ark. In a followup the press association reported that Emory Lamb, the man the dead couple believed to be Jesus Christ, was not certain they would rise from the dead and he did not want their bodies taken to his home.

Among the recent news stories about cults have been the following:

June 20, 1982—The UPI reported from Victoria, British Columbia that a telephone warning that Satanist groups planned to sacrifice a baby was made without evidence by a worried Christian, but not until after security was tightened at all maternity wards and other places where infants could be obtained.

Aug. 15, 1982—The furor caused by passage of a Chicago city ordinance to forbid slaughtering by any religious group except for kosher killing was reported by Michael Cordts in the *Sun-Times*. Complaints were made by the Sabaean order, Santeria cult, and other groups whose membership is mostly former Caribbean island residents. Animal welfare groups said the sacrificial ceremonies often are extremely cruel.

Aug. 16, 1982—The Knight-Ridder Newspapers reported from San Jose that the FBI was investigating the Ananda Marga Yoga Society to determine if it is a foreign-based terrorist organization. Reports of violence in several parts of the world have been traced to sect members. Its guru, Prabhat Ranjan Sarkar, has been banned by the State Department from entering the United States.

Aug. 21, 1982—The AP reported from Fonda, N.Y. that 12,000 people have visited the shrine of Kateri Tekakwitha, an Indian maiden known as the Lily of the Mohawks, who died mysteriously at 24.

Sept. 26, 1982—The *Chicago Sun-Times* began running a four-part series by Paul Galloway, "The Evolution of a Cult," which dealt with a small radical religious group called C-U Ministries at the University of Illinois in Champaign-Urbana. After reciting the details of the group's operations and the deprogramming efforts of parents, among other sidebars Galloway answered, "What is a cult? How to define it," listing some of "the most accepted characteristics."

Oct. 24, 1982—At least two members of the all-black Christ Miracle Healing Center in Miracle Valley, Ariz. were killed when 40 sheriff deputies tried to serve traffic warrants on two church members. Chicago papers streamer-headlined the story, as the sect was formerly headquartered in that city.

Nov. 20, 1982—Ronald Yates reported for the *Chicago Tribune* from Los Angeles that a former member of the Rainbow Tribe testified in a custody suit that the Satanic group subjected small children to excessive cruelty, sexual promiscuity and drug abuse.

Nov. 23, 1982—Don Hayner reported in the *Sun-Times* about his visit to the Nichiren Shoshu Buddhist Temple in DuPage County, one of five such temples in the United States. Hayner sketched the history and beliefs of the cult that has 50,000 followers in the United States.

Nov. 24 and 25, 1982—The Associated Press reported from Wilmot, Ind. about the Faith Assembly Church, which takes seriously James 5:15: "And the prayer of faith will cure the sick." Public officials are frustrated in investigating 25 deaths they believe could have been prevented by medical care.

Dec. 8, 1982—Both Chicago newspapers covered the trials in Rensselaer, Ind. of a husband and wife who admitted beating their 3-year-old son to death on the urging of the leader of a cult in DeMotte, Ind. Three days later the papers reported that the cult leader was found guilty of involuntary manslaughter, battery, conspiracy and neglect of a dependent.

Dec. 19, 1982—Tom McNamee reported in the *Sun-Times* that Charles

L. Scudder, former Loyola University professor, was found gagged and shot five times in a weird "castle" near Summerville, Ga. where he practiced Satanic worship. Three days later McNamee reported that a suspect in the slaying was charged in Mississippi with the murder of a sailor.

Jan. 2, 1983 the *Chicago Tribune* gave a half-page to an article by Andy Knott telling what public officials and neighbors thought of the lifestyle of Scudder and another ex-Chicagoan, Joseph Odom, who lived with him and also was murdered.

May 6, 1983 the *Suburban Sun-Times* used a story by Anne Little about the lecture 92-year-old Sri Suntata delivered to a senior-citizen yoga class near Lombard. The Danish-born mystic says his name means "nobody" and he's not a swami.

21

Cultists

By 1980 approximately 3 million Americans belonged to 3,000 sects, according to the estimates of John Sweeney, director of Citizens Freedom Foundation-Information Service, which attempts "to alert the American public to the dangers of mind control by pseudo religious cults." During the '70s several such groups sprang into being, sponsored mostly by parents whose children had been lured from their homes or by dissillusioned former cult members. One such was the Parents Committee to Free Our Sons and Daughters from the Children of God about which Daniel St. Albin Greene wrote in the *National Observer* for April 15, 1972.

After visiting COG headquarters in San Diego Greene wasn't sure whether COG was "an all-volunteer army for Christ laboring to save us all or are they, as more and more detractors insist, brainwashed anti-American fanatics fobbing off revolution and hate as the gospel." One 20-year-old former member described her captors as "possessed of the devil . . . I was." Greene included numerous anecdotes of parents who made futile attempts to persuade their offspring to come home, including the account by one couple whose son spit and swore at them.

Cultists quote biblical passages such as Matthew 10:35: "For I am come to set a man at variance against his father and the daughter against her mother and the daughter-in-law against her mother-in-law. And a man's foes shall be those of his own household." Or Luke 14:26: "If any man come to me and hate not his father, his mother and wife, and children and brothers and sisters, yea and his own life also, he cannot be my disciple."

The latter biblical quote was cited by Carol Kramer in the *Chicago Tribune* for June 17, 1973. Mostly her article related the deprogramming activities of Ted Patrick, formerly a community relations consultant to Gov. Ronald Reagan of California. Patrick became alarmed when COG attempted to convert his 14-year-old son. When he faced charges of kidnapping, conspiracy to kidnap, assault and unlawful imprisonment, he said he had successfully deprogrammed 125 young adults who belonged to sects ranging from the Children of God to the New Testament Missionary Fellowship, an ultraconservative commune with 30 to 40 followers. During a deprogramming, which might last for ten days, Patrick would say such things as "You have been deceived by the forces of Satan, brainwashed and hypnotized and no longer able to think for yourself or to understand God's teaching." According to Patrick, "We give them back their minds."

Details of the charge that led to Patrick's extradition to New York from California were included in a lengthy article by Lynne Olson of the Associated Press to which the *Chicago Sun-Times* June 24, 1973 gave the headline, "Parents vs. the Cults" with the subhead, "Free Choice for Youth?" The case grew out of the efforts of Eugene and Marie Voll to rescue their son Daniel who quit Yale to join the New Testament Missionary Fellowship, founded in the mid-'60s by Mrs. Hannah Lowe, the widow of a Baptist missionary, and McCandish Phillips, a *New York Times* reporter. Said the father regarding what the sect did to his son: "The change in personality was scary. He became mean, hard and cruel. We weren't able to talk to him any more. We couldn't have a rational conversation with him." To which the son replied: "I love my parents very much. I'm very concerned about them. But they've got to realize I'm not a child. They've got to let me go."

Legal action against him did not stop Patrick from activities in many parts of the nation. The *New York Times* reported from Denver Sept. 2, 1974 that Patrick had organized the Citizens Freedom Foundation earlier in the year; the article revealed Patrick had been found guilty of a charge of false imprisonment involving two girls who had left their homes and the Greek Orthodox Church against their parents' wishes. Helping to recruit parents for the new foundation was Mrs. Henrietta Crampton of Redondo, Calif.

Mrs. Crampton's concern was aroused when Patrick succeeded in abducting the Cramptons' daughter Kathe from a Love Family commune in Washington and returned her to California from where she later escaped. Patrick's indictment by a federal grand jury in Seattle on charges of kidnapping was reported by the UPI Sept. 22, 1974. According to an Associated Press story in the *New York Times* Dec. 13, 1974, he was acquitted after a bench trial before Judge Walter T. McGovern. The judge compared Patrick's situation to that of a pedestrian who rushes into a street against a red light to save a child from an onrushing car and then was cited for violation of the traffic light law.

Some other deprogrammers haven't gotten off so easily. Ten persons, including her parents, a Denver policeman and a professional deprogrammer were indicted for kidnapping Emily Kim Dietz who had been a computer programmer in the national headquarters of the Divine Light Mission in Denver. After her abduction she was taken first to Colorado Springs and then to Akron, Ohio where she escaped by jumping from a second story

window. The indicted persons faced felony charges of second-degree kidnapping and a misdeamor charge of false imprisonment. Frank Moya
reported the indictment for the *Denver Post* of June 12, 1981.

Deprogrammers received a serious setback when the United States
Supreme Court let stand a lower court order to permit Thomas Ward of
New York to sue his parents and two deprogrammers for violating his civil
rights. Ward said he was abducted while visiting a sister in Virginia
Beach, Va. and was held captive for 35 days before he escaped. He belongs
to Sun Moon's Unification Church. The press associations reported the
story Jan. 19, 1982 from Washington.

On the other hand, Wallace Turner reported in the *New York Times* for
Nov. 19, 1981, Judge Ira Brown of Superior Court in San Francisco ordered
officials of the Unification Church to produce Mary Lee Hall in court to
determine if she were being held by the church against her will.

April 12, 1982 Chris Freveletti reported in the *Chicago Tribune* that
Repr. Betty Hoxsey was introducing four bills in the Illinois General
Assembly in Springfield to regulate the activities of religious cults, many
of which she said may not deserve to be tax exempt. Among other things
her bills would permit anyone who believes s/he was deceived into joining a
cult to sue and make "malicious interference with family life" a crime if a
family is denied the right to communicate with relatives. Civil libertarians
said it would be impossible to frame such laws without violating the
freedom of religion clause of the First Amendment.

Before Sun Myung Moon's Madison Square Garden rally, Peter Arnett
of the Associated Press interviewed the young people active in the streets
to promote the event. The *New Orleans Times-Picayune* was one paper that
ran an Arnett story in its issue of Sept. 22, 1974. It dealt mostly with the
case of Tom Grabowski whose mother said, "He's a Moon puppet." Tom
consented to be interviewed only if another Moonie was present but
admitted he joined the church while still in the army. He handed over
checks for $325 every month, giving Moonies a total of $4,150.

In its writeup of the Children of God in its issue of April 5, 1975 the
Chicago Daily News mentioned the organization in Dallas of Thankful
Parents and Friends of the Children of God to oppose the Parents Committee to Save Our Children from the Children of God. In a sidebar it summarized some of the Mo letters, sent from self-exiled David Brandt "Mo"
Berg, the cult's founder and leader. Of the imminent Doomsday Berg
wrote, "We're not out to change the world—we're creating an entirely new
one." Mo approved mutual masturbation by females. He said incest must
be all right because the sons of Cain must have married their sisters, the
only females available. On marriage he said, "Whenever you start living
and sleeping with the one you love, you're married."

Inspired by the paper's series on COG, some parents volunteered
further information. One told Lois Wille for her April 21, 1975 *Chicago
Daily News* article that their two daughters sold belongings and took a

$6,000 inheritance to support the Children of Mercy, run by a grand-fatherly ex-butcher who calls himself Pastor Bob. Earlier the girls had belonged to Young Life, a fundamentalist Christian organization for teenagers originating in Texas. When their parents refused to contribute to the sect the girls returned to Pastor Bob's headquarters in Colorado, presumably never to return.

Parents often are frustrated by the refusal of the courts to support their efforts to wean or force their children from a cult. Courts usually say the freedom of religion clause of the First Amendment protects the young person who wants to repudiate his bringing up and adopt a new life-style. The Associated Press reported from Washington Sept. 14, 1975 that a Superior Court judge rebuked the efforts of Mr. and Mrs. Elton Helander of Guilford, Conn. to win their daughter, Wendy, back from the Unification Church. The judge said they had failed to prove that the church used systematic mind control techniques or held psychological sway over their daughter.

A full-length comprehensive article about the Helander case was written by Robert Signer for his paper, the *Chicago Daily News* of Sept. 30, 1975. For the entire family, Signer wrote, "it has been a time of confusion, turmoil and fright. In the context of the Patricia Hearst case, the Wendy Helander case is a microcosm of our times, of the difficulty of dealing with or understanding new ways of thinking, feeling and behaving." Wendy was a dropout from the University of New Hampshire. She persuaded her parents to visit her at the Barrytown headquarters of the Moonies. They did, but two weeks later they tricked Wendy into taking a ride with them. Instead of taking her to lunch they took her to Ted Patrick for deprogramming. The deprogramming was a terrifying experience for Wendy who quoted Patrick as telling her: "You are worshipping Satan's snake and you are an evil doer and you're stealing money from the people on the street and you're a prostitute, just trying to get money for the church, and all of it going to Moon. All he wants is your money."

Signer quoted Dr. John G. Clark, a psychiatrist, that when the 15 ex-Moonies he had examined left the church they were "somewhat sick, depleted, pale, often anemic, some with skin diseases, looking under-nourished and physically as well as emotionally depleted." Dr. Clark believes "there is a systematic form of psychological control, methods which are brought to bear on the individuals from the time they are recruited until they are completely and successfully inside the organization."

On the other hand Dr. Harold Kaufman, who examined Wendy, found her "very healthy," "a little sunburned" and "extremely confident with people."

That the Moonies' neighbors at Barrytown did not share Dr. Kaufman's opinion was stated by Beth Gillin Pombeiro in the *Philadelphia Inquirer* for Oct. 7, 1975. She reported that many of the neighbors, after two years, were "angry, suspicious and afraid as well." One long time resident of the area said: "They have a certain stare, a fake smile that goes right through you." Another neighbor added, "They are an army of zombies more like androids than people, sort of vague and blank and empty." Pombeiro mentioned James J. Sheeran, New Jersey state insurance commissioner, about whose experience Lacy McCrary wrote a separate story. When he tried to see one of his three daughters in the camp, Sheeran said, he was beaten and physically ejected. He said the church takes advantage of the high idealism of young people like his daughters. Thus, "They are the victims of our own training but we don't blame ourselves," he said. He added, "They have been programmed to believe that we are Satan and would kidnap them if they came home." Sheeran made an unsuccessful attempt to persuade the New Jersey legislature to investigate the Unification Church.

The *Philadelphia Inquirer* Oct. 2, 1975 also ran a comprehensive Associated Press story on the Sheeran case. The three daughters participated in a news conference in New York during which Moonie leaders denied that their father had been attacked physically. They admitted, however, that the father had been bound and gagged in order to remove him from the premises.

In the fourth of his series telling of his experiences as an infiltrator, which the *New York Daily News* and *Chicago Tribune* published Dec. 1, 1975, John Cotter described the deprogramming of a young man whose father and sister lured him to a Bronx apartment where a team of ex-Moonies worked on him for eight days. Mike, the subject, recognized Cotter as having attended meetings in Barrytown and when Cotter asked "Who am I?" Mike replied, "It's obvious." When the reporter asked, "Do you mean I'm Satan?" Mike answered, "Yes." Joe Alexander, Jr., who had been delayed in arriving for the task, needed only a few hours to achieve what others had failed to achieve, the deprogramming of Mike.

In his final installment Cotter summarized the charges against the Unification Church. He concluded with a quotation from one of the church's leaders: "We don't brainwash. We just wash out a few old ideas and replace them with new ones."

In the last of his series, which the AP distributed Dec. 25, 1975, Peter Arnett presented the opinions of a dozen or so former cult members who had tired of the life without need for deprogramming. They all agreed that the main occupation was money raising and the discipline was very tight. One ex-Moonie declared that she was so convinced of the existence of evil spirits that "I thought I actually could see them flying around me."

Similarly Denise Peskin of Plainview, N.Y. said, "I was a robot for Moon. My mind was empty. It was just a reflection of everything they told me." L. H. Whittemore included the quotation in an article, "Sun Myung Moon: Prophet for Profit," in *Parade* for May 30, 1976. He quoted Moon as telling followers: "Kings and queens and heads of state will someday bow at my feet. I will conquer and subjugate the world." One escapee, the godson of then U.S. Sen. James Buckley of New York, said he joined a front group, Collegiate Association for the Research of Principles.

The typical American disciple of Moon is a man or woman, aged 23, from a white upper-middle-class family. Jean Merritt, a psychiatric social worker in Lincoln, Neb., says those who join Moon "are idealistic young men and women who are having difficulty deciding what to do with their lives. Allan Tate Wood, who had been in charge of the church's "political arm," called the Freedom Leadership Foundation, said he left the church "because it's not a church but a fascist political movement. His group is the most powerful analogue to the Hitler youth that we have at this time."

Berkeley Rice began the article "The Pull of Sun Moon" in the *New York Times Magazine* for May 30, 1976 with a detailed account of the Helander case. The Freedom Leadership Foundation actually is subsidized by the South Korean government and has helped cement friendship between that government and the United States. Moon was successful in getting himself in news pictures with several leading American politicians, including Vice-President Hubert Humphrey and Senators Edward Kennedy, Strom Thurmond and James Buckley. Withal the Rice article is an excellent summary of the career of Sun Moon and the operations of his Unification Church.

Equally comprehensive was Michael Putney's article "The Rev. Moon: A Messiah—Or a Menace?" in the *National Observer* for June 12, 1976. Both Rice and Putney mentioned Rabbi Maurice Davis of White Plains, N.Y., who founded Citizens Engaged in Reuniting Families. Putney also compared the Moon movement with the Nazi youth. He quoted Moon's apology for his American crusade: "If there is an illness in your home do you not need a doctor from outside? If your home catches fire do you not need fire fighters from outside? God has sent me to America in the role of a doctor, in the role of a fire fighter." In an accompanying article Putney summarized "Some Issues Viewed in Moon's Light." Typical: "On why Nixon resigned: Communistic power working behind the scenes. They came to threaten to kill him if he did not resign, and that's what compelled him to do so."

In the second of a series of articles in the *Indianapolis Star,* Susan M. Anderson sought the secret of the offbeat evangelism of Sun Moon, based on interviews with a dozen or more ex-Moonies. She reported that local and federal agencies "have begun to suspect that Sun Myung Moon's brand of charity begins at home—at Moon's home, that is." As a result many investigations of different aspects of his operation were underway. She cited especially the campaign headed by Rabbi Davis, who formerly led an Indianapolis Hebrew Congregation.

That deprogramming doesn't always work was indicated by James Robison's article, "Follower of Rev. Moon loses faith—in his Parents," in the *Chicago Tribune* for Jan. 24, 1977. The story was that of Scott Soulman who visited his parents in Danville, Ill. before going on a foreign tour with the church's Go World Brass Band. His father locked him in a room in a motel he managed and four deprogrammers worked on Scott without interruption. Two attempts at escape failed before the son broke a window and yelled for help. Police answered an anonymous phone call. The *Chicago Sun-Times'* account of the incident the same day was similar. It quoted Soulman as saying, "I don't know if I'll ever be able to trust my parents again." The parents said they did all they thought able to do and regretted that the plan was interrupted.

What exponents of deprogramming hope will spread as a legal device to make kidnapping unnecessary was upheld by a San Francisco judge, the *Chicago Sun-Times* reported March 25, 1977. A Superior Court judge granted parents a 30-day conservatorship for five children who belonged to Moon's church. Judge S. Lee Vavuris also refused to forbid deprogramming attempts. He said: "The child is a child even though a parent may be 90 and the child 50."

How an ex-Marine stormed a tiny colony of Druids in New Mexico to rescue his son was related in the *Suburban Trib* for Oct. 26, 1977. With the aid of police and an Indian guide he found the grove and stormed the place shortly before daybreak. He then took his son to Wisconsin where Ted Patrick deprogrammed him in seven hours. As is true of most of the major cults, the Druids required that members break all ties with families, renounce them as demons and take new names. The *Tribune* used fictitious names in its article to protect the family. The father recognized the similarity between the Marines and the Druids. Both worked recruits hard physically. "But," said the father, "the Marines did it to win a war, to save freedom. They (the Druids) are doing it as a money-making scheme. The leaders are rich. That's their motivation."

In a separate article the *Tribune* related some of the history of the ancient Druids and revealed that the contemporary movement began as a joke by Carleton College students who wanted an excuse to skip chapel.

The *Evanston Review* revealed the real family name, Wildermuth, in its issue of April 6, 1978. Since he recovered his son, Mark, the father, Karl, has devoted considerable time to lecturing in the attempt to alert other parents to the dangers of cults. He charged that cults have become big business and that white middle-class youths are attracted to them because of "a great hunger for peer approval" and because "Kids are searching for something that gives them direction, but they're not getting it in society. 'Do your own thing' worked in theory but not in practice."

The risk a deprogrammer takes was illustrated by the case of Joan Stedrak of Pennsauken, N.J. who brought charges of kidnapping against her father, Arthur, and Galen Kelly, lawyer and deprogrammer, who allegedly seized her in a Philsborough, N.J. parking lot and held her captive for five days in Kingston, N.Y. before she escaped. She was a member of a small philosophical group, Circle of Friends, that followed the teachings of George Geza Jurscsek, a self-proclaimed Indian swami, astrologer, philosopher and stock market whiz, according to a UPI story Nov. 19, 1978 from Trenton.

While 90 state and national Unification Church leaders persisted in interrupting witnesses with cries of "liar," Sen. Robert J. Dole presided over a hearing on the mind-control techniques of cults. A star witness was Virginia Mabry, a former bookkeeper and fund raiser, who said she was taught "murder is O.K. if it's done in the name of the cause, specifically world domination by Moon . . ." She was ordered to commit "heavenly deception—a Unification term for fraud and deceit." Most startling revelation was that a nurse instructed her and others how to slash their wrists and were advised to escape a deprogrammer if necessary by throwing themselves in front of a car so the deprogrammer would be blamed for the death. This and more was related in a *Chicago Sun-Times* account Feb. 2, 1979 of an interview with Mabry by Linda Myers.

A side of Sun Myung Moon not generally known was the subject of an article by Daniel S. Greenberg in the *Washington Post* for Nov. 11, 1977. It dealt principally with the Moon-financed International Conference on the Unity of the Sciences. In 1972, its first year, it attracted only 20 participants from eight countries, several prominent scientists having withdrawn when they learned the nature of the sponsorship. Despite the unfavorable press that Moon had been receiving, 363, including seven Nobel laureates from 50 countries, attended the 1976 conference. "What's clean money?" Greenberg quoted one participant as saying. "Others," Greenberg wrote, "insisted that some of our greatest foundations are endowed with the profits of long-ago sweatshops and dubious deals."

The trauma of breaking ties with a strict cult was described by a pseudonymous Jean Vincent in the *Los Angeles Times* for Feb. 12, 1979. On the insistence of her parents she spent 14 years with the fundamentalist Worldwide Church of God, founded by an ex-advertising man, Herbert W. Armstrong. Vincent's disillusionment came gradually at first as she could not understand how an all-powerful deity could bungle human affairs so badly. The church solemnly predicted the end of the world in 1972 or 1975, upsetting to the 70,000 for whom the church offered a psychologically secure life. "Leaving the church was like going off drugs cold turkey," Vincent wrote. "At times I literally felt like dying. The fear that God would strike me down was hard to overcome with mere logic. For months I was deeply depressed, managing to function during the day but staring blankly at the TV and drinking wine all night." Still fearful of retaliation she wrote under a pseudonym.

With the knowledge and consent of the Unification Church, a team of four psychiatrists and psychiatric researchers studied a representative sample of 237 church members. In the February, 1979 issue of the *American Journal of Psychiatry,* they reported that by comparison with 237 non-church members, the Moonies had more serious psychological and emotional problems before their conversions. In her resumé of the article for the *Washington Post* of April 14, 1979, Marjorie Hyer wrote: "At least 90 percent of the Moon followers had dabbled in one of the Eastern religions or in fundamentalist Christianity." The Moonies were 91 percent unmarried, 89 percent white, 61 percent male and with a mean age of 24.7 years. Although 58 percent had started college only 25 percent finished.

Another narrative of a struggle to break ties with the Unification Church is *Hostage to Heaven* by Barbara Underwood. As summarized by Barbara Varro in a full page of the *Chicago Sun-Times* for Nov. 29, 1979, Underwood recalled her four years as a Moonie with bitterness. Despite studies to learn what type of person is most susceptible to the lure of cultists, Underwood felt that anyone, regardless of personality type, could be lured. "It is not a matter of those with low self esteem. Everyone's self esteem is less than perfect. In the cults they promise perfection . . . The cults exploit the realistic view of self and promise you a doubt-free existence." Varro summarized Underwood's suggestions as to how to avoid a cult's clutches.

According to James Franklin in the *Boston Globe* for July 7, 1980, the Unification Church claimed 10,000 members and 40,000 associate members compared to 7,000 full- and 28,000 part-time members in 1978. A former Moonie, Steven Hassan, founder of Ex-Moon, Inc., however, said there are only 4,000 to 4,500 full-time members and 500 associates.

A typical comment by a former Way International follower, according to Zay M. Smith in the *Chicago Sun-Times* for Aug 17, 1980: "I worshipped Wierville without question. So do many others. If he had told me to kill myself, I would have done it. If he had told me to kill someone else I would have done that too." A mother told Smith, "Have you ever seen an animal that's been beaten down? How he cowers when you try to love him? That's how our son looks at us since he joined The Way."

In a followup piece Sept. 14, 1980, Smith quoted several other parents: "My daughter's like a zombie now." "That's what this cult does to people." "Our oldest son was so outgoing. Now he's just nothing. And this year he recruited his brother and they've gone to Kansas." "The Way came along and we became a torn family." "The first thing they ask for is money."

The Way is built on the pattern of a tree. The trunk is in Ohio. The branches and twigs reach out from there. Over 700 took firearms courses over a two-year period. The total Way empire is estimated to be $10 million. Said one ex-member: "I left when I saw people starting to worship Wierville rather than Jesus Christ."

A 14-year-old boy, Jeff Brown, received considerable nationwide publicity when he ran away from his mother seven times because he feared his mother's group, The Way International. According to an Associated Press story July 29, 1982 from Des Moines, a judge decided the sect is not a bad religion and ordered the boy to return to his mother from the home of his grandparents.

One of the most unusual deprogramming cases was reported Aug. 2, 1982 from Winona, Minn. by UPI. It involved a husband and wife. The latter said she was treated well by her captives, who persuaded her to renounce the Disciples of the Lord Jesus Christ, whereas her husband said his deprogrammers broke his left wrist and treated him badly without, however, shaking his religious convictions.

Charging that professional deprogrammers had subjected him to "mental anguish, fright, shock, humiliation and degradation," a University of Michigan student sued for $50,000 and remained a member of the Mara Napha Campus Ministry, the *Chicago Sun-Times* reported Oct. 4, 1982.

For an aggrieved parent to obtain redress is always difficult. A typical case was that of Donald Kieffer of Bedford, N.H., who sued the Unification Church for $1 million for alienating the affections of his stepdaughter. After a five-day trial a jury awarded Kieffer $30,000, but the judge overturned it saying the jury had been swayed by emotions disregarding the failure of the father to provide a burden of proof. The Associated Press reported the event from Concord Sept. 24, 1980.

Perhaps the best success story of a parent's efforts to rescue a son from a cult was that of Morris Yanoff, Chicago labor leader, who exhausted efforts to try to persuade the Hare Krishnas to even tell him the whereabouts of his grandson. By the time legal permission to see the boy was received, the object of the search had disappeared. So Yanoff, the boy's father, other relatives and friends originated the tactic of spoiling the activities of the Krishnas who sell literature and recruit members in public places. They spelled each other off at O'Hare Airfield where they interrupted any soliciting Krishna by informing the prospect of the order's refusal to release his grandson. It worked. The Krishnas gave in, bringing the son back from France. Yanoff dropped the $75 million suit. The *Chicago Sun-Times* gave the story a two-page spread in March 16, 1982; the *Chicago Tribune* gave it a half-page March 26, 1982.

There also was a happy ending to the story Virginia Mabry told Don Bishoff of the *Eugene* (Ore.) *Register-Guard* for his columns of Oct. 12 and 13, 1977. She was a Sonoma University student when she attended a Unification Church meeting and, impressed by the message and by the lavish treatment she received as a potential recruit, she finally joined. Instead of being used as a teacher, as she had expected, however, she was sent to Texas with a Mobil Fund-Raising Team. It was grueling work, sometimes 16 hours daily.

After a year she long-distanced some friends in Eugene who told her to get on a bus and come there. She did, and among the statements she made to Bishoff were: "Once on TV I was asked if I had been brainwashed. I said no, I was heartwashed. A better statement is that your true person is put in the deep freeze . . . I feel that I've been a robot for a year . . . they took away my own belief in God and gave me Reverend Moon's belief in God."

That nobody is immune is what Steve Hassan, president of Ex-Moonies,

Inc., told a conference of Citizens Freedom Foundation Information Services, Herb Gould reported in the *Chicago Sun-Times* for Oct. 12, 1980. Hassan declared the Moonies had caught him at just the right moment, were very friendly, never left him alone. He came to his senses while recuperating for a fortnight in a hospital after an automobile accident. Paul A. Teschner, a lawyer who specializes in constitutional cases, told the conference, "The cult phenomenon has led to massive First Amendment violations but on the part of the cults, not the deprogrammers. The cults have turned the entire thing upside down. The First Amendment protects beliefs, not conduct."

Since 1975 the Spiritual Counterfeit Project, organized by a group of Protestant evangelicals, has operated in Berkeley, Calif. "to research and biblically critique new religious groups and trends and to equip Christians with the knowledge and discernment to enable them to understand the significance of today's spiritual explosion." The group has compiled data on about 200 groups, including the largest—Hare Krishna, Unification Church and Transcendental Meditation.

Increasingly the parents of sons and daughters lured away by a cult are joining such groups. The *Suburban Chicago Tribune* for May 6, 1981 told the story of a family that succeeded in abducting a daughter and successfully deprogramming her despite the efforts of her boyfriend and others to lure her back to the cult led by ex-marine Jim Roberts who calls himself Brother Evangelist. For 11 months the young woman, who deserted the campus of the University of Iowa, traveled about the country eating out of garbage pails. The women in the small group were compelled to bow their heads at all times and couldn't speak to the male members of the group. Women weren't allowed to read the Bible; the men read it to them. No wonder that after 11 months the girl at first didn't even recognize her parents. Said her father, "We saw her as a zombie. Only intelligent people with open minds are attracted to cults." The parents are helping to fight cults through the Citizens Freedom Foundation.

The frustration parents experience, even when they have support, was related by United Press International Sept. 14, 1981 from San Francisco. There, a father from Donegal, Ireland and 50 members of the Irish community of San Francisco unsuccessfully stormed a Moonie campground near Calstoga, Calif. Sheriff's deputies stopped the group's attempt to break down gates and barriers, all rather futile efforts anyway since the young former Dublin schoolteacher whose release was sought had been spirited away to another Moonie site. Sept. 17, 1981 the *Chicago Sun-Times* reported that according to a church spokesman the daughter had left the country.

Most parents of youthful cultists are too worried about their immediate personal family problems to concern themselves with the sociological and philosophical reasons for the phenomenon. Although baffled, professional sociologists, psychologists, psychiatrists, theologians and other scholars have tried to find answers. Lacking the perspective that comes only after years of study and analysis of scientific probes, there seems to be general agreement among the experts that most cultists are in their 20s and previously participated in other movements, either to effect political change (as the civil rights and peace movements) or to withdraw from contemporary society (as a beatnik, hippie, dope addict).

As Gary Wills wrote in his column Aug. 12, 1971, ". . . now the freaks are loose,—chanting, dancing, praying, freaking out," and he predicted, "The religious binge is now in for Hollywood commercialism."

When John Denver mentioned EST in a radio interview, a reader asked the *Chicago Tribune's* Action Express for information. The paper provided it July 19, 1974: EST is Erhard Seminar Training which for two $200 weekend sessions will promise to increase one's self-awareness, described as a combination of various psychological disciplines and Asian philosophies. Dr. Alan W. Schreiber, a New York psychotherapist, defines EST as "a training which involves the use of harsh, authoritarian techniques to tear you down, then put you back together in such a manner that, as its founder Werner Erhard says, you develop the awareness that you are and that the only way to be happy is to do what you are doing. You are perfect the way you are." EST offers "at best a momentary escape from the realities of one's world and one's self," he wrote in the *New York Daily World* for May 12, 1982.

Obviously EST does not fit the definition of a cult as given by many scholars, particularly Carroll Stoner and Jo Anne Parke, who wrote *All God's Children.* In the *Chicago Sun-Times,* of which Stoner is associate feature editor, rules were given Aug. 28, 1977 whereby to determine the legitimacy of a new religion. Accepting the usual dictionary definition of a cult as "a minority religious group regarded as spurious or unorthodox," the authors cited the following criteria:

A cult has *a living leader.* Cult doctrine is based on his or her revelations, which either supplant or supplement traditional religious doctrine and scripture.

The cult leader is *the sole judge* of the quality of a member's faith and he enjoys absolute authority over the members.

A cult *promises* a system in which a convert may work to save the world and humanity but actually sponsors no community improvement programs.

The daily work of nearly all cult members is *demanding* and utilizes little of their potential, in terms of intelligence, training or education.

In religious cults, members are taught to believe that they are "superior" to those outside of the group.

To be a member of a cult, a person must remove himself from society, cut himself off from job, education, friends and family.

Methods of ego-destruction and thought-control are part of a religious cult's recruiting and indoctrination practices.

Cults discourage critical analysis by dictating the suppression of negative thoughts, therefore fostering a dependency on the cult's authority that arrests the maturation process.

The cult rituals and practices are psychologically unwholesome and, in some cases, physically dangerous when they involve the use of drugs or perverse sexual rites.

The same newspaper devoted a page Dec. 22, 1975 to the article "New Messiahs—Holy Beings or Hucksters?" by Victoria Graham of the Associated Press. She began her article: "New messiahs are arising across America, idolized by young converts who seek the truth and reviled by parents who accuse them of brainwashing . . . They reflect a growing impulse to establish an alternative life style that not only provides doctrine but also demands total commitment . . . Many recruits stepped out of the 1950s' countercultrue and the psychedelic experience. Those movements didn't deliver all they promised but they showed the way to other intensely personal ways of relating to the universe."

In his review of the Stoner-Parke book, in the *Sun-Times* for July 10, 1977, Dean Peerman wrote, "The motivations of those who get caught up in the cults are manifold but if there is one characteristic common to almost all the young recruits, it is an undirected idealism—along with the ambience, vulnerability and need for peer approval that seem to mark the crisis that is post-adolescence."

In comment on the Jonestown tragedy, the *Sun-Times* edtorialized Nov. 22, 1978, in part as follows:

At worst it plumbs the worst of the cult phenomenon: desperate people seeking grand answers but finding only deeper sadness. Latter day messianic types, charismatically feeding their adherents easy, quick answers to all questions, temporal and spiritual, have twisted the notion of worship, sometimes for financial gain, sometimes for power. They have tacked new—and wrong—meanings onto old revered ideals of self sacrifice for a greater good.

In the next day's issue of the same paper, Nov. 23, 1978, appeared Carl T. Rowan's syndicated column, "Stealing, killing in the name of God." Asked Rowan: "When are we going to face up to the fact that 'religion' is America's greatest sanctuary for people who engage in systematic theft, tax evasion, rape, torture and even murder?"

Rowan called the "gruesome tragedy at Guyana" an appalling example of governmental failure to act, primarily because governmental officials are timid about breaching sanctuaries of 'religion.' The State Department not only failed to act early against the Jones 'empire' but it fought to prevent FBI involvement."

More caustically, Nov. 29, 1978 in his *Sun-Times* column, Mike Royko wrote he didn't fear a governmental scrutiny of cults would lead to a violation of freedom of religion. He wrote:

With our constitutional safeguards, the only people who would have any reason to feel nervous would be the many Bible-thumping con men, hustlers, scam artists, phony faith healers and assorted gurus who use religion as a means of building personal power, inflating their Swiss bank accounts and getting weird kicks. Almost any glib talker who can memorize Biblical passages can set himself up as a spiritual leader and find lonely, gullible, frightened followers who are looking for something to cling to in this nervous world.

"California cults have seemingly filled the spiritual needs for thousands unable to find salvation or security in orthodox creeds," according to Richard Mathison in the *Los Angeles Times* for Nov. 27, 1978. He cited Guy Ballard's Mighty I Am and Mankind United, founded by Joe Bell, a post-depression dandy who preached that "a race of little men with metal heads who lived in the center of the earth" would tell his cultists what to do through his revelations. Bell ended by claiming a quarter-million of the gullible who mortgaged their homes and sold property before he was grounded with a maze of legal problems.

Mathison generalized: "A successful cult thrives only on such visions of its leader no matter how outlandish . . . They [cultists] seek something exciting, and a new togetherness . . . Their new supernaturalism makes them treat other faiths with disdain, sad indulgence or outright hate . . . It follows that the more outrageous the cult's concepts, the more they will be persecuted from the outside—and that only tightens the leader's control."

In three full pages of its Dec. 3, 1978 issue, the *Chicago Tribune* published the following stories: "What exactly is a cult?" "At Synanon violence is the new god," "How groups use lies, guilt, terror to capture converts," "The need to believe is common to all cultures," "Portraits of the six major cults in America," "Rootless Californians flock to fanatics, false prophets," "With each new life saved, Synanon's fame grew," "Synanon still thriving," "1st amendment guards beliefs." In addition to the standard dictionary definition, the *Tribune,* with Ray Moseley composing, quoted a psychiatrist, "Religions that haven't grown up yet," and Gordon Melton, director of the Evanston-based Institute for the Study of American Religion, "In popular use a cult is a weird group we don't like."

Experts differed as to what effect the Jonestown tragedy had according to Roy Larson who summarized the opinions of several in the *Chicago Sun-Times* for Dec. 12, 1978. Jacob Needleman of the Graduate Theological Union in Berkeley, Calif., thought "New cult formation has tapered off from what it was five, six or eight years ago." On the other hand, Rabbi Maurice Davis of White Plains, N.Y., chairman of a commission on cults of the Central Conference of American (Reform) Rabbis, felt, "I don't perceive for a moment that the cults have peaked," although adopting a "low profile" for the time being. Thomas Robbins, Queens College sociologist, distinguished between total commitment cults that are communal, authoritative and work hard to segregate members from conventional society, and "limited liability groups" that are adaptive and work within conventional society. Examples of the first type, which Robbins said peaked several years earlier, are the Unification Church, Hare Krishna and Children of God. Example of the latter is EST. Several other scholars were quoted pro and con, all agreeing it is difficult to obtain data.

Senate investigations of the cults focus on matters of secondary importance, Edward Levine, Loyola University sociologist, told the *Suburban Chicago Tribune* for May 28, 1979. He said, "Children who have good parenting and a happy family life have their basic emotional and social needs met. Cults can't appeal to such persons when they reach young adulthood."

Criticism of and opposition to the investigation by a committee of the Illinois General Assembly also was expressed by 33 Protestant ministers, Philip J. O'Connor reported for the *Chicago Sun-Times* of Sept. 5, 1979. The Rev. Gordon Melton, pastor of the Emmanuel United Methodist Church of Evanston, spokesman, released a statement that read in part: "We oppose the repetition of unsubstantiated charges against the new religions . . . We oppose as vigilantism the business and practice of kidnaping and physically restraining and coercing citizens of this state to change their faith under the guise of deprogramming."

With a slightly longer perspective, Rabbi James Rudin and his wife Marcia wrote a book, *Prison or Paradise: The New Religious Cults,* which Roy Larson reviewed in the *Sun-Times* for March 1, 1980. Rudin, assistant national director of religious affairs for the American Jewish Committee, wrote that since the Jonestown massacre, the cults have grown, not shrunk. About 9 to 12 percent or more of the membership in the Moonies were Jews although Jews constitute only 3 percent of the population, the rabbi reported. About 20 percent of the Hare Krishna and 30 percent of the Divine Light Mission's memberships were Jewish. The Rudins concluded: "It appears that the most vulnerable target group for cult recruitment is the person, young or old, who has made no meaningful connection with an established religion, who is in search of spiritual values and transcendent meaning, who is willing, even yearning for strict discipline and authority, and who may be burdened with guilt about affluence or sex or drugs."

In an article in the *Chicago Tribune* for Sept. 30, 1980, Rabbi and Mrs. Rudin suggested several ways the legal system could be used to reduce or counter the cults without violating their First Amendment rights. Among the suggestions were these: tighten and enforce anti-solicitation laws; disallow tax exemption for profit-making activities; enforce health and sanitary codes; enforce child abuse and involuntary servitude laws; enforce minimum wage laws; enforce school attendance laws; demand compliance with consumer protection laws; tighten laws against proselytizing;

watch for charity fraud violations and enforce laws against interference with family relationships.

On the basis of an ongoing study of 415 present and former cultists and their families, Prof. Margaret Taler Singer, clinical psychologist at the University of California's Medical School in San Francisco, says the modern cults are using brainwashing techniques that are centuries old. After interviewing her Barbara Varro wrote for the July 8, 1980 *Sun-Times,* "Singer said that cults promote the breakdown of the family because they urge members to forsake their pasts, including family and friends. They are a danger to the fabric of our society because we live in a democracy founded on long-standing Judeo-Christian ethics in which the rights of individuals are highly respected."

Cults find it easier to recruit middle-class young people, Singer had found, because they have been taught to be obedient and trusting whereas ghetto kids are skeptical of anyone apparently offering them something for nothing. "In cults," Singer said, "members become totally dependent upon the leaders for everything. They are totalitarian systems without grievance procedures. There is no way to appeal to an outside authority." Cults generally are formed by a charismatic, domineering, determined male. There are few or no women at the top.

The January 1982 issue of *Science Digest* contained results of a study of 400 former cult members, UPI reported Jan. 4, 1982. The researchers, Flo Conway and Jim Siegelman, found that cult indoctrination procedures approach brainwashing and produce a number of serious, long-term mental and emotional effects. Periods of disorganization were reported by 52 percent; 40 percent suffered from nightmares; about 20 percent showed suicidal tendencies and one in seven had hallucinations or delusions eight years later.

In his syndicated column for April 13, 1981 Garry Wills warned against underestimating the powerful effect of the evangelical movement. He especially extolled Jim Wallis of the Sojourners, an active peace advocate. Wrote Wills: "The great reform movements in America have been religious in inspiration, from the time of the abolitionists . . . Only religious communities have shown staying power since their motives are deep and stable."

In the *Chicago Sun-Times* for July 12, 1981 Roy Larson, religion editor, cited examples to prove that mainline churches and synagogues can command the loyalty of teenagers, thus successfully competing with the cults. Dramatic programs and social affairs have proved successful, but one pastor was quoted as saying, "I can't think of anyone who's bragging about his youth program."

In the meantime the press will continue to give ample coverage to every leader of an esoteric sect who visits their circulation areas, especially those with an Asiatic or Oriental background as the Dalai Lama, exiled god-king of Tibet, regarded by his followers as the 14th reincarnation of the country's original Dalai Lama. When he visited Wheaton, Ill., Billy Graham's bailiwick, the *Chicago Sun-Times* covered his speech in its July 26, 1981 issue. Under the sponsorship of the Theosophical Society of America, he said: "I am not speaking to you tonight as a Buddhist or as a Tibetan but as one human being. I hope that as you listen, you will think of yourselves not as Americans or as Christians or as Theosophists but as a member of the one human society." What a different world it would be if all followed that advice.

"Ex-Moonie Blows Whistle on 'Evil' of Love Bombing," was the headline the *Los Angeles Times* gave Dec. 28, 1981 to a review by Day Longcope that originated in the *Boston Globe* of the first book by an ex-Moonie, Steve Kemperman.

The book condemns the arduous tasks, mostly selling candy and other commodities, to "debilitate you through lack of sleep and fatigue . . . You're put on emotional overload." And for what? "Fund raising is holy. You're taking money away from Satan and giving it to God, giving the contributor the opportunity for spiritual blessing by giving money to establish a financial empire for the kingdom of God, Moon's kingdom on earth of course."

In February 1981 and again in February 1982 the *Waukegan News-Sun* charged that Christian Fellowship, Inc. was a front for homosexual activities. Not waiting for the outcome of a libel suit against the newspaper, after its own investigation, the Great Lakes Naval Training Center ordered the religious group off limits for military personnel, William Currie reported in the *Chicago Tribune* for Feb. 12, 1982.

22

In God's Name

There have always been gods. Archeologists and anthropologists have found evidence of them in drawings in the caves inhabited by prehistoric artists, in the earliest known writings and, especially, in places of worship and/or sacrifice, holy artifacts and burial customs observed thousands of years ago.

It was logical, given their knowledge, for primitive people to believe the sun was alive as it moved from one horizon to another, so sun worship was one of the earliest forms of religion. And how else to explain night and day, the seasons, life and death of both plants and animals and such phenomena as rain, thunder and lightning, earthquakes and the invisible wind? The unseen powers had to be cajoled to prevent harm and to obtain supernatural assistance in almost all of life's activities, particularly in warfare.

Although contemporary religious beliefs and rites are not so brutal as in past generations, more blood continues to be shed in the service of a deity than for any other reasons—in Ireland, the Middle East, the Philippines and at times almost everywhere else. Always the god's favor is sought and obedience to his laws is enforced. No army goes into battle today without the blessing of the lord's emissaries on earth. Christian soldiers go onward into war firm in the conviction that the lord is on their side, despite the contention of the enemy that the exact contrary is so. Meetings of legislative bodies and many public gatherings are opened with prayer and the clergy presides at significant events, such as birth, marriage, illness and death.

Much religious behavior in everyday life is so routine and performed so unquestioningly that it is not considered newsworthy. Nevertheless, there is much suggesting supernatural influence even though routine that gets headlines. It is not only clergymen who insist that they are doing the lord's work. For example, when the first black was elected president of the student body at the University of Arkansas, the UPI reported July 17, 1972 that the young man declared, "God told me what he wanted me to do." About the same time the Chicago press reported that Illinois Gov. Daniel

Walker told a Governor's Prayer Breakfast, "I pray that we dedicate ourselves to resisting these pressures with every ounce of backbone we can muster. With God's help we can do it."

Such typical declarations indicate that there still is widespread belief that the Almighty is actively interested in human events and can be persuaded by cogent appeal, perhaps also by rites and sacrificial offerings, to turn the tide one way or another. So powerful is the belief that God's will must be solicited as well as obeyed that many school districts defy the United States Supreme Court's 1963 order against designated prayers in the public schools. The Associated Press reported Jan. 1, 1976 from Hampstead, N.H. that many schools in the state had a daily reading of the Lord's Prayer as allowed by the state legislature when it defied the Supreme Court with an enabling act in 1975. School officials reported that there had been no protests.

In his syndicated column for Aug. 29, 1979 Carl Rowan cited an example of God's name used as justification for racial injustice. A federal judge in Virginia ruled that a school principal had a First Amendment right to forbid interracial dating.

God's name also can be used to escape blame for some disasters. It was necessary for the Pennsylvania Supreme Court to rule that an "Act of God" defense no longer would be accepted in civil damage cases resulting from storms, heavy rains and other natural causes, the United Press International reported March 14, 1962 from Pittsburgh. The case related to damage to an automobile when a telephone pole fell on it during a snowstorm. Said Justice Michael Musmanno, "There is something shocking in attributing tragedy or holocaust to God. The ways of the Deity so surpass the understanding of man that it is not the province of man to pass judgment upon what may be beyond human understanding."

Nevertheless, the Illinois Cook County assessor noted that many property owners were finding that their insurance companies refused to pay for collapsed roofs because snow is presumably an Act of God, according to the *Chicago Sun-Times* for Jan. 20, 1979.

Most American property owners, furthermore, doubtless agree with such underwriters that such disasters commonly called Acts of God do occur. Some even say, and probably are deeply convinced of its truth, that some action, either good or evil, was the result of direct commands from the Almighty. For example, the *Chicago Tribune* reported May 1, 1937 from Stooping Oak, Tenn. that Jackson Whitlow, a trapper, ended a 52-day fast on a direct command from God after a night during which the devil tried to get him. Whitlow explained the fast thus: "The Lord told me to fast and to purify myself to become ready for His work." Whitlow's cabin became a shrine where religious mountainfolk gathered to pray. Two days earlier, April 30, the *Tribune* had a long story of Whitlow's struggle with the devil until God spoke to him "through his thoughts" and said: "No longer use water—use wine for thy stomach's sake."

At the height of World War II with 27 of every 1,000 soldiers casualties because of mental stress—24 times the number of upsets among civilians before the war—Dr. Charles T. Holman of the University of Chicago declared 200,000 American pastors could change the situation, "By urging families of servicemen and women to commit their loved ones to God's protecting care and to rise above their worries and problems by practicing the religion of faith and hope they can hold the line against stress and strain." William F. McDermott reported the Holman speech for the *Chicago Daily News* of Oct. 25, 1943.

After the black evangelist Father Divine said he was responsible for Joe Louis becoming heavyweight champion, the *Chicago Sun* used a 3-column, 2 line headline over the UP story from New York, Oct. 3, 1946: "This Explains Louis' 'Divine Right' But What About That Satanic Left?" Divine had written that he got the idea of creating a new Negro champion after the defeat of Jack Johnson and did it by the transmission of the spirit of his prophet and reincarnation.

After a cold kept him home for a day, veteran coal miner Albert K. Gates told the *Chicago Times* it was God's way of saving him from an explosion, the paper reported March 26, 1947 from Centralia, Ill.

Gil Dodds, track star and holder of the world's record indoor for the one-mile run, told 700 fundamentalist Protestant youths that he won races because people prayed for him every time he ran, the *Chicago Sun* reported March 31, 1947.

To his horror Vance Timberlake discovered that the derelict whom he had seen struck by an automobile was his brother Cader, who had disappeared nearly 40 years earlier. The *Sun-Times* concluded its account of the tragedy Feb. 4, 1948: "No one could explain the mysterious force that in a city of 3,500,000 persons had led Cader to a spot where his brother could find him."

In Lexington, N.C. the UPI reported Nov. 11, 1982 a 14-year-old boy said God had given him a sign "to come home and live with him," so he discontinued dialysis treatment and died.

After her 9-year-old son collapsed and died while playing football Mrs. Jacqueline Bunn recalled that he had begun to have a sense of God's presence and said it would be up to God to decide his future.

Charles Harraway told Clyde Bolton of the *Birmingham News* that he believed God guided him in coming to the Birmingham Americans from the Washington Redskins, Bolton reported in his paper April 24, 1974. "I made a commitment 2½ years ago to become a follower of Jesus Christ," Harraway said.

After he was drafted by the Chicago Bears football team, Mike Singletary told a *Chicago Tribune* reporter in Houston that he had prayed for just that to happen, John Husar reported in that paper June 30, 1981. When he was not chosen on the first round Singletary left the reporters and went outside "to talk to the Man upstairs." Because he is short he wanted to play with a team he could help. So he said, "God, I wish it could be Chicago. If it's your will that's where I want to go." It was only a few minutes later that the welcomed word came. Said Singletary, "The Lord has always given me things I've asked but never have I gotten results that fast."

The extent of superstition among athletes was mentioned in Chapter 9 (see pages 184 ff.), also their religiosity (see Chapter 17 pages 384 ff.). Coaches and fans on both sides also implore God to bring victory to their heroes. When Notre Dame defeated Southern Methodist to become national football champions, instead of bedlam in the Irish dressing room there was silence as Coach Frank Leahy and the players knelt in prayer. Leahy began: "Something happened to you today for which we've prayed. Lets show our gratitude. I want you all, players and coaches, to go to that church where we prayed this morning and pray again." The AP distributed a photograph of the scene Dec. 4, 1949.

The same service produced a picture Sept. 25, 1946 of the Rev. Benney J. Benson kneeling before an audience on the steps of the Brooklyn Borough Hall to pray for victory for the Brooklyn Dodgers baseball team. Too bad, the St. Louis Cardinals won the National League pennant that year.

The whole custom of prayer in the attempt to enhance the chances of an athletic team is repulsive to some. For example, Mike Royko began his column May 16, 1973:

> I've never understood what religion has to with sports. Why would a coach who leads his football team in a locker room prayer think that a universal deity could have the faintest interest in whether the team can kick, stomp, gouge, bite and fracture its way to more touchdowns than the opposing leg-breakers. At some major events the fans are asked to rise and join a clergyman in prayers for an event on which millions of dollars are being bet with the nation's bookies. And now we are getting the pious preachings of a growing band of muscle-flexers called the Fellowship of Christian Athletes.

The players that Royko has in mind are ones that wear good-luck medals around their necks and cross themselves before they go to bat.

Convinced that they were under orders from heaven a family of six from Kansas City, Mo. spent six months in a parked car near New York's City Hall waiting for a spiritual message to set out for Jerusalem, according to the *Chicago Daily News* Beeline for Aug. 31, 1968.

Also in New York, the UPI reported March 6, 1977, Sister Joan Marese, a Catholic nun, worked in an automobile repair shop in the belief her aptitude was "a gift of God." Back in Kansas City, Mo. the AP reported July 14, 1981, an independent Roman Catholic newspaper reported that a woman was performing as a priest in an unnamed eastern city where the congregation ran things. After she substituted at mass for the regular priest he invited her to do so again, saying "You have been called now. Any other ceremony will only affirm what has already happened."

How "The Holy Spirit talked to me and gave me advice while I was in prison" was relayed to Charles Madigan for publication in the Oct. 28, 1980 *Chicago Tribune*. Tom White, the narrator, had been forced down in Cuba while on a flight to Jamaica. He was imprisoned for more than a year after it was discovered he had been dropping religious literature from the sky.

According to the UPI for June 12, 1981, Mark David Chapman, accused of killing singer John Lennon, told his lawyer that God visited him twice in his cell and directed him to plead guilty. June 23 the AP reported that in New York Judge Dennis Edwards accepted the plea. Since God's visits, the lawyer said, it has been impossible to conduct a rational conversation with his client.

Chapman was not the most prominent figure to believe he was visited by heavenly messengers. In his biography of Lyndon B. Johnson, Ronnie Dugger, longtime editor of the *Texas Observer* and friend of LBJ, revealed that the 36th president believed he was visited by the Holy Ghost during early hours in the White House during the Vietnam war.

Even though there was no prayer of solicitation, recipients or beneficiaries of good luck frequently give thanks to God. That happened when two survivors of a plane crash were rescued after six days on a mountainside in British Columbia. Their comment, as reported May 9, 1949 by the AP, with pictures, was, "Someone upstairs looked after us."

Rescued with five companions after ten days in a 36-inch-high coal mine tunnel, Eugene Martin told the AP May 17, 1968 in Richwood, W.Va., "I went in a sinner and came out a Christian." The men talked and prayed throughout their ordeal. One said, "Jesus kept the water from drowning us . . . we weren't electrocuted when we tried to get out through the water before we turned back . . . and the air stayed remarkably good."

At least two children and maybe more died in an early-morning fire on Chicago's south side. A babysitter and another child survived, however, and the *Chicago Sun-Times* published the adult's explanation Feb. 2, 1972: "The Lord woke me up and I looked where the kids was at. That whole room was nothing but fire. The Lord told me to open the back door. I was dragging little Tony and I was dizzy. But I got to the door and it was all I could do to get to the back porch and say help."

Although the odds against being struck by lightning are supposedly a million to one, a Niles, Ill. man was hit on the street. *Chicago Today* interviewed him in the hospital for a Sept. 19, 1972 story. He said: "There is a God in heaven. Thank God I'm alive to talk about it." The reporter did not push him as to God's reasons for what he did.

After 400 firemen battled a spectacular blaze that destroyed four buildings, Chicago Fire Commissioner Robert J. Quinn told Paul Galloway and Michael Minor of the *Chicago Sun-Times* for May 27, 1973: "The good Lord was with us," as the wind shifted and spread, saving several other buildings from being engulfed.

Forced to land because they violated regulations a group of 32 American and Canadian missionaries were pleased because of their 24-hour enforced stay over in Cuba. The UPI reported from their home base, Alliance, Ohio, Feb. 25, 1974. The group's spokesman told the press: "We knew God had made our plane land for a purpose . . . and we know we made quite an impression on those who saw us. I think they will think twice before they force a plane full of Christians to land in their country again. We caused quite a commotion with our song and prayer services."

On the other hand, when an Anglican archbishop and three cabinet members were killed in an air crash in Uganda, the country's president, Idi Amin, claimed they were killed "as punishment by God."

While kidnapped by terrorists in a remote Ethiopian village a pregnant young American missionary nurse wrote her parents in Freehold, N.J. that she was "well physically, mentally and emotionally. I am praising God and hope you are too," Don Wycliff wrote in the *Chicago Daily News* for June 5, 1974.

In its Dec. 29, 1978 account of a United Airlines crash near Portland, Ore., the *Los Angeles Times* quoted a survivor as follows: "I want you to publish this. The Lord Jesus saved our lives. We were praying and the Lord told me he was going to do a miracle."

By inference, of course, all who died in the crash were undeserving of the Almighty's favor. Nor were hundreds of others mentioned in other journalistic accounts.

The sole survivor of a canoe accident in which three others drowned, Cheryl Steele said it was her Christian faith that caused her to endure 15 hours in Lake Huron, Mary Trueman reported in the *Detroit Free Press* for July 7, 1980. Steele, a "true believer," was sure the accident was God's will and she was happy her companions had accepted the Lord and would be in heaven.

"A plain outright miracle" is what the UPI reported April 6, 1980 from Cincinnati a bus driver said after his runaway bus stopped on his foot without breaking it. Said Elmer Hambauch, Jr., "I don't want to take credit for heroism. I don't want to take credit for saving lives. I just want people to know God is alive."

"Stretching their love for Jesus" was the four-column headline the *Clearwater* (Fla.) *Sun* gave May 29, 1982 to Annette Drolet's writeup of Claudia Dineen's Fitness Fellowship. She wrote, "Mrs. Dineen—constantly smiling, singing and whooping—exhorts them [students] to stretch their bodies to the limit in time to Christian music for the glory of God." Mrs. Dineen considers it her Christian duty to keep her body in shape. She said, "I think we . . . owe it to Him to keep it in good shape."

When he awakened to discover himself trapped by a raging fire in the MGM Grand Hotel casino in Las Vegas, said Randy Howard, as reported by the AP Nov. 24, 1980, "I dropped to my knees and yelled, 'God in Jesus, help me find a way out.' Just then I looked out the window and saw a rope fly by to my left." Howard said his escape by means of the rope was an act of God.

Eighty-four others died in the fire. They evidently forgot to get on their knees and yell.

Following a similar fire in Seattle the UP quoted a survivor as saying he was "lucky to be alive and thankful to God."

Placing no confidence in public officials, trade unionists or anyone else to help, Cardinal Stefan Wyszynski, at a Christmas Day 1980 mass, told his Warsaw congregation, "We can be saved only by God." By contrast the *Chicago Tribune* reported Dec. 5, 1974 the Democratic Party Rules Committee meeting in Kansas City defeated a motion to insert "In God we Trust" in a resolution. Later "Under God" was added.

From Fremont, Calif. the AP reported Oct. 16, 1981 that a hunter, lost 13 days in the Mendocino National Forest, thanked God for his survival. "My prayers were answered," he said, fingering his crucifix.

A "close-grown accord between American medicine and religion" was demonstrated when a heart-attack victim survived after 2½ hours of massaging while a priest and several hospital attendants prayed constantly. The story first was told in the *Journal* of the American Medical Association and reviewed in the *Chicago Sun-Times* for April 12, 1957. A surgeon was quoted, "Actually we never were sure that we were completely alone in this thing. We knew we were getting some guidance."

In the *Chicago Daily News* for July 28–29, 1973 Henry Hanson wrote: "No matter how excellent the medical care may have been some patients are inclined to regard their recovery from illness to be because of their great faith and their prayer." Such cases demand journalistic attention, as when the AP Sept. 19, 1974 quoted an injured motorcycle stunt man who doctors were doubtful ever would walk again: "I have all the faith in the world the Lord is going to let me walk," he said.

After he successfully presided at an eight-hour operation to separate Siamese twins, Dr. C. Everett Koop recalled his nervousness in 1956 when he saw his first such babies and attributed his self-possession in the later case to 18 more years of experience plus what he calls "my anchor—a complete belief in the sovereignty of God." Arthur J. Snider quoted the doctor further in the *Chicago Daily News* for Sept. 23, 1974, "Having that, knowing that someone else is running the show gives me a tremendous amount of comfort."

It is doubtful that any newspaper anywhere would ignore a "God did it" story whether the news source was patient, relatives, friends, doctors or nurses.

A typical example appeared in the *Chicago Daily News* for Jan. 20, 1947 under the top line "Miracle" and headline, "Sight Restored, Vet Gives God Full Credit." A German artillery shell during World War II had destroyed Dick Herbert's right eye and doctors doubted the left ever would be restored. It was when the vet was stoking the furnace in his father's home, suddenly. "Sure it's a miracle of God. What else?" he said.

For the same newspaper Arthur J. Snider obtained about two columns of opinions by medical and religious authorities regarding Tony Cantellope, 8, of Spangler, Pa. who took his first step after prayers and novenas to Mother Cabrini. Medical opinion was that the child already had been cured from a pathological standpoint and needed only an incentive to walk. The symposium appeared Jan. 10, 1949.

Mrs. Louise Slater of Tecumseh, Ontario was convinced it was her prayers for over a year that were answered when her paralyzed son regained use of his limbs and his speech while she became confined to a wheelchair. She had asked God to transfer the young man's afflictions to her, according to Fred Bird in the *Chicago Daily News* for Feb. 15, 1949.

Prayers of 1,000 parochial school children were reported by the *Chicago Sun-Times* of Jan. 12, 1950 to be the only hope for Mary Ann Lindbloom, 13, who had been in a coma for 22 days after an automobile accident.

Two-year-old Randell Wayne was one of two of four to survive liver transplants and the first to recover enough to leave a Denver hospital, Burl Osborne reported from the place for the Associated Press May 20, 1968. "God is responsible for what has happened to Randy," said the child's mother. "It's all in His hands."

"I've a great deal of work to do. That's why God saved me. After all, life is helping other people," is what Mrs. Betty Anick, the second longest-surviving heart transplant recipient, told Karen Hasman for publication in the *Chicago Daily News* for July 28–29, 1973.

In the same paper Oct. 12, 1974 Charlotte Hunt quoted John Miller on his 109th birthday that he thanked God and gin for his longevity.

To explain why at 77 she walked 10 to 20 miles a day, Irene Hoyer told Judy Rosenfield for the Oct. 15, 1974 *Louisville Times:* "I walk to show God my appreciation for being strong enough to be so active."

Jocko Conlan, Hall of Fame umpire, walked out of the hospital and praised "the two finest heart specialists—Dr. Edward Dietrich and the good Lord," the AP reported Nov. 30, 1974 from Phoenix, Ariz.

Jack Mabley headed his daily column in the *Chicago Tribune* for Dec. 1, 1974, "Medical miracle is answer to prayer." What followed was the story of a 12-year-old girl who had come out of a coma six months after a near drowning caused serious brain damage. When told repeatedly by hospital attendants that her daughter would not recover, the mother said, "I hadn't given up. I told them, God's work isn't impossible." No explanation of why God let it happen in the first place.

After 27 years of deafness as the result of spinal meningitis, Bobby Jimenez, 30, of Porterville, Calif. experienced a flash of orange light and an explosion and recovered his hearing. "God has given me back my hearing," he said, but prematurely, because in less than a week he was deaf as before. Doctors were puzzled. William Endicott reported the story March 2, 1979 for the *Los Angeles Times*.

"Son's Brain Surgery Is Christ's Gift for Dad" was the headline the *Grand Rapids Press* gave Dec. 19, 1979 to an Associated Press story from

Philadelphia of a Greek fisherman who brought his 12-year-old son to America for brain surgery of a tumor which all were overjoyed to learn was benign.

After she became Miss America, Cheryl Prewitt told Bob Herguth, conductor of the Chicago *Sun-Times* Public Eye column, "I was crippled in a car accident at the age of 11. It left one leg shorter than the other until I was 17. Then the leg became the same as the other. The Lord healed me. God showed he had great things ahead for me. I needed to be a whole person." Herguth used the item June 12, 1980.

When he tripped over his dog, fell down a flight of stairs and hit his head against the wall, Joseph C. Sardler, 32, regained his sight after six years. The UPI distributed the story from Mount Airy, N.C. March 14, 1981.

James Tassone was an automobile accident victim whose kidneys were transplanted in two other men. Andy Gluck reported in the *Clearwater Sun* for April 29, 1982 that Tassone's father said, "Maybe it was just God's plan. My son died so that two people could live."

In times of sorrow or adversity religious people find comfort and support in their faith and some nonbelievers, especially if they have been caught misbehaving, turn to God and are born again. "God works in strange ways but his will must be done," a grieving person consoles himself. And there presumably are no atheists in foxholes. A stale joke still goes the rounds of an adamant freethinker caught in a precarious predicament, praying, "Lord, I've never bothered you before and I never will again if you get me out of this mess." Not quite so profane are the prayers of promises to reform one's ways or perform some act of attrition in exchange for some petition to heaven. To illustrate these principles:

A father explained that his daughter had been "called by the Holy Spirit" to the waters of Madawaska River where she drowned, the AP reported Sept. 7, 1948 from Bancroft, Ont.

"He's probably smiling now up in heaven," another father, whose seven-year-old son was a leukemia victim, told Philip J. O'Connor for the Dec. 20, 1974 *Chicago Daily News.*

"God has willed it. He knows what he's doing," said a priest as he surveyed the ruins of his church in Balvano, Italy following an earthquake, according to Jil Schmetzer in the *Chicago Tribune* for Nov. 25, 1980.

Entombed and sexually assaulted in an underground dungeon for 181 days, a 13-year-old girl retained her faith in God and at one time wrote her tormentor, "I know you think I'm stupid and, like you say, everybody is entitled to their own thoughts but I do believe in God and I do believe in friends. And I just wish you would be my friend."

Circus people are naturally religious and "There are no atheists on the high wire or in the lion cage," a Barnum & Bailey clown told James H. Bowman for a story in the Oct. 5–6, 1975 *Chicago Daily News.* Dusty said he was converted from Roman Catholicism to Mormonism by a circus ringmaster and found fellow churchmen in every town he visited to keep him from becoming lonely.

A series of misfortunes—a serious automobile accident, a freak accident when a spike destroyed a lung, the death of her baby from pneumonia—left Shena Reed feeling "destroyed, that God had tried every way he could to get me," the AP reported Dec. 20, 1980 from Elkton, Ky. Her love for her husband, however, caused her to carry on. She said: "I've even thought that maybe God was trying to tell us that me and Clark aren't right for each other. But when you've been through as much as we have, you've got to figure you ought to stay together."

The world's oldest adult Siamese twins, attached at the tops of their heads, were photographed by the AP for distribution Aug. 21, 1981. The cutlines explained "Their mother taught them at an early age that they were the work of God."

This was reminiscent of a long feature Paul Malloy wrote for the *Chicago Sun-Times* for June 25, 1973 about a 4-foot, 6-inch dwarf, a hotel clerk who acted as a clown to entertain children in hospitals and other institutions. His mother explained: "The doctors say it is probably hereditary but it could be back in the family 100 years or more. We don't know. It's been said that God sends babies who are disabled to the people He loves, so I guess I consider Jeff one of the gifts of God."

Several of the Nixon administration found guilty in the Watergate burglary and subsequent conspiracy of silence "found God" for repentance, forgiveness or retribution. The *Washington Post's* Timothy S. Robinson and Lawrence Meyer interviewed John D. Ehrlichman, his wife and five children for publication July 13, 1974. One paragraph of their story follows: "When asked what was sustaining them through the trial, Mrs. Ehrlichman and the five children answered almost in unison, Love for God . . . religion . . . love for family." The article did not specify how the love of God operated. Jeb Stuart and Gail Magruder were more specific in talking to Joan Zyda for the June 8, 1976 *Chicago Tribune.* They said they found themselves gripped by something stronger than themselves, something that many see as the inexhaustible power that spins the universe: God. So Jeb joined the staff of *Young Life,* publication of a nondenominational Christian organization based in Colorado Springs. Regarding the Watergate scandal, Mrs. Magruder said that the press didn't unearth it. "Woodward and Bernstein uncovered several miscellaneous facts, that's all. The real hero was God," she said. May 20, 1982 the AP distributed a picture of the Magruders with cutlines to say he had become assistant pastor of the First Presbyterian Church of Burlingame, Calif. He said he "found Jesus" while in prison seven months.

No journalist has ever described the gritty nitty mechanisms by which the Deity functions. There is, however, no greater evidence of most people's belief in God's magic than their attempts to persuade others to join in

prayers to accomplish some desirable end. About the only journalistically
recorded instance of a minister's refusal to join in such a campaign appeared in the *Chicago Tribune* for March 7, 1932. The story told of the
explanation the Rev. Carleton B. Miller gave the congregation of the First
Congregational Church of Battle Creek, Mich. of why he did not join in
prayers for the kidnapped Charles D. Lindbergh, Jr. He said: "If God does
not have it in mind to prevent such crimes, it can do no good to pray for the
child's return." The baby, of course, died shortly after its abduction but the
body was not found for months.

Much more typical was the appeal of the Rev. Eugene Solie of the
Evangelical Mission Covenant Church of Milwaukee who wired his congregation from an Ann Arbor hospital to pray for a miracle to cure his rare
blood ailment. At the same time he expressed "unshaken faith in the
wisdom of God," albeit, of course, it might be contrary to what the sick man
hoped would be the case.

Nationwide attention was aroused when a 9-year-old girl wrote to the
Memphis Commercial-Appeal to ask, "Don't you think praying will save
my hand?" the hand being threatened with amputation to prevent an
infection or spread of bone cancer. The United Press International and the
Associated Press transmitted daily stories from Memphis and Brownville,
Tex., the child's home town. Also published widely was a facsimile of her
letter and pictures of parochial school pupils praying before a statue of the
Virgin Mary and of Betty Lou Marberry herself attending a rural Sunday
school class while waiting for the medical decision.

Dec. 2, 1949 the UPI reported that thousands of persons from all walks
of life answered the little girl. Special prayers were said in several
churches and parishioners were asked to pray for the child's recovery. Dec.
19 the UPI reported that Betty Lou would go to Boston to be examined by a
bone specialist. Dec. 28 the AP reported that the little patient became
reconciled to the surgery and said, "If the Lord wants my hand that's all
right with me."

Another tear-jerker was written by Eileen Ogintz for the *Chicago
Tribune* of Dec. 7, 1981. It concerned Alexis Grotz, a 9-year-old who was
slowly dying from a hereditary disease that was destroying her nervous
system. A 2-column picture showed her and her parents laughing. She
said: "God doesn't say when but I'm in a hurry to go. I'm not afraid. In
heaven I'll be able to walk again. And ride my bike. And my grandpa is
there."

In a letter to all churches in the country, Spain's Cardinal Marcelo
Gonzalez Martin wrote: "In view of the continuing drought under which we
suffer and which has such harmful effects of every kind, I call upon all
priests, together with believers, to direct your prayers to God, our Lord,
that He might grant us the benefit of rain," Deutsche Presse-Agentur's
Rolf Gilpert reported Nov. 11, 1981 from Madrid.

Before the Watergate scandal broke John Cardinal Cody of Chicago asked his congregation to pray for the success of President Nixon's peace trip to China, Bob Herguth reported in his *Chicago Daily News* column for Feb. 17, 1972. Such requests from the pulpit are not rare. In fact, clergymen are constantly asking God to give presidents, governors and other public officials wisdom, integrity and courage. It's not possible to keep a box score to evaluate the results.

When the great Hall of Famer Jerome Herman "Dizzy" Dean, longtime star pitcher for the St. Louis Cardinals, suffered a severe heart attack in Reno, Nev. his wife appealed for prayers "from all those who know and love him," the press reported July 16, 1974. They were, of course, in vain.

Not so the supplications for heavenly assistance for Mrs. Eleanor Daley, wife of Chicago Mayor Richard J. Daley. When she was hospitalized for acute gastroenteritis, the mayor asked a gathering of Democratic precinct captains to pray for her recovery, Larry Weintraub reported in the *Chicago Daily News* for Feb. 4, 1975. She recovered.

Among the most prayerful, as typified by these examples, were athletes and politicians. The religiosity of the former was discussed in Chapter 9 (see page 184). William Eaton did a roundup of Washington, D.C. prayer groups for the *Chicago Daily News* Sept. 24, 1974. The much publicized conversion of Charles Colson, one of the worst Watergate bad guys, and the resignation of Iowa Sen. Harold Hughes to do Christian fellowship work helped the organizers of Senate prayer breakfasts every Wednesday in the Prayer Room for Congressmen "to seek divine strength and guidance, both in public affairs and in their own personal concerns." There also was a House prayer breakfast every Thursday, a Judicial prayer group and, at the Pentagon, a full schedule of religious activities. Eaton believes the initial emphasis was provided by President Dwight D. Eisenhower who wrote his own inaugural prayer. When he was sworn in, President Gerald Ford asked, "Confirm me with your prayers."

Whenever something for which s/he has prayed comes about the true believer takes credit for having helped God make up his mind. To such persons prayer is a form of lobbying and the press reports successes. When Henry J. Mueller was acquitted in San Jose of a murder committed in 1919, his wife in Chicago told Hub Logan for the *Sun-Times* of Jan. 29, 1948: "We prayed every night and kept the Christmas tree up for him. I knew my prayers would be answered."

Unreported, of course, are the instances in which such prayers are not successful. Near misses, however, do interest the press. Fulton Oursler related such a case exclusively for the *Chicago Daily News* of Feb. 18, 1950. A Congregational minister was unable to summon medical help for his son who was suffering from an edema, or swelling of the larynx. So, in desperation, the minister knelt and prayed, "Father in Heaven with all my heart and soul I entreat You to save the life of my little boy, but your will, not mine, be done." He had hardly gone further before his telephone rang with the news of a refugee doctor living in his neighborhood who attended the boy. The *News* headlined the article, "A Modern Parable. Prayer Answered or Lucky Break?"

Polydore Levi had no doubts as to the cause of his escape from death, the AP reported Aug. 16, 1950 from Quebec. A disk harrow cut halfway through his legs, and it was 45 minutes before help arrived. However, Levi said the bleeding stopped as soon as he began praying to Jesuit martyr St. John Breboeuf.

After a *Nashville Tennessean* reporter investigated a two-year-old occurrence, the AP distributed the story from Sherwood, Tenn. Nov. 26, 1961. Despite the gloomy prognoses of doctors, a 4-year-old recovered her sight after four months of blindness. The Rev. Joseph Huske told how the parents prayed daily and declared the happy ending "a miracle!"

Another miracle, Bruce Taylor wrote in the *Chicago Sun-Times* for Dec. 23, 1964, occurred because hundreds of readers prayed and bought a puppy for 12-year-old Sheila Baird who endured 25 hospitalizations and six major operations for an abdominal tumor. The paper gave the story a 4-column, 2-line headline, "Thanks to Hundreds of Prayers Cripple Sheila Shares a Miracle." As ethical journalists must, they kept confidential the heavenly source of their information.

Acting on a tip from a neighbor police rescued a teenaged girl who was a kidnapper's captive for five days. According to the child's father, "I think it was prayer more than anything that brought her back." The story was published in the *Chicago Sun-Times* for April 3, 1967.

For two days an 11-year-old boy and his 12-year-old sister and their father were trapped on Mt. Rainier by a heavy snowstorm. "We kept praying and praying—over and over again, Dear Lord, please bring us good weather," according to an AP story from Seattle June 4, 1968. Their mother was certain their prayers were answered, since the storm lifted. It was discovered, however, that the father had died of exposure because he gave his children all the shelter available.

Skeptics often have difficulty arguing with devout readers about apparently successful pleas to heaven as that told in cutlines for a photograph distributed by the AP May 2, 1971. The picture showed an Indian chief chanting a prayer during a rain dance at Pompano Beach, Fla. Moments after the Comanche chief concluded the performance, a respectable rain began to fall.

Seeing was believing also for an *Asheville Times* reporter and photographer who saw a 9-year-old boy identify objects with a plastic eye, his real eye having been removed after a fireworks injury. The AP distributed the story from Black Mountain, N.C. Aug. 21, 1971. The family was quoted as believing there had been a miracle; the doctor in charge suggested it might be a case of extrasensory perception. The patient himself explained, "Jesus loves me."

Another who believed good fortune resulted from her prayers was Debbie Hamilton whose story the AP told from Royal Oak, Mich. After

Debbie had been photographed in the nude and paid $5,000 by *Playboy*, she decided her religious scruples as a Jehovah's Witness did not permit her to be a magazine's centerfold. She prayed before asking the magazine to cancel her contract and Hugh Hefner capitulated.

When three captured American pilots were released by North Vietnam, *Chicago Today* headlined the AP story Sept. 2, 1972 "Wife's prayers are answered." Said one wife: "We have really been blessed by God. He's really taken care of us and answered our prayers."

Even today, more than a decade later, there are hundreds, perhaps thousands of Americans whose fates are unknown. Possibly they didn't have any loved one to lobby for their release.

Another headline, "Mom prays and there's hope for son, 18," in the *Chicago Daily News* for Jan. 31, 1973 told how a young man who was injured in a train accident came out of a coma three months later after his mother prayed to Mother Mary Theresa, a Franciscan nun being considered for sainthood. "This has proven my faith," she said, and doctors who had considered the case hopeless took heart.

" 'Plea to God' then $50,000" was the *Chicago Sun-Times* headline Aug. 20, 1974 over a story of a meat production company foreman who prayed in his boss' office before a drawing of the Illinois State lottery. "I told him, 'God I don't want the $300,000 [first prize]. Only give me one of the $10,000 prizes so my kids can go to school!'" Shortly thereafter the governor called to tell him he had won $50,000. There was no report on how many losers there were who also prayed.

"The Lord was with us," was the reaction of Vincent Skladany when he found a lottery ticket worth $100,000 unspoiled in a suit of clothes when it was returned from the cleaners. The AP sent out the story Jan. 13, 1976 from Cleveland.

When she read the winning numbers in the *Chicago Sun-Times* Lucky Numbers jackpot, Mrs. Murphy Freeman "just stood there and kept saying 'Thank you, Jesus,' " while her husband laughed because he thought she was kidding him.

Because he believed his research and especially his prayers would be answered, Dan Bowen bought nearly $200,000 worth of stock on little more than a promise and a prayer because he hoped God would help him realize his ambition to become a missionary in the Philippines. Instead, the stock dropped in value and Bowen faced bankrupty, the AP reported in July, 1981 from Valparaiso, Ind.

"Lucky state lottery winners who see their new wealth as an answer to prayer won't find support for their assertions among theologians," James H. Bowman, religion editor, wrote in the *Chicago Daily News* for Sept. 21–22, 1974. There's no way a gambler can pray his way to the bank, Bowman wrote in summarizing the views of a sizable number of clergymen. In fact, praying to win was considered offensive by them. One divine said, "Praying to win a lottery is based on the rather magical notion that God intervenes in events from outside the world."

Nevertheless, the *News'* Beeline July 6, 1973 answered a reader who wanted to know if it was sacrilegious to pray for victory for the White Sox by revealing that such prayers had been said at the Episcopal Cathedral of St. James. Several rabbis said they intended to do the same and the Catholic chancery was asking all priests if they wanted to do it in unison or separately.

In testimony before a Senate subcommittee on the budget, a convicted drug dealer said he had been "saved by Jesus" and had worried unnecessarily that the Internal Revenue Service would detect his laundering of money in Caribbean island banks, the *Chicago Sun-Times* reported Nov. 18, 1981.

"Sign From God, Says Terrorist Victim" headed a story from Jerusalem Jan. 7, 1975 by William J. Drummond of the *Los Angeles Times*. The victim was a 16-year-old member of a group of tourists from the Main Street Baptist Church of Jacksonville who lost a leg when a grenade exploded as the group was boarding a bus near the tomb of Lazarus. The girl, DeJean Replogle, said she felt queer because she did not join others in weeping in the room where Jesus' last supper supposedly was held. "I said, 'hey Man' something is wrong. I'm not right. I prayed that the Lord would do something to me. I honestly prayed that he would do something to me, build my faith in him. It wasn't 20 minutes later that this happened." She was the only one injured.

When her son threatened to jump from the roof of a three-story school building in Boise, Idaho, a mother prayed and shortly thereafter the boy's father and a priest talked him into climbing down. The *Chicago Daily News* used the caption, "Her prayers answered, son is safe" on the AP photograph it published Jan. 9, 1976.

The same newspaper Dec. 1, 1976 used a 2-line 5-column page-1 headline, "I kept on praying I'd get out alive" over an account of two gunmen who robbed a currency exchange and held three women hostages for nearly five hours.

Under a UPI photograph captioned "Tornado hits school: 2 Die," the *Chicago Sun-Times* May 5, 1978 used cutlines that began, "Georgia Novak, her silent prayers answered, hugs her son Richard . . ."

A father whose prayers were not answered was disconsolate when his 17-year-old daughter was found murdered. In the *Chicago Sun-Times* for May 28, 1978, he was quoted as saying: "I'm an alcoholic but I haven't had a drink in three years. I asked God to help me get a job to help my daughter graduate and I got a job. I had really been getting it together. I was doing it for my kid . . . And then my kid dies . . . Now what's the use."

Irving Kupcinet led off his Kup's column in the Nov. 27, 1978 *Sun-Times* with a quotation from Patty Lewis, who said that doctors who relieved the spinal agony of her husband, Jerry Lewis, differed with the evangelist Oral Roberts who "performed a miracle in helping Jerry."

How someone can display superhuman strength in an emergency was related by the UPI in a story from Trout Run, Pa. April 8, 1981. Barbara Sechrist said it was "the grace of God" that gave her the strength to lift a 500-pound tombstone that fell on a 50 pound, 5-year-old girl, a member of a Methodist Bible school study class on a walk.

After she saved a man from drowning in the Chicago River, Marilyn Bees told the *Evanston Review* June 1, 1975, "It was only by God's grace that I had the strength and courage to do what I did."

The AP June 13, 1981 publicized the plans Mayor Charles McMackin of Salem, Ill. was making to thank 24 ministers for their prayers which the mayor accredited with helping to end a long drought.

People are most inclined to thank God when they have close encounters with death. Thus President Ronald Reagan agreed with Cardinal Terence Cooke that "The hand of God was upon you," after he escaped assassination May 30, 1981. The president told the priest, "I know, and whatever time he's left for me is his."

When a would-be assassin seriously wounded Pope John Paul II the AP reported May 15, 1981 that pilgrims at the shrine of Our Lady of Fatima, Portugal believed that the pontiff's life was saved because the attack occurred on the 64th anniversary of the first six apparitions of the Virgin Mary to children there. Said the mother superior, "Naturally it [the attack on the pope] was on Our Lady's day so the pope had the protection of Fatima." Aug. 11, 1981 Herguth reported in the *Chicago Sun-Times* that John Paul II had sent Chicago his apostolic blessing and thanks for Chicagoans' prayers.

Exactly a year later when the pope visited the Fatima shrine a knife-wielding would-be assassin was subdued by security guards in time.

Always good for priority handling is the type of story John Saar and Alfred E. Lewis wrote for the *Washington Post* Jan. 21, 1975. It told of a security guard whose life was saved when a knife-wielding masked man lunged at him with a foot-long butcher knife which did not penetrate the Bible his intended victim had in his left breast pocket.

Nov. 20, 1968 the UPI distributed a picture of a Compton, Calif. minister who displayed a stack of religious tracts that stopped a bullet aimed at him.

Hospital officials called it "a near miracle" when a security guard lived after being shot three times; apparently the bullets were deflected by the man's breastbone, according to the *Los Angeles Times* for Sept. 7, 1981.

One narrow escape that convinced two policemen that there is a power that can protect one occurred at the end of a visit to Chicago of evangelist Billy Graham. Bidding goodbye to the two men who had been his bodyguards, Graham said: "God bless you both. God bless you and keep you from harm." As *Chicago Today* told it June 16, 1961, the next day when a sniper's bullets missed them the two men bowed their heads briefly and said, "Thank you."

When the British commandos embarked for the Falkland Islands, the *New York Times* reported from London that Major John Moore "probably will make it to those bleak islands with a Bible in the left breast pocket of his combat jacket." The *Chicago Tribune* used the story May 19, 1982 under a 2-column headline, "British force's chief is Bible-carrying hero."

The devout are impressed when religious symbols remain unscathed after some disaster. Jan. 30, 1948 the AP distributed a picture of a crucifix, the only object left standing after an earthquake leveled a church in Oton, Philippines. From Centerville, Calif. Nov. 4, 1950 the AP reported that a man's life was saved when a bullet hit a crucifix he wore around his neck and was deflected.

A similar occurrence was the fire that gutted Cyril and Methodius Church but left almost unharmed a statue of St. Joseph on the saint's feast day. Picture and story appeared in the *Chicago Sun-Times* for March 20, 1958.

Prayer never got a better press than when Flight Commander Frank Borman prayed for his home planet a quarter-million miles away: "Show us what each one of us can do to set forward the coming day of universal peace." The *Chicago Sun-Times* reported Dec. 25, 1968 that Borman said this with great sincerity as Apollo 8 raced through the third of its ten planned orbits of the moon. "The Story Behind Borman's Message From Space" was told in a page of *Parade* for Feb. 23, 1969. "It was the evidence that God lives" was the direct quote used as a subhead. According to the unsigned article, however, "For the astronauts the flight through the heavens brought no dramatic changes in their beliefs." Borman was quoted as saying: "I don't believe in miracles. Men make their own miracles. I believe God gave us a free will and free brain to work out our problems. Our flight was a success because of the ability of the NASA team." Sort of inconsistent.

The avidity of the press to publish accounts of persons in all walks of life taking the Lord's name to explain an event or advance a cause has offended some readers and writers who have tired of vainglorious attempts to so use the Almighty. For example, the *Chicago Sun-Times* for July 16, 1968 had a letter from James K. Gandy of Brighton, England: "The so-called 'miracles' of Britain were brought about by prayer all over the country. The war in Viet Nam can be ended in just the same way. Spare a thoughtful prayer every day." To which Eunice Goodchild replied July 20, "No wars are ended by prayer and if we had had to depend on prayer during the Battle of Britain there would be no England today."

After her 19-year-old son was shot and killed by a motorist whom he had asked not to tailgate him, Ms. Carolyn Budde said: "At first I blamed God. But God didn't do it. So who do you blame? They took Kennedy, President Kennedy. They take everybody—Maniacs. Maniacs with guns walking around," as related by Roger Simon in his *Chicago Sun-Times* column for May 19, 1982.

When Rebecca Folder, 18, a bank teller, was shot by a burglar she "cried out to the Lord," her father said, and continued: "I asked her if she told the Lord it was all right if He took her then, and she nodded her head yes. It's hard sometimes to understand what the Lord is doing, but we know His way is best." Anne LaRiviere wrote the story for the *Los Angeles Times* of Dec. 18, 1981.

In a letter to be published after his death the late John Cardinal Cody of Chicago wrote: "I wish to let everyone know that I have forgiven my enemies . . . But God will not so forgive . . . Join in praying for mercy."

The letter was published in the *Chicago Sun-Times* April 26, 1982. The paper had printed several stories of the federal grand jury's investigation of charges the cardinal had diverted church funds to a lifelong woman friend. That friend said the paper should not cover his funeral.

Columnists have greater freedom than most other journalists. In her Dec. 3, 1981 column Abigail Van Buren (Dear Abby) advised a woman reader who told of the severe beatings she received from her husband. To forestall divorce they decided to consult a marriage counselor. When the male counselor pointed out the husband's faults, he said, "Of course he'd stick up for you; he's a man and you're a woman." So they changed to a woman counselor who also said the husband was wrong, so he commented, "You women always stick together."

The reader told Abby: "He says the Bible says I am supposed to forgive him 70 times 7, which is 490. I forgave him three times already. Does that mean I have 487 times more to go? I don't think I could live through it. Help me." Abby's help was: "Pete is sick. 'Forgive him' but have nothing to do with him until he recovers."

Sometimes Abby's mail includes more philosophical queries, as the one she published April 8, 1982. It commented on a reply Abby had given a father whose daughter had escaped death in an automobile accident while under the influence of drugs. Abby had advised telling the daughter that the Lord spared her because he wanted her to live. The new correspondent wrote:

> So you are assuming that the Lord made the decision to spare her life. There is nothing unusual about that. It is very common for people to thank God for the good things, like recovering from a serious operation or a life-threatening accident. Anything good is supposed to come from God.
>
> And who should we blame for having put the girl in a position to lose her life in the accident? Why did the Lord not intervene then? Why don't we say, "The Lord is uncaring about his people." Couldn't he have prevented the accident? . . .
>
> If we are going to thank the Lord for the good things should not we also blame Him or Her for the bad times as well?

That floored Abby, who replied: "Your question brings up an ancient unresolved theological question that would take far more wisdom and knowledge than I possess to answer." Big help.

In his inimitable sardonic style which won him the first Henry L. Mencken prize given by the *Baltimore Sun,* Mike Royko wrote June 21, 1973: "I've always been fascinated by the kinds of events that people attribute directly to God." His interest, he wrote, dates from his childhood when he was told, "God came and took your grandma." As a young reporter he witnessed a kindly neighbor comforting a woman whose husband had just died, "God wanted Joey to come and live with him." Royko also recalled the comments of a lone survivor of a train crash: "God wanted me to live." And when Janet Lynn, Olympic prize ice skater, went professional, at more than $1½ million annually, she explained, "I felt it's what God wanted me to do."

"I can no longer take credit for Rocky," Fred Yager of the Associated Press June 2, 1982 quoted Sylvester Stallone as saying: "The whole thing was preordained by God. I believe my participation in the film was merely as a medium." Which suggests that there should be a further category for judging motion pictures—GO for God Ordained. It ought to pack the theaters, Yager wrote.

In at least four other columns—May 15, 1981, March 2 and 11 and April 8, 1982, Royko has dealt with the same theme. The first column, entitled "Dear God: Why?" was a letter to God, somewhere in the universe, "about how things are going here." Then, "Well, things couldn't be going any better at least as far as your image is concerned. You wouldn't believe how well you are loved on this planet today and how much is being done in your name." A typical extract follows:

> The Irish Protestants are so devoted to you that they do everything possible to make life miserable for the Irish Catholics because they don't think the Irish Catholics have the right approach toward worshipping you. And the Irish Catholics do what they do to make life miserable for the Irish Protestants for essentially the same reasons.

In "God's Wrath vs IRS" with an overline, "Bob Jones' hot line," Royko cited numerous cases of persons saying they talked with God, or saw God, or heard God speak. Most of these are, he said, harmless nuts and to test that fact he suggested telling someone, "God spoke to me this morning. I heard his voice in my ear. He gave me an important message."

Most of the column was about Bob Jones, president of a university by that name, which is denied tax exemption because of its discriminatory racial policy. Royko was particularly shocked by Jones' statement that he saw God in a vision "rolling up his sleeves and doubling up his fists," because, Jones said, the federal government "is just waiting to be socked in the nose by the Almighty." Royko then asked a number of rhetorical questions about God's intentions and concluded, "Despite what Jones said, I would have to ask this question: If God doesn't like the IRS, why did he create so many W2 forms?"

Inspired by angry letters about his Bob Jones column Royko wrote: "We look up to him, Just a Regular Guy." "The thought of God as a brawler intrigued me," he explained. Then he remarked that few if any complained about the growing concept of God as the Avid Sport Fan, as illustrated by such comments as, "If the Man Upstairs wants us to win this big game we'll win it. If he doesn't we won't. It's all up to the Big Scout in the Sky now . . . What they seem to be saying is that God is a fixer."

Then there is God the Fund Raiser, an example being the characteristic appeal by the hot-eyed Bible-beaters: "Last night the Lord came to me and told me that our crisis would pass if you would only send me $10. That's all the Lord wants from You, just $10 and me and the Lord will keep the Devil from comin' in your basement window and messin' up your sump pump and your soul."

"And, of course," Royko wrote, "there is God the Commander in Chief, the Field Marshal, the Generalissimo, the All Supremo . . . Throughout history there have been very few wars in which God was not said to be on one side or the other—usually on both sides."

"God's newest Image" was that of "The Heaviest Hitter." Royko began by wondering about the statement by Bump Wills, Cubs second baseman, that the team won its opening game because "the Man Upstairs wanted it to happen." That made Royko wonder why the Cubs had not been a winning team for almost 40 years. Since Chicago is no more sinful than New York it seemed unfair that New York teams always win championships.

Royko quoted Bob Jones' comments after the Department of State refused a visa to a Northern Ireland Protestant leader. Regarding Secretary of State Alexander Haig, Jones told his followers: "I hope you'll pray that the Lord will smite him, hip and thigh, bone and marrow, heart and lungs and all there is to him, that he shall destroy him quickly and utterly." That meant that Jones wanted Haig bumped off and God was the hit man.

In his syndicated column for April 26, 1982 Richard Reeves told of a student who walked out of a meeting in Washington Cathedral during Ground Zero Week because the movement's founder, Roger Molander, began talking about God and noble causes. She said politics don't belong in churches. But, Reeves pointed out, "In America pulpits have always been political platforms and the name of God has been invoked in a multitude of causes, good and bad." July 4, 1981 Roy Larson, *Chicago Sun-Times* religion editor, reported on a fictitious interview with God. Larson was not surprised that the Almighty had become media shy and refused to be quoted. Wrote Larson:

In May England's "Yorkshire Ripper," accused of slaying eight prostitutes and five other women, told reporters he was acting under orders from God . . . because God had selected him to get rid of "the scum of the earth."

Then, Mark David Chapman disclosed that God, during a legal aid visit to his prison cell, persuaded him to plead guilty to the murder of former Beatle John Lennon . . .

Now God is being dragged into a real estate deal in New York's extremely high rent district. At St. Bartholomew's Church on Park Ave. God, according to one faction of the congregation, has passed the word "Sell." Another faction, however, has the distinct impression that the words were "Don't sell . . ."

Moslem fundamentalists in Iran, having no questions about God's intentions, promised reserved seats in heaven for anyone producing information leading to the arrest of deposed President Abolyassan Bani-Sadr.

. . . it was disclosed by God's self-appointed confidants that the Lord of Heaven and Earth was opposed to the Panama Canal treaty and the Equal Rights Amendment, but strongly favored the Human Life Amendment, prayer in the public schools and a huge defense budget . . .

Like it or not, God is being quoted left and right.

More sarcastic than either of his fellow columnists, Nicholas von Hoffman wrote Sept. 27, 1980:

God, it turns out, is not an equal opportunity listener. The divinity does not automatically lend an ear to the prayers of the afflicted, all who search, according to the Rev. Dr. Bailey Smith, the president of the Southern Baptist Convention.

At a recent gathering of like-minded fundamentalists, including Ronald Reagan, in Dallas, the reverend doctor instructed the multitude thusly: "It is interesting at great political rallies how you have a Protestant to pray, a Catholic to pray and then you have a Jew to pray. With all due respect to those dear people, my friends, God Almighty does not hear the prayer of a Jew." . . . On one point, he [Smith] is wrong. I have it on the best authority from on high, a source of archangelic rank, who must understandably be nameless, that God has long since made it a firm rule not to heed any prayer uttered by any duly licensed minister of religion at any political rally, civic banquet or ribbon cutting. The simple exemptions are the logical statements made by Zbigniew Brzezinski, when he appeared on television squinting down the barrel of a gun looking across the Pakistan border toward Afghanistan and declared, "God is on our side" God decided he had no choice but to back him up and as a sign of divine assent, blow the top off Mt. St. Helens back in Washington.

And there has been the editorial, "Extremism in the name of God," in the *Chicago Tribune* for Sept. 27, 1981 as follows:

Every major religion preaches peace and brotherhood and mercy, yet some of the cruelest and most intolerant repressions in history have been committed in the name of God.

This is the paradoxical threat that arises whenever a revivalist religious group seeks to extend its influence beyond parochial boundaries and to establish itself as an organized force in the world of politics. It is why many Americans worry about the ambitions and influence of groups like Moral Majority even though they may share most if not all of its concerns. It is The Tribune's response to those of our readers who wonder why a normally conservative paper like this should be so critical of people who are a bit more conservative than we.

Throughout history people have turned to religion when they feel that they have lost their bearings in a rapidly changing society. There is abundant reason today to wonder what has happened to the old time values—to family unity, to the work ethic, to self-reliance, to fiscal prudence, and the like.

But there is also reason to worry when religious zeal turns into self-righteousness and intolerance and is used to cloak activities that are essentially self-serving or political. Consider some examples of history.

The Crusades. Though billed as an effort to restore Christian control of the Holy Land, the leading roles were played by opportunists who proclaimed their loyalty to the Pope, recruited troops in the name of the Lord, and set off in the hope of winning their own principalities and a share of the fabled riches of the Orient—or, in the case of the Venetians, to set up trading offices. Whatever conquests these princes achieved dissolved in bickering among themselves (at least one, Conrad of Montferrat, was assassinated in the process). The state was thus set for a new Crusade. This went on for two centuries until Europe and the church were in such disarray that the Mohammedans were able to retaliate by conquering most of southeastern Europe.

The Inquisition. For centuries, the Catholic Church tried to deal with dissent within its ranks (called heresy) by means of an inquisition, a sort of grand jury investigation that often led to confiscation of property. But in 1478 Ferdinand and Isabella of Spain, seeking to consolidate their power, prevailed on Pope Sixtus IV to let them handle inquisitions, ostensibly as a service to the church. They and the "Most Catholic Majesties" who succeeded them used it viciously—not against Catholic dissenters but against anybody who threatened the power of the monarchy, particularly Jews. Spain made the inquisition a political tool and gave it its notorious reputation for cruelty. Not until 1816 was the Vatican able to abolish torture by the Spanish Inquisitors.

The Puritans. The Puritans came over from England in search of religious freedom. But having established themselves as the dominant power in Massachusetts Bay Colony, they proceeded to convert the colony into an intolerant theocracy from which dissenters like Roger Williams were banished. A final orgy of fanaticism led to the Salem witch trials in the early 1690s; but by then the government had made so many enemies that the king of England revoked its charter and established a more liberal government.

The mullahs. True to the pattern of history, rapid social changes in the Middle East have brought a Moslem revivalist or fundamentalist movement dedicated originally to a restoration of traditional Moslem values. It has appeared as a religious movement in many countries, but in Iran it was harnessed by enemies of the shah and has led to a vicious Islamic Republic in which the mullahs praise Allah, recite the Koran (in which brotherhood and mercy figure even more prominently than in the Bible), and then order the execution of a dozen political enemies. More recently the Moslem fundamentalists have appeared as a political faction in Egypt, leftist in ideology and bitterly opposed to President Sadat. They have demonstrated under banners carrying such unbrotherly messages as "Believers do not take the Christians and Jews as friends."

Israel. In recent months the Begin government has been challenged by extreme Orthodox Jews who have become influential in small political parties, who make such religious demands as stricter observance of the Sabbath (no El Al flights, for example), but who have also become an obstacle to the quest for peace—a sort of mirror reflection of the "Moslem Associations" in the Arab world.

The list could go on, but the message is clear. We're not suggesting that the Rev. Jerry Falwell is about to become Chief Inquisitor for the U.S. But when religious zeal is diverted to political ends, it loses its religion and all too often becomes a vehicle for intolerance and divisiveness leading ultimately to the destruction of its own original goals.

23

Artifacts and Visions

No matter how strong one's faith s/he eagerly seeks confirmation through tangible evidence, real or circumstantial. And the press displays no skepticism while reporting the endeavors.

One approach is the archeological—to discover artifacts that substantiate biblical accounts.

Nothing has been the object of more searches than Noah's ark, in which according to Genesis the patriarch and his family lived for 40 days with two of every form of life, coming to rest on the mountains of Ararat near the present Turkish-Soviet border. *Chicago Sun-Times* Action Time told an inquirer July 14, 1979 that Eryl Cummings, a New Mexico real estate agent and an ark expert, examined 37 pre-1961 eyewitness accounts and another 37 post-1961 reports to conclude, "None have produced any actual scientific evidence of a rediscovery."

Typical of the earlier stories were those that Edwin E. Greenwald wrote for the Associated Press from Istanbul. The *Houston Chronicle* used them Nov. 14 and 15, 1948. They were illustrated by pictures of Shukru Asena, a Turkish farmer, pointing to the place on the map where he said he found petrified wood.

Among the more recent stories was that by Russell Chandler of the *Los Angeles Times*, to which the *Chicago Sun-Times* June 8, 1974 gave a page-1 streamer headline "Expeditions still hunting Noah's ark." It summarized the efforts of many searchers.

Neither the Turkish nor the Soviet government has been overly eager to allow explorations. The former Moslem government wants to protect the environment and the Soviets are suspicious that the scientists might actually be anti-Soviet spies.

The most persistent ark searchers have been two Frenchmen, Jean de Riquer and Fernand Navarra. Since the biblical account says mountains (plural) they have sought to explore several peaks in the range. In 1959 they found a beam of wood they believed might have been part of the ark. In a 2-page feature, "They Hope to Find Relics of Noah's Ark," in the *Chicago*

Sunday Tribune for March 29, 1953, Henry Wales, writing from Paris, also told of a document by a Russian aviator, Vladimir Roskovisky, who flew over Ararat in 1916. It states that 200 men climbed the mountains and found the remains of huge timbers. Measurements and photographs were sent to Czar Nicholas II but before he could do anything he was overthrown by the Bolshevik revolution.

In 1969 a six-man expedition climbed Mt. Ararat with simple tools and removed several pieces of hand-hewn wood from under a glacier at the 14,000-foot level. Almet Balan reported for the AP from Istanbul Aug. 11, 1939 that all of the wood found by both expeditions was at least 4,000 years old but there was no clue as to its use. July 13, 1960 the AP reported from Ankara that the Turkish government had refused permission for the Search Foundation of Washington, D.C. to ascend the 16,946-foot mountain with excavation equipment.

Four years later Dr. John Montgomery, a professor at Trinity Divinity School in Deerfield, Ill., was still trying vainly to obtain permission to make the trip. According to a UPI story Feb. 22, 1977 from Salt Lake City, Sen. Frank E. Moss told the American Congress on Surveying and Mapping that Professor Montgomery thinks a dot on a photograph taken by a U.S. space satellite might be the ark.

One of the comprehensive journalistic accounts of the search for the ark appeared in the *Toronto Star* Sept. 15, 1973. Tom Harpur reported, as the headline suggested, "Canadians hoping to prove the ark is on Mount Ararat." Illustrations showed the 5-foot piece of wood Navarra had dug out from beneath a glacier. It was white oak, which doesn't grow within 300 miles of where it was found. Tests established its age as from 1,300 to 5,000 years. It was recalled that as early as 300 B.C. Berossus, a Babylonian priest-historian, wrote that pieces of the ark had been taken up and rebuilt near the peak as a shrine, so believers in Navarra's find conjecture that the newer wood was imported for making repairs at that time.

According to the Rev. Dr. Lloyd R. Bailey, Duke University professor of divinity, scholars have not wanted to dignify reports of discovery of the ark which, he says, date from the 3rd century B.C. However, when the NBC-TV movie "In Search of Noah's Ark" was shown, he wrote the book *Where Is Noah's Ark?* in which he charges that all current reports about the ark are based on hearsay evidence and invalid scientific tests. George Cornell, AP religion editor, reviewed Bailey's book Sept. 16, 1978.

In an interview with Gary Wisby for the *Sunday Chicago Sun-Times* Nov. 2, 1980, Howard Teeple, executive director of the Religion and Ethics Institute of Evanston, Ill., scoffed at all reports that the ark's remains had been found. "How could they be?" he asked, "when the ark never existed?" He then questioned how a boat of the size the Bible stipulated could contain two of every living species, how one family could feed them all and clean their stables, how animals from all over the world—for example, polar bears from Siberia, zebras from Africa and kangaroos from Australia—

managed to travel great distances to the ark and expressed other doubts, many of them in his book, *The Noah's Ark Nonsense.*

Early in August 1982 the AP reported from Colorado Springs that former astronaut James Irwin, who walked on the moon in 1971, would lead a 12-man expedition to seek the ark. Aug. 20 the UPI reported from Ankara that in its 11th day of climbing the group was approaching the top of the highest peak. Aug. 21 the UPI reported from Ankara that Yucel Donmez of Chicago, a member of the expedition, said he had "pure and solid proof" that the ark is there. The next day the *Chicago Sun-Times* gave the same story a page 1 streamer headline. Although Donmez said he could not disclose the nature of his discovery, the newspaper headlined the story, "Solid proof of Noah's ark reported found."

Convinced that God appeared to him three times to warn him of the end of the world, the Rev. Jesse Richard Greene of the Church of the Brethren in Frostburg, Md. is building a $4 million 3,000-seat ark. Roger Simon wrote a column about it in the *Chicago Sun-Times.*

"Plain hogwash" was the answer the *Chicago Sun-Times* Action Time quoted May 12, 1983 in answering the query of a reader whose mother had told her Arkansas got its name because Noah's ark landed there.

Presumably ten centuries of controversy ended with the Italian Franciscans being given jurisdiction over the building in Jerusalem where Christians believed Jesus and disciples ate the Last Supper but which Mohammedans claim was the site of the tomb of David who, like Abraham, is a Mohammedan as well as Jewish prophet.

Helping to keep alive controversy in what used to be called the Holy Land, a Dutchman who signed himself H187 asked the supreme court of Israel to review the trial of Jesus Christ, the AP reported Jan. 30, 1949 from Jerusalem. The name on the envelope containing the petition was that of H. A. Robbe Groskamp of Santpoort, Holland. He cited legal precedents dating from 1486 B.C. to the establishment of the modern nation of Israel in 1948.

Scientists from the Goddard Space Flight Center in Green Belt, Md. denied that their studies confirmed the biblical account of the sun's standing still for a day upon command from Joshua. Harold Hill, president of the Curtis Engine company of Baltimore and a consultant in the space program, made the statement in speeches in Indiana according to a reader of the *Chicago Daily News* Beeline which investigated the rumor and reported in the paper's issue of June 26, 1970.

Astronomical and biblical calculations make it possible to pinpoint the date of Jesus' crucifixion as early evening of April 3, A.D. 33, according to Karlis Kaufmanis, professor emeritus of astronomy at the University of Minnesota, the UPI reported April 4, 1980.

Even more iconoclastic than the failure to discover life on the moon was the conclusion of a Dead Sea scroll scholar, John Allegro, that Moses, Abraham and all the other Jewish patriarchs are myths. This theory, advanced in Allegro's book, *The Chosen People,* followed by a year *The Sacred Mushroom and the Cross* in which he said Christianity originated in mushroom worshipping. The *Columbia* (S.C.) *Star,* in the Bible belt, devoted a column to the story Aug. 21, 1971.

Remains of the original church built in 335 by Emperor Constantine who made Christianity the official religion of the Roman Empire, over the supposed grave of Jesus in Jerusalem were uncovered by a Greek archeologist, the AP reported March 3, 1971.

The foundation stone of Solomon's Temple, on which rested the ancient Ark of the Covenant containing the tablets of the Ten Commandments, still stands on Jerusalem's Temple Mount, the UPI reported Feb. 27, 1983 on the authority a noted Hebrew scholar, at the time in Washington, D.C.

In a copyrighted exclusive story by John Gunther Oct. 19, 1925 the *Chicago Daily News* reported that a solution to the centuries' old debate over jurisdiction of the cenacoio, or place of the last supper, between Jesus and his 12 apostles, had been settled. Gunther wrote that it shortly would be announced that control would revert to the Franciscans as King Robert of Naples had ordered in 1333. The story did not relate how the claims of the Mohammedans, who believe the site is that of the tomb of David, or of the British, then in political control, or of the Jews would be satisfied.

Also controversial is the identity of a body discovered in Egypt's western desert and claimed by two Egyptian newspapers to be the remains of John the Baptist. According to a UPI story from Cairo Nov. 15, 1978 skeptics recalled that John had been beheaded by King Herod to please Salome; thus the body could not be John's, but other remains might be those of Elisha and other unnamed saints.

Perhaps the most iconoclastic newspaper article concerning miracles appeared in the *Chicago Daily News* for Jan. 4–5, 1975. In the piece entitled "Did Jesus Walk on Water?" James H. Bowman, religion editor, quoted several leading theologians that belief in miracles was "beside the point." A Protestant said, "The question is not whether the stories are true but whether the belief they express is valid or invalid." A Catholic scholar said, "If miracles did not happen literally but nevertheless have a theological importance . . ."

Although every scholar whose opinion was asked said "hoax," Tom Croster insisted that he and three others from the Institute for Restoring Ancient History International found the Ark of the Covenant in a sealed passageway inside a cave in Mount Pisgah east of Jerusalem. He refused to release photographs that were to be given to the international banker David Rothschild. The ark, according to the book of Exodus, is a gold-covered receptacle containing the Ten Commandments. The UPI reported the story Nov. 22, 1981 from Winfield, Kansas.

More important than archeological evidence to buttress faith are visions, especially of the Virgin Mary. All over the world there are shrines on the sites of alleged apparitions and millions of believers visit them annually. Especially important are they to persons with physical disabilities. Of stories of miraculous cures there is no end. It is impossible for the press to keep up with any appreciable number of them. Some, however, are deemed to have more reader interest than others and often receive extravagant coverage.

More credence probably should be given to some claims than to some others. For example, as the *London Telegraph* reported March 31, 1978, in a story by James O'Brien, writing from Birmingham, England, the tomb of Jesus has been discovered in a valley in northern India. Rafigg Immam of the London Mosque, British leader of Islam's Ahmadiyya movement (10,000 members in Britain and 11 million worldwide), believes that Jesus did not die on the cross. Rather, he was rescued by his disciples and went to India in search of the ten lost tribes of Israel. The movement was founded in 1890 in Qadian, Punjab by Hazrat Miraz Ghulam Ahmad, who said it had been revealed to him that he was the Messiah and that Jesus had not died on Calvary.

April 24, 1981 the *Chicago Tribune* ran a long article that Marsha Barber and Emmanuel Hadzipetros wrote for the Independent News Alliance. Writing from Srinagar, India they added some facts to the London *Telegraph's* story: that Jesus found the lost tribes in Kashmir. Ahmad's divine revelations included the contention that death by crucifixion usually took three days whereas Jesus was on the cross for not more than six hours.

Another iconoclastic book is *The Holy Blood and the Holy Grail,* by Henry Lincoln, Richard Leigh and Michael Baigent, who said ten years of research convinced them that Jesus married Mary Magdalene and had a child by her so there are living descendants among European noble families today. The AP reported the controversy regarding the book from London Jan. 19, 1982.

Books with such startling claims are newsworthy. Not so any more are most criticisms of the contents of the Bible. An exception was the review of a Canadian Broadcasting Company Christmas program in 1972 in the *Toronto Globe and Mail.* The reporter-critic Blair Kirby intimated that it was bad taste to broadcast a program during the Christmas season to contend that most of the stories about Jesus' birth are legendary.

This is particularly true of what in the Western world is considered the most important of them all: the Grotto of Our Lady of Lourdes in the French Pyrenees. It was there Feb. 11, 1858 that 14-year-old Bernadette Soubious saw the Virgin Mary the first of 17 times. Invisible to townspeople who watched the girl, Mary instructed her to tell the village leaders to construct a chapel on the spot. She also instructed Bernadette to scratch a hole in the sand, from which water then began to trickle, gradually increasing to a large stream. It is in this water that millions of the faithful bathe in the hope that their physical infirmities will be cured.

Replying to the girl's question the vision said, "I am the immaculate conception." The skepticism of the townspeople began to change when a man who had been blind in his right eye for 20 years bathed it in the spring water and regained his sight.

Not many of the millions who seek better health at Lourdes are considered newsworthy in themselves. Some, however, do interest wire services and newspapers because of unusual circumstances connected with their pilgrimages, their public importance or the peculiarities of their ailments. Jan. 24, 1934 the AP reported that Roman Catholic church medical authorities had agreed that the cure three years earlier of a French colonel suffering from a liver abscess could be attributed to miraculous causes. July 17, 1947 the International News Service distributed a short article by a 13-year-old Pittsburgh girl, an infantile paralysis victim. In part she wrote, "As soon as I came out of the three foot deep water I felt so much stronger. I was able that night to follow a procession on foot for about an hour. I attended the blessing of the sick daily." Feb. 22, 1956 there was a story of a 21-year-old Westchester, Ill. woman whose parents took her to Lourdes hoping that the treatment would arouse her from a coma that had lasted for 14 years, ever since she underwent surgery for removal of her appendix.

Occasionally a case is considered big news not only in the principal's home town but worldwide as well. One such case was that of 7-year-old Randy Eckman whose neighbors in St. Joseph, Mich. raised $2,300 to make it possible for his mother to take him to Lourdes. Medical opinion was that Randy's leukemia would result in his death within a year. For a week, beginning Feb. 2, 1956, the *Chicago Sun-Times* gave 5-column streamer headlines to play-by-play accounts of the pilgrimage written by Jack Olsen who accompanied mother and son on their journey. In the first dispatch the mother was quoted as saying: "Randy is one of God's children, and God will look after him. It doesn't matter that we are Lutherans and the shrine is a Catholic shrine. I don't think God cares about that." Olsen told of the expeditious handling Randy got from customs and other officials in Paris where the newspapers played Randy's story on page 1.

Despite the below-zero weather Randy dipped his feet in Lourdes water for about ten minutes. When, however, it was suggested that the boy be immersed, the mother refused to take the risk of pneumonia. En route home, in Paris doctors relieved the mother's anxiety somewhat by saying a rise in the boy's temperature to over 103 degrees was the result of his small pox vaccination and was unrelated to his leukemia.

Throughout the entire escapade the press associations wrote daily stories. Feb. 9 the headlines told of Randy's return to school on the advice of hometown doctors. June 10, 1956 the *Sun-Times* headline was, Randy Romps His Age After Shrine Trip." The mother was quoted as saying her son was 100 percent better than before the trip. Feb. 5, 1957 exactly a year after his departure for Lourdes, Randy was baptized a Catholic and died.

The paper used the story inconspicuously on an inside page.

As the centennial of Bernadette's first vision approached, feature articles appeared in abundance the world over. Feb. 5, 1956 the *Chicago Sun-Times* retold the story of the conversion of a famous doctor, Alexis Carrel, in 1903 when most medical authorities were nonbelievers. Carrel lost a position at the University of Lyons when he said one of his patients had been cured of tuberculosis miraculously at Lourdes. Nine years later, in 1912, Carrel received a Nobel Prize and 3,000 French francs, testified to the value of Lourdes to patients "whom we doctors have been powerless to save."

In a series of daily articles beginning Feb. 8, 1958 Paul Ghali detailed the 100th anniversary ceremonies. He estimated there would be 6 to 8 million pilgrims during the year. Catholic Ireland and the United States topped the pilgrim groups scheduled to come. March 8 Ghali wrote a first person account of his bath in 50-degree icy cold water in one of the outdoor pools, which he called "primitive installations—just holes in the ground 7 feet long and 4 feet wide," each with a crucifix and statue of Mary at the top.

The story of 10-month-old Karen Woods of Gibsonia, Pa. whose mother dipped her in Lourdes water hoping to enable the baby, born blind, to see, was told by S. I. Newhouse, Jr. for the *Syracuse Herald American* July 18, 1958. March 21, 1958 one of the few iconoclastic stories about the shrine was reported from London by the UP. It reviewed an article from the British *Churchman's Magazine* in which David Foot Nash blasted Roman Catholic pilgrimages to Lourdes as a "black, blasphemous lie" believed by millions. The lie, Nash wrote, is that God "will do something for you at Lourdes that he will not do for you anywhere else."

When a reader inquired how she could get some Lourdes water for her son's eczema, the *Chicago Daily News* Beeline Feb. 5, 1973 ran a picture of an Air France hostess holding a bottle of Lourdes water that was to be delivered to the mother.

A *Geo* magazine article, distributed by Special Features, was published by the *Chicago Tribune* May 30, 1981. Calling Lourdes "the single most magnetic place of pilgrimage on Earth," Kevin Buckley described the city that had grown from 4,000 in Bernadette's day to 18,000 today as "a fountain of faith in a forest of gift shops." To accommodate millions of pilgrims—50,000 new ones daily during July and August—there are 402 hotels and "where there are no hotels there are gift shops—hundreds of them" with merchandise "for the most part startingly vulgar."

March 5, 1933 the *New York Times* ran a 75th anniversary story written by Eloise Liddon Soper. During the preceding 60 years, she reported, there had been a reputed 4,000 cures. June 6, 1936 the UP reported that of 88 cases examined during 1934 only 14 were recognized as supernatural. A quarter-century later, Sept. 4, 1971, the *Chicago Daily News* Beeline told a reader that there had been 1.5 million cures since 1858 but that the Medical Bureau said only 62 could be considered miraculous. Still a decade later Kevin Buckley wrote in the *Chicago Tribune* for May 30, 1981 that the number of acknowledged miracles had increased to 64.

Second in importance among shrines is the one at Fatima, Portugal, where Oct. 13, 1917 three illiterate shepherd girls said they saw Mary during a thunderstorm. One girl Lucia dos Santos, 10, later to become Sister Maria Adorata, told church officials that the virgin confided to her three prophecies. Two of them were revealed by the Vatican in 1942. The first predicted the end of World War I, which was waging at the time, and a worse war to break out during the reign of Pope Pius XI. That pope died Feb. 10, 1939. Hitler began his invasion of Poland Sept. 1, 1939.

Prophecy No. 2 was that there would be a revolution in Russia and called for the rest of the world to work and pray for the conversion of the Soviet Union to Christianity.

Prophecy No. 3 has not been disclosed. Sister Mary confided it to a bishop in 1939 when she thought she was dying. Since then the secret has been under strict guard in the Vatican. Rumor has always had it that the prophecy is the end of the world. Jan. 1, 1961 the Associated Press revealed in Vatican City that Sister Maria had directed that the envelope containing the prophecy should be opened upon her death or, if she were alive, in 1960. The Vatican, however, chose to ignore the instructions and so the mystery persists.

Over the years there have been many newspaper and magazine articles and full-length books on Our Lady of Fatima. Oct. 14, 1951 the UP reported from Vatican City that Frederico Cardinal Tedeschini told pilgrims at Fatima that Pope Pius XII had seen the virgin Oct. 30 and 31 and Nov. 1, 1950. Nov. 17, 1951 the AP reported that *L'Observatore Romano* had published two photographs of the "revolving sun" phenomenon at Fatima in 1917. *Life* magazine reproduced the pictures Dec. 3, 1951. In the meantime the AP reported Oct. 18, 1951 that the Vatican had not meant to imply the pope actually had a vision but only that he observed a solar phenomenon similar to that reported from Fatima in 1917. March 10, 1952 the AP reported from Rome that the pictures had been taken years later "during an atomspheric effect at sundown."

In a feature article from Fatima, to which the *Houston Chronicle* gave a column and a half Sept. 5, 1972, the UPI added details to the many-times-told story. During her first visit, "the beautiful lady from heaven" told the children she would reappear at noon on the 13th of each succeeding month for four months. On Sept. 13 approximately 70,000 people accompanied the children who came to the remote mountaintop. Although the children said they saw Mary on a treetop, she was not visible to the other onlookers, who, however, observed the peculiar behavior of the sun.

May 9, 1982 the UPI reported from Vatican City that Pope John Paul II would visit the Shrine of Fatima May 13 to thank the virgin for saving his life exactly one year earlier when a would-be assassin shot the pontiff. On the day of his visit to Fatima another fanatic lunged at him with a knife but was quickly subdued.

Even more important in the Western Hemisphere than Lourdes or Fatima is the Basilica of Our Lady of Guadalupe in Mexico City. There Dec. 12, 1531, the Virgin Mary is said to have appeared before Juan Diego, placed some flowers in his cloak to show the bishop as evidence of her miraculous appearance. When the flowers fell out the Virgin's image appeared on the white cloth made of the fibers of the century plant. Juan M. Vasque wrote from Mexico City for the *Los Angeles Times* Dec. 11, 1981: "Many of the faithful fall to their knees as they enter. Hands clasped in devotion, they inch their way painfully to the altar as millions have done before them . . . Ever since the apparition the Virgin has been associated with the propagation of the faith among the natives of the New World . . . considered to be a sign she loves the Indians just as much as she did the Spaniards who brought the sword and the cross to America."

May 7, 1965 the AP distributed a photograph of a 16-year-old Spanish girl and her mother. They claimed that they and three other sisters had been visited several times by the Virgin Mary. Apparently their evidence did not convince church officials.

When Pope Paul VI attended the celebration of the 50th anniversary of the Fatima miracle, pundits speculated as to whether he would reveal the nature of Prophecy No. 3. He did not. A typical resumé of the entire phenomenon appeared in the *Chicago Daily News* for May 13, 1967 which gave a full page to an article by George Weller.

On two different occasions the *News'* Beeline answered inquiries regarding the Fatima miracle and the prophecies. The lengthy replies were in the issues of June 20, 1970 and Aug. 19, 1976. Sept. 21, 1974 the paper devoted a full column to a story by James H. Bowman that the bishop in charge at Fatima had broadened the message of the prophecies "to reinterpret an original message as times change." In essence he said, "It is not only Russia that needs conversions but all of us, the West included."

Christian refugees from other parts of the country have come to outnumber Moslems in the Beirut district of Nabaa and pilgrims come there to invoke the healing powers of Sharbel Makhlouf, a canonized priest who died in 1808 and in whose name several miracles have been claimed. A paralyzed nun walked after touching a red substance that oozed from the saint's coffin and a blind boy gained his sight when a picture of the priest was passed before his eyes. The story was reported Oct. 23, 1977 for the *Los Angeles Times*.

April 13, 1982 the UPI distributed a 2-column picture captioned "She Says She Sees the Virgin" and cutlines: "Fourteen-year-old Blandine Piegay, who claims the Virgin Mary appeared to her, tells Easter Sunday spectators in LaTalaudiere, a small village in the Loire, France, how the apparition came to her."

In the Western Hemisphere there are shrines aplenty. Most famous in addition to the Basilica of Our Lady of Guadalupe in Mexico City is Ste. Anne de Beaupre on the St. Lawrence River, near Quebec, Canada. It is visited annually by thousands and many cures are reported. Sometimes crowds gather after someone, usually a child, claims to have had a vision. Another outstanding tourist attraction is in the making in Necedah, Wis. where Mrs. Anna Van Hoof announced that the Virgin Mary, whom she said she had seen six times since Nov. 12, 1949, would appear again Aug. 15, 1950. The AP reported June 17, 1950 that 1,000 knelt in silence when Mrs. Van Hoof knelt before the clump of trees where the virgin supposedly appeared to her. She then told the crowd to beware of Russians.

The crowd of 100,000 who gathered at the Van Hoof farm doubtless was made up mostly of Catholics who ignored strong warnings from Bishop P. Treacy of the LaCrosse diocese in an editorial in the church's official paper that "There is absolutely nothing official about Necedah to date," the AP reported Aug. 6, 1950. Furthermore, the AP reported Aug. 10, Bishop Treacy warned Catholics that their presence "may bring dishonor to the traditional devotion to the mother of God." Aug. 11 the bishop said parishioners were not fobidden to attend but were strongly advised not to do so.

The morning of the scheduled apparition, the UP reported, a thousand carloads of pilgrims from all over the nation followed hundreds who had visited the farm since June 15 when Mrs. Van Hoof first revealed she had seen the virgin.

The page 1 streamer headline in the *Chicago Daily News* for Aug. 15, 1950 was: "Wife Sees Miracle: 100,000 at Scene." There followed a 2-column story by the paper's city editor, Clem Lane, a devout Catholic, and a full page of pictures of the multitude. Crucifix in hand Mrs. Van Hoof prayed and asked the spectators to do likewise. The mother of Jesus, she said, told her: "Pray and pray hard. The time is short." Then Mrs. Van Hoof told the crowd that America's time of danger had come, after which she retreated to her house. Her daughter Joan answered reporters' objections that, yes, her mother had seen the virgin that day. Nobody else had done so.

The next day, Aug. 16, the AP reported from LaCrosse that the church had not changed its attitude of doubt, emphasizing that there were no unusual signs to support the farm woman's story.

Feb. 4, 1951 both the UP and AP reported from Rome that an article in the Vatican newspaper, *L'Observatore Romano*, warned Catholics against "uncontrolled" claims of miracles or supernatural events that could discredit real miracles. The article said, "We have been witnessing for years an increase of popular passion for the marvelous, even in religion."

Nevertheless, in the same day's edition of the *Chicago Daily News* the Necedah incident was given as much credibility as a long list of earlier apparitions dating from 1531, when Juan Diego saw the virgin at

Guadalupe, Mexico. Several cases were cited of the church's acceptance of the genuineness of the phenomena years after their occurrence.

Despite the church's negative attitude 30,000 persons saw Mrs. Van Hoof collapse as she delivered what she said was her seventh and last message from the Virgin Mary. A priest in the audience declared he saw the sun whirl clockwise and jump, the UP reported Oct. 7, 1950. The AP estimated the crowd at 50,000 and said Mrs. Van Hoof talked for 25 minutes during which time she announced seeing the erratic behavior of the sun.

On orders from Archbishop Moses E. Kiley of Milwaukee the shrine on the Van Hoof farm was dismantled and so were stations of the cross on a nearby bluff, the UP reported Nov. 28, 1950.

Neither the farmer's wife nor 1,500 faithful followers were influenced by the church's discouragements, however. Oct. 8, 1965 the UPI reported they held an all-night vigil on the 15th anniversary of the day 100,000 descended on the farm. Mrs. Van Hoof told her devotees not to be confused by the church's reluctance to endorse her claims. "Our struggle is far from over," she said as she prayed for peace for an hour.

April 25, 1957 the *Chicago Daily News'* "What Ever Became Of . . ." feature column briefly recalled Mrs. Van Hoof's claims and stated that she still resided in Necedah.

Feb. 4–11, 1980 the *Madison* (Wis.) *Capital-Times* ran a six-part series on "The Necedah Cult" by Rob Fixmer and Dan Allegretti. The first paragraph of the first article read: "I think it's very possible for the thing to go as far as Jonestown went," according to a witness who described the religious fervor and paranoia that marked the Necedah cult. One illustration showed the foundation for a basilica for the cult's new archbishop, Edward W. Stehlick. The rest of the articles, reprinted in 12 news pages, are a devastating exposé of Mrs. Van Hoof and others. As a result, the paper announced, several federal and state agencies began investigations.

There have been many more news stories of apparitions that received more than a flurry of attention but that did not lead to the construction of a shrine or other monument. Among the most newsworthy accounts have been the following:

Oct. 2, 1925—From Nagyszakacsi, Hungary R. R. Decker reported for the *Chicago Daily News* that "Devils are being cast out and the crippled are throwing away their crutches. The wine drinking places are empty and gambling has ceased." The cause: a little girl reported she saw the Madonna and Child in a vision. Calm was restored after the local bishop said the villagers had been hallucinating and the captain of the gendarmes said it was a commercial swindle.

Oct. 5, 1945—Ninabelle Cross, 28, a crippled invalid for 16 years, told the *Chicago Daily News* from her Upper Sandusky, Ohio home that she was cured miraculously after she envisioned God in a beautiful white robe and of his command to "rise and walk." That was what she was doing in the accompanying AP picture. Two days later, Oct. 7, Terry Colangelo, sob sister for the *Chicago Times,* reported from Upper Sandusky that public opinion there was divided on the nature of Ninabelle's cure. The naturopath who attended her illness and the pastor of the Methodist church she attended believed her story.

Nov. 15, 1945—New York newspapers and national news magazines covered the crowd of 25,000 that visited a vacant lot in the Bronx where a 9-year-old boy said he saw the Virgin for the 17th and final time. The *New York Sun* quoted several spectators who said they too saw the apparition. They also visited the home of the boy, Joseph Vitolo. *Life* had two pages of pictures Nov. 26, 1945 including one of a woman who says paralysis left her finger when she touched the child.

June 29, 1949—The *Milwaukee Journal* reported the forthcoming July 4 feast of the Blessed Virgin at St. Nazianz, Wis. The original shrine there was built in 1875 by Frank Lox, an immigrant from Bohemia, to fullfill a promise that if his health were restored through the intercession of the Virgin he would build it in her honor.

Aug. 10, 1951—On orders from the Vatican three young girls who claimed they saw a vision of the Virgin Mary were barred from receiving holy communinion "for the duration of their disobedience," the AP reported from Bamberg, Germany.

Feb. 10, 1955—A 14-year-old girl was showered with presents, including $8,500 cash, when she told of having seen the Virgin Mary in her home town of San Cayetano, Argentina, the AP reported from Buenos Aires. Rumors spread that the child had been given curative powers and could heal the sick, who flocked to her presence.

Oct. 12, 1959—Drawn by word-of-mouth reports that a luminous Madonna-like figure had appeared at the top of a church steeple for three nights, crowds gathered around the church, the AP reported from Warsaw, Poland.

July 21, 1962—Reuters, the British news agency, reported from Hamburg, Germany that 19 villagers had been excommunicated because they persisted in worshipping on Vision Hill, where the Virgin presumably was seen after the Vatican declared the shrine a fake and its followers heretics. The vision reportedly occurred in October 1949 and was seen by three children. Daily crowds of 40,000 were not unusual. Trade was good, especially of "specially blessed rosaries" and "holy earth" from the hill.

Sept. 19, 1967—When an 8-year-old girl said she saw the Virgin, Quebec streets were jammed as word spread. Mary, however, did not reappear as the child said she had promised she would, the AP reported.

Sept. 12, 1969—Shortly before his death, Illinois Senator Everett M. Dirksen wrote: "Man is not alone. I have felt God's presence in my life as long as I can remember," the UPI reported from Washington. "I talk to him about my aspirations every day. Most people call it prayer. I have thought of it as conversation with Him," Dirksen wrote.

Nov. 24, 1970—The *Chicago Daily News* Beeline did research to answer a reader's query concerning 80-year-old Rosa Quattrini of Samdano, Italy to whom the Virgin reportedly appears Fridays and feast days. An article in a Roman newspaper said when the Virgin touched a plum tree it immediately bloomed and bore fruit.

May 12, 1973—Beeline told a reader what happened to a woman who had received the paper's help in obtaining clay from the Shrine of Our Lord of Esquipulas, N.M. The news was good: the woman rubbed the clay on her leg and it did not have to be amputated. Beeline added that she did undergo an operation to bypass a blocked artery. Also, it was noted, the Catholic church does not recognize the clay from the so-called Lourdes of North America as miraculous.

Dec. 18, 1974—Thousands of persons flocked to see 19-year-old Margaret Wangari who said she heard the voice of God and saw a vision, after which she apparently cured two invalids, the AP reported from Nairobi, Kenya.

Aug. 11–12, 1976—The *Chicago Suburban Sun-Times* gave a whole page to Mark Fineman's feature on Joseph Pawlak, who said he saw Jesus walking on the waters of Lake Michigan. "He was as tall as a telephone pole," Pawlak said. "He came toward me and when he got to the hood of my car he blessed me. Ever since then I've seen visions and prophecies sent by the Lord."

Pawlak's Jesus was a midget compared with the 900-foot Messiah that Oral Roberts said he talked with May 25, 1980. The news of the encounter became public with release in September of a letter Roberts sent to his followers asking contributions to complete construction of his City of Faith Hospital in Tulsa. According to an AP story Sept. 1 nearly a half-million followers contributed nearly $5 million in answer to the appeal.

Roberts' story was ridiculed by another evangelist, the Rev. Carl McIntire, president of the International Council of Christian Churches. Both AP and UPI had stories Nov. 28 and 29, 1980 from Collingswood, N.J. quoting McIntire as accusing Roberts of committing a hoax to raise money. "No decent Christian believes that Jesus is 900 feet tall," McIntire said. "Nor does Jesus make such appearances. The Bible says Jesus is seated at the right hand of God. Oral Roberts, I'm afraid, has gone berserk on these visions of his." The *Los Angeles Times* for Dec. 6, 1980 published a painting of the scenes as described by Roberts, with the gigantic Jesus easily lifting the 60-story building that Roberts said Jesus in 1977 told him to build. See page 372 for more details.

Although he disavowed any supernatural power and sought no publicity, the late Brother André is remembered by thousands who visit his grave at St. Joseph's Oratory in Montreal which Brother André, whose real name was Alfred Bessette, built just before World War I and of which he was caretaker until his death in January, 1937. Humbly he always said any cures were the work of St. Joseph. Today the shrine is wallpapered with crutches and other bad memories of onetime illnesses and hundreds of thousands of tourists view them annually. The *New York Times* noted its popularity as early as June 13, 1937.

Sometimes the vision is reported to have appeared in someone's dream. For instance, the AP reported from Rome April 27, 1945 that a convicted murderer, repentant and his prison sentences ended, attended the beatification of his victim, 11-year-old Marin Goretti. Nobody in the crowd of 25,000 recognized Alexandro Serenelli who said that his victim had appeared to him several times in dreams during his 27 years in prison. She was beatified for giving her life rather than submitting to her murderer's sexual advances.

After a friend told her she had had a dream that the dog Spotty was still alive, Mrs. Helen Moderman sued veterinarian Dr. George T. Hart for obtaining money under false pretenses, in that he did not kill the pet as its deceased owner had requested. The doctor said the dog was too friendly and the charges were dropped when Mrs. Moderman said she'd keep the animal, the *Chicago Daily News* reported Feb. 20, 1947.

Spurred by a vision he said he had in a forest preserve near Chicago, the Rev. Hendon M. Harris, 34, of LaGrange, Ill. went to Formosa (now Taiwan) to bring "a message of hope" to the Chinese Nationalist troops there, the *Chicago Sun-Times* reported Sept. 24, 1950.

Because the number 7 kept appearing in his dreams, Billy Rose bet seven dollars on the seventh horse in the seventh race at Hialeah. It came in seventh. In his Feb. 20, 1949 syndicated column, the noted showman also related the superstition the novelist Tom Wolfe had regarding the symbol K-19. He used it in all three of his major novels. When Wolfe's body was loaded onto a train to take it to its resting place in his home town of Asheville, N.C., friends noticed that the car's number was K-19.

A Turin, Italy woman had better luck in the Italian national lottery when she put four dollars on three numbers of which she had dreamed. According to the UP May 12, 1952, she won $16,320.

Because she said God appeared to her in a dream to tell her she would die if she underwent an operation for a heart ailment, eight-year-old Pearl Simon convinced her parents to cancel arrangements for the surgery, the UP reported Oct. 18, 1952 from Boston. Accompanying the story was a picture of the child with hands folded in prayer; some papers used it in three columns.

Just exactly the opposite had been the prediction of Mrs. Edythe Hanson of Redwood, Calif. who for a month after her return from a hospital predicted she would die at 11:45 on Aug. 21. She did, the AP reported Aug. 23, 1951.

Such prophecies are called premonitions. Almost invariably when a celebrity dies without warning, survivors are asked if the deceased had one. Some journalists will include the reply, whatever it is, as an integral part of the obituary.

June 20, 1971 the *New York Times* devoted a quarter-page to a UPI report from Saigon, South Vietnam. It told of the death of a soldier who had been fearful for days that his time had come. "He was scared that morning," one of his fellow soldiers said. "We were all scared. We'd been having it pretty easy for a few weeks and we figured it was time for one of us to get it." The *Times'* headline was: "The Death He Forecast Comes to G.I."

At the funeral of Robert Hannegan, onetime postmaster general and chairman of the Democratic National Committee, Monsignor Kane related that Hannegan told him shortly before his death that he had a premonition of death and had put his affairs in order. The anecdote appeared in Kup's Column in the *Chicago Sun-Times* for Oct. 12, 1949. In his column for July 15, 1965 Kup asked, "Did Adlai E. Stevenson have a premonition of death?" The possibility was seen in the fact that he told friends he was tired and wished he could avoid the London trip on which he dropped dead.

Ever fascinated by the occult the *Chicago Daily News* ran a weeklong series on "Mysteries of the Mind" beginning June 23, 1962. Some of the headlines over the stories by W. M. Newman were: "Lincoln Knew When He'd Die," "Mark Twain Dream—It Came True," "A Woman's Foreboding, Then Death," "Kipling Got a Preview of the Future," "Soldier Acts on his Sixth Sense and Scores a Victory," and "A Royal Brother Rejects News of Death."

The Kipling ancedote, taken from his autobiography, *Something of Myself,* was what usually is called déjà vu, meaning the feeling one may have that he has had the same experience earlier. In Kipling's case he dreamed of having his view in a crowd obscured by a fat man. That is what happened to him soon afterwards when he attended a ceremony at which the Prince of Wales dedicated a plaque to World War I dead. Of the phenomenon Sydney Justin Harris wrote in his syndicated column for Feb. 2, 1953; "It is an eerie sensation as though we were possessed of some alarming magical properties which we ourselves do not quite understand how to use. I am convinced we have such properties—not magical but what we, in our present state of ignorance, called 'super human.' It seems to me merely dogmatic to dismiss the feeling of déjà vu as coincidence or hallucination."

For more on premonitions see Chapter 5, pages 109–111.

A bit more knowledgeable an authority, Dr. Alfred Blazer, wrote in his *New York Daily Compass* column for July 2, 1951: "What you describe is a benign phenomenon that occurs to normal people more often than you think. . . . The psychodynamics of what happened to you is as follows: This phenomenon occurs when an individual is fatigued, emotionally overstimulated or tense. . . . An experience seems to be an exact replica of a previous experience. During the war soldiers under stress occasionally reported such experiences."

Throughout history, of course, soldiers have seen all kinds of omens in the sky. In this century the most interesting case was that of the apparitions that British soldiers saw during the battle of Mons, Belgium. A recent journalistic recall of the incident was written by Doane R. Hoag for the *Atlanta Journal and Constitution* for Aug. 24, 1980. The Indian philosopher Krishnalal Shridharani related numerous historical anecdotes of visions soldiers had and miracles claimed by inhabitants of besieged cities in a feature article, "Miracles in War," in the *New York Times Magazine* for Jan. 28, 1940.

Throughout the centuries there has been plenty of sense and nonsense written about sleep and the meaning of dreams. Dr. Morris Fishbein, longtime editor of American Medical Association publications, wrote in his Family Doctor syndicated column March 12, 1949 that most superstitions related to sleep are the result of belief in magic. He ridiculed sleeping on a piece of wedding cake or any of several prophetic dreams; also the taboo against sleeping with cats or with horseshoes under the pillow and several others. Despite such medical iconoclasts, psychics and others persist in preparing guides to interpreting dreams and newspapers consider them good copy.

The fifth of a series of articles on "Nervous Breakdowns" by Frank S. Caprio, M.D. and Frances Spatz Leighton in *Chicago Today* for March 5, 1970 dealt with the significance of dreams of a person having or about to have a nervous breakdown, which can be very painful. They interpreted 25 dreams: "5. Dreams of being robbed mean insecurity, fear of losing what you possess" and "13. Dreams of success and achievements, dreams of fame mean inferiority complex." There was a half-page of such helpful hints.

Nov. 25, 1973 the *Chicago Daily News* gave about twice as much space to an article by Diana Milesko-Pytel on "The stuff nightmares are made of." She explained that the word *nightmare* comes from *niht,* meaning night, and *mare,* an Anglo-Saxon word that means demons. ".Primitive people," she wrote, "believed that nightmares were monsters or evil spirits that oppressed people. They often thought nightmares suffocated people in their sleep." In 1200 B.C. the mythical Egyptian god Bes was believed to protect sleepers against demons of the night. And in 1518 a soothsayer, Artemidorus, wrote a book in which he warned: "to dream of having one's head shaved signifies the same thing that nudity does; it foretells sudden and dire misfortune." The reporter interpreted a dozen or more common present-day dreams.

The *Suburban Chicago Sun-Times* for June 23, 1976 gave a sympathetic writeup to the (then) new School of Metaphysics' first Illinois branch in Palatine. Debbie Wood reported a list of dreams and their meanings, including: "Murder or death in dreams means you're changing part of your personality" and water means life, so "to dream of bridges over water, or of avoiding water, you may feel you lack experience."

The closest that any journalist has come to a scientific study of the subject is the Central Premonitions Registry, a moonlighting activity of Robert Nelson, a circulation executive for the *New York Times.* Nelson

collects and files predictions of future events sent to him by people all over
the country who want to go on record with their premonitions and visions.
The *Chicago Tribune* Dec. 10, 1972 devoted a half-page to an article by
David Gifford about Nelson's unusual hobby. Although Nelson is skeptical
of professional soothsayers like Jeane Dixon and considers the overwhelming majority of the letters he receives to be of little value, he says
there have been some astonishing coincidences between quite a few predictions and events.

July 16, 1974 the *Chicago Sun-Times* devoted its page 1 Topline to a
report by Jon Ziomek on Nelson's career, "This may be the story of your
dreams."

After the murder of Dr. Martin Luther King the AP interviewed his
widow and distributed an account from Atlanta April 5, 1968. "I do think
it's the will of God. We always knew this could happen," Mrs. King said.
The same day the *Boston Herald Traveler* devoted a full page to "Key
Scenes in the Modern American Tragedy" and headed its story by AP's Jay
Bowles, "Did King Earlier Have Premonitions of Death?" Evidence that
such might be the case was a statement from his Memphis speech, "It
really doesn't matter what happens now. I've been to the mountain top."
That article and a second article declared that King often received threats
against his life. His lieutenant Andrew Young, later United States ambassador to the United Nations and mayor of Atlanta, said, "I don't know
whether it was premonition or not."

Feb. 26, 1968 the syndicated columnist Earl Wilson related that Connie
Stevens told Merv Griffin she and Eddie crash-landed in Frank Sinatra's
jet after she had a dream foretelling it.

And earlier, Nov. 26, 1960, the *Chicago Courier* reported that several
members of the clergy viewed the sudden death of Judge Emory B. Smith,
onetime Congregational minister, as a "devil's warning" to all members of
the clergy. One prominent churchman was quoted as saying, "The act of
forsaking the word of God was a moment of moral descent."

Probably there are quite a few columnists and editorial writers who
believe that they could match the experiences that Joe Natale recounted in
the *Chenoa* (Ill.) *Clipper & Journal* Nov. 8, 1979. Under the caption, "Sixth
Sense" he wrote:

> All week I was debating with myself on whether to write about Jane
> Fonda or New Wave music. Since Chenoa won the Midstate conference title, I
> decided to write about psychic power instead.
>
> Having a sixth sense has helped me get through life so far. I often get
> premonitions of things that happen. In fact, I've called a collision of two 747s
> a few years ago and the last two Popes dying.
>
> By the second week of the football season I was predicting Chenoa would
> win the conference championship.
>
> Also, during the season I predicted Lexington would defeat Gridley by 21
> points, which they did.

On Halloween I was walking in my apartment complex, and a snake crossed my path. Right then I knew something was up. Lo and behold, a few nights later I met Dorothea the Boa constrictor.

Unfortunately, at press time I have not received any premonitions on the Chenoa-Macon football game or what will happen with the economy.

However, I have a feeling Jane Fonda will star in a movie about Wave music.

24

Relics

During Holy Week 1949 the nation's attention was directed by the news media to Syracuse, N.Y., where a broken statuette of St. Anne was reported to weep whenever kissed by 11-year-old Shirley Anne Martin, who had rescued it from a garbage can.

Crowds gathered, the ill and infirm sought a look or a touch of either the statuette or child. There were newspaper interviews and radio and television appearances in Syracuse and New York. Viola Martin, the girl's mother, usually accompanied her daughter while the milkman husband and father sought to discourage publicity. After about ten days, April 13 to 24, he succeeded in restoring order in the family.

For a report in a public opinion seminar in the Medill School of Journalism of Northwestern University, graduate student Mason E. Miller studied the coverage of the story by the local press, press associations and news magazines. He concluded: "On the whole I would say that in covering this news event the press did only a superficial job. The surface miraculous part of the story was reported extensively while attempts to find the natural causes of the tears were not encouraged and even not reported."

Miller said the press was remiss in not following up the announcement by John McMahon, dean of the State College of Ceramics at Alfred University, that he was sending an investigator even though he didn't think the weeping possible inasmuch as plaster of paris absorbs water readily but does not release it except by evaporation. Miller became convinced that "There seems to be no real effort outside of the letters section to find a scientific explanation for the event." He described what transpired in the Letter to the Editor column as "a battle royal."

As a result of inadequate investigative reporting and rumor, Miller concluded, hope was built "in all the credulous and those who desired to believe in a miracle." The only "consistently claimed and yet unverified phenomenon was the curing of the grandmother's neuralgia." No other member of the family verified the old woman's claim and the press made no effort to learn the truth. Likewise there was no followup as to the effect of the visits Shirley made to many sick persons, nor what happened when she held the statue to the cheek of a baby with a blood tumor, a picture of which incident was published throughout the country. Nor was any attention paid to the number of times the statue disappointed onlookers by failing to weep.

In addition to the Syracuse papers, the *New York Times, New York Sun-Times, Chicago Daily News, Chicago Tribune, Newsweek* and *Time* "seemed simply to look on it as a good Holy Week story with a religious angle. They did not weigh the effect of what their stories said from the viewpoint of advancing or refuting superstition and false beliefs."

Doubtless the same could be said about the coverage of many more similar stories. Weeping virgins can become contagious. Two months after the Syracuse phenomenon hysterical crowds stormed the cathedral in Lublin, Poland, where, it was rumored, a portrait of the Virgin Mary was weeping. During the three weeks following July 3 it was estimated a half-million Poles made pilgrimages to Lublin, disrupting train service and resulting in at least one death and 19 injuries when a platform collapsed. Early reports came from the AP in Warsaw. Irving Pflaum, foreign editor of the *Chicago Sun-Times* interrupted a European vacation to cover the story. July 18, 1949 he wrote that he and a colleague, Dennis Weaver, and their wives stood within four feet of the painting when a tear seemed to appear and move down her face. Not all of the four agreed on the movement but all agreed there was a tear-shaped brown spot below the eye. Pflaum concluded that the government's charge it was a deliberate invention intended to goad the Communist government into cracking down on the Roman Catholic church to discredit itself with the populace had validity. Pflaum quoted a government official that the whole affair was "a disgraceful deceiving action" and "a fraud aimed at the Polish nation." The hierarchy of the church ordered the pilgrimages to stop.

Similar occurrences have been reported from many parts of the world. April 10, 1956 the UP reported from Nice, France that a village blacksmith said that blood oozed from the nail-pierced hands of an iron Christ he was fixing to a cross. From Sausalito, Calif. the UP reported Jan. 15, 1957 that crowds gathered to kiss a 10-by-20-inch piece of cedarwood on which a madonna was chiseled. This was after an elderly man on crutches visited an art gallery where the object was exhibited and asked permission to kiss it, after which he insisted he saw tears in the portrait's eyes. Almost the same was reported by the AP March 22, 1960 from Island Park, N.Y. where the highest Greek Orthodox prelate in the Western Hemisphere vouched for some parishioner's story that a portrait of the virgin in a private home was shedding tears.

Other reports included the following:

Aug. 17, 1969—The UPI reported from Johannesburg, South Africa that a wooden cross brought there 50 years earlier mystified forestry experts annually by weeping resin on the anniversary of the World War I battle of Delville Wood in France, during which the 2nd South African Infantry Brigade was virtually wiped out. It was generally believed that black troops were used in dangerous situations to save white lives.

July 20, 1972—During its ten days on exhibit in New Orleans, one of the two existent Pilgrim Statues of Fatima, carved under the supervision of Sister Lucy, only surviving member of the trio who claimed they saw a vision of the Virgin Mary in 1917 in Fatima, Portugal, reportedly was photographed weeping. It did so not in one of the ten churches in which it was displayed but in a motel nearby, the AP reported from New Orleans.

Jan. 15, 1973—When the Fatima Pilgrim statue reached Detroit under the auspices of the Blue Army of Fatima, an international peace organization, Nancy Manser, religion editor of the Detroit News, was given a half-page for pictures and description. She quoted a Blue Army official: "People are beginning to realize they have to ask for help from above and they have to depend on their father."

April 29, 1973—The *Houston Post's* religion editor, Charlene Warnken, reported on what members of the Esmirna Pentecoastal Holy Church of Alvin, Texas insist was a miracle. It occurred Easter Sunday when a man's figure was seen in a bright light that suddenly shone seven feet in front of a landscape painting that heretofore had no image. Said the pastor: "I believe very strongly in miracles. I have been expecting something great since the first of the year. This is an answer to prayers."

Sept. 23, 1975—The AP described crowds that visited a humble house in Marcus Hook, Pa. where a dark substance resembling blood was detected in the palm of the hand of a small statue of Jesus. The housewife owner refused to allow the substance to be tested because "I haven't been directed by God to do so."

July 28–Aug. 10, 1982—*In These Times* reported that a statue of the Virgin Mary began sweating to express opposition to the Sandinista revolution, according to the opposition newspaper, *La Prensa*.

"The woman who has caused more wonder than any other living person," according to the Chicago *Lincoln-Belmont Booster* for Dec, 26, 1945, was Theresa Neumann of Konnersreuth, Bavaria, Germany. She baffled scientists as well as everyone else as she lived without food, drink or sleep. She bore on her body the bleeding wounds of Jesus and had the gift of prophecy and healing.

Shortly after the stigmata first appeared in 1926 crowds gathered every Friday, the largest on Good Fridays, to witness bleeding from the marks of nails in her hands and feet and around her head like those made by a crown of thorns on Jesus' head.

The *Booster* story was of a Chicago soldier stationed in Germany at war's end who visited and was photographed with Theresa. April 8, 1950 the AP reported that thousands passed by the woman, then 52, as she lay in bed in a trance on Good Friday. Six years later, March 28, 1951, foreign correspondent David M. Nichols reported for the *Chicago Daily News* that for the first time in 25 years the stigmata failed to appear on Good Friday, disappointing a crowd of 8,000, 2,000 of them Americans. Five years later, for the second time, visitors (about 6,000) were turned away. According to a UP story March 30, 1956 there are about 300 persons throughout history who have borne the stigmata. The Roman Catholic church never officially recognized the supernatural origin of the stigmata during the lifetime of any person bearing them. However, it said Theresa Neumann's stigmata were "a gratuitous gift of divine grace." A year later, April 12, 1957 the AP reported that the Rev. Joseph Naber, for whom she kept house, told the assembled pilgrims that Theresa's health was better and she could be seen again. The April 14, 1957 issue of the *American Weekly,* a syndicated newspaper supplement, abstracted a chapter on Theresa from Marcus Bach's book, *The Circle of Faith.* It was illustrated with some of the few pictures ever taken of the woman. He attempted to explain her condition as due to her loving nature, which led her to relieve the sufferings of others by assuming them herself. Nobody else has had a better theory.

Stigmata cases are rare enough to be newsworthy when discovered. A United Press correspondent was among a small crowd that was admitted to an orphanage at Cosena, Italy where a nun, Elean Aiello, lay with blood streaming from her forehead as though she wore a crown of thorns. As reported April 10, 1936 it was the 12th consecutive Good Friday on which the phenomenon had occurred. A year later the *Catholic Herald Citizen* warned April 10, 1937 that "This is, so far as we know, the first report concerning Sister Aiello. Caution is advised because press reports of such phenomena are not always reliable."

When a 16-year-old Lemay, Mo. high school girl bled from wounds in the hands, feet and side every day during mass, the church merely announced that the case was being studied in the office of the archbishop, the United Press reported Aug. 25, 1950 from St. Louis.

Both Reuters and the AP reported March 23, 1972 from Oakland, Calif. that a 10-year-old girl had a palm that had been bleeding off-and-on for more than a week without hurting. Doctors were quoted as saying it was an Easter bleeding syndrome. Unidentified medical authorities also were said to believe stigmatization may be caused by auto-suggestion or other emotional condition that upsets the body's chemical balance. The UPI reported March 24, 1972 that a hematologist announced that blood tests failed to show any abnormality.

Even more mysterious is the behavior of the blood of St. Januarius who was beheaded in 305 by the Romans at Pozzuoil near Naples, Italy and has been Naples' patron saint ever since. The faithful believe that two phials on the high altar of the Naples Cathedral contain the saint's dried blood which a woman rescued after his execution. Three times annually—the first Saturday in May, the saint's feast day, Sept. 19 and Dec. 16, the anniversary of the eruption of nearby Mt. Vesuvius in 1631—it liquefies. When the miracle is late in occurring it is believed to be a sign of misfortune, as in 1940 when Benito Mussolini declared war and in May 1976 when 1,000 persons died in the Fruili region despite eight days of constant prayer.

There have been only three occasions on which the miracle did not occur at all: 1527, when bubonic plague followed; 1884, when there was a cholera epidemic; and 1944, when Vesuvius erupted again. All of this historical lore was related by the Associated Press in a dispatch May 3, 1954 from Naples.

When the miracle occurs on schedule there is cheering and demonstrating in the street, which is what the UP reported May 2, 1948.

Sept. 20, 1956 the AP announced the miracle occurred on time and a shouting, cheering crowd almost overran a cordon of police.

In a feature in the *Toronto Sun* for Aug. 16, 1972 Allen Spraggett reported that if the miracle is tardy the parishioners were not averse to cajoling the saint with such admonitions as "Come on old yellow face," referring to the saint's allegedly jaundiced complexion. Spraggett also revealed that a skeptical chemist, Dr. Alberto Albini, made a compound of powdered-chocolate and milk that looked solid in a vial but turned to liquid when he applied the heat of his hands. However, he could not get it to turn bright red as the traditional blood of St. Januarius does. Other scientists have shot light rays through the blood with uncertain results. Concluded Spraggett: "Still, the fact of the phenomenon remains. It cannot be merely shrugged off out of existence."

Sept. 19, 1976, the UPI reported, the crowd exploded fireworks, their joy being enhanced by the fact the miracle failed to occur in May. Sept 9, 1981 the UPI reported that the blood liquefied quickly, giving hope to the thousands of Neapolitans left homeless by an earthquake that it might mean the end of their problems.

Another sacred relic is the right forearm of St. Francis Xavier, one of the original members of the Jesuits, founded by his friend Ignatius Loyola and considered the patron of missionaries because of his extensive missionary work in Japan, China and India. He died on his way to China in 1552 and his body was returned to Italy in 1554. James Supple, religion editor, wrote a brief history of the arm in the *Chicago Sun-Times* Oct. 14, 1949 at a time the relic was to be exhibited in Chicago on its way back from China to Italy.

When it was announced that the corpse had all but wasted away the church declared that miracles need not go on forever, according to an article by William J. Drummond in the *Los Angeles Times* of March 2, 1973. Nevertheless, the village of Old Goa, India was preparing to receive a throng of pilgrims to view the body, to be exhibited for the first time in ten years. Its permanent home is a magnificent silver coffin inside the basilica of Bom Jesus in Old Goa.

More important should be considered the bones found beneath the

Church of St. Peter's in Rome, which the UPI predicted Aug. 24, 1949 would be declared by Pope Pius XII to be those of St. Peter himself.

In order to combat bad weather inhabitants of Limoges, France exhibited the relics of third-century Saint Martial, patron saint of the city, Reuters reported Aug. 19, 1968.

At the end of the holy year of 1976 there was an exhibition, "Treasures of Sacred Art," at the Palazzo della Esposizioni in Rome. Among the 500 objects were a silver gilt "Flight From Egypt," dating from about 1400; a repository of Mary Magdalene's foot, silver-gilt, 1645; the reliquary of St. Matthew's arm and, especially, late 16th-century angels holding the reliquary of Christ's circumcision, the Holy Foreskin preserved by a succession of devout guardians.

Even the non-Christian Soviet Union recognizes the importance of saintly relics. Dusko Duder of the *Washington Post* reported Aug. 9, 1981 from Moscow that there was wide resentment when the Russian Orthodox church announced that relics supposed to be of some of the most revered saints in Russia are, in fact, the bones of Mongol invaders.

On tour in the United States Patriarch Bendictus I of Jerusalem, prelate of the Greek Orthodox church, presented President John F. Kennedy with an engraved box containing the Insignia of the order of the Holy Sepulcher and the Grand Cross medallion said to contain a fragment of the True Cross. The AP distributed a picture of the occasion Oct. 6, 1961.

In 1981 two thefts of sacred relics were reported from Italy. The first, reported by the UPI Nov. 16 after two masked men forced their way into the Church of Germia in Venice and stole the remains of St. Lucy, a third-century martyr, which had been in Venice for 77 years. She was considered the patron saint of eyesight because her eyes were gouged out before she was executed in 303. The second theft was reported by UPI Nov. 16. Burglars cracked open an urn containing the relics of Pius I, stole an ancient ring and scattered the remains on the floor of the chapel.

Despite the precautionary measures that the church takes to avoid being fooled, any tourist who travels from Rome to Istanbul and Jerusalem and environs cannot help becoming skeptical, perhaps cynical. That is because the visitors will be shown enough pieces of the true cross to build a good-sized house and enough mummified remnants of the saints, beginning with John the Baptist and Peter, to dwarf Hercules.

An example of how people see what they want to see and interpret events in accordance with their wishes was provided at Sante Fe Springs, Cal. Kristina Lindgren wrote about it in the *Los Angeles Times* for Jan. 17, 1981. Hundreds gathered to observe a shadow on a garage door that Graziela and Rafael Tascon, the homeowners, insisted resembled Jesus Christ. The image was distinct—a cross, about 3 feet tall and 2 feet wide, surmounted by the face of a man crowned with thorns. The shadow of the cross was cast by a real estate sign planted on the front lawn. The shadow of the head and thorns was cast by a bush closer to the door. The light source for both was a pair of street lamps across from the house.

Even after the phenomenon was explained, Mrs. Tascon persisted in saying the shadow was the spirit of Jesus. "The Lord is talking to all his children," she said. "He has manifested himself in this way." Jan. 10, 1981 the *Times* reported that at least 600 people came to see the garage door even after the grass was cut and the sign removed.

Sometimes the attempts to invent brand new antiques and relics are humorous. When Mrs. Maria Rubio of Lake Arthur, N.M. was rolling tortillas into burritos, she noted the pattern made on one tortilla by skillet burns. "It is Jesus Christ," she cried aloud. When other members of the family agreed, she got a reluctant priest to give the tortilla a blessing and built a shrine for it in her home. Thousands of visitors from all parts of the United States came to see the miracle, often to pray and to seek divine help in curing ailments. Despite the cynicism expressed by Ken Walston of the *Albuquerque Journal*—"It looks more like Leon Spinks to me"—the story appeared in newspapers all over the country.

In his column in the *Charleston* (W.Va.) *Gazette* for June 13, 1982, L. T. Anderson revived the tortilla story and considered the question of why Catholic miracles are newsworthy whereas Protestant miracles are ignored. His Catholic wife suggested that it might be because Catholic miracles are more imaginative and Anderson admitted that during his many years as a city editor he rejected at least 50 stories of Jesus' face appearing on the wallpaper of non-Catholic homes.

Because they thought the foliage of a vine-covered tree resembled a profile of Jesus Christ, large crowds gathered at Holden, W.Va. The *Charleston Mail* streamer-headlined the AP story Sept. 9, 1982 and used a picture by a staff photographer. The *Charleston Gazette* used the UPI story and photo the next day. The latter paper's columnist, Don Marsh, said the vision was first noticed by one of three boys who were drinking beer. "They said it shook him up so that he quit drinking and joined the church," Marsh wrote. In its story the paper quoted a sheriff's lieutenant: "I wouldn't know about any signs, but in my opinion Jesus ain't going to come in any tree."

More than 10,000 persons were attracted to the Walker County Medical Center after the father of an ill boy said he saw an image of the face of Jesus on a wooden door to the recovery room, the UPI reported April 17, 1983 from Jasper, Ala.

In June 1980 the AP reported from San Antonio that a cactus fiber coat bearing the image of the Virgin Mary and thought to be more than 450 years old will undergo scientific tests to establish its validity. The relic is enshrined in the Basilica of Guadalupe in Mexico City on the spot, tradition has it, the Virgin appeared to an Indian youth, Juan Diego, on Dec. 9, 1531 and told him to advise the bishop to build a church in her honor on the site.

However explainable, more reliable were reports of incredible occurrences, miracles, involving prayer. April 9, 1936, for instance, the UP reported from Calumet, Mich. that three roses, their delicate petals exuding a blood-red fluid, were discovered in a communion ciborium after the congregation had prayed to the Little Flower to "give us a tangible proof of her power with God and her love for us."

Within a week after Saint Frances Cabrini was canonized, the Vatican reported that a 5-year-old boy, blind since birth, gained his sight. The UP distributed the story July 15, 1945 from Rome.

The growing trade in antiques with a religious meaning was noted by Anne Gilbert in the *Chicago Daily News* for Sept. 23, 1972. Popular items, she said, are tall brass altar candlesticks, usable as fireplace accessories, baptismal fonts and minorahs, all potential miracle workers. Who can predict what myths may be created about them?

What Pope Paul VI called "the most important relic in the history of Christianity" is a piece of linen cloth 14½ by 3½ feet that is guarded safely in a silver box in the Giovanni Cathedral in Turin, Italy, where it has been since 1478. On it is imprinted the full length figure of a man, said variously to be from 5 feet 10 inches to 6 feet one inch tall and weighing from 165 to 185 pounds. The hair is long with a pigtail in back, the beard pointed. Experts agree that wounds on wrists and feet and in the side indicate that the man had been scourged, crowned with thorns and crucified.

Because of the obvious resemblance to artists' portrayals of Jesus Christ many believe that the cloth was the shroud in which Jesus was wrapped after his descent from the cross to be taken to a tomb of Joseph of Arimathea, according to the scriptures.

Reconstructing the shroud's history is difficult. It has been traced to Lirey, France in 1354, the property of Geoffroy de Charny. Some historians think it was taken there by some crusading Knights Templar. It also is known that some shroud was taken from Jerusalem to Edessa and from there to Constantinople in 944. There is no evidence, however, that the shroud said to have been in Constantinople from 900 to 1200 was the shroud of Turin.

It is known that in 1395 Pierre d'Arcis, Bishop of Troyes, called the shroud a fake and said that its forger had confessed. Also known is the fact that Geoffroy de Charny was killed by the English in the battle of Pointiers Sept. 19, 1356 and in 1453 his granddaughter gave the relic to the Duke of Savoy. For years it belonged to former Italian King Humberto, who lived in exile in Spain and left custody of the relic to the cathedral in Turin. When he died March 18, 1983 it was revealed he willed the shroud to the Vatican, the *Washington Post* reported April 2, 1983.

Although several popes have spoken lovingly of the shroud, the church has never accepted its validity officially. As recently as 1911 the *Catholic Encyclopedia* tended to discredit the cloth on the basis of the bishop of Troyes' statement.

For more than 500 years majority opinion was that the image was a painting. In 1898, however, an Italian photographer, Secondo Pia, discovered on developing his plates that the image was a photographic negative. Since then there has been no cessation in the controversy over the authenticity of the shroud. The press has played a large part in keeping interest in it alive. Although question marks are usual over stories of new developments and although the statements of critics are published, the overall impression the journalistic endeavor makes is sympathetic to those who believe the cloth actually was used to cover Jesus' body.

A typical headline was that in the *Catholic Herald-Citizen* for April 10, 1937: "Are Imprints of Christ's Body on the Holy Shroud at Turin?" with a subhead, "Scientists No Longer Satisfied That Impressions Are 14th Century Paintings." That was almost 40 years after Pia's startling discovery. The story reviewed an article that *Reader's Digest* had condensed from the *Scientific American* by Paul Vignon, Sc.D., professor of biology at the Catholic Institute in Paris and secretary general of the Italian and French commissions on the Holy Shroud. The author described how the different markings could have been made and pointed out the similarity to New Testament versions of the death of Jesus.

Accepting the evidence of the shroud as valid Prof. Lorenzo Ferri, Roman artist, made a three-dimensional clay model of what Jesus must have looked like. *Parade* syndicated a picture of it March 13, 1955.

In the United States none has studied the shroud longer, to become a true believer and strong advocate of it, than the Rev. Francis L. Filas, S.J., professor of theology at Loyola University in Chicago. In the '40s annually on Good Friday he told the shroud's story on WGN-TV. The press gave good advance notice of the programs. The *Chicago Daily News* March 26, 1950 quoted him regarding the authenticity of the relic, "That is up to the individual." Over the years as the results of scientific studies were announced, Father Filas became more positive in his endorsement of the cloth. March 24, 1955 that paper used a picture of Filas with a blown-up photograph of the shroud.

Typical of scoffings from skeptical laymen was a letter Ann Landers reprinted in her syndicated column for Sept. 5, 1971. The correspondent wrote, "If one more long-haired hippie tells me Jesus had long hair I will personally kick him in the teeth. Nobody knows what Jesus looked like. They did not have photographers 2,000 years ago and no artist ever painted a picture of him. The pictures we see hanging in hospitals and churches are based on somebody's imagination." The writer quoted I Corinthians 11:14, "Does not even nature itself teach you that if a man has long hair it is a shame unto him?"

Landers declared that she received 2,000 sworn statements and 1,000 pictures of Jesus. One writer declared that Jesus was from Nazareth, also the home of the hirsute Samson, and quoted Numbers 6:5. Other correspondents quoted I Samuel 16:7, other biblical passages and other authorities.

In answer to a reader's letter the *Chicago Tribune's* Action Line March 14, 1973 gave a thumbnail summary of the shroud's history and nature and exclaimed the shroud was "one of Italy's many questionable relics, which reportedly include everything from angel feathers to the house that Mary and Joseph supposedly lived in in Nazareth."

The first public showing of the shroud in 40 years was announced by the *New York Times* Nov. 23, 1973. About 40 experts from many countries attended but the church authorities refused to permit an all-out scientific examination.

Except for a few advertisements, an entire page of the *Chicago Sun-Times* for March 28, 1975 was devoted to a feature by David Anderson about Father Filas' interest in the shroud, illustrated by a picture of the priest with an enlarged picture of the face on the linen, headlined, "Shrouded in mystery: Did this cloth touch Christ's Body?" Father Filas was quoted as favoring scientific tests. The same picture reduced from two to one column, was used in the paper's Action Time column May 31, 1976. July 25, 1977 the paper ran a UPI story from the U.S. Air Force Academy in Colorado Springs that computer studies of photographs of the shroud revealed some buttonlike objects that might be coins placed in the dead man's eyes, a Jewish custom of the time. Jan 8, 1978 the *Sun-Times* ran a half-page feature, "The Shroud of Turin—a true photo of Christ?" illustrated by the same closeup of the face on the cloth, with the subhead, "No one can come up with a better explanation." Philip Nobile interviewed Robert W. Wilcox, former religion editor of the *Miami News* who traveled to faraway lands and examined about 2,000 shrouds, none of which had impressions. Wilcox said, "The shroud strongly implies the resurrection."

An even stronger statement was that of Father Filas, first reported by John Justin Smith in the *Chicago Daily News* for Feb. 11, 1978: "There's one chance in a billion times a billion times a billion" that the shroud is not authentic. He revealed that a Swiss photo expert had determined that scrapings of the linen disclosed eight fragments of pollen fossils from some plants that existed in the Holy Land in Jesus' time. Also, there are no brush marks on the cloth, thus discounting the idea it might be a painting. Smith's article was headed "Mystery Still Surrounds Turin Cloth," with the subhead "New findings support belief that the Shroud of Turin is indeed the burial cloth of Jesus Christ, Chicago prelate says." Smith mentioned a book, *The Shroud of Turin: The Burial Cloth of Jesus Christ?* by a Britisher, Ian Wilson, to be published soon. April 23, 1978 the *Chicago Tribune* began a series of three articles entitled, "Is image of Christ preserved on Shroud?" extracted from Wilson's book. In it the suggestion was made that possibly a "flash of energy" at the moment of the resurrection changed a physical body into a spiritual, resurrected body. He also told of the use at the Air Force Academy of a VP 8 Image Analyzer, a machine used by the U.S. space program for reconstructing from photographs the relief of the moon and the surfaces of distant planets. The shroud's image showed up in perfect 3D, proving it was a body, not a painting.

In the second installment from Wilson's book more than 80 thumb-nail-shaped markings all over the back were what would come from whipping with the Roman scourge of flagum. In a sidebar, Dr. John Robinson, dean of chapel at Trinity College, Cambridge, England, was quoted as believing the burden of proof had shifted to those in favor of the authenticity of the shroud of Turin.

In another story from Turin, John Justin Smith wrote Aug. 20, 1978 for the *Sun-Times* that 3 million persons were expected when the shroud was exhibited publicly for the first time in 45 years. The question-mark headline for this story was " 'Turin's shroud' proof of Easter?" Aug. 27 the UPI confirmed the predicted attendance, giving it as 6 to 9 million, in celebration of the 400th anniversary of the arrival of the shroud in Turin. The same day the *Chicago Tribune* quoted the Religious News Service in London that a scientific commission advised against allowing a carbon-14 test to determine the shroud's age. Aug. 29 the UPI reported that in two days 140,000 people had viewed the relic. From the Jet Propulsion Laboratory in Pasadena Donald Lyon, who makes computer enhancements of photos, was quoted: "If the shroud is a forgery it would be a greater miracle than if it is real."

George T. Will's syndicated rehash of the story Sept. 19, 1978 was headlined "Was Jesus Buried in the Shroud of Turin?" Sept. 29, 1978 the UPI elaborated on its Pasadena story. Lyon said there was no known way to duplicate the negative photograph. Lyon was to be among the 30 scientists permitted by the bishop of Turin to examine the relic for 24 hours beginning at midnight Oct. 9. That day the UPI reported from Turin that 3.3 million persons, including 20 cardinals, had viewed the shroud. A group of scientists were to engage in testing by radioaction, X-rays and flourescence studies. They would not, however, be allowed to do carbon-14 tests.

Covering a meeting sponsored by the Council for the Advancement of Science Writing, William Hines reported from Gatlinburg, Tenn. for the Nov. 11, 1978 *Chicago Sun-Times* that Harry E. Gove, University of Rochester physicist, believes a new process for carbon-14 dating will be permitted at Turin. It enables the test to be done with only a few threads whereas the older method required a sample about the size of a pocket handkerchief. May 6, 1979 the AP reported that the scientists who ran tests for two weeks last fall had not yet drawn any conclusions. The experts had determined the image was not painted or stained, not caused by a body "contact print" or by fluids or other elements and is not a vaporograph from ammoniac chemical reaction to body vapors and burial unguents. Oct. 10, 1979 the AP reported from Los Alamos, N.M. that the scientists planned a closed meeting to compare their notes within a short time. After only 5 of the 40 scientists invited showed up, the *Sun-Times* reported from Los

Alamos "Turin shroud Christ?" Proving it unlikely it was revealed that the scientists had been allowed only 96 hours to work in Turin with representatives of the Catholic church and Italian scientists watching.

Nov. 20, 1979 the *Los Alamos Monitor* ran an AP story that stated in part, "The scientist who led the team . . . says evidence so far indicates the linen did in fact wrap the crucified body of Jesus Christ." That stirred Marvin Mueller, a Los Alamos physicist, to become "devil's advocate" by means of an article in the *Monitor* for Dec. 16, 1979. He charged that the scientific committee was under the auspices of the Holy Shroud Guild, a longtime Catholic organization.

Dr. Mueller in particular challenged the conjecture that "a short burst of radiation" had caused the image. That, he said, means only that there was a miracle "and in all history of natural science never has a supernatural hypothesis been necessary to explain the existence of objects or events."

Undaunted, Father Filas told the *Sun-Times* Nov. 12, 1979 that the coins detected in the eyes of the corpse were minted only between 29 and 36. Jesus presumably died in 33. The priest had been aided by two numismatists. Reporters expressed difficulty in detecting any markings on the supposed coins.

Editorially Dec. 24, 1979 the *Grand Rapids* (Mich.) *Press* complained because the findings regarding the shroud were not included in anyone's list of the outstanding happenings of 1979. It quoted approvingly the surmise of Thomas D'Muhala that the three-dimensional image was projected onto the cloth's surface, perhaps by a burst of some kind of radiant energy emanating from all parts of the body in a flash lasting two-thousandths of a second.

April 5, 1980 the *Chicago Sun-Times* Action Time gave a reader Donald Lyon's address because s/he wrote, "I have news of significant importance to him." The editors expressed doubt that the reader had something that he had eluded the scientists. In comment on Action Time's reply, another reader wrote to quote the Gospel of John that a facecloth was placed on Jesus' dead body and that there were wrappings, not a single sheet. Father Filas replied that the confusion resulted from numerous translations from one language to another.

The euphoria of the faithful received a jolt when microscopist Walter C. McCrone, who examined particles taken from the shroud, said he found traces of an iron ore used in an artist's pigment. He was quoted as telling the British Society for the Turin Shroud, "I believe it is a fake but I can't prove it." Two days later the UPI reported from Hartford, Conn. that one of the scientists, Thomas D'Muhala, said that McCrone's views were not those of the group as a whole. No official report had as yet been issued by the group. As expected, the *Sun-Times* reported Sept. 23, 1980, Father Filas denounced McCrone's statement as unscientific. It, he said, "blithely passes by all the positive evidence for the authenticity of the shroud." Nov. 2, 1980 the *New York Times* reported that members of the scientific team unanimously rejected the idea that the image was painted. It quoted 4 of the 32 involved.

Christmas Day, 1980, Frederick M. Winship wrote for the UPI, physicist Samuel Pellicori categorically denied the image was painted and is certain it was caused by contact with a human body. He directed microscopic examinations of the shroud.

Although the full report of the investigative committee was still unpublished, the AP reported Feb. 8, 1981 from Santa Barbara that Samuel Pellicori of the Hughes Research Laboratory, had written in the magazine *Archaeology* that his microscopic examination of the linen fibers in the shroud convinced him that the image was produced by direct contact with a body. How it could happen, he said, was still unknown.

From Switzerland came the news April 3, 1981 that the criminologist Max Frei said he had proof that the shroud was wrapped around Jesus.

Finally April 18, 1981 the AP reported that the Vatican agreed to permit carbon-14 testing provided there was a guarantee that damage to the shroud would not exceed one square centimeter. The next day the contents of the forthcoming report of the experts leaked out. Presumably it would say that the image is not a forgery but whether it is an image of Jesus Christ is still unknown, the UPI reported from Santa Barbara.

Although the news had been reported several times before, in the *Chicago Tribune* for June 11, 1981, Bruce Buursma, religion editor, wrote that Father Filas had released new evidence. It pertained to the coins the priest said were in the image's eyes. Another oft-told bit of news was retold in the *Tribune* for June 21, 1981, namely, details of an interview with McCrone by the science editor, Ronald Kotulak. McCrone's background, it was told, included his discovery in 1974 that the Yale University map showing that the Vikings discovered Vinland centuries before Christopher Columbus was a forgery.

If any Chicagoan remained ignorant of the history of the shroud of Turin it wasn't because the city's papers had neglected to retell the story time and time again.

The same day, June 21, 1981, the *Sun-Times* retold Father Filas' story of the coins. Sept. 25, 1981 it used a long article by George W. Cornell, Associated Press religion editor. Cornell reviewed a book, *Verdict on the Shroud,* by a computer engineer, Kenneth E. Stevenson of Dallas, onetime official spokesman for the 1978 scientific team, and a philosopher, Gary R. Habermas of Lynchburg, Va. The authors concluded: "The historical arguments and the scientific arguments are very probable empirical indicators that Jesus did rise from the dead."

The next day, Sept. 26, 1981, the *Chicago Tribune* ran a short piece on page 19 that quoted from the book, incorrectly identified as the report of the scientific group as a whole. Sept. 27 the *Tribune* gave a full page to an article by Michael Coakley headlined "Shroud of Turin gains scientific support." The article asserted that the Shroud of Turin Research Project subjected the relic "to the full range of tests possible through modern science," a palpably false statement since the church had not allowed carbon-14 testing, the most important possible.

The same day, Sept. 27, 1981, the rival *Sun-Times* devoted two full tabloid pages to the first of three articles by Cullen Murphy on "What the experts discovered." In the series the entire history of the artifact was retold and the 1978 tests described in detail. Almost half of the last of the three installments was devoted to a picture of the Rev. Francis Filas with the headline on one sidebar strangely uncertain: "Chicago theologian: Shroud may be real."

The avidity of the press for any new angle was demonstrated Sept. 28, 1981 by the *New York Post*. It ran a story by Robert Weddle who interviewed Frank Smith, a Long Island accountant who said he could prove the shroud was that of Egypt's King Tutankhamen, not Jesus Christ He argued that there is no proof of how Jesus looked whereas King Tut's mummy shows features detectable on the shroud.

About 50 scientists who had done some research on the shroud, mostly with the project, met in New London, Conn. Oct. 9, 1981 bitterly divided, Michael Oakley reported for the *Chicago Tribune* the following day. At the team's crowded press conference, he reported, "it became clear that their differences go beyond the judgemental." The immediate controversial matter was the book by Stevenson and Habermas. A lawyer for the project read a statement saying the book was not authorized by the team and that Stevenson's resignation from the project had been requested.

Despite their expression of regret for not being able to make the carbon-14 tests, the group agreed on the following short summary of its report: "We can conclude that for now the shroud image is that of a real human form of a scourged, crucified man. It is not the product of an artist. The bloodstains are composed of hemoglobin and give also a positive test for serum albumen. The image is an ongoing mystery and until further chemical studies are made, perhaps by this group of scientists or perhaps by some scientist in the future, the problem remains unsolved."

Despite this statement the *Tribune's* 3-column headline was: "Report on Turin Shroud 'Real Image of Crucified Man,' " accompanied by a picture of the face on the image. Much less misleading was the heading the *Grand Rapids Press* used Oct. 10, 1981, "Turin Shroud Image Human, Study Says," with the hanger head "Researchers said science can't determine whether the image on the shroud is that of Jesus Christ."

The same day the AP reported that a federal judge in Detroit had dissolved a one-day restraining order to prevent distribution of the Stevenson and Habermas book issued by a state court judge on the motion of the

Shroud of Turin Research Project. Whereas the *Sun-Times* played the AP story prominently on page 1, the *New York Times* waited until Oct. 12 and then ran a two-inch UPI account on a back page.

The breach widened between the convinced and the still-skeptical scientists when Dr. Walter C. McCrone spoke up again—strongly. Larry Weintraub reported in the *Chicago Sun-Times* for Oct. 24, 1981 that McCrone, who had been working on the problem before the project began, declared: "We tried to get together and for a while we were getting along pretty good. They actually gave me the samples [from the shroud] that I was looking at. But then I started getting results that they didn't like and from that point on our paths started to separate."

McCrone said that he was able to examine much smaller areas of the relic at higher magnification. "I can't sit still while my findings are ignored—worse yet, said to be incorrect."

Support for the skeptics was included in a latter to the *Chicago Tribune*'s Voice of the People column for Oct. 31, 1981. Norman Paradis said Father Filas cannot offer proof that the coins were not used for years, no matter when minted.

Nov. 27, 1981 the *Sun-Times* quoted Father Filas as saying the findings of another coin with similar misspellings "should eliminate all doubt" that the coins existed at the time of Christ's crucifixion. However, an ancient coin expert, Robert D. Leonard of New York, called Father Filas "a biased observer who was wrong with this second so-called discovery just as I believe he was wrong with his earlier ones. Father Filas is a Biblical expert but not a coin expert—and it showed."

One of the first and possibly the only editorial in a major newspaper to belittle the claims of authenticity appeared Dec. 4, 1981 in the *New York Times*. After quoting the Bishop of Troyes and Walter McCrone, the editorial concluded: "We excel over our medieval forefathers in many things, no doubt, but should try not to outdo them in credulity."

Dec. 21 the Rev. Vincent J. Donovan of Oswego, N.Y. was given more space in which to reply. He did so by saying there was no proof of the Bishop of Troyes' allegation and McCrone made an inadequate examination.

In his syndicated column for Dec. 25, 1981 William F. Buckley, Jr. wrote: "To the dismay of the skeptics the evidence mounts incontrovertibly that it is legitimate." He chastised the *Times* for accepting weak witnesses.

So that "the public can now decide for itself where the truth resides" Father Filas released a new half-hour film-strip that emphasizes the importance of the misspelled coins. The *Chicago Tribune* gave him publicity in an article by Bruce Buursma in the issue of Jan. 13, 1982. Support for the importance of the coins came from Alan D. Whanger, a Duke University psychiatrist, the AP's religion editor, George Cornell, reported April 10, 1982. Eric Meyers, a Duke University archeologist and editor of *Biblical Archeologist,* remained unconvinced, saying the coins could have been in circulation for 200 years.

April 20, 1982 a display of 150 photographs of the artifact from several military laboratories about the country opened in New Trier High School, Northfield, Ill., both Chicago papers reported.

When he visited Stevens Point, Wis. for an American Chemical Society meeting, Prof. Eric Jumper of the Air Force Institute of Technology at Dayton, Ohio told reporter Bonnie Bressers that now that it is possible to carbon date using only a small sample it is likely that such a test will be made. In the *Stevens Point Journal* for May 14, 1982, Bressers quoted Jumper, co-director of the 1978 investigation, as saying even if the cloth is dated there is no way to prove that it is the burial cloth of Jesus Christ.

The three-dimensional image apparently was caused by X-rays, Giles F. Carter, a Michigan scientist, told the American Chemical Society's annual meeting in Kansas City, Mo., the *Chicago Sun-Times* reported Sept. 15, 1982. High-energy X-rays, he said, could have reacted with chlorine and silicone in salt and dirt on the surface of the skin. Such molecules emit soft X-rays that could have made images of the body on the cloth.

A generally favorable view was expressed by retired Vice Admiral John T. Hayward in a speech at the Naval War College, the Field News Service reported Nov. 26, 1982 from Newport, R.I. The *Daily Oklahoman* streamer-headlined the story to say the former member of the examining committee was convinced the shroud had wrapped Jesus' body. Dr. John H. Heller's book *Report on the Shroud of Turin* and a con view expressed by McCrone were included under the heading "The Shroud of Turin Mystery" in the *Chicago Sun-Times* for June 3, 1983.

For a sympathetic description of most of the phenomena mentioned in this and preceding chapters one should read the series of five articles in the *New York Daily News* March 14 to 18, 1982 inclusive. Author was D. Scott Rogo, parapsychologist, and the articles are extracted from his book *Miracles*. Enumerated uncritically are numerous cases of snake worship, faith healing, stigmata, visions, levitation, shrines and relics.

The eagerly awaited *Inquest on the Shroud of Turin* by Joe Nickell, an iconoclastic member of the University of Kentucky faculty, was published in 1983 by Prometheus Books.

Encouraging to scoffers also was the Associated Press story from Stockton, Calif. that the *Christian Science Monitor* used June 8, 1983. It stated that the Roman Catholic diocese had declared the "weeping Madonna," a large statue in a Thornton church, to be a hoax.

26

Clairvoyance

Not many generations ago one sought advice and/or comfort from relatives, clergymen and friends. As Irene Juno told Frances Leighton for an article in *American Weekly* for Nov. 29, 1957: "When I was a child nobody spoke of ESP—they hadn't given it a name, but the process was going on just as effectively. Mother would remark that 'her bones' told her a relative would come to visit on a given day and usually the relative arrived."

How times have changed was emphasized by Robert Lindsey in the *New York Times* for Dec. 27, 1976: "More people are owning up to consulting psychics today, and in some social groups it is as fashionable to tell about one's favorite psychic as it is on New York's upper East Side to talk about a favorite psychiatrist."

In the attempt to break down the cynicism that the overwhelming majority of scientists still have regarding ESP (extrasensory perception) believers cite evidence of its antiquity and quote many of the world's leading thinkers as believers or at least open-minded. Mortimer J. Adler, director of the Institute for Philosophic Research, wrote in his syndicated column for Jan. 24, 1965: "Extrasensory perception (ESP) is a new term for an ancient form of thought and belief. Simply speaking, it means perception of things by means other than those of our senses of sight, hearing, touch, etc. It includes what used to be called divination, clairvoyance and telepathy. It refers to the perception of or prevision of events at a distant place or future time or to the transmission of thoughts without external material means."

In the rest of the piece, as in an earlier one April 15, 1962, Adler asserted that all were "a matter of common belief in ancient times." According to the Bible, he said, "where even though extraordinary psychic powers are denounced as evil—when in the service of mere magic or false gods—they are nevertheless regarded as actual." Prophecy and divination also played an important role in ancient Greek religion. One of Aristotle's followers, Moses Maimonides, analyzed the phenomena by separating people into three psychological types: the intellectual, the imaginative and the combined intellectual-imaginative.

In *Life* for Jan. 11, 1954 the famous British philosopher and scientist, Aldous Huxley, wrote that psi, the term modern scholars use to include all manifestations of psychic power, "is as old as human experience. Prophets and oracles, ghosts and haunting, poltergeists and apparitions, thought reading and second sight—we find them everywhere and at every period of history, in the Atomic Age and in the Bronze Age, in great cities and in the jungle and the tundra, among the most highly civilized as well as the most primitive of peoples.

"Up to about 1650 practically everyone in the Christian world accepted the reality of psi, and practically everyone attributed its manifestation to the intervention of supernatural agencies, in the main diabolic," Huxley wrote.

It was not until 1882 that enough scholars thought the phenomenon, whether real or imaginary, should be studied scientifically. That year the British Society for Psychical Research was founded and in 1888, largely with the help of the great philosopher William James, the American Society for Psychical Research was organized. It was not until 1969, however, that parapsychologists [psi scholars] were admitted to the American Association for the Advancement of Science. Foremost advocate of the move was the eminent anthropologist Margaret Mead. The displeasure of many members culminated in an effort by Dr. John A. Wheeler, a leading theoretical physicist of the University of Texas, to drop the division of parapsychology, the *New York Times* reported Jan. 9, 1979.

Modern parapsychologists are fond of citing hints in the writings of scholars of the past that they experienced or believed in extrasensory experiences. Among the most often named are Francis Bacon, Increase Mather, Thomas Huxley and Mark Twain.

One of the best journalistic attempts to define parapsychology was John Peterson's article "Science and Psychic Power," in the *National Observer* for Oct. 20, 1973. He quoted Allen Cohen, a clinical psychologist in Berkeley, Calif. and director of a drug abuse institute at John F. Kennedy University in Martinez, that there are three traditional types of psychic phenomena: mind-to-mind, mind-to-matter and matter-to-mind. His classification of the phenomena was: mind reading, or the ability to receive telepathic messages; clairvoyance, of the past, future and present; vibrational empathy, the most complex, includes the ability to heal, read another person's aura, and perceive others' spiritual guides; psychometry, the ability to know the past of a person or object through touching; and mind-force control, the most dangerous ability, which includes both the projecting of thoughts into another person's mind—as in voodoo—and the rare psychokinetic power to bend or alter metals and to make objects dematerialize and rematerialize.

More succinctly Barbara Varro wrote in a 2-page article, "Taking hocus-pocus out of parapsychology" in the *Chicago Sun-Times* for July 6, 1981: "It is a science involving the investigation of evidence for such psychic abilities as clairvoyance, telepathy, precognition and psychokinesis. It is concerned with an individual's ability to mentally picture places he has never seen, to foresee the future, to know that an event is about to happen before it occurs and to move objects without physical means."

Varro makes it easier to understand by preparing a list of terms used in parapsychology as follows:

Extrasensory perception (ESP): the ability to perceive knowledge about people, places or objects without help of the ordinary senses.

Psychokinesis (PK), telekinesis: mind moving matter. It involves movement of a physical object without use of physical means.

Precognition: perception of a future event that is not known through rational inference.

Clairvoyance: perception of an event that's hidden from ordinary senses.

Telepathy: involves a thought that is transferred extrasensorially.

Psychic healing: healing that is achieved through mental processes.

Aura: energy radiating from living things, usually perceived in color.

Remote viewing: perceptual ability. Information about a remote location is obtained via telepathy from one individual to another.

Out-of-body experience (astral projection): a sense of the consciousness leaving the physical body and being transported to another time and place.

Near-death experience: involves individuals who, after suffering near-fatal crises, claimed to have left their bodies before regaining consciousness.

Parapsychological research received its greatest impetus with the establishment in 1938 of the Parapsychology Laboratory and the Foundation for Research in the Nature of Man at Duke University, Durham, N.C. by Dr. Joseph B. Rhine, unquestionably the most outstanding name in this field to date. There are today, however, scores of other organizations in the field, many with new special interests. Withal they have had a sympathetic press and news stories of incidents that might be the subject of their inquiry have been increasingly numerous. Adverse comment or critical analysis has been left mostly to scholarly publications.

One of the first journalistic publications to actively champion the new science was *This Week;* a weekly supplement subscribed to by hundreds of papers. In its issue of March 25, 1950 it excited interest by the recitation of several baffling incidents by Fred Rosen in an article, "Are You Psychic?" Accompanying the article was a test prepared by members of the American Society for Psychical Research by which readers could determine if they appeared to have psychic power. Those who got a significant score were invited to write a description of their psychic experiences to be analyzed by society members. Typical test question: "Do you frequently snatch up a ringing telephone and say without thinking, 'Hello———'; and find you've greeted the right person?"

One of the earliest converts to a belief in parapsychology was Gardner Murphy, director of research of the Menninger Foundation and a former president of the American Psychological Association. Beginning with its issue of Feb. 17, 1957 *This Week* ran a series of three articles by Murphy on mental telepathy, clairvoyance and spiritualism. The author cited several case histories "among the classics in the field, those considered over the years from earliest research to the present to be the most substantial and most significant." One was of a businessman driving home from Minnesota and influenced by an inner feeling went to Fort Wayne instead of South Bend. At a hotel where he had no reservation there was a message for him from his wife that their daughter was dying.

Murphy also extolled the work of Rhine and several others.

All of the major television networks at one time or another have had programs to startle watchers with bizarre accounts of unexplainable occurrences. The press, ordinarily not given to free promotion for broadcasters, has helped advertise such programs. As early as July 5, 1968 the *New York Times* ran a 2-column picture of a young boy participating in a new program about ESP over the ABC network.

Nov. 13, 1958 the *Chicago Sun-Times* had a 3-column headline over a column-long story of a contest between ten man teams of the University of Chicago Para-Psychology Society and a similar group at Cambridge University, England. Stephen Abrams, captain of the Chicago team, was chagrined that he scored only 47 on the trans-Atlantic test, whereas he should have scored at least 40 by chance.

As related in an article by William Stoneman from Oxford, England in the *Chicago Daily News* for June 7, 1962, Abrams claimed to have proof of ESP as a result of research in both the Soviet Union and Great Britain. The column-long article did not explain the basis for the young man's conviction, but it did cite some of his experiments, including hypnosis induced by thought transference.

In the meantime, Gardner Murphy resumed his *This Week* articles. In the issue of Jan. 11, 1959 he described "Six Amazing Cases of Mental Telepathy." One told of a sailor on leave who had to break a date to go to Coconut Grove. He awoke choking to realize that a couple of his buddies to whom he had recommended the nightclub were among the 491 casualties in the fire that destroyed it.

Other *This Week* features included:

Jan. 28, 1962—"Can Twins Read Each Other's Minds?" summarized the conclusions of Dr. Robert Sommer, University of Alberta psychologist, that identical twins and, to a lesser extent, fraternal twins "report unusual ability to communicate with one another through ESP." The article was written by Jhan and June Robbins.

Sept. 8, 1963—"The Great Nautilus ESP Hoax," in which the paper debunked a story, originating in a French magazine, that the U.S. Navy had communicated with an atomic submarine by ESP. The story was pure fiction, including even the name of the submarine.

March 27, 1966—"Yesterday, Today and Tomorrow," by Jess Stearn, subtitled "An uncanny ESP report on predictions that often came true and what the future may hold," related mostly to the presidencies of Kennedy and Johnson.

Oct. 8, 1967—"I Didn't Ask to Be a Psychic," a collection of anecdotes of clairvoyance, telepathy and precognition, related by Mrs. Patricia Baxter to Jhan and June Robbins.

Oct. 15, 1967—"I Can See Tomorrow," by Taylor Caldwell. Considered "fey" as a child, the famous writer forecast many events in later life, but resolved not to make unhappy predictions because, when they came true, she got the blame.

Oct. 22, 1967—"The ESP Gap," in which Lawrence Blochman told that the Nautilus hoax had stimulated research in the Soviet Union. This rumor, as well as a 1963 *Chicago Tribune* story by Norma Lee Browning telling of Soviet experiments, was debunked by Daniel Cohen in the *Nation* for May 9, 1966. Blochman also told of thought and emotional impulses being transmitted across the campus of the Newark College of Engineering to affect the vascomotor nerves of a subject connected to a plethysmograph, an instrument that measures changes in the hand or one finger.

Nov. 11, 1968—"Lila's Got The Power" by Jhan Robbins, a collection of anecdotes of clairvoyance practiced by a fruit seller in London.

Another early series that promoted belief in the occult was "Mysteries of the Mind," written by W. H. Newman for the *Chicago Daily News* in June and July 1962.

During the past half-century similar series have appeared in newspapers in all parts of the country. Uncritical articles about the experiments and theories of parapsychologists are favored by editors. Especially newsworthy are accounts of the exercise of clairvoyance or similar psi phenomena. For years *Coronet* magazine specialized in presumed true stories of such incidents, with no indication they had been investigated to prove their authenticity. Alexander Woollcott, dilenttante actor, lecturer and author, held audiences spellbound with his tales of miraculous occurrences for which he offered no explanations. The following are typical examples of what has received favorable attention from the press in recent years.

Emulating *Coronet*, which specialized in such stories, Henry W. Pierce, in his column in the *Pittsburgh Post Gazette* for Oct. 14, 1971, told of a woman who felt the presence of her daughter's cat at the time the pet died many miles away.

Feb. 13, 1971 the Associated Press reported from Houston that Apollo 14 astronaut Edgar Mitchell during his flight to the moon and back conducted a private ESP experiment with Olof Jonsson of Chicago, a clairvoyant. The next day, Feb. 14, the *Chicago Sun-Times* had an interview with Jonsson by Cecil Neth, in which Jonsson expressed displeasure that news of the supposedly secret test had been leaked. No results of the test were revealed.

May 19, 1971 the Associated Press reported from Little Rock, Ark. who the speakers were to be at the third annual God-Mind-Spirit Workshop sponsored by the ESP Research Associates Foundation, of which Howard Sherman is founder and president. Included were Russell Whitesell, former test pilot for Howard Hughes, who can cause his spirit to leave his body, and Jeane Dixon, astrological prophetess.

There were many protests worldwide when the United States announced it would test new nuclear bombs on uninhabited Amchitka Island. Nov. 6–7, 1971, the UPI reported from Davis, Calif. that a group of University of California students urged people to join a "psychic power protest" just before the explosion to bring about a failure of the project.

Sept. 24, 1972, Roy Larson, *Chicago Sun-Times* religion editor, described the growth of occult book stores and departments, some serving as fronts for religious groups. Clifford M. Royce, Jr., radio and television Mr. Psychic, lectures on ESP at the Chicago Psychic Center in Oak Park, Ill.

Because "thousands of today's earthlings have traveled to the planets via astral projection," Countess Ilelen De Suaghi announced the establishment of a cosmic center where "they can discuss other dimensional phenomena; where they can settle down to some serious research," Jay Carson wrote for the *Toronto Globe and Mail* for Nov. 9, 1972.

"For those deep into psi phenomena—and who isn't these days?—or if you're even just curious," George Gent began his "Going Out Guide" in the *New York Times* for May 8, 1973 to announce the first showing of the motion picture "Psychics, Saints and Scholars" at a local church.

Aug. 29, 1973 the *Chicago Daily News* Beeline advised readers to enroll in psychic Irene Hughes' course in ESP Spiritual Awareness.

Jan. 28 to 30, 1974 *Chicago Today* had articles by James Pearre on "ESP—Fact or Fiction?" Believers and nonbelievers both may receive subconscious ESP input to influence their decision-making, some scientists think. Northeastern Illinois University is the first American college to offer psychology students a bachelor's degree with emphasis on parapsychology.

The extent to which the public has been influenced by the parapsychologists has been measured by several polls. Peter Corner began his story on the *Chicago Tribune's* survey in the issue of Jan. 11, 1977:

It is unlikely, had the *Tribune* surveyed Chicagoans on religious beliefs and practices ten years ago, that any questions about psychic phenomena would have been included.

And it is only recently that the fledgeling issue of parapsychology has come out of the closet.

The headline over his more than a half-page report was "The 'wizards' of another age come out of their closets as parapsychologists." The percentage of believers in various phenomena were: psychokinesis, 5; clairvoyance, 17; mystical/ecstatic, 19; spiritualism 21; precognition, 32; telepathy, 35; déjà vu, 5. Comparable figures reported by a Gallup poll June 15, 1978 were: Loch Ness monster, 10; Bigfoot, 10; witches, 10; ghosts, 11; astrology, 29; déjà vu, 37; devils, 39; ESP, 51; UFOs, 57; angels, 54.

The most important anti-superstition organization is the Committee for the Scientific Investigation of Claims of the Paranormal. Michael Kernan wrote a lengthy article, "The Unexplained-Profitable Nonsense" with a topline, "Scientist Battles Occult's Magnetism," for the *Denver Post* of June 18, 1978, in which the committee objectives and policies get considerable mention; he also debunked "parlor magic, wildly promoted 'mentalists' and 'psychics' [who] perform tricks that a few decades ago were standard vaudeville turns." The article also considered the Easter Island monoliths, Erich von Däniken's ideas about ancient astronauts, and other matters.

Even more iconoclastic was the article "Phooey on Psychic Phonies" by Dennis Breo in the *Chicago Tribune Magazine* for Aug. 20, 1978. It was about Thomas Gray Sexton who teaches courses in "Miracle Workers Unmasked" at Indianapolis Free University. A professional magician, Sexton exposes how some tricksters who claim to have supernatural powers perform their illusions. He believes human credulity is higher today than at any other time in history.

The annual predictions of several of the best-known psychics were satirized and exposed by Tony Kornheiser in the *Washington Post* for Jan. 1, 1981. A new course, "Pseudoscience: Crackpots, Cults and Con-Men" was announced in *On Campus,* a University of Texas weekly, for Dec. 7–13, 1981. Instructor was Dr. Rory Coker, the subject of an article by Kerry Gunnels in the *Austin American-Statesman* for Dec. 8, 1981. His only reservation about offering the course, Coker said, is, "If you discuss it you give it validity. You should just ignore it. The only problem is that it doesn't work."

The UPI distributed a picture Feb. 2, 1974 of a mother and the two young daughters who were restored to her after two years when she consulted a psychic who provided the license number of a pickup truck owned by the children's father who had kidnapped them in New York state and taken them to North Carolina.

March 3, 1974 the *Chicago Tribune* gave a half page to Georgia Sauer's writeup of Peter Jewett and the Inner Peace Movement, which operates on the belief that everyone has a sixth sense that needs development. It teaches that everyone has an aura about him, an energy field that shows itself in different colors. Jewett also teaches levitation and telepathy.

April 24, 1974 Nancy Roberts described biologist Lyall Watson's belief that mental telepathy is better when subjects are meditating, thus increasing the oxygen in the brain. The story appeared in the *Chicago Sun-Times*.

July 15, 1974 the *Chicago Daily News'* Beeline suggested that the notorious erasures on a Nixon tape could have resulted from the tape's editor not understanding the meaning of psychokinesis.

To advertise their abilities 34 New York and London psychics and clairvoyants chartered a Staten Island ferry and performed for $10 per onlooker. Proceeds went to the Hampton Animal Shelter, the *New York Post* reported July 17, 1974.

Beula Brown, an ordained minister in Spiritual Science is executive director of "Happy Days," which opened at the Lincoln Art Theater, to be dubbed by some critics as a porn "American Graffiti." Brown claims to have predicted the murders of both John and Robert Kennedy, *Variety* reported July 31, 1974.

Peter Jewett reached Dallas on his nationwide tour for the Inner Peace Movement in time for Nancy Jones to interview him for the *Daily Morning News* for Jan. 12, 1975. Jones summarized Jewett's views: "What the soul is to the theologian and the electromagnet field is to the scientist, the aura is to Jewett, who insists that it not only exists but can be photographed." Auras are energy fields that surround all living things. In her July 6, 1980 piece in the *Sun-Times* Barbara Varro wrote up Ruth Berger, whose specialty is aura reading at her New Era Psychic Center in Glenview, Ill.

Jan. 26, 1975 the *New York Times* magazine had a lengthy piece, "Are we a nation of mystics?" by the Rev. Andrew Greeley and William C. McCready, both associated with the Center for the Study of American Pluralism at the National Opinion Center of the University of Chicago. Four out of ten Americans in a survey reported experiencing a "powerful spiritual force which seemed to lift them out of themselves."

The First International Psychic Film Festival over, plans were begun for next year, *Variety* reported Oct. 29, 1975. Among the judges for the festival were famous anthropologist Margaret Mead and astronaut Edgar Mitchell.

"I've found the terms for aura, ESP, astral projection and psychic healing in the Bible," Rabbi Alvin Jacob Bohroff told *Village Voice* for Nov. 17, 1975. "These terms," he elaborated, "have always deliberately been misinterpreted and mistranslated because Judaism wanted to destroy the power of the occult. The funny thing was that most of the great prophets were psychics and magicians. When Elisha 'saw with his heart' he was having an out-of-body experience. When Moses saw the burning bush it was probably an aura."

Dec. 17 & 18, 1975 in the *Chicago Sun-Times Suburban Week* Barbara

Hill wrote an interview with John Bisaha, a Mundelein College assistant professor of psychology who claims to be able to take Kirlian photographs of colorful bursts of light emitted by living objects when they are placed in a field of high frequency electrical currents.

Don Ethan Miller wrote a full-page article, "Can Kirlian Photography Start a Revolution in Biology?" for the Jan. 5, 1976 *Village Voice*. An important extract was as follows:

> A healthy leaf . . . placed in the Kirlian apparatus and photographed immediately, showed a stunning pattern of halos and flares. Several days later the same leaf showed a diminished pattern of radiation; and finally, after further passages of time, the leaf would produce no image whatsoever.

The article was illustrated with a picture of a leaf. The caption was: "A leaf from which a small portion has been cut shows up whole in Kirlian photography. This suggests a non-material organization of living organism." The cutline was: "Is this halo the leaf's 'etheric body'?"

Other Kirlian photographs were displayed at a Conference About Energies and Consciousness at a New York Baptist Church, Tom Buckley reported for the *New York Times* June 2, 1976. Exhibitor and lecturer was Dr. Lyman Fretwell, holder of a doctorate from the California Institute of Technology. According to Buckley some of his pictures looked like closeups of Lifesavers, X-rays of a row of defective molars or an overexposed photograph of a snowdrift.

There was hardly an issue during a two- or three-year period that the *Chicago Sun-Times* Suburban News did not have some article related to the supernatural. In one, in the issue of Feb. 4 & 5, 1976, Ken Swoyer, Jr. told that he participated in a Bisaha experiment that failed. It was one in precognition; the professor was unable to say where he was.

Announcement of a forthcoming Students for Esoteric Thought conference entitled New Age Festival '76 was made by Howard Smith and Brian Van Der Horst in the *Village Voice* for July 12, 1976. Among the "bona fide heavies" to attend were Swami Satenidananda, researcher Dr. Stanley Krippner, Kirlian photographer Prof. Douglas Dean, author Charles Berlitz and psychic Uri Geller. Sept. 15 & 16, 1976 Neil Goldstein related his experience as the subject of a parapsychological experiment conducted at the Illinois Center for Psychological Research in Park Ridge, Ill. He was correct 8 times out of 25 chances, supposedly above average but hardly conclusive evidence.

Bisaha of Mundelein College was the subject of a full-page feature in the *Evanston* (Ill.) *Review* for Sept. 25, 1980. Marilyn R. Abbey, the author, wrote, "Psi is fuzzily defined as the process of perceiving the environment in a way seemingly independent of the five senses." Nevertheless, Bisaha and others she mentioned say they can observe it, quantify it and repeat experiments with similar results.

Eveything from ESP and biofeedback to split-brain research and rein-carnation was to be discussed at a conference at Governors State Univer-sity, Park Forest, Ill. featuring Chris Velissaris, executive director of the Illinois Center for Psychological Research, the *Chicago Sun-Times* re-ported April 14, 1977.

June 29, 1977 Michelle Stevens wrote an article for the *Chicago Daily News* about Joe East, who in 1966 founded the Group Foundation for Psychical Research. He received the first annual award of the Illinois Society for Psychic Research.

The First International Congress of Paranormal Phenomena was to begin in Acapulco, the *New York Times* reported Nov. 13, 1977. It was to deal with the mysteries of hypnosis, magic rites and religions, cosmic medicine, telekinesis, poltergeist and "things that go bump in the night."

May 26, 1978 Rick Kogan gave a thumbnail description of the Inner Peace Movement for the *Chicago Sun-Times*. IPM was founded in 1964 by Francisco Coli and has instructed 400,000 persons worldwide. Kogan quoted Nancy Seyburt, a leader: "Everything is inside us. We are all beautiful people. The only problem is that most people don't know who they really are."

The Amazing Kreskin unsuccessfully challenged two of the world's top chess players, playing both while blindfolded, and lost. "It was the tough-feat I've ever attempted," he said according to the *New York Post* for March 21, 1979.

Sept. 28, 1980 the *Chicago Tribune* ran a story by Carol Oppenheim from Atlantic City, N.J. of the reunion of triplets separated at birth to be adopted by three different sets of parents. At 19 they not only looked alike but had similar mannerisms, tastes, habits and ideas. They told of ex-periencing similar physical discomforts before they knew of the existence of the others.

Tony Schwartz wrote a story for the *New York Times* for March 13, 1981 about Beverly Dean, who was employed for two years by Fred Pierce, president of the American Broadcasting Company, to advise regarding scripts and programs the network was considering. Two days later, March 15, 1981, the *Chicago Tribune* ran a lengthy article about the contract written by Deborah Caulfield, for the New York Times Feature Service. It was revealed in the longer article that Dean's contract was kept secret and she was forbidden to make known her relationship with ABC. Dean also was quoted as explaining how she started studying the occult after a stranger told her in the London Heathrow Airport that she would become a world-famous psychic.

June 20, 1981 the Knight-Ridder News Service distributed a story by Gary Swan from San Jose, Calif. about Mary Palmero and her Association of Psychic Practitioners. Psychic certification may require 2,400 hours of training and two years of experience, Palmero said. Certificates of ordina-tion from mail-order religions are discouraged.

Aug. 6, 1981 the *Tacoma Facts* gave a full page to a feature about Mrs. Evon, the only licensed extrasensory perception reader in Seattle. A fifth generation reader she tells a person's past, present and future by studying the shape of the face, especially the eyes.

April 4, 1981 Dean Meg in the *New York Post* thanked a reader for congratulating her on a column sympathetic to premonitions. Meg wrote, "I do recognize the existence of extrasensory perception which is strong enough in some people that they are often maligned for their gift."

Liza Minnelli did not marry Peter Sellers, to whom she was engaged for three weeks, because Frederick Davies, a London clairvoyant, advised against it, according to Walter Scott's column in *Parade* for Dec. 13, 1981.

The *Madison* (Wis.) *Capital Times* devoted a half-page Feb. 8, 1983 to the hit scored by Alleen Cummingham, dubbed "the psychic Ann Landers," who spent a day on a talk show giving advice to hundreds who called. Author of the article, Debra Carr, wrote that Cunningham says she can judge personality by a person's voice and in 10 years has advised 65,000.

A full-page feature by Tracey Harden in the *New York Daily News* for Feb. 13, 1983 related the successes of Beatrice Lydecker, who treats the emotional problems of animals with whom she says she communicates by ESP.

By means of a power he calls telekinesis, David Gurrdino "makes things happen," according to a long profile by Mark Schwed that UPI distributed March 13, 1983 from Nashville. Gurrdino often uses his psychokinetic energy to "put the whammy" on someone blocking a client's ambitions.

March 17, 1983 the Associated Press reported from London that the author Arthur Koestler, a recent suicide, left $600,000 to promote the university study of psychic phenomena.

Newspapers seldom publish stories about specific psi experiences. Whereas they assign reporters to investigate haunted houses, sea or land monsters and visions of the Virgin Mary, they are unimpressed by callers who say they were emotionally upset at the exact hour that a friend or relative was injured or died hundreds of miles away.

The closest the press comes to such coverage is to state, as the *Chicago Daily News'* Beeline did July 2, 1974, that a psychic friend of Thomas Gatch "saw" him alive on an Atlantic island after the balloonist was believed lost on his flight across the ocean. Gossip columns also often satisfy a reader's curiosity about some celebrity as the *News'* "Just Ask" column did July 29, 1972 regarding entertainer Karen Black who insisted, "I can go a whole day and know who's going to call me or who'll answer the phone when I make a call. I also see other people's memory pictures— photos in my mind of what a person is thinking." She said Joan Blondell had similar power.

The exception to the policy of avoiding news of parapsychological demonstrations is when foul play or crime is involved. Then psychics often assist others in recovering lost or stolen articles and help police search for lawbreakers. This practice has been a development of the past few decades only. A *Chicago Tribune* copyrighted story by Sigrid Schultz in Berlin Oct. 16, 1925 indicated how the evolution occurred. Because of protests from townspeople the trial of a schoolteacher and a medium in the small town of Bernburg on charges of occultism was delayed two years. Witnesses for the defense testified that the two helped them recover stolen geese, sheep, linen and jewelry by going into trances.

In the Ozarks Jean Wallace, known as the Mystery Woman, was able to advise neighbors and the sheriff where to search for missing objects. She insisted that she was not a fortune teller and could not predict the future, according to a half-page article from Roaring River, Mo. by A. B. Mac-Donald in the *Milwaukee Journal* for July 9, 1936.

As late as 1948 some clairvoyants were still calling themselves fortune tellers even though they hardly ever prophesied except as to where a lost article or person would be found. April 28, 1948 the Associated Press reported from LaSalle, Ill. that the body of a 19-year-old who had drowned in the Illinois River was found just where three seers, consulted separately, had told his mother it would be.

Other accounts of successes and failures have included the following:

The Associated Press reported Aug. 5, 1975 from Spencer, N.Y. that a small boy missing overnight in a heavily wooded area was found alive by a young man claiming to possess psychic powers. He said he knew he was on the right track after touching the 5-year-old's sneakers.

A member of the Church of the New Jerusalem was not so lucky when he tried to find the bronze bust of the founder of his sect, the 18th-century philosopher and mystic Emanuel Swedenborg, which was stolen from Chicago's Lincoln Park. Robert Flaherty reported for the *Chicago Sun-Times* of Feb. 10, 1976 that the police, in lieu of ESP, were going to distribute a picture of the statue.

Using an artist's drawing of what a psychic said the murderer of three looked like, police of South Gate, Calif. arrested an acquaintance of one of the victims. The incident caused some police officials to attempt to determine what value to them there might be in parapsychology. In a column-long article on the subject Nov. 26, 1978 the *New York Times* cited the skepticism of Dr. Martin Reiser, director of the behavioral science laboratory of the Los Angeles police department, and his plans to conduct a scientific study of the problem. March 9, 1980 the *Times* reported that two groups of psychics did no better than two other groups, one of police and the other of college students. No one, Dr. Reiser reported, gave any information of value in criminal hunting. Most reports, he said, seemed to be mere guesswork, but the psychics were much more positive in their beliefs.

Nevertheless, in nearby San Andrea, Calif. a psychic's tape-recorded visions were used to find the body of an elderly man missing for five months, Bill Denscore reported for the AP Feb. 4, 1979.

An unnamed Dutch psychic helped Equity Service Corporation select sites to drill oil wells but the Securities and Exchange Commission stated in a civil suit filed in Philadelphia that investors in the company were not so informed, the *Wall Street Journal* reported April 28, 1977.

Some residents of the section of Brooklyn nearest New York Harbor said they had a premonition that the psychopath dubbed Son of Sam would invade their territory on the anniversary of his first murders. They turned out to be right, while police guarded other areas where previous killings had occurred. Richard Goldstein wrote a story for the UPI about it July 31, 1977.

M. Kathlyn Rhea, who says she tunes in her mind "like a television set," received plenty of attention from the press when she told police where to find the bodies of an 8-year-old girl who had been raped and murdered and a 78-year-old man who had a heart attack or stroke in solitude. Joan Sweeney broke the story from Fresno in the *Los Angeles Times* for Feb. 7, 1979. The parents of the slain child gave Rhea credit but the police chief said finding the girl's dog nearby had been the principal factor. Feb. 11 the reporter interviewed the psychic in her home in Cupertino, where the seer elaborated on the instructions she gave the police and discussed her own psychic powers. "I actually see things as they happen," she said. "What I do is go to where that person was, what they were experiencing and describe the scenery related to the stimuli of what happened and that triggers my conscious mind into giving me picture and thought forms." .

The same day the *Times'* human behavior writer, Lois Timnick, defined and described psi and PK and reviewed the research that has been done by Dr. J. B. Rhine and others. She also reported the skepticism of a number of scholars. Feb. 18 the AP distributed a picture of Ms. Rhea who said she expects to help find the child's murderer.

March 27, 1979 the UPI reported from Cupertino that a search party of 50 volunteers failed to find the body of a chauffeur missing 20 months. Ms. Rhea had a vision of a blood-splattered workshirt. Such a shirt was found but no body. Nevertheless, John C. Eaton reported July 8, 1980 from Cupertino for the AP that Ms. Rhea receives from one to six calls for help from police every week. She regrets always being called in as a last resort. To improve the public's opinion of psychics she believes they should be licensed by the state as are doctors.

Hindsight often is better for psychics as it is for everybody else. This becomes evident after some cataclysmic news occurrences. Editors as well as police and other public officials receive calls from psychics claiming to have known what was to happen. After the worst airport disaster in American history, at Chicago's O'Hare field, one woman called to say she knew why it occurred: a mechanic was in the engine.

Detectives said it was coincidence that the rope-bound body of John Sugar was found exactly where an unnamed Philadelphia psychic said it would be. Fred Kerber and Michael Daly reported for the *New York Daily News* of Aug. 30, 1979.

One of 16 psychics she consulted after police had hunted in vain for two months told Ms. Katherine Scott that her daughter, Madonna Hernandez, was dead in a wooded spot near water. Just before she discovered her daughter's decomposed body the mother heard her daughter scream "Mama, mama," Robert Weddle reported July 22, 1980 for the *New York Post*.

Another psychic, Bobby Drinnon of Morristown, Tenn., wasn't so lucky when he failed, as did police and about 100 volunteers in Knoxville, Tenn. After scouring the countryside for miles around there was no trace of 6-year-old Avery (Peaches) Shorts, who disappeared after buying a bottle of soda pop at a store near her home in an integrated housing project. So the search was discontinued.

Another time the psychics joined police in failure was after 6-year-old Etan Patz disappeared on the way to catch a school bus in New York's Soho district. May 30, 1979 the *New York Post* ran a story and a 4-column cut of psychic Robert Petro in a trance, which caused him to say the boy was with a woman who speaks with a Spanish or Cuban accent.

Oct. 9, 1979 on Etan's seventh birthday the *Post* had a 2-line streamer headline to report that Doris Stokes, who allegedly helped Los Angeles police solve a baffling case, had arrived with the revelation that the boy was abducted a few blocks from home, which everyone already knew. Mrs. Stokes, shown in a photograph with the boy's mother, conjectured that the abductor might be seeking to hurt the parents.

Publication in 1982 of the novel *Still Missing* revived memories of Etan Patz. The author is Beth Gutcheon, a neighbor, who says her book is not a fictionalized version of the Patz case, even though the abducted child in the novel is six years old and there is a sympathetic detective, as was true in the search for Etan. The novel has a happy ending, which unfortunately the real-life drama has not yet had. Glenn Collins wrote nearly a full-page review of the novel, and of a forthcoming motion picture based on it, in the *Chicago Tribune* for Aug. 5, 1982.

The New York Civil Air Patrol obtained the aid of a woman psychic, who preferred to remain anonymous, to search for a TV reporter and a restaurateur missing for more than a week on a flight to Fall River, Mass., Cynthia R. Fagen reported July 19, 1982 for the *New York Post*. The psychic described the accident scene but didn't tell where it was. A posse of 100 could not find it.

Only a few psychics who play the role of prophet, advisor or human bloodhound receive much attention in the press outside their home territory. A few of the lesser ones were the following:

Mrs. Richard Broman, subject of a feature interview by Genie Campbell in the *Arlington Heights* (Ill.) *Herald* for July 20, 1970. She regards herself as merely a channel for God, "the true source of all psychic phenomena."

She explains, "The only thing that makes me different is that I hear the beat of a different drummer." She is able to give readings, dehaunt houses, contact spirits and see auras. She believes in reincarnation, is a follower of Edgar Cayce and can interpret dreams.

Mrs. Beverly C. (Bevy) Jaegers of St. Louis, about whom Edward J. Presberg wrote a feature for the Newhouse News Service that the *Kansas City Star* used Aug. 16, 1976. She attracted attention when she tried to stop the *St. Louis Globe Democrat* from using an Associated Press story that the body of a missing travel agent, Mrs. Sandra Fronczak, had been found in a lagoon south of Acapulco. A few hours later the AP sent a correction; it was not Mrs. Fronczak's body. Her children raised, Mrs. Jaegers makes a business of her psychic operations. She is a private investigator, business consultant, investor, book author, magazine article writer and teacher, all lucrative activities.

Karen Getsla, who, according to Larry S. Finley's article in the *Chicago Daily News* for Sept. 11, 1977, has discovered unknown passages in the Sphinx in Egypt and rediscovered a lost city in Honduras. He interviewed her at a two-week conference on parapsychology at Mundelein College, where panels considered ESP, out-of-body experiences, meditation and psychokinesis.

Greta Alexander's success record was examined by Harry Eagar for the *Des Moines Register* for Sept. 3, 1981 after police indicated they might consult her about a year-old unsolved murder. It was a devastating account of failure. Several law enforcement officers were quoted as saying that Alexander's predictions, even if the vague language she used to make them proved correct, were nevertheless of little or no value in solving murder cases.

The first clairvoyant activist and still perhaps the most famous is a Dutchman, Peter Hurkos (real name, Peter van der Hurk), who came to the United States from Holland in the early '50s and was tested by Dr. Henry K. Puharich, director of the Round Table Foundation in Glen Cove, Me. Hurkos' phenomenal success in matching pictures while blindfolded indicated why he was called "the man with the radio brain" in Europe. One of the first eulogistic articles about him in the United States was written by Sid Ross for the Oct. 7, 1956 *Parade*. The article stated that Hurkos had assisted European police in solving several crimes, including the theft of the Stone of Scone from Westminster Abbey. Although the article did not say so, Scotland Yard is known to have denied vehemently that the Dutch psychic was of any help in the case. Ross described Hurkos' supposed power thus: "Hurkos can pick up an object belonging to an unknown person, finger it for a few minutes and rattle off detailed—and often accurate—facts about the owner." It should be noted that neither Hurkos nor other clairvoyants are astrologers although there are some parapsychologists who claim to be both.

Hurkos says he acquired the ability to receive brain waves from others in 1943 when he was 32 years old and hospitalized in a coma for three days after falling from a scaffolding while plying his trade as a house painter. He claims to be 80 percent successful in his predictions of where objects, including corpses, can be found.

A leading journalistic fan of Hurkos has been Nancy Lee Browning of the *Chicago Tribune*, who actually wrote a biography of him, *The Psychic World of Peter Hurkos*. In August 1970 *Chicago Today* ran a six-part series taken from the book. Browning made Hurkos the feature of a 2-column story, "Psychic Boom Rolls on From Tearoom to Campus," in the *Tribune* for March 15, 1964. She reported that he made "splashy headlines" with his psychometric manhunt of the Boston Strangler but failed to mention that the Boston police resented Hurkos' interference; they arrested a suspect not named by the Dutchman who asserts the wrong man was convicted of strangling 11 elderly women.

Browning did not mention that Hurkos was arrested in New York for extradition to Milwaukee where a federal grand jury indicted him for impersonating an FBI agent. Browning also reported Aug. 19, 1969 that Hurkos was working on the Sharon Tate murder case "and what he came up with you wouldn't believe!" Neither did the police whom Hurkos told the Manson Family crimes were committed by three men whom he named and described.

More details of Hurkos' part in the Tate case, in which he became involved through a lawyer, not the police, were included in an Ivar Davis story in the *San Francisco Examiner* for Aug. 29, 1969. The police told Davis, "If we resorted to calling him in officially we would probably be the laughing stock of the entire world."

Undaunted, the press has continued to run the risk of ridicule by giving Hurkos plenty of free publicity. Sept. 24, 1970 *Chicago Today* quoted the Dutchman, now living in Studio City, Calif., as regretting that Illinois Sen. Charles Percy had not asked him to solve the fatal stabbing of his daughter Valerie Sept. 16, 1966. During his interview with reporter Frank Von Ark, Hurkos predicted that the Vietnam war would go on "for a long time," said President Nixon would not incur danger, that the American people would come to realize demonstrations by college students were inspired by Communists and Black Panthers.

To her chagrin Browning had to report Feb. 20, 1974 that Hurkos' prediction that his first child would be a boy was wrong, but she quoted him as saying, "What I saw was a boy but what I really wanted was a girl."

"Psychic Hurkos' Tormented Mind" by Colin Dangaard in the *Chicago Daily News* for May 24, 1974 related Hurkos' success in picking a spot on a map only six miles away from where a private plane crashed near Mount

Laguna, Calif. During the preceding five years, the article stated, Hurkos located 32 missing light aircraft on the West Coast, often without leaving his living room in Los Angeles. His fees ranged from $2,000 to $5,000 per plane.

When five murders remained unsolved after three years, Dr. E. Regis Riesenman of St. Elizabeth's Hospital hired Hurkos to come to Washington. Beginning June 12, 1960 the *Washington Star* had several articles on his activities. Within five days a suspect was in a mental hospital and Dr. Riesenman thought the cases solved although police had insufficient evidence to file charges. Hurkos had visited the lovers' lane where Mrs. Margaret V. Hall was found shot to death June 23, 1957 and the sites where the bodies of Mr. and Mrs. Carroll Jackson of Apple Grove, Va. were found a year and a half after they disappeared Jan. 11, 1959. Hurkos said he received brain waves and visualized the same person as responsible for the killings.

May 16, 1975 the UPI reported from West Salem, Wis. that Hurkos had said the missing Patty Hearst was in Wisconsin and would be taken without a shootout. When that fact became public, the FBI reported, it was deluged with calls from persons who said they had seen the missing heiress.

In its issue on Feb. 19, 1961, *This Week,* always ready to accept a manuscript about the occult, had an article, "Holland's Incredible Mind Readers," by Jack Harrison Pollack. The principal subject of the eulogy was Dr. W. H. C. Tenhaeff who, although not a psychic himself, occupied the world's only chair of parapsychology at the University of Utrecht. His most important paragnot (his name for clairvoyants) was Gerard Croiset who could help find missing objects and persons by telephone clues only. He received worldwide attention when he designated a house in Yonkers, N.Y. where, he said, New York Supreme Court Judge Joseph Force Crater had been murdered 25 years earlier. News magazines gave the story more attention than did newspapers. *Harper's* had an article by Murray Teigh Bloom November 1959 and *Life* followed with one Nov. 16, 1959. Judge Crater, a Tammany politician who may have had gang connections, vanished Aug. 6, 1930.

After all other efforts failed Mrs. Elizabeth Lagerstedt consulted three psychics in a search for her father who had been a German soldier in World War II a quarter-century earlier. All three said her father was alive although ill, but they could not say where. Paul Malloy wrote a fascinating story of Mrs. Lagerstedt's wartime experiences for the *Chicago Sun-Times* April 17, 1971.

Sometimes a journalist goes out on a figurative limb to his regret. That happened to Bob Herguth, gossip columnist for the *Chicago Daily News.* He gave a Gary, Ind. clairvoyant, Anne Rose, publicity June 3, 1971 when she said she was going to find $98,000 worth of buried gold, loot from Indiana's last great train robbery June 7, 1868. June 8, 1971 another reporter, Robert W. Billings, sadly related that the tin box exhumed from the Hobart, Ind. city dump, contained only a few tintypes, a pen knife, a small canvas money bag and $20.30 in Confederate money.

A touching account of how a bereaved mother sought a solution to the murder of her daugher was related by Margo in her Oct. 5, 1972 column in the *Chicago Daily News*. The mother was Essee Kupcinet, wife of columnist Irv. Their daughter Karyn was murdered in her Los Angeles apartment nine years earlier. In desperation, after the police admitted to being stalemated, she consulted more than 20 psychics, including Hurkos, Croiset and Arthur Ford. After they all failed to provide clues leading to detection of the murderer Mrs. Kupcinet turned to spiritualists in the attempt to communicate with her dead daughter.

When Mrs. Letitia Shindo of Scottsdale, Ariz. had a premonition that Jim Grundy, a fellow member of Astara, an organization of ESP enthusiasts, was in trouble, she summoned her son and his friend and drove to Grundy's isolated cabin. There they found him being held hostage by two murderers who had just escaped from the Arizona State Prison in Florence. She soft-talked the convicts into taking all four of them as hostages rather than just him. They drove to Tempe where the escapees said they had friends and parted company amiably. Jerry Cohen wrote the story Nov. 24, 1972 for the *Los Angeles Times*.

When three boys, aged 11, 12 and 14, disappeared while presumably attending a movie Oct. 16, 1955, to be found strangled to death two days later, a Chicago postal employee who believed in ESP wrote Croiset giving as many details of the crime as he could. Promptly Croiset answered describing a house northwest of Chicago, with sides patched with corrugated tin, with a tree that had been struck by lightning nearby. It was one of about 4,000 letters on the case to which the police paid attention. No house or location to fit Croiset's description could be found, however, and police gave the letter no publicity at the time. In fact, it first became known when the *Chicago Tribune* ran a story by James Long Oct. 24, 1961 in which a police officer was quoted as saying. "This doesn't mean there isn't any such place. We just may not have found it or it could have been torn down."

Nancy Lee Browning wrote a feature on Croiset for the *Chicago Tribune* of March 22, 1964. When Croiset died the AP reported July 22, 1980 from Utrecht that he had assisted Dutch police on many cases of missing persons and murders and was credited by Japanese police with having found a murder victim.

According to Jack Harrison Pollack in *Parade* for Aug. 26, 1964, the psychic who had helped the most people in America was Florence Sternfels of Edgewater, N.J. Pollack digested several homicide cases in which law enforcement authorities gave her credit for help. One anecdote pertained to a prominent gangster, Dutch Schultz, who ignored her advice to stay out of Newark. He went there and was shot to death.

Few predictions by a psychic, no matter how wild, are ignored by the press. If the city desk doesn't assign a reporter, a columnist is likely to have a scoop. Such was the luck of Earl Wilson, whose syndicated Broadway column, "On the Light Side," was published in the *Salt Lake Tribune* for Aug. 21, 1969. The news was that Broadway's "white witch," Cindi Bulak, went into a trance and decided from her vibrations that Sharon Tate was murdered by the 13th member of a coven of Hollywood "black witches."

Usually the press can be trusted to make news even when there isn't any in this field. Such was the case when the UPI reported on an interview with Mrs. Grace Porter of Lubbock, Tex., whose son, Karl Schneider, was reported shot by some airplane hijackers in Thailand where he was working March 29, 1981 for an American oil-drilling team. Mrs. Porter said she had a premonition that her son was in trouble hours before she learned of it officially. Then she said, "The good lord has taken care of him before. Now I've put it in God's hands where it belongs."

Another spooky UPI story told of the chagrin police of North Yarmouth, Me. experienced when the skeleton of an 11-year-old girl missing ten years was found in a barn. The locale corresponded to sketches that they had received at the time from an old man who lived in a trailer camp with four cats. The old man died in 1973 but the police kept his sketches to which they had paid little or no attention at the time.

Movie critic Carol Kramer awarded first prize for "the most questionable publicity campaigns so far this year" to Paramount Pictures for the film, "Man on a Swing," the story of a clairvoyant's role in solving a murder. Since the viewer is led to suspect that perhaps the investigator is the murderer, for her review in the *Chicago Tribune* for March 10, 1974 Kramer asked the real-life clairvoyant on whose experiences the picture was based whether the implication disturbed him. It didn't.

Nationwide attention was directed to Lake Park, Ia. Sept. 6 and 7, 1981 when use of a psychic's map led 4,000 rescuers to where a 2½-year-old boy was huddling in a cold cornfield. The posse had stopped at a fence that they thought the child would be unable to surmount; the psychic's map directed the hunt beyond the fence and the rescue occurred just after the father had told the rescue party, "Justin will no longer be with us." After the rescue the parents insisted that a miracle had occurred; it was a "miracle of God" working through a Christian psychic.

After police and Civil Air Patrol officials had sought Chester William Martin, Jr. for a week after he disappeared, his family consulted a psychic and offered a $5,000 reward for anyone who solved the disappearance of the former president of the Pepsi Cola Bottling Company of Washington. The *Washington Post* reported the situation Aug. 26, 1982.

Five months after she disappeared May 15 the body of 23-year-old Lorraine Borowski was found in a Clarendon Hills cemetery, Thomas Powers and Don Meinhert reported for the *Chicago Sun-Times* Oct. 10,

1982. "The dead woman's body would be found within 18 miles in a shack in a cemetery."

When a psychic in Bremerton, Wash. had a dream in which a busload of schoolchildren was struck by a train with considerable loss of life, she phoned the Wyoming Highway Patrol. She described the railroad crossing, presumably in the Casper area. Believing there was such a spot in their town, Mills, Wyo. police were especially alert. According to a UPI story Sept. 20, 1981 from Cheyenne, all law enforcement officers in the state were put on alert. The *Bremerton News* reported that in her vision the psychic, whose name was withheld, saw a little girl reading a newspaper dated Nov. 11, when there supposedly would be a blizzard. When the fatal date came and went the *Casper Journal* reviewed the incident and said it had directed attention to a dangerous crossing in Mills, of which the paper printed a picture. Dec. 8, 1981 the *Laramie Daily Boomerang* used a UPI story from Cheyenne that insisted the deaths of two teenaged Kemmerer, Wyo. girls in a railroad crossing accident in Utah were not related to the accident envisioned by the Washington psychic in September. She had said small children, not teenagers, would be killed during a blinding blizzard. Not the weather but faulty brakes caused the real accident.

Although police still are reluctant to admit it and some still condemn it, psychic assistance is utilized by a majority of them. At least such is the case in Cook County, Ill., according to Mark Fineman, who wrote a comprehensive article on the subject for the *Suburban Sun-Times* of Oct. 6–7, 1976. One of the rewards of discovering or developing psychic power is the opportunity it gives to assist law enforcement agencies in solving crimes, especially murder. And there's nothing that succeeds like success and it is not uncommon for the press to give psychics credit for their contributions. Using the size of press clipping books as a criterion it is difficult to challenge the claim of Mrs. Dorothy Allison of Nutley, N.J. to being No. 1. Since her first case in 1968 through 1979 she claims to have helped find 26 bodies of murder victims.

The first case that brought Allison into the journalistic limelight was when she dreamed of a child in a green snowsuit, his shoes on the wrong feet, lying drowned by a drainpipe. She called the police and they found what she had reported. April 3, 1977 the Associated Press reported from Waynesboro, Pa. that the police followed Allison's directions and found the body of 18-year-old Deborah Sue Kline in a trash dump. Nevertheless, the local police said she provided only psychological help. The same article revealed that Allison had been asked by William Randolph Hearst to assist in finding his kidnapped daughter, Patty. The psychic told the Pennsylvania police that Patty was in their state months before her hideout was discovered in Scranton.

When the body of Susan Jacobson was found in a 55-gallon oil drum at the bottom of a 12-foot shaft in a Staten Island shipyard, the Associated

Press recalled March 29, 1978 that two years earlier Allison had predicted she would be found in a marshy area in sight of two bridges. There even were the letters M A R on a rock nearby as the psychic had said there would be. March 18, 1979 the *New York Daily News'* reporter Brian Kates wrote that she had the name and description of the man who murdered Yoran Hashmonal, a cabby and former Israeli Army tank driver. His mother came to America and sought out Allison, whom she had read about in a Jerusalem newspaper. Before the body was retrieved from a marina, Allison had predicted its whereabouts.

In an advisory to editors March 23, 1979 the AP cited the disappearance of skepticism on the part of police, a characteristic attitude now being "When you know you haven't any good leads and you want something, you try anything and everything." There followed a lengthy trend piece by Dolores Barclay datelined Nutley, N.J., mostly a profile of Allison at home. Recalled were both the Jacobson and Kline cases. Also her failure to find the body of 18-year-old Robert Piest despite many 16-hour days in which she covered 1,000 miles. The body never was found but after 29 bodies, not all identifiable, were found in his home, John Gacy was charged with Piest's murder too by Des Plaines, Ill. police.

In her profile, "Dorothy Allison's Special Gift" in the *New York Daily News* for July 5–6, 1979, Constance Rosenblum recalled Allison's correct directions that led police to the grave of Ronald Stica of Lodi, N.J. and mentioned her work on the Etan Patz case. Allison entertains policemen in her kitchen, where they discuss cases. Her billfold bulges with pictures of "her babies," whom she has known only in death. Of her world she says, "I never said I was God. All I say is that I try and I have had some success. I don't know what makes me psychic. All I know is that I find bodies."

On Allison's advice divers were to search a small waterfall in an attempt to find the body of Ruth Dorsey, missing for five years. The New Jersey psychic said the child would be found under running water near a cemetery and a restaurant, the AP reported July 15, 1979 from Opeluka, Ala.

Allison entered the case of 10-year-old Lorraine Pacifico of Oakwood, James Duddy reported for the *New York Daily News* July 1, 1980. She began by asking the names and birthdates of all the family.

Allison told the family of Bruce Lindsey that his body would be found near a deadend road and a body of water. Although an informer's tip led to the finding of the body in a wildlife area near St. Charles, Mo., her information was correct, Kieran Crowley reported Oct. 30, 1980 for the *New York Post.*

Even when the police follow the advice of a psychic a crime may remain unsolved. That was the case when skillful burglars got nearly a million dollars worth of gold and jewelry from a Chicago jewelry company. Allison gave detailed descriptions of two burglars and of the offices of the company sustaining the loss. Nevertheless, in a followup feature a year later, Aug. 23, 1981, the *Chicago Sun-Times* reported the crime remained unsolved.

Shortly before she entered the case of the murdered black children in Atlanta, she told the Associated Press Sept. 14, 1980, "I can understand why people doubt psychics. There are a lot of frauds around. But no one can call me a fraud when I've been working 18 hours a day for the past 12 years for the police. I don't go to them. They come to me."

Allison said in that time she solved 13 murders and found more than 50 missing children. She said she became aware of her power at age 14 when she had a vision of her father's death. Her sister has the same power but is afraid to use it.

Between July 1979 and June 1981 in Atlanta 28 black children and young adults disappeared. Ultimately the skeleton remains of all but a few were found and identified. The newspaper coverage accelerated as each new crime was committed. Crime experts, including the FBI and at least three psychics became involved in the search for victims and killers. Foremost was Dorothy Allison who was invited by the police and paid her own expenses for a week in late October 1980 in the city. Promptly upon her arrival she told a news conference, "I can guarantee he won't murder while I'm here. I will control him. I have seen who he is. I see where he is. I follow him." She refused to reveal names to reporters but described the killer as a black male from the metropolitan Atlanta area. At least one of the victims knew his murderer, she said. And she promised to stay in Atlanta until the crimes were solved.

But she didn't. Within a week she was back in New Jersey. As would be expected the wire services and newspapers grabbed for every small detail to provide fresh angles and new leads almost daily. Oct. 22 the *Chicago Tribune's* Charles Madigan wrote about "Atlanta—a city of fear." He told of the avidity of terrified people to believe any accident was linked to the murders and that there was a conspiracy, possibly involving the Ku Klux Klan. Opinion was divided as to whether the crimes were all committed by one person or by several. Ordinarily, it was pointed out, there are eight child murders annually in Atlanta. Sunday, Oct. 26, 1980 the *Chicago Sun-Times* wrote about "Atlanta's agony" and reprinted Herbert H. Denton's article in the *Washington Post*. That article was based on a nationwide survey of "a rash of murders [that] has fallen like hot embers on a patchwork of school racial battles, cross burnings and other strife."

Increasingly the account mentioned the citywide tension. Madigan reported in the *Tribune* for Nov. 9 that Atlanta Mayor Maynard Jackson blamed the FBI for not offering enough assistance. Nov. 17 the same paper devoted almost a full page to a review by Elaine Markoutsas of Dorothy Allison's participation in the cases and her previous record of assistance to police. She recalled Allison's boast that the killer would not strike again while she was around and noted that a little more than a week after the psychic left there was another murder. Whatever clues Allison had given police, however, had not led to any solutions.

Nov. 20 the UPI reported that a second psychic, Pat Gagliardo of Norwich, Conn., had told police to seek clues in Lincoln cemetery. They did, using dogs provided by a tracker, Don Laken, and discovered some items that they refused to describe. Jan. 18, 1981 the *Chicago Tribune* headlined Charles Madigan's story, "Massive hunt in Atlanta hasn't cracked case." It reported charges of negligence on the part of the missing persons bureau in following complaints.

Feb. 16, 1981 the *New York Post* headlined, "Jeane Dixon tried to psych out the Atlanta killer." The story told no more than the heading and no more was reported anywhere of the famous seer's participation, if it occurred.

In his *Washington Post* syndicated column for March 6, 1981 William Raspberry belittled Washington's Mayor Marion S. Barry who told a meeting of citizens concerned over the Atlanta killings that the tragedy was part of some anti-black conspiracy that involved, at least because of their unconcern, the Reagan Administration and, by implication, the FBI. Raspberry pointed out that both Atlanta's Mayor Maynard Jackson and his chief of police are black.

Raspberry also revealed that the *Washington Post's* astrologer, Svetlana, had cast the charts of 12 of the Atlanta children and concluded that the killer probably was a woman or a man dressed as a woman. If she knew the exact birthdates of the principals, she said, she could tell more.

June 20, 1981 the *Sun-Times* reported that Wayne Williams, 23, was seeking a judicial restraining order to prevent 17 newspapers from referring to him as a suspect in the murders. Especially objectionalbe was a *New York Post* headline, "Atlanta monster seized." The next day, June 21, Williams was arrested and charged with 2 of the most recent of 28 murders. July 17 he was indicted on the charges.

Feb. 5, 1983 the *New York Daily News* reported that the family of a 15-year-old epileptic had asked Dorothy Allison to help in the search for the boy, believed missing in a mountainous park. Two days later the *New York Post* reported that Allison, who it said has a "good track record" in such cases, was on the job.

As in many, perhaps most, other aspects of American life, the warning "The Russians are coming" is a spur to American parapsychologists, with the federal government eagerly awaiting results. Among the first intimations that the Soviet scientists were making progess in psi research was an article by Robert K. Plumb in the *New York Times* for Jan. 26, 1964. It told of three Russian women who possessed extraocular vision, the ability to read and, especially, to detect colors in the dark with their fingertips. The Russian news agency, Tass, was quoted as saying they were tested with a spectroanomaloscope. Soviet scientists verified the ability but could give no explanation.

From Moscow March 25, 1968 Lars-Erik Nelson reported for Reuters that a former Russian Army master sergeant, Helya Mikharlova, was gifted in telekinesis, the transmission of motion without any evident use of physical force or energy—or mind over matter. She, alleged the Soviet newspaper *Pravda*, can cause objects to move by staring strongly at them.

At the second Western Hemisphere Conference on Acupuncture, Kirlian Photography and the Human Aura, Dr. Stanely Krippner, director of the Maimonides Dream Lab in Brooklyn, talked about Kirlian photography, according to a story by Tracy Young and Howard Smith in the *Village Voice* for Jan. 19, 1979. The luminescence that is photographed surrounds only living things, plant or animal. It may be useful in medical diagnoses and, since no two auras are alike, may be a substitute for fingerprints.

An awestruck James Warren reviewed the book *The New Soviet Psychics Discoveries,* by William Dick and Henry Gris, a former UPI foreign correspondent, in the *Chicago Sun-Times* for Jan. 13, 1979. The article, headlined in 96-point type, "Mind Control," got a half-page. Warren related some of the book's anecdotes, as the Russian ability to throw rice into the air and have it come together in midair. Mention was made of the arrest of a *Los Angeles Times* reporter, Robert Toth, to whom a stranger handed a file containing secret reports on parapsychological research.

Details of the Toth incident had made headlines two years earlier. The *New York Times* had a long article by Flora Lewis from Paris June 19, 1977. Also a Soviet emigré, August Stern, was quoted as saying the Soviet Union had been doing secret work in parapsychology for what appeared to be military and police purposes. In an accompanying piece, Boyce Rensberger quoted the Menninger Foundation as believing the United States should study parapsychology, but it and other American scientists doubted that the Soviets had learned very much of importance to date.

What might happen if there was found to be anything to the matter was postulated in a page-and-a-half article by John L. Wilhelm in the *Washington Post* for Aug. 7, 1977. Entitled "Psychic Spying?" it was subtitled, "The C.I.A., the Pentagon and the Russians Probe the Military Potential of Parapsychology." Wilhelm gave a condensed summary of just about every aspect of the research at the Stanford Research Institute by Harold E. Puthoff and Russell Targ, by Dr. Anrija Puharich, formerly with the Army's Chemical and Biological Warfare Center at Frederick, Md., by Joseph B. Rhine at Duke University and by a score or more experimenters. The article is, as far as secrecy permits, a who's who and what's what.

Whatever it is Dorothy Allison and others have, there are quite a few newspaper readers who would like to know how to get it. One of them who thinks he already has it asked the *Chicago Daily News'* beeline how to get a license to practice as a clairvoyant. Feb. 5, 1969 Beeline advised that neither a city nor state license is required. However, the Spiritual Church certifies mediums. Fortune telling is prohibited by law.

There are many books for anyone interested. The reviews in the *New York Times* are especially good if only because they are long enough to describe the nature and contents of the books. Aug. 23, 1975 Peter Grose recommended reading both sides of the controversy concerning the occult, the adversely critical *Mediums, Mystics & the Occult* by Milbourne Christopher and the sympathetic *Psychic Exploration, a Challenge for Science,* by Edgar A. Mitchell and John White. In the Oct. 30, 1975 issue of the *New York Review of Books,* the iconoclastic Martin Gardner reviewed *Superminds: A Scientist Looks at the Paranormal* by John Taylor and *The Magic of Uri Geller* by the Amazing Randi. Gardner predicted that Taylor "now runs the risk of being remembered only as the British boob of the century." One of the most hilarious anecdotes in Randi's book was his visit to the office of *Psychic News* in London where he moved around "Gellerizing" one object after another to get his picture in the paper.

Robert Ornstein's review of *Scientists Look at Psychic Ability* by Russell Targ and Harold Puthoff, the Stanford University researchers, was generally favorable, calling for open-mindedness by recalling the resistance to the ideas of Copernicus, Ptolemy, Harvey, the Wright brothers and others.

Similarly Donald J. Lapore was quoted by Jill Smolowe in the *New York Times* for Nov. 13, 1977: "What is impossible today will exist tomorrow. You can call these things divine revelation. Many creators don't know where they got their ideas or innovations, and perhaps this helps to explain it."

Lapore is director of a 12-week seminar at the YWCA in Jersey City, where 35 people gather twice weekly to discuss their out-of-body flights or their premonitions or other eerie experiences. Similar study groups are to be found in virtually every city of any size in America.

As for the attributes essential for success as a parapsychologist, the *New York Daily News* reported Jan. 27, 1982 that *Omni* magazine said that anyone possessing any kind of psychic ability probably suffers from a vitamin deficiency condition known as a psychic burnout. More specifically the *Chicago Sun-Times* Action Time recommended that two readers, concerned because they lose things, contact the American Society for Psychical Research, the Spiritual Brothers Fellowship, Sybil Leek or the Illinois Society for Psychical Research. "Be aware, however," the editors warned, "the cost of hiring such experts may outweigh the losses."

In a story from Peoria, Ill. announcing the Psychic Fair at Peoria's Exposition Gardens, the AP quoted Betty Livingston, an Urbana psychic, as saying a psychic is a person who is able to see more than ordinary people by utilizing a part of the brain that most people leave closed.

More amusing if not enlightening was the answer in the *Chicago Sun-Times* Action Time for Nov. 4, 1982. A reader signing him or herself as "No Name" wanted to consult a clairvoyant to learn if the operation is a hoax. No Name wrote: "A friend and I have an $11.50 bet that Action Time will either state in the paper that you people are not in the clairvoyancy referral business or you will throw this in the wastebasket." The column's reply was: "You flunked the clairvoyancy test because we've done neither. But we're sports and you deserve another chance. While we do not have a list of clairvoyants, we do have access to several groups that can help you. The names and addresses are tucked away in a dark corner of a staff member's desk. Guess what's written on the slate."

To assist anyone wanting an answer to "Am I psychic?" in *Parade* for May 1, 1983 Dr. S. V. Didato listed some traits typical of persons with high ESP ability. They included: a tendency to trust rather than suspect others; calm and placid rather than active, tense or excitable; a liking for people; no neurotic tendencies; no depressions; happy-go-lucky, carefree, etc. making one wonder why anyone with such traits would care about psychic ability. One of the strongest attempts to dissuade people from belief in or practice of psi was Jack Smith's column in the *Los Angeles Times* for Nov. 17, 1982.

26

ESP

The parapsychologist is concerned with psi (psychic) phenomena. Psi occurrences belong to two physical types: (1) subjective experience or (2) physical effects. The subjective or mental is studied under the heading of extrasensory perception, or ESP. This means awareness of something outside of one's self, acquired without the use of the senses. It includes *clairvoyance,* or the ESP of an objective event, and *telepathy,* the awareness of the thoughts or mental state of another person. There may be ESP not only of a current event but also of those that have not yet happened. Such foreknowledge is called *precognition.* Psi phenomena, when there is a physical effect, are known as *psychokineses,* or PK.

The foregoing is almost verbatim the first paragraph of a monograph, *A Brief Introduction to Parapsychology,* by the late J. B. Rhine of the Parapsychology Laboratory at Duke University. Research for the Foundation for Research in the Nature of Man goes on despite Rhine's death at 84 in 1980. Already mentioned in the preceding chapters have been other research and teaching institutes, including the following:

Parapsychological Foundation, New York, headed by Dr. Karlis Osis.

London Society for Psychical Research.

Psychic Research Foundation.

Parapsychology Foundation, headed by Eileen E. Garrett and financed by Rep. Frances Bolton of Cleveland.

Dreams Laboratory at Maimonides Medical Center, Brooklyn, where Dr. Montague Ullman is director of psychology and Dr. Gardner Murphy experiments.

New Era Psychic Center, Glenview, Ill., run by Ruth Berger.

Committee for the Scientific Investigation of Claims of the Paranormal.

Stanford Research Institute, Stanford, Calif., with Professors Russell Targ and Harold Puthoff.

Midwest Psi Research Institute, directed by Nancy Solomon.

Illinois Center for Psychical Research, Park Ridge, Ill., directed by Dr. John Bisaha.

ESP Research Associates Foundation of Little Rock, Ark., founded by Howard Sherman.

Institute for Noetic Sciences, founded by ex-astronaut Edgar Mitchell.

Association of Psychic Practitioners, run by Mary Palermo in San Francisco.

Chicago Psychic Center in Oak Park, Ill.

This is just a sample listing of such facilities which are increasing steadily in all parts of the country. In addition, in 1974 it was estimated that 100 colleges and universities were offering courses in the subject. Many more have sponsored lectures and workshops.

Within the ranks of the psychics themselves there are wide differences of opinion as to whether psi is an inborn or acquired trait enjoyed by all or only a few. In the *Suburban Chicago Sun-Times* for Nov. 3–4, 1976 Steve Ginsberg told about Carolle Bailey who said she discovered she had psychic power when she was 8 years old, as did Florence Steinfles. "I concentrate, touch a person's hands and pick up psychic impulses about a person's past and future," Bailey said.

On the other hand, according to Edward J. Presberg in an article the Newhouse News Service distributed Aug. 14, 1976, Mrs. Beverly C. (Bevy) Jaegars of St. Louis was not born with a psychic gift. Wrote Presberg: "She did not fall on her head, get struck by lightning or acquire her talent in a moment of revelation. Bevy wanted to be a psychic so she practiced. She was 31, the mother of six and bored with her secretarial job, so she studied and practiced to become one of the nation's leading psychics."

The article was not specific as to what Bevy's self-imposed discipline was. There has been available since 1937 the *Journal of Parapsychology*, today only one of many periodicals in the field. In the *Chicago Sun-Times* for Sept. 24, 1972 Roy Larson, religion editor, reported on the proliferation of occult book stores in the Chicago area, and the avalanche of paperbacks catering to the same trade.

Imogene Coca has said she became interested in the occult at an early age, largely because of an uncle by marriage. Larry and Flora Frink and their daughter, Jackie, who operate the Mystic Eye, an occult book store, believe "Everyone has ESP or psychic abilities. They've just laid dormant. No one develops them. Psychics are people who have noticed their abilities and have learned to use them," according to the *Arlington Heights* (Ill.) *Herald* for July 10, 1974.

In the same suburban area seven women calling themselves the North Shore Psychic Researchers believe that by tapping their unconscious people can be taught to program themselves into positive thinking by concentration and meditation to help solve the problems of everyday life, the *Evanston* (Ill.) *Review* reported Nov. 30, 1972.

One of the first persons prominent in the public eye to dabble in ESP was Alan Jay Lerner, who wrote the libretto for the musical about ESP, *On a Clear Day You Can See Forever*. Milton Esterow wrote a profile of him for the *New York Times* of Jan. 27, 1966 to reveal Lerner was deluged with letters from people telling of their telepathic and other supernatural experiences.

May 19, 1968 the *Chicago Tribune* had a story by Robert Cross about the addition of a course called Workshop on Occult Sciences to the adult education program of Chicago's YWCA. The teacher was a former dancer, Libby Chartok, who said she engaged in automatic writing by which she received clues as to the whereabouts of British Col. P. H. Fawcett who disappeared somewhere in a South American jungle in 1925.

Chicago Today reported Jan. 28, 1974 that Northeastern Illinois University was the first college to offer a bachelor's degree in parapsychology. James Pearre wrote a 1½-page article, "What Science Has Discovered," under the larger head, "ESP—Fact or Fiction." It described classwork at Northeastern, especially in hypnosis.

When the *New York Times* published an editorial "Paranormal Science" Nov. 6, 1974, it received some sharp criticism that clarified the issue dividing the believers and skeptics that permeates any consideration of the presumed phenomenon. The editorial criticized scientists for not paying enough attention to ESP. "Scientific orthodoxy has grown increasingly remote from the interests of and believers of a generation of Americans," the editorial stated.

In reply Marvin Margoshes of Tarrytown, N.Y. wrote Nov. 21, 1974 that the editorial had "little basis in fact." He explained:

> Scientists have spent inordinate amounts of time on paranormal "phenomena." . . . the distinguished physicist and chemist Michael Farady [performed] ingeniously simple experiments by which he demonstrated that table movements in seances were anything but supernatural . . . a letter said to have been written by M. Chevreuil . . . debunks the theory, apparently believed by much of the public, that a pendulum held in the hand would swing of its own volition without movement of the hand or arm.
>
> The burden of proof in science has traditionally been on those who bring forth a novel theory. Adherence to a theory by some portion of the public, or even by some scientists, does not constitute proof.
>
> In times since 1854 individual scientists have spent the time to debunk one or another "phenomenon." One case that comes to mind is Professor Rhine's card experiments that purported to prove extrasensory perception. We stopped hearing about that when it was shown that his results were entirely due to faulty experimental design. Can you blame those of us who recall such past events for being skeptical this time?

Another correspondent, Leon M. Lederman, Columbia University professor of physics, chastised the *Times* for its mention of ". . . the strange object 'scientific orthodoxy,' but in fact that has not existed in any effective sense since Galileo's troubles . . . Einstein, Bohr, Lee and Yang received rapid recognition for radical and iconoclastic innovations. To be recognized in science you must be unorthodox."

Scientific experiments to test the validity of mind reading or mental telepathy have been undertaken for centuries. Impetus to the studies in Europe came from the successful demonstrations of hypnotism by Dr. Franz Anton Mesmer, 1733–1815. Among the 20th-century Americans interested in the phenomena were Charles Richet, Frederic Myers, Edmund Gurney, James H. Hyslop and William James. It remained, however, for Joseph Banks Rhine to supply "what appears to be the first genuinely scientific evidence to support telepathy and clairvoyance," to quote Edwin C. Hill's column, "The Human Side of the News," which the *Boston American* used Oct. 22, 1937.

Hill's comment was typical of that of the journalistic world as a whole. In his review of Rhine's book, *New Frontiers of the Mind* in the *New York Times* for Oct. 10, 1927, Waldemar Kaempffert, science editor, concluded: "He [Rhine] has made extra-sensory perception a respectable psychological discipline by stripping it of the mysticism and occultism in which it has been draped by quacks, charlatans and the selfdeluded."

The *Kansas City Star* didn't even wait for *New Frontiers of the Mind* to be published. Perhaps it was familiar with Rhine's 1934 *Extra-Sensory Perception,* a scientific treatise intended for scientists. The *Star* cited an October 1936 *Harper's* article by Dr. Ernest Hunter Wright and another in *American* magazine by Gardner Murphy. Aug. 15, 22 and 29, 1937 the tabloid *Chicago Sunday Times* ran a series of articles labeled "Telepathy—The Laboratory Tests It."

According to a full-page feature, "Strange Experiences No One Can Solve—Or Can They?" in the *American Weekly* in 1937, Joseph Banks Rhine became interested in unorthodox psychology when the prophecy of a neighbor that her brother had died was fulfilled. In 1927 he and his wife Louisa went to Duke University as assistants to Dr. William McDougall who in 1930 established the Parapsychology Laboratory there. In 1933 he shocked the scientific world by announcing that a divinity student could predict with 40 percent accuracy the symbols on cards flipped in a building 100 yards away. In 1965 Dr. Rhine resigned his Duke professorship and established his own institute, which became known the world over for its experiments in clairvoyance, telepathy, psychokinesis and precognition.

Rhine's methodology was very simple and easily emulated by others. Many newspapers and magazines described and explained it. Among the recent of such articles were "Arguing the Existence of ESP" by Malcolm W. Browne in the *New York Times* for Jan. 29, 1980 and "Are You Psychic?"

by Thomas J. Majerski in the *New York Daily News* for Jan. 18, 1982. The method consists of a deck of 25 cards, each bearing one of five symbols: star, rectangle, cross, circle or wavy lines. In the telepathy test, as James R. Newman described in it his Dec. 15, 1947 *New Republic* review of Rhine's *The Research of the Mind,* after the cards have been shuffled the experimenter picks up the first and concentrates on its symbol; the subject, from whom all the cards are concealed, usually by means of a partition between the two persons, is then asked to identify it. The process is repeated until the pack has been exhausted.

The clairvoyance test is similar except that the experimenter does not look at each successive card until after the subject has identified its symbol. Presumably this makes it impossible for the experimenter to send telepathic messages to the subject.

After less than a decade Rhine was making lavish claims of success. He cited numerous subjects who had made scores considerably above what would have resulted by chance. One subject, a psychology student named A. J. Linzmyer, beat odds of 2,000,000 to 1 by naming nine cards straight more than once; in 600 trials he scored 238 correct answers, or 10 cards correct of every 25. Even more remarkable was the feat of a divinity student, Hubert Pearce, who averaged 10 correct of every 25 cards during 5,000 tests day by day for two years; once he named all 25 cards correctly. Presumably he beats odds of 298, 023, 223, 876, 953, 125 to 1. There never has been any explanation of why a psychic person can't have 100 percent correct scores.

All over the country scientists rushed to share the limelight by repeating Rhine's experiments. The results were mixed. Jan. 15, 1936 Rhine told the Boston Society for Psychical Research that thought transference had been demonstrated over a distance of 1,000 miles, from North Carolina to Arkansas. According to the *New York Herald Tribune* for the next day, he also said that out of 77 persons tested 18 had the ability to engage in extrasensory communication. July 20, 1947 Alton L. Blakeslee, Associated Press science writer, reported from New York that new experiments indicated that some psychics' abilities may work better in normal light than in the darkness usually preferred by spiritualists for seances. J. M. Bevan, one of Rhine's assistants, gave his reasons for so believing in the *Journal of Parapsychology,* published at Duke. In a very lengthy review of Rhine's findings Dec. 5, 1937 the *New York Times* reported, "Strange as it may seem, the statisticians of note find no fault with his conclusions, though they criticize his mathematical methods. It is the psychologists who object." The *Times* itself, however, ridiculed the objections of Dr. Chester Kellogg, professor of psychology at McGill University, who pointed out that he once held a hand at bridge that consisted of all spades, "an event to be expected only once in 779, 737, 580, 760 times." The anonymous *Times* writer said the analogy was fallacious.

Among the first experiments to determine the validity of ESP were conducted at New York University's School of Commerce, Accounts and Finances. Beginning in March 1936 a total of 126,075 trials were made with 69 student volunteers. Girl students achieved a 50 percent higher score than boys. Of the total, 46 had positive deviations from chance whereas 23 had negative deviations.

ESP buffs received a boost when Dr. Alexis Carrel, Nobel Prize–winning biologist, granted his first interview after becoming associated with the Rockefeller Institute for Medical Research. Willian Engle quoted him in the *New York World-Telegram* for Oct. 8, 1935 as believing that thought transference, intuition and clairvoyance are logically provable phenomena.

When *Thoughts Through Space* by Sir Robert Wilkins and Harold Sherman appeared, A. C. Spectorsky was converted to a belief in thought transference. In his review of the experiment the two authors conducted in 1937 when Wilkins was searching for a Soviet flier, Sigismund Levanevsky, lost in the Arctic Spectorsky wrote in the *Chicago Sun-Times* for March 21, 1942: "Coincidence simply will not explain the number of 'hits' Sherman made." He gagged, however, on accounts of predictions of events to come.

Another reporter who came to believe was Pence James of the *Chicago Daily News* who covered a performance by Dr. Frank J. Polgar before the Oak Park Community Lecture Forum and then followed the eminent mind reader to his hotel where Polgar found hidden objects. James shared his bewilderment with the paper's readers Nov. 17, 1942.

Still another reporter who accompanied Polgar on a search for a revenue stamp from a package of cigarettes was Hyman Goldberg who related his adventures in a page-long story with seven illustrations in the New York *PM* for Feb. 21, 1943. The hiding place was on the thigh of a pulchritudinous waitress named Helen. Goldberg lost a $500 war bond when Polgar found it.

A fourth bewildered reporter was William J. Manly of the *Milwaukee Journal* who followed "Doc" Ralph Passer around for a day to obtain a sizable feature for the July 21, 1943 edition of his paper.

Impossible to ignore was Rhine's claim, which the Associated Press reported he made in a speech in Buffalo, that mankind can really gain precognition or knowledge of future events. To accompany its publication of the AP report Feb. 4, 1939 the *Christian Science Monitor* ran a background piece by its natural-science writer (unnamed) stating it as a fact that Rhine has proved the existence of extrasensory perception.

Another scientific bombshell was Dr. Rhine's announcement that "there is a great accumulation of evidence that strongly favors the possibility that there is something about human personality that could survive." In reporting the announcement from Durham Jan. 31, 1949 United Press International explained that Rhine was "not yet ready to tell in precise terms what that evidence is."

Feb. 5, 1956 the *Chicago Tribune* began a series of articles on extrasensory perception by its mystical writer, Norma Lee Browning. The editor's note described the purpose and contents thusly: "The series deals with the strange findings of scientists at Duke University who have explored psychic phenomena and supernatural manifestations." Browning's first article began: "Man has harnessed the atom. The day may yet come when he can trap his own soul in a test tube."

Most of the articles related to eerie case studies. Browning wrote: "Stories of such uncanny behavior are common. So are stories of haunted houses, ghosts and poltergeists. Are they merely hallucinations of man's physical mind or actual evidence of a nonphysical world?" In her installment Feb. 8, 1956 Browning wrote, "The experiments have proved beyond any reasonable doubt—at least in his own mind—that there is something in man that transcends the law of matter, that man is more than a physical machine, that Psi, as he calls it (short for psychic capacity), is a natural function of normal personality."

When controversy was at its height over *The Search for Bridey Murphy* (see page 130), Louisa Ella Rhine wrote a three-part series that the *Chicago Daily News* ran Oct. 29, 30 and 31, 1956. She ducked a direct answer to the question of the reality of reincarnation, saying that Duke experiments into the matter were still in process. She did review other activities and cited numerous anecdotes of clairvoyance, telepathy and precognition that she said were as remarkable as the Bridey Murphy tales.

The suburban *Arlington Heights* (Ill.) *Herald,* then a weekly (now a daily) devoted a page of its May 5, 1960 issue to a comprehensive account by Dick Hoffman of Rhine's theories and findings as he related them to an audience at Forest Hospital in nearby Des Plaines.

Two years later the ever-sympathetic *Chicago Daily News* announced a series of articles on "A Deeper Look Into Dark World of ESP." The project ran from June 9 to 23 inclusive. There were daily installments from Louisa E. Rhine's book *Hidden Channels of the Mind* and a parallel series by reporter Richard T. Stout in Durham, N.C. In introducing the series the *Daily News* said it did so "not as endorsement or criticism of ESP, but only in the interest of fully informing its readers of a fact of life that is attracting more and more serious attention."

All of the 12 extracts abound with accounts of clairvoyance while Stout reported on work in progress in Durham, with special attention to the participation of any from Chicagoland as either researchers or subjects. There were no articles with any adverse criticism of Rhine.

As a followup of Mrs. Rhine's series, the paper ran scores of accounts of ESP contributed by readers in response to a request that they do so.

Scripps-Howard papers reported from Washington April 2, 1942 that Rhine said 500 cases of "puzzling animal behavior" studied over 12 years "strongly suggest" that some animals are psychic.

About the most startling report from Durham during the '60s was that

Dr. E. E. Barnard, who the AP reported Sept. 13, 1966 was convinced, as the result of his research at Rhine's laboratory, that the minds of many individuals can leave their bodies and drift away uninhibited by physical barriers or distance. Called astral (out-of-body) projection, it is "like lying on a sofa, getting up and seeing your body still lying on the couch," Barnard said.

Ten years later Rhine told the Chicago chapter of the American Statistical Society that laboratory mice develop the ability to know which side of their cage is safe from electric shock. He said, "We're beginning to suspect the whole animal world has this power," according to Bob Olmstead, reporter in the *Sun-Times* for Oct. 29, 1970.

No matter what the reporter's motive may have been, an Associated Press story from Durham, N.C. Aug. 7, 1971 amounted to a pitch for financial support of Rhine's Psychical Research Foundation. It quoted Director W. G. Roll of Stanford University as explaining the slow progress of the work resulted from too many scientists thinking it all a waste of time, with the result that potential donors ignore it.

The appeal for support should have influenced a sizable element in the population after Rhine told Steve Cady of the *New York Times* that "Picking horses through ESP is entirely possible in view of what we've found in other cases. Many winners have been predicted in dreams." According to the *Times* for Aug. 2, 1974, however, a test by that paper of the ESP ability of Majorie May resulted in a theoretical loss of $67 if $2 had been bet on every one of the 95 horses the subject selected.

In announcing Rhine's imminent appearance on the program of the 16th annual conference of the Spiritual Frontiers Fellowship, the *Chicago Daily News* May 12, 1973 said, "More than anything else his studies have brought the subject into the arena of respected scientific research."

That attention didn't always mean accolades. A formidable critic from the beginning of his work was Harold O. Gulliksen, one of whose critical analyses appeared in the *American Journal of Sociology* for January 1938. Among the few newspaper journalists who scoffed was Dr. George W. Crane of Northwestern University who syndicated "Case Records of a Psychologist." June 30, 1936 in answer to a letter about a man and wife who recalled an old friend independent of each other, Dr. Crane wrote: "If there were real thought transference existing between himself and his wife, then he should be able to write a name on a slip of paper and his wife should be able to call out the name even though she had never seen the original person whom he had in mind. This is obviously impossible and has never been capable of demonstration thus far in any psychological laboratory. Some people believe in thought transference—the thing which is called telepathy—but it has never been capable of proof."

Years did not mellow Dr. Crane on the subject. June 7, 1950 he wrote in his syndicated column, "The Worry Clinic": "Telepathy doesn't exist as popularly conceived, though husband and wife may start humming the same tune, or two people who have the same type background may be led to the same idea when both encounter the same new situation."

Edgar Allan Poe related incidents of two or more people reacting similarly to the same situation in what he called tales of ratiocination; A. Conan Doyle's Sherlock Holmes did the same.

After the *New York Times* eulogized Rhine editorially, it also published Jan. 30, 1938 a letter by Henry Hart that was a scathing denunciation of Rhine's methodology, basically his selecting "from the whole field of the probabilities involved only that portion which will conduce to a desired result." Two pertinent paragraphs from the column-long letter follow:

> In his book Rhine naively confesses, and boldly *aggrandizes, these facts:* (1) those who did not score high averages were not utilized for further tests (because, Rhine reasoned, since they obviously lacked "extra sensory perception," it was silly to test them for it), and (2) persons who originally scored well later lost their ability so to do (which Rhine misinterprets as the loss of "extra sensory perception" instead of as examples of the late appearance of minuses in a series in which the pluses appeared early).
>
> Thus, if out of twenty-six persons taking the tests only A, B and C make an average (5.0), only these three are given further tests. And, what is worse, when, according to Rhine's own statement, A, B and C stop making better than chance averages, they stop taking the tests. It is obvious that A, B, and C, instead of possessing "extra sensory perception," are merely the preponderant pluses in a series in which D, E and F are the initial medians or minuses. If Professor Rhine were to test X, Y and Z (who initially made the poorest showing) long enough, he would find their average to be a value very close (but not quite) to the chance average for the cards on the normal probability curve, as will A, B and C if tested long enough.

Another heretic was Dr. John L. Kennedy, fellow of psychical research at Stanford University. According to the report James O. Leary wrote for the *Chicago Daily News* Dec. 29, 1937, Kennedy told the American Association for the Advancement of Science that tests with 100 students resulted in scores much lower than those claimed by Rhine.

Still another disbeliever was Dr. Eugene Adams, assistant professor of philosophy at Colgate University, who, the *New York Times* reported Feb. 13, 1938, after 30,000 experiments over two years in emulation of Rhine, concluded that extrasensory perception cannot be established and that telepathy and clairvoyance are not scientific facts.

Rhine's experiments tending to prove the existence of psychokinesis were challenged at the twenty-third annual meeting of the Eastern Psychological Association by a group of professors and research students from Yale University who claimed they repeated the Duke experiments and obtained very different results. Robert K. Plumb reported in the *New York Times* for March 30, 1954 that Rhine's volunteers resented being called cultists and accused of fooling themselves as well as others.

John Crosby, one of the first and, many think, the all-time best critic of radio, adversely criticized an ABC-TV program on ESP. There was, he wrote July 17, 1958, nothing remarkable about correct wild guesses regarding cards. "We were," he wrote, "doing that well taking wild stabs in our living room."

That some of the original supporters of the Foundation for Research on the Nature of Man, which is what Rhine called it when he founded it in 1965, had lost interest was indicated in an article by Patrick O'Keefe in the *Greensboro* (N.C.) *Record* for April 25, 1975. One of the two principal contributors, Chester F. Carlson, inventor of xerography, had died and the other, W. Clement Stone, had found other interests. Also, O'Keefe wrote, "Unfortunately the Rhines had no (product) as such; in other words, no application of the pure research."

About the same time Mrs. Rhine's book *Psi* appeared. Reviewing it for the *Tallahassee* (Fla.) *Democrat* for June 29, 1975, Brenda Jones wrote: ". . . its primary accomplishment may well be that parapsychology will be taken out of the dark, misty realm of fantasy and the supernatural and brought into the daylight of scientific research for the general public as it was for the researchers many years ago."

Skepticism bordering on cynicism was present in several answers the *Chicago Daily News'* Beeline editors gave readers Dec. 27, 1972. A reader wanting to know where to be tested was given the names and addresses of Ansul (Answers Unlimited) and Psychic Research Foundation and, since one already had attested to the inquirer's psychic ability, slyly asked, "If you are really psychic, how come you didn't know this yourself?"

Aug. 29, 1973, however, Beeline referred another reader to Irene T. Hughes, widely known psychic, who stresses, however, that "if you do not have natural psychic ability to begin with, she can't teach you the art." Sept. 12, 1974 Beeline answered a query, "Is there a test for ESP?" with a description and illustration of Rhine's five cards and also referred the reader to Irene Hughes. May 20, 1977 there apparently was a new Mr. and Ms. Beeline who answered a reader who wrote, "I think I have ESP. How can I tell for sure?" by advising him or her that most scientists and psychologists disbelieve in ESP; nevertheless, Beeline provided Irene Hughes' address.

In two *Chicago Daily News* columns, July 25 and Aug. 24, 1972, Norman Mark lambasted the American Broadcasting Company's series "The Sixth Sense," because it was "pure entertainment and disregarded any description or interpretation of serious experimentation of ESP." Jan. 17, 1973, shortly before he was replaced as the *News'* television critic, Mark said the ABC series "Sixth Sense" was "vying for honors as the worst TV series ever created" because it presented ESP as possible to transmit instructions to an American prisoner of war on how to escape.

In his Oct. 20, 1973 *National Observer* article, John Peterson warned, "Most people who are excited about the psychic get involved through such methods and practices as transcendental meditation, hypnosis, yoga, drugs, scientology and several different mind control programs. By altering their consciousness they hope to open their minds to deeper insight into the meaning of life."

One of the most virulent opponents of parapsychology is Martin Gardner, iconoclastic author of books, articles for *Scientific American, Skeptical Inquirer* and similar publications and book reviewer, especially of books in support of the supernatural. In the *New York Review of Books* for May 16, 1974 he commented on *Uri: A Journal of the Mystery of Uri Geller* by Andrija Puharich and *Arigo: Surgeon of the Rusty Knife* by John G. Fuller: "It's hard to say which of these two books is the nuttier." The first is about the Israeli who bends keys and the second a Brazilian psychic healer.

In the same publication March 17, 1977 Gardner reviewed *Mind Reach* by Russell Targ and Harold Puthoff, the Stanford University testers of clairvoyance. July 14, 1977 Gardner printed letters from three mathematicians dealing mostly with the work of Charles Tart at the University of California at Davis and his reply. All four communiques dealt with the mechanics of the experiments of which all four were skeptical.

An exchange of letters between Tart and Gardner appeared in the *New York Review of Books* Oct. 13, 1977 and in the issue of May 15, 1980 Gardner reviewed a recent article by Tart.

In the United Press International's "People Talk" by Joan Habauer for March 25, 1982 a satirical effort to discredit parapsychologists by James "The Amazing" Randi was reported. The stunt was announcing that Uri awards for outstanding accomplishments in parapsychology and the supernatural would be announced on April Fool's day in the mansion of the publishers of *Penthouse* and *Omni*. Winners would be notified telepathically and are free to announce their awards in advance by precognition if they so desire. In 1983 there were four Uris for psychic foolishness, the AP reported April 2, 1983 from New York. Winner in the media category was Paul Bannister of the *National Enquirer,* who answered the question of whether he believed in psychic powers: "I don't have to believe in it. All I need is 2 Ph.D.'s who will tell me it's so and I have a story."

On the other hand there were some important converts to parapsychology.

In a lenthy article in the *Washington Post* for Aug. 20, 1970 Russell B. Pulliam told of the conversion to a belief in the possibility of ESP of a psychiatrist, Dr. George Sjolund, after a patient correctly forecast an automobile accident a month before it occurred. After three years of study and experimenting on his own, Dr. Sjolund concluded, "All the evidence indicates that ESP does exist." His experimental method was to have 50 subjects try 100 times each to determine what colored lights would go on; there were 1,070 correct answers out of 5,000, he said. Dr. Sjolund believes that everyone has the capacity but some are more open, spontaneous, relaxed and trusting than others. He says that our understanding of ESP today is about the same as the understanding of electricity a century ago.

A similar opinion was expressed by William Braud who, with his wife, Lendell, conducted experiments at the University of Houston. In the *Chicago Daily News* for Jan. 6, 1976, William J. Cromie reported that the Brauds concluded that ESP comes easier to a relaxed body and a mind turned off to its surroundings. Another researcher, D. Scott Rogo, is quoted as believing that people who achieve an ESP state of mind easiest are happy extroverts, sensitive to their own internal processes, well adjusted to the world and apt to open themselves up to others.

In the first of a series of four articles that began in the *New York Daily News* for July 22, 1971, William Rice reported that 48 of 67 corporation presidents believed they had ESP. Mostly the articles consisted of anecdotes of precognition, déjà vu, poltergeist and other experiences and laboratory experiments by Dr. Helmut Schmidt and Dr. H. Roll, both of the Rhine organization. The fourth and final article gave instructions for self-testing for ESP.

Among the strong defenders of parapsychology and critic of most scientists for not taking it seriously is the columnist Sydney J. Harris. June 10, 1974 he wrote: "The evidence in favor of ESP is far stronger than the evidence for some other theories that psychologists believe in—yet hardly a reputable psychologist will concede the probability of ESP existing . . . the fact is ESP is not respectable."

The cause of at least the Durham operations received quite a shock when the experimental data that presumably ascribed ESP ability to mice were discovered to have been faked by Walter J. Levy, director of the Institute for Parapsychology who Rhine had thought would be his successor. The *New York Times* reported the calamity Aug. 25, 1974 and had a longer account Sept. 30, 1974. Levy resigned and Rhine apologized to the scientific world.

Undaunted, the devotees have proceeded to act on the advice of Dr. Henry Morgenau, Yale University professor of physics and natural philosophy, who told the American Society of Psychical Research to "go out and build your own body of research and study scientific theory to account for it." That was reported Nov. 21, 1965 by the *New York Herald Tribune*, which also quoted Morgenau as believing physicists who have had to change their views on several matters as a result of atomic research should be openminded.

The *Durham* (N.C.) *Sun* for July 30, 1975 and the *Boston Evening Globe* for Aug. 3, 1975 both used a *Los Angeles Times*-originated article by Al Martinex that began, "Parapsychology, once ridiculed as a doctrine of the occult, is winning new interest among hard-nosed physical scientists who never before have believed in goblins or in fairies dancing on the lawn." The page-long article listed many governmental agencies that show an interest in the subject, explained the experiments being conducted by many colleges and industries and traced the history of unorthodox scientists who overcame skepticism and opposition.

Feb. 28, 1976 the *Daily Illini,* student publication at the University of Illinois, published a ten page special section on "The Mysterious World of the Psychic." It had special articles on the Indiana Association of Spiritualists and its Camp Chesterfield, palmistry, "ESP for Fun and Profit," fortune telling, prophecy and UFOs.

Joseph B. Rhine's name, of course, overshadows those of any and all others in this field. There are, however, several other experimental centers that receive a modest amount of publicity. One is the Psi Communications Project of Newark College of Engineering. Aug. 31, 1969 the *New York Times* had a long article by Robert A. Wright who quoted Prof. John Mihalasky that there is a correlation between superior management ability and an executive's extrasensory perception, or ESP. Among the subscribers to the Times Service who used the Wright article were the *Lancaster* (pa.) *Intelligencer Journal* Sept. 1, 1969 and the *Riverside* (Calif.) *Press* Sept. 3, 1969.

Dec. 28, 1970 the *Chicago Daily News* had an account by Karen Hasman that company presidents who say they believe in ESP are likely to have better profit-and-loss statements than those who do not so believe. This on the authority of E. Douglas Dean, research director of the ESP project at Newark, who spoke to the convention of the American Association for the Advancement of Science.

The results of ten years of study of 9,000 businessmen were reported June 11, 1971 by the Associated Press from Newark. Mihalasky was quoted: "I was skeptical at the outset, but I've been converted to a firm belief that telepathy, clairvoyance and precognition play a large role in the function of management and can be made to play a larger one yet." The *York* (Neb.) *News-Times* used the piece, by Henry Gottlieb, July 19, 1971.

When Lynn Schroeder and Sheila Ostrander teamed up with Dean and Mihalasky to write a book, *Executive ESP,* the *Atlantic Constitution* gave Helen C. Smith about a half-page Nov. 20, 1974 to eulogize it. She stressed the extent to which the authors cited hunches by businessmen that turned out happily.

Another on-going institution is the Maimonides Medical Center's Division of Parapsychology and Psychophysics in Brooklyn. There in 1963 Dr. Montague Ullman established a dream laboratory that in 1973 received a $52,000 grant from the National Institute of Mental Health, the first major grant awarded for parapsychological research.

One of the first journalistic mentions of the dream laboratory was by Dr. Joyce Brothers in her syndicated column for Aug. 3, 1970. She reported that research by Dr. Stanley Krippner indicated that it is possible for a dreamer's mind to be influenced by others' thoughts.

In a story announcing the grant to the center Gordon T. Thompson wrote in the *New York Times* for Nov. 25, 1973 that what distinguishes the ESP effort at Maimonides, according to Charles Honorton, senior research associate, is its focus on "altered states of consciousness," mostly dreaming, during which 65 percent of spontaneous (not in a laboratory) ESP experiences occur.

In *Chicago Today* for Jan. 30, 1974 James Pearre quoted Dr. Ullman's statement that opposition to parapsychology is softening and then interviewed several Chicago psychologists for their opinions. Typical reply was that of Dr. Theodore Millon of the University of Illinois, "I don't think that the more hard-nosed scientists in psychology are any more inclined to buy this than they were before."

Upon his return from a trip to the Soviet Union Krippner was interviewed for the Aug. 8, 1974 *Village Voice*. He related many significant experiments by Soviet scientists. One was their discovery that if a chicken embryo is bisected and one half injected with a deadly virus the other half will wane sympathetically.

Establishement of the international quarterly *Psychoenergetic Systems* with Dr. Stanely Krippner as editor was announced in the March 17, 1975 *Village Voice*. Among Krippner's credentials was his position as senior research associate at Maimonides. The paper described the magazine as rough going, written in dense technical jargon with a forest of footnotes. It demonstrated "how far science has gone in the direction of what used to be called witchcraft."

In the *New York Daily News* for April 17, 1977 Edward Edelson described some of the dream experiments, quoted Honorton as explaining the two-year grant-supported project failed because subjects were selected too hurriedly. However, Ullman said, "I think our work has added to the evidence that establishes definite proof." The iconoclastic Paul Kurtz was quoted: "The data from parapsychological claims have to be checked very carefully. Often data are left out of published reports and what has been left out are the negative findings as a rule."

What Stuart Nuerbach wrote in the *Washington Post* for Dec. 28, 1970 caused ESP researchers to "hope that they had finally moved from the world of fortune tellers into the respectability of prescience" was the admission of the Parapsychological Association as a division of the American Association for the Advancement of Science. That was in 1969 when the eminent anthropologist Margaret Mead championed their cause. Since then, as the *New York Times* reported Jan. 19, 1979, Dr. John A. Wheeler, of the University of Texas, has campaigned for their expulsion.

The debate between Wheeler and some parapsychological researchers was carried on in the *New York Review of Books*. After Wheeler called parapsychology a "pathological science . . . a pretentious pseudo-science," four scholars answered him at great length, in the issue of June 26, 1980. They were Olivier Costa da Beauregard, University of Paris; Richard D. Mattuck, University of Copenhagen; Brian D. Josephson, Cambridge University, England; and Evan Harris Walker, Johns Hopkins. They made a technical attack on Wheeler's article, reproduced in "Quantum Theory and Quack Theory" by Martin Gardner in the May 17, 1979 issue. Gardner made a two-page reply to their three-page critique.

For Ted Rockwell's criticism of Wheeler, see page 85.

Because of his much publicized background Capt. Edgar D. Mitchell, Jr. received journalistic attention second only to that accorded Rhine when he resigned from the navy to form an organization "to study the psychic potential of man and other forms of life." The Associated Press reported Oct. 1, 1972 from Houston that Mitchell, the lunar module pilot on the 1971 Apollo 14 flight and the sixth man to walk on the moon, during his rest periods on that flight carried on an ESP experiment with four persons on earth, one of them Olof Jonsson of Chicago. Mitchell used specially made Duke University cards during six sessions of six minutes each. The results were uncertain as Jonsson said the images he received were fuzzy. The Associated Press June 22, 1971 from Durham and the UPI story the same day from New York were essentially the same.

In an article, "Comedown from the Moon—What has happened to the astronauts," in the *New York Times Magazine* for Dec. 3, 1972, Howard Muson told of visiting Mitchell in his Houston office. He displayed a broken ring that he says a friend in New York broke in his hands without pressure. Mitchell didn't know how psychokinesis works. "It seems," he said, "to relate to conscious states which somehow interact with the physical world, with things like electromagnetic and electrostatic fields."

Feb. 20, 1973 the *Times* reported that Mitchell said in Davis, Calif. that he wanted to start an institute in Palo Alto for noetic sciences, hoping "eventually to have to embrace the subjectivity of the Eastern scholars in order to discover the secret of conscious energy—a name I give to all the things we do not yet know about the nature of man and living systems."

In his "It Happened Last Night" column in the *Post* for Aug. 10, 1973, Earl Wilson noted that the sixth man to set foot on the moon, Captain Edgar D. Mitchell, had completed a 1,000-page manuscript on *Psychic Exploration.*

By the time Pat Colander interviewed Mitchell for the *Chicago Tribune* Oct. 18, 1973, the Institute of Noetic Sciences was in operation. What he is searching for, the story went, is the key that will unlock the potential of the human mind. In an article he wrote for the *New York Times* for Jan. 4, 1974, Mitchell said the success of his experiments from space could not be duplicated by chance in one out of 3,000 experiments. He also wrote: ". . . the evidence of psychic research suggests that awareness can operate externally to the body and that therefore it is not unreasonable to hypothesize that mind may be able to operate independently of the body."

In a *New York Times Magazine* article, "Parapsychology and beyond," Aug. 11, 1974 Francine du Plessix Gray described the work by numerous parapsychologists, including Dr. Montague Ullman in Brooklyn, the Menninger Foundation in Topeka, Joseph B. Rhine and some Russians. She explained, "I began with Captain Mitchell because few Americans offer a more striking symbol of the newest high in our culture—our shift from outer to inner space, our avidity to explore the mythic and mystic areas of consciousness."

Other journalistic mentions of the existence of organized research efforts follow:

Robert C. Toth reported in the *Los Angeles Times* that Westinghouse Electric Corporation scientists were seriously studying the possibility of harnessing mental telepathy for long distance communications systems. Dr. Peter C. A. Castruccio, director of the company's Astronautics Institute, said he was convinced that telepathy and brain-to-brain telepathy is real.

Aug. 26, 1970 the *New York Times'* religion editor, Edward R. Fiske, wrote that Robert E. L. Masters and Jean Houston, directors of the Foundation for Mind Research in Manhattan, discovered that ordinary people can have profound religious experiences like those of the great Eastern and Western mystics without the use of drugs. They used psychedelic sounds, lights, pictures and other devices.

Sidney Fields wrote a short profile of Dr. Karlis Osis, director of the American Society for Psychical Research, for the *New York Daily News* of June 9, 1971. A native of Riga, Latvia, Osis became interested in ESP through study of the experiences of ill persons who survived their death beds, and studies that convinced him meditation makes for better ESP.

Because he believed "there is no truly replicable experiment in this field," Robert G. Jahn decided to do psychic research, mostly into ESP. He made the announcement at a meeting of the Council for the Advancement of Science Writing at Palo Alto, Edward Edelson, science editor, reported in the *New York Daily News* for Nov. 11, 1979.

ESP also is essential "because economic analyses have been so wrong," the Maha Yogi A. S. Narayana was reported to believe by Carol Mathews in the *New York Post* for March 7, 1980. Mathews cited several predictions by the Toronto yogi, who received $10,000 annual retainers from financial companies.

Despite the mild iconoclasm of such articles, journalists have persisted in demonstrating their belief that psychics make good copy. Characteristically Don Bishoff, *Eugene* (Ore.) *Register-Guard* columnist, gave Jamil fulsome treatment Jan. 14, 1977. Jamil, who calls himself a psychic, discovered his talent in Vietnam. He lives off the freewill donations of those who answer his magazine ads offering to "bewitch (mesmerize) loved ones, others to do your bidding." Jamil believes his power is a gift from God, who would take it away if he became unethical.

In a "topic advisory" to managing editors and wire editors Dec. 31, 1980 the Associated Press wrote:

James Hydrick has at various times in the presence of reporters, done the following:

Turned the pages of telephone books from ten feet away by giving them hard stares.

Blocked punches while blindfolded.

Sneaked up on deer at night and grabbed them around the neck.

Hydrick makes no claim to mystical or psychological power. "I think it's an energy I put out," he says.

Now, what's stranger than Hydrick's peculiar power is the story of how he came by it. As AP writer Vern Anderson reports in today's topic: strange odyssey for master of mind over matter.

The 1,500-word article datelined Salt Lake City was an elaboration of the memorandum with mention of Tibetan high priests, reform schools, penitentiaries, adventures and demonstrations of psychic power.

In the program "That's My Line," telecast Feb. 24, 1981 on the Columbia Broadcasting System, Hydrick failed to win the $10,000 that the professional magician James Randi has made as a standing offer for anyone able to perform a psychic act that he cannot duplicate by normal means. The Parapsychological Association was represented by one of the three scientists who voted that Hydrick's power to move objects resulted from skillful blowing of his breath. Randi described the incident in the Summer 1981 issue of the *Skeptical Inquirer*.

What anyone with only a modicum of knowledge of theatrical magic knows but which few newspapermen understand is that it is impossible to blindfold a professional magician so that he is helpless in the performance of his wonders. June 23, 1935 a Dr. A. J. McIvor Tyndall received a full column in the *New York Times* telling of his triumph over a roomful of reporters at New York's Park Central Hotel. With a heavy black band to reinforce a white blindfold about his eyes, the veteran spiritualist found objects hidden by the newsmen. He described in turn the colors of a silk handkerchief, a wallet, an ivory and cloth compact and, without touching it, the necktie a man was wearing.

Unfortunately journalists haven't become much smarter over the years. For the May 3, 1968 issue of the *Daily Report* of San Bernardino County, Calif., Willard Hatch did a column piece on a demonstration-lecture by Russ Burgess at Chaffey College. The entertainer made several predictions, such as that a ticket of Richard Nixon and Charles Percy would win the 1968 presidential and vice-presidential election and that Ronald Reagan would never be president. He identified objects in the possession of members of his audience and climaxed the performance by having a college officer open an envelope that Burgess had sealed a week earlier. In it was a correct prediction of what the day's headline in the *Los Angeles Times* would be.

The headline prediction trick is as old as the blindfolded magician driving an automobile. Editors all over the country have been fooled by it over the years. The details of how Lee Fried, a Duke University student, successfully performed the trick was told in Chapter 3 (see page 61). Another incident was reported by the *Chicago Daily News* April 14, 1950. A picture showed Evanston's Mayor Samuel G. Ingraham and North End Club members holding a box in which magician Jack Gynne, also pictured, had placed a piece of paper more than a month earlier. When opened April 13, the box, which had been in the mayor's safe in the meantime, was found to contain a prediction of what the wording of the top headline of the newspaper would be on that date. The words were exactly correct.

Similarly July 17, 1977 the Associated Press reported from Seattle that the *Post-Intelligencer* of that city had been the medium for the same trick, an easy one for any experienced magician to perform. The perpetrator of the Seattle deception was attending the convention of the Pacific Coast Association of Magicians.

Over the years there have been several who made the headlines because of their alleged possession of X-ray eyes. One such was Kuda Bux, who failed a test witnessed by a committee of ten, including A. C. Marks, president of Bucknell College, and Albert Edward Wiggam, famous psychologist. The *New York Times* for July 8, 1938 reported that when a simple paper bag was substituted for dough, cotton and bandages Bux said, "I can't. I think we had better stop here." It was Joseph Dunninger, president of the Universal Council for Psychical Research, who insisted on the paper bag, so he went home with the $10,000 he had offered to pay the alleged psychic if he had succeeded.

No other claimant to possession of X-ray eyes received so much journalistic as well as scientific attention as Patrick Marquis of Glendale, Calif. when he was 12 years old. Even with the most secure blindfold he traced drawings, imitated gestures, played pool and in general seemed to see as well blindfolded as he did normally. His talent was discovered by his physician, Dr. Cecil E. Reynolds, who said Pat performed his feats while in a trance with part of his brain under the control of an 11th-century Persian named Napeji. In introducing a half-page account of the boy's achievements, the *Milwaukee Journal* June 6, 1936 declared:

Nearly every celebrated medium who has been investigated by scientific persons has eventually been proved a fake. Houdini spent years and much money fighting fakers and proved time and time again that he could duplicate any so-called supernatural stunt that he saw a medium perform. But every now and then cases of so-called mediumship puzzle scientists for a long time and many famous and educated persons are firm believers in spirits and spirit messages.

The following account is not printed with the idea of defending or attacking mediums. It is simply a straightforward account of the amazing performance of a boy only 12 years old and the report of a committee of scientific men.

The report, signed by 12 medical men, called the demonstration one of "supernormal vision and cognition." The report, much of which the newspaper reproduced, was descriptive of the boy's behavior before an audience of 150 at the Hollywood Hospital.

June 11, 1936 the Associated Press reported from Los Angeles that Pat's strange powers did not help him much in his studies at school. "I wish they did," he said.

Alma Whitaker followed Pat for the *Los Angeles Times*, beginning with an account May 7, 1936 of his blindfold tests at Hollywood Hospital to dumfound 150 doctors. In a feature, "The Other World," June 7, 1936 Whitaker asked rhetorically, "Are the spirits of the legions of the dead making a concerted effort to communicate with us?" She answered by telling of how Pat shook the experts, including the former cynic Hamlin Garland, author of *Forty Years of Psychic Research*. In a trance during which he presumably was controlled by Napeji, Pat fenced skillfully, the *Times* reported June 21, 1936. In all of these accounts the many-layered blindfolds were described.

May 1, 1937 Whitaker wrote more than a full-page profile, "Boy Wonder Baffles Science" for the *Times*. In it she related many baffling anecdotes of the boy's ability, including his speaking and writing Persian while in a trance, correctly stating that a baby in a picture had died, identifying the key to a letter box with exact description and many more.

After *Life* gave three pages, mostly of pictures, April 10, 1937, Lewis Browne, rabbi and author who had witnessed the demonstration, wrote a letter that *Life* used May 3, saying that Dr. Joseph Rhine had tested Patrick to conclude the boy could loosen the adhesive tape and had no psychic ability. The *Life* editor's note confessed it did not know of the Rhine tests. In a long rejoinder in *Life* for May 17, 1937, Dr. Reynolds wrote that Rhine's tests were inappropriate and that he could not emulate Pat's performance when Hamlin Garland blindfolded him. *Life* then humbly commented: "Obviously *Life* cannot attempt to determine the scientific authenticity of Pat Marquis' performance. That controversy must be settled between Dr. Reynolds and his critics."

The case of Rosa Kuleshova, who claimed to be able to read printed matter through her fingertips, was told in America by the UPI, which broadcast story and picture from Moscow Jan. 31, 1931. Rosa also supposedly could distinguish colors by the toes of her right foot and the tip of her tongue while blindfolded. In his book *Myths of the Space Age*, Daniel Cohen tells how Lev Teplov, a reporter for the *Novosti* press agency, arranged for scientifically controlled tests for Rosa and several of her imitators. They all failed. Teplov's vitriolic condemnation of the women might well be emulated by some American journalists who too often are either gullible or too polite.

Another tantalizing use of eyes was to transmit thoughts onto a Polaroid camera. That, at least, is what Ted Serios, a bellhop at the

Chicago Hilton Hotel, asserted was the case. Development of the power to produce thought photography came after hypnotic searches for treasure buried by Jean Lafitte, notorious pirate who helped General Andrew Jackson defeat the British at New Orleans. George Johannas, a hypnotist friend, suggested trying to photograph Ted's visions. The foremost believer in Serios' power was a psychoanalyst, Dr. Jule Eisenbud of Denver who wrote a book, *The World of Ted Serios.* As James Randi explained in his book *Flim-Flam!* the secret of psychophotography was the gimmick or tube that Serios held before the lens, a small device easily hidden by use of paper covering.

Ted Serios was the darling of the psychics for almost two decades. Two of the best newspaper features were by John Davy, written for the *London Observer* and reprinted in the *Chicago Sun-Times* for May 28, 1977, and a piece by David Miller, "Psychic snaps pictures you wouldn't believe," in the *Chicago Tribune's Suburban Trib* for June 23, 1976 under the headline "Mind Images If a Fraud, Where Are the Loopholes?"

Stories of extraordinary performances making unorthodox use of parts of the body always are newsworthy. April 30, 1949 the Associated Press reported from Godhra, India that a 3-year-old boy had second sight and had restored the sight of a man who had been blind for three years and converted water into sweet wine.

At least a dozen Chinese children were able to read through their ears and at least two by pressing the material into their armpits according to a story by Timothy McNully in the *Chicago Tribune* for Feb. 3, 1980.

Feb. 6, 1938, in an exclusive story, the *Boston American* reported that the celebrated medium Margery (Mrs. L. R. G. Crandon, wife of a surgeon) had challenged Dr. Rhine and Prof. William McDougall of Duke University to match her telepathic talents in a tournament of psychic phenomena. She had been provoked by statements by Rhine and McDougall that she lacked the ability to name cards by extrasensory perception and that fraud had been detected in her performances, during which she claimed to be in a trance under the control of her dead brother Walter. Although the article did not include the background, the fraud had been detected by the great Harry Houdini on whose proof of fraud a committee of scientists representing the *Scientific American* denounced her and refused to award her $5,000 that was on deposit in the office of Boston's mayor, to be paid to anyone able to perform in public any mystery that Houdini could not satisfactorily expose and explain. The play-by-play account of how Houdini exposed Margery is included in the biography *Houdini,* by Harold Kellock, based on the documents and recollections of the widow, Beatrice Houdini.

According to the *American* the adverse comments of Dr. Rhine and McDougall surprised Margery who said that the former had previously commended her at the University of Virginia. She probably forgot that McDougall was on the *Scientific American* committee that condemned her.

Feb. 7, 1938 the *Boston American* reported that Rhine refused to accept Margery's challenge unless she agreed to "certain conditions." This prompted her to retort that "Dr. Rhine is making thought transference so complicated it might as well be the Einstein theory so far as the public is concerned. That's smart of Dr. Rhine; as long as people can't make out what he's doing he'll gain the reputation of being a superman."

Nobody ever collected the Houdini $5,000 prize or the $10,000 offered by Joseph Dunninger, who for 25 years performed as a magician and then turned to professional mind-reading, admitting his magic was trickery but insisting his mind reading was real. For most of his career he was president of the Universal Council for Psychic Research.

Dunninger was a student of magic. He wrote an article on the origin of some outstanding tricks and the contributions of many American greats. The article appeared originally in *Today* magazine and was reprinted, among other places, in the *Milwaukee Journal* for Sept. 16, 1936. It began: "The best way to give an old trick real flavor is to ship it to India and let it come back again." Levitation, walking on hot coals and climbing a rope to disappear into the atmosphere all originated in the United States." He related the contributions of Herman (Comars) the Great, Harry Keller, Howard Thurston and, of course, Harry Houdini who began life in Budapest, not Appleton, Wis., as Erik Wisz.

What Dunninger did that almost everyone qualified to have an opinion said was impossible was related by Betty Burns in the *Chicago Sun* for Nov. 14, 1943. The supposedly impossible feat was to conduct a successful mind-reading act on radio. When he reviewed Dunninger's book, *What's On Your Mind?* for the July 16, 1944 *Chicago Sun-Times,* Harold M. Sherman lauded the "master mentalist" for exposing hundreds of spirit mediums, psychics and fortune tellers, but was obviously saddened by Dunninger's espousal of mental telepathy. The review concluded, "It is often difficult to tell where magic ends and telepathy begins."

A similar tone of regret permeated the feature Larry Lawrence wrote for the Dec. 30, 1955 *Milwaukee Journal.* He recalled a small social gathering attended by Mayor Daniel and Mrs. Hoan at which Dunninger entertained informally. Then Lawrence asked rhetorically, "Was he just tired of being a skeptic?" He quoted without comment Dunninger's own defense of himself.

The respect that such geniuses as Herman, Houdon, Keller, Thurston, Houdini, Dunninger, Blackstone, Sr. and Jr. and others have earned enabled Isaac Bonewitz to persuade the University of California at Berkeley to permit him to take a special course leading to a bachelor of arts in magic, believed to be the first and only such degree granted by any American college or university. The students defined magic as "phenomena which occur and do not fit in with any of the known laws of the universe." His individualized curriculum included courses in sociology, psychology, anthropology, various religions, folklore and mythology.

Another who declares he's riding the wave of the future is Stanley Poulton. According to Dave Canfield in the *Chicago Daily News* for Feb. 24, 1970, Poulton told the Spiritual Frontiers Fellowship: "Rather than escapism, I think it is facing reality and preparing ourselves for the journey that sooner or later all of us are going to face."

An outstanding magician, Milbourne Christopher, was interviewed by Philip Nobile, his Q & A story appearing in the *Chicago Sun-Times* for March 10, 1974. Wrote Nobile: "Christopher's pet peeve (and mine) is illegitimate deceptions—seers, psychics and the ESP crowd. As chairman of the Society of American Magicians' occult investigating committee, he delights in puncturing the pretensions of pretenders." He deplores Uri Geller and wishes Kreskin would stop making believe he has supernatural powers.

Perhaps the three greatest living magicians are Harry Blackstone, Jr., George Kresge, Jr., who calls himself Kreskin, and James Randi (real name, Randall James Zwinge). Blackstone is a masterful all-round actor carrying on for his great father; an entertainer, he steers clear of debates about ESP and relative matters. Kreskin, on the other hand, says he's psychic although his colleagues are unconvinced that he is anything but an extremely clever sleight-of-hand performer and, especially, judge of human nature, meaning his audiences. He told Philip Nobile, who wrote about him in the *Midwest Magazine* of the *Chicago Sun-Times* for March 23, 1975: "As a performer I try to dramatize whatever ability I have. That's why I refuse to state that my entire act is based on ESP."

By contrast James Randi is a crusader, going after frauds and charlatans even more vigorously than Houdini or Dunninger ever did. He is on the editorial board of the *Skeptical Inquirer,* quarterly publication of the Committee for the Scientific Investigation of Claims of the Paranormal. There is hardly an issue that does not have at least one article by Randi debunking some myth or superstition. One of his main targets has been Uri Geller, the Israeli who claims he bends keys, forks and other metal objects by will power rather than physical strength. Geller's psychokinetic achievements have received international attention.

Geller was cited by Robert C. Cowen in the *Christian Science Monitor* for April 23, 1971 as one who raised "an awkward research question, Can the traditional coldly objective methods of the laboratory effectively probe phenomena that seem to need a 'favorable mental atmosphere' to appear? Is science being asked to investigate something beyond its powers?" He mentioned four scientists at London's Birkbeck College who thought they saw Geller cause part of a vanadium carbide crystal to vanish.

Geller came to the United States in 1972 and almost immediately was a sensation. "The man who came to dinner played havoc with the forks," James H. Bowman wrote in the *Chicago Daily News* for June 30, 1973. The story told of a dinner party given by Dr. John S. Long, among whose guests were Marshall Field, a publisher of the *Chicago News* and *Sun-Times,* and

Lt. Gov. Neil Hartigan. Uri amazed everyone by bending rings and forks
and making a broken watch work.

A typical example of how Geller bewildered journalists was Helen
Kruger's long profile, "The man who bends forks with his eyes" in *Village
Voice* for April 19, 1973. She wound up dumfounded when Geller bent a
fork in her presence. This was after she had reported that the Israeli once
turned rosé wine to red, made milk into water, experienced an astral
projection to Brazil to seek coins and bent a fork on the Jack Paar show. On
the negative side she cited *Time's* report that the Stanford tests of Geller
were sloppy and unreliable.

Six months later James Pearre began his story in *Chicago Today* for
Jan. 29, 1974, "Uri Geller is the biggest thing to hit the psychic world since
Bridey Murphy." In between his two Chicago visits Geller had spent
several months being tested at the Stanford Research Institute (SRI) at
Menlo Park, Calif., which reported that it could find "no scientific explana-
tion" for Geller's mind boggling feats.

Another Chicago paper, the *Sun-Times,* gave Jane Gregory a page May
14, 1974 to amplify her lead, "After an hour with psychic Uri Geller I
simply don't know about his power. Certainly he has something going. But
how it works, to say nothing of where it comes from, sure beats me. I am not
a true believer. But I do have this crazy bent key."

The *Chicago Tribune* reported Oct. 27, 1974, "Uri Geller's detractors
aren't going to like this very much, but he's dignified now." The story
reported on the results of some of the Stanford tests, especially drawings
that he made presumably by telepathy. The *New York Times* had an
extensive story, with illustrations, Oct. 22, 1974 and the *Sun-Times* used
an Associated Press account Oct. 23 under the headline, "2 Say ESP a
possibility." The two were Harold Puthoff and Russell Targ of the SRI. In
the *Times* Boyce Rensberger quoted them as believing that Geller, and
probably most people, have an ability to send and receive information by
some "as yet unidentified perceptual modality."

Amost the same words were used by a group of scientists, Reuters
reported from Paris May 5, 1975. Albert Ducrocq, who arranged for the
tests, said, "When Curie discovered radioactivity before the turn of the last
century, people used to laugh and treat her like a charlatan. But now that
radioactivity has been explained people have ceased to be skeptical. They
will stop considering Geller to be an illusionist when his powers are
understood."

In her Personalities Plus column in the *Chicago Tribune Magazine* for
Sept. 1, 1974, Robin Adams Sloan answered the query of a reader who
asked the status of confidence in Geller's claims. She mentioned the exposé
by Randi and an article in *Psychology Today* by Andrew Weil, once a Geller
true believer but now disillusioned.

On the other hand in the *Village Voice* for Oct. 17, 1974 Howard Smith
and Brian Van Der Horst reported that Geller convinced a team of English

investigators, including David Bohm, John Hasted, Arthur A. Clarke and Arthur Koestler, and *Nature* magazine intended to publish the favorable Stanford report.

When Geller went to Chicago to advertise his book *Uri Geller, My Story* he completely fooled reporter Patricia Shelton and Pulitzer prize–winning photographer John White by bending two keys by stroking them gently, by the power of his mind according to him. The story and picture appeared in the *Chicago Daily News* for June 2, 1975.

One journalist who remained skeptical after interviewing Geller was Bob Greene who reported May 19, 1975 on the experience. The *Sun-Times* columnist stumped Geller with ten questions, such as the capital of Idaho, is Mike Royko going to transfer to the *Washington Post* and who wrote the Philep Dream Girl Song. When Greene asked Geller to straighten his key, the entertainer answered, "You fix your own key."

In the same newspaper Aug. 12, 1975 it was revealed that 50 or so viewers who held broken watches before the television screen as advised by Geller on Kup's show over WMAQ-TV kidded themselves that it helped. They either lied or were self-hypnotized, because the program had been taped three months earlier and had been televised at least once previously.

Growing opposition to Geller's claims of supernatural power was evidenced by an increase in articles, interviews and books by professional magicians who, Boyce Rensberger reported in the *New York Times* for Dec. 13, 1975, were "long irked" by the Israeli's claims. They have duplicated almost all of Geller's tricks using ordinary conjuring methods and, Rensberger wrote, "they believe that Mr. Geller is demeaning their craft by saying that his powers are beamed to him from a space ship sent by a superior civilization in outer space."

The article mentioned several of the methods Randi used to belittle Geller in England. At Birkbeck College in London, for instance, he taped a magnet to his leg to make a Geiger counter click wildly as Geller had done before him.

Feb. 25, 1980 Michele Stevens reported in the *Chicago Sun-Times* Public Eye column that Uri would make a visit to a New York restaurant to teach women how to use ESP to propose to men. April 10, 1981 the *New York Post* reported that for 15 minutes during a flight from New York to Los Angeles Uri would draw a paper image and—using telepathy and telekinesis—transmit messages to people nationwide.

In his books *The Magic of Uri Geller* and *Flim-Flam!* James Randi destroyed whatever credibility Geller had. At a reception at an American Booksellers convention in California Randi, in disguise, bent the keys and stopped the watches of delegates. The *New York Times* for Sept. 24, 1982 summarized his case against Uri Geller.

For the *Chicago Sun-Times* of May 9, 1976 Philip Nobile interviewed "Tricky Uri Geller," who he called "the hottest thing in occult showbiz since Houdini." Geller said he was indifferent to criticism from magicians and others as long as scientists supported him. Asked why he didn't sue some of his detractors, he replied, "Why should I sue? They've made me a millionaire."

Editorially Dec 22, 1976 the *Village Voice* expressed mock sympathy for Uri who will have to certify that every bent key to be marketed by Ancillary Enterprises, Inc. was bent by his exercise of mental prowess. A three-column photograph of Geller accompanied a story in the *New York World Herald* for Oct. 27, 1978 that Geller and three other psychics would compete with four newspaper sports writers in selecting the winners of the forthcoming horse races at Aqueduct.

Randi's most important triumph over the parapsychologists to date was his infiltrating the McDonnell Laboratory for Psychical Research at Washington University in St. Louis. Two teen-agers, selected, trained and directed by Randi during three years convinced Dr. Peter R. Phillips and his staff that they had psychic powers. By means of standard magic tricks they bent wires by stroking them, knocked a clock off a table without touching it and performed other startling acts. Bella English covered a Randi press conference on the episode for the *New York Daily News* of Jan. 30, 1983. William J. Broad wrote a half-page article for the *New York Times* of Feb. 15, mostly on the furor the hoax caused among scientists. After the detailed report appeared in the March *Discover,* the *Washington Post* ran a lengthy piece by Philip J. Hilts in its issue of March 1, 1983. Randi said he masterminded the hoax to show that scientific research on psychic powers is not as scientific as it should be and that psychic researchers refuse the help of magicians to design experiments that prevent fakery.

What the future holds in store if, undaunted by critical opposition, the true believers persist, may be surmised in part by considering plans for further research as they have been announced in recent years. For example in the *New York Times* for July 29, 1971 Israel Shenker reported the awarding of $297,000 to the American Society for Psychical Research to accelerate its search for proof of the existence of man's immortal soul. The money came from the estate of a prospector, James Kidd, who designated in his will that the court determine who the recipient should be. Dr. Gardner Murphy, president of the society, persuaded Arizona Superior Court Judge Robert L. Myers that his organization was the most worthy of 130 contenders.

"Psychic power as weapon of tomorrow" was the headline the *Chicago Sun-Times* used Aug. 14, 1977 on a story by John L. Wilhelm, written originally for the *Washington Post*. It revealed that the Central Intelligence Agency and the National Security Agency were sponsoring secret research conducted at the Stanford Research Institute to determine how ESP could be used as a weapon against the Soviet Union. Two subjects, Ingo Swann and Pat Price, allegedly were successful in describing remote sites. Wilhelm wrote: "There is particular concern about Soviet psychical capabilities, including allegations that the Russians are able tele-pathically to influence the behavior of others, alter their emotions or health, knock them out or even kill by directing a kind of psychic double-whammy at them.

A followup *Washington Post* article by Wilhelm, "ESP is for espionage," appeared in the *Sun-Times* for Sept. 3, 1977. It contained more details on the places that Price described from afar, causing one security officer to exclaim, "Hell, there's no security left." The nature of the document given to Robert Toth of the *Los Angeles Times* to cause him to be expelled from the Soviet Union was revealed as containing a theory of psychic function-ing called mitogenetic radiation. Wilhelm quoted Dr. Pucharich as saying Geller could erase magnetic tapes, levitate tiny weights, materialize and dematerialize small objects.

The avidity with which the American press accepts any evidence of Soviet failure in any undertaking was illustrated in the 400-word story the Associated Press distributed April 28, 1968 from Moscow. It told of the exposé of a woman who had received considerable publicity for apparently being able to move objects without touching them. Similar iconoclastic pieces about American magicians seldom appear.

That the CIA in the early '50s seriously considered extensive re-search in the use of ESP in spying and espionage work was revealed when memoranda were made public under the Freedom of Information Act, the UPI reported from Washington March 12, 1979.

It is not surprising that Cold War rumors should circulate to spread suspicion and fear of the Soviets and enchance the chances of passage by Congress of huge military expenditures. In the May 9, 1966 *Nation* Daniel Cohen mentioned several of them, including that the Soviets had eight large laboratories experimenting with ESP with considerable success. The *Nautilus* and eyeless vision rumors have been mentioned (see pages 525 and 566).

Consistent with their centuries-old behavior in response to new scien-tific claims some religious leaders have changed their attitudes regarding ESP from rejection to advocacy of experimentation to benefit the church. One such religious leader is the Rev. Morton Kelsey, an Episcopal priest on the faculty of the University of Notre Dame. John Dart, religion editor, reported in the *Los Angeles Times* for Oct. 22, 1977 that Father Kelsey believes ESP is a door that opens people to believe that they are in contact with something material, not illusory. "I would describe the supernatural as the natural which we have simply shut out. If the mainline churches integrate their present scientific views with the one parapsychological facts suggest, Christianity will again be in a position of central influence on modern culture," he said.

Almost the same time Michael I. Malloy reported in the *National Observer* for Sept. 4, 1976, both the International Brotherhood of Magi-cians and the Society of American Magicians were growing at the rate of

100 per month. Malloy covered the 54th annual convention sponsored by Abbott's Magic Company in Colon, Mich., the small town that Harry Blackstone made his winter headquarters in the '20s. The 1,314 who came outnumbered the 1,172 permanent dwellers in the host city. Wrote Malloy: "Uri Geller is a bad word here. 'Magicians are more skeptical about ESP than anyone and they hate people who step over the line,' says Warren Stephens. The Israeli psychic bends keys with the power of his mind. For four bucks I can buy a gizmo that lets me bend keys too. The directions contain a request, 'All we ask is that you do not claim supernatural powers; one is enough.'"

Another small town, Galveston, Ind., with 1,300 souls, is the site of another mecca for magicians and fans. There the son of the late Mysterious Lawrence, the Phenomenal Prestidigitator, alias Reginald B. Lawrence, operates the International Magicians' Hall of Fame. The hall, opened in 1971, has the largest, if not the greatest collection of historical magical apparatus in the world. Blackstone's working tools, Houdini's caps and even the steel playing card Bill Bixby used in the old television show "The Magician" and much, much more is there, according to Bill Shaw who wrote it up for the Nov. 5, 1981 *Chicago Tribune*.

In the same paper Oct. 29, 1981 Monroe Anderson paid homage to Mrs. Frances Marshall, 50 of whose 71 years were spent performing magic or operating the largest magic shop in Chicago, called the magic capital of the world. In her honor more than a dozen magicians planned shows at several high schools on Halloween. The change of notes is the decline of theater performance and a sizable increase in restaurant and barroom entertainers. Thus the disappearing elephant gives way to the card shark.

The growing interest in ESP had made more business for newspaper advice columnists. Dec. 8, 1981 Dr. Joyce Brothers replied to a reader worried about the advice she received from a neighbor, who claimed to possess ESP, that she should leave her husband. Wrote Brothers: "While there's some scientific evidence for ESP, talking with your husband would be a far better way to get information about how he feels about you and your future together than talking with your neighbors."

In the *New York Daily News*' "Your Dreams" column for March 9, 1982 Katy advised Curious Sister that her 12-year-old brother might have nightmares because by ESP he knew other members of the family frequently dreamed that he was injured or killed. In the same column May 31, 1982, Katy gave an either-or reply to Appreciative that the dreams she and one sister had about another sister were similar not because of ESP, but she was equivocal in how to interpret several aspects of the dreams. For example, she wrote about the birth of twins: "Either you feel she is about to realize a favorable potential or she's in for added burden or 'double trouble.'"

In his Lyons Den column Leonard Lyons told of Hans Holzer's work on a pilot TV series, "Haunted," in a house where a knife was seen rising slowly from the floor. Called in to investigate Holzer brought a film crew with him.

Other newspaper pieces about or of interest to ESP buffs included the following:

Two doctors at Jefferson Medical College in Philadelphia tested 28-year-old identical twin brothers to discover that when one closed his eyes the brain waves of the other changed as if he too had closed his eyes. In a lengthy article in the *New York Herald Tribune* for Oct. 25, 1965 Joseph R. Hixson described in detail the test that convinced the researchers that the mind has channels of comprehension other than the five senses.

In the *Chicago Tribune* for July 11, 1971 Stephanie Fuller wrote about the proliferation of ESP games, among the most popular being Kreskin's ESP, Testing Color Perception and Switched-on-ESP.

The possible resurrection of the ESP television series, "One Step Beyond," possibly under a different name in England, was reported Aug. 8, 1981 from London in *Variety*.

Jane Gregory gave the game Switched-On-ESP a plug in the *Chicago Tribune* for Dec. 1, 1971. The game is a spinoff of the book *Psychic Discoveries Behind the Iron Curtain* by Sheila Ostrander and Lynn Schroeder. The article was headlined in three columns, "If you're bored with Ouija, here's a switch."

The *Corpus Christi Callum-Times* for June 9, 1972 had a true-false test of one's knowledge of ESP. Question 1, "People who are nervous and highstrung have the edge over the rest of us when it comes to ESP ability" was false. But No. 2, "ESP works best with people who are congenial with each other" was true.

In the *Chicago Daily News* for Aug. 12–13, 1972 Peggy Lipton answered a query concerning the truth of the rumor that the Las Vegas Flamingo Hotel bars Kreskin from the gaming tables because of his ESP prowess. The casino's manager was quoted as saying Kreskin had been telling that lie for years, adding, "Kreskin is as psychic as your average oyster."

Roger Verhulst reported in the *Chicago Tribune* for Sept. 15, 1972 that an experiment in trying to project a six-word message by silent meditation, attempted daily for a week, was a complete failure.

In two articles more than a year apart the *Wall Street Journal* told of what happens when the Securities & Exchange Commission disbelieves someone who advertises he uses his ESP power to advise investors. The May 7, 1973 article told of the SEC's calling of four hearings to determine if Stuart A. Schwalbe, a San Francisco investment advisor, defrauded his clients. Jan. 30, 1974 the paper reported that Schwalbe's license had been revoked and a psychic healer was the subject of Eugenia Sheppard's "Inside Fashion" column in the *New York Post* for Jan. 15, 1973. Maria Cooper Janis is the daughter of the late Gary Cooper and Mrs. John Converse. She expected to be on Barbara Walters' show with Uri Geller who twisted tableware when she had breakfast with him. She also got mention in

Suzy's column for Feb. 5, 1978 in the *New York Post*. Then she was in demand for comment in connection with the motion picture *The Fury*.

George Gent wrote in the *New York Times* for May 8, 1973 that there would be a first public showing in a Universalist church of a documentary film, "Psychics, Saints and Scholars." Subjects covered included ESP, spiritual healing, Kirlian photography, clairvoyance and similar aspects of psi.

An all-day program, "Paranormal Experiences," sponsored by the School of Continuing Education and the Foundation for Parasensory Investigation to examine tangible evidence of intangibles, including ESP, was announced in the *New York Times* "Guide to Going Out" column for March 1, 1974.

As the House Judiciary Committee began hearings in April 1974 that eventually led to President Nixon's resignation, Marcie Kuhn had a party for 40 fellow clairvoyants. Although the supposed guest of honor, Jeane Dixon, didn't come, the others exchanged prophecies to make a sizable story for Judy Van Bachrach in the *Washington Post*.

An anonymous reporter for *Village Voice* told Aug. 15, 1974 of using an ESP teaching machine recently invented by the Stanford researchers. It has the usual 25 symbols and the subject punches his guesses. When one gets 8 of 25 right a sign lights up "A Good Beginning." For better scores there are signs "Outstanding ESP Ability" and "Psychic Medium/Oracle." The article does not say how many times it is necessary to make the high scores to maintain the title.

More than 100 films from 22 countries were to be shown at the New York–Montreal Film Festival in New York, the *New York Times* reported Sept. 4, 1975.

Sylvia Disher of Staunton, Va. has had 50–55 percent success in ESP experiments with her Labrador retriever, sending him mental orders while he slept in the bathtub and she was in another room with the TV loudly drowning out all other sounds. "Dogs," she says, "have a super-sensory awareness much more acute than a human." She has sent test booklets on ESP to dog owners with instructions and a request that she be sent the results. Walter R. Fletcher reported on the situation in the *New York Times* for April 8, 1976.

Prime Minister Eric Gairy of Grenada, a small Caribbean republic, urged the United Nations General Assembly to establish a department or agency to conduct psychic research, the *New York Post* reported Oct. 9, 1975. Exactly a year later, Oct. 9, 1976, the *Post* reported that Gairy repeated the suggestion and asked why the existence of flying saucers was kept a secret. He called for the acceptance of a universal god.

Another *New York Times* article on Fisher and her dogs, written by Pat Gleeson, was published May 12, 1977. It was a report of a speech Ms. Fisher delivered to a dog fanciers' club. She cautioned about not confusing ESP with a dog's supersensory awareness. She cited examples of clairvoyance and precognition involving owner and dog.

At an ESP Psychic Fair Jane Perlez, *New York Post* reporter, was most impressed by Komar, who lay on a bed of nails with a 230-pound man squatting on top of a sheet with more nails that covered him. There also were specialists in many different aspects of psi that she described May 8, 1977.

The "predicting newspaper headlines" stunt failed in Philadelphia when a sharp radio reporter saw how the trick was done and threatened an exposé, *Variety* reported Aug. 24, 1977.

April 15, 1979 the Associated Press reported from Metairie, La. that when his 9-year-old daughter Wendy disappeared, in addition to notifying the sheriff, Ronald Hitchcock called an astrologer, two psychics and the newspaper.

That parapsychology is coming of age was indicated when James S. McDonnell, president of McDonnell-Douglas Corporation, gave a half-million dollars to Peter R. Phillips, a Washington University physicist, for research in parapsychology. The *New York Times* quoted McDonnell Oct. 23, 1979: "Man is approaching the evolutionary point where he is beginning to realize there is a possible merging of matter and mind and a priority item for current scientific research is the understanding of human consciousness." Randi's hoax followed.

Organizers of a mass meditation experiment said perhaps a million persons worldwide tried by telekinesis to get the orbiting skylab back on course, Stacy Jolna reported from Brookline, Mass. for the *Washington Post* May 26, 1979. The Brookline Psychoenergetics Institute arranged for a 42-station international hookup originating in a Florida radio station. Nothing happened during the 7½-minute test.

Jacqueline Trescott made Mental Magic parties seem like fun but not much different from group gossip sessions on psychic matters, as she described the new phenomenon in the *Washington Post* for Jan. 5, 1982. Psychics acted like professional mind-readers to provide fun for everyone.

Many ESP buffs believe in the Corsican Brothers syndrome, meaning that twins, even though separated, share each other's psychical pains and are likely to have identical tastes. Edward Edelson related several anecdotes of such happenings in the *New York Daily News* for March 2, 1982. The immediate news was the refusal of a judge to hear a case in which a surviving twin claimed damages when her twin was killed in an airplane crash. Experts pro and con are cited in the article.

The *New York Daily News* devoted two pages June 13, 1982 to "New York Psychics," mostly biographical sketches of five of the most important, by Cynthia Raymond. The subhead was "Do they know what's in the cards for you?"

27

UFOs

Heavenly bodies, also known as stars, planets, comets and meteors, were not all that our ancestors saw when they surveyed the sky. The mythology and folklore of just about every human society tell of flying objects that terrorized many but often were interpreted as signs and portents to guide the behavior of earthlings. Both the Old and New Testaments have such accounts and there are legends about what famous warriors and others throughout history saw to cause hope or despair.

Sometime in the late 1940s or early 1950s, exact date lost, Barry O'Flaherty of the *Chicago Daily News* discovered a rare book in Newberry Library, *Book of the Damned,* by Charles Fort, in which are included the accounts of four mysterious sightings, the first in 1731 when a "luminous cloud moving at high velocity" was observed over Florence, Italy.

May 16, 1808 as "The sky turned brick red," there appeared on the western horizon a number of round objects, dark brown in color and seemingly about the size of a hat crown, according to a report from Skeninge, Sweden.

March 22, 1870 a sea captain reported "a remarkable cloud or object in the sky" off the west coast of Africa. And, Fort reported, "An object that looked like the moon in the three-quarter aspect" appeared over County Wicklow, Ireland.

Unquestionably during the past century as before there were many persons who reported seeing mysterious objects overhead, but newspaper editors apparently did not take seriously what any of them might have reported. The contemporary era of bewilderment, wonderment and terror over unidentified flying objects began June 24, 1947 when a Boise, Idaho businessman, Kenneth Arnold, told the press that he was piloting his own plane near Mt. Rainier, Wash. when he observed, 50 miles away, a formation of nine objects moving at perhaps 1,200 miles per hour "like saucers skipping over water," which description caused an Associated Press reporter to dub them "flying saucers," which is what they continued to be called for more than a decade until "disk" was substituted, as it was shorter and easier to fit into headlines. There was dispute as to whether it should be "disk" or "disc." In 1957 the Air Force adopted "Unidentified Flying Objects" to designate its Project Blue Book. UFO fits nicely into any headline and has survived.

When Arnold first made the headlines I was on an automobile trip in the East, which accounts for the fact that I have no clippings about flying saucers dated earlier than July 7, 1947 when the *Chicago Tribune* had a page 1 streamer headline, "Reports Seeing Disk Land," followed by a hanger, "Woman Says 8 Fluttered Down in Idaho," over a 2-column story datelined San Francisco.

Since then to date I have accumulated thousands of clippings, to digest which would make a book much larger than this one. So, of necessity, here are the headings of just a few typical stories from 1947 on, classified by their major interests:

Sightings

July 8, 1947, UP undated streamer was headlined by the *Chicago Sun:* "Flying Disks Pass Up Kansas: After All, It's a Dry state." The lead was: "The fantasy of the 'flying saucers' was growing hourly across the country last night amid a flood of bizarre reports, many of which were attributed to pranksters."

In the same issue of the paper "Those Flying Saucers" were belittled in what was a typical journalistic viewpoint at the time.

> After a hard Fourth of July weekend, the nation finds itself jittery over the subject of "flying saucers." Some people claim they are jet-propelled and roar like mighty bombers. Others have seen them flying in formation, heading north. A gentleman in Denver says he saw the American flag painted on one of them. If true, this is certainly the most encouraging report to date. It will bring merciful relief to many people who feared the disks might be of foreign origin.
>
> Human suggestibility being what it is, a lot of people didn't see what they think they saw. But in these days of Buck Rogers miracles, nobody can be sure that nobody saw anything. It is easier to ask "what brand d'ya drink" or suggest a switch to Calvert, and to note that the Russians apparently have not yet seen a single "flying saucer."
>
> All this, of course, is just the beginning. One day the American people will wake to read in their morning papers that the Russians have developed an atomic bomb. It seems hardly premature to ask ourselves what effect this will have on the national digestion. Nor does it seem repetitious to point out that we have roughly five years to work out some form of international control of atomic energy. Otherwise this jittery world may face the possibility of a conflict in which Prof. Einstein estimates only one third of the human race will survive.

July 8, Frederick C. Othman, who identified himself as United Press Sea Monster and Saucer Correspondent, also satirized the situation in his syndicated column, to which the *Sun* gave the headline "When You're in Your Cups the Flying Saucers Appear," another indication of the skepticism widespread in journalistic ranks at the time.

July 9, the *Sun* gave multiple-column headlines to two Associated Press stories, one from Fort Worth, "Army's Flying Disk in New Mexico Turns Out to be Weather Balloon," and the other from Richmond, "Blast It, Says Admiral, Why Blame Bikini Test?"

July 10, 1947, the *Chicago Daily News* editorialized on "Who's Loony Now?" It began: "The sky disk mania appears to have wound up in a busted balloon. Since it started it has provided sophisticates with a delightful excuse to denounce the common herd for its susceptibility to mass hysteria."

Also July 10, the *New York Compass* ran one of Albert Deutsch's masterpieces, "On Seeing Flying Saucers or the Cloud That Looked Like a Whale."

July 11, 1947, the columnist Kenesaw M. Landis II elaborated on "A Streamlined Terror Ousts Witches of Old."

July 12, 1947, Philip Wylie wrote, "The Disks Show Our Hysteria".

July 20, 1947, Howard Q. Blakeslee, Associated Press science editor, wrote, "Great Flying Disk Mystery May Start New Folklore," with a subtitle, "Mankind on Alert for Threat From Skies, Scientists Say in Explanation of Puzzle."

Nov. 4, 1947, the North American Newspaper Alliance distributed an article by Lionel Shapiro from Geneva, Switzerland: "Say Spy Saga Franco Linked to Air Disks," with a hanger, "New Weapons Made by Nazis in Spain."

July 6, 1948, the *Springfield* (Ill.) *State Journal and Register* streamer-headlined an AP story "Atom Energy Behind Discs?"

July 25, 1948, a United Press story from Atlanta was headlined: "It Had Windows, 2 Pilots Report. See in Sky Huge Fiery Flying Cigar."

July 7, 1949, the *Chicago Times* reported, "Discs 'Sighted' in 39 States." The same day the *Chicago Sun* had a page-1 streamer, "Silly Season Is Here! Planes Hunt Flying Discs.' " over an AP story from San Francisco that had the lead: "Military aircraft hunted the skies over Pacific coast states today for sight of the mysterious 'flying saucers' that for 12 days have puzzled the entire country."

March 10, 1950, the *Chicago Sun* reported: "Disc Reports Start Jitters."

March 26, 1950, the *Chicago Times* had a story by William I. Hathaway, "Claims Disks Are His," he being the famous balloonist, Jean Piccard, whose picture was used with the story. In an adjacent column was a story from Rome: "Professor Says Hitler, Mussolini Had Disk Design."

April 29, 1950, the *Chicago Daily News* headlined a story, "Saucers Flight or Fancy? Scientists Here Disagree."

Feb. 10, 1952, *Parade* had an article, "Who's Throwing Fire Balls at US?"

July 20, 1952, Associated Press story, "Disks Trick Radar. Atmosphere, Says Air Force—But Probe Continues."

July 23, 1952, the *Chicago Sun-Times* used a full-width page-1 headline, "Flying 'Objects' Chased By Jets. Picked Up Via Radar at Washington Airport."

Aug. 3, 1952, for the *New York Times* Waldemar Kaemffert wrote: "Those Flying Saucers Not What They Seem. There are Various Explanations for Them But More Can Be Learned."

Aug. 5, 1952, Arthur J. Snider wrote for the *Chicago Daily News:* "Ghosts or Real: Often Fooled Public Sticking Neck Out Again on Saucers. They're Seeing Something Sums Up Attitude of Men on Street."

Nov. 4, 1952, the *Chicago Tribune* used an AP story from London under the headline "British Tie up Flying Saucers to Comic Books."

Feb. 4, 1955, the *Chicago American* devoted a full page to "Visitors From Space? Saucer Folk Called Harmless. Astronomer Says Ships Are Unarmed."

April 24, 1961, the *Chicago Sun-Times* reported from Eagle River, Wis. that a flying saucer with three live pigmylike men had landed there. A citizen displayed three pancakes he said the spacemen gave him. The paper gave the story almost a column of space.

Sept. 8, 1966, Peter Reich wrote a full-page article, "Flying Saucers—Fantasy or Grim Fact?" for the *Chicago American.*

Oct. 18, 1966, the *Kent Stater,* student publication at Kent State University, headlined its page-1 story, "Kent Students Perpetuate Hoax?" and the next day ran "UFO Hoaxer Named; Explains Saucer Details." The details were that Donald David Wymer and an unnamed friend created a flying saucer out of weather balloons and a hinged frame made of balsa; they obtained helium from discount stores presumably to blow up fraternity balloons. April 17 two sheriff's deputies chased the contraption 86 miles into Pennsylvania. The *Wooster Daily Record* ran the story Oct. 14 after the mother of one of the boys tipped it off. The Wooster paper's sister publication, the *Kent-Ravenna Record-Courier,* also had it and the student paper followed up. A fortnight later an anonymous reader followed up the *Kent Stater* by charging that the story of a hoax was a hoax in itself and raised several questions testing the account's credibility. The *Kent Stater* editorially supported the demand for a confession. None had come when this book went to press.

Oct. 28, 1967, Isaac Asimov wrote an article for the *Chicago Tribune Magazine,* "Nobody Loves You Unless You Believe in the Great Flying Saucer Myth."

Dec. 27, 1967, an AP story from Moscow was headlined "Russians Sight UFOs, Ask World Study" in the *Chicago Sun-Times.*

March 8, 1973, Dr. J. Allen Hynek, professor of astronomy at Northwestern University and director of the Center for UFO Studies, told an *Evanston* (Ill.) *Review* reporter that "All UFOs are not hoaxes." For many years he was an advisor of the Air Force which sponsored Project Blue Book from 1948 to Dec. 17, 1967, during which time it investigated 12,618 UFO sightings, only 701 of which remained unexplained. Before it discontinued its operations the Air Force asked the University of Colorado to undertake an intensive two-year study under the direction of Dr. Edward U. Condon, former head of the National Bureau of Standards. In the *New York Times* for Oct. 21, 1973 Walter Sullivan quoted Dr. Condon: "If you define a UFO as a visitor from outer space, there's no evidence they exist. I've never seen one. I think further study of UFOs would be scientifically useless. I think my own study of UFOs was a waste of government money."

Hynek violently disagreed and he established the Evanston Center to continue the investigation.

Sullivan wrote that the flurry of sightings at the time was the greatest since 1947. He related numerous anecdotes and explained a few as pranks or resulting from the "chasing" effect whereby a bright planet like Venus is mistaken for a UFO. He explained that at their brightest the planets change color, especially near the horizon. Such color changes are a feature of UFOs.

During the flurry of sightings that Sullivan mentioned, "the most unusual and spectacular" was reported by the UPI Sept. 16, 1973 from Griffin, Ga. where Russ Clanton said he saw a golden, egg-shaped object descend to earth, burn a hole in the ground and disappear in a cloud of steam. An official soil chemist said something definitely elevated the temperature of the soil which was 200 degrees nearly two and a half hours later.

The article also recalled that Jimmy Carter reported seeing a UFO before he became Georgia's governor. He has often been quoted as saying, "It was the darnest thing I ever saw. I don't scoff at people any more when they say they have seen UFOs."

Another prominent governor was added to the list of UFO reporters. He was Gov. John H. Gilligan of Ohio whose statement appeared in the press Oct. 12, 1973.

Another student hoax was reported Oct. 26, 1973 by the Associated Press. The preceding day the *Advance-Titan,* student publication at the University of Wisconsin–Oshkosh, devoted its entire first page to a picture and story, "UFOs Sighted in Oshkosh!" The story of eight flying saucers flying in formation was pure poppycock. The picture was obtained by pasting portions of paper cups together and painting windows on them, then superimposing the result on a picture of a campus building. Police and school authorities were deluged with calls from anxious parents and other citizens.

Oct. 28, 1973 the AP reported from Corvallis, Ore. that Bob Houglum, owner of radio station KLOO, offered $10,000 to the first person who would bring him a live animal, thing or person that has never been on Earth before.

Nov. 29, 1973 the American Institute of Public Opinion, commonly called the Gallup poll, reported:

> An astonishing 11 percent of the adult population, or more than 15 million Americans, say they have seen a UFO, double the percentage reported in the previous survey on the subject in 1966.
>
> In addition, the latest survey shows approximately half of the persons interviewed (51 per cent) believing that these flying objects—or "flying saucers"—are real and not just figments of the imaginations or hallucinations.

Chicago Today for Feb. 5, 1974 had a story by Peter Reich, "Pilot Tells of Takeover of Helicopter by UFO."

The next day Reich wrote, "Why UFO People Are Hoaxers" and Feb. 6 he wrote, "Pursuit of UFO Ends in Death." That was a recall of the still-unsolved crackup of Air Force Captain Thomas F. Mantell, Jr. who resigned to investigate reports of a flying disk near Franklin, Ky. and lost control of his plane which exploded at 10,000 feet.

April 21, 1975 Don Bishoff devoted his entire column in the *Eugene* (Ore.) *Register-Guard* to the story of a dairy farmer who said he saw a huge rectangular-shaped UFO hovering over the farm where he works.

When a reader asked, "Have there been any recent sightings of UFOs?" the *Chicago Daily News* Beeline replied April 29, 1975: "Indeed there have," and referred the reader to J. Allen Hynek's Center for UFO Studies. Illustrated was one of the drawings two North Carolina policemen made April 3 and 5 of a boomerang-shaped object.

Reports of sightings multiplied and so did the descriptions of what was observed in the sky. Newspapers couldn't possibly cover them all but did mention reports like the one UPI sent Jan. 24, 1976 from Clovis, N.H. that a reporter took a picture of a cigar-shaped white object without any detail. Dr. Herbert Strentz, now journalism dean at Drake University, who worked with Dr. Condon and wrote a doctoral dissertation on the press handling of UFOs under my direction at Northwestern University, found that papers of more than 80,000 circulation used only 20 percent of the reports they received whereas papers with less than 20,000 circulation used 56 percent of the available material. Strentz estimated that during the period of 1947 to 1968 newspapers printed more than one million UFO stories.

One publication that was sympathetic to flying saucers was *Village Voice*. In a two-page article, "Sane Citizen Sees UFO in New Jersey," March 1, 1976, Budd Hopkins wrote: "A common misconception about people who report encounters like these is that they believe in UFOs. The fact is very few witnesses have a prior belief." The article pertained to what

George O'Barski said he saw in January 1975 and again in February 1976: a spaceship landing in New Jersey, apparently to collect soil samples.

July 25, 1976 the *New York Sunday News* began a series on UFOs by Edward Edelson entitled, "Flying Saucers Still Alive," with a jump head, "UFOs still swooping across the sky—or so say 15 million Americans," replete with reports from all parts of the country.

A 2-column picture of Warren Berbit displaying drawings he made of UFOs appeared on the front page of the *New York Times* for Oct. 11, 1976 with an article, "U.F.O. 'Invasion' of Rockland Starts Round of Explanations," the explanations including about every theory anyone else ever advanced. That the objects of awe and fear were of Russian origin appeared less likely when David K. Shipler wrote a column-long story from Moscow for the *New York Times* of Dec. 26, 1976. It began: "A flying saucer craze has been flourishing in the Soviet Union. In classrooms and around dinner tables, on buses and in offices it has infected conversation like a ubiquitous germ, sometimes dividing friends into hostile camps of believers and unbelievers."

Nobody knew what to believe about the Great Ice Caper, about which the *Washington Post* used an AP story from Wakefield, N.H. Jan. 11, 1977 and the *New York Post* had an AP story from Concord, N.H. Jan. 13, 1977. The excitement followed the discovery by farmer William McCarthy of a round hole with a diameter of 3 feet in his 18-inch-thick pond. National Guard and state Civil Defense authorities remained baffled. Outstanding sightings during 1977 included: an AP report from Danbury, Conn. of an object with flickering lights, seen by three police; pulsating lights of many shapes and colors, reported by the AP from Punxsutawney, Pa; a Piper Aircraft employee took pictures on a moonlit night of a teardrop-shaped object near his Clearfield County home, the AP reported April 5, 1977. Unfortunately the Pennsylvania Center for UFO Research said the photos were too underexposed to be of any value. The *Chicago Sun-Times Midwest Magazine* for May 1, 1977 had two 2-page articles, "UFOs Over Hollywood" and "Inside UFOs," the former by Roger Ebert, movie critic, and the latter by Bill Barry, a Florida free-lancer. Both were based largely on interviews with Hynek, who was serving as consultant for the film *Close Encounters of the Third Kind*. Hynek said he never had seen a UFO but reported that many who did described the crewmen as four feet high with large heads and rather spindly bodies.

A fantastic tale of a Chilean soldier who went to investigate one of two bright objects that landed a quarter-mile from camp, returned after 15 minutes and collapsed, losing consciousness for 2½ hours, after which it was noticed his watch had stopped and the date on it advanced five days, all reported from Santiago by the AP May 23, 1977. *Star Wars* and similar science fiction movies were accredited with increases in believers who Gallup said numbered 57 percent of the population, with 46 percent believing there are people like us on other planets, the *Chicago Daily News* reported June 24; the next day Reuters reported that Gallup found 15 million Americans who have seen flying saucers, 100 of which are reported every night; Reuters covered the first International Conference on Flying Saucers held in Chicago with Arnold, Hynek and many other speakers; "The Great UFO Debate" consumed three pages of the *Christian Science Monitor* for Aug. 24, 1977, the debaters being Hynek, pro, and Philip J. Klass, con; the effect of science-fiction movies, especially *Close Encounters of the Third Kind,* was analyzed by Dick Brass in articles Nov. 27 and 28 in the *New York Daily News,* entitled, "UFOs: Close Encounters of the Local Kind"; in the *New York Times* for Dec. 9 Boyce Rensberger also noted the increase in UFO sightings and blamed it in part on the motion pictures. He also reported that pressure was being brought on NASA to begin another investigation and that Sir Eric M. Gairy, prime minister of Grenada, was persisting in his demand that the United Nations study the phenomenon.

During 1978 the *Harrisburg* (Pa.) *Patriot News* reported March 14, in its Cumberland County edition, that there were sightings in Dauphin and Cumberland counties immediately after a visit to the area by Samuel T. Freedman, authority on extraterrestrial life, who told a Harrisburg area community college audience that he was convinced this planet is being visited by alien spacemen. The UPI reported May 18 that sailors told of seeing UFOs near Ocala, Fla.; Gallup's latest poll, announced June 12, revealed 57 percent of Americans believe in UFOs, whereas nonbelievers outnumber believers by three to one in England; the *Chicago Sun-Times* editorialized on "Paranormal Percentages," to point out that twice as many British believe in ghosts and that only 10 percent of Americans believe in witches; the AP reported Sept. 25 from Logan, Utah that "An unidentified object was seen in the sky over parts of Idaho, Utah and Wyoming but reports differed as to whether it was one or more objects and whether it moved." The *New York Post* reported Nov. 2 that 50 people told of seeing "a silvery, circular reflecting object" hovering over the southern end of Central Park at twilight. It didn't stay long and it's not clear what it was: Oct. 24 the AP reported from Melbourne, Australia that a pilot vanished after he radioed he was being pursued by a large object; the UPI reported Nov. 14. "The first-ever flying saucer on Kuwait came without sound, was as big as a jumbo jet, cylindrical, with a huge dome and a flashing red light." It spent seven minutes over an oil field and took off without a trace. Nov. 29 Reuters reported from Rome that Italy was stricken with a saucer fever, tales being circulated of tidal waves, red lights over the Adriatic and cigar-shaped disks; the same day the AP reported from Naples that UFOs had been sighted over the Isle of Capri and other places in southern Italy. Nov. 29 the AP reported several weird experiences from Buenos Aires. Two lagging stock-car racers said after they noted yellow and violet lights a strange force shut off their motor and headlights, lifted the car 15 feet off the road and set it down a minute later 75 miles away. Another man said a huge saucer swallowed his car, after which five bulky figures stuffed his 13-year-old son into a box while a sixth interviewed him. This was supposed to be witnessed by unnamed others. There were other similar stories in the AP account, written by Richard Boudbreau.

Early in 1979 reports from "down under" increased in volume. Jan 2 the AP reported from Auckland that the New Zealand Royal Air Force had ordered an alert after television news camermen filmed what they said was a UFO. The afternoon *New York Post* used a followup AP story under the headline "New Zealand's UFO Sightings may only be Venus—Experts." Nevertheless, reports of sightings continued to be made. Pictures taken of them were most unconvincing and an Air Force pilot sent to investigate reported all he saw was the lights on Japanese fishing boats, the AP reported Jan. 4. By then, Reuters had reported from Sydney, Australia what the *New York News World* headlined Jan. 3, "UFO fever sweeps Australia." And the *New York Post* used the headline "Jersey UFO upstages New Zealand" over a news picture the UPI sent from Auckland showing a large white sphere with a small indistinct dot in the exact center. The news story reported that a UFO had hovered for 40 minutes over Barnegat Bay, N.J. A Brick policeman described "the weirdest thing" he ever saw as resembling a balloon with lights around it. The next day, Jan. 5, the *New York Daily News* printed an interview with Lt. Joseph DeAngelo who declared, "I can only tell you what I saw," which was a white circle of light with blue lights at either end, and motionless for 40 minutes. "At about the same time," Brian Kates,*News* reporter, wrote: "At the other end of the world, six police officers in New Zealand stood before their bosses and said the same thing." Added Kates: "What they saw depends on what you believe."

March 25 lights like a meteor were seen over five western states, the AP reported from San Francisco; July 21, the *New York Times* used a story from Moscow by Craig R. Whitney who wrote that almost all Russians apparently believe in UFOs and think they come from outer space. A widespread rumor was that a flying saucer landed on the moon next to Apollo 11 but the news and pictures were suppressed by the American government.

July 23 the UPI reported from Mt. Rainier, Wash. that the New Age Foundation said the spacemen were afraid to land on the special airfield provided for them, so it was planned to build a signal tower to help allay fears.

"Chronicle of a U.F.O. Sighting: Investigation Leading Nowhere" was the streamer headline over a half-page piece by Matthew L. Wald in the *New York Times* for Aug. 21, 1979. It related the attempt of police to investigate three reports by sober citizens of a fiery red ball in the sky in the vicinity of Stamford, Conn. Some policemen speculated that the military was experimenting. Air Force officials responded that the Blue Book study ended Dec. 17, 1969 after covering 12,618 reports, 701 still unexplained. Reasons for abandoning the project were: (1) no UFO ever reported was a threat to national security; (2) no evidence the UFOs represented any new scientific knowledge and (3) no evidence that any UFO is an extraterritorial vehicle.

Deputy Sheriff Val Johnson of Warren County, Minn. and Henry Johnson (no relationship) of South Vermilion, Minn. both reported within two days of each other that they were rendered unconscious and burned by bright white lights. The first account was by the AP Aug. 31 from Warren. Allan Hendry of the Evanston center called it "a most incredible case" and cited as unusual clues the two bent antennas, shattered windshield, broken headlamp and a small dent in the hood of the patrol car. The UPI reported Sept. 6 from Minneapolis and Sept. 11 the AP reported that Val Johnson repeated his story on ABC's "Good Morning America" program.

Sept. 10 the UPI reported from Dresser, Wis. that five men claimed they saw a large football-shaped object with a brilliant metallic sheen hovering about 40 feet off the ground. One of Hynek's inspectors said it was a "close encounter of the first kind" because the witnesses were within 200 meters of the UFO.

Notable foreign reports during 1979 included UPI's report from Manila of a disk-shaped object with a flashing light that changed color as it disappeared over the horizon; a situation story from Moscow by Craig R. Whitney in the *New York Times* for July 31 telling of the widespread interest in UFOs in the Soviet Union; an AP account Sept. 18 of three UFOs that hovered briefly over Ingelstadt, West Germany and a UPI story Nov. 13 from Valencia, Spain of a passenger plane bound for the Canary Islands pursued for four hours by four red fireballs. Nov. 14 the AP reported the pilot successfully landed the plane that came from Salzburg, Austria.

During 1980 the AP reported from Melbourne that UFO researchers said a UFO landed in a tree, but police had no comment except that they found only some unexplained broken branches. April 6 the AP reported that a round brightly glowing object was observed flying at a high altitude over Jerusalem on Holy Saturday. April 10 the AP reported that strange flashing lights, said to be almost as bright as the sun, were reported from several spots in Northern England. June 15 Reuters reported from Buenos Aires a spherical UFO with a halo was sighted in western Argentina.

Almost all of the first page of the *Anderson* (S.C.) *Daily Mail* for Sept. 11, 1980 was devoted to several stories under the two-line streamer headline, "Town buzzes with excitement after possible UFO sighting." The first few paragraphs of the principal story provide a perfect example of how a newspaper can lose perspective and attempt to capitalize on a sensational occurrence.

By Louise Ervin

Did a vehicle from another world pay a visit to the Broadway Lake area this morning?

Jerry McAlister of Parnell Road is not sure. But he is positive he saw something strange in the back yard early today. And since the 4:20 A.M. sighting, the news media [have] beaten a path to his door.

Radio stations from over three states have kept him busy on the telephone, relating the experience for an "on-the-spot broadcast." Television camera trucks from area stations rolled up and down the country roads, asking directions to the remote rural section as they drove to McAlister's house.

What McAlister saw was a terrifically bright light in his backyard preceded by a crashing noise. His wife and daughter also saw the object, of which he made a sketch, turn and disappear.

Sept. 12 the *Anderson Independent* also ran the sketch of an elongated balloon with a row of lights on all sides. The story by Tom Kiss added little, except that the object was about 70 feet long and two stories high. The day's headline was "Strange Noise Marks Beginning of 'Close Encounter.'"

Bright flying objects, with Saturn-like rings were reported from northeastern Tibet by an official Chinese newspaper in Peking, the UPI reported from there Aug. 6, 1981. A month later, Sept. 13, the AP quoted the *Peking Evening News* that it received many calls from persons who said they saw such objects over their cities. The same day the UPI reported that Chinese officials thought a UFO cited in Tibet July 24 might be the same as the one seen in San Diego a few hours later.

Contact

Not all UFOs go about minding their own business, possibly seen by humans but not especially interested in communicating with them. There have been exceptions and anyone who says he has seen, talked to or been entertained by little green men in a UFO is bound to get his name in the paper. A few examples follow:

After Tad Jones tried to investigate a ball-shaped UFO with legs and antennas, it shot straight upward and disappeared. The next day Jones received a note, shoved under his door, "We were here and if you don't keep your mouth shut, we'll be back." Jones left town but was safe in his new location. The president of a UFO investigative Society said: "People who get to know too much either vanish or are silenced." All of this was reported March 27, 1968 by the *Charleston* (W.Va.) *Gazette*.

A large orange circular object hovering just above the trees caused Greg Faltersack's car to skid off the road and put the car's radio, lights and horn out of commission, the *Chicago Daily News* reported Aug. 24, 1972 from Waukesha, Wis.

Two shipyard workers said they were taken aboard a fish-shaped, 10-foot-square space craft by three creatures with pale silvery-gray skin, no hair, long pointed ears and noses, the UPI reported Oct. 13, 1973 from Pascagoula, Miss. The sheriff said, "These are reliable people and they were stone sober at the time," Oct. 15 the UPI reported that after the men underwent hypnosis J. Allen Hynek announced, "There is no question in my mind that these men had a very terrifying experience."

In his "The Unexplained" column in the *Phoenix Arizona Republic* for Dec. 12, 1971 Allen Spraggett recalled the Sept. 19, 1961 experience of Betty and Barney Hill of Portsmouth, N.H. The columnist met Betty on a radio show and she elaborated on her book, *The Interrupted Journey*. The story was that the Hills were chased by a UFO, lost consciousness for two hours after which they found themselves 35 miles away. What happened during the amnesia period was revealed under hypnosis. Mrs. Hill described the spacemen as about 5 feet tall, with nostrils but no noses and eyes that slanted across the face. They said they were from a distant star system and meant no harm. The book was a best seller.

When Mrs. Hill repeated her story for the benefit of 1,000 persons at the first International Unidentified Flying Objects Congress in Chicago, Mile Anderson gave her a 2-column story in the *Sun-Times* for June 26, 1977.

Hypnosis and truth serum also were used to diagnose the nervous attacks that plagued an Argentine trucker. The UPI reported Feb. 21, 1974 that he had been taken aboard a spaceship for an hour and a half.

For ten days newspapers all over the nation headlined stories of the attempts to solve the mystery of the disappearance of 20 persons from the vicinity of Waldport, Ore. When the mother of one received a postcard from Fruitto, Colo. saying, "I am leaving this Earth and will not see you any more," the blame pointed to a man and a woman, known as Bo and Peep, who spoke to about 200 persons Sept. 14, 1975 at Newport, Ore. According to a UPI story Oct. 6, 1975 from Portland, Ore., the duo advised the audience to give away all their possessions, including children, so a UFO could take them to a better life.

Oct. 7 the AP reported from San Jose, Calif. that the *San Jose Mercury-News* carried an advertisement for a meeting to learn how to follow two persons to a higher form of life. A week later the focus of interest shifted to Illinois. Paul McGrath reported in the *Chicago Sun-Times* for Oct. 14 that from Oct. 2 to 7 a group of 50 to 70 persons who resembled the missing UFO people camped in Chain O'Lakes Park near Fox Lake. By means of automobile license plates and postcards sent to Oregon the peregrinations of the group were traced through Oregon, California, Colorado and Nebraska to Illinois. McGrath reported that persons who attended the Sept. 14 meeting said the group was called Human Individual Metamorphosis.

Oct. 15 McGrath reported that two cows were found slaughtered near the site of the UFO people's camp and it became known that about 100 cattle were reported mysteriously dead in Colorado. Oct. 16 McGrath reported that he had interviewed two of the sect whose pictures the paper used. They called themselves Vicki and Seymour Morgenstern and were one of many teams of two into which the group was split to do missionary work in all parts of the country.

The identity of Bo and Peep was revealed by the UPI in a story Oct. 17 from Portland, Ore. The man was Marshall Herff Applewhite, son of a Texas Presbyterian minister, and she was Bonnie Lu Trusdale Nettles, a nurse from Houston. The *Houston Post* revealed that the woman's astrology charts showed that the two knew each other in previous incarnations.

Wesley Pruden, Jr. did a comprehensive roundup story for the *National Observer* Oct. 18, 1975, after which the press seemed to lose interest in the story.

Feb. 2, 1976 the AP reported from Los Angeles, "Deserters from the Great Lost UFO Cult are straggling back after a summer and fall of spiritual wandering, settling gently to earth in a pleasant rustic half-way house in the seclusion of Topaganda Canyon." The house is run by two of the first dropouts among the 24, leaving Bo and Peep almost alone.

Despite one successful lie detector test and several television and motion picture appearances, law enforcement officials remained skeptical of the story of Travis Walton who said he was kidnapped for five days, during most of which he was an amnesia victim. Four companions corroborated his story, Jon Halverson reported Feb. 19, 1976 for the AP from northern Arizona. The story was of worldwide interest, reporters coming from as far away as Australia. Walton did not appear for a second lie detector test at which reporters were to be present. He was richly rewarded, however, with the *National Enquirer's* $10,000 prize given annually for the best UFO story.

Then, however, Philip J. Klass, senior avionics editor of *Aviation Week and Space Technology* magazine, investigated. First he found that Walton had not passed the first polygraph test and the *National Enquirer* knew it all the time. In his 17-page report on the Walton case Klass, author of *UFOs Explained,* used the word "hoax" numerous times. In the *New York Daily News* for July 28, 1976 Edward Edelson reviewed Klass' investigative work.

Two very tall humanoids with large feet and no necks shined a blue light at a woman near Nashville, Ill., the AP reported Feb. 26, 1978. One of Hynek's deputies said, "The fact that they did not have any necks is especially significant."

The father of a young pilot missing in a small aircraft told the UPI he believed his son was being held alive by people from another planet, the press association reported Oct. 25, 1978 from Melbourne, Australia. His radio had gone dead shortly after he reported a mysterious object was hovering over him. The incident revived reports of UFOs in the area.

Anyone having a close encounter with a UFO understandably has butterflies in his stomach. Sometimes entire communities share the jitters. A few additional examples follow:

So many citizens became alarmed that police notified the *New York Daily News* April 30, 1977 about spinning white lights moving across the Throggs Neck Bridge.

An old-fashioned railroad lantern glowing under water in a silt pond kept residents of Carbondale, Pa. on the alert for UFOs, the AP reported Nov. 12, 1979.

Almost all 5,500 inhabitants of Chester, Ill. were figuratively up in arms when the January 1978 issue of the magazine *Official UFO* appeared with a story that the town had been wiped out by aliens from outer space, the *Wall Street Journal* reported Dec. 21, 1977. Apparently without checking the facts, the magazine accepted a manuscript by someone it insisted was reliable, stating that a flying saucer had laid waste Main Street, destroyed homes and cars and been brought down by an Air Force plane, all of which the television station presumably had photographed. Investigation revealed Chester's principal street is not called Main, there is no TV station and the radio station has no camera. Despite the evidence that Chester still existed, the magazine did not retract.

Another example of how widespread rumors can be was provided by Kevin Klose writing from Moscow for the *Washington Post* of March 16, 1979. A question asked him by natives was why the United States government censored the news of a UFO that followed the astronauts to the moon and landed near them. Study of the occult, astrology and similar matters seemed to be on the increase in the Soviet Union as everywhere else.

To allay fears that American or Iraqi planes were flying overhead, the Iranian Air Force announced it was pursuing a UFO, the UPI reported from London the Iranian radio was reporting.

Organizations

As reports of sightings and encounters increase so do the groups interested in UFOs. The number probably now is in the hundreds or thousands but most are manned by volunteer members. The best-financed, equipped to investigate and report, is the Center for Unidentified Flying Objects Studies at Northwestern University. One of the best profiles of the director, Dr. J. Allen Hynek, was "The Flying Saucer Man," written by Richard Lewis for the *Chicago Sun-Times* Dec. 22, 1966, shortly before the center's establishment. The center's activities were updated in Dennis Byrne's article, "UFO center alive and well, but interest lags," in the *Chicago Sun-Times* for Oct. 31, 1982 and in Howard Witt's article, "UFO's star needs close encounter with money" in the *Chicago Tribune* for Feb. 27, 1983. Then there is the UFO Investigators of Charleston, W.Va. founded by J. Ralph Jarrett, whose speech before the Charleston Exchange Club was covered by the *Charleston Gazette* for March 26, 1968. Although it has no investigative bureau the *National Enquirer* specializes in UFO news and gives awards for important sightings. The *New York Times* for June 8, 1974 told of $5,000 being given Major Larry Coyne and his helicopter crew for a sighting in October 1973. Among its readers the *National Enquirer* has a credibility rating of 3.6 on a scale of 5, the *Wall Street Journal* reported Jan. 26, 1983. The survey was conducted by the *National Enquirer's* advertising department. Another pollster found the paper's credibility among advertising agencies to be only 1.3.

The *Chicago Daily News'* Beeline April 24, 1973 advised an interested reader to contact the Public Education Group of the Adler Planetarium, "where you also can learn about the sky's nonidentified objects." The "greatest cause of excitement in Missouri since last year's Missouri Monster, upriver at the town of Louisiana" have been sightings in Grand Tower, Ill. and Piedmont, Mo. Jan. 8, 1975 the *Chicago Sun-Times* Action Time gave a reader the address of the Mutual Unidentified Flying Objects Network then in Quincy, Ill.

The National Spiritual Science Center, with a nucleus of 100 members, sponsored Washington's first Psychic Fair at American University that Emily Fisher covered at length for the *Washington Post* of May 5, 1975.

A short notice, typical of many throughout the country, advertised a UFO seminar at Purdue University in the *Chicago Sun-Times* for May 4, 1976.

The UFO Education Center at Appleton, Wis. was given a perceptive writeup by Ann Beckman in the *Madison* (Wis.) *Capital-Times* for May 20, 1976. Its director, Charlotte Blob, believes that the truth about UFOs is being suppressed not only by the federal government but also by "the power companies, the oil companies, that control the world economy and the Atomic Energy Commission." She charges that until the mid '60s Air Force pilots who saw and reported UFOs faced dishonorable discharge, court martial, up to two years in prison and a $10,000 fine.

Blob is a disciple of the late George Adamski who wrote several books on contacts in the deserts of the southwest with visitors from outer space. His books are illustrated with pictures of spaceships; two are really enlargements of Christmas tree ornaments.

And there's the ongoing Society for the Investigation of the Unexplained at Columbia, N.J., whose organization was announced Aug. 8, 1968 in the *National Observer*. Interest at that time was heightened by a rainstorm of falling stones on Long Island. According to the paper falling stones "have dropped down from the sky for ages. One that fell on Luce, France in 1772 puzzled scientists who analyzed it. In 1963 flying rocks descended on San Bernardino, Calif. There's never been a satisfactory explanation for these or numerous other similar occurrences."

The First International Congress of the UFO Phenomenon in Acapulco made obvious the growing conflict between scientists who study UFOs and self-described ufologists who describe the spacemen who they believe are bringing "divine intelligence" to earth. Even Hynek deplored "the religious nuts [who] muddy the waters for everyone," also commenting on so-called abduction cases: "I haven't found anyone who said he had been taken on a trip by a UFO to be credible." On the other hand, the Rev. Salvadore Freixedo, a Spanish-born Jesuit, thinks the explanation lies in parapsychological phenomena. He said, "If we wait for the scientists we'll never get an answer." Construction of a model flying saucer capable of much destruction was announced at the conference, the UPI reported April 23. Few reputable scientists attended the conference, probably fearing ridicule if they did. However, Hynek and others said that interest in ufology was increasing, the *New York Post* reported April 29. Alan Riding covered the conference for the April 25, 1977 *New York Times*. Marlise Simons did so for the *Washington Post* May 1, 1977. She was more optimistic, saying that ufology "may finally be coming out of the scientific closet and gaining some respectability." A survey by the American Astronomical Society showed 53 percent of those answering to believe there should be further study of UFOs.

Another First International UFO Congress was held in Chicago with 1,500 attending, Henry Hansen reported for the *Chicago Daily News* of June 24, 1977. To minimize the "ridicule factor" the call for the gathering emphasized that President Carter believed. Curtis G. Fuller of *Fate* sponsored the affair and the keynote speaker was Kenneth Arnold on the 30th anniversary of his first sighting. Among the other headliners were Hynek, Betty Hill and J. Gordon Melton, a United Methodist minister and director of the Institute for the Study of American Religion, who talked on "The Virgin Mary—Ufonaut Extraordinaire."

Ronald Kotulak, *Chicago Tribune* science editor, reported June 25, 1977 that the number of serious scientists interested in ufology was increasing. Prof. James Harder of the University of California told him he was converted to the possibility of UFOs by the finding of three metallic objects in Brazil associated with a UFO sighting; they could have been extraterrestrial.

In an editorial, "A Cosmic Call-in," inspired by the Chicago gathering, the *Sun-Times* admitted the possibility of life elsewhere in the universe and approved the plans of the National Aeronautics and Space Administration to send recorded greetings in 13 languages into outer space and the proposed five-year planetary probe to begin in 1984.

In a separate article from the convention, Jon Ziomek interviewed Kenneth Arnold for the *Sun-Times* of June 25, 1977. Arnold said he never described the objects he saw 30 years earlier as shaped like saucers; rather, he said, they skipped as saucers do on water.

One of the last speeches at the conference was by Ted Phillips, an inspector for the Missouri Highway Department. He pointed out common characteristics of UFOs: circular objects with lights flashing around them, dehydration of trees and soil, stalling of automobile engines and disruption of electrical appliances. He said there's no explanation other than extraterrestrial visitors.

From Cape Girardeau, Mo. the UPI reported June 16, 1978 that the Southeast Missouri State University was offering two hours of university credit and a scientific kit to anyone helping to detect UFOs.

The organization interested in open-minded study of the unexplained that existed before UFOs became popular is the Fortean Society, named for the journalist-scientist maverick Charles Fort. It holds an annual convention. Don Barkin covered one for the Aug. 7, 1978 *Washington Post*. Most of the speakers were anonymous and the reports pertained to the status of investigations of the Bermuda Triangle, UFOs and other phenomena. It was revealed that the FBI was interested in UFOs briefly before 1947.

The Scientific Bureau of Investigation was formed by Pete Mazzola, a New York policeman, and Jim Fillow, a New Brunswick, N.J. carpenter, the *New York Daily News*' Frank McKeown reported May 19, 1979. Both had been working for another UFO study group but felt their reports were ignored.

What began as a hobby for John Lutz mushroomed into Odyssey Research, a nonprofit organization headquartered in Baltimore and operating with 15 members in several nearby states as well. The Associated Press distributed a story about the enterprise March 7, 1980. In ten years the group checked 480 reports of UFO sightings; about 75 percent of them were identified but many remained mysteries.

An older and more active private organization is the International UFO Bureau, directed by Hayden Hewes of Edmond, Okla. In 1967, a decade before Kenneth Arnold's sightings, Hewes founded the Interplanetary Intelligence of UFOs and was the recipient of considerable attention by the Oklahoma City newspapers, the *Daily Oklahoman* and the *Journal*. Kay Cavanaugh of the former wrote a long piece Aug. 6, 1960 about the 16-year-old Hewes who was learning Russian in order to read Soviet announcements about flying saucers. April 30, 1964 Jack Taylor of the *Daily Oklahoman* reported that Hewes would probe some sightings in New Mexico. July 15, 1974 his news was that the Air Force offered to let him study its files in Dayton, Ohio. July 25, 1965 he told the New Age Center that UFOs were probably spaceships. July 28, 1965 Jack Taylor reported that Hewes believed Earth to be under surveillance by beings from another planet. Dec. 18, 1969 the news was that Hewes had been asked to play himself in a documentary by Crossfield Productions of Los Angeles. Feb. 22, 1970 the *Journal* printed a long profile of Hewes by Richard Boggs of the UPI. In the *Journal* for May 30, 1973 Hewes was quoted as believing that metallurgists were stumped by metals discovered after an aircrash in 1897 near Aurora, Tex. Although 70 percent iron they had no magnetic properties. March 11, 1974 Hewes was announced as the main speaker during Engineers' Week at the University of Oklahoma at

Norman. Oct. 14, 1975 Kevin Donovan reported that July 12, 1974 Hewes was visited by a man and woman who called themselves Bonnie and Herff, seeking publicity for their plan "to save mankind." They told him how to use a "thought code sequence" if he ever wanted to get in touch with them. Hewes reported, "They were very sincere . . . They claimed powers of dematerialization . . . the ultimate proof of their mission would be their assassination and their physical resurrection three and a half days later." The later exploits of Bonnie and Herff, also known as Bo and Peep, were related on page 589.

Oct. 5, 1976 Steve Sloan did a long profile on Hewes for the *Daily Oklahoman.* April 30, 1975 the Associated Press had reported from Washington that President Carter had sent Hewes a detailed account of his sighting of a UFO for 10–12 minutes in October 1969 at Leary, Ga. In its account of the announcement the *New York Post* stated that Carter had also filled out a form from the National Investigation Committee on Aerial Phenomena in Kensington, Md. In his story of the announcement Thomas O'Toole recalled in the *Washington Post* for April 20 that during his campaign Carter had laughed off a report that he had seen a UFO. He said then, "A light appeared and disappeared in the sky . . . I have no idea what it was . . . I think it was a light beckoning me to run in the California primary."

May 1, 1977 the AP had a longer piece stressing Hewes' possession of the report. May 10, 1977 the *Washington Post* quoted UFO debunker Robert Sheaffer that examination of the astronomical reports for Jan. 8, 1969 made it clear that what Carter saw was the planet Venus, at the time 100 times brighter than a first-magnitude star and just about where Carter said he saw the UFO.

Aug. 27, 1978 the *Sunday Oklahoman* had a special 14-page section, "The Strange World of Hayden Hewes." Malinda Walkup-Sloan filled two pages of it with, "Since He Was 13, UFO Fan Has Been Tracking Mysteries." UPI's Kay McCarthy's "Carter Sights UFO" was included, as were several other articles by and about Hewes over the years. Creation of the Hewes Lecture Agency was announced by Cindy Anderson in the *Oklahoman* for April 8, 1983. It offers information on UFOs, ghosts, reincarnation, the meaning of dreams, psychic power, holistic healing, astral projection and a number of other unusual subjects.

Spotting his first UFO when he was 14 years old led Timothy Beckley to become a student of the phenomenon. In the *St. Petersburg Times* for May 8, 1982 Ronald Boyd told the conclusions to which Beckley has come. In the first place there have been too many unexplained sightings to ignore, and Beckley tells audiences there are at least three types of the ETs (1) those who resemble Earthlings; (2) the "little alien man" type—short, basically human but with high indented foreheads, thin lips, pointed ears and saucerlike eyes and (3) "strange saucerians," like bigfoot creatures, hairy humanoids and monstrous animal creatures. He has a plastic head of the alien type to use when he speaks. He is the editor and publisher of *UFO Review,* the only publication of its kind.

In four years the National Science Foundation for UFO Research spent $15,000 on research, sued and obtained the release of 3,000 pages of documents from the CIA and NASA, according to what Fred Whiting, director, told the *New York Times* for June 23, 1982.

"More hard evidence demanded by UFO skeptics; mere belief rejected" was the headline the *Christian Science Monitor* gave July 29, 1981 to John Worrall's report of a conference sponsored by the Mutual UFO Network at Massachusetts Institute of Technology in Cambridge, Mass. Calling for "hard evidence," Hynek said "the crackpots, the charlatans and the mentally tilted" provide "a marvelous excuse to dismiss the whole matter."

At the height of the popularity of the movie *E.T.* the *Los Angeles Times* Service distributed a roundup of opinion by viewers that the *Madison* (Wis.) *Capital-Times* used July 23, 1982. Many were found who said they had had close encounters with spacemen. One praised the movie, saying: "A lot of it is hokey but it also invites the audience to be less afraid of the so-called paranormal. And what better place to start than with the children?"

One of the wildest stories of UFO activities was reported Aug. 19, 1982 from El Paso, Tex. by the UPI. A woman told Monahans police that she had been traveling with retired Army Gen. William Westmoreland when spacemen kidnapped him and disappeared in a flying saucer. It took four hours before the Army was able to find Westmoreland safe and sound and cancel an all-points bulletin.

A pathetic tragedy was reported Nov. 19, 1982 by the AP from Grand Marais, Minn., when a 48-year-old woman was found starved to death in a snow-covered car where her 28-year-old male companion was in critical condition. They had been waiting for a flying saucer to rescue them.

Investigations

Most of these private groups investigate as well as record individual sightings, but none engages in thorough studies of the phenomenon as a whole. Only government could do the kind of job that many want. From 1948 to 1966 (see page 582) the Air Force conducted Project Blue Book which it was glad to terminate when the University of Colorado study was undertaken. Six months before that project began Richard Lewis wrote in the *Chicago Sun-Times* for April 19, 1966 that J. Allen Hynek, the Air Force's consultant, and a committee of outstanding scientists had agreed on the need for a study not under military auspices. Some wanted a project to involve numerous universities; Hynek recommended that the effort be concentrated on a single campus and his idea was accepted.

Announcement of the project was made in a *Los Angeles Times* special that the *Chicago Sun-Times* ran Oct. 8, 1966. With a $300,000 budget Dr. Edward C. Condon, formerly director of the National Bureau of Standards, would direct it for two years at the University of Colorado, the Air Force announced. In 18 years, the news release said, the Air Force received some 11,000 reports of sightings and was able to explain all except 655.

In a resumé of Dr. Condon's career the *New York Times* for Oct. 8, 1966 quoted him on UFOs, "I guess I'm an agnostic. I simply don't know." The articles related the attacks on Condon's loyalty that led to House Committee on Un-American Activities hearings. Condon was cleared of any suspicion several times but quit both government and private industry for academia in disgust. Condon also was quoted, "I raise a little hell when I run things." And so he did; some of the aides when the project began were not there when it ended and Condon made the statement quoted on page 582. Dr. Condon's report concluded:

> . . . nothing has come from the study of UFOs in the past 21 years that has added to scientific knowledge. Careful consideration of the record . . . leads us to conclude that further extensive study of UFOs probably cannot be justified in the expectation that science will be advanced thereby.

The official title of the Condon project was *The Scientific Study of Unidentified Flying Objects*. It was released to the press Jan. 8, 1969. Bantam Books published it with an introduction by Walter Sullivan, science editor of the *New York Times,* in which he related the internal squabbling that opponents of the conclusions magnified in their criticisms. A prestigious committee of American scientists with Dr. Gerald M. Clemence of Yale as chairman, unanimously endorsed Condon's report.

Expansive as the report of the University of Colorado UFO project was, there was quite a large-sized army of UFO buffs who weren't satisfied then or at any time since that the federal government was paying sufficient attention to the phenomenon. In the *National Observer* for Dec. 1, 1973 August Gribbin wrote, "By now enough trained and responsible observers have reported UFOs to credibly establish existence of a scientific mystery." He said Project Blue Book was not good and made no mention at all of the Condon report.

An example of journalistic skepticism is illustrated by the first paragraph of an AP Story by T. Lee Huges Oct. 22, 1974 from Quincy, Ill. "A Quincy-based citizens group says it is stepping where the Air Force fears to tread, investigating and publicizing flying saucers reports and urging the public to take them seriously."

The group, the Mutual UFO Network, through its director, Walter H. Andrus Jr., charged the CIA with downplaying reports and covering up findings.

To keep the crackpots out membership in the Mutual UFO Network, headquartered in Seguin, Texas, is by invitation only. According to Andrus, a retired Motorola executive from Quincy, Ill., there are 1,100 members worldwide. They interview persons who report they have seen a UFO and make reports; about 10 to 20 percent of all cases are said to be unexplainable. The group believes that visitors from outer space are studying earthlings as scientists would guinea pigs from vantage points in all parts of the world. April 24, 1983 UPI distributed a 600-word story on the group.

Robert Barry, executive director of the 20th Century UFO Bureau of Collingswood, N.J., was quoted by Harry McLaughlin in the *Harrisburg* (Pa.) *Patriot-News* for Feb. 5, 1978: "I believe the CIA and NASA have urged the president to withhold public announcements about their findings at this time." By "their" was meant, "beings from the Milky Way and other galaxies that have visited Earth in space crafts." "The Air Force," he said, "had been conducting a debunking policy" that NASA now has adopted.

Nov. 26, 1977 the AP reported from Washington that President Carter had asked NASA to take up the project the Air Force abandoned, but a NASA official said the agency was not eager to do so because "it's not wise to do research on something that is not a measurable phenomenon."

Ground Saucer Watch, Inc., a nonprofit organization of scientists and UFO enthusiasts headquartered in Arizona, explained, through its attorney, Henry Rothblatt, why it was bringing suit against the Central Intelligence Agency. In the *New York Post* for Dec. 1, 1977, the lawyer was quoted as saying the CIA conspired and covered up documents related to UFOs without adequate reason.

A similar suit was brought by the Citizens Against UFO Secrecy against the National Security Agency, the CIA and the Defense Intelligence Agency under the Freedom of Information Act. Ward Sinclair wrote of it in the *Washington Post*.

In the midst of the growing pressure for the American government to do something, the UPI reported the attitude of the English magazine *New Scientist,* of which Robert Musel wrote from London Sept. 3, 1977: "Despite the years of study the infield of Ufology has failed to produce one concrete example of alien visitation from any dimension."

Still, the AP reported Nov. 25, 1977 from Washington, the White House was exerting pressure on NASA to investigate. The response of Dave Williamson, NASA assistant for special projects, was: "Give me one little green man—not a theory or memory of one—and we can have a multimillion dollar program. It's a scientific dilemma, how do you prove something that doesn't exist?"

Dec. 27, 1977 the AP reported NASA's formal rejection of the White House request terming it "wasteful and probably unproductive." NASA said it stood ready to investigate "bona fide physical evidence from reliable sources."

In a resume of the situation in the *Wall Street Journal* for Feb. 10, 1978, Arlen J. Large quoted a letter from an irate Pennsylvania woman to President Carter accusing him of covering up the truth about UFOs. She voted for him because she thought he was a man of truth and now demanded, "I feel the time has come for you to lay it on the line now and TELL THE PEOPLE THE TRUTH."

The campaign of Sir Eric Gairy, prime minister of Grenada, to persuade the United Nations to investigate took on steam, the *New York News World* reported Oct. 14, 1978. Speaking, he said, for all plants and animals, he appealed to the entire human race through the UN General Assembly to take necessary steps to protect nonhuman life. His campaign ended in March 1979 when he was overthrown while in New York by the Revolutionary Provisional Government that revealed Gairy had placed huge orders for guns and ammunition to protect the 100,000 islanders, the AP reported from St. George, Grenada March 17, 1979.

Nov. 6, 1980 the UPI reported that the University of Pittsburgh was embarrassed by a news release announcing a coming address by a UFO expert that said the government had officially admitted the existence of UFOs. So the appearance of Clark McClelland was postponed.

UFO believers were pleased with the special 8-page section, "UFOs and Other Cosmic Phenomena." in the *New York News World* for Nov. 21, 1981. Among the articles were "Britain's Lords Studying UFOs," "Science Fiction Comes to Life," "ABC Eyes UFOs on TV Programs" and "The Nagora Photos: A UFO's Strange Dance."

A charge that documents obtained under the FOI Act indicate "a huge coverup" has been going on for years, a graduate student told a Northern Illinois University audience in DeKalb, the UPI reported Dec. 2, 1981.

Despite defeats in a U.S. District Court and the Circuit Court of Appeals for the District of Columbia, the Citizens Against UFO Secrecy appealed to the United States Supreme Court to compel the National Security Agency to release 135 documents it admitted it had, Robert Sangforge reported for the UPI from Washington Feb. 14, 1982. Without comment the highest court rejected the appeal, the *Chicago Tribune* reported March 8, 1982.

In comment on the court decision, George O. Fawcett of Lincolnton, N.C., an officer in CAUS, was quoted by the *Suburban Chicago Sun-Times* as saying the government is inconsistent. It abandoned the Blue Book project saying UFOs were no danger to security, yet now they contend exactly the opposite to prevent the public's knowing what has been learned. The article dealt mostly with Sherman Larsen of Glenvies, cofounder of the Evanston Center with Hynek.

Formation of a new Society for Scientific Exploration, to include both believers and nonbelievers, was announced April 24, 1982. The AP story from Stanford, Calif. that the *Washington Post* used said the group also would study ESP and other on-the-fringe matters. Paul Kurtz and Ray Hyman, foremost disbelievers, and Allen Hynek and Targ, believers, will belong.

Almost simultaneously, as reported May 20, 1982 by AP's Marcia Dunn from Greensburg, Pa., the Pennsylvania Association for the Study of the Unexplained said it is ready "in a moment's notice to investigate reports of UFOs, Bigfoot-like creatures or some seldom-seen wildcats." Of 1,000 Pennsylvania reports, 95 percent had natural explanations and fewer than 5 percent were deliberate hoaxes.

Believers

Just about all of the leading proponents of UFOs have been mentioned. Another is Prof. Harley D. Rutledge, head of the physics department at Southeast Missouri State University in Cape Girardeau, about whom Ed Schafer wrote a feature Nov. 26, 1977 for the Associated Press. Rutledge was a skeptic in 1973 when he was asked to investigate a rash of sightings. After four years, 140 sightings and 700 photographs he said, "Now I know they are up there, what they are or where they come from I have no way of knowing."

There also is Michael K. Schutz, an assistant professor of sociology at St. Ambrose College in Davenport, Iowa from which place the UPI sent a story about him Sept. 22, 1980. He was converted by his father who saw some UFOs on a plane trip in Oregon. He thinks the most credible sighting occurred Jan. 16, 1968 on an island off the coast of Brazil.

No. 1 expert in this field, of course, is Dr. J. Allen Hynek, longtime chairman of the astronomy department at Northwestern University, who founded the Center for UFO Studies in Evanston after his dismissal as consultant for the Air Force's Project Blue Book. In addition to the many mentions of his publicity in earlier pages, the following newspaper stories are important: "UFO Shots Don't Look Like Hoax: NU Expert," by Richard Lewis in the *Chicago Sun-Times* for Jan. 17, 1967; Hynek's comments on pictures by two teenagers over Lake St. Clair; "Close Encounters With Hynek and his UFOs," by Patrick Goldstein in the *Chicago Daily News* for Nov. 22, 1977, in which Hynek comments on the motion picture *Close Encounters of the Third Kind,* for which he was advisor. He said: "I think it's going to have a tremendous impact. It will be a real sociological event, a movie that intrigues people, not just entertains them." "Evanston scientist alters views," by Jim Ritter in the *Sun-Times Suburban Week* section for Feb. 29, 1980 in which Hynek said he feels like a latter-day Moses, leading the way toward an eventual scientific breakthrough that he won't live to see; and "UFO expert still claims some sightings are real," by Jack Mabley in the *Chicago Tribune* for April 14, 1981 with the news that Hynek's picture was to appear on the cover of the second issue of a new UFO magazine in China.

An indication of the erosion of fears as regards UFOs was the offbeat bicentennial year plan of Lake City, a suburb of Erie, Pa. It was a runway where spaceships could land, constructed on an acre of donated land surrounded by red, white and blue lights. A spokesman explained: "Everyone else is looking back 200 years and restoring buildings and writing books. We wanted to look in the other direction—to the future." John Bronson's story for the AP was used or plagiarized widely Jan. 23, 1976.

Another place extending extraterrestrial visitors hospitality was the village of Ares, near Bordeaux, France. According to the AP Aug. 17, 1976 it announced the opening of the first UFO landing field.

"Fate, Official Journal of the UFOs, Other Beasties," has been mentioned earlier (see page 593). The article with this title was written by James Klass for the *Chicago Daily News* for Sept. 12, 1977. It was followed by "A Magazine That's Out of This World" Dec. 14, 1978 in the *Chicago Sun-Times' Suburban Week* and by the March 25, 1982 piece by Grant Pick in *Parade* for March 23, 1982.

The article is based on an interview with Curtis and Mary Margaret Fuller, founders, owners and editors of the longest lasting periodical in the Chicago area, now 35 years old, with 120,000 subscribers. The original concept was to present the unexplained, the bizarre, the extraordinary and "make the incredible seem credible," Fuller said. "We don't say we believe everything we publish but we say it has to be capable of belief," according to Mary Fuller, and she added: "Oh yes, I believe in ghosts. Ghost stories are my favorite. Of course I don't know what a ghost is." Except for the *National Enquirer,* which has a wider scope, *Fate* has no important competitor.

Skeptics

From the start there have been many skeptics and cynics to counterbalance the wishful thinking and gullible majority. College student-newspaper editors solicited the opinions of faculty members. The *Summer Northwestern* of Northwestern University used the comments of four professors July 11, 1947. Bergen Evans, professor of English and author of *The Natural History of Nonsense,* said the flying saucer reports were "an indication of the gradual rising tide of imbecility." He said bluntly, "People tell lies and disks don't fly."

In the same symposium Dr. R. L. French, psychologist, said it's quite possible people saw something in the sky but very unlikely that it was a real disk. Dr. R. K. Summerbell, chairman of the chemistry department, said the problem "belongs in the field of psychology rather than the field of natural science." And this book's author was quoted that the wave of reports is "another case of the tremendous power of mass suggestibility."

When the sightings continued to be reported from all parts of the country the *Chicago Daily News* solicited the opinions of Evans and Mac-Dougall. The former said, "People are ready to believe anything when it comes to the sky," and the latter commented, "It's another case of mass hysteria." In the *Summer Northwestern* for Aug. 1, 1952 MacDougall said it was an improvement to be seeking a scientific explanation rather than a supernatural one. In the same issue Dr. Kaj A. Strand, director of Dearborn Observatory, said, "Anything we have seen so far can be explained by natural causes."

To counteract the claims that UFOs were extraterrestrial, three students at the California Institute of Technology created their own homemade saucers from plastic balloons with red flares dangling from rotating blades. For several days residents of Pasadena and other nearby suburbs were alarmed. The hoaxers said: "These UFOs were launched by persons of superior intelligence. There is indeed such intelligent life on Earth."

Dr. William Markowitz, Marquette University physics professor, wrote in *Science* magazine that UFOs from outer space would violate natural laws. The *Washington Post* digested his remarks Sept. 16, 1967.

After he failed a polygraph test commissioned by the *Houston Post,* Carroll Wayne Watts, a Loco, Tex. farmer, confessed that his story and photographs of his contact with little gray men from Mars was a hoax. Hynek had said of the pictures, "If this is a hoax it is a very, very clever one." The Associated Press reported the incident from Amarillo Feb. 26, 1968.

In a lengthy piece, "Hoax a Risk That Haunts Newspapers," David Shaw cited an Atlanta case involving UFOs as the lead of his story in the *Los Angeles Times* for July 7, 1975. He recalled that to win a bet that he could get his name on the front page of the *Atlanta Constitution* a man—whose name didn't make page 1 of Shaw's paper—recalled that July 7, 1953 the little creature run over by a truck was not a spaceman who failed to get back into his spacecraft in time but a dead rhesus monkey that had been shaved. The story appeared in many newspapers throughout the nation.

Not all citizens of the Soviet Union are believers, an AP story from Moscow Jan. 14, 1977 indicated. It quoted Bladimir Migulin, director of the Institute of Earth Magnetism, debunking the rumors of spacemen as "without serious foundation."

And from London the UPI reported Sept. 3, 1977 the magazine *New Scientist* said that after 30 years of sightings almost all the incidents had perfectly natural explanations.

"Two down-to-earth views of UFOs" took a full page of the *Chicago Daily News* for Dec. 8, 1977. One article by Jon Hahn said the fact that Professor Hynek and President Carter were believers made necessary further studies. Dan Miller, however, summarized: "The history of flying saucer phenomena has been characterized by hoax, chicanery, mischief and swamp gas, and the impending eruption will be no different. In point of fact there is no reason to accept the idea that Earth ever has been visited by extraterrestrial life." The "impending eruption" means several motion pictures, especially *Close Encounters of the Third Kind.*

In the belief that many viewers of the movie would result in a rash of reports of having been abducted, Glenn Collins composed a satirical piece, "Tips for Intergalactic Travel, Sturdy Walking Shoes Are a Must" for the *New York Times* of Feb. 12, 1978. Among the questions for which answers were given were: "Do I need a passport or visa?" "Can I drink the water?" "Is there adequate parking?" "Is tipping permitted?" and 12 other similar humorous questions.

Another newsman who saw the *Encounter* movie was Roger Simon, who apologized to People from Outer Space in his May 11, 1978 column in the *Chicago Sun-Times.* Previously Simon had expressed doubt of their existence; now he headed his piece "How about a lunch encounter? UFOs you won a convert." Most of the article takes not so subtle digs at believer Prof. Harley Rutledge of Southeast Missouri State University.

"UFO buffs resort to hoaxes, frauds and advertising tricks in a bid to win respectability for their belief in UFOs," was the way the AP summarized the winning essay in the *New Scientist* magazine. Winner, the UPI account from London Oct. 14, 1979 said, was James Oberg, an engineer for NASA headquarters in Houston.

The reactions of reviewers to books, motion pictures and television shows have been mixed. In the *New York Times* for Dec. 13, 1974 John J. O'Connor wrote the National Broadcasting Company's program, "UFOs: Do You Believe?" provided "too much credibility." Frank Segers cited the unprecedented demand of Columbia Pictures that an exhibitor pay $150,000 for a license as indication of the success of *Close Encounters of the Third Kind.* In the *New York Times* for Nov. 17, 1977, Vincent Canby said the picture was far better than any of its predecessors in the same category. Feb. 17, 1978 John J. O'Connor reported that Jack Webb's forthcoming "Project UFO" on NBC was "a dramatization inspired by official reports of governmental investigations of claims of reported sightings of UFOs on file in the National Archives of the United States. In an article Feb. 20, 1978 in the *Chicago Daily News,* from Hollywood, AP's Jay Sharbutt reported that Webb obtained the reports of 13,000 sightings, after the Air Force's Project Blue Book files were made available to the public.

Adding to the rave notice that the motion picture *E.T.* obtained, helping it to earn $13 million in three days, Roger Simon entitled his *Chicago Sun-Times* column for June 17, 1982, "Space aliens, show us your stuff." He called the movie charming but remained unconvinced regarding the reality of UFOs and thinks it's time the extraterrestrial denizens "come on down," as they say on quiz shows.

Explanations

As indicated in the preceding pages there has been no lack of explanations for the epidemic of UFO sightings. At one extreme are those who believe they fulfill biblical prophecies; at the other are those who say they are hallucinations. Aug. 4, 1952 the *Evanston* (Ill.) *Mail* quoted me as believing people see flying saucers because they want to see them. Jan. 9, 1969 the *Chicago Daily News* stated in a streamer headline, "Unidentified Flying Objects Identified." It published three pictures that the UPI reported the University of Colorado researchers had branded as fabrications.

In most sightings, the Pennsylvania Center for UFO Research reported witnesses mention an odor of sulfur, disappearance of pets, and strange sounds, like that of a crying baby. The *Harrisburg* (Pa.) *Patriot* reported June 1, 1976 that the Center was investigating the Glenolden (Pa.) Gorilla allegedly wandering about the town's streets. The *New York Daily News* for July 26, 1976 asked, "Do UFOs Spring From the Devil?" For one and a third pages Edward Edelson, science editor, enumerated most of the theories regarding the identity of UFOs without answering the headline's question.

The eminent actor and producer, Woody Allen, wrote a half-page article, "The UFO Menace," for the *Washington Post* of June 26, 1977. It was mostly a historical resumé of sightings from early biblical days to the present, the menace apparently being the annoyance the subject causes many people.

A publicity stunt to advertise the movie, *Close Encounters of the Third Kind* in Tokyo was a failure, *Newsday* reported Feb. 26, 1978. UFOs were not lured by the use of red, white and blue spotlights and sound trucks.

The most profound psychological evaluation of the phenomenon was made by Carl Gustav Jung, the great Swiss psychologist and psychoanalyst. The streamer headline summarized the viewpoint: "Flying Saucers—Perhaps a 99 Percent Psychic Product." Jung saw the discs as symbols of totality, "well known to all students of depth psychology, namely the mandala (Sanskrit for circle). Marginal notes on the article were: "If the round shining objects . . . in the sky be regarded as visions, we can hardly avoid interpreting them as archetypal images" and "Anyone with the requisite historical and psychological knowledge knows that circular symbols have played an important role in every age."

The sheriff's office was deluged with calls with reports ranging from sightings of a UFO to a plane crash and fire, the AP reported May 30, 1978 from Brewster, N.Y. Actually a balloonist from Ridgefield, Conn. was landing his balloon. Similarly a scare in Brooklyn and Queens quieted down when the object was identified as a pilot doing some night advertising for a restaurant, Hugh Braken reported in the *New York Daily News* for June 3, 1978.

Nocturnal swarms of insects glowing like "a discotheque in the sky" from electrical discharges in the atmosphere could be responsible for many nighttime UFO reports, according to Dr. Philip S. Callahan of the Agricultural Research Service laboratory in Gainesville, Fla., Al Rossiter, Jr. of the UPI reported Nov. 2, 1978 from Washington.

Then again on the other hand the nocturnal visitors might be UFOs intent on studying the nation's supersensitive nuclear missile launch sites and bomber bases, according to an article by Ward Sinclair and Art Harris in the *Washington Post* for Jan. 19, 1978. Defense Department records show that in 1975 objects, maybe helicopters, aircrafts and brightly lighted fast-moving vehicles hovered over such places in Montana, Michigan and Maine and evaded pursuit efforts.

"Although it's not a popular point of view to espouse, the truth is that there are many explanations for 'unexplainable' lights and objects in the sky that don't depend on foreign forms of life," the *Harrisburg* (Pa.) *Patriot* for Jan. 23, 1979 quoted Dr. Hershel W. Leibowitz of Pennsylvania State University, with Dr. Allstair B. Fraser agreeing. Among the human factors are poor perception, motivation, lights and objects originating within the eye for normal and abnormal reasons and hallucinations. Among atmospheric causes are reflection and refraction of light, unique cloud patterns, electrically charged insect swarms and optical illusions and mirages.

The first verifiable picture of a UFO was taken by a camerman hired by an Australian television station over New Zealand in December, 1978. Reuters reported March 26, 1949 that the National Investigative Committee on Aerial Phenomena made the announcement in New York. Principal sponsor of the photograph's authenticity was J. Allen Hynek.

"Just Russian junk" is what the North American Air Defense Command named the UFO reported over west Washington state, the UPI reported Oct. 7, 1979 from Spokane. Specifically the agency said it probably was the rocket body of a Soviet satellite entering Earth's atmosphere.

The spaceship that was to return four earthlings from Jupiter to Brazil did not land because there were 10,000 persons waiting, according to Edilcio Barbosa, whose TV announcement attracted the audience. The UPI reported the tragedy from Rio de Janeiro March 1, 1980.

A rare natural occurrence similar to ball lightning was postulated as the identity of what Linda and Trent Anderson saw, Joe Mosley reported in the *Eugene* (Ore.) *Register-Guard* for Oct. 31, 1981. That was the explanation given by an investigator from Hynek's Evanston center. Ball lightning is a rare lightning form emitted in glowing balls rather than bolts, the article explained. Several recent sightings in the area might be so explained.

Spacemen, Past and Present

Contemporary spacemen, if they exist, are certainly reticent about making their presence known. Except for the few who say they were kidnapped, those who say they saw spaceships land claim that, as soon as the occupants saw they were being observed, they took off presumably for home, leaving nothing behind except some burned-out grass. There are those who believe it wasn't always so. In many parts of the world there are artifacts that stump modern scientists and certainly were beyond the ability of any primitives of which anthropologists have knowledge: the pyramids of Egypt and Yucatan, Stonehenge in England, Aku Aku sculptures on Easter Island, runways in Nazca, Peru and more. Arthur Gorlick wrote an overall introduction to this field of study, "Who flew prehistoric skies?" for the Aug. 25–26, 1973 *Chicago Daily News.*

The discovery of new artifacts or promulgation of a new theory of the nature of any of the mysteries is newsworthy. There is, however, no day-by-day coverage of sightings by laymen as with UFOs. The scholarly debates and popular interpretations for laymen are mostly in magazine articles and books. It was, in fact, started by a book by a Swiss writer, Erich von Däniken, whose *Chariots of the Gods* was published in 1969 to be followed by *Gods From Outer Space* and *The Gold of the Gods.* His thesis is that invaders from a far distant planet visited Earth and either built the pyramids and other architectural marvels or taught humans how to do so, imparting to them their own advanced knowledge of mathematics, engineering and other skills.

Inspired by von Däniken other authors produced at least 100 other books. Best known of them were written by Rod Serling, chiefly *In Search of Ancient Mysteries.* There also were *We Are Not the First,* by Andrew Toman and *Those Gods Who Made Heaven and Earth,* by Jean Sendy.

Fans of von Däniken have not been dissuaded by revelations of their hero's unsavory past. A good resumé of it was written by Richard R. Lingeman in the *New York Times* for March 31, 1974. Before coming to the United States von Däniken was convicted of embezzlement, fraud and forgery, fined $1,000 and sentenced to 3½ years in prison. The *Miami News,* Lingeman wrote, disproved von Däniken's claims of having discovered a treasuretrove of gold and a metallic library in Ecuador, as related in *Gold of the Gods.*

Inspired by von Däniken's book and NBC's first special program based on it, a Highland Park, Ill. lawyer, Gene M. Phillips, founded the Ancient Astronaut Society. It held its first annual conference in late April 1974 in Arlington Heights, Ill. F. K. Plous, Jr. covered it for the *Chicago Sun-Times.* April 28 he said the attendance was 300 and speeches by John W. White and Peter Tompkins, author of *The Secret Life of Plants* and *Secrets of the Great Pyramid,* were well received. As a followup of the convention

Ronald Yates wrote a 2-column article for the *Chicago Tribune* of May 3, 1974. He wrote:

> It is this small but imaginative and prolific band that has produced a prodigious number of books, engaged in numerous lectures across the country, sparked formation of a society and challenged the conventional wisdom of academia.

Yates quoted von Däniken as follows:

> I claim that our forefathers received visitors from the universe in the remote past. Even tho I do not yet know who these extraterrestrial intelligences were or from which planet they came I nevertheless proclaim these strangers annihilated part of mankind existing at the time and produced a new, perhaps the first Homo sapiens. This assertion is revolutionary.

As he usually did Daniel St. Albin Greene wrote the most comprehensive article, "God Flies a Saucer. Or at least Some Space Cultists Think So," in the *National Observer* for July 6, 1974. He characterized the "new pop cosmology" as ". . . a mind-stretching jumble of flying saucer conjecture, space age interpretation of the Bible and antiauthoritarian zeal. For want of an official name, let's call them the Saucer Cosmologists."

Greene not only pointed out liberties von Däniken took with the truth but also cited the views of several others of his followers. For instance, the Rev. Barry H. Downing of Binghamton, N.Y. believes that the clouds mentioned in the Scriptures were really spaceships by which angels spread Christianity. And Wallace Spencer, a former UFO investigator, thinks there's an unworldly colony living under the Atlantic Ocean that occasionally abducts planes and ships for examination. God, von Däniken asserts, is "the quintessential astronaut."

Another refutation of von Däniken was provided by Ron Story in his book *The Space-Gods Revealed: A Close Look at the Theories of Erich von Däniken*. In one of his "Conversations" that the *Chicago Sun-Times* used July 25, 1976, Philip Nobile cited Story's revelations that von Däniken is not a scholar but a college dropout, that he was convicted of fraud, embezzlement and forgery and, despite the popularity of his books, has had no effect on the scientific community.

When an Easter Islander, Edmund Edwards, came to Chicago he was interviewed by Rick Soll for the *Chicago Tribune* of March 30, 1975. He recalled von Däniken's visit to the island, describing him as extremely excitable and scornful of scientific theories regarding the Aku Aku monuments. Finally Edwards showed him a rock with some writing and jokingly said, "Here is your man from Venus." When *Gold of the Gods* appeared Edwards was astonished to note pictures of the rock and von Däniken's insistence that it was an early drawing of a ram-jet propulsion unit—a section of a combustion rocket. "I couldn't believe it," Edwards said.

When the fifth annual convention of the Ancient Astronaut Society was held in Chicago the attendance had grown to 650, the *New York Times* reported July 31, 1978. Speakers from all over the world theorized about ancient times. For example, an English engineer, Rodney Dale, said that the manna that fed the children of Israel on their trek to the Promised Land was actually a form of green algae produced by a nuclear-powered machine from outer space.

According to the AP Sept. 30, 1979 in a dispatch from Moscow, a Soviet scientist believes that there is archeological evidence in a remote section of Siberia to prove there were visitors from outer space in ancient times.

John S. Robinson sent the *Christian Science Monitor* a story, "Deciphering the figures of Nazca," from Peru for use Oct. 11, 1978. He interviewed 78-year-old Maria Reiche, longtime student of the ground markings. Robinson wrote:

> . . . the manner in which the lines and drawings were made seems reasonably clear. Small dish-brown stones cover the pampa. When these are removed light-colored sand is exposed underneath. To create the lines and drawing stones were simply taken away. To produce all of them hundreds of tons must have been displaced.
>
> One of the most baffling puzzles about the lines and drawings is the fact that they appear to have been designed to be viewed only from the air. This, together with their bizarre, curiously disquieting quality has convinced many people that they were not made by mere humans.

A sad case illustrating the possible consequences of fanaticism, religious or scientific or both, was that of Dr. Charles A. Laughead, campus physician at Michigan State University, East Lansing, Mich. It first hit the front page Dec. 16, 1954 when the Associated Press reported that the administration was considering acceptance of the doctor's resignation after students complained of his holding meetings at his home to teach "the beliefs of some peculiar religion," as President John A. Hannah put it.

Dr. Laughead went to Oak Park, Ill., where he and Mrs. Dorothy Martin issued a joint statement: "It has come to our attention that the flying saucers or, more correctly, the Guardians of Earth, are here for a definite purpose." In the meantime Dr. Laughead's sister, Margaret V. Laughead of Des Moines, filed a mental competency suit against her brother, the *Chicago Sun-Times* reported Dec. 13, 1954.

Dec. 17 the same paper headlined, "Denies World Ending Tuesday But Insists We'll All Be Wet." In the page-1 story which, with pictures of him and Mrs. Martin, consumed half the page, Dr. Laughead said that a tidal wave would hit Chicago Dec. 21 but the world would continue. The message came from "connoiters" who dwell on another planet. Dec. 22 the *Sun-Times* quoted him as saying he was through prophesying. He insisted, however, that Mrs. Martin had accurately received the messages on which he made his forecast. He said: "It was just that the 'general'—you may call him a god—changed strategy at the last moment."

Dec. 19, 1954 Marvin Quinn reported for the *Sun-Times* from East Lansing that Dr. Laughead's interest in extraterrestrial beings began when he accompanied the Michigan State football team to the Rose Bowl Jan. 1, 1954. Upon his return he said he had made contacts with persons who, with ESP, received messages from outer space. He put a telescope on the rooftop of his house where many students joined him in stargazing. He was fired because he disturbed some students. Dec. 28 the *Sun-Times* reported Dr. Laughead's disappointment when no spacemen came to escort him into outer space. A crowd of about 100 sang carols and jeered outside the Oak Park home of Mrs. Martin, where they both were.

Jan. 7, 1955 the AP reported that Margaret Laughead had filed a writ of attachment in Lansing court against both her brother and sister-in-law to prevent their moving to Florida. She charged that they had not repaid $3,000 she loaned them in 1950.

Thereafter the press stopped keeping readers abreast of the psychiatric history of the Laugheads.

"Are We Alone?" was the headline the *St. Louis Globe-Democrat* used Jan. 21–22, 1978 over the first of a series of three articles by Marcia Seligson following her attendance at the Acapulco convention. The hanger head summarized her viewpoint: "Though crank stories of UFOs will abound, writer says the only way many sightings can be explained is by accepting the idea they are extraterrestrial."

Jan. 31, 1979 the *New York Daily News* began a series of articles, "Who Goes There? The Search for Life in Space," excerpted from the book *Who Goes There?* by the paper's science editor, Edward Edelson. The first installment contained a formula whereby Earth scientists hoped to communicate with other civilizations if they exist. These scholars have nothing to do with UFOs in which they do not believe. Rather, they belong to the group that the *New York Times*' science editor, Walter Sullivan, described in his book *We Are Not Alone*. An article based on Sullivan's book, "The Universe Is Not Ours Alone," appeared in the *New York Times Magazine* for Sept. 29, 1968. There have, of course, been some newspaper stories and features but the work has not reached fruition and sober scientists do not go in for statements that make flashy headlines as do the tales of the saucer fans. Nov. 21, 1954 the Associated Press did distribute a long article quoting Harlow Shapley, Harvard University astronomer, that there might be 100 million planets capable of supporting life. The *Miami Herald* Tropic section for March 31, 1974 had an article, "Can We Talk to the Stars?" by the eminent Carl Sagan. Isaac Asimov wrote, "Let's Not Turn Our Backs on Space" for the *Chicago Tribune Magazine* for Oct. 18, 1981.

When 30 of them participated in a two-day meeting at the University of

Maryland most challenged the prevailing scientific belief that intelligent life is widespread, Malcolm W. Browne reported in the *New York Times* for April 9, 1979. Carl Sagan and other supporters of the majority view did not attend.

Dec. 3, 1979 the *Sun-Times* used a story from the *London Daily Telegraph* about the abduction by Martians of a French youth, Franck Fontaine of Cergy-Pontoise, a suburb of Paris. A schoolmaster told a French newspaper that he believed the spacemen had had his town under surveillance for a long time. Eyewitnesses said the spacecraft landed on Franck's car and sent two other youths home to get cameras "so the Earthmen can see we are real." No pictures accompanied the story. The UPI reported Dec. 4, 1977 that the youth returned home after a week, saying he remembered nothing after a glowing sphere about the size of a tennis ball appeared near the hood of his car.

The *New York Post* gave good space to an announcement of a National UFO and New Age Conference in a Manhattan church. Don Gentile covered a similar conference for the *New York Daily News* of Sept. 27, 1981, at which Mark Gershon used a crystal ball and a contact on Saturn to put people in touch with extraterrestrials, aliens or anyone else in outer space—"or so he said."

And as for what I say, here's what I wrote for my Observation column in the *Chicago Skyline* for Jan. 11, 1979:

SOME DAY presumably a low-flying UFO will travel the length of Pennsylvania Avenue, or Fifth avenue or State Street, in broad daylight, slowly enough for hundreds of thousands or millions to be witnesses.

When such happens, but not before, I shall become a convert, especially if the flying disk or saucer lands, the little green or purple people alight and demand to be taken to our leader.

Up to now visitors allegedly from outer space have chosen to come down in darkness in obscure places, such as a Nebraska cornfield, New England highway or southwestern desert. Books have been written by the select few who were examined by the interlopers. Sometimes they were rewarded with rides in spaceships, even visiting the homelands of their captors way out in the bright blue yonder somewhere.

This UFO nonsense should have ended with the publication in 1968 of the results of a two-year University of Colorado project financed by the Department of Defense and directed by Dr. Edward Condon, noted physicist and former head of the Bureau of Standards.

It concluded:

"Nothing has come from the study of UFOs in the past 21 years that has added to scientific knowledge. Careful consideration of the record . . . leads us to conclude that further extensive study of UFOs probably cannot be justified in the expectation that science will be advanced thereby."

Obviously what needs study are the millions who have had visions, hallucinations and errors of perception. It is they who make jubilant reports to assorted crackpots and wishful thinkers who write popular and learned articles. Proof of the existence of extra-terrestrial messengers exists entirely in the imaginative reports of frustrated, deluded or publicity-seeking persons.

"If so many people believe they have seen them they must exist," is the rationalization of believers, an attitude which no true scientists could possibly accept. Nor any cross-examining lawyer or investigative journalist.

For many years the Air Force investigated with completely negative results. For decades the entire planet has been blanketed with electronic devices to detect virtually every activity in and beyond the earth's atmosphere. No UFOs have been intercepted.

Nor has anyone provided any common sense reason why space ships would travel millions of light-years just for a few minutes' inspection. The craziness unfortunately has been encouraged by the press, other journalistic media, TV and motion pictures.

The gullibility of the masses is symptomatic of the insecurity and fear of our times. People seek surcease in the supernatural—astrology, esp, spiritualism, witchcraft and other manifestations of anachronistic human ignorance. It would be great if magical help were available in these troublesome times. Unfortunately, however, man is still on his own and the sooner he stops seeking relief in fantasy the better for him.

July 29, 1983 the *Chicago Sun-Times* reported that U.S. District Judge Oliver Gasch in Washington dismissed a suit brought on behalf of the Citizens Against UFO Secrecy charging the Air Force was holding bodies of outer space aliens whose flying saucers landed in New Mexico in 1950.

Index